Western Civilization
to 1660

WESTERN CIVILIZATION

TO 1660

J. Kelley Sowards

WICHITA STATE UNIVERSITY

ST MARTIN'S PRESS · NEW YORK

To my wife, Ardis

Preface

IT IS, I suppose, a truism to observe that a book of this kind invariably grows out of one's own experience in the college classroom and a lack of complete satisfaction with the available texts. Most of us who have spent very many years teaching basic civilization courses have experimented widely with a variety of teaching aids, including "problem" books and paperbacks. But no matter how excellent many of these are in themselves, and useful as supplementary reading (I have listed many of them in the Suggestions for Further Reading lists that follow each chapter) they generally prove inadequate to the specific purpose in hand—the teaching of a beginning college course in history.

For most of the students who take this course, the cultural terrain of Europe, western Asia, and the Ancient Near East is virtually unknown ground. Given the limitations of three or four fifty-minute hours a week and the highly structured setting of the classroom, the instructor cannot do all that needs to be done to achieve even the minimal expectations he has for his course: presenting the basic factual outline, pointing out the connections among various historical developments, speculating about cause and meaning. A textbook can go a long way toward filling in and drawing together material that the instructor can do no more than sketch in lightly. It is with this aim in mind that I have written this book.

It has been the vogue in recent years to offer courses in World Civilization. Given the time available in an introductory course, this seems hardly realistic. My own decision to concentrate on western civilization stems not only from this practical consideration but from the conviction that this is the single most important theme for an introductory course in history. It is the subject most germane to the American college student. The tradition of western civilization is his tradition, and the purpose of this book is to help provide him with a cultural orientation in the history of that tradition.

Moreover, I have organized the material in an "integrated" rather than compartmented manner. Diplomatic, political, economic, military, intellectual, and cultural history are, after all, artificial divisions. One cannot separate the flowering of medieval Scholasticism from the rise of the universities, nor the rise of the universities from the role of the church and the needs of a revitalized society; nor can any of these be separated from the account of the restoration of political order under the great medieval dynasts or the burgeoning of economic life in the High Middle Ages.

Like all instructors, I have come to realize that even if one's students were to share one's own special interest in, say, the Sumerian dynasties, or Renaissance art, or the subtleties of Calvinist theology, there simply is not time to dwell in detail on any one theme, period, or people. One must resign oneself to the knowledge that the enormous amount of detail which history is compounded of will be little noted nor long remembered by students. Thus, in writing this text I have tried to draw out and trace the major threads, the dynamic patterns, in the development of western European civilization.

It is my conviction that among the few items a textbook writer has to offer are a clear and straightforward style and a coherent, easily followed organization of material. I have striven for both.

The author of a text owes so many debts that he is virtually pauperized. Obviously I owe an incredibly heavy debt to my professional colleagues throughout the world whose articles and books I have read and absorbed over the course of some twenty years. Most of these now enjoy for me a pleasant kind of anonymity, for I have cherished their ideas for so long that I have come to consider many of them my own. I address a plea for charity to those who may find their ideas and insights embedded in my work. In every case it is the sincerest kind of flattery.

I owe almost as large a debt to the literally thousands of students who, by their very presence, questions, and interest, and the bond I have felt with them, have helped to form my thought as a historian. I am grateful to them.

Finally, I must acknowledge the more immediate and tangible help of my friends and colleagues on whom I have "tried out" many passages and chapters of this work, and whose criticisms and suggestions have saved me from many a greater embarrassment, and my family, whose endurance has been beyond measure.

I am indebted for their advice and for their reading of portions of the manuscript to my friends and colleagues Professors Paul Tasch, Lowell D. Holmes, Martin A. Reif, Robert W. Frazer, Albert R. Parker, and William Nelson; and especially to my friend Professor Roger L. Williams, the author of the companion volume to this book.

I also wish to express my thanks to Theodore R. Miller, not only for the original maps, but also for many suggestions incorporated elsewhere in this text.

J. K. S.

Contents

1 THE PREHISTORIC BASIS OF CIVILIZATION
[5]

ix

LIST OF PLATES

xix

LIST OF MAPS

[Maps planned and executed by Theodore R. Miller]

Western Civilization

to 1660

Introduction

HISTORY is the cumulative record of human experience; the human animal lives by experience. These two assertions contain both the basic definition of history and the prime argument for its utility. To test this claim we need only dwell for a moment upon what would happen if all the children to be born in the next instant should be born into "the state of nature" rather than "the state of history." Quite simply they would be illiterate savages living in a pre-Paleolithic Age with nothing to serve them but the few meager tools of survival that man has by virtue of nature. They would have to recapitulate all the long and painful process by which man created civilization; they would have to rediscover fire, the wheel, the bow and arrow; they would have to struggle once more to build and sustain societies; and eventually they would have to contrive some form of writing to perpetuate their thoughts and keep their records.

But history does exist, and precisely because generation after generation men have kept records, both intentional and unintended ones—artifacts, buildings, statues and paintings, letters, diaries, novels, chronicles, public documents. Historians call these records sources, and it is upon them that they base their reconstructions of the past. Yet it is important to remember that the sources for different periods differ radically, both in quantity and quality. In the first chapter of this book we speak of prehistoric man, that is, man before he had begun to keep any self-conscious records, and consequently our knowledge of him is maddeningly fragmentary and inconclusive. We know considerably more about the civilizations of the ancient Near East, which were the earliest sites of life complex enough to demand the keeping of records and thus the invention of writing. But even here the story is not all in. Only in the last half century archaeology has added immensely to the sources for this period with, for example, the discovery of the Dead Sea Scrolls and the identification of the Linear Minoan B script as an early form of Greek. Indeed, in a number of cases, such discoveries have led to profound reappraisals of the past, as in the belated recognition of the Hittites as one of the great peoples of the Ancient Near East. Fifty years ago they were simply one of the numerous "lesser" peoples who flow across the pages of the Old Testament. But the gaps remain and the errors remain in the tattered records of the ancient peoples.

In sharp contrast we have the sources of our time. Think only of the records of World War II, literally a mountain of records—millions of public documents of all the governments involved; records of requisition and supply for every item used by the armed forces, from pencils to airplanes; military personnel records, test records, performance records, medical records, and death records; correspondents' dispatches, newspaper stories, interviews, diaries, memoirs, and official regimental histories.

Yet the quantity of records for an age or an instant is only part of the problem. Even where there is an abundance of material the historian must examine his sources with the greatest care, knowing that the report of an event may be sympathetic, naive, or hostile, depending not on the event itself but on the reporter, for the records of history are human records, subject to human error, frailty, ignorance, and spite. This is true even of supposed official records, which are sometimes distorted by national pride, religious zeal, motives of personal advancement, or "company policy." It is even more true of the literary sources historians often have to depend on. Julius Caesar's own account of his exploits in Gaul is the only substantial account we have of those events, and we have every reason to believe that he was using his dispatches deliberately to keep his name and military reputation before the eyes of the voters "back home." We know that the Roman historian Tacitus was bitterly hostile to the very imperial house that was the subject of his history. We know that the good Bishop Gregory of Tours, on whose account virtually our whole knowledge of early Merovingian history depends, was convinced that the Catholic orthodoxy of the house of Clovis was sufficient justification for any crime or enormity. In our own time we have only to think how Nazi and

Soviet historians have distorted historical fact in the interests of national and party apology.

There is, however, an important and sometimes subtle distinction between distortion and interpretation. Interpretation, the ordering of the raw materials of history into a meaningful account, is essential to the historian's task. The mere accumulation of facts, even irrefutably established facts, is a variety of antiquarianism, not the writing of history. The historian is properly concerned with finding the relationships among ideas, institutions, actions, and events. He is concerned with questions of meaning and cause. He will ask of the past not only "What happened here?", but "How did this happen?", "Why did it happen?", and "Why in this particular way?". Such questions of purpose, cause, and meaning have always intrigued historians of whatever age. Moreover, every age has tended to view history in terms of some large framework of meaning. The ancients saw history as a part of the law of nature and thus subject to the inevitable cycle of nature. The great Thucydides wrote of the devastating Peloponnesian War with a view to "the like events which may be expected to happen hereafter in the order of human things."[1] The medieval Christian historian saw history determined by the will of God, unfolding as the expression of His inevitable plan. With the proliferation of thought in more recent times the varieties of historical determinism multiplied. This was especially true of the great historians and historical theorists of the nineteenth century, with their theories of progress, of cycles, of heroes, of social Darwinism, and a great many others including the Marxian dialectic. Today's historians have reacted strongly against the whole concept of determinism. Perhaps the events of the past half century have made impossible the kind of thinking about the overall order and meaning of history that men of less anxious times could indulge. But more than that, modern historians have generally come to the conclusion that when one begins by looking for patterns in history one frequently ends up by forcing patterns upon history and making it conform to one's own theories. History is ultimately the story of what men have done to themselves, to each other, and to the world in which they live. It is enough to tell that story, to find meaning where and when we can, and to draw whatever circumspect lessons we may within the knowledge that the choices that open to human action and human ingenuity are virtually endless. This is a modest claim, and yet it is one that is not to be despised. When the present awes and the future frightens us, there is some comfort

1. *The Peloponnesian War,* I, 22.

in the knowledge that we are not alone in the experience of living, that other men and other times have known their agonies and survived, and that our alternatives of action are extended by the knowledge of what they thought and did. History is a teacher of reality, and the reality it teaches us is that truth is never quite conclusive, that men and things can seldom be all good or all bad, that even the simplest events may have complex causes, some of which we will never know. All of this is of value in that the mind which is exposed to the discipline of historical study will not be hasty to praise or blame, will not be quite so easily captivated by "isms" of any sort, and will have had some experience at the immensely important business of discriminating the more true from the more false.

This book is a history of western civilization. It covers the enormous span of time from the dawn of time itself to the eve of the modern age. It is concerned with many facets of human activity. But the main thread of its story is what we might call the process of western civilization—how it has developed and grown and been transmitted and enhanced by the peoples who have contributed to it, and how it has spread its influence to every corner of the world. It is a fascinating story; but more, it is an important one. For it is the story of the basic tradition to which the men of the western world belong. It is the sum of *our* experience. Wise old Cicero once said, "The man who knows only his own time remains forever a child."

The world of the twentieth century is no child's plaything.

❧ 1 ❧

The Prehistoric Basis
of Civilization

THE COMING OF MAN

The Setting

Geologists have determined that the earth was millions of years old before even the most remote ancestors of man appeared. Its surface had cooled and wrinkled into mountains and valleys; it had separated into land masses and oceans. The cycle of seasons had begun. Life had sprung up in the ocean and spread to the land, where millions of species had flourished and become extinct. As the age of the great reptiles gave way to the age of mammals, the first members of the primate order from which man was to develop appeared. But since he did not begin to record his history until long after, most of what we know about prehistoric man—including his origins— is conjecture.

Fossils that have been discovered in Africa, southeast Asia, China, and western Europe[1] suggest that humanoid (manlike) creatures probably ap-

1. These fossil remains have been descriptively named, and great care has been taken to place them in some sort of order in time. The oldest, and most recently found, is an East African form called Zinjanthropus, which has now been dated rather conclusively at 1.7 million years ago. Several other African species (Australopithecinae—southern ape family) date to nearly 1 million years ago. All of these are classed in the shadowy area of *Hominidae* (manlike, but not yet man). The Java specimens (Pithecanthropus erectus—erect ape man), the Chinese (Pithecanthropus pekinensis—Peking ape man), and possibly the earliest European specimens (Homo heidelbergensis—Heidelberg man), while widely separated, are roughly contemporary

5

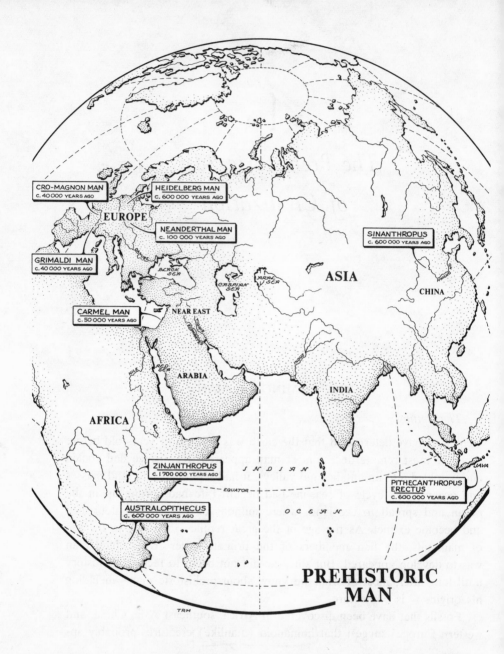

CRO-MAGNON MAN
c. 40 000 YEARS AGO

HEIDELBERG MAN
c. 600 000 YEARS AGO

EUROPE

NEANDERTHAL MAN
c. 100 000 YEARS AGO

SINANTHROPUS
c. 600 000 YEARS AGO

GRIMALDI MAN
c. 40 000 YEARS AGO

ASIA

CHINA

CARMEL MAN
c. 50 000 YEARS AGO

NEAR EAST

BLACK SEA

CASPIAN SEA

ARAL SEA

NILE

RED SEA

ARABIA

INDUS

INDIA

AFRICA

ZINJANTHROPUS
c. 1 700 000 YEARS AGO

INDIAN

EQUATOR

PITHECANTHROPUS
ERECTUS
c. 600 000 YEARS AGO

AUSTRALOPITHECUS
c. 600 000 YEARS AGO

OCEAN

JAVA

**PREHISTORIC
MAN**

TRM

peared over 25 million years ago, at the end of the Miocene geological period, and separated from the anthropoid line to develop in a new biological direction. Apparently a number of different species—semi-erect, short and massive, beetle-browed and heavy-jawed—were clearly adapted

(about 600,000 to 500,000 years ago) and are comparable in their stages of physical development.

FORMS OF EARLY MAN

ZINJANTHROPUS	*1,700,000 years ago*
AUSTRALOPITHECENES	*600,000 — 1,000,000*
HEIDELBERG MAN	*c. 600,000*
PEKING MAN	*c. 600,000*
JAVA MAN	*c. 600,000*
NEANDERTHAL MAN	*c. 100,000*
MT. CARMEL MAN	*c. 50,000*
CRO-MAGNON MAN	*c. 40,000*
GRIMALDI MAN	*c. 40,000*

to an upright posture with arms and legs resembling those of man. These species adapted to the Pleistocene ice flows of the northern hemisphere, whose advances and retreats radically changed the climate in every part of the world, and the species continued to increase in number and differentiate in form.

At the end of the glacial age—over 20,000 years ago—*Homo sapiens* (knowing man) originated either in Asia or Africa, overlapping the development of such less advanced species as Neanderthaloid man.[2] Homo sapiens rapidly replaced his predecessors on every continent, to become the only surviving species of the human family.

Though skeletal remains do not reveal skin color or hair texture, they do suggest that there were different races among the earliest of Homo sapiens. The remains of Cro-Magnon man, found in Europe, show that this tall, well-knit, and fine-featured creature may well have resembled the modern European; those of Grimaldi man, found on the European coast of the Mediterranean, give evidence of Negroid characteristics; and still

2. Neanderthal, probably the best-known fossil man preceding our own species, lived throughout the Old World and for a time was probably the dominant species. Like Homo sapiens, he represents an evolutionary "end product." The fact that later Neanderthal specimens show much more marked Neanderthaloid characteristics than the earlier ones suggests that Neanderthal man was evolving in a distinctive direction away from the line of development taken by Homo sapiens, which doomed him to extinction.

another race, or group of races, whose remains were found in central and northern Europe, may have been the ancestors of the Eskimo and perhaps of all Mongoloid people.[3] Whether each race descended directly from a certain fossil species or whether its development was influenced by such factors as climate, isolation, and inbreeding is not known, but the basic biological unity of all mankind is clear. Compared to the similarities, racial differences are insignificant, and there is truly only one kind of man: we are all "fed with the same food, hurt with the same weapons. . . . If you prick us, do we not bleed? If you tickle us, do we not laugh? If you poison us, do we not die?"[4]

The Basis of Human Culture

While other species may have had some specialized protective attributes—great physical strength, natural camouflage, speed, the ability to climb or swim—each was endowed with only one or two such qualities. Man, on the other hand, though not especially fleet of foot, agile in climbing, or powerful in swimming, was sufficiently adept in each of these skills to cope with a greater variety of environmental challenges. Most important, even the humanoids who preceded Homo sapiens had a greater cranial capacity than other animals—including the related anthropoids. Because Java ape-man's brain was twice the size of a gorilla's for example, he could reason his way to the solution of many problems of physical survival. More adaptable than other species, man could (and can) live in almost any climate and thrive on a varied diet.

Not only can man remember and generalize his experience, but, because of his capacity for articulate speech, he can pass that experience on to others. The human species can thus preserve what it has learned; it can, in other words, develop cultures by transmitting the accumulation of learned behavior from generation to generation within a given social group.

Significantly, the settings in which all the remains of prehistoric man have been found—amid the litter of a camp, by the broken bones of game animals, or alongside the coals of a communal fire—suggest a culture and a society. The earliest cultures were probably no more than instinctive groupings—not unlike the banding of wolves into a pack or reindeer into a herd—based on the sex drive and the bonds of family feeling. But presumably at a very early stage these prehistoric "societies" became more

3. There is every indication that the Mongoloid represents an adaptation to extreme cold. His stocky, corpulent, short-limbed body tends to conserve heat, and the scarcity of body hair and the oily skin are protection against frostbite.
4. William Shakespeare, The Merchant of Venice, III, i.

complex as man was able to speak his thoughts, instruct his children, and build up a tradition within his own group.

Thus man created, within the framework of his natural physical environment, an artificial environment of his own—a culture that affected even his biological and psychological needs by dictating the foods he ate, the clothing or ornaments he wore, his methods of courting his mate, and his relation to his family and to the rest of society. In fact, man's conception of himself and of his world has always been shaped by the culture of which he was a part: simple as the cultures of prehistoric man must have been, they were the precondition of civilization.

The Paleolithic Age: Material Culture

The term usually applied to man's earliest culture period, "paleolithic" (old stone), refers to the crude stone tools and weapons that are almost the only objects surviving from the period that predates the appearance of Homo sapiens by many thousands of years. Some experts have conjectured that the ancient and primitive South African Australopithecus of almost a million years ago, and the even earlier Zinjanthropus, at least used as tools whatever natural objects came to hand (tree limbs, stones, animal bones), but the earliest consciously shaped stone implements—the primitive hatchets and digging stones of the Abbevillian culture[5]—can probably not be dated before 600,000 years ago. Through countless cultures such forms as axes, blades, scraping and piercing tools, gravers, and pounders were slowly developed, improved, and diversified. The rudimentary Paleolithic technology was well suited to the life of a hunter, and his extremely circumscribed life was not likely to suggest extensive technical innovation.

All Paleolithic artifacts made by Homo sapiens or his prehuman ancestors were created by chipping and flaking and were used for hunting and food gathering. At first the shapes of natural stone were modified to make more convenient hand-holds or to sharpen their edges, but event-

5. This is the earliest of a series of prehistoric subculture periods, based almost entirely upon stone artifacts. The Abbevillian culture, lasting roughly from 600,000 to 500,000 years ago, was followed by the Acheulian, which lasted, in some areas, until the end of the last glacial period some 20,000 to 30,000 years ago. This overlaps the more advanced Levalloisian and Mousterian periods, which date from about 250,000 years ago until after the last glaciation. The last significant periods of Paleolithic technology were the considerably more complex and diversified Aurignacian, Solutrean, and Magdalenian. These were cultures created by various races and groups of Homo sapiens, such as Cro-Magnon man. The periods are often differentiated by the most minute variations of technique and form and are named usually from the site where the first find was made.

ually a few blows against a flint or obsidian "core" could be so calculated that a handful of blades, arrowheads, spear points, or scrapers could be flaked off.

Paleolithic man also learned to control and use fire. He must have been familiar with forest and prairie fires before he himself generated flame, first for warmth and protection against predatory animals and then to cook otherwise indigestible foods. Gradually he also learned to use fire to fell trees, to shape wood, and to sharpen and harden wood points. The fossil bones of Peking man (dating back more than 500,000 years) were found by the ashes of a fire; indeed, the evidence suggests that he may have been a cannibal and used his fire to cook his fellow Peking men.

The Paleolithic Age: Social and Intellectual Context[6]

The prehistoric hunters traveled in small groups of related families, limited by the scarcity of food to about fifty or sixty persons. Although these groups may have been connected in certain ways, the social universe of the individual was largely confined to his own little band, every member of which contributed to the survival of all. When the hunt was successful, the meat was shared and gorged in gluttonous haste; when it failed, all suffered.

The development of new ideas or techniques in such small and culturally homogeneous groups was extremely slow, and the inflexible demands of survival provided little stimulus to innovation. Nevertheless, Paleolithic technology gradually became sufficiently complex to call for the development of artisan "skills." The discovery of stone chips, broken or imperfect blades, and discarded cores and hammer stones littering the ground at many places where flint or similar material was available indicates that "factory" sites or "flaking" floors were established comparatively early. There is evidence that flint and obsidian were traded over considerable distances, and the ancient "arrow makers" may have played some role in this first anticipation of commerce.

Since most of the activities of each member of the primitive group were specified by tradition and necessity, few occasions requiring arbitrary leadership arose. But direction was needed at times, above all in the im-

6. Many of the conclusions presented in this section are based upon analogy with what is known about present-day primitive peoples, since fossil bones, tools, and weapons, and a few specimens of prehistoric art provide the only direct evidence of life in the Paleolithic Age. This method clearly must be used cautiously, but it does provide a general picture, probably true in its large outlines, of the life of prehistoric man.

portant business of hunting the great herd animals—mammoth, bison, musk-ox, and reindeer. Individual hunters, armed with the poor weapons available to them, would have been unable to kill enough game to keep the group alive, but the animals could be trapped in skillfully concealed pits toward which they were maneuvered, or could be stampeded over cliffs. The discipline and direction obviously called for in such cooperative hunting was probably provided by the oldest male in the group, who acted as chief on the model of the father as head of the family.

Since religion was one of the most important and all-pervasive aspects of primitive life, the *shaman* (the religious practitioner—priest, witch doctor, or medicine man) was one of the prominent figures in the Paleolithic band. Serving as the link between the ordinary individual and the fearful host of spirits that crowded in upon his world, the shaman was probably almost as terrifying to his fellows as the spirits with which he dealt. It is likely that the usual shaman possessed intense psychic powers: indeed, he was probably able to induce seizures and states of self-hypnosis, during which his soul was thought to have departed on journeys to the supernatural world.

The shaman's two important functions—tending the sick and charming game—grew out of the whole complex of interest, fear, superstition, and faulty understanding of causation that were the basis of primitive religion. His "objective" knowledge of physical symptoms and healing herbs, perhaps even of crude surgery, was mixed with his command of magic, spells, and charms, which could help the hunter as well as heal the sick. His supposed ability to control the spirits of buffalo or reindeer forced the herds into the range of the hunter's weapons and guided the spears and arrows to their marks. Indeed, the shaman's dances, chants, and rattles were considered fully as important as the hunter's skill in assuring food supplies.

The Religious Experience of Paleolithic Man

Traces of religion can be found as far back as we can see into the prehistory of man. The primitive made no clear distinction between the natural and the supernatural, and his religious practices were invariably related to his attempts to gain some measure of control over the vast number of events and forces he could not explain. The fire that burned nightly in his camp or at the entrance to his cave had the perfectly natural function of keeping preying animals at bay, but it also provided a light by which malevolent, prowling spirits could be seen. Though the hunter used every natural skill in stalking and killing game, he believed the amulet around his neck and the mysterious markings on his spear or throwing stick to be fully as responsible for his success as his own intelligence. Without understanding the mystery of conception and birth, primitive man knew that the survival of his band depended upon the fertility of its women, which he tried to assure by magical means; excavated small figurines from many levels of the Upper Paleolithic cultures are obviously female effigies, faceless and globular, coarsely carved, and the exaggeration of their sexual parts indicates that they were connected in some way with fertility magic.

As mysterious as conception and birth must have been to primitive man, he must have stood in even greater awe of death. In Neanderthal and Cro-Magnon burial sites the bodies may have been painted with red ochre and other earth colors to simulate the "color of life." Indications that head-hunting and cannibalism were practiced have also been found in several levels of prehistory, but both these practices may have been death rather than burial rituals (as they tend to be among modern primitives) intended to transfer strength or vitality from one individual to another.

Since the life of the Paleolithic hunter was circumscribed by fear and hunger, and he was too preoccupied with basic necessities to take pleasure in purely aesthetic or academic pastimes, most, if not all, prehistoric art is clearly religious. The association of the many fertility figures with a type of "Venus" goddess is clear, as are the religious meanings of the decorations on bone and horn weapons—largely scratchings of game animals. Prehistoric savages, like present-day primitives, may have painted, scarred, or tattooed their bodies, combining their sense of magic with a desire for adornment.

By far the most impressive and mysterious art works of prehistoric man are the Cro-Magnon paintings found high on the walls and ceilings in the dark rear chambers of cave galleries at such sites as Altamira in northern Spain and the Dordogne valley in France. Created in natural earth colors mixed with water or animal fat, these well and carefully executed paintings, like the more modest carvings on weapons and tools, almost exclusively portray game animals. They must represent a long development of artistic technique and are perhaps the work of tribal shamans. Whatever aesthetic motivation may have been present, their chief purpose appears to have been to involve religiously the likeness of an animal with the animal itself, thereby facilitating the kill.

THE AGRICULTURAL REVOLUTION

Hunter into Farmer

The most decisive revolution in prehistory was undoubtedly the development of agriculture. It ushered man into a new culture period, known as the "neolithic" (new stone) age because of its characteristic technology. Primitive and uncertain as early agriculture must have been, its results were still more predictable than those of even the most skillful hunting, and the new technology was itself determined by the new mode of life that agriculture demanded.

Well before 7500 B.C. bands of blade-carrying hunters in the Iranian highlands of southwest Asia began to supplement their diet from the abundant seed-bearing grasses of that region. As they came to rely more on reaping than on hunting, their weapons were gradually modified into crude agricultural implements. More significantly, the causal connection between planting and reaping was established after it had been observed —probably by the women who tended camp and gathered berries, nuts, roots, and wild seeds—that the wind "sowed" the seeds from which the grain sprouted.

After agriculture had freed man from the need to keep on the move, his camp gradually became a village and the wanderer settled into the role of town-dweller. The earliest traces of settled village life have been found in southwest Asia on the fringes of the Fertile Crescent, at sites in modern Iraq, and in Palestine at ancient Jericho. The remains of the Iraqui finds can be dated about 5000 B.C. and those of Palestine two to three thousand years earlier.[7] At first rock ledges or caves probably con-

7. This date was fixed by one of the new methods of scientific dating, in this instance, the now rather widely known and accepted radiocarbon technique. The technique depends upon the constant rate of deterioration of a radioactive element known as carbon 14. This can be measured and, since its "lifespan" is known, the amount that is found in any specimen containing organic material often provides an astonishingly accurate figure for its age. There is, however, a time limit of about 50,000 years to the carbon 14 method. A newer method has been developed, the so-called potassium-argon technique. Again, this is based upon a slow but constant rate of atomic change, but in this case the "lifespan" of the elements involved is much longer. It was this technique which established the date of Zinjanthropus remains in Kenya. Other techniques are being developed; one such depends upon the standard declination of the earth's magnetism and has been tested on baked clay remains. Another depends upon the microscopic amounts of water and certain exotic chemical elements trapped in ancient salt deposits. Such techniques are, of course, extremely useful to archaeologists, anthropologists, paleontologists, and historians who work in very early periods for which reliable dates are almost nonexistent.

Top: Rectangular House of the Neolithic period at Knockadoon, Lough Gur, Ireland.
Above: Paleolithic Cave Paintings. c. 30,000—10,000 B.C. Lascaux.

Above: The Stones of Stenness, England, built by Prehistoric Man.
Below: Skulls of Prehistoric Man. Left to right: Pithecanthropus, Neanderthal, Cro-Magnon.

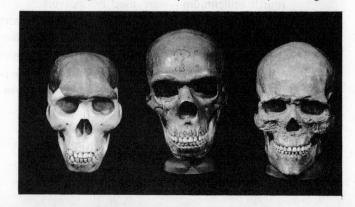

tinued to shelter the transitional farmer, as they had the hunter. Where no natural shelter existed, mud and wattle huts were clustered together, with a mud or bramble wall probably encircling the village to ward off marauding animals.

Outside the village lay the fields that provided the new staple of man's diet. Largely primitive forms of barley, millet, and wheat were ground or crushed and cooked into a gruel and, later, cooked on hot stones into thin cakes of unleavened bread. Hunting and fishing continued to be the important sources of meat, but eventually man learned to domesticate animals. Thus he guaranteed the regularity of his supply of meat and, even more important, turned the animals' milk into an endless variety of cheeses. Neolithic man also learned to ferment grain and at an early time produced one of the most universal of beverages, beer.

The Urban Revolution: Technology

The basic technological shift from Paleolithic chipping and flaking techniques to grinding and polishing, which marked the coming of the Neolithic Age, actually resulted from the far more fundamental change implied by agriculture and settled village life. Only after survival had become somewhat easier, after man had been freed from the limited and impoverished life of the hunter, could the laborious Neolithic technology develop. Since farming demanded new and different kinds of tools, the adz, the ax, the sickle, and the hoe were added to the hunter's blade. Thus the basic Neolithic technology was a function of what has been well called "the Neolithic urban revolution."

Similarly, once hunting had ceased to be man's primary activity, the animal skins from which Paleolithic man had made his clothing became less abundant, and new techniques of cloth weaving were developed to meet the different clothing needs of the farmer. The old techniques of knotting fish nets and snares from vegetable fibers were gradually refined and transformed until the simple loom was invented and became part of Neolithic technology. Eventually a great variety of vegetable and animal fibers—including flax, which was grown in Egypt at least as early as the fourth millennium—were used by weavers.

The invention of pottery also was almost certainly a response to the new demands of agricultural life. The Paleolithic hunter had roasted his meat over a fire and had probably eaten it only half-cooked. His vegetable foods were eaten raw or pounded into a paste and cooked in the ashes of the fire. He heated water by placing it in a skin or bark bag into which he dropped hot stones. This "cooking" bag may have been strengthened or waterproofed with mud or clay, but the molding and firing of pottery were not developed until the village dweller discovered that vegetables, especially grains, were most easily prepared by boiling. At first the split gourd, the egg shell, and other forms of natural containers were imitated, but gradually the cooking pot, the flat dish for curd-cheese making, and the large vessel for the storage of grain were developed, along with many other pottery forms.

Only a settled, sedentary life could allow such fragile and cumbersome equipment as pottery vessels or such an unwieldy implement as a loom to become part of man's cultural equipment. As each technological advance suggested another, new needs multiplied the demands on human ingenuity, and the expanding skills of the artisan were passed on from father to son in the relative permanence of village life.

The Urban Revolution: Its Social and Intellectual Consequences

Neolithic man's social forms and modes of thought were also altered by his new conditions of life. Tradition, a sense of history, and myth began to provide continuity and to embody values to be passed on to each generation. Customary, time-proven modes of behavior became the raw materials of law and social order.

Religious practices, which earlier had focused upon the animals that were the hunter's prey, now came to bear upon the farmer's crops and fields. Sexual rites were based on the identification of the cycle of vegetation with the cycle of man's life and on the obvious relationship between the fertility of woman and that of the earth. Though the magnificently expressive religious art of the Paleolithic Age had no counterpart in the Neolithic village—perhaps the need for such representation had gone—figurines of the "mother goddess" type have been found in the earliest village sites excavated. As the primitive shaman became the priest of the vegetation cult, his supernatural skills were put to the new work of coercing the yield of the fields in order to sustain life. Vestiges of the deities he called upon have exerted a potent influence upon all subsequent religion.

Neolithic man also became, for the first time, economic man in the modern sense. Problems of ownership, distribution, expansion—and greed—were created by the agricultural revolution, which brought about a new social order. Land, which to the hunter had been simply the area over which he and his game passed, gradually took on intrinsic value. Though at first many of the processes of agriculture remained communal, requiring the cooperation of the entire village in clearing the land, seeding, and harvesting, the development of the notion that a certain piece of land "belonged" in some way to those who cared for it was inevitable. The owners of the more productive fields seemed more able or more favored than their less lucky fellows.

Family units held together by economic as well as by biological ties gradually became the nuclei of political organization based upon blood relationship. In a squalid village of the Neolithic peasant the "state" came into existence for the first time; its outlines had been implicit in the Paleolithic hunting band, but the organizational imperatives of agricultural society called it into its full and complex form. Clan families served as units of power, and decisions were made by a council of family elders. The laws that represented the traditions of the group were protected by the sturdy sons of the village peasants. While most matters fell easily within the scope of village-clan-tribal-family tradition, in many areas final arbitration, judgment, and decision were required, and the halting intermittent leadership of the earlier hunting chief took on more permanent form as the headman or chief of each village was empowered to make "executive" decisions of a primitive sort. Frequently he must have been one of the council, and he may often have been only a figurehead, though his office may well have had supernatural sanction.

Cain and Abel

Paleolithic man, precariously balanced between subsistence and starvation, had been the most widely dispersed but also one of the rarest of animals. After agriculture brought about an abundance of food, the human population began to swell, and waves of people went out from the original village centers of southwest Asia. Taking their techniques with them, they overwhelmed and absorbed their less advanced neighbors until population began to outstrip productivity. Land was soon overcrowded and quickly exhausted by the crude and wasteful methods of primitive agriculture, as Neolithic culture spread into the steppe lands of Eurasia, the wooded Danube valley and the north of Europe, the Near East and North Africa.

As Neolithic man pressed into every corner of the earth—traveling the land bridges and island chains and taking to the sea in crude boats and rafts, until he made his culture nearly universal—war came into existence. The more primitive hunting bands, while dangerous and efficient, had been too small to be an effective army and, more importantly, had found

THE CRADLE OF AGRICULTURE

250 MILES

BLACK SEA

LAKE URMI

LAKE URMIR

ARAXES

CASPIAN SEA

MESOPOTAMIA

EUPHRATES

SYRIA

SYRIAN DESERT

Jericho

Jarmo

ZAGROS MTS.

IRANIAN HIGHLANDS

SUMER

PERSIAN GULF

ARABIA

MEDIT. SEA

500 MILES

NORTH SEA

ATLANTIC OCEAN

IBERIA

ELBE

VISTULA

CENTRAL EUROPE

ITALY

BALKANS

DANUBE

BLACK SEA

ASIA

CASPIAN SEA

IRAN

APPROXIMATE ROUTE OF MIGRATIONS OF PEOPLES & TECHNIQUES

MEDITERRANEAN SEA

AFRICA

PALESTINE

SYRIAN DESERT

SEA

FERTILE CRESCENT

PERSIAN GULF

ARABIA

LIBYAN DESERT

NILE

EGYPT

TRM

NEOLITHIC URBAN REVOLUTION
10 000 - 4 000 B.C.

little or nothing to fight over. Furthermore, Paleolithic man was probably not especially warlike by nature; even today the few true nature people who have survived the ravages of civilization are normally as peaceful as they are simple. But the large bands of Neolithic conquerors seized the lands they invaded and were driven into conflict with one another by necessity. The demands of war stabilized and strengthened the primitive state that had been brought into existence by the complexities of settled life; leadership became more constant and authoritative as defense against invasion became necessary.

The extensive domestication of animals was almost certainly another consequence of settled agricultural life. The Paleolithic hunter could not remain settled long enough to tame and provide pens and enclosures for any animals except the dog, who was his constant companion, and he was unwilling to impede his movements with the encumbrance of a herd. Animal husbandry probably began in the long period of transition to full-time agriculture, and the Neolithic villager gradually domesticated the pig, the sheep, the goat, and the cow, as well as a few animals that have since reverted to a wild state.

As hordes of people poured out from the original agricultural centers into the surrounding lands, migrants, in regions where local conditions made agriculture unrewarding or impossible, turned increasingly to their flocks and herds. Thus the animal economy became a dominant pattern of life in the steppe lands of Eurasia, where the prairie turf and heavy clay could not be turned with the crude plow that had been adequate for the light soils of lands farther to the south, and in such dry areas as North Africa and the more arid parts of western Asia.

The separation of animal husbandry from the actual tillage of the soil, which had developed in parallel lines for many centuries, resulted in a shift in cultural values that was one of the most significant forces in the history of the world. Time and again the hungry and warlike descendants of nomadic herdsmen descended upon the ancient urban centers, destroying, modifying, and assuming the forms of civilization that had already been achieved. This hard pattern of pastoral life produced the Tartar-Mongols of Genghis Khan; the Bedouin followers of Mohammed; the Huns; the Magyars; and even the earliest ancestors of the Greeks, the Romans, and the Hebrews.

SUGGESTIONS FOR FURTHER READING

*Ruth Benedict, *Patterns of Culture* (New York: Mentor, 2) a classic study of anthropology.

M. Boule and Henri V. Vallois, *Fossil Men*, tr. by Michael Bullock (New York: Dryden Press, 1957), detailed and authoritative account of the ancient primitives.

R. J. Braidwood, *Prehistoric Men* (Chicago: Chicago Natural History Museum Popular Series, 1948), Anthropology, No. 37.

V. Gordon Childe, *The Dawn of European Civilization* (New York: Knopf, 1948).

*————, Man Makes Himself (New York: Oxford University Press, 1939), an exciting and readable classic of cultural anthropology and prehistoric archaeology.

————, Prehistoric Migrations in Europe (Oslo: H. Aschehough, 1950).

*J. D. Clark, *Prehistory in Southern Africa* (Baltimore: Penguin, 1959).

*W. E. LeGros Clark, *History of the Primates* (Chicago: Phoenix, 1959), readable survey, stressing the relationship of early man to his prehuman antecedents.

Carlton S. Coon, *The Origin of Races* (New York: Knopf, 1963), a modern revival of the thesis that suggests a separate evolutionary line for the races of man, as opposed to the more generally accepted diffusion theory.

*Raymond Firth, *Human Types* (New York: Mentor, 1958), a standard work on the matters of race and the bases of human differences.

W. W. Howells, *Back of History* (Garden City, N. Y.: Doubleday, 1954), a standard work by one of America's most distinguished scholars.

*H. Kuhn, *On the Track of Prehistoric Man* (New York: Modern Library, 1955).

*L. S. B. Leaky, *Adam's Ancestors* (New York: Harper, 1960).

Ralph Linton, *The Tree of Culture* (New York: Knopf, 1955), a brilliant and provocative summary work bridging anthropology, archeology, and early history.

Robert H. Lowie, *Primitive Religion* (New York: Grosset and Dunlap, 1952).

*Bronislaw Malinowski, *Magic, Science and Religion* (New York: Anchor, 1954).

————, *A Scientific Theory of Culture and Other Essays* (Chapel Hill: University of North Carolina Press, 1949), a basic book by one of the pioneers of modern cultural anthropology.

Margaret Mead, *Male and Female* (New York: Morrow, 1949).

A. Montagu, *An Introduction to Physical Anthropology* (Springfield, Charles C. Thomas, 1951).

*————, *Man: His First Million Years* (New York: Mentor, 1957).

*Kenneth P. Oakley, *Man the Tool-Maker* (Chicago: Phoenix, 1957).

Paul Radin, *The World of Primitive Man* (New York: Abelard- Schuman, 1953).

Robert Redfield, *The Primitive World and Its Transformations* (Ithaca: Cornell University Press, 1953), the application of the findings on modern primitive peoples to the study of prehistoric man.

*G. G. Simpson, *The Meaning of Evolution* (New York: Mentor, 1956), a popular and authoritative summary of the evidence of evolution and the human species.

Charles Singer, E. J. Holmyard, and A. R. Hall, eds. *A History of Technology* (Oxford: Clarendon Press, 1956), a massive multivolume work of multiple authorship, each article written by a recognized authority; Vol. I, is especially good on the prehistoric subcultures and their technologies.

*Paperbound edition. In the case of reprint editions, publisher and date of publication given will be that of reprint rather than the original.

❧ 2 ❧

The Cradles of Civilization

THE LAND BETWEEN THE RIVERS

The Challenge of Environment

About 7000 B.C. southwest Asia felt the effects of a long, slow cycle of climatic change which eventually extended a desert belt across the Middle East into central Asia, and across North Africa to the Atlantic coast. The drying up of the highland areas as well as the pressure of growing population and the exhaustion of arable land, forced Neolithic farmers to seek fertile land elsewhere. Some made their way to Mesopotamia, settling in the alluvial plain between the Tigris and Euphrates rivers, in the land they called Sumer.[1]

The villagers cleared the riverine jungle, drained the marshes, and, above all, learned to control and direct the rivers, which would flood suddenly and violently. This last called for the highly organized cooperation of many villages, which pooled their strength under the central authority of a "superchief," who rapidly became a full-fledged monarch.

1. These early people are simply called Sumerians, from the name they themselves gave to their place of settlement. The Proto-Sumerians can be traced by pottery remains from the highlands of Turkestan in slow stages through the sixth and fifth millennia. In spite of all we know about them, they remain mysterious in many ways. Their physical type, so well displayed in their art, is generally like that of any number of Neolithic peoples of western Asia but is specifically unlike that of any historic people in that area. Their language is not related to any other known language.

20

The Sumerian monarchy was not only a political but also a religious authority. By the early fourth millennium there was established what was to remain for thousands of years a characteristic form of political organization: a cluster of cooperating villages that became a city-state governed by a priest-king.

The origins of the city-state dynasties are obscure, but there were kings in Sumer from the earliest recorded times. The king ruled and protected the state, upheld the law, punished transgressors, and led his citizen armies. But beyond this the king stood at the pinnacle of the structure of authority. The extent of Mesopotamian royal power is dramatically illustrated in the remains of the royal graves of the city of Ur in the twenty-sixth and twenty-fifth centuries B.C. A tomb might contain as many as seventy persons—courtiers, ladies-in-waiting dressed in their finest clothes and jewels, musicians with their instruments, a guard of soldiers with their wagon-chariots, mules, and oxen—all sacrificed to honor the dead king.

As earlier villages had merged into city-states on the alluvial plain, so city-states—such as Lagash, Kish, Erech and Ur—merged with one another, their ambitions unimpeded by natural geographic frontiers as the weaker capitulated to the stronger and the units of political power grew larger. But at no point did a single political authority embrace all the Sumerian cities.

About 3500 B.C. a flood swept over Mesopotamia, so devastating that it found a place in the folklore of many Near East peoples.[2] The survivors thrived, however, and by the late fourth millennium a handful of Sumerian city-states held sway from the Persian Gulf to the river narrows. The greatest of these was Ur; the early history of Sumer is sometimes reckoned in terms of its dynasties. There developed among the city-states a remarkably homogeneous culture.

The Cosmos and the Image of Society

All phases of Sumerian life—political, economic, and religious—were closely centered around the priest-king, whose authority was all-pervasive.

---

2. Flooding was more usual than unusual in Mesopotamia, and much of Sumerian canal building, earth moving, and hydraulic engineering was concerned with flood control. The Tigris in particular was a savage river, and the whole river system was highly responsive to excessive snow in the mountains, heavy rains in the back country, or a sudden thaw. The flood plain of Mesopotamia was relatively narrow, and the Sumerian cities had no high ground to protect them. Geologists have read the flood record in the soil levels, and their findings confirm both the severity and the approximate date of the "Great Flood."

Deference to authority became a prime value in Sumerian society; it was even identified with virtue.

To the Sumerian, as to all men, the rhythms of nature were reassuring: vegetation returned to life in season; the sun took its accustomed daily course across the sky; the stars and planets made a familiar map of the heavens. But these regularities were upset by unpredictable floods that swept away his dikes, destroyed his canals, inundated his cities; and burning wind and drought spoiled his fields. Indeed, nature was capricious and mysterious to him, and he felt insignificant in the face of it. He saw worldly phenomena, not as a complex of things, but as a complex of beings. The animism of the savage had developed into polytheism (the belief in many gods). The Sumerian conceived his gods in terms of the social order in which he himself lived; thus the cosmos was a gigantic mirror of his own state. As he was subservient to his king, so was his king subservient to the gods. The hierarchy of creation extended from earthly beings upward; heaven and earth existed together, men and gods sharing a universe composed of the natural and the supernatural.

The Sumerian lived in a theocracy; it was no pious fiction, but a reality of life that the city-god and his cosmic circle literally owned the state. Man's actions and institutions served. not his own ends, but those of the gods:

> "I will form man," says the god Marduk,
> "Let him be burdened with the toil of the gods,
> That they may freely breathe."

In the city-states of Sumer there were two focal points—the palace of the city-king and the temple of the city-god. The king, as the representative of the gods and the warden of the interests of heaven, implemented the will of the gods. He mediated between gods and men, he was the high priest of the god. Below him ranked some thirty categories of lesser priests. The temple was a shrine; the king's palace and the city were the estate of the god. The temples were thus more than centers of worship; they were also economic centers, holding vast tracts of land and employing hosts of officials and thousands of slaves.

The First Master Builders

The temples and palaces of the Sumerians were the earliest structures of their sort, and the people who built them were the founders of the art of architecture. The temple was normally dominated by a great structure, not unlike a mountain, terraced on the sides and graced by a ramp which led upward around the tower, or *ziggurat,* and marked the point of transition between heaven and earth. The walls of the temple were made of clay bricks; some walls were twenty-eight feet thick at the base. The bricks might be glazed and painted, relieving the monotony of the otherwise seemingly endless wall space. The complexity and magnificence of these buildings are difficult to visualize, for time and weather have tumbled them into the now anonymous mounds which still dot the plain of Sumer. Here and there, however, there are remains—the great Arch of Nippur and the Babylonian Gate of Ishtar—more than five thousand years old.

The Invention of Writing

Writing was developed by the Sumerians probably as early as 4000 B.C. In a thousand years it was in wide use. Many people more primitive than the Sumerians had already anticipated writing with pictographs— pictures grouped to convey a meaning or tell a story—but the Sumerians developed "script."

The Sumerians first wrote on tablets made from river-bottom clay. Once its plastic surface had hardened, the record inscribed on it was durable and unalterable. To "draw" on the wet surface, the Sumerians developed the technique of pressing the point of a sharpened stick or reed into the clay; the resulting impressions were wedge-shaped, or *cuneiform*. These impressions could be grouped to indicate different objects and meanings. /

Even this script was probably a relatively late convention, and the early cuneiform inscriptions are obviously stylized pictographs. If a man, for example, owed three oxen to the temple, his record tablet would show his identifying mark (made by a carved cylinder seal which left a distinctive signature impression when rolled across wet clay), a crude picture of an ox, and three marks to indicate number. Such a record would be sealed and notarized by the temple officials. Even with the degree of stylization displayed by the early cuneiform pictographs, the technique was still clumsy and had the limitation of being able to represent only object and quantity, and not such abstract qualities as cold, hot, good, bad, and so forth.

The next important development was the ideograph, in which certain conventional picture symbols came to represent abstractions. Then simple representations became stabilized as phonetic building blocks; that is, the sound was separated from the original meaning of the symbol, and the symbol was used whenever the particular sound needed to be indicated, so that it could stand as a word or as a sound occurring in a longer word. This technique is known as *rebus* writing. Thus, beginning with simple pictures of sensible objects, the Sumerians evolved a system of sound equivalents by which all the syllabic sounds in their language were reduced to a few hundred conventional symbols. Anything that could be said could now be written.

The Sumerian Culture

The Sumerians had a mania for keeping records, and much of the vast volume of surviving clay tablets (many still in their baked clay "envelopes"—stamped, sealed, and unopened) are devoted to the daily transactions of a busy and literal-minded people. But writing was put to other uses as well. The tablets reveal a considerable literature: epics and mythological tales, hymns, religious incantations, rituals, and prayers. Among their other myriad functions, the temples maintained scribes' schools, and thousands of the "exercise books" of their pupils have survived.

The tablets also reveal an extensive use of two separate number systems: a decimal system derived from finger-counting and a second system based upon six and its multiples. The standard tables of reference developed by the Sumerians for their reckonings revealed that they could carry out simple arithmetic operations and work with fractions and square and extract roots; they even conceived of the fundamentals of algebra. They knew the "Pythagorean Theorem" 2000 years before Pythagoras lived and calculated π closely enough to make practical use of it.

These mathematical skills were applied to the creation of the earliest calendar, based on both a lunar and a solar year. The year was subdivided into twelve lunar months of thirty days each, and the solar difference was adjusted by adding special months at periodic intervals. The day was divided into twelve double hours, and the hour into sixty minutes. Since the agricultural cycle was celebrated in a host of magico-religious observances and festivals, an accurate calendar was a most important element in the Sumerian's control of nature.

But many other uses of mathematics developed in response to the needs of an increasingly complex society. Fields and portions had to be divided and allocated accurately; precise and standardized measures of weight, distance, and time were more necessary than ever before. In short, civilization demanded a system of numerical and quantitative records fully as much as it demanded writing.

Though Sumerian legal and medical records reveal that they had trained and knowledgeable physicians, architects, and engineers, their great accumulation of accurate empirical knowledge and useful skills nevertheless ran easily into the magical, the supernatural, and the theological. Indeed, all knowledge was subordinate to theology, since the apprehension of the holy, from which everything else flowed, was the most significant pursuit in Sumerian life. The vault of heaven was regarded as the book of the universe, and astrology was used to discover its record of every event— past, present, or future. Since the learned man who could read the stars enabled the Sumerians to know, anticipate, and thus control the future, he was a highly honored member of society. The future was also divined by such methods as examination of the livers of sacrificial animals which had been dedicated to a particular god. Famous predictions, based on the officiating priest's "reading" of the thoughts of the god that had entered the animal's liver, were kept in the form of metal or clay models and diligently studied for centuries.

The Coming of the Bronze Age

In time the cities of Sumer needed trade and exchange, and they pushed upriver, where they could sell their farm products and the goods of their artisans. Barges and boats crowded the waterways, and overland caravans went upriver to trade for raw materials—stone, wood, and crude metal—with less civilized peoples.

Though the reduction of metallic ore was probably not first achieved in Mesopotamia, the process had a revolutionary impact on Sumerian technology at a very early date. Between 5000 and 4000 B.C. copper became the first metal purposely and systematically smelted and worked by man. We will probably never learn exactly how the process of metal fabrication was discovered, but copper can be reduced by comparatively low temperatures, and a great variety of techniques for handling it quickly developed, reaching their climax in the control of ingredients that produced the highly serviceable alloy of tin and copper called bronze. So general and important was this material that it justifies our speaking of Sumerian culture as the first great Bronze Age civilization.

Quite apart from any uses to which the metal itself could be put, bronze played a most significant part in Sumerian trade, since copper was not readily available in all parts of Europe and southwest Asia. Bronze goods, tools, and especially weapons were shipped out from the urban centers to be traded to the barbarian and semibarbarian world in exchange for the raw ores or ingots of copper from which more goods could be manufactured. This trade allowed the city to develop as an economic unit and, in turn, permitted it to become the primary unit of civilization.

The Semitic Conquest: The Akkadian Empire

Even as the Sumerians extended trade to other areas and brought them under control, they were themselves threatened by hard-pressed peoples from the surrounding marginal lands who were attracted by the wealth and luxury of Mesopotamian civilization. Successive waves of nomads were to descend periodically upon the fertile plain of Sumer for thousands of years.

The first to come were the Akkadians, one of the numerous subgroups of fierce Semitic peoples in the Near East, who had migrated from the deserts of Arabia and settled upriver. As internecine conflicts weakened the Sumerian city-states, the Akkadians grew stronger until they finally completed the conquest of Sumer about 2400-2350 B.C. City after city fell as one of the first great personalities of Near East history, King Sargon I, pushed his conquest through the lower plains to the Persian Gulf. Having subdued the world, as he himself put it, "from the upper to the lower sea"—that is, from what is now Iran to perhaps even as far as the islands off the coast of Asia Minor—he founded the first of the great territorial states of the Ancient Near East.

Sargon ruled from his capital of Akkad, which, keeping pace with his conquests, had grown in magnificence. It is surely ironic that we do not know the exact location of the capital city, though it has been established that the heart of the Akkadian Empire was on the fertile lower plain where ancient Sumer had been established.

The Akkadians were forced by necessity to maintain the water-control system that had been established by the Sumerians, and they adopted Sumerian techniques of rule and civilization. They learned to express their Semitic language in cuneiform script and extended the principle of sacred kingship throughout the entire empire. Thus, Sumerian civilization became the basic subculture of the Akkadians, as it would be that of every other people who conquered Mesopotamia.

"Babylon, the Glory of Kingdoms"

As the Akkadian Empire grew older, still another barbarian people, the Amorites, who for centuries had lived in scattered tribes on the Syrian frontier, prepared to inherit the riches of Mesopotamia. About 2000 B.C.

they pressed south and east, and in the area of the upper valley where the Tigris and the Euphrates flowed toward each other they established a strong point at the insignificant mud village they named Babylon. By 1900 B.C. they had conquered all of Mesopotamia and had transformed the Akkadian Empire into Babylonia.

The city of Babylon, the greatest that Mesopotamia was ever to know and the most fabulous center of art and culture in the Ancient Near East, was dominated by its temple ziggurat. Rising two hundred feet into the air from a gigantic base, the tower was faced with glazed brick that glistened in the sun and reflected dappled patterns of the rich, exotic foliage that made a shaded park of each of its stories. It is no wonder that such a structure, which may have been remembered in the biblical Tower of Babel, became for the primitive Hebrews the symbol for the vaunting ambition and arrogance of "sinful Babylon," whose people would challenge God and thrust their man-made mountain into the sanctuary of His Heaven.

Below the tower was the huge, sprawling temple of the Babylonian god Marduk, and beyond it lay the teeming capital city, which was a prototype for every city of the east. Broad avenues contrasted with fetid, crowded alleys, market-place bickering could be heard everywhere, and the scents of offal and perfume floated over all. A sacred avenue lined with one hundred twenty bronze lions ended at the Gate of Ishtar.

The greatness of Babylon is linked with the name of King Hammurabi (*fl. c. 1700* B.C.), who brought peace and order back to Mesopotamia after more than a century of turbulence. He replaced petty local kings with royal governors, and his vast correspondence reveals his painstaking concern with the thousand social and economic details of a complex civilization: taxes, the renting of land, the management of royal estates, the the work of bondsmen in the fields and on the systems of transportation and communications. As new canals tied the Tigris and Euphrates together and extensive irrigation work brought more land under cultivation, the old areas of trade and exploitation were extended; one canal, the greatest in antiquity, was some two hundred miles long and four hundred feet wide.

As Babylonian civilization grew to maturity in the peace and prosperity provided by a powerful empire, the old Sumerian subculture was expanded and enriched. The fame of the astronomers and mathematicians who devised a system of the heavens and a catalogue of the stars was worldwide. As the Babylonians attained international prestige, the cuneiform Sumero-Akkadian writing, which had been adopted by the new empire, became the language of diplomacy as far away as Egypt and Asia Minor, and perhaps even the distant coast of the Greek peninsula. Though the names of the Sumerian gods were changed, the basic mythological tales were retained, for their moral implications gave supernatural sanction to the established order; for the first time the complex fragments of Mesopotamian mythology were organized and reduced to a system that became a political bulwark of the Babylonian Empire.

The most striking achievement of the systematization of Babylonian civilization was the famous uniform code of law proclaimed by Hammurabi as chief priest and earthly agent of the gods. Though it may have been drawn in part from earlier local regulations, the Code of Hammurabi is the earliest recorded attempt to set down the full and complete body of law for a great imperial state. The nearly three hundred paragraphs of its text treat virtually every facet of life—crime and punishment, domestic relations, building codes and standards, military action and obligations, medical practice, court procedures, and much more. If civilization may be said to represent the regularizing of human relations, the Code of Hammurabi is a significant milestone in the history of civilization.

The Code literally stated, as its leading principle, "an eye for an eye." An individual who caused the blinding of another was himself blinded; if a house collapsed and the owner was killed, the architect forfeited his life; a thief who was caught stealing from a burning building was himself burned. The Code frankly assumed social inequality: the fee for a specific eye operation, for example, was ten shekels of silver for a free citizen, five shekels for a subject, and two for a slave. The Code was also paternalistic, setting wages for builders, brick makers, stonemasons, carpenters, tailors, boatmen, ox drivers, herdsmen, shepherds, and so on. Indeed, it reflected the hierarchic nature of the society for which it was designed at every point: the shopowner was responsible for his employees, the husband for his wife, the father for his children, and the master for his slaves.

The series of Babylonian epics that stem from this rich and creative period are also significant intellectual remains of Mesopotamian civilization. Like most epics and folk literature, the basic stories had long been a part of a stock of adventure tales, ancestral histories, and fables that loosely and inconsistently explained the cosmic order. In the age of Hammurabi these tales were re-created as a means of dealing with urgent philosophic questions. The Tale of Ludlul bel nemeqi, a primitive Job story, examines the problems of the righteous sufferer; the Tale of Adapa, "the seed of mankind," is somewhat related to the theme of the biblical

Adam legend; but the greatest of the Babylonian tales—a long, rambling epic of Gilgamesh—focused primarily on the problem of death.

No doctrine of personal immortality had been developed in Mesopotamia. The belief that the soul descended below the earth, where it eked out an unsatisfactory eternity, may have implied an idea of reward for virtue and punishment for vice, but the supreme injustice of death was never overlooked. The Babylonians, like most men, regarded the deprivation of earthly life as the last and greatest evil, but the adventures of the ancient hero Gilgamesh, which had long been part of the Sumerian tradition, provided some explanation and consolation.

THE SUCCESSION OF
POLITICAL POWER IN MESOPOTAMIA

SUMERIANS	*c. 4700* B.C.—*c. 2400* B.C.
AKKADIANS	*c. 2400* B.C.—*c. 2000* B.C.
AMORITES	*c. 2000* B.C.—*c. 1600* B.C.
KASSITES	*c. 1600* B.C.—*c. 1100* B.C.
ASSYRIANS	*c. 1200* B.C.—*605* B.C.
PERSIANS	*550* B.C.—*331* B.C.

Gilgamesh, whose name meant "man of fire and ax," was a strong, brash "man of his hands" who nevertheless also personified wisdom. The episodes in his story had been taken over by each culture that had inherited the riches of Sumer until he had become a symbol of their achievements. As the Promethean figure who had brought and upheld the gifts of civilization, he could be regarded as a personification of the Sumerians themselves.

At the end of the epic of Gilgamesh the hero and his companion, who have succeeded in overcoming all their enemies, are so invincible and proud that they do not hesitate to offend a powerful goddess. After his comrade has been slain by the goddess, Gilgamesh, resolving to seek eternal life, goes in search of the only human ever granted immortality by the gods—a figure analogous to Noah—who tells Gilgamesh about the

Flood. Ordered to stay awake as a condition for gaining his wish, Gilga-mesh is easily overcome by sleep—the twin of death and its symbolic form—and is thus defeated. Then he seeks and acquires at the bottom of the sea a miraculous plant that could renew life. But after a serpent takes the plant from him and eats it, Gilgamesh has to face, with all men, the bitter fact that death is universal and inescapable.

The city of Babylon, which reached its highest peak in the age of Hammurabi, was to remain the center of Mesopotamian civilization for another thousand years. Its achievements gradually became part of the growing legacy of civilized man and were to be passed on to one culture after another up to our own day.

EGYPT, GIFT OF THE NILE

The Step into History

The drying up of the grasslands that had forced the Sumerians into Mesopotamia drove the Egyptians into the valley of the Nile before 5000 B.C. They settled in scattered villages where the reeds and brush that grew beside the narrow, swift stream were least dense and where the soil was most easily reached. On either side and to the south of their green strip of valley lived tribal peoples who seldom threatened them. To the north and east, separating Egypt from Asia, lay another desert gap, which the Egyptians managed either to close or control during most of their long history.

Egypt was, indeed, in the happy phrase of Herodotus, "the gift of the river"; nature had fashioned this land for isolation and for unity. Though with proper husbandry, two, and even three, crops a year might be har-vested, the Nile could bring disaster if its annual flood came too soon or too late, if it were too full or too meager. The river had to be controlled by canals, and only irrigation works could extend the farmland into the bordering desert.

Large-scale authoritarian government was necessary for such elaborate projects in Egypt as in Mesopotamia, and it is probable that a strong family in the narrow, upland section of the river gradually assumed leadership of the village settlements. By about 2850 B.C. this dynastic authority had been pushed to the north into the more thickly settled delta. One of the oldest Egyptian political titles, "king of the two lands," indicates that the ruler controlled both upper and lower Egypt.

The founder of the First Dynasty of the Old Kingdom, Menes, established his capital at Memphis near the junction of the "two lands." By controlling traffic on the Nile, he subdued the settlements that crowded along its banks. Nevertheless, it was only in the Third and Fourth dynasties —nearly four hundred years later—in the middle of the third millennium that a permanently unified state and a common "national" culture appeared.

The Stimulus to Civilization

At the end of the Predynastic period a cluster of basic tools, civilized skills, and ideas appeared along the banks of the Nile. Exactly how they developed we do not know, but there was unquestionably some influence from the already developing civilization of Mesopotamia. Egypt was launched into history with the advent of the cylinder seal and the potter's wheel, advanced techniques of woodworking, metallurgy, and monumental building, definite artistic motifs and identifiable myths, and, above all, writing, the one indispensable tool of true civilization.

Egyptian *hieroglyphics* differ from Mesopotamian writing in that even the earliest of them show no trace of the elementary pictograph. Instead, they were governed by the relatively advanced notion that a standardized picture symbol could stand for a word. The naturalistic hieroglyphics were not stamped or scratched in clay but from the first were precisely carved on stone monuments and, with the stubborn conservatism so characteristic of Egypt, tended to retain their form over the centuries. Even the cursive hieratic script that was later developed by temple scribes for use on papyrus "paper" was simply a "rounded" form of the same picture system.

Many other aspects of Egyptian culture were similarly borrowed from Mesopotamia, but in a remarkably short time foreign institutions as such had disappeared. By the time the political strife of the early dynasties had ended, such formative influences had been completely assimilated into a fundamentally Egyptian culture that was to last for thousands of years.

Pharaoh: Man—King—God

The civilization of Egypt, which reached its fullness in the first few dynasties of the Old Kingdom, was remarkably homogeneous. As in Sumer, an essentially hierarchial structure of power developed in response to the need for a highly organized agricultural system. But, whereas in Sumer and all subsequent civilizations of Mesopotamia the king had served as the warden of a city-god, the Egyptian rulers were themselves understood to be gods. The divinity of the Pharaoh, which was established in the early dynasties, transformed the Egyptians into a people "of the god" and thus set them apart from other cultures.

All Egyptian law, in its broadest principles and most petty details, stemmed from the king-god, who not only ruled but *was* the state. Since the Pharaoh's commands had to be unquestionably obeyed, there was no need for an explicit code of law like that of Hammurabi. At times the Pharaoh consulted with his fellow gods by means of oracles, dreams, and portents, and sometimes he amazed even them by the wisdom with which he demonstrated *ma'at,* "right ways."

Unity, Death, and Eternity: The Shaping of Egyptian Civilization

The Egyptian, secure in his "God-chosen" land, regarded his universe as determined by divine plan. The Nile might be too low or too high, a few days late or early in flooding, but every July the river began to rise in the lower valley. At first its water was green with the scum of jungle growth carried from far upstream, but about two weeks later it took on a reddish color as its load of silt began to appear. This "Blood of Osiris"—evidence of the god's sacrifice from which the new life of the coming year would spring—spread out over the land. It was held in basins by dams and dikes and allowed to flow through intricate artificial waterways, depositing as much soil as possible over the greatest distance. By the end of October it had returned to its banks, and the Egyptian could sow his seeds in the warm mud. The rich crops were ready for harvest in mid-April or May, and by the end of May or June the riverbed was again a cracked and parched plain, watered only by a shrunken stream. The regularity of this cycle, like that of the sun which ran its daily course in the copper sky with barely a cloud to shadow it, was assurance that the world was a good and right place.

These natural regularities shaped the two basic religious systems that stretch back into the earliest period of Egyptian prehistory. In one the sun-god Ra—who, as the creator-god, was known in many forms and worshiped in many sacred animals such as the hawk, the ram, and the bull—was peculiarly the god of the king, who was regarded as his son. In the other system the god Isis, the great and mysterious principle of fertility, was the wife-sister of Osiris, the Nile. The myth that after Osiris had been killed by Set, the god of darkness and evil, Isis restored him to life with the help of the other good gods was re-enacted each year in the cycle of the life-giving river.

The catalogue of Egyptian gods, including many who were in no way involved in the two principal systems of belief, is almost inexhaustible. Indeed, the ancients regarded the Egyptians as the most religious of all people. Gods manifested themselves in human, animal, and mixed forms, and they governed every act and virtually every thought. But, in the long run, the most conspicuous feature of Egyptian religion was the doctrine of personal immortality, which was clearly influenced by the recurring rhythms of nature and was closely associated with the concept of the divinity of the king. The awe-inspiring monuments that are the very symbol of Egypt, the pyramids, were tombs intended to insure that the king could rejoin eternity in proper royal style.

The earliest Egyptian monumental structures were built of the mud bricks typical of Mesopotamia, and with borrowed Mesopotamian technical skills; but by the third dynasty stone was being used. The great solid mass of rock cliffs on either side of the Nile seemed to present a veritable plan of nature to the Egyptians. The Step Pyramid at Saqqara of the Third-Dynasty king, Zoser (*fl.c. 2700* B.C.) is the first great stone monument in the world. Only fifty years later in the Fourth Dynasty—at a still early stage of Egyptian history—architectural, engineering, and artistic skills had developed to such a degree that the pyramids of Giza could be conceived, built, and decorated. These pyramids required an immense amount of labor during the fourth dynasty (*2650–2500* B.C.). For example, one hundred thousand men worked for nearly twenty-five years on the Tomb of Khufu, which is now known as the Great Pyramid. But the precision of their construction is perhaps even more striking than the brute force of their labor: this huge structure, whose base deviates from true plane by only .004 per cent, has stood with its companions for thousands of years, though the workmen did not even have the advantage of the wheel. Structural blocks, some weighing as much as one hundred fifty tons, were dragged into place on earthen ramps, carefully engineered and sloped, and then "floated" together on a slime of mortar which, when dried, helped to cement them into place.

The white and glistening surface of the pyramid was carved and painted, and the tomb was surrounded by temples and statuary. Within it were placed all the furniture, trappings, and food necessary to mirror eternally the image of life on earth. There is even evidence that servants and retainers sacrificed themselves in early dynastic tombs, as in Mesopotamia, so that they might continue to serve the king.

Since the Egyptians believed that, upon burial with the proper rites, the body was reunited with the soul, and that both were then immortalized, they developed the curious and elaborate art of embalming. Every phase of mummification was controlled by magico-religious sanctions and was accompanied by the reading of a sacred text; the chief embalmer carried high priestly rank. Egyptian embalming was essentially a process of dehydration in which the body was eviscerated, prepared, and then slowly dried, possibly by salting or even over a slow fire, traditionally for seventy days but sometimes for nearly a year.

During the earliest periods of Egyptian history only kings were granted the hope of immortality. As gods, they were simply translated into another sphere, where their fellow divinities received them in a manner related by the pyramid texts:

> This is my son, my first born . . .
> This is my beloved with whom I have been satisfied.
>
> .   .   .
>
> He lives, king of Upper and Lower Egypt,
> beloved of Re, living forever.
>
> .   .   .
>
> Thou hast come into being, thou hast
> become high, thou hast become content![3]

The mass burials during early dynasties may possibly attest to the belief that immortality could be gained by others through continued association with the king in death, but it was not until considerably later that the privilege came within the grasp of the ordinary Egyptian: whoever could then afford the services of the embalmers availed himself of them.

Though the fact that much more is known about the Egyptian dead than alive may seem paradoxical, the decoration of the tombs and mortuary temples is evidence of his belief that life and death were inevitably wedded. The fascinatingly detailed paintings and carvings mirror every phase of life —its trades and occupations, its tools, its vegetation, its beliefs, and its frivolities. Despite the limitations of time, distance, and records, a complete reconstruction of the Egyptian way of life is available to modern man.

As the age of the pyramids passed—whether for economic reasons or because of some subtle reorientation of religious beliefs—the massiveness of the tombs was carried over to the temples and palace-temple complexes which reached their height during the Empire (1500–800 B.C.). The temples still standing at Luxor and Karnak, both sacred to Amen (one of the forms of the sun-god), were clearly designed to impress and overawe

3. Eric Voegelin, in *Israel and Revelation,* Vol. I of *Order and History* (Baton Rouge: Louisiana State University Press, 1956), p. 75.

and thus to symbolize the eternity and power of the state in its gods and kings. Such temples were constructed, like most Egyptian buildings, on the extremely simple principle of the post and lintel, two uprights supporting a capstone. The equally simple ground plan, a series of long rectangles, gave full scope to the architect's sense of space and size. The temple at Karnak is thirteen hundred feet long and some of its columns are seventy feet high and twenty feet in diameter. The statues decorating the various temples—sometimes as many as two hundred separate pieces—were equally colossal. At the entrance to the rock-cut temple of Ramses II at Abu-Simbel, for example, the seated statues of that ambitious king are almost seventy feet tall. But size and monumentality were always subordinated to the Egyptian sense of style: the orderly forest of columns, the rigid poses of statuary, the repetition and multiplication of forms, all contribute to a geometrically ordered whole that suggests sublimity and eternity.

As might be expected, Egyptian literature consists primarily of religious writings, usually more magical than spiritual. Lyrics and short stories were written, and several collections of homely maxims have been found, but even these seem labored and heavy-handed. Throughout every period of Egyptian history literature aimed principally at sententiousness—in which it succeeded with tedious frequency—and reflected very little of everyday life. Even the handsome hieroglyphic inscriptions seem largely to symbolize bare and prosaic formulas.

Egyptian Society

Since Egypt's geography securely isolated the entire country from outside interference, its civilization was not concentrated in small city-units resembling those centers of protection that had grown up in Mesopotamia. The dense village settlements which had developed in Predynastic times served throughout Egyptian history as the basis for its entire culture. The lives of the farmers who kept the land under intense and almost constant cultivation remained unchanged from generation to generation. The essence of that life, patient and unremitting labor, was determined by nature rather than by culture or government, and the king and his court were separated from the vast, anonymous, recordless mass of agricultural laborers by a difference, not of degree, but of kind.

The palaces and gardens of the court, the homes of the nobility, and the temples were first centered at Memphis and later at Thebes. Since Egypt was a sacred state, the temples were an important factor in every phase of existence in these centers of political and religious administration. In fact, temple cults and priestly groups controlled more of the social, economic, and political life than they had even in Mesopotamia. The temples owned vast tracts of land and represented the greatest concentration of wealth in Egyptian society; in the later Empire, for example, one person in every ten and one acre in every eight were the property of the temples, the sun-god Amen alone owning more than 400,000 cattle, which were tended by 971 herdsmen who also belonged to him.

In such a society no clear distinction could be made between the sacred and the secular. The colleges of priests blended with the high nobility to form, immediately below the Pharaoh, a privileged order of great power and importance. It is the members of this group who are pictured and represented in Egyptian art; they, and not the peasantry who worked the fields, were thought to constitute the true Egyptian population. Living easy, comfortable lives, these wealthy and sophisticated individuals were handsome and proud of their physiques. They considered slimness a virtue to be courted diligently: "Most of what we eat is superfluous. Hence we live off only a quarter of all we swallow: doctors live off the other three quarters."[4]

Within this religious framework, a rich and varied culture was centered upon the operations of the temples: the word *Hieroglyphic* ("sacred carving") itself indicates that writing was the work of the temple scribes. Early empirical mathematical, engineering, and architectural skills were necessary for the construction of the impressive monuments, and Egyptian physicians were justly famous for their skill and knowledge.

The labor force of craftsmen was carefully divided into specialists in the various arts and trades. Egyptian metal goods, glass, and jewelry were widely sought in the Near East as well as ivory, gold, slaves, and other goods of the African hinterland.

The Sequence of Egyptian History

In the twenty-second century B.C. disturbances in the deserts that served as the trade route to Asia and challenges to the god-king by many ambitious nobles and by the rich and powerful priesthood of Ra brought an end to the Old Kingdom, which had created the unity of Egyptian culture and political life. Not much is known of this "time of troubles," but it is apparent that the kings were weak and insecure. (An exaggerated

4. Quoted in Lissner, *The Living Past* (New York: Putnam, 1957), p. 79.

tradition states that the Seventh and Eighth dynasties consisted of seventy kings in seventy days.) By 2050 B.C. stability had returned, and a new King of the Two Lands was established as the period known as the Middle Kingdom began.

OUTLINE OF EGYPTIAN DYNASTIC HISTORY

PREDYNASTIC PERIOD
c. 5000 B.C.—*c. 2850* B.C.

OLD KINGDOM
c. 2850 B.C.—*c. 2200* B.C. (*1st.-6th. Dynasties*)

FIRST INTERMEDIATE OR "FEUDAL" PERIOD
c. 2200 B.C.—*c. 2050* B.C.

MIDDLE KINGDOM
c. 2050 B.C.—*c. 1750* B.C. (*11th.-13th. Dynasties*)

SECOND INTERMEDIATE OR "HYKSOS" PERIOD
c. 1750 B.C.—*c. 1550* B.C.

NEW KINGDOM OR "EMPIRE"
c. 1550 B.C.—*c. 650* B.C. (*18th.-22nd. Dynasties*)

During the consolidation of the Middle Kingdom, Egypt had been so absorbed in her own problems of reunification that she had either not foreseen or had been unable to control the alteration of the political balance that was occurring on the Asiatic frontier. The nomadic Hyksos had been a disturbing force in the Near East for some centuries and, just as the Kassites had earlier overcome Babylonia, they conquered Egypt in the mid-eighteenth century B.C. Despite the fact that this barbarian minority ruled Egypt for more than a century and a half, very little is known about their culture.

The Egyptians finally rose against the Hyksos, having learned the lessons of hardihood, brutality, and military organization. Though hitherto they had not even used the wheel to any extent, since their river was the chief means of transportation, they became expert charioteers and learned to wield the slashing sword and the laminated bow and to employ the tactics of their savage masters.

In rising to the challenge of the Hyksos, Egypt had not only demonstrated an amazing national vitality but had also learned that she was not forever secure and sealed against troubles. As a great military power, the Egyptians began to assert themselves in the complex tangle of Near East politics during the period known as the Empire, which reached its peak of international prestige during the reign of Amenhotep III (*c. 1411– 1375* B.C.).

Ikhnaton and the Search for God

The reign of Amenhotep's son and successor, who had inherited a great and dynamic Egypt, was marked by a dramatic, internal religious crisis. From his magnificent new capital at Amarna Ikhnaton launched an attack upon the sun-god Amen and upon all the other traditional gods. He declared Aten, the disk of the sun, to be the sole divinity, and the names of all other gods were hacked out of inscriptions. This highly spiritual and intellectualized worship, the most monotheistic religious development prior to Mosaic Judaism, grew logically out of the sun worship that had already appeared in many forms during Egypt's long history. Ikhnaton's "Hymn to Aten" as the source of life, thought, and knowledge best expresses its nature:

> When thou settest in the western horizon,
> The land is in darkness like death. . . .
> Every lion comes forth from his den;
>
> All creeping things, they sting.
>
> At daybreak, when thou arisest in the horizon . . .
> Thou drivest away the darkness . . .
> Men awake and stand upon their feet. . . .
>
> How manifold are thy works!
> They are hidden from man's sight.
> O sole god, like whom there is no other,
> Thou hast made the earth according to thy desire.[5]

Since the worship of Aten was the result of the Pharaoh's dictates and not a revolutionary democratization of religion on the part of the general populace, it could not survive Ikhnaton's death. The old, familiar, comfortable religious system had been destroyed and the vested interests of

5. John A. Wilson, *The Culture of Ancient Egypt* (Chicago: University of Chicago Press, 1951). p. 227.

many gods, with their powerful priesthoods, had been briefly threatened, but political affairs had been neglected and no broad popular base for thoroughgoing reforms had been provided. Even when the Hittite Empire menaced and finally conquered northern Syria and the coastal powers of the eastern Mediterranean became restless, Ikhnaton did not reassert Egyptian supremacy, and his immediate successors were too busy with the internal consolidation necessary after the religious upheaval to attend to outside threats.

The Decline of Egypt

When a new dynasty came to power at the end of the fourteenth century, it was determined to win back the empire and prestige that Egypt had lost. It soon reconquered the Asian frontier and claimed northern Syria and, about 1280 B.C., concluded a peace with the Hittites in the face of renewed threats to both of them, but Ramses III (c. *1195–1164 B.C.*). was to be the last Pharaoh to claim an Asiatic empire.

In the twelfth century B.C. the "Peoples of the Sea" were moving, and the final ethnic spasm of the Ancient Near East began. Less than two centuries after the thwarted religious revolution of Ikhnaton, Egypt retreated behind her frontiers into the geographic and cultural security that had already been hers for more than two thousand years. The future of the Near East belonged to the new nations that were then arising.

THE ANCIENT BALANCE OF POWER

For many centuries power politics in the Near East focused primarily upon the Fertile Crescent—a strip of relatively productive land running along the Mediterranean coast through Palestine and Syria, bordering the deserts to the east and the rugged mountains to the north, and stretching like a highroad between the Egyptian frontier and upper Mesopotamia. This area attracted the marginal, nomadic peoples who were constantly being forced out of Arabia, Asia Minor, and Iran. Moreover, Mesopotamia continued to extend her frontiers upriver, and Egypt found it necessary to protect the Sinai Peninsula that separated her from Asia. In the middle of the second millennium the dynasty established by Hammurabi was toppled when the Kassites, a barbaric tribe from southwest of the Caspian Sea, entered Mesopotamia. Their kings reigned in Babylon for more than five hundred years, but eventually they were unable to maintain the Syrian hinterland against the other invaders who pushed hungrily into this area.

For several centuries Syria, Palestine, and northern Mesopotamia were held by shifting combinations of invading peoples, such as the Hurri and the Mitanni, whose cultures are only imperfectly known. After the Egyptians had expelled the Hyksos (*c. 1580* B.C.) they expanded northward along the Fertile Crescent, embracing dozens of fragmentary peoples. But they soon encountered the Hittites, an Indo-European people whose southward expansion from Asia Minor, across the Taurus range, had brought them into the contest for Syria. As the third great political concentration in the Near East, the Hittites came to rival both Egypt and Babylonia.

The Indo-European Migrations

The surge of new peoples that began to press along the northern frontiers of the Ancient Near East civilizations between 2000 and 1500 B.C. did not take the form of intermittent raids and transient settlements. Rather, they were mass migrations of whole nations. Some went west to become the Celtic, Italic, and Germanic peoples; others traveled as far east as Iran and India; and still others moved southward into the fringes of the old Near Eastern civilizations.

They are collectively known as the Indo-European peoples. Almost nothing else is known of them before their migrations carried them into contact with older civilizations. They appear to have been loosely related tribes of nomadic herdsmen who had originated in the steppe land of central and western Asia and spread widely across much of central Eurasia. Though they may have shared a rough common culture, they certainly never created either a "lost" Indo-European empire or an "Aryan culture."[6]

In spite of the diversity of their places of settlement, the immense distances and lengths of time covered by their migrations, and their contact with other peoples and cultures, striking similarities in the basic structure and even in the vocabulary of their languages are still evident.

6. The term "Aryan" was used by nineteenth-century philologists, who first recognized the wide linguistic kinship of the Indo-European languages, to designate the parent language. Since in Sanskrit, the ancient Indo-European language of India, the word actually means "noble," it eventually was used, with a cluster of other meanings, by racist propagandists to refer to a "superior" white or Caucasian people, blond "noble savages" of pristine virtue and racial purity. The importance of this concept in one of the favorite Nazi German myths has hindered the usefulness of the term in dispassionate, scientific argument.

These hardy barbarians appeared on the frontiers of the civilized world armed with the battle-ax, the spear, and the deadly Asiatic bow, whose use they had learned from the nomads farther to the east. More importantly, they also brought the light horse-drawn chariot from Asia into the Near East and the Mediterranean.

The Growth of the Hittite Empire

Although the vanguard of the Indo-Europeans and the numerous other peoples pushed ahead of them probably reached the upper edge of Babylonia before the death of Hammurabi it was not until the fourteenth century B.C. that one of the Indo-European peoples, the Hittites, rose to imperial power in the Near East. They had probably filtered across the Caucasian land bridge between the Black Sea and the Caspian as early as 2000 B.C. and had settled in small, independent, fortified cities as a dominant military aristocracy, at the expense of any number of lesser peoples. During the long and obscure period of expansion, consolidation, and penetration of Asia Minor, the military and religious power of small Hittite tribal kings and war chiefs increased until they had obtained the same priest-king status that had so long been familiar in the Ancient Near East. Such royal titles as "my Sun" and "Hero, beloved of the gods" became common, and one Hittite king, in his account of a successful battle, recorded, "And the gods stood by me, the proud storm-god, my lord, the sun-goddess of Arinna, my lady, . . . And I destroyed the enemy."

Under such kings the Hittites extended their control over almost all Asia Minor and, by the middle of the fifteenth century B.C., their states were well on the way to unification. Formerly independent fortress cities had become military and administrative centers for a single royal dynasty that began to claim imperial authority. A great capital city built of massive hewn stone rose at Hattusas, a strategic site to control the crossing of the principal overland trade routes in north central Asia Minor. As newly won territories were organized under royal governors, client kingdoms and vassal states were bound to the growing empire, under military threat and by terrible oaths in the name of "the thousand gods of the Hittites."

By the middle of the fourteenth century B.C. the Hittites had pressed down into northern Syria, aided by the jumbled international affairs in that area and the cancellation of Egyptian power in nearer Asia after the reign of Ikhnaton. Under the leadership of Suppilulimas (*c. 1380–1340 B.C.*), the greatest of Hittite kings and probably the most powerful ruler of his day, their armies engulfed Syria, throwing the cities of Palestine into confusion, and pressed on to the threshold of Egypt. Pharaoh Ramses II rashly engaged them at Kadesh, and in one of the great pitched battles of the ancient world (c. 1295 B.C.) was resoundingly defeated. Though his ambushed army had been cut to pieces, he later devoted his energies to a series of monuments proclaiming his victory at Kadesh. Eventually he entered into diplomatic relationships with the Hittites, and an alliance between the two powers was sealed by his marriage to a Hittite princess. Thus the Hittites were, for the moment, the undisputed masters of the Fertile Crescent.

The Hittite Civilization

The Hittites, like all Indo-European peoples, developed their particular culture only as they came into contact with more highly developed, older civilizations. The most important of these was Babylonia, whose goods, tools, weapons, ideas, beliefs, and gods had for almost a thousand years been carried upriver until their influences had spread into the no-man's land of Syria and the wild limbo of the northern frontier. As the semibarbaric Hittites expanded into these areas, it is almost certain that they appropriated the idea of the sacred monarchy and many of the trappings of Babylonian religion, and it is probable that the evolution of the early Hittite fortified garrison towns into complex cities followed the Babylonian pattern of urban life. The populous and wealthy city of Hattusas was, like Babylon, centered around its temples and state treasury. Its royal archives contained more than three thousand clay tablets, on which both cuneiform characters borrowed from Babylonia and complex hieroglyphic writing, possibly developed from contact with Egyptian influences in Syria, were scratched.[7]

Though Hittite art was marked by a distinctive quality and style, the animal forms in low relief, both naturalistic and imaginative, bear a strong resemblance to Sumerian and Babylonian forms, and the stilted profile poses of their processional friezes and statuary also suggest Babylonian influences.

---

7. In spite of this double borrowing of the tools of literacy, the Hittite language retained its Indo-European substance. Many, if not most, of its words were also borrowed, with the result that the remarkable affinities of vocabulary in the other Indo-European languages are less clear in Hittite. The linguistic structure, however, is distinctly Indo-European. It is so crude and archaic that some scholars insist on calling it "Proto-Indo-European" but, nonetheless, the Hittite documents represent the earliest written form of any of the languages of this important group.

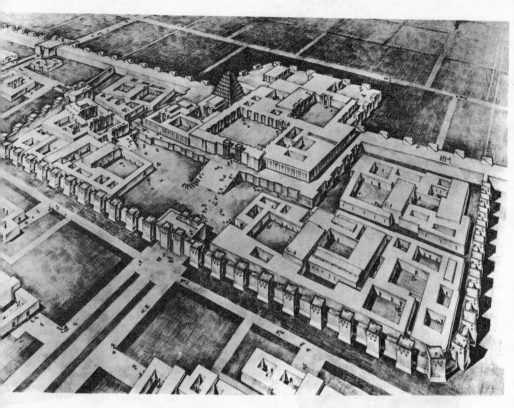

Above: Reconstruction Drawing of the Citadel of Sargon II. 742—706 B.C. Khorsabad.
Below: Hittite Stone Relief. c. 1200 B.C. Tell Halaf.

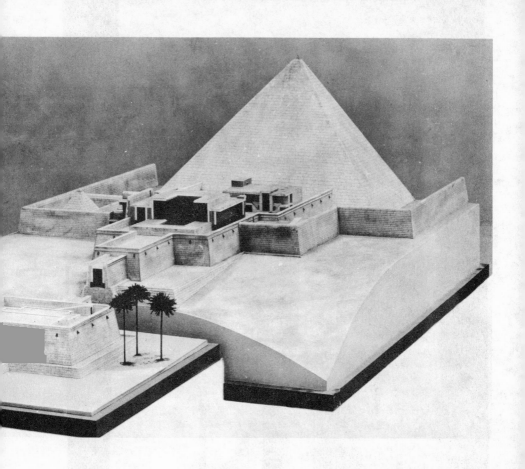

Above: Lotus Pillars
Representing Lower and
Upper Egypt, at the
Al-Karnak Temple.
Right: *Lion,* from an
Achaemenid Palace, Susa.
5th century B.C.

Their art works indicate that the Hittites were of a strikingly different physical type from any of the earlier peoples in the Near East. Their short and powerful figures, with prominent facial bone structure may be classified as Armenoid. The sloping forehead, strongly curved nose, and short chin led one scholar to call the Hittites, rather unflatteringly, "parrot-faced."

The heroic and muscular poses found in Hittite art reflect their preoccupation with war, the one area in which they were innovators rather than borrowers. Military skills necessary for survival during the long period of seminomadism had been perfected by conquest and settlement until the Hittites as a whole constituted a military class whose principal occupation was soldiering. Below the king were ranked, in a feudalistic order, his relatives, companions, and vassals, all of whom were military commanders; the entire structure probably rested upon the labor and tribute of the conquered peoples. Their civilization is marked by roughness and urgency, showing little evidence of the contemplation and orderly intellectual life so apparent in Egypt and Mesopotamia.

The Age of Iron

Even while the Hittite Empire was attaining the height of its power, a new wave of migrations convulsed the entire Near East. Indo-European groups were again moving along a front that extended at least as far west as Italy and Greece and east to India. Many peoples of other linguistic and ethnic stocks were carried along with or driven before the impetus of their migration. Egypt managed to hold the entrance of the Nile against these "Peoples of the Sea" for a time, but the Kassite Empire in Mesopotamia was conquered. The Hittite Empire fell with cataclysmic suddenness when Hattusas was overthrown and destroyed by fire about 1200 B.C. Its remnants were consolidated in Syria, where a Hittite succession state survived for several centuries, but throughout the ancient centers of civilization the darkness of a new barbarism reigned.

Perhaps the most significant cause and one of the most important effects of this destructive wave of migrations was the spread of the use of iron. Though evidence suggests that the smelting process had been discovered early in the second millennium—possibly in Armenia at the base of Asia Minor—the peoples of the Ancient Near East had remained fundamentally in the Bronze Age. Perhaps they were unable to discover a suitable method of reducing iron ore in large quantities, though the Hittites seemed to have had some knowledge of iron and a few ornamental pieces have been found in Egypt. In any case, the technological processes for producing bronze were familiar, and that metal had long been identified with the weapons and armor of the military aristocracies who dominated war and politics in the old centers of civilization.

But copper, a basic ingredient of bronze, was a relatively scarce metal, while usable iron ore could be found almost anywhere. As soon as even a rudimentary process for its reduction in quantity had been discovered, the vast numbers of people beyond the old frontiers of civilization could arm themselves with weapons fully as effective as those which had held the frontiers for centuries. As the technology of iron spread and developed, the hordes of barbarians who swept over the Ancient Near East at the end of the second millennium, destroying the political order of the great states, brought the Bronze Age to an end.

Because the new invaders were, in general, politically unsophisticated and of relatively low culture, they were unable to maintain the complex civilizations they had conquered. They merely imposed their own familiar pattern of tribal life and village settlement upon the ruins. The old states and civilizations were fragmented, and it was not until the Assyrian Empire had arisen that a true political balance of power was reconstructed.

The Rise of the Assyrian Empire

For centuries before the great upheaval of the Iron Age, the Assyrians, a tough, hardy race of mountaineers, had menaced the borderlands of Mesopotamia from their buffer state (the land of the god Ashur) to the north of Sumer and Babylonia. At the same time, they had provided a defense against the intermittent pressures of the Indo-Europeans and other peoples along the open frontier to the north and west. In the centuries following 1300 B.C., however, they expanded from their capital fortress of Nineveh on the Tigris into lower Mesopotamia, and by the ninth century B.C. they were moving westward into Syria.

Though their striking art and many aspects of the culture that they borrowed from Mesopotamia exhibit great vigor (modern scholars are indebted to them at least for their transcription of a considerable volume of Mesopotamian literature, which they stored in their royal libraries), the essential characteristic of the Assyrians was their total devotion to war. Even their art works tend overwhelmingly to depict the hunt, warfare, and siege. The strong, thick-set, muscular bodies of the Assyrians themselves appear in scene after scene, along with strings of mutilated prisoners; scenes of torture and death and devastation are lovingly detailed.

Like the Hittites, the Assyrians, whose social system had resulted from a necessity of self-preservation and had been perfected during the early imperial expansion, were an aristocratic military minority among the dozens of peoples whom they had conquered. They themselves were largely unproductive, living off the loot, tribute, and taxes of the conquered, and bringing the techniques of warfare closer to perfection than they had ever been before.[8] Since their system constantly demanded fresh conquests and new sources of revenue, they developed a unique policy of calculated terror. They often wiped out entire nations, such as Israel, and moved conquered peoples bodily from their homelands in order to destroy their traditional sense of identity. Sennacherib, one of the kings of the late empire, destroyed a total of 89 towns and 820 villages and carried 208,000 prisoners into exile; in crushing a rebellion in Babylon in 689 B.C. he placed the city under harrowing siege, burned it to the ground, and slaughtered almost its entire population.

At its height, the brutal Assyrian police-state was the largest unit that had yet appeared in the expanding political order of the Ancient Near East. It had spread out to include the trade and culture of Mesopotamia; then it moved from Syria north into the body of Asia Minor and down through Palestine, conquering the kingdom of Israel (722 B.C.) and dominating the Fertile Crescent; and it completed the conquest of the desert gap into Egypt by 661 B.C. But it shortly began to topple before the uprisings of its conquered and allied nations, and the rise of Persia during the sixth century B.C. completed its destruction.

The Phoenicians

Amid the wreckage of the great states of the Ancient Near East, after the overthrow of the Hittite Empire and before the triumph of Assyria, the Phoenicians, along with several other peoples, raised themselves to limited power and independence. The land comprising Phoenicia—the coastal strip of Syria, Lebanon, and Israel, including the seaport cities of Tyre, Byblos, Sidon, Marathus, Ugarit, Beirut, and others—lay in the heart of the Fertile Crescent, but its frontiers were never clearly estab-

---

8. The Assyrians profited from the military lessons of all the peoples with whom they came in contact, both civilized and barbarian. Having learned chariotry from either the Mitanni or the Hittites, they perfected its use as a striking arm. To the concept of mass warfare borrowed from the barbarian hordes of their borders, they added the elements of discipline and tactics, using specialized weapons and services much like those in modern armies. Their common soldiers carried iron arms, and their siege trains and engines were not to be improved upon until the successors of Alexander the Great.

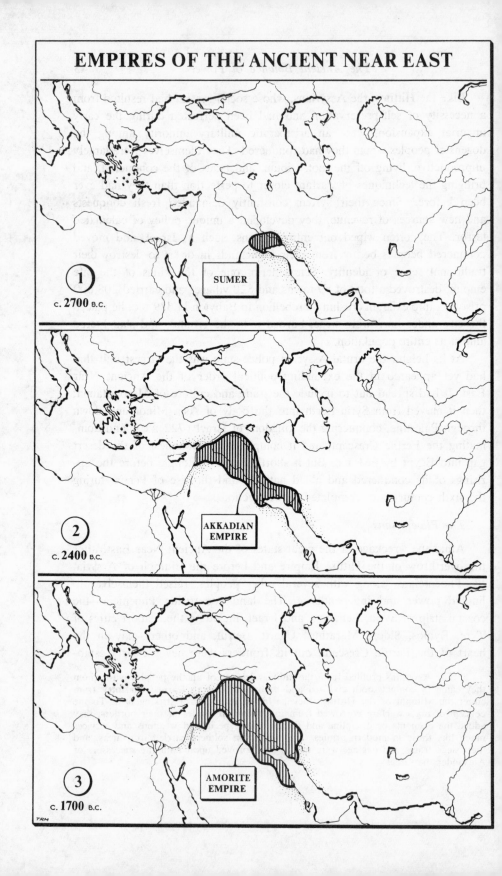

EMPIRES OF THE ANCIENT NEAR EAST

1

c. **2700** B.C.

SUMER

2

c. **2400** B.C.

AKKADIAN
EMPIRE

3

c. **1700** B.C.

AMORITE
EMPIRE

TRM

EMPIRES OF THE ANCIENT NEAR EAST

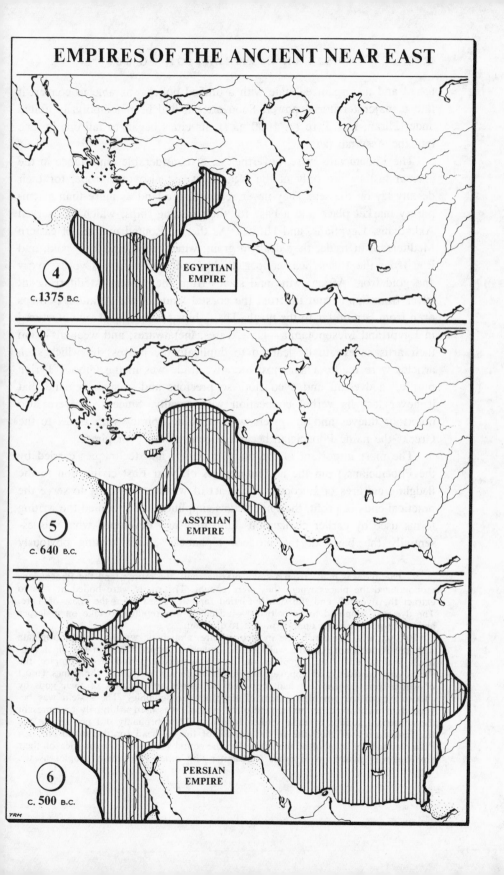

4
c. 1375 B.C.

EGYPTIAN
EMPIRE

5
c. 640 B.C.

ASSYRIAN
EMPIRE

6
c. 500 B.C.

PERSIAN
EMPIRE

TRM

lished and no organized state with a unified policy was able to convert it into a major territorial power. Soon after it had been temporarily united under Hiram I of Tyre (*c.* 1000 B.C.), its cities began to fall one by one into the Assyrian net.

The Phoenicians were, nevertheless, of considerable importance in the ancient history not only of the Near East but also of Europe, for their destiny lay on the sea. They never regarded the land as more than a temporary market place and a base for their trading ships, which had served Akkadians, Egyptians, and Hittites. As the undisputed masters of eastern Mediterranean trade, they dealt in grain, wine, and cloth; lead, gold, and iron from the Black Sea; copper, timber, and grain from Cyprus; ivory and gold from Africa; wine and slaves from the western Mediterranean; silver from Spain; and tin from the coastal lands of the Atlantic, perhaps even from Britain far to the north. Their ships carried goods manufactured in Egypt and Mesopotamia—glass, vases, metalwares, and weapons—and their artisans eventually learned to duplicate the process by which such articles were made. Their most lucrative trade was in the famous Tyrian purple,[9] a dyestuff and dyed cloth so precious and in such demand that it never lost its verbal connection with royalty. Since they were also notorious thieves and sharpsters who combined piracy with trade, to the Greeks the name Phoenician became a general word for pirate.

The most important of the many products and techniques carried by the Phoenicians from the ancient centers of Near East civilization to the fledgling cultures of Europe was the art of writing. Primarily to serve the practical ends of profit, the Phoenicians simplified and modified the writing forms used by earlier civilizations until they had developed what was essentially the basis of the modern alphabet.[10] Such writing obviously

9. The dye was made from a small marine snail, the murex, and the Phoenicians monopolized the places where they were caught. The snails were boiled in vats to extract the dyestuff, and the stench carried far out to sea from the coast of Tyre. The dye was supposed to be colorfast—indeed, it was reputed to take on a deeper and more perfect color upon exposure to the sun.

10. Actually, like much else in their culture, alphabetic writing did not originate with the Phoenicians. On the walls of the extensive copper mines in the Sinai Peninsula maintained by the Egyptians during the aggressive period of the Empire, the slaves, war captives, and impoverished local laborers who worked the mines (most of whom were Canaanites) had scratched the names and pictures of their gods by choosing from the complex system of Egyptian hieroglyphics. The system was beyond their understanding, but a handful of symbols was used arbitrarily to represent the consonant sounds of their spoken language. They probably did not realize the full implications of their use of the symbol of the ox head for the sound *alif,* for example, and the symbol of the house for the sound *bet,* but the basic idea of their alphabet was passed on to other Canaanites and other Palestinian peoples as the

facilitated the rapid and accurate keeping of accounts, and bills and payments could be noted anywhere. An alphabetic inscription was placed on the sarcophagus of a king of Byblos as early as approximately 1200 B.C., and the multitudinous advantages of the alphabet were quickly passed on to the other peoples of the Mediterranean world.

JUDAISM AND ITS GOD

"In the beginning . . ."

The Hebrews were never one of the great powers in the Ancient Near East. Only once in their history did they achieve the political and territorial unity of a nation; yet despite the fact that their story is largely one of exile, enslavement, and degradation, the religious force flowing from them through Christianity can be said to constitute one of the most significant currents in the heritage of western man.

The epic tradition from which the history and religion of the Hebrews grew pictured a heroic age during which the sons of Noah overspread the earth and became the founders of peoples and nations. The races of men found in the Ancient Near East thus came to bear the names of the patriarchs who were believed to have established them. Jacob, for example, won for himself the name of his nation, Israel, and his twelve sons gave their names to its tribes.

The epic incidents in which the patriarchs passed through experiences that gave them a stature above that of ordinary mortals—such as Jacob's wrestling with an angel, Isaac's survival of his father's ritual sacrifice, and Abraham's speaking with God—were interwoven with folk tales common to many peoples and were combined with elements from other mythological systems. A large part of the Hebrew tradition is based on folk memory of actual events, but almost none of it can be called history in any modern critical sense. Nevertheless, the history of the Hebrews is inseparable from the development of their religious beliefs.

The pre-Mosaic Hebrews were presumably one of a large number of Semitic peoples who were constantly forced from the south into the frontiers of Mesopotamia by the pressure of growing population. The records of the great peoples of the Ancient Near East speak of a nomadic folk generally located in the lands between the horns of the Fertile Cres-

population flowed through these turbulent coastal lands. Eventually it reached the Phoenicians.

cent whom the Egyptians called, contemptuously, the Khabiri ("wanderers"). The first Biblical reference to Abraham places him in "the land of his nativity, Ur of the Chaldees," a Mesopotamian city that was destroyed by the Elamites about 1950 B.C.

After Abraham and his family had fled Ur, perhaps after it had been destroyed, his people followed their flocks across much of the land of the Fertile Crescent for some three centuries. During the period between the founding of the Amorite dynasty in Babylonia and the Egyptian Empire, such small groups were able to move with some freedom and to preserve themselves among and between the great powers.

Each family-tribal group had its own social framework within the nomadic life of the early Hebrews, and each had its own god (or possibly a number of gods ranking below a superior who was the heavenly counterpart of the patriarch of the entire tribe). Thus the Hebrews' god, like the Sumerian's city-gods, simply stood above the other members of his "chosen" people as a figure of authority. The Old Testament, for example, speaks of a covenant struck between "the God of Abraham" and the patriarch's family and tribe: "And I will establish my covenant between me and thee and thy seed after thee in their generations for an everlasting covenent, to be a God unto thee, and to thy seed after thee" (Genesis 17:7). The protective deities of other tribal patriarchs were probably variants of the same type of god, though nothing is now known of most of them.

As the children of Abraham, protected by their god, traveled westward from Mesopotamia, they brought with them a great cultural store. Their cosmogony, known to us from the Book of Genesis, was remarkably consistent with the traditions and mythology of Mesopotamia, where variants of the Hebrew stories of Creation, Eden, the Flood, and the Tower of Babel had long been in existence. Nevertheless, though the religion of Israel began with eclecticism, its most dynamic feature, ethical monotheism, was peculiar to the Hebrews.

The God of Moses and His Holy Nation

It is probable that at least one group of Hebrews—the people of Joseph—were among the conglomerate Hyksos bands who invaded and ruled Egypt at the end of the Middle Kingdom (c. 1750–1550 B.C.). After the collapse of Hyksos rule, many remnants of these people remained in such border lands as Goshen, where they probably served as mercenary troops, border guards, or impressed laborers. As Egyptian strength grew, some Pharaoh or Pharaohs "which knew not Joseph" further depressed the condition of these foreigners until, about 1200 B.C., a group of them fled into the desert of Sinai under the leadership of Moses.

During the forty-year period following their departure from Egypt, Moses and his people were transformed into a nation every phase of whose existence was bound to the religion that was finally created by its leader. Though the God of the Hebrews had earlier said, "There shall no man see Me and live," Moses actually saw, heard, and was transformed by Him. It was this transformation that he passed on to his people: as God overpowered Moses, so the vision of God dominated the Israelites.

The God's name, *Yahweh,* seems appropriate, for it probably meant, "He causes to be."[11] Cosmic force was the most apparent and universal characteristic of this God: He was the answer to every question about the beginning and end of the world, the very cause of nature itself. As a single God, ruling aloof and alone, He controlled the universe but was not to be identified with its transient matter. Like the tribal gods of the patriarchs, he might appear on the mountain top, in the tabernacle, or in many other places; He was the God of everywhere and nowhere. Though His thought and will were understandable to men, He was hidden from them and was never to be represented in any form. The existence of such a deity could ultimately be expressed only by the phrase, "I am that I am."

Nothing, great or small, could escape such a universal force. Because of his very perfection, God was necessarily separate from everything in the universe derived from Him, including man. But He nevertheless demanded that sinful man lead a blameless life, and out of this virtually impossible condition came much of the strength and vigor of Judaism.

Striving constantly with his own imperfection, man did not question the justice of God, who took cognizance only of his sin—not of his weakness—and punished him for infractions of His law. Even the greatest religious heroes of Judaism writhed and suffered in the knowledge of their imperfections, and the calamities that befell the hard-pressed life of man and nation were regarded as God's visitations upon His disobedient people.

The absolute and awful authority of this God was forever recorded and established in Exodus and the other four books of Moses known as the Pentateuch or the Torah ("The Law"):

And it came to pass on the third day in the morning, that there were thunders

11. Since the written form of His holy name contained no vowel symbols, we cannot be sure how it was actually pronounced. Its incorrect but time-honored transliteration, however, is our word Jehovah.

and lightnings, and a thick cloud upon the mount, and the voice of the trumpet exceeding loud; so that all the people that was in the camp trembled.

And Moses brought forth the people out of the camp to meet with God; and they stood at the nether part of the mount.

And Mount Sinai was altogether on a smoke, because the Lord descended upon it in fire: and the smoke thereof ascended as the smoke of a furnace, and the whole mount quaked greatly (Exodus 19:16-18).

The Holy Law "handed down" to Moses on Mount Sinai made no clear distinction between secular and religious demands. As we have already seen, the Code of Hammurabi and the laws of other peoples and kings of his age similarly sanctified modes of behavior that were actually prescribed by social necessity, and all of the complex details of the Judaic law as it was committed to writing could not possibly have related to a people as primitive as the Hebrews in the time of Moses. Some elements in it—notably the holy ethic—seem to reflect the patriarch's lofty religious conceptions, and still other elements were undoubtedly borrowed from earlier codes with which the wandering Hebrews had come in contact, but the great bulk of detail must have been added after they had gained the "Promised Land" and become a settled people.

Dominion and Bondage

After spending a generation consolidating themselves in the wilderness, the tribal nation of Israel slowly moved northward and gradually occupied Palestine. Though the historic view of the leaders of this period, such as Joshua, has been obscured by time and the traditional tales of great and majestic deeds that have always tended to accumulate around such heroes, the occupation probably incorporated many kindred peoples, perhaps even other Hebrew tribes who had lived in Palestine since patriarchal times. The triumph of Israel and its God swept away the cultures of these peoples, most of which had reached a higher level of civilization than the desert Hebrews.

As Israel slowly gained its unity as a nation—with small groups fighting, bypassing Canaanite strongholds, moving into the promised land, and settling down—its leadership was furnished by its judges. Individually these half-legendary figures may have been the heroes of local settlements or shifting federations rather than the leaders of a united nation, but collectively they represent an important and characteristic phenomenon in Hebrew history. God had clearly conveyed a special power and grace to such a bold assassin as Ehud, to such an able soldier as Gideon, to such a legendary strong man as Samson, and even to such a possessed woman as Deborah: "The Lord raised up judges, which delivered them out of the hands of those that spoiled them" (Judges 2:16). Moses had created a nation that was also a religious community, and during the halting conquest of Palestine the God of the Israelites became their leader in war, as Barak and Deborah sang: "Lord, when thou wentest out of Seir, when thou marchedst out of the field of Edom, the earth trembled, and the heavens dropped, the clouds also dropped water" (Judges 5:4).

But the military and political success of Israel was partly due to the fact that the great powers of the Ancient Near East were unable to oppose its battle for nationality in Palestine. By the mid-twelfth century B.C. Egypt had withdrawn from Asia, and the growth of Assyria was faltering on the Syrian frontier. The power of the Hittites had been so reduced that even in Syria they could do little but preserve themselves. The "People of the Sea" were powerful and disruptive, but they quickly broke apart and offered concerted resistance only as the coastal people of Palestine, whom the Hebrews knew as the Philistines.

The final phase of the conquest of Palestine began about 1000 B.C., when Israel became a nation under the leadership of vigorous young Saul, and was concluded by the final defeat of the stubborn Philistines in the reign of the shepherd-warrior David (*c. 1012–972* B.C.). Under the leadership of David, the greatest king of Hebrew history, Israel became a power among the lesser states of the Syrian-Palestine coast. The ethnic and territorial base of the kingdom was broadened by the addition of Judah to its lands, whose frontiers were successfully guarded against the surrounding peoples. Even Hiram of Tyre recognized David's monarchy, and his people flourished in the shadow of his success. The narrative of his reign in the second book of Samuel reveals the power and personality of this remarkable man, the hero-king favored of his God.

After the work of war had been done, a long and prosperous period of peace came to Israel during the reign of David's son, Solomon (*c. 960– 932* B.C.): "Then sat Solomon upon the throne of David his father; and his kingdom was established greatly" (I Kings 2:12). Faced with the new demands of peace, Solomon became a great figure of wisdom, whose legends are part of the golden age of Hebrew history: Jerusalem became a great walled city centered about his palace and the temple, and his harem represented a cluster of treaties sealed in royal marriages.

In a sense, however, the fabled glory of Solomon sealed the economic and political fate of his nation. After the loot of the Philistine and Canaan-

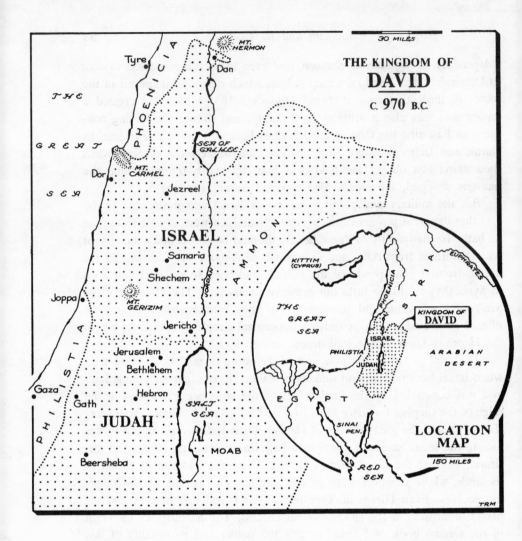

The Kingdom of David c. 970 B.C.

ite conquests had been exhausted, Israel could not support herself through agriculture, for rugged mountains and deserts filled most of Palestine, as they still do today. Opportunities to develop seagoing commerce, like that on which the civilizations of the Phoenicians and Philistines had been based, were severely limited. In any case, the eminence of a kingdom that had come into existence mainly because the great powers had withdrawn their authority from a territory lying in their midst was bound to be ephemeral.

After the death of Solomon ten of the twelve tribes fatefully weakened the kingdom by breaking away to establish the independent state of Israel:

"What portion have we in David? Neither have we inheritance in the son of Jesse: to your tents, O Israel: now see to thine house, O David" (I Kings 12:16).

In the late eighth century B.C. the brutal and warlike Assyrians pushed into Palestine, and the terrorist policies that had demoralized their enemies elsewhere were visited upon Israel. Some twenty-seven thousand people of the ten "lost tribes" disappeared from history as they were transported across the vast empire of Sargon II somewhere in Asia. The southern kingdom of Judah was carried into captivity in 586 B.C. by Nebuchadnezzar, who had temporarily revived the Babylonian Empire. The wrath of God had seemingly been visited upon them, and the Hebrews were never again to be a great nation:

By the rivers of Babylon, there we sat down, yea, we wept, when we remembered Zion.

We hanged our harps upon the willows in the midst thereof.

For there they that carried us away captive required of us a song; and they that wasted us required of us mirth, saying, Sing us one of the songs of Zion.

How shall we sing the Lord's song in a strange land? If I forget thee, O Jerusalem, let my right hand forget her cunning.

If I do not remember thee, let my tongue cleave to the roof of my mouth; if I prefer not Jerusalem above my chief joy (Psalm 137:1-6).

The Achievement of Judaism

Even after the Israelites had ceased to exist as a specifically covenanted nation, their symbolism and their traditions passed into a universalism that was to find its ultimate expression in Christianity. The Hebrews might well have been merely another of the hundreds of obscure peoples who passed across the lands of the Ancient Near East in the two millennia before Christ had it not been for their belief in Yahweh. Though the God of Israel had no history, properly speaking—in the words of the Psalmist, "Before the mountains were brought forth, or ever thou hadst formed the earth and the world, even from everlasting to everlasting, thou art God" (Psalm 90:2)—He provided the Hebrews with their focus and identity, which continued to exist long after they had lost their territorial claim to Palestine. New aspects of His nature were constantly being revealed to them. At first He was a jealous, vengeful God as narrow as the ignorant desert people who worshiped Him:

If I whet my glittering sword, and mine hand take hold on judgment; I will render vengeance to mine enemies, and will reward them that hate me.

I will make mine arrows drunk with blood, and my sword shall devour flesh; and that with the blood of the slain and of the captives, from the beginning of revenges upon the enemy.

Rejoice, O ye nations, with his people: for he will avenge the blood of his servants, and will render vengeance to his adversaries, and will be merciful unto his land, and to his people (Deuteronomy 32:41-43).

But the Jews in Babylon were sustained by the belief that, though God punished them, He would ultimately respond to the needs of His chosen people:

Therefore thus saith the Lord of hosts, the God of Israel; Behold, I will punish the king of Babylon and his land, as I have punished the king of Assyria.

And I will bring Israel again to his habitation, and he shall feed on Carmel and Bashan, and his soul shall be satisfied upon mount Ephraim and Gilead.

In those days, and in that time, saith the Lord, the iniquity of Israel shall be sought for, and there shall be none; and the sins of Judah, and they shall not be found: for I will pardon them whom I reserve (Jeremiah 50:18-20).

The Hebrew captive took grim and sanguinary joy from the thought:

Remember, O Lord, the children of Edom in the day of Jerusalem; who said, "Rase it, rase it, even to the foundation thereof."

O daughter of Babylon, who are to be destroyed; happy shall he be, that rewardeth thee as thou hast served us.

Happy shall he be, that taketh and dasheth thy little ones against the stones (Psalm 137:7-9).

Half a millennium later His existence could be expressed only in the most universal terms:

And he shall judge among many people, and rebuke strong nations afar off; and they shall beat their swords into plowshares, and their spears into pruning-hooks: nation shall not lift up a sword against nation, neither shall they learn war any more.

But they shall sit every man under his vine and under his fig tree; and none shall make them afraid: for the mouth of the Lord of hosts hath spoken it.

For all people will walk every one in the name of his god, and we will walk in the name of the Lord our God for ever and ever (Micah 4:3-5).

The ethical monotheism of Judaism thus bound every man to every other man in justice and mercy, and every man to God: "and what doth the Lord require of thee, but to do justly, and to love mercy, and to walk humbly with thy God."

Communication with a God who was conceived of as an omnipresent spirit was perfectly feasible—indeed necessary—and the plans of God were revealed to the last great formative figures in the Judaic tradition, the prophets. Confident that they were the instruments of His will, they spoke with the sure knowledge that their words were His.

The history of Hebrew prophecy began when the authority of the aged and saintly Samuel sanctioned the monarchy of Saul. Later prophets encouraged the kings who "walked in the law of the Lord" and fearlessly excoriated those who fell from His way. But such bearded, staring mystics as Elijah—whose staff and rough mantle of hair made them familiar figures in Israel—also represented the conscience of the entire society.

During the declining years of the monarchy, as morality loosened and luxury sapped national vitality, the great Judaean prophet Isaiah (*fl.* 700 B.C.) saw that his land, the chosen nation of God, would be destroyed by the power of Assyria that was ominously rising in the north and regarded this fate as God's judgment upon a "sinful nation, a people laden with iniquity . . . they have forsaken the Lord, they have provoked the Holy One of Israel unto anger, they are gone away backward" (Isaiah 1:4). Yet he also looked forward—beyond the time of trouble, blood, and enslavement—to an age of gold, when the remnant of the Jews should again turn to God and receive their inheritance: "And it shall come to pass in that day, that his burden shall be taken away from off thy shoulder, and his yoke from off thy neck . . ." (Isaiah 10:27). This message of doom was echoed by Jeremiah, whose life ran through the last years of Judah's independence and who witnessed the sack of Jerusalem. Through him the Lord said: "I will make Jerusalem a heap of ruins, a lair of jackals; and I will make the cities of Judah a desolation without inhabitant," explaining that this punishment was necessary "Because they have forsaken my Law which I set before them. . . ." During their exile the later prophets kept the hope of redemption alive in the Hebrews.

When the Persian Empire began to rise in the sixth century B.C. after the victory of Cyrus, the Hebrews were restored to their land. But, though the experience of exile had renewed their faith and had established the pattern of their religious life, they were never to regain the power and independence they had first achieved under David. Rather, they were simply one of the hundreds of peoples subject to Persian rule.

After the fall of Persia, Palestine passed first into the hands of the Hellenistic kings and then into those of the Romans. From time to time Palestine was to play a part in the common history of the great states of the Mediterranean world as she was granted an ephemeral freedom or achieved the status of a semi-independent client state. But her history as a separate power had ended, and the unique religious experiences already developed by the Hebrews were to remain their major contribution to western civilization.

SUGGESTIONS FOR FURTHER READING

≫≪

General Works and Works on Special Topics

Cambridge Ancient History (New York: Macmillan, 1923-26), Vols. I-III, the standard work on ancient history, somewhat in need of revision but still the most readily available major work on its subjects.

C. W. Ceram, *Gods, Graves and Scholars* (New York: Knopf, 1951) a now famous book popularizing the "romance" of archaeology.

*V. Gordon Childe, *What Happened in History* (Baltimore: Penguin, 1946), a far-ranging and provocative work by a great authority, imaginative and readable.

*Leonard Cottrell, *The Anvil of Civilization* (New York: Mentor, 1957) an exciting account of the clash of ancient civilizations by a competent amateur enthusiast.

*Henri Frankfort, *Birth of Civilization in the Near East* (New York: Anchor, 1959), a brilliant and pioneering work.

————, et al., *The Intellectual Adventure of Ancient Man* (Chicago: University of Chicago Press, 1948).

————, *Kingship and the Gods* (Chicago: University of Chicago Press, 1955), an important "thesis" book on this crucial topic.

*Arnold Hauser, *The Social History of Art,* tr. in collaboration with the author by Stanley Godman (New York: Vintage, 1952), 4 vols; relates art history specifically to the creative forces of civilization; see especially Vol. I for this period.

Ivar Lissner, *The Living Past,* tr. by J. M. Brownjohn (New York: Putnam, 1957), interesting and readable, an up-to-date general treatment in a series of brief "profiles"; suffers somewhat from popularization.

*S. Moscati, *Ancient Semitic Civilization* (New York: Capricorn, 1958).

*Herbert J. Muller, *The Loom of History* (New York: Mentor, 1961), a "linear" account of the history of Asia Minor; particularly good on the early history; exciting and readable.

Eva M. Sanford, *The Mediterranean World in Ancient Times* (New York: Ronald Press, 1951), a standard work emphasizing geographical determinants.

Singer, Holmyard, and Hall, eds., *A History of Technology,* cited for Chap. 1.

Mesopotamia

*Edward Chiera, *They Wrote on Clay,* ed. by George G. Cameron (Chicago: Phoenix, 1957), an account of "topics" in Mesopotamian civilization and archaeology, with an exciting I-was-there flavor.

L. Delaporte, *Mesopotamia, the Babylonian and Assyrian Civilizations* (New York: Knopf, 1925), a somewhat outmoded volume of a famous series, but still a fine "overview" of Mesopotamia.

The Oldest Code of Laws in the World, tr. by C. H. W. Johns (Edinburgh: T. and T. Clark, 1903), the standard edition of the Code of Hammurabi.

A. T. Olmstead, *The History of Assyria* (New York: Scribner, 1923), the standard work on the subject.

C. L. Wooley, *The Sumerians* (Oxford: Clarendon Press, 1929), a pioneer work by a great archaeologist, the virtual "discoverer" of the Sumerians.

Egypt

J. H. Breasted, *The Dawn of Conscience* (New York: Scribner, 1933), a classic if somewhat overly enthusiastic account of the monotheistic "revolution" of Ikhnaton.

————, *A History of Egypt* (New York: Scribner, 1909), a classic work on the subject; badly in need of revision but still a useful and readable book.

*I. E. S. Edwards, *The Pyramids of Egypt* (Baltimore: Penguin, 1947).

K. Lange and H. Hirmer, *Egypt: Architecture, Sculpture, Painting in Three Thousand Years* (New York: Phaidon Press, 1956), detailed, comprehensive; a rich and beautiful book.

Margaret A. Murray, *The Splendour that was Egypt* (London: Sidgwick and Jackson , Ltd., 1954), massive work, standard treatment.

*John A. Wilson, *The Culture of Ancient Egypt* (Chicago: Phoenix, 1956), one of the finest recent works on Egypt; probably the best modern reinterpretation of the subject.

Asia Minor and Syria

C. W. Ceram, *The Secret of the Hittites* (New York: Knopf, 1956) a popularization of much recent scholarly work; a topical survey rather than a connected narrative.

*O. R. Gurney, *The Hittites* (Baltimore: Penguin, 1952) almost the only up-to-date, connected history of the Hittites.

R. Weill, *Phoenicia and Western Asia to the Macedonian Conquest,* tr. by E. F. Row, (London: Harrap, 1940).

The Ancient Hebrews

*William F. Albright, *From the Stone Age to Christianity* (New York: Anchor, 1957), a study of the history, setting, and culture of the biblical Hebrews in the light of modern archaeology and scholarship.

A. Lods, *Israel from Its Beginnings to the Eighth Century* (London: 1952).

H. M. Orlinsky, *Ancient Israel* (Ithaca: Cornell University Press, 1954), a good general account of Old Testament history.

T. H. Robinson, *Hebrew Religion, Its Origins and Development* (London: 1952).

Eric Voegelin, *Israel and Revelation* (Baton Rouge: Louisiana State University Press, 1956) Vol. I of *Order and History,* an elaborate interpretation of history; demanding reading, heavily philosophical, with difficult vocabulary.

*Paperbound edition. In the case of reprint editions, publisher and date of publication given will be that of reprint rather than the original.

❧ 3 ❧

The Miracle of Greece

THE BRONZE AGE AND THE DAWN OF HELLENISM

The Minoans of Crete

During the thousands of years while great empires had risen and fallen in the Ancient Near East, Europe had remained a barbaric, recordless, silent appendage to the land mass of Asia. Eventually Crete—a long, narrow island about fifty miles off the southern tip of the Greek mainland— became heir to the earlier civilizations. It was there that the mysterious culture known as Minoan developed.[1]

It may be surmised that the same slow climatic changes that drove the predynastic Egyptians and the Proto-Sumerians into their forbidding river valleys forced early seafarers to settle in Crete, where the surrounding sea provided them with isolation and a certain degree of security. But the land itself, unlike the valleys of Egypt or Mesopotamia, held no promise of agricultural riches, and the Cretans turned of necessity to the sea. A full thousand years before the Phoenicians, they came to dominate the waters of the eastern Mediterranean.

Century after century Cretan ships sailed farther from their home ports to touch the islands near the mainland to the north and Cyprus and Asia

---

1. Named for the legendary King Minos who is so indelibly fixed in Cretan mythology—though whether this name belonged to a single king or a dynasty or was simply the word for king is not known.

Minor to the east. Usually they carried goods manufactured by other peoples, for neither Egypt nor Mesopotamia had easy or natural access to the Mediterranean, though both had expanded to the coast by the middle of the third millennium.

Enriched by material wares and inspired by ideas and techniques developed by these earlier civilizations, Crete became one of the great centers of the Bronze Age. Minoan craftsmen learned to fashion beautiful metal goods, and highly diverse and well-developed pottery became a distinctive item of luxury trade. The great mountains of Egyptian potsherds (broken fragments of common pottery) accumulated at Cretan sites attest to the volume of her trade with Egypt, where wealthy households prized Cretan ceramic ware. The jewels of Minoan ladies were placed in delicate Egyptian faïence boxes, and their perfumes were stored in tiny Egyptian stoneware bottles.

The learning and religious beliefs of the Ancient Near East poured into Crete with the stream of trade. Elements of the older and more mature cultures were certainly used in the creation of a new and fundamentally distinctive civilization.

The Minoan Monarchy and the Golden Age

The Cretan population increased and cities were developed to such an extent that Homer's Odysseus would call Crete "a fair, rich land, begirt with water, . . . therein are many men, past counting, and ninety cities." But the fact that life on the island was dependent on and protected by the sea affected every aspect of Minoan culture: no walls were needed to defend cities from invaders, for example, and the political organization granted preeminence to a merchant-aristocracy, the "Sea Kings." Many of the Minoan gods were associated with the sea, and the dead were believed to sail off to the "Happy Islands" of the west in soul ships. Even the cult of the bull, which is so prominent in both the art and later the mythology of Crete, was probably related to the raging, wild, and unpredictable character of the sea.[2]

2. The specific religious connection of the so-called Minoan Snake Goddess is less certain. As represented in several beautiful and characteristically posed statues that have survived, she is obviously either a snake priestess or goddess, but the specific religious practice cannot be ascertained. The snake was usually associated with the gods of the underworld in later cults, and this goddess may have been a Persephone-like figure. Apparently several goddesses in Minoan religion or several manifestations of the same goddess were of the same type as the later Greek Artemis, the virgin huntress; one at least was a "fisher-goddess," or patron of the nets, and another could well have been the snake goddess or patron.

The Lion Gate. c. 1250 B.C. Mycenae, Greece.

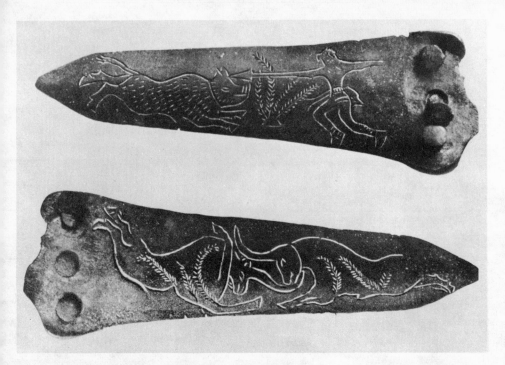

Above: Engraved Bronze Dagger Blade Showing a Boar Hunt and a Fight between Bulls. Knosses, Crete.
Below: *Cup*, from a tomb in Vaphio. c. 1500 B.C.

Toward the beginning of the second millennium B.C. Crete came increasingly under the domination of a single authority, centered in the palace-city of Knossos on the northern side of the island. The name of the legendary King Minos is associated with this period of unification, the great age of Minoan civilization, though less is actually known about him than about even Hammurabi or Ramses II. However, nearly every later Greek myth that involves Crete—such as those of Europa, Theseus, and Daedalus—mentions Minos or his family, and it was in his palace that Minoan art reached its apex.

The excavations at Knossos have laid bare a magnificent, complex structure to which units were apparently added over several centuries. It served as a political capital, storehouse, factory, workshop, and shrine. At the height of Minoan civilization more than a thousand chambers, rooms, and passages rambled over the top and sides of its hilltop site, their walls richly colored with lively frescoes depicting many aspects of everyday life with a subtle blend of naturalism and decorative style.

The expansion of the Egyptian empire and the contest for Syria, the rise of the strong Amorite empire in Mesopotamia, and the growth of Hittite power in Asia Minor and northern Syria created new areas for Cretan trade. Their fleets pushed into the Black Sea and along the coast of the western Mediterranean, traveling beyond the Pillars of Hercules at the eastern end of the Strait of Gibraltar to the Canary Islands, and possibly journeying north as far as the British Isles.

The Coming of the Greeks

Directly to the north of Crete lies the peninsula of mainland Greece, the point of the great European hinterland; and Crete moved in to exploit it. In this period it was a cultural and economic vacuum, and the comparatively primitive native peoples were easily subdued by the Minoans. The fingers of Cretan domination searched into every corner of the peninsula—setting up trading stations, citadels, and outposts; victimizing and at the same time civilizing this part of the barbarian world. Settlements grew into cities and Minoan culture struck deep into the soil of the mainland, creating a separate Bronze Age civilization of great vigor.

About 2000 B.C. the Minoan frontier outposts on the mainland began to feel the slow but relentless pressure of the mass movement of peoples. The same Indo-European migrations that had disjointed the political power-structure and culture of the Ancient Near East now pushed down along the Greek peninsula. The invaders came by slow stages, settling for

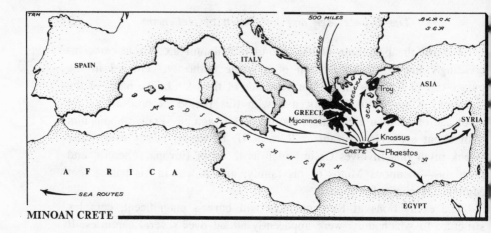

MINOAN CRETE

a generation, then moving on, driving their crude chariots, ox-drawn wagons, and herds of cattle. They spoke a language the Minoans had never heard, the earliest form of Greek;[3] for these Indo-European tribesmen were the most remote ancestors of the historic Greeks. The Proto-Greeks of the great migration penetrated to the edge of one of the most advanced civilizations of the ancient world and the process of cultural assimilation began again.

The Greek Civilization of the Bronze Age

During a period of more than five hundred years the culture of one of the most advanced civilizations of the ancient world was gradually assimilated to that of the most remote ancestors of the historic Greeks. Earlier cities and towns were overwhelmed, and many of them burned. As the basic population changed and increased, the new centers grew in wealth, power, and complexity.

During this time Minoan civilization on Crete itself reached its zenith

3. This "simple fact" was discovered in probably the greatest archaeological breakthrough of our century. The existence of a mainland, Bronze Age culture, comparable to the island culture of Crete, had long been an established fact; but its creators remained mysterious for the lack of written records. Then in the early 1950's, caches of clay tablets were found at several mainland sites. They were written in what Sir Arthur Evans (1851-1941), the pioneer of Minoan archaeology, had called Linear Minoan B. For the moment these discoveries seemed to tie the mainland closer to Crete and substantiate the earlier thesis that its culture was purely Minoan "colonial." Then almost immediately this thesis was destroyed. An English amateur archaeologist, linguist, and cryptographer, Michael Ventris (with the aid of the classicist John Chadwick), proved that these tablets were not Linear Minoan but Linear Greek! That the creators of the mainland culture, in spite of their cultural debt to Crete, were Greeks, speaking Greek, and writing it in the borrowed characters of the Minoans. In one stroke the history of the Greek language—and of Greek civilization—was pushed back more than a thousand years.

and began to grow weak and effete. Its vulnerability eventually attracted the mainland warriors, who sacked and burned Knossos about 1400 B.C. The Egyptian records that had often spoken of the Kefti, "the men of Crete," mentioned them no more, for the Minoan empire, with its dominion of the sea, had passed into the hands of the "Achaean" Greeks.[4]

A vigorous and forceful people, the Achaeans pillaged and traded until great hordes of gold and treasure accumulated in their storehouses and accompanied their leaders to sumptuous tombs. The center of their world was Argolis, with its great citadel-city of Mycenae. The stone lions that still guard the ruins of its main gate symbolized the strength and power of the kings who dwelt behind the cyclopean walls, which were ten feet thick, and constructed of rude stone blocks, some weighing more than a hundred tons. Traders, farmers, artisans, merchants, and the rest of the populace lived in hamlets scattered over the plain below, under the shadow of the king's authority.

Throughout the mainland similar castles and fortresses grew up at Sparta, Tiryns, Pylos, and elsewhere. Together they formed a loose network or confederation, the organization of which was essentially feudal. Each castle-city was the stronghold of some local king or quarrelsome baron. They distrusted each other, and veiled their mutual hostility only when all were greatly threatened or expedient action was absolutely necessary. Since no great power in the eastern Mediterranean challenged their supremacy, the Achaeans were able to expand their empire widely. The epic story of the Trojan War is a poetic example of their most famous exploit.

The later Greeks, like modern historians, learned of this period from the pages of Homer. Though he (if he was indeed a single man) probably lived some three centuries after the end of the age of heroes about which he wrote, the basic narrative material of the *Iliad* and the *Odyssey* had been handed down by bards and minstrels as elements in a tremendous body of folk stories and primitive songs. Since the late nineteenth century archaeological excavations have confirmed the broad outlines of his poems in a rather striking fashion: they have established that a city known as Troy was actually destroyed by the Achaeans about 1185 B.C. and have

4. This term, which was sometimes used in Homer to describe all the Greeks, is now used as a general term for the Greeks of the Bronze Age. The archaeological term "Helladic" is purely descriptive, and "Mycenaean" derives from the name of the leading city among the Homeric Greeks, Mycenae. In fact, however, the early Greeks may have had no collective name for themselves since they had no overall political unit with which to identify.

provided most of our specific knowledge about the Greeks of the Bronze Age.[5]

Shortly after the Trojan War, near the beginning of the first millennium B.C., the pattern of Achaean civilization was shattered by another wave of invasions. A more backward and barbaric branch of their European subfamily—now known as the Dorian Greeks because they called themselves the sons of Dorus—entered Greece during the great migrations that brought the Iron Age and engulfed the eastern Mediterranean and the Ancient Near East in destruction. The details of their invasion are lost, but the glory of the vanished Bronze Age was replaced by a long and troubled interlude, sometimes called the Greek Middle Age.

The Emergence of Ionia

The Dorian invasions, even as they brought about the destruction of the earlier civilization of the Greek mainland, were largely responsible for transplanting the seeds of Greek civilization to the land of Ionia, across the Aegean on the coast of Asia Minor. Through much of the preceding age a steady migration into Ionia had been encouraged by both the hope of gain in war or commerce and the pressure of population. A number of towns and cities had been founded at commercially advantageous spots on the broken western coast of Asia Minor, where immigrants from central Greece, especially from Attica, had arrived after moving outward across the islands of the Cyclades. The Trojan War may have been part of this late Bronze Age movement of colonization. When the disruptive force of the Dorian invasions precipitated a general relocation of the Greek people, the wave of migration to Asia Minor was strengthened.

Though little is known of the early growth of Ionia, it is apparent that the territory did not suffer the decisive break with the past undergone by Greek settlements on the mainland. A continuing tradition gave the Asiatic Greeks direction and a sense of community even in an alien land. Moreover, the wealth of Asia Minor poured into the market places of their cities, which lay across the major trade routes of that wealthy subcontinent.

5. The founder of Aegean archaeology was Heinrich Schliemann (1822-1890), a wealthy German merchant and amateur Homeric enthusiast who set out to prove the historicity of Homer. He succeeded in finding and excavating the site of Troy (not one city but several, each one built upon the ruins of the others). Later he excavated several Bronze Age sites on the mainland, including Agamemnon's city of Mycenae. While his methods were crude and sometimes destructive, his judgments hasty, and his conclusions often wrong, he opened the field of Aegean archaeology and Greek "prehistory" to the more cautious and scientific workers who followed him.

Perched on the edge of the old culture world of the Near East, the Greek cities of Asia Minor were inevitably influenced by the ancient wealth of ideas, techniques, beliefs, and superstitions. It was not simple chance that the pattern of historic Greek civilization distinctly emerged for the first time in Ionia. As merchants and mercenary soldiers traveled to Egypt, Mesopotamia, and beyond, and foreign travelers arrived from Syria, Phoenicia, Egypt, and Babylon, the Ionian civilization was invigorated.

The Ionians subjected the pious confusion of Greek mythology and religion to criticism for the first time, and Greek philosophy, history, and science came into existence. It was probably in the Ionian cities that the crude Canaanite-Phoenician alphabet was first adapted to the Greek language, and it was certainly there that most of the forms of Greek poetry were experimented with and developed. Homer, the earliest name in Greek literature, was an Ionian.

Thus began the Greek contribution to western civilization. Over the next four centuries Hellenism was to reach its zenith of creativeness and pass in time to become the most important cultural determinant in the heritage of western man. In virtually every area of the life of the mind the starting point is with the Greeks. In philosophy they created the vocabulary and the categories of speculation: we think as we do because the Greeks taught us. They invented both the language of logic and the subject of ethics. In both philosophy and literature they placed man at the center of the universe. They did not find him always good or always fortunate—indeed their plays and poems tell us the reverse; but they never found him commonplace. Through their literary art they examined every problem and every condition of man, raising literature from the charming and the ordinary to a magnificent humanism, stripped of the particular and the irrelevant, focused upon the essential and the pertinent, and expressed in a variety of forms which, if their masters had created nothing more, would have made a permanent place for them in literary history. Through their art they taught us to see beyond visual reality, to the essential, whether in a pot, a temple, or a statue. They thus invented classicism with its enormous train of influences, its insistence upon clarity, order, and harmony in life as in art or letters.

In everything they did the Greeks competed with each other and taught each other. Practically every form of Greek literature and many forms of Greek art were judged in competition, at athletic or artistic contests that were part of their cycle of games and festivals. Every notion or system of philosophy had its opposing notion and countersystem. The Greeks loved argument as no other people. They were passionate, narrow, and provincial. They refused to learn any language but their own and regarded those who did not speak it as barbarians. Perhaps they were right.

The Pattern of the City-State

Though citadel-cities had certainly existed during the Bronze Age, the Achaeans, even at the height of their power, had never developed more than the most vagrant notion of a large political authority resembling those in the great empires of the Near East. During the dark centuries following the end of the Bronze Age the tradition of local power they developed was passed down into the *polis,* or city-state, one of the most important and characteristic of all Greek institutions.

As transportation became increasingly difficult and dangerous throughout much of the Greek world, and communication between settlements broke down with the collapse of political order, the spirit of localism was intensified. The population of settlements in the rugged terrain typical of mainland Greece, and even of Ionia and the Aegean Islands, could turn to no central authority. Each city, with its protective fortress, its walls, and its outlying fields, represented the limit of loyalty for its citizens, and the agriculture which was its basis could support only a limited number of people. Even the greatest Greek city-states in much later times would be regarded today as only moderately sized cities; indeed, we would consider most of them small towns.

In such circumstances the life and effort of every citizen gained particular significance. Each man knew, for example, that if the civic militia was reduced by the dereliction of a single individual, the safety of the city would be appreciably diminished, and, conversely, that any conspicuous courage displayed by a member of that militia would be immediately known by his fellow citizens. Thus each citizen developed a feeling of responsibility to and for his city and a conviction of his own worth and the value of his participation in the life of the state—qualities that were intimately related to that cluster of virtues often simply referred to as the "Greek spirit."

The young citizen was thoroughly trained in the tradition of the past and had before him the example of the honors accorded men who served their state well. Under the critical eyes of their elders, the young were drilled in the hard skills of war—spear-throwing, wrestling, running, and jumping—in the city square or public exercise field. Moral precepts and examples of heroism, culled from the heroic tradition and its poetry, were passed along from generation to generation. Every youth learned the responsibility of citizenship as he listened to the debates on public questions in the city square. Basically, the city itself was the schoolmaster of the young. Political participation in the life of the polis was based upon tightly knit associations of families, clans, and tribes that were also sanctioned by religion. Each group was favored or protected by a certain god or gods. Thus, even his family life and worship bound the Greek citizen to the political life of his city.

A handful of families that had provided leadership in war and counsel for longer than anyone could remember held the choicest land in the estates beyond the city walls. Their wealth gave them the leisure to participate more fully and continually in public life, and they belonged to the proud traditions and blood lines that flowed from the warrior kings and heroes of the Bronze Age. Even the assembly of the people, which was the basic institution of government, was swayed and intimidated by the council of nobility, which existed under different names in different Greek states. As the aristocratic view of life became deeply ingrained in Greek civilization, the values of the nobility became those of the entire state.

Colonization and the Rise of Tyranny

About 750 B.C. the cities of the Greek world began to prosper once more. Though there were vast material differences from one state and one region to another, trade began to quicken generally and in some locations to thrive. The pressure of population in the old settlements and the fear of economic exploitation and debt also stimulated thousands of Greeks to leave their home cities and plant colonies all around the Mediterranean Sea. Greek cities dotted the coast of the Black Sea and grew up in the fertile soil of Sicily and southern Italy. The trade of the western Mediterranean enriched such colonial settlements as Syracuse in Sicily, and Tarentum, Sybaris, and Neapolis (later Naples) in Italy.

As colonization accelerated, the earlier simplicity of the isolated, static farm villages rapidly disappeared from much of the Greek world. Metallic coinage, which was "invented" in the kingdom of Lydia during the eighth century B.C.—or perhaps copied from farther east—was quickly adopted by the Ionian cities. It facilitated commerce and, at the same time, provided a new source of wealth which could be quickly accumulated in a form distinct from property. A new class of citizens whose wealth came from trade began to arise, and rumblings of discontent were heard against

THE IONIAN GREEKS, c. 750 B.C.

the long-established and inviolable class structure based on the ownership of land. As lower classes demanded political, social, and economic concessions, the ancient nobility clung doggedly to their privileges. These social tensions were especially serious in cities where trade, commerce, and industry flourished and contact with other peoples and ways of life fed discontent.

The series of revolutions that took place along the routes of trade in the expanding Greek world culminated in the rise of "tyranny"[6] in almost every commercial state of the late seventh and sixth centuries B.C. Swept

6. The term "tyranny" was not originally the totally negative word it has become. To the Greeks of the preclassic period "tyrant" meant simply one who ruled without traditional sanctions. And, since such sanctions were usually controlled by the old aristocracies, the tyrant might well be—and often was—a champion of the people. It was only in later time, and with the abuse of power by tyrants themselves, that tyranny gained the taint we associate with it.

into power by the hopes and enthusiasm of the populace for whose discontent he provided a voice and a rallying point, the tyrant could rule as long as he pleased them. Sometimes he was a man of the people, more often a noble turned democrat, and his usual policy was to despoil the nobility of power, position, and wealth. Most of the tyrants were themselves men of taste and ability, and in many cities the period of tyranny was one of great material and cultural progress. Public works of every sort—temples, theaters, harbor works, and fortifications—were constructed, and art and literature were lavishly patronized. This period of boldness and experimentation in the arts of civilization proved to be a transition between the rule of the few and the rule of the many.

The Growth of Greek Religion

The earlier Greeks brought with them into the lands of the Mediterranean the refractory family of their typically Indo-European gods, ruled by Zeus. The deities of the older Mediterranean religions, too powerful to be ignored, were assimilated into this family—often rather uncomfortably and sometimes incongruously. The completely humanized gods lived on the cloud-draped height of Mount Olympus in a social framework that was a heavenly counterpart of human society, and the Greeks wove about them a fascinating and intricate web of mythology.

The gods were no more moral, wise, or beautiful than man, and they were capable of base behavior and petty emotions. As members of a higher order than man could attain, however, they were powerful and, above all, eternal. As the poet Pindar stated it:

> One is the race of Gods and of men; from one
> mother we both draw our breath. Yet are our
> powers poles apart; for we are nothing, but
> for them the brazen Heaven endures for ever,
> their secure abode.

Even the shade of the great hero Achilles, when Odysseus visited Hades, said:

> Nay, speak not comfortably to me of death, oh
> great Odysseus. Rather would I live on ground
> as the hireling of another, with a landless
> man who had no great livelihood, than bear
> sway among all the dead that be departed.

Since in early Greece, as in the Ancient Near East, religion and politics were inseparable, the formal state religion contributed to the political advantage of the nobles, who often claimed descent and special favor from the gods and who probably monopolized the priestly functions. When the conflicts of nobles and commons swelled to revolution at the close of the Greek Middle Age, resentment was directed against the Olympian gods, and "popular religion" began to manifest itself in a variety of mystery cults. Secret societies met in the name of some god—usually not one of the Olympians—and engaged in practices often bloody and orgiastic, aimed at identifying the worshiper with his cult god. Based on the belief that personal immortality could be attained through participation in the god's immortality, such practices were related to the ancient belief in the efficacy of earth and fertility magic; many of them arose directly from pre-Greek, Minoan religion, and some Asiatic and Egyptian influences are also apparent.

The Origins of Philosophy

The search for order and unity in nature and the universe outside the context of religious belief led to the earliest development of a type of speculation that modern man is able to call "philosophy." In the Ionian cities, whose wealth provided the leisure and freedom for productive thought, the nature and origin of the universe and the physical world were first investigated by Thales of Miletus (c. 640–546 B.C.). A widely traveled man of means, Thales was influenced by the learning of the earlier Egyptian and Near Eastern civilizations, especially by their mathematics, as he set about to explain the rigorous regularities he observed in the universe and its apparent unity. His orderly, rational search for a "first matter" out of which everything else had been made led him to conclude that the primal substance was water. Some of his followers contended it was air, others earth, and still others different substances, but more important than their specific conclusions is the fact that they were the first "cosmologists" of western civilization. In their search for unity and their drive to organize and simplify the chaos of human knowledge, they developed a naturalistic orientation of thought that was to become a characteristic of Greek philosophy, finding its summation in the system of Aristotle.

The Ionian search continued, becoming more abstract and mathematical, until Anaximander (611–547 B.C.) conceived of a unity so vast that it could contain and produce all things and every change could be contained within it. This "boundlessness," the never-ending, expressed the concept of infinity for the first time, and the idea that a cosmic purpose moved through that infinity necessarily presupposed an active force for order in the universe. This supposition formed a second basic strand of Greek philosophy, the "mystic tendency," expressed most clearly by Pythagoras in the mid-sixth century B.C.

Pythagoras is usually remembered for his mathematical discoveries, and his search for universal unity culminated in the abstract, mathematical concept of ratio. This one constant in a world of change imposed a unity upon opposites: just as chaotic sound subjected to ratio became music, so other unlike things could be brought together harmoniously. Pythagoras also applied the concept of harmony, which was to have great significance in later Greek civilization, to man and his mode of life. By relating it to religion, he became the first philosopher to introduce an ethical content into the complexities of myth and ritual.

At the school he founded in the Greek city of Croton in the south of Italy, Pythagoras taught a religious philosophy of purification and salvation. His system propounded the existence and transmigration of the soul and incorporated the cult of Orpheus, one of the mystery gods. After his school was destroyed in the bitter social conflicts of the period of tyranny, much of what he taught disappeared into legend, from which it still cannot be clearly separated. Nevertheless, though his ideas, as they are known to modern man, seem fragmentary and often incoherent, they had a tremendous and continuing impact upon Greek thought. By opposing and balancing such ideas as body and soul, good and evil, nature and supernature, Pythagoras devised the first system of philosophic dualism in western philosophy.

The Foundations of Greek Art

During the same period that produced the beginnings of philosophy Greek art developed its most characteristic features. The basic forms of architecture and sculpture had their source in religious inspiration, and the artistic tradition of the Bronze Age was apparently handed down only in the most fragmentary manner, the influences of Egypt and the Near East being more important.

No separate temple structure had existed during the Bronze Age, but by the classical period the only significant architectural works created by the Greeks were temples. Once the temple had been established as a distinct entity of set shape, the drive to perfect its beauty and religious effectiveness began. The development of temple architecture was also a function of civic patriotism, for worship was intimately connected with every aspect of Greek life. The city itself was protected by certain gods, as were tribal and family units and workmen in the various crafts and trades; even street corners, wells, doorposts, and hilltops had their gods. When the Greek citizen lifted his eyes to his city's temples, he partook of the greatness and prestige they represented.

Sculptors also turned to the gods, presenting their figures as the perfection of human form and beauty. Models for their works could be found everywhere: in the naked young men performing their military drill and gymnastics in the city square, in the superb athletes of the physical contests that were part of the year's round of festivals in every Greek city, and in the chaste young women growing to maturity in the practice of domestic virtue. Their coolly noble statues were generalized representations of both perfect virtue and perfect form; they were designed to set before the eyes of men in eternal substance the values by which they should live. Thus Apollo, the god of young men, became every vigorous, handsome youth, and the dignity and power of Zeus or Poseidon expressed the bearing of the civic leader or the captain of the city militia.

No Greek statue was designed to represent any one man, no matter how individually perfect in form. Rather, the idealized figures of the perfect man, or god, were enhanced by the sublime quality that is now known as "classic." In early temples, statues, and vase figures, the balance essential to classic art was crude and obvious, mathematical and stiff, but later it became a wonderfully subtle interplay of space and form. The idea of limit or moderation was also essential to classic art. Taking a few relatively basic and pleasing forms—a handful of flower and leaf shapes, statuary of various types and poses, and temples of various construction— the Greeks polished, refined, and developed them to perfection.

The Encroachment of Persia

Forming a loose and jealous confederation on the edge of the great ruined empires of the Ancient Near East, the Ionian city-states, the richest and most progressive in the Hellenic world, had grown to maturity secure from external threat. At the height of their prosperity, however, in the early seventh century B.C., the Kingdom of Lydia in Asia Minor grew strong enough to absorb most of them. Lydian domination was apparently not oppressive, and as the two cultures gradually fused, the Ionians profited from their inclusion in the economic and cultural sphere of a great and wealthy Oriental state.

About the middle of the sixth century B.C., the Persian Empire began its expansion far to the east, in the highlands of present-day Iran. Under a dynasty of able kings, the first of whom was Cyrus the Great (*550–529* B.C.), they embarked on a conquest of the known world. The brutal, short-lived Assyrian empire quickly crumbled, and in 546 B.C. the Persians overwhelmed Lydia and the Ionian cities. By the reign of Darius I (*521–485* B.C.), "the Great King," as the Greeks called him, the realm spread from the Mediterranean to the Indus River; from the homeland of the Cimmerians on the steppes of southern Asia to the Indian Ocean. With the incorporation of Ionia into the vast Persian Empire, the formative period of Hellenic civilization came to an end.

ATHENS, WONDER OF THE WORLD

The Growth of Athens

Greek civilization reached its apogee in the city-state of Athens. From a remote little market town on the rocky Attic peninsula, Athens developed into a typical polis, dominated by an aristocratic oligarchy. By the beginning of the sixth century B.C. the effects of the commercial revolution sweeping the Greek world had made themselves felt in Athens, and a new merchant class rose to challenge the vested interests of the landed aristocracy. Another threat developed in the discontented peasant class, which was pressured both by the aristocratic engrossment of land and by the inflationary tendencies of the new money economy.

In 594 B.C., faced with mounting political tensions, Athens took a decisive step, giving dictatorial power to the eminent statesman, Solon (*c.* 638–559 B.C.). An aristocrat but also a well-to-do merchant as well as a man of learning and cultivation, Solon promulgated a series of reforms which embraced all classes and the social, economic, and political institutions and practices of Athens.

Solon recognized in his economic reforms that the future of Athens lay in commerce and that the economy must be adapted accordingly. He saw that it was necessary to turn from stable land values to the expansive values of trade and fluid capital, and to effect this he shifted Athens to another standard of coinage that brought her into the trade network of other growing mainland cities. To provide a valuable export crop that could be exchanged for the agricultural necessities that the poor and rocky soil of Attica could not yield, Solon encouraged the large-scale development of olive culture, since olive oil was a highly prized staple of ancient trade. He reformed the existing laws and removed some of the most serious burdens

THE GREEK CITY STATES
AND THE AEGEAN
ABOUT 500 B.C.

150 MILES

THRACE
Byzantium
Calchedon
BOSPORUS
PROPONTIS

MACEDONIA
Pella
Thessalonica
CHALCIDICE
THASOS
SAMOTHRACE
IMBROS
MT. ATHOS
HELLESPONT
PHRYGIA
Troy

EPIRUS
MT. OLYMPUS
THESSALY
THRACIAN SEA
LEMNOS

CORCYRA
AMBRACIA
LESBOS
MYSIA
PERSIAN

AEGEAN
SCYRUS
LYDIA
Sardis

LEUCAS
AETOLIA
LIS
LOCRIS
PHOCIS
Delphi
EUBOEA
Eretria
CHIOS
EMPIRE

CEPHALLENIA
BOEOTIA
PLATAEA
SEA

ACHAIA
Megara
MARATHON
Athens
ANDROS
SAMOS

ELLIS
ARCADIA
Corinth
ARGOLIS
ATTICA
SALAMIS
AEGINA
TENOS
ICARIA
Miletus
CARIA

ZACYNTHUS
Olympia
CEOS
MYKONOS
DELOS

MESSENIA
LACONIA
CYNTHUS
PAROS
NAXOS

Pylos
Sparta
PELOPONNESUS
SIPHNUS
IOS

MELOS
RHODES

CYTHERA
CRETAN
CARPATHUS

AEGILIA
SEA

Knossus
Tanais
TRM

CRETE
Phaestus

Massilia
ILLYRIA
DANUBE
BLACK SEA

CORSICA
ITALY
Rome
ADRIATIC SEA
THRACE
Byzantium
Sinope
Trapezus
Ph

SARDINIA
Naples
MACEDONIA
LYDIA
PONTUS

MAGNA
Croton
GREECE
ASIA
CAPPADOCIA

Carthage
Selinus
SICILY
GRAECIA
Syracuse
AEGEAN
SEA
PELOPONNESUS
Athens
Sparta
Miletus
CARIA
Tarsus
Phaselis
Soli

AFRICA
Knossus
RHODES
CYPRUS
PHOENICIA
SYRIA
Tyre

CRETE

GREEK CITY STATES
AND COLONIES
Cyrene
NILE
DELTA

500 MILES
LIBYAN DESERT
Naucratis
EGYPT

THE GREEK WORLD ABOUT 550 B.C.

of the peasantry by abolishing slavery for debt and by forbidding a man to give either his land or his person for security. He further bolstered the Athenian economy by encouraging the immigration of skilled craftsmen and artisans from other cities by liberal grants of citizenship.

Perhaps the most important reforms instituted by Solon were those affecting the machinery of government. Prior to this, the class to which a citizen belonged, and consequently the degree to which he was enabled to participate in government, depended upon the ownership of land. By translating land ownership into monetary values, Solon opened participation in government to the growing class of merchants and artisans. The assembly of the people was accorded the basic power of decision and consent. Above the assembly Solon created a council of four hundred, its members drawn equally from the four ancient Athenian tribes. This body formulated the issues to be considered by the more unwieldy assembly and took a large part in the routine of government. It almost replaced the older council of nobility which retained, however, a vague and semireligious function as the "guardian of the laws." He created large popular courts, comprising some six thousand jurors drawn from all property classes, as a judicial check upon those who made and administered public policy. The overall effect of Solon's reforms was to create a state adapted to exploit the economic opportunities which lay before Greece and which accorded all classes some responsibility for the welfare of the state.

Excellent and far-reaching though these reforms were, they did not succeed in solving two major problems: the continued political dominance of the nobility and the economic distress of the peasant farmers. There was still no instrument of government that the nobility could not influence, either directly or indirectly. And the peasant problem remained unsolved because only a redistribution of land would make it possible for them to survive, and this the nobility was able to prevent. As the situation became progressively worse, the way was opened for the rise of a tyrant, in this case a spokesman for the peasantry, an ambitious and persuasive politician named Pisistratus.

In 560 B.C., with the aid of an armed band, Pisistratus seized the Acropolis and established a tyranny in Athens. The pattern so often set in other Greek cities was repeated. Pisistratus ruled in the interest of the poor and the many at the expense of the wealthy and the few. By exploiting the nobles, he solved for a time the problem of the land-hungry peasantry. Like Solon, moreover, he recognized that Athens had to be a commercial state and encouraged the new economy as well. Commerce and business flourished. Great building projects gave employment to hundreds of citizens. The shrewd economic diplomacy of Pisistratus extended the markets for Athenian goods; and the prestige of Athens rose in the Greek world.

Under Pisistratus and his sons the tyranny lasted for half a century of peace, growth, and prosperity. In 510 B.C., however, the vengeful nobles organized a coup that ended the tyranny. But it was no longer possible to turn back the clock and restore the narrow oligarchy of a few conservative, aristocratic families.

The Persian Wars

The Ionian cities flamed into revolt against Persia in 499 B.C. and appealed to the other Greek states for support. Athens (joined by the small city of Eretria) sent twenty-five ships against the greatest empire in the world.

By 493 B.C. the revolt had been crushed and the Athenians' effort had succeeded only in affronting the Persian Empire. Herodotus, the Greek historian of the Persian Wars, recounts that on being informed of the intervention of Athens, Darius shot an arrow high into the air and swore an oath, " 'Grant me, Zeus, to revenge myself on the Athenians!' After this speech, he bade one of his servants every day, when his dinner was spread, three times repeat these words to him, 'Master, remember the Athenians.' "[7] He remembered them; in 491 B.C. Darius sent a task force against both Athens and Eretria. These states sought help from their fellow Greeks and got little or none. While Eretria was being besieged, the Athenian militia marched across the Attic peninsula to the Aegean coast and faced the superior Persian force which had been landed at Marathon. The Athenians, fighting with desperate courage, won their victory at Marathon.

This Persian defeat encouraged revolts in other parts of the empire. Before order could be restored, Darius died and was succeeded by his son Xerxes I (c. 486-465 B.C.). It was ten years, 480 B.C., before Xerxes could marshall the kind of force that would make victory seem certain. Every detail was methodically organized, and the army marched to the Hellespont, where a bridge of ships had been built for their transit to Europe. When a storm destroyed the bridge, the king punished the sea with three hundred lashes which were delivered while the scourgers chanted, "Thou bitter water, thy lord lays on thee this punishment because thou

7. *The Persian Wars,* George Rawlinson (trans.) Bk V, ch. 105.

hast wronged him without a cause. . . ."[8] The bridge was rebuilt and the army crossed.

The Persian grand strategy was a double attack by land and by sea— the army marching around the Aegean to attack Greece from the north, the fleet skirting the coast supporting the army and prepared to blockade the coastal cities and destroy their fleets. Heralds had been sent into Greece and dozens of states had given earth and water as symbols of their submission to Persia. The remaining states met in desperate conference to decide how best to meet this threat.

The council was dominated by the Athenian general, Themistocles (*c.* 527-460 B.C.), who advanced a plan based on the hope of a naval victory. For years Themistocles had advocated a powerful Athenian navy. His policy represented a blend of high patriotism and personal political ambition. Envisioning Athens as the supreme maritime power of the Greek world, he had wooed support from the shipping and commercial interests of the city and organized them into a political party. By 480 B.C. he had succeeded in his design and Athens had a powerful fleet.

As the Persians advanced in the north, Themistocles convinced his fellow Greeks that if the Persian fleet were defeated, the Persian army could not be provisioned and would have to retire. It was decided that a small land force would fight a holding action in the north while the combined Greek fleet attempted a decisive defeat of the Persian navy. The land force under the leadership of a few hundred Spartans took up a defensive position at the pass of Thermopylae, which commanded the approaches to central Greece. They bought time with their lives: after two days of heroic resistance, they were betrayed and mainland Greece lay open to the Persian advance. Furthermore, the battle at sea had not been decisive.

As the dispirited Greek fleet sailed south toward Athens, pursued by the Persian navy, and the victorious Persian land forces marched unimpeded through the Greek states, the end seemed inevitable.

Aware that Athens was the special object of Persian vengeance, the citizens began to abandon their homes. From across the bay of Salamis and the nearby islands they watched as the Persian army swept into their city and set it on fire. The Greek ships milled in the bay and Xerxes had a great throne built on the shore from which to watch his fleet administer the final blow. But the policy to which Themistocles had devoted his life

8. *Ibid.,* VII, 35

was dramatically vindicated. In this moment of desperation he rallied the Greek ships to join in battle with the enemy. In the crowded bay the vast, unwieldy Persian fleet was unable to maneuver, while confusion of command further hampered their efforts. The Battle of Salamis was an overwhelming Greek victory. What was left of the Persian fleet sailed for Asia. The Persian army, having destroyed the crops in its advance, had to abandon Athens and retreat to the north. Xerxes returned to Asia. In the following year a pitched battle was fought at Plataea and the combined armies of the Greek states defeated the Persians who were left in Greece. On the same day—according to tradition—their ships delivered a comparable defeat to the last of the Persian fleet in the harbor of Mycale in Asia Minor. Greece had defeated Persia in one of the great military reversals of history. David had again met and toppled Goliath.

The Creation of the Athenian Empire

The Golden Age of classical Hellenism may be dated from the end of the Persian Wars. It was an age dominated by Athens. With the defeat of Persia the entire Greek world was swept by a wave of enthusiasm, a surge of indomitable optimism. Nowhere was it more marked than in Athens, largely responsible for the victory through Athenian policy, Athenian ships, Athenian leadership. But the city gained more than a new prestige from the war; she gained a new economic position. The Ionian cities of Asia Minor had been virtually destroyed by the long war which had involved them for some twenty years. Their fleets had been appropriated, their economies shaken, and their web of commerce torn apart. As a result, the center of Greek economic life shifted to the mainland and to Athens.

The Greek world realized—and no state more than Athens—that, though Persia had been defeated it had not been destroyed. Therefore, in 477 B.C., the major maritime states and the smaller states of the Aegean formed a defensive alliance under the presidency of Athens. Each state was bound by treaty to Athens and was assessed a proportionate tribute for naval construction and defense. The league was placed under the protection of Apollo and its treasury located on the sacred island of Delos.

From the beginning the Delian League was endangered more by Athenian ambition than by Persia. In 454 B.C. the treasury was transferred to Athens. Then in 449 B.C. the Athenians negotiated a formal peace with Persia, ending both the Persian threat and the need for a defensive league. Yet in the next year, Athens reimposed the tribute upon the member states. What had begun as the free alliance of states for mutual defense had become the basis for an Athenian empire. The league fleet became an Athenian navy, the league fund an Athenian treasury. The league territory was expanded and, within a few years, by 443 B.C., divided into tributary districts. Thus Athens secured the economic base on which to build her civilization.

Pericles and His Policy

Both the imperial policy and the cultural achievements of Athens in the fifth century are associated with the name of Pericles. From 461 to 429 B.C. he virtually ruled the city as the dominant member of the Board of Generals, which had become the chief executive power after Themistocles. A wealthy aristocrat, Pericles dedicated himself—in the best tradition of his class—to public service. When he spoke men called him "the Olympian." Paradoxically, his party was the democratic party created by Themistocles. He gave to Athens a unique way of political life; as Plutarch says, "an aristocratic government, that went by the name of a democracy, but was, indeed, the supremacy of a single man." No one has expressed it better than Pericles himself, speaking from the pages of Thucydides:

. . . we are called a democracy, for the administration is in the hands of the many and not of the few. But while the law secures equal justice to all alike in their private disputes, the claim of excellence is also recognized; and when a citizen is in any way distinguished, he is preferred to the public service, not as a matter of privilege, but as the reward of merit. Neither is poverty a bar, but a man may benefit his country whatever be the obscurity of his condition.

. . . a spirit of reverence pervades our public acts; we are prevented from doing wrong by respect for authority and for the laws.

Our city is thrown open to the world, and we never expel a foreigner or prevent him from seeing or learning anything of which the secret if revealed to an enemy might profit him. We rely not upon management or trickery, but upon our own hearts and hands.

For we are lovers of the beautiful, yet with economy, and we cultivate the mind without loss of manliness. Wealth we employ, not for talk and ostentation, but when there is real use for it. To avow poverty with us is no disgrace; the true disgrace is in doing nothing to avoid it. An Athenian citizen does not neglect the state because he takes care of his own household; and even those of us who are engaged in business have a very fair idea of politics. We alone regard a man who takes no interest in public affairs, not a harmless, but as a useless character; and if few of us are originators, we are all sound judges of policy.

The great impediment to action is, in our opinion, not discussion, but the want of that knowledge which is gained by discussion preparatory to action. For we have a peculiar power of thinking before we act and of acting too, whereas other men are courageous from ignorance but hesitate upon reflection.[9]

No loftier statement of the virtues, goals, rewards, and responsibilities of democracy has ever been made. But Pericles here pictured the ideal rather than the actual, for the period of his rule was marked by a continuation of class warfare and intense party strife. Though democracy triumphed, it was at the cost of bitterness and division. Moreover, the success of the democratic party in Athens was tied to the exploitation of the empire—for it was tribute from the empire that was used to reward the people and thus assure their support. The glory of Athens at home was based on repression abroad. But, at the same time, the wealth that poured into Athens from the empire made possible the highest achievement of Greek civilization. It virtually created a patronage class of the entire Athenian citizenry. It gave unprecedented leisure to that citizenry to cultivate the refinements of art and argument. It paid the elderly a form of relief for service on the mass juries of the Athenian courts. It defrayed for the poor the cost of attending the dramatic festivals which, it was asserted, instructed citizens in virtue. The wealth of Athens attracted talent, commercial and artistic, from all over the Greek world and beyond—and resident aliens called *metics* swelled the population into the hundreds of thousands and infinitely enriched the city in goods as well as in ideas. Moreover, the rise of Athens to political and economic power coincided happily with the end of the preparatory phase in the development of practically every form of art and thought the Greek world had developed. These forms, created in the many centers of the archaic culture, tended to drift to Athens where one after another they were given their classic form, in the Attic Black Figure vases, the cast metal sculpture of Myron (possibly Corinthian in origin), the originally Asiatic Ionic temple style, the Ionian epic, or the preclassic form of the tragic drama. Athens became indeed "the school of Hellas."

The Realization of Classic Art

When the people of Athens returned to their city after the Battle of Salamis, they found it in smoking ruins. Yet this seeming disaster

---

9. *The Peloponnesian War*, B. Jowett (trans.) II, 35-36.

became a challenge and opportunity for Athens to cap her victory with the most magnificent creations of Greek art. A new Athens began to rise, crowned by the Acropolis, the hilltop fortress which had been the refuge of the Athenians in the early days of their history. It had long since been abandoned for human habitation and given over to the gods, its temples and statuary associated with all the traditions that gave Athens her proud identity. But the whole venerable complex had been burned by the Persians with the rest of the city. Thus, when the Athenians set about to rebuild their city, the Acropolis was their special concern. It was to be the symbol of the spirit and greatness of Athens.

The most imposing structure of the Acropolis, the Parthenon, was the temple dedicated to Athena Parthenos, the virgin goddess and namesake and patron of the city. The Parthenon was built between 447 and 438 B.C. It was a large temple by Greek standards, one hundred feet in width and two hundred twenty-eight feet in length. All its proportions were carefully set—from the dimensions of its typical rectangular base to the small carved pegs under the edge of the overhanging roof. The Parthenon was the most perfect of Doric buildings, the end product of the historic evolution of that architectural style. Greek architecture had developed not only a sense of structure but a sense of appropriateness and style. The Parthenon is the perfect sum of many perfect particulars. This perfection and unity were gained, in part, by the self-conscious employment of irregularities. These are called "refinements," and they have the same subtle effect in a work of architecture as modeling and the calculated play of light and shadow do in a piece of sculpture. The columns of the Parthenon have a slight *entasis,* or "swelling," which makes them seem to "give" under the weight they bear and thus avoid the appearance of rigidity and strain. They were placed closer together as they approached the corners of the building, again satisfying the eye's demand for the appearance of greater support. The columns and the walls were inclined inward a few inches to enhance the impression of stability and the long sides of the temple base gradually rose several inches toward the middle to correct the visual sag of an absolutely straight line of that length. Even the pattern of shadows cast by the fluting of the columns was carefully contrived for the same subtle, organic effect. The whole edifice was of Pentelic marble; both inside and out it was lavishly decorated with bright gilt and paint. No expense was spared— the finest architects, the finest artists, the finest craftsmen and materials were summoned for this monument to art and to Athens.

The smaller temple of the Erechtheum represented the perfection of the Ionic style. The columns of the north and east porches are the most beautiful and perfectly proportioned Ionic columns in all the ruins of Greek architecture. All the parts of the building are superbly finished. The Porch of the Maidens, where a series of sedate, standing statues of young women (caryatids) gracefully and effortlessly bear the weight of an overhanging roof, expresses the Ionic love of decoration.

In fifth-century Athens the two styles met to close a magnificent chapter in the world's architecture. One smaller temple, the Temple of the Wingless Victory, was completed; other structures such as the Propylaea, a monumental gateway with portico and gallery, were only partially finished. Even the roof of the Erechtheum remained unfinished, the money that would have been used for its completion being diverted to war.

Much of Greek sculpture had always been associated with architecture and, just as the classic orders reached their perfection in the Acropolis, so Greek sculpture realized its completion there also. In its final period of transition to the classic style, in the generation of the Persian Wars, sculpture at last achieved the conquest of technique in rendering the form toward which it had been striving for centuries. The work of such artists as Myron, Polyclitus, and Phidias crowned the sculpture of the fifth century B.C. The greatest of the sculptors was Phidias, who had been called the sculptor of gods; Polyclitus had been called the sculptor of men. It is not surprising, therefore, that Phidias was given general charge of the Parthenon. Some of the statuary was his own work, notably the famous and expensive cult image, Athena Parthenos, some forty feet high and made of gold and ivory. But his unifying direction was everywhere apparent.

The scheme of decoration was appropriately connected with Athens and Athena. The Parthenon was her temple and the structure in which the conscious pride of Athens found its symbol. Athena was a war goddess, and in the ninety-two *metopes,* the alternate spaces of the exterior Doric frieze, were depicted pairs of struggling figures illustrating episodes from legendary wars. In each metope the figures achieved perfect balance within their restrictive space. Inside the building a continuous Ionic frieze more than five hundred feet long depicted the Pan-Athenaic procession, the solemn conclusion of the great quadrennial festival of Athena.

The outside of the building was completed by the pediment groups. Fifty sublime figures were balanced and set in faultless proportion in the flat, triangular spaces under the gables of the east and west ends of the

"Temple of Poseidon" detail. c. 460 B.C.

Above: *Battle of the Gods and Giants,* from the north frieze of the Treasury of the Syphnians, Delphi. c. 530 B.C.

Left: Archaic Ephelic Torso.

Below: Black-Figured Amphora showing Warrior Arming. Attributed to the Amasis Painter. c. 550—540.

OPPOSITE

Right: *Poseidon (Zeus?).* c. 460—450 B.C.

Left: SKOPAS? *Battle of Greeks and Amazons*, from the Mausoleum of Halikarnassos. c. 355—330 B.C.
Right: *Dying Gaul*. c. 240—200 B.C. Roman copy.

Right: *Three Goddesses*, from the east pediment of the Parthenon. c. 438—432 B.C. Athens.

13

Porch of the Maidens (Caryatid Porch) from the Erechtheum.
421—406 B.C. Athens.

building. The long battle of Greek sculpture to deal effectively with this difficult space was won in the Parthenon. It was customary for the west pediment of a Greek temple to depict violence; the east, repose. The east pediment of the Parthenon presented the birth of Athena; the west depicted the mythological strife of Athena and Poseidon for the domination of the Acropolis. In each case the figures were confined within their limited space, yet appeared to move entirely free of its restriction.

Other famous works of art dotted the Acropolis and Athens became a museum of the finest of Greek classic art. Her wealth and prestige attracted talent and ability from every corner of the Greek world. The workers, craftsmen, and artisans who flooded into the city brought their own techniques, their native crafts and skills which acted as a leaven for the skills and arts native to Athens. Metalwork in bronze, gold, and silver, pottery of great delicacy and brilliant design—every form of art flourished.

The Market of Ideas

The very nature of Athenian public life made men aware of ideas and led them into discussion and debate. Rhetoricians made schools of the street corners. Soothsayers and astrologers rubbed shoulders with physicians and philosophers. Men who had things to say came to Athens. Every form of literature was represented, as was every form of thought. Poets, scholars, prose writers, and charlatans all had their hearing in the *agora,* or market place, of this brilliant city. The strands of Greek philosophy were gathered into Athens.

On the eve of the Persian Wars, Greek philosophy was beginning to mature. The gap that had separated the semireligious, mystic Pythagorean philosophy from the semiscientific thought of the Ionian cosmologists had begun to close and two new, though opposing, schools developed, propounding in general the philosophy of stability on the one hand and the philosophy of change on the other.

Stability had its great advocate in Parmenides, who lived about 500 B.C. He radically changed the course of philosophy with his conclusion that nature, the very subject matter of Ionian philosophy, was merely the product of illusion. The very processes of nature are change—the coming to be and passing away, growth and decay. Parmenides rejected the possibility of change; he saw no way that "being" could become "not being" without altering its condition, for if these are ultimate, polar condi- the very "facts" of nature by the "facts" of logic and Greek philosophy tions, then they cannot alter themselves. This striking conclusion invalidated took a momentous turn away from observation toward pure reason. This path was to lead to many absurdities, but it also led to some of the most abstract and lofty speculations in the history of philosophy. Faced with the two states of "being" and "not being," Parmenides and his followers turned to "being," giving it an almost religious importance. "Being" was eternal, immovable, ubiquitous; a unity interconnected, indivisible, homogeneous, boundless, impenetrable. In short, this was "the one" that philosophy was to be occupied with for centuries.

Just as surely and as logically as Parmenides and his school had found stability as the essential condition of reality, his irascible contemporary, Heraclitus "the obscure," came to the opposite view. He boldly accepted what his senses revealed, which was that the only constant is the constancy of change; that, for example, a moment of time is gone even as one notes it or that one cannot put his foot in the same river twice.

Both Parmenides and Heraclitus had their followers and their opponents. The endless debates of these schools and subschools were symptomatic of the richness of Greek intellectual life, for there was not only contention but creation. The Greeks investigated every significant field of philosophic speculation and every subsequent philosopher or philosophic system has had to begin with some aspect or tenet of Greek thought.

Yet, the greatest achievement of Greek philosophy was not part of this golden, Periclean age but of a later time. Perhaps the Athens of Pericles was too busy with the art of living to afford time for contemplation. The typical Athenian was too much a practical man of affairs to pay much heed to the abstract speculations of philosophy. It remained for a more troubled and less confident age to bring Greek philosophy to its completion and to grapple at last with the problems of human nature and behavior.

The Poetry of Drama

Periclean Athens sought wisdom not from her philosophers but from her poets. For centuries poetry had been the teacher of Hellenism and it continued to be in Athens of the fifth century B.C. The men who most persuasively expressed the eternal quest of mind were poets, and their form was the tragic drama.

It is typically Greek that the most profound of questions should have been expressed within the framework of an art form. It is also typical that both the substance and the form should have been intimately associated with religion. Tragedy originated long before the fifth century. It had its beginnings in the turbulent times at the end of the Greek Middle Age and in the religious revolution expressed in the development of the mystery cults. Its earliest form was the wild and bloody passion play associated with the widespread worship of the fertility god Dionysus. During the tyranny of Pisistratus, the performance of this became part of an annual festival, the Great Dionysia of the City, celebrating the rebirth of vegetation and human hope in the rebirth of the god.

Gradually the religious ritual became an art form. The unrestrained chanting and singing took a definite literary pattern. Unrelieved choral monotony was broken by the introduction of actors. Without losing any of its basic religious character, the drama came to deal with other myths and sagas as the great storehouse of Greek traditional literature was opened to dramatic treatment: the cosmic tragedy of Prometheus, the fate of Agamemnon and his family, the house of Oedipus, and others. In less than fifty years from its establishment as part of the regular cycle of Athenian festivals, the drama had developed from a crude and simple ritual to the richness and variety of the classical tragedy—staged, understandably, in the Theater of Dionysus on the southern slope of the Acropolis.

Yet, the religious connection remained basic. Indeed, this was the very reason that tragedy developed as tragedy: it had to depict suffering and destruction. The tragic hero was a ritual substitute for the suffering god, and the play was his passion. The same strong bond continued to exist between the play and its audience that had existed between the ritual and its participants. The essence of tragedy was the ritual purification of the audience, what Aristotle called *catharsis*. This was achieved through vicarious suffering with the tragic hero.

Although many fragments of dramatic verse have survived from this period, the canon of classical tragedy is largely the work of three men: Aeschylus (525-456 B.C.), Sophocles (c. 496-406 B.C.), and Euripides (c. 480-406 B.C.). Aeschylus, a veteran of Marathon, was a stern moralist who wrote with force and directness. His tragedies include *Seven against Thebes, Prometheus Bound,* and a cycle of three plays, *The Oresteia,* dealing with the fate of Agamemnon and his family. Sophocles, a man of wealth, culture, and sophistication, spoke for the expansive, confident Athens that emerged from the Persian Wars. His long life spanned her Golden Age and for more than half a century his plays impressed and informed her people. His *Oedipus the King, Oedipus at Colonus,* and *Antigone* have not, even today, lost their power to move an audience.

Euripides, whose own life was a tormented tragedy, wrote, among others, *Medea, Alcestis, Iphigenia in Aulis,* and *Iphigenia in Tauris.*

Within the restrictive compass of the tragic form, the works of all three tragedians dealt with the same intricate cluster of problems, and above all the same basic question—the eternal quest for the cause of human suffering. Sophocles posed it in this famous choral speech from *Antigone:*

> Blessed are those whose life no woe doth taste!
> For unto those whose house
> The Gods have shaken, nothing fails of curse
> Or woe, that creeps to generations far.
> E'en thus a wave (when spreads,
> With blasts from Thracian coasts,
> The darkness of the deep)
> Up from the sea's abyss
> Hither and thither rolls the black sand on,
> And every jutting peak,
> Swept by the storm wind's strength,
> Lashed by the fierce wild waves,
> Re-echoes with the far-resounding roar.
>
> .   .   .
>
> Thy power, O Zeus, what haughtiness of man,
> Yea, what can hold in check?
> Which neither sleep, that maketh all things old,
> Nor the long months of Gods that never fail,
> Can for a moment seize.
>
> But still as Lord supreme,
> Waxing not old with time,
> Thou dwellest in Thy sheen of radiancy
> On far Olympus' height.
> Through future near or far as through the past,
> One law holds ever good,
> Nought comes to life of man unscathed throughout by woe.
>
> For hope to many comes in wanderings wild,
> A solace and support;
> To many as a cheat of fond desires,
> And creepeth still on him who knows it not,
> Until he burn his foot
> Within the scorching flame.
> Full well spake one of old,

That evil ever seems to be as good
   To those whose thoughts of heart
   God leadeth unto woe,
And without woe, he spends but shortest space of time.[10]

This emphasis upon suffering is not misanthropy or grimness. To the Greek tragedians there was really only one inexorable conflict, the struggle of life, conquered and dismembered by death. This is what Greek tragedy is about. And it implies, as it deals with this conflict, that there is something in the eternally destroyed life which returns to life again and that death's job is never done; that like Charon, it is doomed to the eternal frustration of a work that can have no end. It says that life is tragic, that it is filled with suffering, but—and this is its great moral point—man can rise above the common lot of his suffering and learn wisdom and virtue from it.

Greek comedy, like tragedy, reached its fullness in Athens. It had the same religious origin, perhaps representing the exultation and joy at the return of Dionysus from death. Its frankly sexual emphasis is closely tied to the fertility magic of that god. But although they had a common origin in religious festivals, tragedy and comedy differed widely in form, theme, and purpose. The great tragedians had taken the theme of a crude and ancient passion play and transformed it into a means for expressing moral truth and posing the most profound psychological and philosophical questions. The comic writers took a loose, ancient form of sex play and transformed it into a devastating device for social criticism. As tragedy took upon itself the function of teaching morality to the people of Athens, so comedy assumed the function of flaying them for not having learned it well enough.

Though we are at a disadvantage in making generalizations about comedy because the substantial work of only one comic writer has survived, we do find in the works of Aristophanes (*c.* 448–380 B.C.) keen and perceptive satire at its best. Aristophanes was a dedicated conservative who both feared and despised the decline he saw in public morality, the innovations he saw in the arts, the trends he perceived in public policy. His plays are a catalogue of his prejudices. In *The Clouds* he attacked what he saw as alarming tendencies in the teaching of philosophy, and pilloried the philosopher Socrates; he used *The Frogs* to contrast the

10. Quoted in Edwin M. Everett, Calvin S. Brown, and John D. Wade (eds.), *Masterworks of World Literature* (New York: The Dryden Press, 1947), I, pp. 216-17.

dignity and morality of Aeschylean tragedy with what he regarded as the degeneracy of Euripides; in *Lysistrata* he attacked the confusion of democratic leadership, which he thought was unnecessarily prolonging the war with Sparta. The plays of Aristophanes were never subtle; they are fast-moving, rollicking, and at times their lewd humor depended not only upon outrageously farcical situations, but upon cruel characterizations. In the hands of Aristophanes this acid literary form came to perfection.

Aristophanes and most of his contemporaries witnessed the waning of Athens, just as most of their fathers had seen her ascendancy in the victory over Persia. The end of Athens' Golden Age was in war as had been its beginning.

THE NEMESIS OF WAR

The Dragon Seeds

The achievement of Periclean Athens seems a triumph for the human spirit to us who stand so greatly in its debt. However, to the rest of the Greek world of the fifth century B.C. it symbolized the imperial chains with which Athens would bind them. As the growth of Athenian power provided the wealth and leisure conducive to cultural achievement, it inevitably aroused the envy, resentment, and fear of other states. The expansive quality of Athenian policy opposed the most deep-seated tradition of Greek political life, the autonomy of the city-state. The result was a thirty-year war that ultimately involved nearly every state in the Greek world. By its protraction, bitterness, and destructiveness it not only brought about the end of Athenian civilization but also the end of the Hellenic world. In what many scholars consider the greatest history ever written, Thucydides the Athenian has left a stirring record of this in his *The Peloponnesian War*.

The war took its name from the Peloponnesian League, a group of city-states constituting a competing center of power to Athens. The alliance was the more formidable because of its domination by the city of Sparta, whose influence directed both its spirit and its policies. The conflict came to be more than a clash of ambitions: it reflected a clash of ideologies and of two different ways of life—the Athenian and the Spartan. To understand the war, one must note the radical differences in the traditions and circumstances of these two cities. Ethnically, Athens was Ionic and Sparta, Doric. Athens was a rich maritime state; Sparta, a backward agricultural state. And, highly significant, Athens was a turbulent, broad-based democracy; Sparta, a conservative, narrow oligarchy.

Sparta and Her System

Before the middle of the eighth century B.C. Sparta had already begun to commit herself to the way of life that was to bring her to the Peloponnesian War. In this early period most of the Greek states solved their internal economic and social problems by turning to commerce or colonization. Sparta turned to conquest, and invaded the territory of her neighbor, Messenia. The conquered land was divided into lots and awarded to Spartan families; the conquered population was enslaved and Sparta's dependence on her slaves—called *helots*—began. This repressive system led to a revolt which was crushed with the greatest difficulty.

This was the moment for a crucial choice: Sparta could abandon her system of helotry and seek another economic expedient or she could keep it and condemn herself to eternal vigilance over a captive people. She chose the latter. The implications of this crucial choice are evident in the Spartan constitution which dates from this time and carries the name of the legendary lawgiver, Lycurgus. This constitution made of Sparta a perpetual armed camp, in which everything was subordinated to military needs. Ironically, this system, designed to maintain slavery, made the Spartans themselves the slaves of their system, molding the life of the Spartan from birth. Only physically fit children were permitted to live. At the age of seven they were placed in military barracks under brutal discipline and taught by painful lessons to be strong and resourceful. The Spartan youth grew up in a band of youths like himself who would later be fellow members of his military unit. As he grew older, he could marry but could not maintain a home. His home was his barracks, his family the band of his military companions. His table was the common mess to which he brought his share taken from his helot lands. Life was a military exercise. There was no place for art, luxury, and ease, and beauty was not given any value. It is not surprising that Sparta became the foremost military power in the Greek world; nor that she came to dominate the Peloponnesian League, which was constituted as a series of alliances between Sparta and the other member states.

The Peloponnesian War

The rivalry between Sparta and her league and Athens and her empire came to a head in the Age of Pericles. All that was needed for an open clash was a pretext, and this was provided by the commercial rivalry between Athens and Corinth, the chief merchant city of the Peloponnesian League. Beginning as a petty outbreak, the conflict spread from one minor state to another. In the spring of 431 B.C. Sparta entered the conflict and the Peloponnesian War began.

Pericles had long anticipated war with Sparta and his careful strategy dominated its early years. Athens was a well-fortified city and her ships commanded the sea. Thus, she could protect herself, provision herself, and police her empire. She could also blockade the Peloponnesian coast.

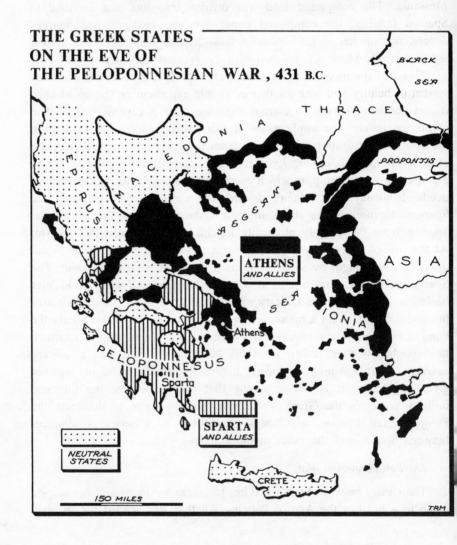

THE GREEK STATES
ON THE EVE OF
THE PELOPONNESIAN WAR , 431 B.C.

BLACK SEA

THRACE

PROPONTIS

EPIRUS

MACEDONIA

AEGEAN SEA

ASIA

ATHENS
AND ALLIES

IONIA

Athens

PELOPONNESUS

Sparta

SPARTA
AND ALLIES

NEUTRAL
STATES

CRETE

150 MILES

TRM

Pericles' strategy was to gather the outlying people within the protecting walls of the city and to allow the Peloponnesians to campaign fruitlessly through a land they could not win. This policy was successful through the first year of the war but during the summer of its second season a fearful plague broke out in the besieged and overcrowded city, carried from the east by Athenian supply ships.

Faced by ubiquitous and sudden death, the people panicked; rioting and looting broke out, and a demoralized populace gave itself to licentiousness. More than a third of the people of Athens died of the plague, including Pericles. With his death, the moderate policies he had advocated were abandoned. The war settled down to grim and costly attrition.

In 422 B.C. the most aggressive leaders of the war parties in both Sparta and Athens were killed and an uneasy peace was made the following year. After ten years of war none could claim victory. The Peace of Nicias was negotiated to last for fifty years; before it was a year old, the warring forces were at work again.

Athens found a new leader in Alcibiades (*c.* 450–404 B.C.), a brilliant young man with every gift but virtue. He broached a dramatic scheme, the conquest of Sicily, by which Athens would be able to corner the long-coveted western Mediterranean trade which had enriched Corinth and the Peloponnesian League. The venture was mishandled from the beginning. Alcibiades was removed from command on a charge of impiety and fled to Sparta. The expedition continued to be mismanaged with incredible consistency, and what had begun as the great Athenian stroke to win the war ended catastrophically for Athens. The proud fleet of the expedition was utterly destroyed; the men of its broken army were held in open pits for the better part of a year, and the few who survived sold into slavery. Forty thousand men perished.

An immediate reaction set in. The few states which had remained neutral rushed to ally themselves with the Peloponnesian League. The Athenian navy, severely depleted, was for the first time seriously menaced. Even Persia, the ancient enemy of all Greeks, was solicited by Sparta. As the military fortunes of Athens crumbled, a frenzy of partisan politicians seized the city. First one faction, then another, rose to power while the war dragged on. Finally, in 405 B.C., the remaining Athenian fleet was destroyed and the war was over.

Athens had thrown everything into the last desperate years. Even the treasures of the temples had been melted down and turned into money. Not only was the empire lost but the city fortifications were destroyed and what was left of the navy surrendered. The end had also come for Athenian democracy, for the victorious Spartans restored the Athenian oligarchy. Athens was to remain a cultural center in the ancient world for nearly another thousand years, but she was never again to be a great power. Sparta, although she had destroyed the imperial designs of Athens, was unable to assume the leadership of Greek affairs, for which she had fought Athens. Indeed, there was no winner in this suicidal war.

More than a quarter of a century before its end Thucydides had written at the opening of his work, "Thucydides, an Athenian, wrote the history of the war in which the Peloponnesians and the Athenians fought against one another. He began to write when they first took up arms, believing that it would be great and momentous above any previous war. For he argued that both states were then at the full height of their military powers, and he saw the rest of the Hellenes either siding or intending to side with one or other of them. No movement ever stirred Hellas more deeply than this; it was shared by many of the barbarians, and might be said even to affect the world at large. . . . The Peloponnesian [War], if estimated by the actual facts, will certainly prove to have been the greatest ever known."[1]

It was not, of course, the "greatest ever known" in terms of its territorial extent or its cost in lives, property, and misery. Yet while not the greatest of wars, in the hands of Thucydides it became every war, with its account of the causes of conflict rising out of the stubborn pride of states, the passions of party politics inflamed by news of victory and defeat, the opportunism of demagogues, the pain, the loss, and the grinding despair of eventual defeat. Again, in the sense that the Peloponnesian War marked the beginning of the end for the most momentous cultural moment in European history it can perhaps be counted the "greatest," or most tragic, of wars.

The Sophists, Socrates, and the Philosophy of Man

It is a seeming paradox that philosophy, literally, the love of wisdom, should have come to its maturity in the Greek world out of the consummate folly of war. Yet it did, and the great Greek philosophers—Socrates (470–399 B.C.), Plato (427–347 B.C.), and Aristotle (384–322 B.C.)—lived and taught in the period of Athens' decline. Perhaps it is natural that this should have been the case, since philosophy is the diversion of

1. Thucydides, *The Peloponnesian War,* Jowett Trans., Bk. I, 1.

maturity, and the work of these men represents the summing up of Hellenic thought.

The Athens of Socrates was profoundly affected by the calamities of the closing years of the Peloponnesian War. The general cost and horror of more than a quarter century of conflict had succeeded in undermining all positive values and in leaving a disillusioned society which could point to no absolute ideals.

Most characteristic of this mood were the Sophists, who represented an important shift in Greek philosophy, though, strictly speaking, they were not philosophers. As paid, professional teachers, they taught the techniques necessary for public life to rich and ambitious young men: rhetoric, argumentation, politics. They were not concerned with metaphysics or cosmology, nor were they even generally concerned with morality. Their concern was with the means of obtaining success. In their scale of values, success was placed above virtue, glibness above profundity, and the appearance of things above their reality. Disreputable as their methods were, and questionable as their aims, they succeeded in introducing into the stream of philosophy an interest in man and his behavior.

It was in such a climate of ideas that Socrates lived and undertook to examine the principles of human conduct. Socrates did not come from among the rich and powerful families of Athens; for most of his life he was an unemployed stonecutter. But he became one of the most influential teachers of all time. He founded no schools, wrote no formal treatises. But, by his discourse in the streets of Athens, he attracted a following of intelligent young men from the most distinguished families. Most of what we know about Socrates we owe to the writings of one of these men, Plato, his foremost pupil.

Socrates declared that, like the Sophists, he was not interested in "search[ing] into things under the earth or in heaven." Indeed, there was a superficial similarity between his ideas and those of the Sophists on a number of points. But his notion of values was fundamentally different. He was not concerned with worldly success nor with the means of achieving it. His purpose was to arrive at definite and unchanging principles of conduct.

His technique of philosophic discourse was to be of great significance in the development of philosophic methodology. The essence of the so-called "Socratic method" was to pose questions, eliciting answers which would then be questioned and debated until a logical conclusion was reached. In this way he revealed to his students his ideas about man, his conviction that evil was above all a failure of knowledge, that man could be turned to goodness and truth and the practice of virtue through knowledge, that he must live not by giving way to shifting expediency but by adhering to absolute principles of conduct.

Inevitably Socrates questioned the morality of his own society. Alarmed by the effects of these criticisms the people of Athens charged Socrates with corrupting the morals of the youth and brought him to trial. In 399 B.C., at the age of seventy, Socrates was condemned to death. His eloquent defense at his trial can be found in Plato's *Apology*.

Plato had wanted to be a poet but, under Socrates' influence, he devoted himself instead to the study of philosophy. Of his teacher he wrote, ". . . I may truly say, that of all men of his time whom I have known, he was the wisest and justest and best."

Platonism and the Ideal State

After the death of Socrates, Plato left Athens to travel widely through the Greek world. On his return he founded the Academy which became a center of learning and philosophy. Here he developed the first of the great western philosophical systems.

The Platonic system survives for us in a series of dialogues in which, by the Socratic method of discourse, the various questions with which philosophy deals are examined. The *Protagoras* and *Gorgias* (the dialogues are usually · named for one of their participants) deal in part with the varieties and meaning of pleasure. Knowledge and reality are the subjects of the *Phaedrus, Theaetetus,* and *Parmenides.* The *Timaeus* is concerned with cosmology, the *Philebus* with the "good," the *Symposium* with love, the *Phaedo* with the soul. These dialogues are not only philosophy but literature of the highest order.

Plato, like Socrates, placed man at the center of his system; and, again like Socrates and the whole Greek tradition, he could not visualize man apart from the state and the exercise of citizenship. Thus, the greatest of the dialogues and the most complete statement of the Platonic system is the *Republic*. In the *Republic,* Plato constructed an ideal state. It is austere and puritanical. It has no commerce, no wealth, no luxury—not even the luxury of family life. Its only beauty is the beauty of philosophy; its only pleasure, the exercise of virtue. The citizens of the *Republic* are divided into three classes—workers, soldiers, and rulers—to perform the basic tasks of the state. The class structure is based upon an elaborate educational system which places every person in the class to which his abilities entitle him. The result is a balance of classes comparable to the Pythagorean idea of harmony.

Closely related to Plato's concept of the state, the individual, and the "ideal" education is the "doctrine of ideas," which is central to the Platonic system. The "doctrine of ideas" is Plato's theory of reality. He rejects the apparent reality of sense impressions as only pale reflections of eternal, unchanging forms or "ideas." These exist for all things substantial and insubstantial. There is an ideal form which is the reality, such an abstraction as a triangle, such a virtue as justice. The highest of all ideas is the idea of the "good," and all the rest are ranked in an order of value below it. Man is able to know this transcendental world of ideas by virtue of his soul, that part of him which can touch the eternal because it is itself eternal. Plato expresses the complex relationship between man, soul, education, and "ideal" reality in an allegory, "The Myth of the Cave." "Behold! human beings living in an underground den."[11] Imagine that they have been there since birth, chained with their faces to the wall of the cave. As men, animals, and objects pass the mouth of the cave their shadows, dancing on the wall, are all the reality the prisoners know. Then

when any of them is liberated and compelled suddenly to stand up and turn his neck round and walk and look toward the light, he will suffer sharp pains; the glare will distress him, and he will be unable to see the realities of which in his former state he had seen the shadows.

. . .

And suppose once more, that he is reluctantly dragged up a steep and rugged ascent, and held fast until he is forced into the presence of the sun . . .

then he will know the source of all light and feel compassion for his former companions in the cave. The men whom Plato would have rule the *Republic* are those who have seen the sun—the "idea of the good." Having mounted the pinnacle of education to perfect knowledge, these "guardians" then must return to the mundane state to govern it by their wisdom. Then will "philosophers be kings."

Plato's ideas represented the final statement in Greek philosophy of

11. *The Dialogues of Plato*, B. Jowett transl. (New York: Random House, 1937), I, 515ff.

the mystic strain which began with Pythagoras. His system became a cornerstone of western thought, and his ideas have remained an integral part of the western philosophic tradition.

Aristotle and the World of Reality

Through his long life, the teaching of Plato touched many young men; none more productively than his pupil Aristotle, who studied at the Academy for twenty years. Aristotle was as much a scholar as a theoretician and the whole of knowledge was his province. He wrote on natural history, anatomy, logic, metaphysics, meteorology, aesthetics. Though he revered Plato, he created a philosophic system of his own, in many ways antithetical to that of his teacher. The Aristotelian system was equally if not more influential in the development of western thought.

There were many points of difference between Aristotle and Plato, and most of them stemmed from the diametrically different orientations of their systems. Plato was a mystic; Aristotle, a scientist. Plato's concern was to know the "one" and identify with it; Aristotle was content to define and accept it. His main interest was the natural, the intricate mechanics of "being." His work may be regarded as the logical conclusion of that search for physical principles begun by the Ionian philosophers.

Aristotle started with the sense impression that Plato rejected; he observed, collected, and classified—beginning with the specific and mounting to the general. Universal quantities were to Aristotle generalizations derived from a multitude of observed similarities. Yet, the universe was no less impressive for the rejection of Platonic absolutes.

Man, the "Good," and the State

Applying this method to the order of the universe, Aristotle sought the force that stood behind every other force, the generalization that contained all the rest. He viewed the universe as essentially meaningful. The unceasing activity which he observed had to be going somewhere. It must have an end, a cause, a purpose. Such a conclusion is thoroughly Greek; it is also thoroughly Greek that that end, cause, or purpose should have been viewed as ethical. Aristotle assumed the universe to be good. It was a universe of "becoming," a constant dynamic process of fulfillment, and Aristotle could not accept the notion that this was meaningless. Everything has within it the potential of its completion and is constantly moving toward completion. This led him to the conclusion that there had to be some force which had no potential, which was pure form, completely realized. This was the Aristotelian God, the "prime mover," the first cause, himself uncaused.

Into his orderly scheme of the universe Aristotle fitted man. As a creature of body, a biological complex, man was subject to the same general pattern of development as all nature. His physical potential was constantly realized through growth. But man was more than a physical being. He possessed a soul which had its potential also; and this was a potential for the "good." Here again is the ethical assumption. As the meaningful universe is understandable only as it moves from worse to better, so the faculty in man which enables him to understand its progress is oriented toward goodness. The same faculty makes man's end, the purpose to which he moves, the enjoyment of the good life. This is a thoroughly practical conclusion that accepts the limitations which all nature has. The good life is equated with happiness, understood not as mere animal pleasure, but as the fullest development of man's spiritual-intellectual potential for the good.

Human potential can only be realized within the framework of political society. But Aristotle did not follow Plato to the *Republic*. He was not concerned with idealizing the state. He was concerned rather with understanding it as it actually existed and seeing how it could be practically perfected. At the moment in history when the life of the polis was about to come to an end, Aristotle looked back at the course of its growth. Man, by his nature and the endowment of his highest faculty, aims at the good; ". . . man is [also] by nature a political animal." Therefore, he can attain the highest good only in the state "which is the highest of all, and which embraces all the rest, [and] aims at good in a greater degree than any other, and at the highest good." By the state, Aristotle meant the polis, the small, self-sufficient, intimate context of the Greek city-state. He saw man as the citizen achieving happiness by meeting fully his civic obligations. Yet, Aristotle was to witness the passing of the world in which this was possible.

MACEDONIA, GREECE, AND THE HELLENISTIC WORLD

The Peloponnesian War had shattered the Greek world but had not instructed it in political wisdom. The states and leagues of the early fourth century B.C. continued to fight bitterly for the fragments of that world. The principle of city-state sovereignty had reached its logical conclusion in interstate anarchy. The hegemony that Sparta had won from Athens was won in turn by Thebes, but Thebes was no better able to dominate and order the chaotic affairs of the Greek states. The reconstitution of Greek political life lay outside the abilities of the Greeks themselves.

The Creation of the Alexandrian Empire

On the northern flank of mainland Greece lay Macedonia, the power that was to impose upon the Greek states the unity they could not achieve for themselves. The Macedonians were a crude and backward people who had had little or no influence upon the Greek world. They were ethnically related to the Greeks but had not shared in the development of those institutions of public life and refinements of culture which had created Hellas.

In 359 B.C. Philip II came to the throne of Macedonia. A man of enormous ability and ambition, Philip could be brutally cruel or insidiously clement as expediency dictated. Within a short time he became a power among the Greek states. In Athens the great orator, Demosthenes, warned the Greeks against this potential danger but was ignored. When the crisis came, a hastily assembled army met Philip at Chaeronea in central Greece in 338 B.C. and was defeated. Philip created a league of the Greek states under his own presidency and from this time the life of the polis was joined to that of the territorial monarchy of Macedonia.

Philip was murdered in 336 B.C. In less than twenty years he had created a great state and an invincible army. He had engulfed the squabbling Greek states and conceived a plan for the conquest of the Persian Empire which was, to the Greeks, the remainder of the world.

His power and plans were inherited by his son Alexander III, (336–323 B.C.), fitted both by temperament and training to assume them. He had many of the characteristics that had accounted for Philip's success but he had even greater ambition and capacity. The natural gifts of the young Alexander had been carefully cultivated. When Alexander was thirteen, Philip, who had great respect for Greek education and culture, had invited Aristotle to come to his court to tutor his son. Aristotle stayed with his pupil until Alexander succeeded to the throne. We must assume that Alexander learned much from his teacher, though his life and career did not reflect many of the virtues—especially that of moderation—which Aristotle preached. Certainly Aristotle contributed to Alexander's enduring devotion to Greek civilization.

On ascending to the throne, Alexander consolidated his position in

Macedonia and Greece and, in the spring of 334 B.C., crossed the Hellespont to Asia to confront the Persian king, Darius III. The Persian Empire
was a typical Asiatic monarchy whereby the king was the state and whoever defeated the king assumed his powers. In 333 B.C. Alexander defeated Darius at Issus and acquired the western part of the empire. He
set up a system of administration and tax collection under Macedonian
generals and then, in 331 B.C., again fought Darius at Gaugamela, where
he won decisively. Darius, who had escaped after both encounters, was
murdered soon after, and with him died the Persian Empire.

With his victory Alexander had also assumed the obligations of rule,
but his genius for war had no opportunity to mature and develop into a
genius for peace and political consolidation. As he led his men on eastward
to complete the piecemeal conquest of his empire, the strain of long
marches and constant fighting began to affect both leader and army: one
of his generals rebelled and was executed and in a drunken brawl Alexander murdered an old friend who had once saved his life. After eight
years of battle, having marched more than eleven thousand miles through
strange and hostile lands, the army finally mutinied and demanded to
return home. Bitterly Alexander agreed and began the trek back.

A little more than a year later, at Babylon, Alexander was struck
down by a fever and died on June 13, 323 B.C. He was not yet
thirty-three years old. In thirteen years he had won the largest empire the
world had ever seen. He had scattered thousands of men and, reputedly,
seventy cities—all of them named Alexandria—through that empire.
Alexander had planned to unify his empire, to make it the meeting ground
of Greek and Asiatic civilizations, but though he had done whatever he
could to bring this about, it remained a dream not half realized. There
was no successor: he left a "foreign" wife carrying an unborn child; a
feeble-minded, illegitimate half-brother; a vengeful and scheming mother;
and a handful of able and rapacious generals. One source recorded that
as Alexander lay dying, his generals pressed close and asked to whom
the empire should go. Alexander replied, "to the best." The story is probably false, but the contest to determine who that "best" might be scarred
the history of the next two centuries.

The Political, Economic, and Social Foundations
of the Hellenistic World

Following Alexander's death, the only effective power lay in the hands
of his generals, none of whom intended to yield any part of it. Alliances

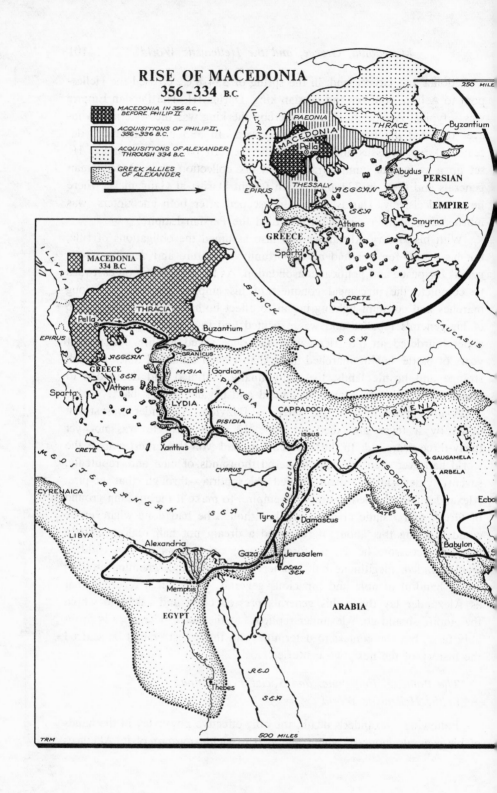

RISE OF MACEDONIA
356-334 B.C.

MACEDONIA IN 356 B.C.,
BEFORE PHILIP II

ACQUISITIONS OF PHILIP II,
356-336 B.C.

ACQUISITIONS OF ALEXANDER
THROUGH 334 B.C.

GREEK ALLIES
OF ALEXANDER

250 MILE

ILLYRIA
PAEONIA
THRACE
MACEDONIA
Pella
Byzantium
Abydus
PERSIAN
EMPIRE
EPIRUS
THESSALY
AEGEAN
SEA
Smyrna
GREECE
Athens
Sparta
CRETE
CAUCASUS

MACEDONIA
334 B.C.

ILLYRIA
THRACIA
BLACK
Pella
Byzantium
EPIRUS
GRANICUS
SEA
AEGEAN
GREECE
SEA
MYSIA
Gordion
CAUCASUS
Sparta
Athens
Sardis
PHRYGIA
CAPPADOCIA
ARMENIA
LYDIA
PISIDIA
CRETE
Xanthus
ISSUS
MEDITERRANEAN
CYPRUS
TIGRIS
GAUGAMELA
ARBELA
MESOPOTAMIA
Ecbo
SEA
CYRENAICA
PHOENICIA
SYRIA
EUPHRATES
Babylon
LIBYA
Tyre
Damascus
Alexandria
Gaza
Jerusalem
DEAD SEA
Memphis
ARABIA
EGYPT
NILE
Thebes
RED
SEA
500 MILES
TRM

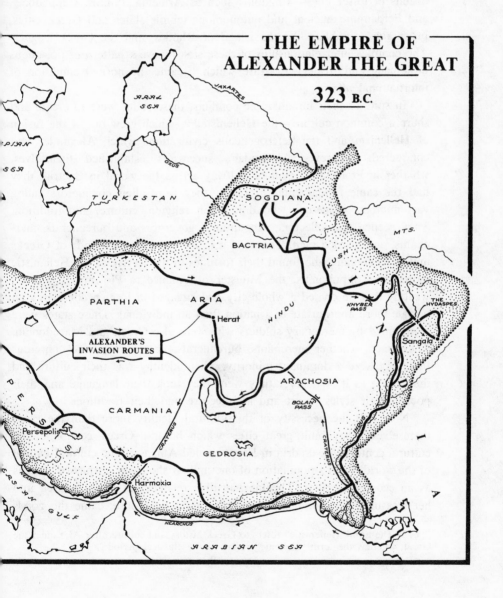

THE EMPIRE OF
ALEXANDER THE GREAT

323 B.C.

ARAL SEA

JAXARTES

CASPIAN SEA

OXUS

TURKESTAN

SOGDIANA

BACTRIA

MTS.

PARTHIA

ARIA

HINDU KUSH

KHYBER PASS

THE HYDASPES

Herat

ALEXANDER'S
INVASION ROUTES

ARACHOSIA

Sangala

CARMANIA

BOLAN PASS

CRATERUS

INDUS

CRATERUS

N

I

A

PERSIS

Persepolis

GEDROSIA

PERSIAN GULF

Harmoxia

NEARCHUS

ARABIAN SEA

were formed and broken as each skirmished for advantage: open fighting alternated with diplomatic intrigue. After two generations of struggle a balance of power was finally achieved at the beginning of the third century B.C., with the emergence of three great succession states: Egypt under Ptolemy, Asia under Seleucus, and Greece and Macedonia under the family of the Antigonids. Around the edges of these three states were dozens of lesser ones—kingdoms such as Armenia, Pontus, Cappadocia, and Pergamum; ancient and autonomous temple states and Greek cities; prosperous republics like the island of Rhodes, and the Greek leagues. The complex interrelationships of these states wove a pattern of poisonous diplomacy and strategic warfare which became the normal condition of international affairs.

In spite of their innumerable conflicts, these states were to create and share a common culture—the Hellenistic[12]—which grew out of the fusion of Hellenism and the heterogeneous civilizations which Alexander had conquered. Wherever Alexander's successors established themselves, whether in Ptolemaic Egypt or halfway across the world in Bactria, they had the same fundamental problem: they were alien conquerors ruling vast numbers of people who differed in religion, culture, and tradition. They needed tax collectors, accountants, governors and bureaucrats, merchants, and learned men. The need was answered by thousands of Greeks and Macedonians who found their fortunes in the service of the Hellenistic monarchies. Apollonius, the Minister of Finance to Ptolemy II, was so wealthy that he owned a whole city and engaged in foreign commerce on a scale more appropriate to a nation than an individual. These states were maintained by mercenary soldiers who were also Greek and Macedonian. These men, whether merchants, bureaucrats, or soldiers, were conscious that they were a dominant minority. Their identity was their culture and they clung to it. Wherever they went they took their language and their poetry, their styles of art and architecture and their traditions.

None felt the necessity of this cultural identity more than the kings themselves. They built great cities which became Greek economic and cultural centers. Alexandria in Egypt rivaled Athens as the cultural capital of the world. With a population of one million she easily surpassed Athens as an economic center. The inexhaustible revenues of Egypt poured into her treasury; into her harbor, past the great lighthouse, came the goods

12. The term "Hellenistic" refers to Greek history and culture after Alexander the Great, whereas the term "Hellenic" refers to the classical period.

of the entire world. Her people were as cosmopolitan as her goods; in the broad streets of Alexandria mingled Greeks, Persians, Jews, Syrians, Anatolians, Indians, Arabs, Africans, Etruscans, all the peoples and races known to antiquity. Cities like Alexandria (Antioch in Syria, Seleucia on the Tigris)—but none her equal—were founded throughout the Hellenistic states.

The Hellenistic world was dominated by cities, wealth, and commerce. Its trade was a world trade bringing cedar for shipbuilding from Syrian Lebanon, wool from Asia Minor; salt fish from the Black Sea, woolen cloth from Miletus, linen from Egypt, carpets from Sardes, and silk from China. Grain, the staple that fed the teeming cities, came from Egypt and coastal North Africa, Sicily, and the Crimea. Trade stimulated the growth of a money economy. The great treasures of Persia had been coined and released into circulation by Alexander and the wealth of this empire continued to be exploited by his successors. In turn, money and trade stimulated credit, and banking grew into a lucrative and regular practice. In the countryside of Egypt and on the limitless crown lands of Asia the peasants led the same drudging lives they had always led, filling the treasuries of kings and laying the material foundations of Hellenistic civilization.

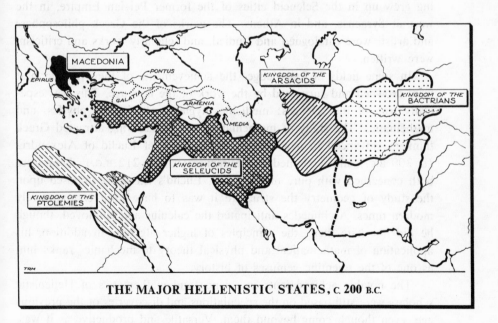

THE MAJOR HELLENISTIC STATES, c. 200 B.C.

Hellenistic Civilization

Despite the almost continuous wars and dynastic rivalries, the stream of Hellenistic culture flowed as easily as its trade, breaking down the intense parochialism which had characterized Hellenic civilization. Men of learning traveled from city to city, court to court, supported by the patronage of the wealthy empires and opulent states which comprised the Hellenistic world. Though the self-conscious Greek culture of the rulers set a certain tone and imposed a certain cultural unity, Hellenistic civilization was heavily influenced by the deep-rooted Asian civilizations on which it was built. Inevitably the blending of these diverse influences made for many contrasts: scientists, mathematicians, and physicians practiced side by side with astrologers and magicians; the Greek monuments of the Ptolemies rose side by side with the ancient monuments of Pharaonic Egypt.

Alexandria under the Ptolemies was the greatest center of Hellenistic civilization. Here Ptolemy I founded the famous library and museum which contained nearly five hundred thousand volumes in the form of papyrus rolls embodying the scholarship of the ancient world. To Alexandria came scholars and artists from all parts of the world, and other centers of learning grew up in the Seleucid cities of the former Persian Empire, in the west at Syracuse, and in Athens. The works of the Greek philosophers and artists were catalogued and studied, and scholarly works and criticism were written.

In some fields of knowledge, the achievements of the Hellenic past were crowned and surpassed by the work of the new age. This was especially true of the sciences: medicine, hygiene, physiology, physics, and mathematics. The study of mathematics, which had long attracted Greek thinkers, advanced to new heights in the work of Euclid of Alexandria (c. 300 B.C.) and Archimedes of Syracuse (c. 287–212 B.C.). They were both concerned with pure mathematics. Euclid's *Elements* imposed upon the study of geometry the structure it was to have until comparatively modern times. Archimedes anticipated the calculus and employed, though he did not state them, the principles of higher algebra. In addition, his application of mathematical and physical theory to mechanics ranks him as one of the scientific geniuses of history.

The notable achievements in science and mathematics of Hellenistic scholars were still based on the speculations and discoveries of the previous age, even though going beyond them. Versatile and productive as it was,

Hellenistic civilization remained deeply indebted to classical Hellenism. The civilized world was still Greek, but it was separated from its own past by more than the passage of time. The basic institution of the old Greek world had been the polis. It no longer existed. After Alexander, the Greek found that he was no longer a political animal in the sense that he had been before. The Greek cities of Hellenistic times, both the famous old cities and the new ones founded in distant lands, maintained the same appearance as before, but the dynamic vigor of their political independence was gone. This lack had a profound effect upon nearly every aspect of the Hellenistic civilization.

In sculpture and architecture it was coupled with another factor, the exhaustion of classical forms. Classical building styles had reached perfection in the fifth century B.C.; there was nothing else to be said in the artistic language of the basic orders. Though they remained the predominant architectural styles throughout the Hellenistic world, they were pushed beyond their classical perfection both in size and function. The Hellenistic age was grandiose in its tastes. The structural forms that had been developed for the usually modest and severe Greek temple were expanded and adapted to palaces, municipal buildings, and elaborate tombs for divine kings.

In sculpture as in architecture there was no failure of technique, but a fundamental change of purpose. Classic sculpture had been tied to the public worship of the state religion and the state religion had been tied to the seminal idea of civic patriotism. The whole cluster of ideas and practices which had initiated and supported the achievement of classic art collapsed under the forces that brought the Hellenistic world into being. Statues had once represented to the citizen-man the idealization of form and bearing of the civic patriot. There was, in the world of vast, impersonal empires and mercenary soldiery, no employment for such patriotism and no need for its idealization in art. The strong, male statuary types of the best Hellenic sculpture were gradually changed. They became on the one hand the heroic, Herculean type which was regularly used to represent the Hellenistic kings and princes; on the other they tended to such a delicacy of rendering and finish as to represent a languid, introspective, almost feminine ideal. Both tendencies had appeared gradually in the fourth century B.C. The Hellenistic world, in the catholicity of its tastes, broadened Greek art even as it corrupted it.

The sense of the sublime and the severe began to give way to theatricalism and emotionalism. Though the techniques and many of the forms remained unmistakably Greek, the Hellenistic sculptor belonged to a new age which demanded new things of his craft. The new art achieved its own glories as it freed itself from the limitations and motivation of the past. Never before in the history of Greek civilization had there been such wholesale demand for beauty or such means to buy and patronize it. Hellenistic sculptors traveled widely and absorbed a greater variety of influences than their masters of the former age.

The glorious age of Attic drama closed with the generation of Euripides, for the poet was no longer called upon to teach wisdom. Greek tragedy had been a blending of religious and civic drama, and the tragedian's intention had been to remind his fellow citizens of the necessity for virtue. Neither the polis nor its religion were meaningful to the Hellenistic world. The old comedy which Aristophanes had turned into a satiric conscience of the civic soul gave way to new forms, especially the comedy of manners, with its durable types and stock situations.

Hellenistic Philosophy—The Emergence of Stoicism

In no area of artistic or intellectual activity was the difference between the Hellenic and the Hellenistic age more marked than in philosophy. Like Hellenistic art, Hellenistic philosophy was the heir of a long tradition. Its summation had come in the work of Plato and Aristotle. Different as the Platonic and Aristotelian systems were from each other, they shared one important assumption: that the study of man was the prime concern of philosophy. And they both assumed that man found the meaning of his life as an active participant in politics. The end and being of philosophy were associated fundamentally with the ideal of the polis.

When the city-state lost its significance as a political reality, philosophy had to take a new direction, for the old philosophy had taught men how to think and behave in terms of a world-view that was no longer relevant. Hellenistic philosophy had to find a new motivation for human thought and behavior. It found it by attaching prime importance to the individual. All of post-Alexandrian speculation was keyed to the individual—not as a citizen or a responsible member of a group, but as a single person alone in an uncaring universe.

Beginning with this assumption, a number of groups developed divergent theories. The Cynics preached the practice of virtue by self-denial to give the individual an inner security derived from himself, independent of external circumstances. The Skeptics were nihilists, that is, they believed in nothing, maintaining that there was no possibility of knowledge, that man must accept the world as it is, that there are no values except the conviction that no value exists. The Epicureans held that the gods existed in another world, neither knowing nor caring about man, and that the atoms which comprised man, body and soul, would dissolve upon death, leaving neither trace nor memory of him. Because of this, happiness was the greatest and the only good. Only in the freedom from fear and pain was there any value. Even though the Epicureans did not disdain virtue, the system as such recognized no tribunal higher than the pleasure of the individual.

The most characteristic and influential of the Hellenistic philosophies was Stoicism. After Platonism and Aristotelianism, it is the third and last of the great classical systems. It was founded by Zeno, who came to Athens to teach in the last years of the fourth century B.C. In common with the other Hellenistic systems its basic intention was to help man become a happy and self-sufficient being in a world from which external ties, responsibilities, rewards, and predictability had been removed; and it shared the notion that happiness was the greatest good. But the Stoic concept of happiness was placed in a larger and more meaningful context.

Other philosophies taught the acceptance of the world. Stoicism went beyond this to argue the existence of a "world soul," a kind of god that motivates the universe and everything in it. It further argued that this power was a benevolent power. The problem of evil was resolved for the Stoic by holding that the apparent evils of the world—sickness, misfortune, calamity—were beyond human understanding and that men must accept their burdens as a part of the enigmatic goodness of nature and the world. This acceptance of adversity became one of the identifying characteristics of Stoicism. The idea of obligation inherent in the system also set it apart from the prevailing tone of Hellenistic philosophy. The happiness it sought to gain for man was not a selfish pleasure. The soul of man was viewed as part of the soul of the world, and to gain his happiness man had to live in conformity with this world soul, making the happy life the virtuous life.

The Stoic notion of right conduct and the life of virtue merged with another leading Hellenistic idea, the notion of one world, one human race, and a common brotherhood. This emphasis was not limited purely to philosophy for, as we have seen, it existed in the arts and indeed expressed the general spirit of the age.

In comparison with the elaborate systems of Plato and Aristotle, the Stoic system seems truncated and even banal in some of its concepts. Its saving grace was neither its logic nor its consistency, but its spirit, which made of it as much a religion as a philosophy.

For centuries philosophy and religion had alternately merged and drawn apart in Greek thought; in Stoicism they came together again. The Stoics taught man to submit to the will of god and to conform to a moral standard which had the sanction of god and nature. The reward for virtue was virtue itself. There was a minimum of supernaturalism and no promise of personal immortality. The scope and adaptability, the uncomplicated and unequivocal ethic of Stoicism made it one of the most influential philosophic systems. Its very simplicity enabled men to make of it whatever they desired.

When the Romans came to include the Hellenistic states within their empire and to appropriate the achievements of Hellenistic civilization, no small portion of their inheritance was the Stoic system.

SUGGESTIONS FOR FURTHER READING

☙❧

Primary Sources and Original Works

All the following are available in almost numberless editions, and most are now to be had in inexpensive paperback form.

Homer, *The Iliad*
Homer, *The Odyssey*
Hesiod, *Poems*
The Greek lyric poets such as Sappho, Alcaeus, and Pindar and works of the dramatic poets Aeschylus, Sophocles, Euripides, Aristophanes, and Menander are either in separate works or in several anthologies.
Herodotus, *The Persian Wars*
Thucydides, *The Peloponnesian War*
Plutarch, *Parallel Lives of Noble Greeks and Romans*

The works of Plato and Aristotle, especially in the following editions:

From Thales to Plato, T. V. Smith, ed. (Chicago: Phoenix, 1956).
From Aristotle to Plotinus, T. V. Smith, ed. (Chicago: Phoenix, 1956).
The Stoic and Epicurean Philosophers, ed. and intro. by W. J. Oates (New York: Random House, 1940).

General Works

G. W. Botsford and C. A. Robinson, *Hellenic History* (New York: Macmillan, 1956).

Cambridge Ancient History, Vols. IV-VII, first three vols. cited for Chap. 2.

Will Durant, *The Life of Greece* (New York: Simon and Schuster, 1939).

*Edith Hamilton, *The Greek Way to Western Civilization* (New York: Mentor, 1939), a famous "appreciation" of the Greeks, largely based on and dealing with literature.

*H. D. F. Kitto,*The Greeks* (Baltimore: Penguin, 1957).

The Bronze Age and Early Greek History

A. R. Burn, *The World of Hesiod* (New York: Dutton, 1937), still one of the few works on the so-called Greek Middle Age.

C. W. Ceram, *Gods, Graves and Scholars,* cited for Chap. 2.

*Leonard Cottrell, *The Anvil of Civilization,* cited for Chap. 2.

*M. I. Finley, *The World of Odysseus* (New York: Meridian, 1954).

J. Forsdyke, *Greece before Homer* (New York: Norton, 1957).

Hilda Lorimer, *Homer and the Monuments* (New York: St. Martin's Press, 1950).

George E. Mylonas, *Ancient Mycenae* (Princeton: Princeton University Press, 1957), a report of the recent archaeological work and reconstruction by a leading modern authority.

*Robert Payne, *The Gold of Troy* (New York: Paperback Library, 1962), Schliemann and the rediscovery of the Aegean Bronze Age.

J. D. S. Pendlebury, *The Archaeology of Crete* (London: Methuen, 1939).

Michael Ventris and John Chadwick, *Documents in Mycenaean Greek* (Cambridge: Cambridge University Press, 1956), the definitive report on the decipherment of Linear Minoan B; a scholar's book, but exciting material even for beginning students.

A. J. B. Wace, *Mycenae* (Princeton: Princeton University Press, 1949).

Special Topics in Greek History

*V. Ehrenberg, *The People of Aristophanes* (New York: Schacken, 1962).

Kathleen Freeman, *Greek City States* (New York: Norton, 1950), studies of some of the lesser states of the Greek world.

*Robert Graves, *The Penguin Greek Mythology* (Baltimore: Penguin, 1955-57), 3 vols., the best modern collection with exhaustive notes and exciting commentary.

W. K. C. Guthrie, *The Greeks and Their Gods* (Boston: Beacon Press, 1955).

Werner Jaeger, *Paideia* (New York: Oxford University Press, 1934-44), 3 vols., Greek education and culture in brilliant interrelationship.

A. H. M. Jones, *Athenian Democracy* (Oxford: Oxford University Press, 1957).

*H. D. F. Kitto, *Greek Tragedy* (New York: Anchor, 1955).
*C. A. Robinson, Jr., *The Spring of Civilization: Periclean Athens* (New York: Dutton, 1959).
H. J. Rose, *A Handbook of Greek Mythology* (New York: Dutton, 1929).
*A. E. Taylor, *Aristotle* (New York: Dover, 1956).
*———, *Plato* (New York: Meridian, 1956).
*———, *Socrates* (New York: Anchor, 1959).
*Edward Zeller, *Outlines of the History of Greek Philosophy* (New York: Meridian, 1957), a reprint of an older standard work with brief, lucid explanations of the various sytsems.
A. E. Zimmern, *The Greek Commonwealth* (Oxford: Clarendon Press, 1939).

The Hellenistic Age

*Arrian, *Life of Alexander the Great,* tr. by A. de Selincourt (Baltimore: Penguin, 1961), the standard ancient biography.
M. I. Rostovtzeff, *Social and Economic History of the Hellenistic World* (Oxford: Clarendon Press, 1941), 3 vols., a massive, heavily documented standard work, but so brilliant and provocative that it can be read with profit by the beginning student.
*W. W. Tarn, *Alexander the Great* (Boston: Beacon Press, 1948), almost the only serious modern study of Alexander; not a connected biography but a series of topical essays.
———, *Hellenistic Civilization* (London: Arnold, 1936).

*Paperbound edition. In the case of reprint editions, publisher and date of publication given will be that of reprint rather than the original.

❧ 4 ❧
The Roman World

EARLY ROME: FROM VILLAGE TO EMPIRE

Roman Origins

The remote ancestors of the Romans, like those of the Achaean Greeks, were part of the great migration which brought the Indo-European peoples into the Mediterranean world in the centuries following 2000 B.C. Throughout the second millennium they drifted across the Alps and down into Italy from central Europe, bringing the use of bronze and later of iron, and settling in crude agricultural villages. One of these called itself Rome and occupied the roughly fortified height of the Palatine Hill on the rolling plain of Latium above the Tiber River. There was no Roman or Latin state at this early time and the Romans were simply one loose tribal confederacy among many. Unlike the Achaean Greeks, who had the advantage of cultural contact with the high civilization of Crete, the early Romans went through a long period of relative cultural isolation among kindred peoples little different from themselves.

Like their neighbors, the Romans were farmers and their lives followed the cycle of the agricultural year. The chief social unit was the family, ruled by the father; the heads of families in turn formed the decision-making body of the village. The basically paternal flavor of Roman government probably originated in this domestic pattern of primitive Roman life.

The religion of Rome was deeply influenced by the soil, the seasons,

113

the crops, and the family. While the Romans seem to have brought with them into Italy their typically Indo-European gods (there were early cults of such gods as the king-father Jupiter), these gods were not humanized until many centuries later under Greek influence. They were conceived rather as spirits in a thoroughly animistic way. Many of these spirits were connected with agriculture. The *lares* and *penates,* the spirits of the hearth and cupboard, were identified with all the important decisions of the household (and later of the state). The spirits of the grain and the field and the boundary stones were scrupulously invoked. The *genius* or spirit of the father presided over the entire family, and the father was the chief priest of his family worship. Later this domestic worship was extended to the Roman state and the chief magistrates became the fathers and priests of the nation. The rituals and formulae, if not the specific substance, of this primitive religion were among the most tenacious forces in Roman life and some of them persisted, in spite of decadence, cynicism, philosophy, and myriad foreign influences, until the very end of Roman history.

Perhaps even more than the Greeks, the Romans made a religion of patriotism and, from the beginning of their history, were as much soldiers as citizens. The early history of Rome was a struggle for survival among the various peoples fighting for living space and arable land on the plain of Latium. Much of this ancient struggle is lost in legends but the legends themselves reflect the military virtues and deify such warrior leaders as Romulus, the founding father of Rome.

These obscure early centuries were the time of the founding of the great myth of Roman character. As the Romans came eventually to dominate the Mediterranean world and brought dozens of other peoples and cultures under their sway, they sought to explain their phenomenal success by looking back into their national origins. They found their answer in what they chose to regard as the moral character of the primitive Roman, comprising a cluster of virtues such as frugality, sobriety, hardihood; respect for elders, for tradition, and for religion; and a sense of duty, discipline, and responsibility.

The Etruscans and the Monarchy

The formative period of primitive isolation ended (probably about the end of the seventh century B.C.) when the Romans came under the influence of a more highly civilized people, the Etruscans. In spite of archaeological unearthings, the Etruscans have remained a mysterious people because we have not deciphered their language, though it was known in

Rome as late as the empire and was studied then as an "ancient" language. But, with the help of the few available classical documents and the remains of Etruscan material culture, we can eke out the broad outlines of Etruscan civilization.

The Etruscans invaded Italy probably some time after 800 B.C., coming most likely from Asia Minor and settling in Italy north of Latium. They came by sea and easily imposed themselves upon their comparatively backward Italian neighbors. Their fleets enabled this commercial people to maintain contact with the economic and cultural fertility of the Aegean world and the eastern Mediterranean. They organized themselves into cities controlling limited economic spheres, and later into city leagues. These leagues shared with their Greek counterparts the apparent inability or unwillingness to form larger units of political authority. But, as in Greece, Etruscan municipal life was extremely vigorous and productive.

The flow of commerce that enriched the Etruscan cities provided cultural connections with the east, and Etruscan civilization showed both Greek and Asiatic influences. As Etruscan power grew, it expanded north into the Po Valley and south to engulf Latium and Rome about 600 B.C. For almost a century Rome was subjected to Etruscan domination.

There is little historical evidence for this period of Etruscan domination, which overlaps the age of the kings in Roman history, only legends carried down to much later times. However, there does appear to have been a positive connection between the Etruscans and the Roman monarchy. At least two of the Roman kings were almost certainly Etruscans. A strong tradition tells of the Roman hatred for their "foreign" kings. But, at the same time, Rome profited immensely from this association. Etruscan influence appeared in countless ways—in Roman religious practice, building forms, military organization, even in many Roman words and names. Rome's chief debt to the Etruscans was twofold: in the first place the Etruscans, themselves already deeply indebted to Greece, introduced the backward Romans to the powerful influence of Hellenism and drew them within the network of a high civilization; in the second place the Etruscans transformed Rome from a simple village into a state. Under Etruscan domination Rome gained a self-conscious political structure, most of the features of which were to pass into the Roman republic.

The Founding of the Republic

Near the beginning of the fifth century, traditionally in 509 B.C., the last Etruscan king, Tarquin the Proud, was expelled and the Roman Republic established. The overthrow of the monarchy may have been the heroic achievement that republican tradition honored, or it may have been part of a widespread revolt of various subject peoples against Etruscan authority. But the principal agents in the successful expulsion of the king were the leaders of the Roman nobility. This fact determined to a great extent the kind of state that succeeded the monarchy. The Roman nobility was known as the *patrician order,* and with the expulsion of the last Etruscan king, the patricians came forward as a unified social and economic class to establish and dominate the Roman republic.

The power of the king was divided and vested in two officials drawn from the patrician order, called *consuls,* who held office for a year. They were the military and civil heads of the state and each could veto the decisions of the other. As circumstances demanded, other offices were splintered off from the consulship in the following centuries, but they always shared with the consulship two essential features: they were plural offices and they were held only for a year. An exception to this general rule was the emergency office of the dictatorship. A dictator could be chosen for a period not exceeding six months but the office was hedged with safeguards. It was never regarded as a regular magistracy and probably seldom used—the memory of the rule of the kings was too strong. It might seem then that, under the republic, executive power was constitutionally weak and so limited as to be completely ineffective. Actually, this was not the case; the nobility was such a cohesive group that a continuity of policy prevailed in spite of magisterial veto powers and limited tenure of offices.

Continuity, moreover, was supplied by another institution, the senate—the citadel of patrician power. It was primarily a deliberative body, composed of the three hundred heads of the patrician families. (It was probably also a holdover from the regal period when it had been an advisory body to the king.) The constitutional powers of the senate were never clearly defined, but its actual powers were considerable. The very nature of the senate made its dominance almost inevitable. Its members were the men who had the greatest experience of government and leadership. They were by birth, age, and experience the "natural" leaders in public affairs. Furthermore, this body was the only continuing source of policy. Senators served for life while magistrates changed yearly. Ex-magistrates became members of the senate and brought to it their wisdom and experience.

Ranked below the senate in power, prestige, and effectiveness was the tribal assembly. It represented the able-bodied citizenry as a whole, but was not a "popular assembly" in any real sense, for it clearly reflected the Roman class system. By far the greatest number of its members belonged to the lower class, the *plebeian order,* but even so they were dominated here as elsewhere by the patricians. The assembly was convoked by tribal voting units and these were easily manipulated by their most wealthy and powerful members. Yet this body was the source of consent in Roman government. Theoretically, all basic decisions of the state flowed from it— the nomination of magistrates, the decisions of war and peace. But there was no ready channel through which this fundamental authority could be exercised. The assembly could not initiate legislation; it could vote only "yes" or "no" on items presented to it by the magistrates; and its decisions could be vetoed by the senate.

The centuries during which the republic assumed its final form were centuries of phenomenal growth and change in every aspect of Roman life. It was the time during which the Romans began the conquests that led them to a world empire. Every step in that conquest had its impact upon the development of the constitution. The demands of almost continuous wars in the fifth century B.C. forced a reorganization of the tribal assembly to broaden the base of military service. War had brought loot and profit, and the older division of the citizenry, based upon the holding of land, was changed to a monetary division.

As Rome expanded to become an increasingly important power in Italy, the problems of government increased. To meet the needs of a growing state, new magisterial offices had to be created. The *quaestor* became an assistant to the consuls; the *aediles* took charge of much of the city administration; the *censor* kept the citizen rolls, let public contracts, and in time, came to have a great influence upon public morals; the press of public business brought about the office of *praetor,* primarily a judicial office but second only to the consulship in prestige. These magisterial offices came to be known as the *cursus honorum,* "the sequence of distinctions." The holding of the offices in order, from the lowest to the highest, became the normal political career for an ambitious member of the privileged class. The Roman politician would slowly gain experience in finance, military life, the rendering of justice, administration and leadership—all the facets of public life—until he might, at the top of his career, hold the coveted consulship. No finer training school for statesmanship has ever been created. Thus, the Roman constitution grew in range and complexity in response to the demands of expansion.

It grew also from a more subtle but equally decisive pressure—the social tensions inherent in the Roman class system. The problems of expansion turned these tensions into open conflict. The plebeians had virtually no political voice. They were at the mercy of patrician justice under law administered by patrician officials. Their economic condition rapidly deteriorated as conquered lands and booty fell into the hands of the privileged. But the very expansion that had intensified their problems gave them the means to their solution. Rome needed these men for her armies and the taxes from their lands for her treasury. As Rome expanded, the plebeians bargained.

The office of *tribune,* a distinctly plebeian office, was created. Tribunes could veto any senatorial legislation touching plebeian interests and they could offer sanctuary to any citizen, even against legally constituted authority. Surrounded by legal and religious sanctions, the next step was the codification of the law, which occurred about the middle of the fifth century B.C. To gain this concession, the plebs were alleged to have withdrawn from Rome, refusing to bear arms or participate in civil life until their request was granted. The codification was undertaken by a senatorial commission and resulted in the Twelve Tables of Law, cast in bronze and posted in the *forum,* the public meeting place. The code was very primitive and similar to the early Greek municipal codes. However, it did not soften the legal inequities the plebeians endured; it merely represented a crystallization of the harsh and unequal justice they knew. The significant advance was that, once written down, the law could no longer be arbitrarily administered. Shortly thereafter, the law against marriage between plebeian and patrician—which was part of the Twelve Tables—was abrogated. In the later fourth century B.C. the Sexto-Licinian Laws, which opened even the consulship to plebeians, were passed. The same body of legislation limited the amount of public land that any individual could hold, and thus struck at the most important source of patrician wealth and power. In 287 B.C. the Hortensian Law proclaimed that all legislation passed by the assembly could become law even without senatorial approval.

It is ironic that even as the plebeians won their struggle for rights and justice from the patricians, the social basis of Roman life was beginning to shift. Many of the proud, old families had been depleted by war, for they had borne the brunt of military leadership. Furthermore, the sharp distinction between plebeian and patrician was beginning to be blurred. Not only legal but economic differences also began to break down. Roman expansion had opened up opportunities for capable and ingenious plebeians; many became wealthy and joined their interests increasingly with those of the patricians. Inequality persisted, but the distinctions of birth and rigid social caste were joined to distinctions of wealth and service.

The Conquest of Italy

The fundamental reason for these far-reaching changes in every aspect of Roman life was expansion. And expansion was the product of war. Rome was almost constantly at war during the two and one-half centuries that separated the founding of the republic from the passage of the Hortensian Law. Not only did Rome gain her independence by the successful revolt against Etruscan kingship; she also lost the protection of Etruscan power. Almost from the moment of the expulsion of Tarquin, Rome was desperately pressed. For a century she struggled to subdue the other minor states in central Italy. Out of this came the Latin League with Rome as the leading power. Wars were fought with the remaining centers of Etruscan authority. About 390 B.C. central Italy was invaded by the savage Gauls, who broke across the Apennines (they were already established in the Po Valley) and laid waste much of central Italy, even burning the city of Rome. The member states of the Latin League attempted revolt. Rome's situation was often precarious, but though she was not invariably victorious, she always had the reserves of strength to come back from defeat. By the middle of the fourth century, Rome had subdued the peoples who had opposed her in central Italy and had secured firm allies. She could now control the whole of peninsular Italy.

That control was disputed in 343 B.C., as Rome entered a fifty-year period of war with the Samnite people of the hill country to the east and south. The conflict began when Rome reached out for the rich Campanian plain to the south of Latium. The Samnites had already begun to infiltrate this land with no resistance from the weak and disunited Greek colonial states in the south of Italy. Thus, the Romans and Samnites conflicted in their brigandage. The war was long and intermittent, gradually assuming the character of a fight for Italian independence against Rome.

Before the Samnites finally sued for peace in 290 B.C., the Romans had involved themselves deeply in the affairs of the various Greek states at whose borders and through whose lands the Samnite wars had been fought. Within another twenty years, Rome was the major power among them. She stood ready to face her first conflict outside Italy and to take the first uncertain steps toward a Mediterranean empire.

Carthage and the Greek East—The Punic Wars

Centuries before the rise of Rome in Italy, a complex balance of power had been formed in the western Mediterranean. We have already noted that the Etruscans traded actively there, and the Greek states, founded as colonies in southern Italy and Sicily, had also flourished and prospered in trade. A third center of Mediterranean economic life was the great city of Carthage on the coast of North Africa. Carthage had been founded about the end of the ninth century B.C. as a Phoenician colony but, while the Phoenician homeland lost out in the power struggle of the Near East, Carthage, virtually unmolested in the west, created a great commercial empire. Carthaginian fleets tapped the rich resources of the backward hinterlands of North Africa and Spain and much of barbarian Europe to the north.

By 270 B.C. Rome had overshadowed both the Etruscans and the Italian Greeks and was the undisputed mistress of Italy. Now she fell heir to the rivalry with Carthage. The island of Sicily divided Roman Italy from Carthage across the narrow waist of the Mediterranean and it was over this rich and strategic island that the two powers finally came to war.

The Greek cities of Sicily and the south of Italy had never been able to achieve any really effective political unity and Carthage had played upon their disunity to gain a strong position in western Sicily. As Carthaginian strength in Sicily increased Rome found a pretext—the affairs of the Greek city of Syracuse—to intervene in Sicily on behalf of her allies against Carthage in 265 B.C. The war party in Rome was led by a group of rich men who had a vital interest in removing the Carthaginian obstacle to the expansion of Roman trade. Thus began the series of Punic Wars (from the Latin word *Punicus,* "Phoenician") which lasted intermittently for more than a century.

Rome was able to invade Sicily but there could be no decisive victory as long as Carthage maintained control of the sea. This led to Rome's decision to become a sea power: Roman fleets besieged the coast of North Africa and blockaded Sicily; Roman armies took most of the strong points on Sicily. But the initiative in the war seesawed back and forth. When it ended, with a crushing Roman naval victory in 241 B.C., the First Punic War had gone on for nearly a quarter century. The cost had been immense in both wealth and loss of life and the original cause had been obscured. The conflict with Carthage had assumed the proportion of a great national and ethnic crusade.

The terms of the peace and Rome's brutal treatment of her conquered enemy made inevitable a Second Punic War of vengeance. It has been called the war of one man against a nation. The man was Hannibal (247–183 B.C.). His father, Hamilcar Barca, had been the leading Carthaginian general in the closing years of the First Punic War and from him Hannibal inherited an intense personal hatred of Rome. For years before the Second Punic War actually began the family of Barca had been engaged in building a massive military machine in Spain, which had long been a Carthaginian dependency and which was to serve as a base of operations in the new war against Rome. In 218 B.C. Hannibal, having assumed command of the forces in Spain, began his march overland to strike at Rome across the Alps. He was confident that he could defeat Roman armies in the field. But he also knew that he could not destroy Rome simply by defeating her armies. He hoped by defeating Rome to induce the various allied peoples of Italy to break their alliances and the ambitious Hellenistic power of Macedonia to invade on a second front from across the Adriatic.

After a harrowing march across the Alps in winter Hannibal's army poured down into Italy.[1] In lightning succession he defeated a series of Roman armies sent against him. In the summer of 216 B.C., shamed by defeat and impatient with delay, the Romans forced a battle at Cannae in south-central Italy. It was the worst disaster Roman arms ever suffered. There were, by report, more than eighty thousand Roman casualties and only a fraction of her troops escaped. As Hannibal had hoped, cracks began to appear in the Roman alliance system. The Gauls of the Po Valley had already joined him. After Cannae they were followed by other peoples. But Rome was far from defeated. There was scarcely a house that did not have a son or father dead, but the state forbade public show of grief. Contributions were solicited to raise another field army. Families gave their fortunes and women their jewels. Moreover, Rome now changed her tactics.

A more cautious army harried Hannibal's lines and kept him moving.

1. In this Alpine crossing Hannibal lost a great number of men and animals, including all but one of his much-discussed elephants. He had taken the use of war elephants from the Hellenistic states whose armies used them regularly. Hannibal probably counted more on their shock value than their actual military utility since the Romans were not used to fighting against them. The loss of the elephants apparently had little effect on Hannibal's strategy.

On the diplomatic front Rome worked to strengthen her alliances and was able largely to regain control of the subject peoples and allies who had defected earlier; she also forestalled Macedonian intervention. But, above all, her command of the sea frustrated the rest of Hannibal's grand design. The war was carried to Sicily with steady success, culminating in the capture of Syracuse, an ally of Carthage. The Romans finally succeeded in reducing Hannibal's base in Spain, and his brother, forced out of Spain, made a dash for Italy to join Hannibal. But before he could do so he was defeated in the Po Valley and Hannibal was forced to withdraw to the heel of Italy. The Roman hero of the Spanish war, the young Publius Cornelius Scipio, carried the war to Africa, and Carthage was compelled to recall Hannibal under truce in 204 B.C. For nearly fifteen years Hannibal had maintained his army and his military initiative in a hostile land. Now he returned home to face his young Roman opponent and was finally defeated—at Zama in 202 B.C.—ending the second Punic War.

Rome had won again, and she exacted from her enemy the full price of victory: Carthage lost the lands of her empire; she was committed to a huge annual indemnity to be paid for fifty years; her fleet was reduced to ten vessels; she was forbidden to make war without Roman consent and left at the mercy of her African enemies with whom Rome concluded alliances.

With the conquest of Carthage, Rome had won the western Mediterranean. The same long conflict that had brought her this rich inheritance had already brought her directly into the affairs of the Hellenistic states. The always precarious balance of power among them was threatened by the accession of two vigorous and ambitious young sovereigns to two key states. Philip V came to the throne of Macedonia in 221 B.C. and Antiochus III became king of the Seleucid Empire in 223. In 202 B.C. Ptolemy IV of Egypt died and was succeeded by an infant heir, inviting aggression from both Philip and Antiochus. The lesser states of the east, certain of their own involvement, called for Roman intervention. The Romans were bound to these states—such as Rhodes and Pergamum—by a web of treaties and obligations dating from the war against Hannibal. But the decision to intervene was made on more fundamental grounds. If Antiochus and Philip succeeded in their designs, Rome might have both to contend with, and either might be another Hannibal. Rome could not afford to allow such concentration of power in the eastern Mediterranean. This, rather than compassion or the sanctity of treaties, made her the champion of the weak against the strong.

From 200 to 197 B.C. Rome successfully waged war against Philip. Having held Antiochus by diplomacy, Rome was forced into war with him in 192 B.C. With the defeat of Philip Rome had placed temptation before Antiochus, who began to push into Asia Minor and Thrace, becoming exactly the kind of threat Rome could not tolerate. Antiochus had been defeated by 189 B.C., and the several Greek states that had been his allies were also under the heavy Roman hand. Perseus of Macedonia, son of Philip V, taking advantage of the general discontent with Roman arrangements, forced war again in 171 B.C. Again Rome responded and Perseus was defeated and carried off in chains to die in a Roman prison. Macedonia was looted and dismembered and Roman settlements fixed the condition of most of the states of the Hellenistic world. In 148 B.C. Macedonia was made a Roman province under direct rule and two years later the city of Corinth was sacked and burned as a symbol of the end of Greek independence. Roman power now encircled the Mediterranean.

The winning of the world had not been all success and glory, for Rome had not won every battle, nor had her decisions been invariably right. She had put together a patchwork of empire that she had yet to subdue and which it would take her more than another century to learn to rule. Expensive and bitter wars continued and others remained to be fought. Carthage was finally destroyed in a brutal aggression that is called the Third Punic War (149–146 B.C.). Rome had won Spain from Carthage but its pacification was to take much longer. The land of the Gauls in the Po Valley—those who had allied themselves with Hannibal—was gained in the same slow and costly way. The task of empire-building was not done; its effects had only begun to be felt. But Rome, the backward agricultural village, had become the ruler of a significant portion of the known world.

THE CENTURY OF REVOLUTION

Rome and Hellenism

One of the most subtle yet pervasive changes which Rome underwent in this time of growth and expansion resulted from the impact of Hellenism. Rome had been half prepared for this by her long association first with the Hellenized Etruscans and then with the Greek states of Italy. She had long since begun to feel the economic effects of commercial contacts with the Hellenistic states. But with their conquest Rome was exposed for the first time to the full effects—both good and bad—of the highly sophisticated culture of the Greek world. Thousands of Romans had served in the eastern wars. They had seen a way of life completely different from their own—undreamed-of wealth and luxury evidenced by temples, palaces, and statuary. They had heard conversation, poetry, and speculation that represented another order of existence.

Not only did the Romans find Hellenism; the Greeks found Rome. The city of Rome was becoming the focal point of the Mediterranean world. The adventurous and acquisitive Greeks who had followed the conquests of Alexander to all the corners of the east turned toward Rome. In addition, Rome took hostages by the thousands as a result of the various peace settlements among the Hellenistic states. The wars had produced countless slaves and the slave market of Delos, at the height of its prosperity, poured ten thousand slaves a day into the streams of Mediterranean trade. Most of these were Greeks or Hellenized Orientals. Wealthy and noble Romans were impressed by the achievements of Greek learning, philosophy, and rhetoric. Under their patronage, Greek scholars and teachers opened schools in Rome, spreading education among the Roman ruling class. The influence of Greek humanism began to create a new type of Roman gentleman: it became fashionable to speak and write Greek; households bought learned Greek slaves to tutor their sons and to accompany them to schools of rhetoric and philosophy; they bought other slaves—physicians and pharmacists to cure and attend them, poets and musicians to amuse them.

From the looted cities of the east came thousands of works of Greek art which virtually created Roman artistic taste; a host of Greek artists followed in its wake. Greek gods, in the superb artistic forms evolved by generations of sculptors, were adopted wholesale by the Romans and made part of the eclectic system of Roman religion. Greek statuary and temple forms were copied, admired—and vulgarized. Greek epics, lyric poetry, and drama began to mold Roman literature. The first figure of Latin letters was the Greek slave Livius Andronicus who, in the middle of the second century B.C., translated popular Greek plays into Latin. Even Plautus (c. 254–184 B.C.), the greatest Roman literary figure of this period, wrote comedies frankly borrowed in theme, tone, and treatment from Hellenistic comedy. The Hellenistic philosophic systems were translated to Rome with comparable effect, on the one hand contributing civilizing influences, on the other shaking the traditional Roman values. Even the Latin language did not escape Greek influences. As Cicero was to say in a later time, ". . . indeed it was not a little rivulet that flowed from Greece into our city, but a mighty river of culture and learning." Along with the culture and learning that flowed from the east to enrich Roman civilization came the delicate vices to undermine the old, naive beliefs—Greek and oriental mystery cults, magicians, astrologers, and charlatans to corrupt the ignorant and fleece the foolish.

Conservative voices were raised in protest and laws were passed from time to time to curb the fertile influence of Hellenism. Its most vigorous opponent was Marcus Porcius Cato the Elder (234–149 B.C.). During his censorship, in 184 B.C., he tried without conspicuous success to combat Hellenism and those who espoused it, but the trend was too strong. From this time to its end, Roman civilization was bound to Hellenism. In the final analysis the fusion of Greek and Roman is one of the important contributions of Rome to western civilization. The Greeks had created a magnificent culture but had been unable to create a socio-political framework stable enough to endure. But even as the Romans were absorbing and adopting the influences of Hellenism, they were in the process of creating a system of political order in which it could grow and flourish.

Constitutional Change

Rome had started upon her career of conquest armed, in part, with the simple, balanced constitution of an archaic city-state. But as a consequence of expansion problems arose that strained the Roman political system to the breaking point.

The army which had begun as a simple citizen militia had grown into a vast and complex military machine. Prolonged campaigns overseas made it manifestly impossible to rotate an army back to Rome and send another into the field. The hard-fought conquest of Spain and the chain-reaction wars in the east kept thousands of Roman soldiers in foreign lands for twenty years and more. Offices created to care for the limited domestic needs of a small and static community were called upon to cope with the problems of an empire; the primitive financial system was clogged with the flood of tribute and loot; corruption thrived despite makeshift safeguards; civil law was forced to create precedents; magistracies were doubled and redoubled.

In the rapidly moving affairs of a growing state, governing policies had to be formulated and administered on a continuing basis, which enhanced the importance of the senate even more. This period of imperial expansion was the golden age of the senate. It was conservative, its policies were often selfish and cruel, and it made serious errors of judgment; but, by and large, it supplied Rome with a vigorous and patriotic leadership.

The Latin and Italic allies, the related peoples who had been joined to Rome in the early days of her expansion, had contributed their share to further expansion. More than half the troops in the scattered Roman armies were contingents of allies. While they had contributed a full share to Rome's victories, they were denied a full share of prestige and profit. This became a smoldering cause of resentment.

The more distant conquered lands had been crudely appended to the state as provinces. Expedients were patched together to govern them. Ex-magistrates of the highest rank were sent to these provinces as governors, endowed with legal authority as proconsuls and propraetors (those who stand "in place of" regular officials). The assignment of provincial governorships was controlled by the senate and were regarded as the rewards of political and military careers given to members of the closed senatorial aristocracy. It was the lot of the wretched provincials to line the purses of a succession of ruthless governors. Rome had gone halfway to empire in the sense that she had won the Mediterranean world. Recognition of the responsibility that went with conquest was many years in coming, and the provinces were to pay heavily for the privilege of Roman rule.

Social and Economic Pressures

For Rome itself, expansion and conquest were profitable. The conquest of Carthage had brought into Roman hands the great resources of the western Mediterranean; the trade of the barbaric hinterland of Europe, the grain of Sicily, gold from the Spanish mines that Hannibal had used to such effect. The conquest of the highly developed Greek east had laid open the seemingly endless riches of the Hellenistic monarchies. Yet, these very riches were a source of turmoil and class strife. The greatest share of the profit of empire was claimed by the privileged class, which also dominated the senate and provided Rome with her consuls and generals. The winning of the world widened rather than closed the gulf of the Roman social order.

The patrician families who had established their leading position in Rome from its beginning had been joined by plebeian families who had risen to wealth and prominence. Many of them ventured into the lucrative trade which Rome's conquests had quickened and redirected; many more invested their wealth in great tracts of "public land" leased from the state. The same families held these lands generation after generation, building homes and even villages on them, and eventually considering them as personal property. They were worked by huge gangs of slaves purchased in the flourishing markets glutted with the victims of Roman wars. There was no commodity so cheap as human life, and seldom has brutality been so nearly systematized as on these estates. Slave labor proved extremely profitable for the owners of the great estates, but in the long run it changed the Roman economy as a whole, with serious social and political results.

Agriculture had been traditionally and predominantly in the hands of independent peasant farmers, who had provided not only agricultural products but sturdy, stolid, and sober soldiers to fill the ranks of the legions. Now several factors combined to threaten the very existence of this class. Prolonged absence in foreign wars resulted in the neglect of their land. Moreover, domestic agriculture found itself in unfavorable competition on two fronts: against the slave-produced commodities from the plantation-estates and against government-purchased grain from abroad, this latter the result of Rome's need to feed a growing population. The inflationary tendencies in the economy as a whole—resulting from the constant flow of tribute and loot from conquered lands—completed the destruction of the peasant farmers. By the thousands they abandoned their homes, some to become tenant farmers, others to become colonists. But great numbers of them flocked to the cities, especially to the city of Rome, to merge with the growing city populace, the instrument and victim of every politician's ambition.

Not only was the traditional class conflict intensified by the growth of the empire, but a new class appeared to complicate it further. As Rome became the center of a complex economic world, a new business and financial class evolved and pushed its claim for acceptance. Called the *equestrian order,* its origin was the class of men wealthy enough to afford the cost of cavalry service in the military. The equestrians early lost their military connection but the association with wealth remained. They were the bankers, magnates, investors, and manipulators who followed the legions. As the soldiery won Rome her domination of the Mediterranean world, the equestrian financiers took over its systematic spoliation and rapidly rose in power as well as wealth to a position inferior only to the senators.

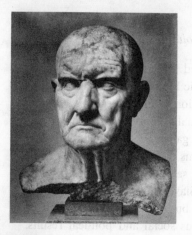

LEFT
Top: Roman bust. 1st century B.C.
Center: Brutus. Below: Cicero.

15

The Forum, Rome.

16

The Colosseum. 72—80 A.D. Rome.

Arch of Titus. 81 A.D. Rome.

Domestic Politics and the Men on Horseback

The rapid economic and social changes which accompanied the conquest of the empire contributed to the century of civil war that brought an end to the Roman republic. The long-existing tensions erupted into open violence in the years following 133 B.C.

In that year Tiberius Gracchus, a fiery young aristocrat, stood for the plebeian office of tribune, deserting his class to become the first of a long series of Roman popular leaders. He championed the cause of the dispossessed peasantry and demanded land reforms. His motives were noble and his proposals were statesmanlike, but the senate feared any encroachment on its privileges. When Tiberius appealed to the sovereign power of the people over senatorial opposition the senate feared not only the loss of its privileges but the creation of a popular despotism, and Tiberius Gracchus was murdered. The senate thus set a dangerous precedent for the solution of civil problems by resorting to violence.

Tiberius Gracchus' program, methods, and office were taken up by his younger brother, Gaius, in 124–123 B.C. But in addition, Gaius formed a full-fledged popular party which he set in direct opposition to the senate. Once more violence flared and Gaius was killed.

The problems which had aroused the Gracchi in Rome needed solution in the empire at large as well. Between the polar forces of the turbulent Roman assembly and the narrow, class-bound senate appeared a new force, bred of imperial growth and successful war—the ambitious general with an army at his back.

The first of the military dictators was Gaius Marius (c. 155–86 B.C.), a rough and able soldier who rose to prominence by crushing a native rebellion in North Africa and defeating a horde of German and Celtic barbarians who streamed across the Alps to menace Italy in 102 B.C. Marius turned military reputation into political fortune and, as leader of the Gracchan populist party, was elected consul six times.

Another series of military crises—a civil war of Rome's Italian allies and a general uprising in the east led by Mithridates VI, the Hellenistic king of Pontus—produced the next dictator, Lucius Cornelius Sulla (138–78 B.C.), who had been one of Marius' lieutenants. Once more a successful general translated his military strength into political advantage. Sulla's dictatorship was accompanied by the most savage reprisals against the Marian populists. But although Sulla was aristocratic in sympathy, the senatorial party profited little from his measures and he failed to destroy the populists.

In spite of both Marius and Sulla, Rome's fundamental social, economic, and constitutional weaknesses remained—and produced their successors. Spain had been driven to revolt and other provinces were ready to strike for freedom from Rome; Mithridates was again a power in the east; Marcus Lepidus, the consul for the year 78 B.C., had attempted a coup which proved unsuccessful; and a slave rebellion in Italy threatened to become a serious war. The senate turned in despair again to an ambitious general and, abdicating civil authority, granted almost unlimited power to Gnaeus Pompey (106–48 B.C.), who had given himself the title *Magnus*, "the great." He almost deserved his title: he had pacified Spain by 72 B.C. and six years later received powers against Mithridates such as no Roman had ever held. Pompey defeated Mithridates and made an equitable and wise settlement in the eastern provinces that was to be the basis of Roman rule there for the next five hundred years. But the price of his success was another dictatorship.

One Empire, One Ruler

As Pompey moved from success to success, another figure was gaining power in Rome. Gaius Julius Caesar (c. 100–44 B.C.), like Sulla, was an aristocrat and a member of one of Rome's most ancient families. But, like Marius, he was committed to the popular faction rather than to the aristocracy. During the years of the Sullan dictatorship and the rise of Pompey, he had held a number of offices and gained wide experience in public life. His contemporaries knew the young Caesar as a man capable of decisive, though often questionable, political action. He showed great acumen on occasion and as an orator was ranked only below Cicero (106–43 B.C.). Yet Caesar was also a man of fashion, a passionate gambler, and the associate of some of Rome's most dissolute men. He seemed much too concerned with the fads of fashion to cherish the burden of real political power, but significantly he was suspiciously popular with the irresponsible mob of the city proletariat.

In 62 B.C. Pompey returned in triumph from the east. He had been so successful that the senate now feared him and refused to ratify his arrangements or to grant his soldiers the lands they had been promised. In this dangerous impasse, Caesar approached Pompey and the ambitious financier, Marcus Crassus, who was already his creditor, for enormous sums of money. The result was the formation of the informal personal alliance known as the First Triumvirate—combining the power and prestige of Pompey, the wealth of Crassus, and the political connections and abilities of Caesar. With this support, Caesar virtually seized the consulship for the year 59 B.C. with a colleague so weak and shadowy that Roman wags referred to the year as the consulship of Julius and Caesar. He forced the acceptance of the eastern settlement, secured the rewards for Pompey's troops and, looking to the entrenchment of his power when the consular year ended, gained for himself the governorship of Cisalpine Gaul (northern Italy) as well as barbarian Gaul across the Alps for five years. This was a master stroke, for it gave him constitutional immunity and put a large army at the disposal of the triumvirate.

With the political situation in Rome fully under control, Caesar departed for his province in 58 B.C. Almost immediately, the suspicious movements of one of the tribes to the north gave him a pretext and he set out upon the famous conquest of Gaul. His career to this point had been that of a politician with only the most limited military experience. He was already a middle-aged man. Yet, in the ten years that followed, Caesar gained an immortal place among the world's great generals. Victory followed victory as Caesar subjugated the tribes of Gaul and the German frontier. He pushed as far as the area of modern Holland and Belgium and crossed the Channel to establish the first bridgehead of Roman authority in Britain. The reports of his fame—among them his own account in *The Gallic Wars*—reached Rome and his two comrades, already distrustful of each other, began to fear Caesar's rocketing prestige. In 53 B.C. Crassus was killed in an inept campaign against the Parthians, who had reared a dangerously strong state across the frontier of the Euphrates. Caesar and Pompey faced each other across the resulting gulf. Their personal relations rapidly disintegrated and the watchful senate, rightly concluding that it had more to fear from Caesar than from Pompey, drew close to the latter. The First Triumvirate was broken. As Pompey and the senate aligned against him, Caesar's command in Gaul was running out. Since it would expire at the end of the year 49 B.C., he demanded the consulship for 48. His demand was refused unless he first surrender his proconsular authority, and this he would not do. Thus, in January 49 B.C., Caesar took the fateful step into open revolution and crossed the Rubicon, the little stream that separated his Gallic province from penisular Italy.

During the years of his absence, Caesar had not neglected his political fortunes. His agents and his own dramatic conquests had kept his name before the Roman people. He posed successfully as the popular champion. His long identification with the old Gracchan and Marian factions and the entente between Pompey and the senate lent credence to his pose. Rome and Italy welcomed him as a deliverer and Pompey's troops began to desert to Caesar. Pompey withdrew across the Adriatic to Greece to prepare to meet Caesar, and the majority of the senate joined him in provident flight. A newly packed senate granted Caesar vast emergency powers; he hastened to Spain and, in a quick campaign, won over the armies still held there by Pompey's subordinates. Then, in the summer of 48 B.C., he crossed to Greece and defeated the Pompeians at Pharsalus. Pompey fled to Egypt, where he was murdered, and Caesar, with expedient clemency, forgave the numerous senators now his captives.

Pompey still had allies in the east and Caesar moved through Asia Minor and Syria to defeat them. In Egypt the aging Caesar was delayed not only by the settlement of the valuable Ptolemaic succession, but by the charms of the young princess Cleopatra (the rake had not completely died even in the conqueror). Redoubts of Pompeian force remained in North Africa and Spain, and the conquest of the empire was completed just a year before Caesar was assassinated. In the chaotic four years since he had routed Pompey from Italy, Caesar had been principally occupied in war. His prodigious energy and his great administrative grasp had enabled him to make many policy decisions of great importance, but only the vaguest outlines of a "Caesarian reform" can be made out.

The plot that took his life was formed by many men with many motives. Some of the assassins were sincere republicans; some, outraged aristocrats or reckless opportunists; others were simply jealous or fearful of his power. They were led by Gaius Cassius and Marcus Brutus. In the senate chamber on the Ides of March, 44 B.C., pierced by more than twenty wounds, Caesar fell at the feet of a statue of Pompey.

Though the assassination had been done in the name of the republic, the only real concern was what dictatorial power should succeed that of Caesar. In the moment of confusion following his death the strongest claimant was Marcus Antonius (c. 83–30 B.C.), consul for the year and one of Caesar's henchmen (as was practically every public official in the state). But there was another claimant. Shortly before his death, Caesar had adopted his nephew, Octavian (63 B.C.–A.D. 14), and this young man, armed only with the magic of his adoptive name, hastened to Rome to face Marc Antony in what seemed an unequal contest.

The senate, largely under the whip of Cicero, had begun to recover its position. Fearing Antony, it turned to Octavian as it had turned before to Pompey. The young Caesar Octavian, quite without legal authority, had collected a large army of his uncle's troops. Cicero, meanwhile, hoped to use one menace to destroy another. He hoped that he could weld the frightened factions of the senate into a moderate majority under his own leadership and thus return the state to the control of the senate and the law. Octavian, with the senate's blessing, faced Antony in the north of Italy where the latter, also illegally, had taken up a proconsular command. Octavian defeated him. Now, his usefulness done and his strength growing, the senate tried to ignore Octavian. The result was simply to drive the two enemies, Antony and Octavian, together. They joined with another powerful Caesarian commander, Lepidus, and the senate found itself the captive of the Second Triumvirate.

Need, not love, held the triumvirs together. The assassins who had fled Rome under an amnesty were in the east raising troops; their friends and sympathizers were everywhere in Italy. Before Antony and Octavian could risk the pursuit of Brutus and Cassius they had to have a secure base in Italy and money for their armies. They gained both by a systematic proscription. Not only the proven conspirators and partisans, but all who might conceivably be a danger to them were outlawed and their property confiscated. Murder and denunciation made a jungle of Italy. The weak and aged Cicero, one of the republic's most devoted statesmen, was among the thousands of their victims. Cicero had been a great senatorial leader in an age of senatorial degeneracy. Although his policies were often questionable, he had been the faithful advocate of peace and legality in an age of military terrorism and anarchy.

In 42 B.C. Octavian and Antony crossed to Greece to defeat the assassins. This done, the need that bound them together began to fade and their inherent enmity to grow. As the First Triumvirate had done, they divided the empire, Antony taking the east and Octavian and Lepidus sharing the west. In the years that followed, Antony squandered his opportunity: he failed against the Parthians and lost the prestige that he might have had; he fell under the charm of Cleopatra and of her kingdom's wealth; and he lost the support of Rome and Italy, which increasingly swung to Octavian. This young man was more than the shadow of Caesar, and the abilities that were to make him the founder of the empire began to appear: he kept the support of the vast number of military veterans and he promised peace and order to the growing middle class of Italy and the western provinces. Lepidus was pushed into the background and Antony and Octavian faced each other again in the contest for supremacy. Their relations deteriorated until, in the fall of 31 B.C., they met in pitched battle at Actium off the coast of Greece. The fleet of Antony and Cleopatra broke and dissolved and their land forces joined the victorious Octavian. Antony and Cleopatra fled, and the world once more had come into the hands of one master.

THE WORLD EMPIRE

The Pax Romana and the Founding of the Principate

After tightening the Roman convenants in the east and confiscating the riches of Cleopatra's Egypt, Octavian returned to Rome in 29 B.C. to celebrate a lavish three-day triumph. The doors of the Temple of Janus were closed as the symbol of peace for the first time since 235 B.C. For a century the huge and hungry armies of rival generals had fed upon the empire; whole provinces had been reduced to desert, cities had been ruined. The recognition of Rome's need for peace and stability motivated Octavian's policies.

Octavian was now the sovereign of the Roman republic, and peace could be maintained only by his remaining so. To relinquish his powers and "restore the republic" would have been unrealistic, for it was clear that the republic could no longer maintain itself against military dictatorship. On the other hand a legal, hereditary monarchy on the lines of the Hellenistic states was equally unrealistic, for against this the tradition of the republic was too strong. Octavian's solution was to retain the powers that made him the ruler of Rome—*within* the framework of the republican constitution. It was a complex compromise, the varied parts of which slowly developed over the years of his rule.

The first necessity was the continued control of the military. In 27 B.C. the senate and the assembly solemnly granted Octavian the authority they had no power to deny him. He was given an extended military command, *imperium,* so vast and of such duration that it made him the commander-in-chief of the Roman military establishment. It was granted for ten years and subsequently renewed for the rest of his life. Every army commander was his subordinate. In keeping with this power, he was given the title *Imperator,* "commander" (which became in time our word "emperor").

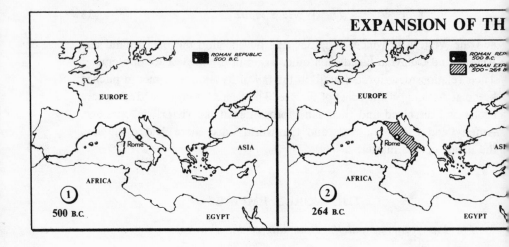

He was also given the title *Augustus,* "consecrated and worthy of honor."

The imperium was the military prop of the Augustan rule; but Augustus needed a strong and legal civil authority as well. The doubtful legality of the triumvirate sustained him until 33 B.C. In that year he received from the senate and the people an oath of military allegiance as a stop-gap power. In addition, he held the consulship annually until 23 B.C. In that year, on the precedent of Caesar, he was given the power of the tribune, the tribunician authority, separated from the actual office. This became his chief civil prop. It gave him the tribune's traditional jurisdiction and control of legislation. Other powers and rights were granted from time to time and he held many customary republican offices.

The total result was the creation of the form of government called the principate. The name comes from an old republican title of honor, *princeps senatus,* "first citizen." This was the title Augustus preferred and it accurately expresses his concept of his role in the state. It was that of a supermagistrate, drawing authority from traditional powers and governing within the constitution of the revered republic. The Augustan system of the principate provided a government for the empire through the most brilliant and productive centuries of its existence.

The Augustan Reforms

Armed with enormous legal powers and a personal prestige few mortals have enjoyed, Augustus set about his reforms. He reduced the swollen lists of the senate to six hundred men. The old aristocracy which had monopolized the senate for so long had survived the civil wars in a bare handful of families, and the new senate was made up largely of those

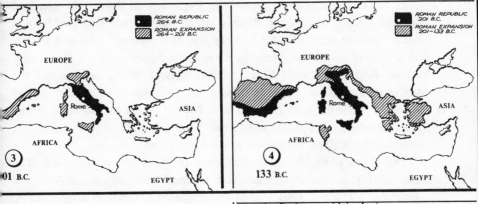

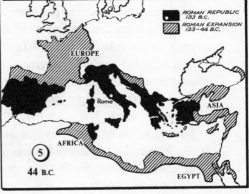

who had some stake in the future of the Augustan empire. Its traditional authority and prerogatives were continued and Augustus scrupulously shared with the senate the burden of ruling the empire.

This sharing of authority was nowhere more evident than in the management of the provinces. Augustus returned to the senate control of those areas which had been longest under Roman rule. Such provinces continued to be governed by senatorial promagistrates and their revenues continued to pour into the state treasury. The newly acquired provinces, the border areas where wars still had to be fought, Augustus retained himself (he had no intention of ceding extended legionary command to some ambitious senator). The frontier wars in the imperial provinces to the north along the Rhine and Danube were hard fought and costly. The commands were given to trusted lieutenants and members of the imperial family, notably the two stepsons of Augustus, Tiberius and Drusus, who were luckily able commanders.

He was not always so fortunate in his generals. In A.D. 9 the arrogance and mismanagement of Quinctilius Varus, the commander of the German frontier army, provoked a coalition of tribes along the Rhine, which defeated Varus and destroyed his army. The frontier was held, by the good efforts of Tiberius, but Roman authority never again penetrated into Germany much beyond the Rhine.

In the east, Augustus accepted the Euphrates as Rome's frontier and made no attempt to conquer Parthia, which had already cost two Roman armies. He was satisfied with a shaky line of influence along that border and a tier of client kingdoms to serve as a buffer between Rome and Parthia. Rome's authority held in other sections of the empire and the modest conquests of Augustus along the frontiers gave to the empire essentially the boundaries it would have for the rest of its existence. Along those boundaries Augustus conducted vigorous and shrewd diplomacy, supported by legions encamped at strategic points.

The military establishment itself was overhauled and reformed. The great armies of the civil wars had reached 500,000 in number and constituted a ruinous burden upon the empire. Immediately after Actium, Augustus had mustered out more than 300,000 of his veterans and settled them on farm land, where their industry and loyalty made them another prop to his rule. In their place he organized a small, highly disciplined, and well-paid professional army. It numbered only about 150,000 and was supplemented by an equal number of provincial auxiliaries. In determining the number and disposition of these troops Augustus considered not only defensive needs but also what the empire could afford. Above all, he wanted to make the army the servant of the civil state, not its master.

Within the frontiers of the empire Augustus regularized the machinery of administration. In his own provinces he began to create an imperial civil service, attracting men in search of careers rather than fortune hunters. In this policy he found an important ally in the equestrian order; and in the service of the princeps, the equestrians found new and honorable careers. Even in the purely senatorial provinces, the worst abuses of the republican provincial administration were abolished, for the senate itself increasingly reflected the new outlook of Augustan Rome.

The efforts of the emperor were aided by time and peace. One world and one culture were beginning to appear. It was bound together by the ribbon of Roman roads that extended from Italy to every center of military concentration or trade. In the forum at Rome stood the golden milepost from which every distance was measured—all roads literally led to Rome.

Augustus attacked a multitude of problems with the same diligence he showed in the reform of the provinces, and there were few areas of Roman life untouched by his efforts. He overhauled the administration of the city of Rome itself, giving it its first police force and regular fire brigade. He regulated the supply of public grain. He created a special corps of elite troops, the Praetorian Guard, who were stationed at various places in Italy and commanded by high-ranking prefects. In an attempt to reform the republican legal system he initiated a vast body of legislation. Both by law and example he tried to encourage a return to the native simplicity and vigor of Roman social life. Such a return to traditional values implied a revival of traditional religion. Augustus sponsored the worship of a host of old Roman gods: he built temples; reestablished dozens of priestly colleges; and participated himself in countless cult duties, combating the Oriental religions which had taken hold during the misery and uncertainty of the civil wars. Augustus' conception of religion was thoroughly Roman; it had little if anything to do with supernaturalism. For him religion was a social force, an indispensable tie with the traditions of the past.

The Golden Age of Latin Letters

The Augustan Age was not only a time of brilliant and significant political achievement, it was also one of the world's golden ages of literature.

Roman literature began to flower during the years dominated by Caesar and Pompey. The political turbulence of the last years of the republic had not inhibited the growth of a vigorous intellectual life. We have already noted the important influence of Hellenism in early Roman culture. That powerful force continued but, by the time of Caesar, Roman culture had reached a healthy young maturity of its own. Its most vigorous expression was in oratory and the prose forms that grew from it. Roman government was a government by discourse. Every day in the senate, the assembly, and the courts, the members of the ruling class had to present their arguments to each other and the people at large. This was the principal source of the development of Latin prose. It owed little to Greek influence and much to the give and take of politics so central to the life of Rome.

Catullus (87–54 B.C.) was the first of the great Latin lyric poets. Taking the varied forms of the Greek lyric, he adapted them with consummate perfection to his own language. His themes were love and hate, and he became the spokesman for the young libertine group in Rome.

An older contemporary of Catullus was the poet Lucretius (96–55 B.C.) who, with equal perfection, adapted Hellenic forms to expound the Epicurean philosophy. In his *De Rerum Natura* (On Nature), Lucretius produced the greatest philosophic poem of antiquity. Like the earlier Epicureans, Lucretius wanted to present man with a system that would permit him to live the good life, a life in which pleasure was present and pain absent. But before this was possible man had to accept the mechanics of the universe and acknowledge that nature was impersonal, orderly, and unswayed by prayer, hope, or susperstition. Only with this acceptance could he attain a life of happiness. This is the burden of Lucretius' poem.

This terror then and darkness of mind must be dispelled not by the rays of the sun and glittering shafts of day, but by the aspect and the law of nature; the warp of whose design we shall begin with this principle, nothing is ever gotten out of nothing by divine power. Fear in sooth holds so in check all mortals, because they see many operations go on in earth and heaven, the causes of which they can in no way understand, believing them therefore to be done by divine power.[2]

He went on to present a completely mechanistic explanation of the universe, man, death, and even the human soul. In the passion of his disbelief, Lucretius created a magnificent monument, but one that was bypassed by the main current of Roman philosophy.

To the cultured Roman of the upper classes the conclusions of Lucretius were largely unacceptable, even to those of his own circle who applauded his work. The life of pleasure, no matter how well argued, could not compete with the life of duty. In a little treatise, On Duty, written in the next half century after Lucretius, Cicero said:

. . . whatever we go about, whether of public or private affairs, whether at home or abroad . . . we lie constantly under an obligation to some duties: and as all the virtue and credit of our lives proceed from the due discharge of this, so all the baseness and turpitude of them result from the non-observance of the same . . . nor can he ever be a man of courage, who thinks that pain is the greatest evil; or he of temperance, who imagines pleasure to be the sovereign good.[3]

The author of this rather stuffy advice brought Latin prose to its highest point of perfection. Cicero was an exemplar of the last phase

2. *On the Nature of Things*, H. A. J. Munro transl., Dutton, 1896.
3. *Offices, Essays, and Letters* (London: J. M. Dent and Sons, Ltd., 1942), p. 3.

of republican culture. In him were met all the prejudices, attitudes, and virtues of the Roman ruling class. In accordance with his values, Cicero was a politician, for the good life was the political life, and the nature of man was inseparable from the state. In the moments he could take from a busy life and in his last bitter years of forced retirement, he wrote a library of philosophic and didactic works. The most consistent strain in all his writing, as the above quotation on duty will attest, was Stoic. But philosophically, Cicero was an eclectic with a typically Roman lack of concern for systematic consistency. He was a practical man who saw himself guided by the values of the Roman fathers of the republic. Cicero drew from the Greek philosophers and schools almost impartially to support those values—honor, honesty, virtue, patriotism, and duty—which the Roman honored even when he did not practice them. The apparent time-serving and vacillation of Cicero's political career were actually an attempt to serve through political expediency the ideals of republicanism and constitutionalism to which he subscribed in his writings and which he saw so desperately imperiled in his lifetime. It was his tragedy that he labored in the service of an ideal already dead.

The republic passed in the blood and horror of the last civil war that ended at Actium. Most men of wisdom did not lament its passing, for its abuses had come to outweigh its blessings. Republicanism remained, but it became increasingly an academic thing and Augustus, sublimely tolerant in his strength, not only allowed but encouraged it.

Men of letters sought new themes, and the greatest lay before them— the reconstitution of the world in the founding of the principate. The greatest figure of Augustan literature was the poet Vergil (70–19 B.C.). The course of his life ran with that of the new order of Augustus. In 41 B.C. his modest family farm in the north of Italy near Mantua was confiscated in the allotment of land to veterans. He appealed to the young Octavian and was taken under his protection. This happy meeting of poet and protector is reflected in Vergil's *Eclogues*. These are a beautifully polished series of idyllic, rustic poems on Greek models. In one of them, the fourth, he addressed these words to an unborn child of the Caesarian family, perhaps to the nascent spirit of the Augustan Age itself:

> The last age told by Cumae's seer is come.
> A mighty roll of generations new
> Is now arising. Justice now returns
> And Saturn's realm, and from high heaven descends

A worthier race of men. Only do thou
Smile, chaste Lucina,[4] on the infant boy
With whom the iron age will pass away,
The golden age in all the earth be born;
For thine Apollo reigns. Under thy rule,
Thine, Pollio,[5] shall this glorious era spring,
And the great progress of the months begin.
Under thy rule all footprints of our guilt
Shall perish, and the peaceful earth shall be freed
From everlasting fear.[6]

The moving spirit of the Augustan literary circle was Maecenas, one of the emperor's closest advisors. In addition to his personal interest in literature, Maecenas, like Augustus, saw the advantage of courting the Roman literati. Under sensitive and abundant patronage, literature flourished and men of letters turned their pens to the willing service of the new age, none with more feeling than Vergil.

At the request of Maecenas, Vergil wrote his *Georgics,* a series of long poems celebrating Roman agriculture. But his greatest poetic gift to the new order was his epic poem, the *Aeneid,* named after Aeneas, the legendary founder of the earliest civilization in Italy to which Roman tradition traced its own origins. Aeneas escaped the burning ruins of Troy, laid low by the Achaeans, leading a small band of refugees. After many years of wandering in strange lands, driven by the cryptic will of the gods, Aeneas reached Italy and there, near the site of Rome, founded his predestined city.

The *Aeneid* is an elaborate tapestry of allusion and allegory. Its allegorical subject is Rome itself. Vergil saw the story of Rome as the unfolding of destiny, the *fatum Romanum,* and as fulfilling that destiny in the age of Augustus. In the central book of the *Aeneid* Aeneas is taken to the underworld. There the ghost of his father, Anchises, leads him to a high hill and they look out over the waiting company of Rome's great men, from the son of Aeneas, Romulus, and the great traditional heroes to

. . . Caesar Augustus, a god's son, who shall again establish the ages of gold in Latium over the fertile fields that once were the realm of Saturn, and carry his empire afar to Garamant and Indian, to the land that lies beyond our stars,

4. The poet is referring to the birth goddess.
5. He was Vergil's friend and consul for the year 40 B.C.
6. T. F. Royds (trans. and ed.), *The Eclogues, Bucolics, or Pastorals of Virgil* (Oxford: Basil Blackwell, 1922), pp. 43-45.

beyond the sun's year-long ways, where Atlas the sky-bearer wheels on his shoulder the glittering star-spangled pole.[7]

Anchises delivers an encomium of Roman destiny and Roman character:

> Others shall beat out the breathing bronze to softer lines, I believe it well; shall draw living lineaments from the marble; the cause shall be more eloquent on their lips; their pencil shall portray the pathways of heaven, and tell the stars in their arising: be thy charge, O Roman, to rule the nations in thine empire; this shall be thine art, to ordain the law of peace, to be merciful to the conquered and beat the haughty down.[8]

The other luminary of the Augustan sphere, second only to Vergil, was Horace (65–8 B.C.). He also was enthusiastic about the new order and, like Vergil, became a protégé of Maecenas. Horace lacked the Olympian loftiness and stern seriousness of Vergil; his forte was the small form, the lyric. His poetry celebrated sensual delights—love, wine, companionship —and expressed his disdain for the stench and scurry of the city, his joy in the quiet indolence of the countryside. He had been an idealistic republican but, like many another, transferred his allegiance to Augustus, for he saw in the strong rule of a single man the only hope of preserving the virtues of the Roman tradition. His poetry was less directly and obviously an apologia for Augustus than that of Vergil, but beneath every well-turned line shone gratitude for the Augustan peace and order. Only under such circumstances could the things that Horace loved exist.

Many lesser poets and artists were attracted to the circle of Augustus. Most of them, like Vergil and Horace, honored the new age. An exception was the poet Ovid (43 B.C.–c. A.D. 17) who exemplified in his life and verses the very libertinism that the emperor was trying so diligently to check. With his polished obscenities he was the literary soul of a considerable circle of rich debauchees. When the influence of this group reached the imperial house and the free-spirited daughter of the emperor, Ovid was exiled to the remote eastern end of the empire and his most pitiable appeals were systematically ignored. This is almost the only example of despotism over letters in this remarkable age. Indeed, censorship was disdained and patronage was given freely to worthy talents.

Another member of the Augustan circle was the historian Livy 59 B.C.–A.D. 17), the greatest prose writer of the age. Taking as his

---

7. Vergil, *The Aeneid*, J. W. Machail transl. (New York: Modern Library, 1934), pp. 123ff.

8. *Ibid.*, 438.

subject the history of Rome from its origin to 9 B.C., Livy's object was to show the men of his time the greatness of their own tradition, to set before them the ideals of their forefathers. Livy wrote glowingly of the republic, though not at the expense of the Augustan dictatorship. His point was that the very Roman accomplishments represented in the deeds of the republic were threatened unless the Roman world accepted its new "founder" in Augustus.

The End of an Era

As the years of prosperity and peace passed, men began to feel that the Age of Gold had actually come again. Augustus himself became an institution. He was revered, and in the provinces he was worshiped as a god in the twin cult of Augustus and Roma, the personification of the state. Nor did he discourage the spread of the cult in Italy and Rome, for these practices, like the Roman roads, helped to bind the empire together.

Augustus died in A.D. 14, having been undisputed master of the Roman world for almost half a century, and having done much to give solidarity and permanence to the imperial system he had created. A new generation had grown up without knowing the republic. Yet, the last years of Augustus' life were clouded by the issue of succession. The fiction of constitutional magistracy that he had played so long and so well had to be laid aside. There was no power to decide who should succeed Augustus except Augustus himself. He had favored many men—old friends like Maecenas and Marcus Agrippa, and members of his own family. He had joined them with him in his enormous authority and groomed them for his tasks—but he had outlived them all except his stepson, Tiberius. Already a middle-aged man, Tiberius had been one of Augustus' most capable and loyal generals but had been passed over in imperial favor many times. For years he had lived in self-imposed retirement, devoting himself to philosophy. Shortly before his death Augustus recalled Tiberius to Rome as his successor. At the death of Augustus, Tiberius held most of the powers that made up the principate. The senate hastened to confirm them, for there was no serious thought of a return to the republic.

In these last years of the Augustan reign, while the whole world looked to Rome, Christ was born in Palestine, one of Rome's eastern dependencies. His brief life would be ended in the reign of Tiberius, but his cult and influence would eventually be established over the ruins of the empire.

THE FULFILLMENT OF EMPIRE

The Julio-Claudian Dynasty

For the half-century following the death of Augustus, the imperial power passed through the line of his family in the Julio-Claudian dynasty. His stepson Tiberius was a conscientious and probably an able ruler; he was an experienced general and competent administrator; but he was neither an attractive personality nor a facile politician. His naturally gloomy and suspicious character darkened over the years and he became increasingly despotic. Tiberius was followed, in A.D. 37, by his grand-nephew Gaius, nicknamed Caligula. Caligula had every opportunity to be a popular emperor but the corruption of power destroyed his sanity. He was the first of the "imperial monsters" and was assassinated in A.D. 41 by a member of the Praetorian Guard. It was an ominous commentary on imperial government that murder had become the only way of removing an incompetent emperor.

THE JULIO-CLAUDIAN EMPERORS

AUGUSTUS	*31. B.C.—A.D. 14*
TIBERIUS	*14-37*
GAIUS (CALIGULA)	*37-41*
CLAUDIUS	*41-54*
NERO	*54-68*

Moreover, the Praetorians, by this step, became the "king-makers" of Rome, for it was they who chose the next emperor, Claudius, the middle-aged, pedantic, bumbling uncle of Caligula. Surprisingly, he turned out to be a fairly effective ruler. But his death (he was probably poisoned by his wife) brought to the throne the last and most infamous of the Julio-Claudians, his stepson Nero (A.D. *54–68*).

The first five years of Nero's reign gave the promise of brilliance. Then the madness that was the curse of the imperial house came to the surface. Nero threw over the responsibilities of government for debauchery, extravagance, and the indulgence of his own mediocre talent for music and dramatics. He wasted the state resources and turned to wholesale confiscations. Rome was filled with the victims of his tyranny. In A.D. 64 a disastrous fire broke out that nearly destroyed the city. Popular hysteria blamed the small and hated sect of the Christians and Nero was happy enough to have a scapegoat and encouraged their persecution.

For thirty years the sect had been slowly growing. Attracting many converts in the eastern cities Christianity—like everything else in the empire—finally spread to Rome. There could not have been many Christians in Rome, but their nature rather than their number made them the objects of suspicion. They consciously set themselves apart and showed a high disregard for the common social patterns of the pagan world. Their exclusiveness, their antisocial behavior and strange actions, made them easily identifiable and readily suspect. Mob hatred followed suspicion and Christians were lynched or dragged before tribunals for summary trial. They were savagely tortured—crucified, covered with the skins of animals and torn to bits by dogs, burned as living torches. The aristocratic historian Tacitus (c. A.D. 55–117) had little good to say for them, calling them "criminals who deserved extreme and exemplary punishment," and assuring us that their crime was, more than anything else, "hatred against mankind." Peter and Paul, the leaders of the embattled sect in Rome, were executed about the same time. The reign of terror seems to have been limited to the city of Rome and not to have spread across the empire.

In A.D. 65 Nero uncovered a plot against him and in vengeance and panic, instituted a reign of blood. Every eminent person was suspected and many were killed whose only crime was excellence. The plot failed but its temper moved to the frontiers: the governor of Gaul raised a revolt; this was followed by another in Spain; the frontier armies marched toward Rome to name their own emperor. In A.D. 68 Nero died by his own hand, allegedly with the words, "What an artist dies in me!"

The Flavian Dynasty

The year that followed, A.D. 68–69, was known as "the year of the four emperors." In the words of Tacitus, ". . . now had been divulged that secret of the empire, that emperors could be made elsewhere than at Rome." In rapid succession Galba, Otho, and Vitellius rose and fell. Finally, the eastern and Danubian legions declared for Titus Flavius Vespasianus (A.D. 9–79), the Legate of Judea, and the fearful interlude of the "war of the legions" ended.

The new emperor had nothing to commend him except ability. Vespasian was not the son of an ancient and noble family, he came from the tough and solid stock of the Italian municipalities and from the army where he had made a distinguished career for himself. He began to repair the ruin that was the principal legacy of the Julio-Claudians. Vespasian richly deserved the name of the second founder of the principate, for he consciously took Augustus as his model and consistently hewed to his policies. He restored military discipline, disbanded legions of doubtful loyalty, and reconstituted the troublesome Praetorians. Both on the German frontier and in the east he carried through the campaigns that had begun during the previous reign. But, like Augustus, he wasted neither troops nor money in military vainglory. He extended Roman citizenship and drew from the provinces an increasing number of distinguished men to serve the state. His careful and honest policies of administration and finance brought new security to the empire. Despite increased taxation, the general level of prosperity rose with peace and order and public confidence. Although Vespasian restored the prestige of the senate and filled its rolls with honorable men, he made no attempt to share with it the responsibility of his rule. The shadow of monarchy lengthened.

Vespasian was the founder of the second imperial dynasty, the Flavians. Long before his death he assured a dynastic succession by associating his elder son with him. At his death, in A.D. 79, Titus succeeded him, assuming all the honors, powers, and titles of his father, including the name of Caesar, which had become by this time simply another imperial label. Titus gave every indication of capping the excellence of his father. Men called him "the delight of mankind," but his promise was cut short by an untimely death after scarcely two years of rule.

His place passed to his younger brother, Domitian, and Rome learned that imperial madness was not the exclusive disease of the Julio-Claudians. Domitian flaunted his powers and openly despised the senate. He was assassinated in A.D. 96, and the senate, impotent while he lived, took vengeance upon him dead. His memory was solemnly cursed and his name removed from public documents.

The "Good Emperors"

Rome had seen the failure of two dynasties: the first ending in a disastrous civil war; the second, in assassination. The weakness of hereditary rule, when men placed their world at the mercy of biological caprice, was evident. In the four emperors who followed Domitian, another principle of succession appeared, the principle of adoption. This, at least in part, was responsible for what the eighteenth-century English historian Gibbon called the ". . . period in the history of the world during which the condition of the human race was most happy and prosperous," the Age of the Antonines, the "good emperors."

The senatorial clique which had plotted the assassination of Domitian placed one of its own members on the throne, the distinguished senator Marcus Cocceius Nerva. In the two brief years of his reign Nerva did much to repair the damage of Domitian's tyranny, but he realized that the key to imperial rule was the control of the military. Thus, shortly before he died, Nerva adopted as his son and successor Marcus Ulpius Trajanus (A.D. 98–117), the commander of the German frontier armies and one of Rome's most honored generals.

Trajan was a man of singular energy and ability who deserves to rank among Rome's greatest emperors. While he handled the endless detail of imperial administration with wisdom and patience, Trajan was primarily a soldier, and it is for the military accomplishments of his reign that he is chiefly remembered.

Since the days of the late republic, Rome had faced two principal dangers across her frontiers—the Germanic tribes beyond the Rhine and the Danube and the Parthians in the east. Rome had fought no conclusive war with either and the emperors since Augustus had been content simply to maintain and repair the frontiers he had established. Both the Germans and the Parthians had grown stronger in the years of the principate and Trajan resolved to deal decisively with them. He waged a series of wars against the Dacians, the most aggressive and pressing of the Germanic peoples, and added the province of Dacia to the empire; it was the land across the previous frontier in the great bend of the Danube. Then he moved to the east to secure the Parthian frontier, but before he could really begin this campaign, he died in A.D. 117. On his deathbed he adopted as his successor his cousin, Publius Aelius Hadrianus (A.D. 117–138).

Hadrian abandoned the ambitious eastern policy of Trajan and in general dedicated himself to a reign of peace. He saw more clearly than his warlike predecessor that the empire as a whole faced serious internal economic problems. He tried to shore up the integrity and independence of the crucial network of cities throughout the empire. He was an indefatigable traveler, moving constantly to check on conditions and correct abuses. He tightened the imperial bureaucracy and succeeded in centralizing and regularizing administration.

Trajan's aggressive foreign policy and Hadrian's knowledgeable domestic policy had prepared the way for Titus Aurelius Antoninus Pius, the successor Hadrian adopted shortly before his death in A.D. 138. The long reign of this emperor—he did not die until A.D. 161—was a time of general peace and order, remarkably free of the crises and emergencies of which most history is made. Long before his death he had adopted his successor, Marcus Aurelius Antoninus (A.D. *161–180*), and granted him imperial powers.

THE GOOD EMPERORS

NERVA	*96-98*
TRAJAN	*98-117*
HADRIAN	*117-138*
ANTONINUS PIUS	*138-161*
MARCUS AURELIUS	*161-180*

Marcus Aurelius set the tone of his age and men called him the philosopher-king, the embodiment of the dream that Plato had expressed so long before. Marcus was a Stoic philosopher and, in the imperial palace, he lived with the simplicity and humility he had learned through a youth spent in the study of philosophy. He accepted the burdens of rule with genuine reluctance but with the sense of duty which was a leading characteristic of Stoicism. He regarded his position as the earthly counterpart of the divine reason and his function to care for the well-being of his people as constantly and as selflessly as the divine reason tended the order of the universe. Always accessible to any citizen, he spent hours of every day in rendering justice and answering petitions. In every way he attempted to fulfill the arduous role he set for himself.

Ironically, almost the entire reign of this gentle philosopher was consumed in war and strewn with disasters. In A.D. 162 a campaign was necessary to hold the Parthian frontier. It was a limited success, but the troops brought back from the east the germs of a terrible epidemic which then swept through the western empire. The eastern campaign was hardly over when the Danube was breached by a dangerous alliance of Germanic peoples. Time and again they came and Marcus turned them back; he died in camp on the frontier at the site of Vienna.

The supreme tragedy of Marcus Aurelius was reserved for the end. The humane philosopher had sired a monstrous son—evil, cruel, and inclined to madness. Some three years before his own death, the emperor had associated Commodus with him in imperial power. Perhaps he hoped that responsibility would sober and reform his son. He knew that, even should he set Commodus aside, the claims of heredity would be raised. Perhaps he preferred one bad emperor to general civil war. Thus, in A.D. 180 the age of the Antonines came to an end and the dynastic principle raised Marcus Aurelius Commodus Antoninus (A.D. *180–192*) to a despotic tenure of the imperial throne.

Rome and the Empire

The conquests of Trajan had extended the empire to its greatest limits. The wise and benevolent policies of the Antonines had extended the blessings of peace to every person who lived within its borders. Careful concern for public affairs had assured an age of general prosperity; peace and plenty had worked to draw the diverse pieces of the Roman Empire into a single world, policed and ruled by the power of Rome, connected by the intricate web of Roman roads, economically unified by a reliable imperial currency.

Trade flowed freely through the empire, impeded only by a modest imperial customs duty. The Roman world was essentially one great free-trade area. The goods of every corner of the empire were available to any person who had the price. The bulk of this trade was in basic goods, much of it in foodstuffs. Great centers such as Antioch, Alexandria, and Rome consumed huge quantities of grain; in fact, one-third of the vast and unfailing grain yield of Egypt was reserved for the city of Rome alone.

In spite of this ceaseless movement of goods, methods of production had improved only slightly. A few items—commercial brick and pottery, for example—were truly mass produced. But most of the goods that were bought and sold in the markets of the empire were produced in small family shops or were the products of "cottage industry." Increased demand was satisfied by more shops and more hands. The real economic advance was the untrammeled opportunity to trade on virtually a world basis. The economic revolution of the Roman Empire was commercial rather than industrial.

The social and political counterpart of the network of imperial trade was a network of urban communities. Where cities had long existed, as they had in the east, they had become administrative centers. Villages and rural communities had been organized where there were no cities. Roman colonies and garrison towns dotted the backward areas of the empire. The imperial system was rather loosely imposed upon this pattern of civic life: local government was substantially in local hands and the cities of the empire were its basic units of administration. Each city was a miniature Rome, with its local form of magistrates and legislative and deliberative bodies. In the imperial cities these institutions were monopolized by an office-holding class, proud and responsible citizens who made the well-being of their communities part of their own lives and fortunes.

In the two centuries of the principate the provinces had become extensively Romanized. This was truer of the western provinces than of the the east, where Rome made little impression against the powerful imprint of centuries of Hellenism. But even in Egypt, Syria, and Asia Minor the imperial order brought unparalleled prosperity in its wake and bound the Hellenized east to the Latin west. The principate was the golden age of the provinces. Neither the ineptitude nor even the madness of some of Augustus' successors had impeded the continual increase of provincial prosperity.

As the years of the principate passed, a gradual leveling process became inevitable. Trade, communications, culture, and a growing sense of imperial community worked to destroy old distinctions. Business, litigation, and curiosity brought thousands of provincials to Italy and Rome. Generations of liberated slaves stayed and bred in Italy. Emperors such as Claudius and Hadrian extended the rights of citizenship to vast areas of the empire and drew upon the services of able men from the provinces. Trajan and Hadrian themselves had come from Spain and some of the finest administrators and creative people of the first two centuries of the principate were provincials. In the age of the Antonines nearly one-half the members of the senate were provincials, and within a generation of the death of Marcus Aurelius this proportion had increased. To a remarkable degree the "good emperors" were truly rulers of the entire Roman world. Their concerns and their policies—as broad as their dominions— flowed from a philosophic conviction of universal human brotherhood. The distinction between Italy and the empire, between Rome and the provincial cities, was becoming one only of degree and tradition.

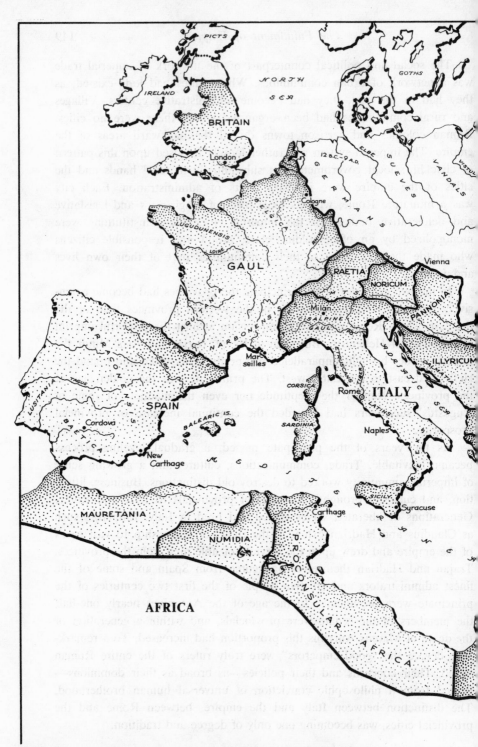

THE ROMAN EMPIRE, 117 A.D.
AT ITS GREATEST EXTENT

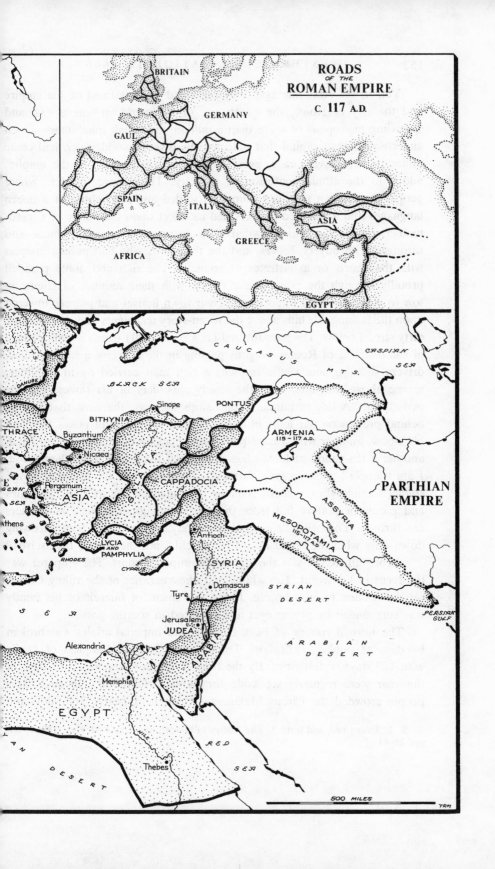

ROADS
OF THE
ROMAN EMPIRE

C. 117 A.D.

BRITAIN

GERMANY

GAUL

SPAIN

ITALY

ASIA

GREECE

AFRICA

EGYPT

CAUCASUS MTS.

CASPIAN SEA

DANUBE

BLACK SEA

Sinope

PONTUS

BITHYNIA

Byzantium

ARMENIA
115 - 117 A.D.

THRACE

Nicaea

PARTHIAN
EMPIRE

GALATIA

CAPPADOCIA

ASSYRIA
115 - 117 A.D.

Pergamum

ASIA

TIGRIS

MESOPOTAMIA
115 - 117 A.D.

Athens

Antioch

EUPHRATES

LYCIA
AND
PAMPHYLIA

RHODES

SYRIA

CYPRUS

Damascus

SYRIAN
DESERT

S   E   A

Tyre

PERSIAN
GULF

Jerusalem
JUDEA

ARABIAN
DESERT

Alexandria

ARABIA

Memphis

EGYPT

NILE

RED

DESERT

SEA

Thebes

500 MILES

TRM

Yet, in the Antonine age, Italy remained the heartland of the empire and the city of Rome, the queen city of the world. It was a vast and sprawling metropolis of more than a million and a half inhabitants, a rich and cosmopolitan capital that reflected the diverse world which had come under its rule. Every race, every type, every nationality of the empire, added to the ethnic confusion of the city. There were quarters where people of common race or occupation settled and the babble of a dozen languages and a hundred dialects had its effect upon the purity of Ciceronian Latin. Rome was crowded with forums and market places and thronged with buyers, sellers, and the thousands who had public business with the courts or magistrates or councils. The rich and noble paraded proudly through the press of the crowd with their retinues of clients in tow to dramatize their importance. Their town houses and palaces towered upon the fashionable hills above the seven-story tenements and the winding, dirty streets below. The poet Juvenal (c. A.D. 60–140) paints a vivid picture of those streets of Rome—wagons passing in the curve of a narrow alley, drivers shouting and traffic snarled; a rich man carried by in his litter, serene above the tumult, on the sturdy shoulders of his slaves. But the pedestrian! "A tide of human beings stops the way; the mass that follows behind presses on our loins in dense concourse; one man pokes me with his elbow, another with a hard pole; one knocks a beam against my head, another a ten-gallon cask. My legs are coated thick with mud; then, anon, I am trampled upon by great heels all round me, and the hob-nail of the soldier's caliga [heavy shoe] remains imprinted on my toe." Broken tiles and pieces of pottery fall from the roofs and upper stories; and others are thrown. You wish ". . . that they may be contented with throwing down only what the broad basins have held," not the vessels themselves.[9]

Above all, Rome was the city of the imperial court. The emperor was the focus of the world. The whims and idiosyncrasies of the ruling Caesar set the fashion for the empire. Every movement of himself or his family was surrounded by prying eyes and reported in soaring gossip.

The normal routine of busy city life and imperial affairs was broken by days of public celebration. Trajan celebrated his conquest of Dacia with 123 days of festivities. By the time of Marcus Aurelius, 135 days of the year were regularly set aside for public celebration. On such days people crowded the Circus Maximus—which held nearly 200,000—and

9. L. Evans (ed. and trans.), *The Satires* (Philadelphia: David McKay, 1896), III, pp. 28-43.

other race courses to shout for their favorite charioteers, to bet, and occasionally to riot. They thronged such amphitheaters as the Colosseum to watch huge and extravagant animal shows and the brutal spectacle of hundreds of teams of gladiators engaged in bloody combat. They crowded the theaters to watch dramatic spectacles as brutalized and tasteless as the shows of blood, and to view licentious comedies and pantomimes and variety shows of the most obscene sort. The puritanical Tacitus called Rome the "cesspool of the world."

The Zenith of Imperial Art

Antonine Rome was as grand and beautiful as it was sordid and brutal. For centuries wealthy men, conquering generals, officials, and rulers had filled the city with buildings and useful works and decorated it with art.

We have already noted how the republican conquerors of the east had returned from their triumphs laden with the spoils of Greek art. Hellenism was the most significant factor in Roman art. In most important respects Roman sculpture, painting, the minor arts, even most of the decorative features of architecture, remained fundamentally Hellenistic. In fact, few of the creators of Roman art were actually Roman. Most were Greeks and many of them slaves or freedmen. The worship of beauty remained basically alien to the Roman character. The statues and paintings that crowded Rome—and every provincial city in imitation of Rome—were largely copies or adaptations of actual Greek works or Greek style. Nearly every public building and monument was surfaced with Greek façades and decorative columns. Rome gave to Greek art a world in which to flourish, and Greek art gracefully accommodated itself to the demands of Roman taste.

It was chiefly in such accommodation that the Roman contribution to Roman art was made. By far the most important result of the Roman taste was the creation of some of the most powerfully realistic statuary in the history of art. We know in detail what the Romans "looked like"; something we shall not know again until the great portrait art of the Renaissance. Yet, even this Roman realism had been anticipated in the genre and portrait sculpture of the Hellenistic schools. Again, Roman taste demanded a workmanlike attention to detail. This, too, fell in readily with the high technical attainments of Hellenistic art. Finally, Roman taste demanded the grandiose and the imperial. The Hellenistic art which had served the divine kings of the east was able to satisfy this Roman demand. In all, while the Romans added something to Greek art, Greek art remained a Roman appropriation.

However, the Romans did make a great and lasting contribution in one general area, that of architecture, construction, and engineering. In contrast to the sculptors and painters, the leading architects and engineers of Rome were Romans, many of them distinguished or even noble men.

Perhaps the most impressive remains of this expression of Roman art are the roads, bridges, and aqueducts. In the late fourth century B.C., during the Samnite wars, the Appian Way was built to connect Rome and Capua to the south—this the first of the great Roman roads. The chief purpose was to facilitate the rapid movement of troops to points of danger in any kind of weather. After Augustus had defined the imperial boundaries, the road system was completed by a series of garrisoned rampart roads, *limites,* along hundreds of miles of the frontier. These roads separated civilization from barbarism with impressive finality and were to mark the frontier of the empire for centuries. Behind the limites a network of highways threaded back to Rome and by the age of the Antonines the empire had more than 50,000 miles of paved, primary roads. They were built slowly and carefully, running as straight as possible, bridging streams and rising over mountain ranges. They were surfaced with heavy paving blocks set in a base of stone and concrete.

The Roman aqueducts were as impressive and almost as enduring as the Roman roads. By the end of the second century A.D., more than a dozen of them supplied Rome with millions of gallons of water daily. The same was true of many provincial cities. The aqueducts were superbly surveyed: in some places they tunneled through mountains; in others they spanned rivers, valleys, and marshes with a uniform gradient of two feet to a mile over distances that ranged from ten to sixty miles. They reflect the minds of their builders. Frontinus, the greatest of Roman hydraulic engineers, expressed it: "Who will venture to compare with these mighty conduits the idle Pyramids, or the famous but useless works of the Greeks."

The same spirit of utility and practicality invested Roman architecture. Many architectural superficialities were borrowed from the Greeks. The Greek column orders were taken over completely and Roman temples generally were Greek or Hellenized Etruscan in form. The differences were largely in size and finish. But in secular building the Romans made unique contributions. In such structures as the huge public baths, the arenas and theaters, public buildings and law courts, and in such architectural complexes as the forums, the unprecedented demands for size and functional space created a new architecture with its basic form the round arch.

Earlier peoples had used the arch and the Romans probably took it from the Etruscans. But the Romans used it more extensively and more skillfully than any builders before them. By placing arches behind each other in sequence, they developed the tunnel or barrel vault. By intersecting one barrel vault with another, they created the cross vault, supported only at its corners and held in place by the stresses of its intersecting groins. By rotating the single arch, Roman builders developed the dome. With these basic devices they could construct buildings with great unobstructed floor space to meet the demands of public affairs. Greek architecture had been an art of form, akin to sculpture; Roman architecture was a true art of space. Space and size were natural and necessary to Roman architecture. The vast structures which resulted were built with skill and economy. The Romans developed the use of concrete. Indeed, the typical Roman structure was of concrete poured in forms reinforced with a core of rubble, then faced with stucco, brick, or stone.

Rome ruled, taxed, and administered more people on a larger scale than any empire before her. Roman architecture reflects this not only in its scale but in its self-conscious grandeur and massiveness. The works of Roman architecture and engineering made a truly imperial art. With the peace and prosperity of the empire and with the progress of Romanization, by the Antonine age, the typical forms of Roman art—like the Latin language and the structure of municipal government—had spread to the provinces.

It is curious that the practical sense of the Romans which created great engineering and a great art of structure did not also create a great age of science. Actually, Roman science made little advance over the previous Hellenistic age. In some areas, such as medicine and scientific agriculture, the Romans carried science into technology. But they made almost no contribution to theory or "pure" science. Many Roman writers were interested in science and some, like Pliny the Elder (A.D. 23–79), had a genuine spirit of inquiry. But little that was either original or systematic was produced in this field. Perhaps the very orientation of the Romans upon practicality made them more naturally interested in immediate effect than in ultimate cause.

The Structure of Roman Law

The Romans were the greatest ruling people of western civilization and, even more than the practical problems of building and engineering, the practical problems of government attracted the Roman genius.

Roman law was as old as the Roman state and, like the state, reached its zenith in the age of the Antonines. It was only with the stability and order and the leveling of the high empire that a full and rational formulation of the legal system could be made. But its roots reached back more than half a millennium.

Its first written form, as we have seen, was the ancient collection of the Twelve Tables, a codification of existing custom and practice in the early Roman state. But as Rome expanded, a substantive law that took cognizance of new conditions was called for. Under the republic the basic source of law was the people themselves gathered in their assemblies; it flowed also from the senate, whose "recommendations" had the force of law, and from the administrative decisions of elected magistrates— the consuls, the lesser officials, and especially the praetors. Indeed, the day by day, case by case judgments of the praetors became the chief source of Roman law. During the last bloody years of the republic, however, the demands of a succession of military dictators took the force of law, foreshadowing the legal role of the future emperors.

As order was restored in the early principate, the tendency for increased authority to accumulate in the hands of the emperor made him a primary source of law. The creation of a single imperial government stimulated the growth of Roman law to similar universal scope. Not only did the imperial system necessitate this growth, the emperors themselves consciously fostered it. The jurists and legal experts who had flourished in the late republic were given semiofficial status in the early principate. They commented upon the tangled wilderness of precedent and conflicting precepts of the law. They searched beneath its particulars for guiding principles of justice and equity, and where they did not find such principles they turned to moral philosophy for suggestions. These men gave to law a structure and a system it had not before possessed.

Earlier Roman law had been cluttered with a religious formalism in procedure which often violated the spirit of justice; but a growing and realistic law of procedure had slowly broken this down. Gradually the cruelty and harshness of the old law was moderated and, by the early empire, the concepts of law and the precepts of moral philosophy were no longer widely separated. Roman law began to consider extenuating circumstances and the intention of illegal acts, not simply the acts themselves. The principle of the presumed innocence of the accused made headway against the presumption of guilt.

For centuries Rome had been developing a law applicable to foreigners, those ineligible for the coveted rights of Roman citizens under the civil law. With the extension of the empire, the necessity of ruling dozens of non-Roman peoples had brought into existence a genuine Law of Nations. This was in essence a "common law" of the empire, compounded of principles and practices generally acceptable and understandable to the populace. This, too, along with the civil or citizen law, was brought to its highest peak in the Antonine age. Thus, by the time of Marcus Aurelius, the Roman structure of law was complete. It represents the most fully developed and impressive legal system created by any of the peoples of western civilization until comparatively modern times.

The Decline of Roman Letters

Nearly every educated Roman had some smattering of philosophy by the time of Marcus Aurelius, and some were deeply committed to it. For many more it offered a reasonable substitute for religion, and philosophers and philosophic schools of all the classical systems flourished everywhere. By far the most popular of these systems was Stoicism.

It had won almost universal acceptance among enlightened and educated Romans by the time of Marcus Aurelius in the second century A.D. From the beginning, as we have seen, it had appealed to the public spirit and sense of responsibility as well as to the straightforward morality of the Roman character. At this time Stoicism had absorbed substantial parts of other philosophic systems. As it became broad and comprehensive, it also became vague and general. Rather than a philosophic system, Stoicism became a way of life. As the concentration of imperial rule had dried up the Roman political spirit, Stoicism ceased to preach an active political doctrine. It had little more than an academic concern for duty in the older sense. It did, however, extend the notion of individual duty to a genuine doctrine of human brotherhood and concern for one's fellow men. It preached the reward of inner peace and comfort for those who lived the philosophic life.

No one expressed this late Roman Stoicism better than Marcus Aurelius himself. All through his life, in the evenings when the responsibilities of the court had been put aside or the day's fighting done, whether in Rome or on the frontiers, Marcus wrote down his "meditations," some of them short epigrams, others small treatises, among them some of the noblest statements of the philosophic life to come down to us from antiquity. They claim to be no more than they are, simply the reflections of a philosopher upon the days and problems and thoughts of his life. There is no system to them; they do not represent the dogma of a school. They may have been no more than the consolation of a harried and lonely man. Thus Marcus reflected on his ideal of the reluctant philosopher-king:

. . . let the deity which is in thee be the guardian of a living being, and of ripe age, and engaged in matter political, and a Roman, and a ruler, who has taken his post like a man waiting for the signal which summons him from life, and ready to go, having need neither of oath nor of any man's testimony. Be cheerful also, and seek not external help nor the tranquillity which others give. A man then must stand erect, not be kept erect by others.[10]

But in the exercise of his power, the philosopher was often as tried as the king. In another place he wrote:

Begin the morning by saying to thyself, I shall meet with the busy-body, the ungrateful, arrogant, deceitful, envious, unsocial. All these things happen to them by reason of their ignorance of what is good and evil. But I who have seen the nature of the good that it is beautiful, and of the bad that it is ugly, . . . I can neither be injured by any of them.[11]

In spite of the general acceptance of philosophy among the literate and the general rise in the level of learning, there had been a steady decline in the quality of Latin literature from Augustus to Marcus Aurelius. This period is generally called the Silver Age to distinguish it from the golden period of Augustan letters. There is no simple explanation for the gradual decline of Roman literature. The fountainhead of thought and art in the last years of the republic and the Augustan Age had been politics and the state. Once the new order was achieved, its existence was obvious and its consolidation a rather mechanical process—a something less than heroic theme for literature. The literati had less cause to celebrate the "good life" characteristic of the Augustan period, for the successors of Augustus failed to fulfill the promise of an age of gold. Men found less to evoke their literary enthusiasm in Gaius or Nero or Domitian than in the divine Augustus.

10. Oates (ed.), *The Stoic and Epicurean Philosophers,* p. 504.
11. *Ibid.,* 497.

Moreover, autocracy tended to cast a shadow over literature. Many of the great themes were dangerous to explore and caution replaced freedom of inquiry and criticism. Authors turned to trivial themes. Juvenal and Martial, who flourished in the late first and early second centuries A.D., were two of Rome's greatest satirists, but their satiric genius was nonpolitical; they did not direct their barbs at the state or state policies, but at the foibles and absurdities of human nature. One of those absurdities was literature itself. It had become fashionable to write. Juvenal opened his satires with the comment that everyone else writes poetry, why shouldn't he! In every corner of Rome poets declaimed themselves hoarse with their own dreary epics and closet tragedies. One could not even escape them in the bath! Roman literature had exchanged quality for volume.

The historical writings of Tacitus, who flourished about 100 A.D., were embittered and marred by his hatred of autocracy. There is some relief in the letters of Pliny the Younger, which give a glimpse into the life of a highly articulate, urbane, and kindly man. Yet they have charm rather than force, and those addressed to the emperor Trajan betray a servility curiously at odds with the Roman tradition. Latin prose generally declined in vitality. It had always drawn its strength from the forum, from the discourse and debate of public affairs. That source of strength no longer existed. Public policy was not a debatable matter. It was dictated by the emperor and quietly and efficiently carried out by an official bureaucracy. The oratory that once was the tool of politics and a rich source of Roman literature had become an academic discipline. Rhetoric was the universal subject of instruction in the schools. It is significant that Quintilian, one of the most honored writers of the age, was a professional rhetorician. The preoccupation with rhetoric, which tended to dominate most of the writing of the Silver Age, made for poor literature. Writers were too concerned with mere form. Rhetoric put a premium upon conscious artfulness, producing elegant emptiness and banality. By the time of Hadrian the vitality of Latin letters, so striking in the Augustan Age, had lapsed, and even the Silver Age was slowly drawing to a close.

SUGGESTIONS FOR FURTHER READING

⨳⨯

Primary Sources and Original Works

All the following are available in many editions and most are now to be had in inexpensive paperback form.

Cicero, various works

Caesar, *Gallic Wars* and *Civil Wars*

The works of the poets Catullus, Horace, Vergil, and Ovid; and the plays of Plautus, Terence, and Seneca.

Suetonius, *The Lives of the Twelve Caesars*

Plutarch, *Parallel Lives of Noble Greeks and Romans*

Tacitus, *The Annals and the Histories*

The *Histories* of Livy and Polybius, the *Satires* of Juvenal and Lucian, and the *Letters* of Pliny the Younger.

N. Lewis and M. Reinhold, *Roman Civilization* (New York: Columbia University Press, 1951-55), 2 vols., an excellent sourcebook, containing selections from most of the standard classical writers as well as some obscure sources not otherwise easily available.

W. J. Oates, ed., *The Stoic and Epicurean Philosophers* (New York: Random House, 1940).

Early Rome, the Etruscans, and the Republic

*F. R. Cowell, *Cicero and the Roman Republic* (Baltimore: Penguin, 1956).

W. W. Fowler, *Social Life at Rome in the Age of Cicero* (New York: Macmillan, 1910).

*T. Frank, *Life and Literature in the Roman Republic* (Berkeley: University of California Press, 1956), a reprint of the Sather Classical Lectures for 1930.

F. B. Marsh, *A History of The Roman World, 146-30* B.C. (London: 1951).

*M. Pallotino, *The Etruscans* (Baltimore: Penguin, 1955).

D. Randall-MacIver, *Italy before the Romans* (Oxford: Oxford University Press, 1928).

G. M. Richter, *Ancient Italy* (Ann Arbor: University of Michigan Press, 1955).

R. E. Smith, *The Failure of the Roman Republic* (Cambridge: Cambridge University Press, 1955).

*C. G. Starr, *The Emergence of Rome as a World Power* (Ithaca: Cornell University Press, 1954), brief and readable survey, designed specifically for beginning students.

*R. Syme, *The Roman Revolution* (Oxford: Oxford University Press, 1939), a large and difficult but brilliant and important book.

The Empire

John Buchan, *Augustus* (Boston: Houghton Mifflin, 1937), perceptive biography by a great modern man of letters.

J. Carcopino, *Daily Life in Ancient Rome* (New Haven: Yale University Press, 1940).

M. P. Charlesworth, *The Roman Empire* (Oxford: Oxford University Press, 1951), good short account.

Samuel Dill, *Roman Society from Nero to Marcus Aurelius* (London: Macmillan, 1904).

Robert Graves, *I Claudius* and *Claudius the God* (New York: Vintage), novelized biographies but accurate in fact and spirit; the work of a careful and imaginative modern classicist.

*H. Mattingly, *Roman Imperial Civilization* (New York: Anchor, 1959).

M. I. Rostovtzeff, *Social and Economic History of the Roman Empire,* 2nd ed. by P. M. Frazer (Oxford: Oxford University Press, 1957), 2 vols., one of the standard classics of imperial history; a large but extremely readable and important book.

C. G. Starr, *Civilization and the Caesars* (Ithaca: Cornell University Press, 1954).

Special Topics in Roman History

F. E. Adcock, *The Roman Art of War under the Republic* (Cambridge: Harvard University Press, 1940).

Cambridge Ancient History, Vols. III-V, VII-XII, cited for Chaps. 2 and 3.

H. N. Couch and R. M. Geer, *Classical Civilization: Rome* (Englewood Cliffs, N.J.: Prentice Hall, 1940), good treatment of almost every aspect of Roman culture.

W. W. Fowler, *The Religious Experience of the Roman People* (London: Macmillan, 1911).

M. Hadas, *Roman Literature* (New York: Columbia University Press, 1952).

G. Highet, *Juvenal the Satirist, A Study* (Oxford: Clarendon Press, 1954).

A. Maiuri, *Roman Painting* (Geneva: Skira, 1953).

G. T. Rivoira, *Roman Architecture* (Oxford: Oxford University Press, 1925).

F. Schulz, *Classical Roman Law* (Oxford: Clarendon Press, 1951).

H. D. Sedgwick, *Horace, A Biography* (Cambridge: Harvard University Press, 1947).

*Paperbound edition. In the case of reprint editions, publisher and date of publication given will be that of reprint rather than the original.

$\approx 5 \ll$
The Great Transition:
The Decline of Rome and
the Beginning of the Middle Ages

THE PATTERN OF ROMAN DECLINE

In the four centuries between the accession of the Roman emperor Commodus in A.D. 180 and the death of the Ostrogothic king Theodoric in 526, one of the most profound transformations in the history of western man took place. In 180, Roman legions held the frontiers of a flourishing Graeco-Roman civilization, an empire vast in extent and unified politically, economically, and culturally. By the sixth century great stretches of the western empire, including even Italy, had passed into the hands of a succession of Germanic peoples. The eastern empire had split off and was developing a unique and separate civilization. The vigorous domestic economy of the Mediterranean world no longer flourished in its ancient framework. The rich urban life and unhampered communication system of the Roman Empire had been virtually destroyed, and in many areas life had been reduced to subsistence and trade to primitive barter. Inevitably, the spiritual unity of the classical world had also been shattered, and on its ruins medieval Christianity had established itself.

The Growth of Autocracy

Even during the age of the "good emperors," destructive internal forces were already at work below the surface of a prosperous and orderly society. These forces, as much as external factors, were to be responsible

162

for the ultimate collapse of the great organism of the classical empire. We have already noted the growth of autocracy which began with the usurpation of power by the military dictators of the late republic and which was eventually regularized in the principate. Inevitably autocracy undermined every institution of popular government and consent: the senate was reduced to the impotence of a social club; the popular assemblies disappeared altogether; the republican magistracies were absorbed into the growing imperial bureaucracy. The imperial household governed fashions in dress, literature, amusements, and perversions. Schools were opened and closed, teachers rewarded or banished at the whim of the emperor.

Under able and responsible rulers the empire enjoyed the benefits of benevolent paternalism; under weak or dissolute ones it suffered the penalties of inefficiency and arbitrariness. But apart from the personalities or abilities of individual emperors, the central problem lay in the impossibility of one man's being able invariably to choose the right course for a complex state of millions of people.

The Economic Problem

One of the chief problems of the empire—latent, but present from the time of its founding—was economic. The Roman economy was based upon expansion. Each new land that fell to Roman arms contributed its share of booty and tribute to her growing wealth. But excepting the final conquest of Britain under Claudius and Trajan's conquest of Dacia, no major area had been permanently added to the empire since Augustus.

Under the Pax Romana the economic as well as the social and political distinctions between conqueror and conquered slowly disappeared. Ironically, as Rome came to accept the responsibilities of imperial rule, she destroyed the basis of her own economic supremacy. Though at first the backward regions, especially of the western provinces, depended on Roman goods or the goods of the eastern empire traded by Roman merchants, eventually these lucrative provincial markets were lost. As the raw provinces of the west matured under Roman tutelage they tended to become economically independent. By the second century, Gallic and African pottery, Gallic wines and textiles, African olive oil, Spanish and Danubian metal wares, began to compete with and, in some instances, to replace the goods of older centers. And now there were no new provinces to exploit.

With the elimination of lateral economic expansion the only alternative to ensure continued prosperity would have been economic expansion in depth, that is, increasing internal markets by increasing the number of people who could afford to purchase a greater variety of goods. But the social structure of the empire prevented this: the purchasing class did not become larger; it became smaller as wealth was increasingly concentrated in the hands of small groups. In the urban centers a prosperous middle class exploited a growing proletariat. In the countryside the concentration of land in the hands of the wealthy continued while the peasants were increasingly expropriated. (In the reign of Nero, for instance, half the province of North Africa was owned by only six men.) The peasantry was either driven off the land or reduced to the hopeless poverty of the share-cropper. Since the broad base of the economy was still agricultural, the impoverishment of the peasantry was relatively more significant than the ruin of the urban laborers. As a result there was, throughout the Julio-Claudian, Flavian, and Antonine periods, a steady impoverishment of the mass of the population. Not only did this create the economic problem of dangerous underconsumption, it also created a political problem by intensifying bitter class division. The imperial government made no systematic attack on this problem. From time to time agricultural colonization in marginal lands of the empire was encouraged, or economic aid in the form of money or remission of taxes granted to needy areas. But in essence the empire remained a laissez-faire state.

Gradually the precarious balance of the imperial economy became more obvious. The sources of imperial revenue declined, producing chronic financial crises. Various emperors tinkered with the monetary system, creating a steady inflationary trend. By the time of Commodus the basic silver coin had been debased fifty per cent, the gold some twenty-five per cent. Moreover, imperial revenue declined further because of the flourishing trade in luxury goods with Arabia, India, and China—a one-way trade which took precious metal out of the empire.

The decline in imperial revenue was all the more serious because the need for such revenue was constantly increasing: the cost of maintaining government services and a pyramiding bureaucracy became ever greater. Imperial defense, above all, made ruinous demands on public funds. Augustus had tried to establish a sound basis for military expenditures, carefully balancing such factors as the length of the frontiers and the financial resources of the state. But with the stabilization of the frontiers the army ceased to be the profitable tool of expansion it had once been, becoming instead an economic liability while remaining a political necessity. The aggressive wars of Trajan and the defensive wars of Marcus Aurelius had necessitated a steady increase in the size of the army. By the end of Marcus' reign there were nearly half a million men under arms and their support placed an almost unmanageable burden on the imperial economy.

As the imperial government demanded more money, the financial ruin of the lower classes was completed and eventually the provincial nobility and the well-to-do of the cities were also affected.

The Military Monarchy and Civil War

These internal problems were intensified by renewed pressures along the frontiers. In 180 Commodus made peace with the Germanic tribes that his father, Marcus Aurelius, had brought almost to defeat, and returned to Rome to enjoy the unlimited power that had fallen into his hands. He proved himself more despotic than Domitian and as blindly extravagant as Nero. He pampered the military, especially the Praetorians, but merely earned their contempt. Indeed, the commander of the Praetorian Guard joined the conspiracy to assassinate him in 192.

This act of violence, following twelve years of irresponsible rule, produced a military crisis known as the Second War of the Legions and recapitulated the bloody events that ended the reign of Nero. The senate, long abused by Commodus, seized a momentary advantage to elevate a candidate to the throne. He was murdered by the Praetorians who then openly disposed of the imperial title to the highest bidder. Once more the frontier armies had declared for their respective commanders. The closest to Rome was Septimius Severus (*193–211*), the commander of the Danube legions, who marched on the capital and established himself without difficulty and with the senate's swift approval.

Within a short time he had dispatched the rival claimants to the throne and ruled unchallenged. It was the story of Vespasian once more, but with crucial differences. Vespasian, though a professional soldier, had modeled his domestic policies upon those of Augustus. Septimius Severus remained a soldier, and his solution to the manifold problems of the empire was basically a military one. With total disregard for the dangerous financial consequences, he increased the already swollen army and raised its pay. The provinces were divided into smaller, essentially military, units of administration so that no large provincial command could be held by a single officer whose political aspirations might threaten the emperor. Septimius tightened the chain of military and administrative command which bound these provincial subdivisions to the imperial throne. A provincial from North Africa—as well as a professional soldier—he had little sympathy for the civil tradition of Rome. He was suspicious of the senate and savagely persecuted the senatorial order throughout the empire. His systematic proscriptions and confiscations made him the wealthiest of all Roman emperors and his terror undermined the wealthy, responsible upper classes everywhere.

The disciplined and militarized imperial system of Septimius Severus had the apparent virtue of efficiency: it enabled the state to exact from every man the full measure of his tax obligations and services. This efficiency temporarily masked the lack of sound, long-range policies to deal with the growing economic problems.

THE SEVERAN DYNASTY

SEPTIMIUS SEVERUS	*193-211*
CARACALLA	*211-217*
(USURPER, MACRINUS *217-218*)	
ELAGABALUS	*218-222*
ALEXANDER SEVERUS	*222-235*

In addition to the other burdens of the state, there was almost constant fighting along the frontiers. Septimius himself took command in Britain, where trouble had broken out in 205. In 211 he died there, bidding his sons, "Make your soldiers rich, and do not bother about anything else." It was not only a summation of his own reign, but a prophecy.

The Severan dynasty continued. Septimius' son, Caracalla, succeeded him and was assassinated in 217. He was followed by a dissolute and immature youth, Elegabalus—who was the high priest of an orgiastic Syrian cult—then by Alexander Severus. Both the latter were dominated by the vigorous and ruthless women of their household. The reign of Alexander Severus gave promise of some return to the practice and policy of the good emperors but Alexander was murdered in 235 in a military revolt.

Septimius had made the army the equal of the throne and now the army attempted to rule the empire. Following the murder of Alexander

Severus, a fifty-year period of military anarchy began in which the fabric of the empire was torn apart: central government failed, the economy faltered, the material basis of civilization was very nearly destroyed, and large sections of the empire broke away to become practically independent states. In this half century no fewer than twenty-six emperors mounted the throne and only one of them escaped violent death. There were, in addition, literally dozens of pretenders, one emperor alone having to deal with eighteen such rivals.

This time has been called the Age of the "Barrack Emperors," for emperors and pretenders alike were almost invariably successful generals raised to imperial office by their troops. The menace of the army had been growing since the days of Marius during the last century of the republic. But while previous emperors had used the army to gain or keep the throne, now the emperors themselves tended to be the instruments of their soldiery.

Yet, never before had the soldiery been less prepared for such a decisive role in the affairs of the state, for, as the military establishment had grown large, it had also grown away from the civil state. Through the centuries of the Augustan peace military careers had become less and less attractive to Romans, Italians, and the inhabitants of the most civilized portions of the empire. Consequently, the armies were recruited from the most backward provinces and warlike peoples in the empire. Domitian, with his fear of military plots, had decentralized the army and stabilized its units in small frontier garrisons. The soldiers who served their whole lives on a remote frontier became identified with the local barbarian or semibarbarian populations. In a matter of a few generations there was little distinction between the "Romans" on one side of the frontier and the "barbarians" on the other. Furthermore, units of barbarian fighting men had been recruited directly for frontier service in many areas. Marcus Aurelius had brought entire tribes over into the empire to take up lands that had been abandoned in the wake of war and pestilence. In return for their land they were to defend it. By the third century the huge, overgrown, Roman army was thoroughly barbarized and felt no obligation to protect the empire which lay behind the frontiers. There was a complete separation of interest between the army and the state, and the army turned upon the empire to loot and spoil.

The spirit of military unity had long since disappeared and regional armies appropriated great sections of the empire under their local commanders, each one proclaimed emperor by his troops. They contested with each other in bloody, destructive wars, always at the expense of the helpless people of the provinces. Commanders rose and fell, killed in battle or assassinated by their troops when they could no longer satisfy appetites grown insatiable. At the same time, hordes of barbarians flowed across the unprotected frontiers to ravage some of the richest lands of the empire.

The half century from 235 to 284 was the lowest ebb of imperial fortunes. Yet by 270 there were signs of recovery. In that year the troops raised to the throne a commander named Aurelian, an able general who also possessed the strength of character necessary to dominate the soldiery. Furthermore, the soldiers themselves, after a generation of chaotic spoliation, had begun to realize that they had a stake in the integrity of the empire. There was some sentiment for the return of discipline and order. This was especially true of the Illyrian legions along the Adriatic coast, which came to form the nucleus of a loyal imperial army once more. Under the emperor Aurelian a disciplined Roman army began to win victories for the empire rather than against it; the barbarian invaders were cleared out of the northern provinces and Roman authority reestablished. Aurelian fought successfully against the separatist tendencies within the empire. His work was ably carried on by his successors, Probus and Carus.

In 284 the choice of the soldiers was Diocletian (*284–305*), another Illyrian commander, who finally ended the half century of military anarchy. The accomplishments of Diocletian represent a fundamental dividing line in Roman history. Not since the paralyzing civil wars at the end of the republic had Rome been so nearly destroyed. Augustus had founded the principate upon the ruins of the republican constitution and created a new order for the Roman world. A task of similar magnitude faced Diocletian, for just as the system of the republic had failed by the time of Augustus, so the system of the Augustan principate had failed by the end of the third century.

The Price of Recovery

The reforms of Diocletian, which gave a new shape and direction to the Roman world, could not ignore the events of almost a century of military monarchy and anarchy. Government continued to be based directly and openly upon the military, for an essentially civil state was no longer possible. Thus, Diocletian's government represented a refinement of the Severan system, structured around a tightly organized military and administrative hierarchy. At the top of the system stood the emperor, separated from the people. He ruled not only by his vast and complex official bureaucracy and his army, but by his own divinity. The trend set in motion by the posthumous deification of Julius Caesar and the worship of the genius of Augustus was finally realized in the divine monarchy of Diocletian.

Almost immediately upon his accession Diocletian named a colleague, Maximian, to share his powers; he too was an Illyrian and a successful general. The two emperors were designated *Augusti*. Then each Augustus took a junior colleague—called *Caesares*. Diocletian chose Gaius Galerius and Maximian chose Flavius Constantius. It was Diocletian's hope that this "tetrarchy" would solve the problem of succession by making the Caesars the obvious heirs of the Augusti by grooming them in office. But there were other pressing reasons for this division of the empire. With the failure of communications, the collapse of imperial trade and money exchange, and the general decline of imperial unity, it was no longer possible for one man to rule the empire. The northern frontiers were still not completely reestablished and barbarians still menaced the empire at many places. In the east, Parthia had been replaced by the rise of the Neo-Persian or Sassanian Empire (developing out of an internal revolt against Parthian domination after the Parthian Arsacid dynasty had been defeated, first by Trajan and then by Septimius Severus). The new empire was revitalized by a line of able kings and by a vigorous revival of the ancient Persian religion of Zoroaster. During Rome's troubles in the third century the Persian king, Shapur II, actually captured a Roman emperor in battle and delivered a serious blow to Roman prestige in the east. In addition to the dangers from outside the frontiers the empire still had serious military problems within. Local and regional rebellions were still smoldering in many areas. Thus, military necessity commended the division of the empire. Diocletian established his capital at Nicomedia in Bithynia, where he could command the eastern frontier; Maximian went to Milan in northern Italy, where he could move quickly to protect either the upper Danube or the Rhine provinces. A further division was made of the two great halves of the empire: Galerius was given Illyricum and Constantius, Gaul. Below the four princes and within their divisions of the empire there was further subdivision of territory and responsibility.

The major military forces of the empire were four large, mobile armies which were held closely under the control of the princes. These armies (nearly half a million men in all) were supplemented by militia and large tribal bands of barbarians (which were frequently as much a burden as a blessing to the unfortunate areas that supported them). This huge and

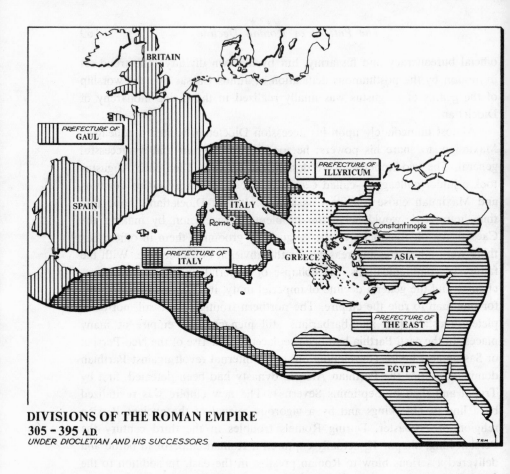

DIVISIONS OF THE ROMAN EMPIRE
305 – 395 A.D.
UNDER DIOCLETIAN AND HIS SUCCESSORS

costly force had one essential tie with the civil state: government existed primarily to support the army. The army and the civil administration of the empire joined to become the deadly enemies of the people. The state of Diocletian was fundamentally a police state and the burden of both its administration and its army rested with oppressive weight upon the people of the empire.

The exchange of goods on anything but a local basis had virtually ceased in the mutinous half century which had preceded Diocletian's reign. Some luxury trade continued but the great slow pulsations of exchange in basic commodities had ceased. Coins had been debased to fractional parts of their face value. They were issued locally and regionally as well as by the imperial mints and none was universally accepted. There was no such thing as public confidence.

Cities had been deserted or reduced to villages. This was especially true in the western empire but even the great city of Alexandria had lost sixty per cent of her population. Nearly all the cities that remained had acquired walls, signifying the end of imperial security. Some, such as the cities where the emperors resided, still flourished. But fundamentally, the city as the economic unit of an empire of cities was dead. The failure of the city was a basic symptom of the passing of classical civilization. In the cities that remained and in the towns and villages that passed for cities in the economic ruin of the empire, the domestic policies of the government systematically completed the destruction of the vital municipal middle class.

It was to this class that Diocletian turned with his ruinous demands for taxes, demands which it could not satisfy. The basis of middle-class prosperity was destroyed as productivity failed and inflation upset economic values. Yet, the demands of the state had to be met. Diocletian and his colleagues could cope with the direct and immediate problems of political unity and the military integrity of the empire, but they failed completely to understand the less palpable forces which were destroying the empire from within. The economic necessity of the state was itself so desperate that, even had they fully understood the underlying causes of decline, they probably could have done little to correct them. Thus they turned the increasing demands of government upon those who were, with each moment, less able to satisfy them. The *curiales* (provincial office-holding class) were made responsible for the collection of taxes. When their communities could not pay, they were forced to make up the deficits themselves. Men sought to escape the destructive honor of membership in the curiale class but the government fixed the membership and forbade defection. When they could no longer pay, many once-prosperous men abandoned their homes and fled—some of them across the frontiers to the barbarians. They were hunted down and returned to the prison of their class; petty bureaucratic officials harried and spied upon them; and often torture was used to discover where wealth was hidden, even when there was none left to hide.

This bedeviled class was not alone. All trades and occupations were organized into hereditary corporations under the control of the state. Scarcely a person escaped; those who worked in such essential trades as mining or military manufacture were actually branded with hot irons like slaves or gladiators for ready identification in case of escape.

The countryside was as impartially pressed as the cities, since the earlier disasters of the third century had also been destructive to the agricultural productivity of the empire. Foodstuffs had been regularly confiscated and farm villages burned by marauding soldiery. Vast areas had been depopulated by barbarian raids and epidemics. Under the police system of Diocletian's government a major part of the burden of feeding the huge and hungry army fell upon the free landowner: his taxes were paid in kind and the produce stripped from his land; his animals were taken for military supply and his sons were impressed into army service. The peasants in increasing numbers fled their land and sought servitude as *coloni* on the estates of those great and powerful enough to maintain themselves. The country villas with their spreading lands, self-sustaining villages, and semifeudal lords were a typical manifestation of the decentralized natural economy and way of life to which much of Europe was returning as the Roman world collapsed.

In an attempt to halt the economic decline for which his own policies were in part responsible, Diocletian issued his famous Edict of Prices in 301. It was an attempt to fix the price of virtually every commodity in the Roman world by decree. It listed a thousand items—perhaps even more—and carried the death penalty for violation of any established price. It was an arbitrary and clumsy expedient which was never generally obeyed because it was both too simple and too inflexible. Inflation continued to mount and it soon became clear that even the most truculent enforcement of the edict was useless.

This abortive attempt at price "fixing" was part of a larger pattern of strictures which fixed not only prices but occupations and, as we have seen, even social position and responsibility. The municipal middle class had been taxed out of existence. Peasant farmers had become serfs. The only free men who remained were friends and favorites of the emperors, high-ranking imperial officials and those who were rich and powerful enough to be immune even from the exactions of the state.

In 305, perhaps hoping to establish a precedent for constitutional abdication, Diocletian retired from the imperial office and forced the reluctant Maximian to do the same. Within five years the mechanism of Caesarian succession had collapsed. Five Augusti ruled in various parts of the empire and the state was torn again by civil war. Constantine (*306–337*), the son of the Caesar Constantius, had been declared emperor by his father's army in 306, following the death of Constantius. He was challenged by rival claimants—even old Maximian came out of retirement to support the claim of his son, only to be killed for his solicitude. It was 324 before Constantine clearly established his claim to the throne. More than half his life had been spent in war.

THE RISE OF CHRISTIANITY

The Bankruptcy of Paganism

The disastrous events of the third century had shaken the beliefs, the worship, and the philosophies of the ancient world as profoundly as its political and economic systems. For centuries there had been a slow but steady decline in the vigor of Roman intellectual and spiritual life. The efforts of many emperors to reinvigorate the old Roman public religion had failed: the cult of the emperor and Rome, and those of the Capitoline gods were merely patriotic exercises with little spiritual substance. Poor and simple people had the precarious comfort of their superstitions; the rich and learned sought comfort in the vague disbelief and nondescript moralism of late Roman philosophy.

The ancient philosophers, whatever their specific systems, had maintained a deep-seated, optimistic materialism, assuming that the cosmos was moving toward a "good end" and that man could find his reward for virtue in the worldly happiness of the "good life." Now men were beginning to turn instead to a hope whose satisfaction lay outside this life—the hope of immortality. And this hope was supplied by the Oriental mystery religions. While essentially nonclassical, the mystery religions had long been a force in the classical world: indeed, the seminal idea of the year god and his annual defeat of death was much older than classicism.

The mystery religions had flowed into Rome from Greek popular religion. By the third century they had become the most active intellectual and spiritual force in the Roman world. Numbering in the hundreds, they appealed to all classes: in them the poor found emotional transport and momentary relief from hunger and despair—a foretaste of happy immortality; the intelligentsia found a whole new philosophic frame of reference.

Along the highways and sea lanes that bound the Roman world together, the mysteries from the east had traveled to every corner of the empire. At first they had made their converts chiefly among the poor and the outcast and had been merely tolerated by the ruling classes. As early as the Second Punic War the cult of Cybele, the great mother-goddess of Anatolia, had been established in Rome itself. In Rome and in every other city of the Mediterranean there were temples and shrines of the Egyptian cult of Isis and Osiris. The armies in the east had adopted wholesale the Persian cult of Mithra and carried it to every frontier.

The multiplicity of the mystery cults concealed a remarkable core of similarity: all drew their strength from the promise of personal immortality; all offered emotional release; all promised reward for virtue and punishment for wickedness; all expressed their promises in a system of symbolic sacraments. Each based its promises and its doctrine upon the story of the founder of the cult—Dionysus, Mithra, Attis, Adonis, Osiris. Each of these gods had suffered, died, and risen from the dead and each offered his worshipers the hope of participating in his triumph over death. Apart from these common elements, however, there was a striking diversity in the cult practices. Many of these were bloody and orgiastic; some included the emasculation of priests and temple prostitution. Almost invariably their dogma strained the most elastic credulity. Yet unsatisfactory and incredible as they seem to us they offered to the people of late antiquity the only hope they could find of a better life.

There had long been, even in classical philosophy, a recessive strain of mysticism beneath its more characteristic strain of rationalism. In the third century this philosophic mysticism asserted itself in the form of Neoplatonism. The moving spirit of this school was a Hellenized Egyptian, Plotinus of Alexandria (c. 205–270). Plotinus' position, highly speculative and transcendental, derived from Plato's notion of the Good. He held that, all created things and, above all, the human soul, derived from the Good and strove, through purification, to return to the contemplation of the Good. Other philosophers turned to the ancient mystic ideas of Pythagoras, as did Apollonius of Tyana, an ascetic and visionary preacher remarkably like the Christian Jesus. Thus, even philosophy became mystical.

The Origins of Christianity

Like the mystery cults, which it so closely resembled, Christianity was born in the eastern empire, within another religion, Judaism. We have traced the development of the parent religion from a simple tribal cult to a high ethical monotheism. We have noted the growth of its beliefs, forms, and law and the extension of its tradition. Into that already elaborate tradition Jesus was born. His life and work were contained with the framework of traditional Judaism. The very foundation of Christianity was Judaic: "Think not that I am come to destroy the law, or the prophets: I am not come to destroy, but to fulfil" (Matthew 5:17). With his small company of disciples, Jesus walked the roads and hills of Palestine. He was a familiar and commanding figure in its cities and countryside. He went about in the immemorial manner of the wise men of the east, preaching of things already long familiar to his Jewish listeners. Like the prophets, he promised the coming of the Kingdom of God and warned of divine judgment. And, like them, he came at a time of internal peril and bitter division in Judaism.

Palestine had been one of the areas of contention in the interminable wars of the Hellenistic kings, and the Jews had fought for two centuries to keep their identity. Each conflict had spawned its parties and its hatreds. With Pompey's settlement of the east in 63 B.C. Judea came under Roman authority. On the eve of the birth of Christ, Herod the Great (*37–4* B.C.) ruled as king and puppet of Rome, hated by every party in Judea. Under his sons, who divided the kingdom, partisan division continued. There were territorial parties and theological factions whose enmities crisscrossed an already divided land with further division. To these varied groups the small following of Christ added another.

Like the prophets, Christ preached a return to the essentials of godliness in a time of troubles, insisting upon obedience to the law of God. In his concept of the law of God he picked up a thread which had been nearly lost in the perilous centuries since the division of the kingdom of Solomon. He turned his back upon the formalism and legalism, upon the specific requirements of the law which had come to characterize the leading parties in Judaism. He demanded that man love God and demonstrate that love of God through the love of his neighbor. This was the "good news" that his disciples were to go forth and preach before all men.

More than by what he taught, Jesus moved men by what he was. He felt that in him the prophecy of Isaiah was come,

For unto us a child is born, unto us a son is given: and the government shall be upon his shoulder: and his name shall be called Wonderful, Counsellor, The Mighty God, The Everlasting Father, The Prince of Peace. Of the increase of his government and peace there shall be no end, upon the throne of David, and upon his kingdom, to order it, and to establish it with judgment and with justice from henceforth even for ever (Isaiah 9:6-7).

This was the concept of Messiahship, the idea of a deliverer for the chosen people. It had grown in the dark days of captivity and persecution and the Jews nourished the hope of his coming. They were strong in adversity, strengthened by the conviction that a new kingdom would be made and another David come to destroy their enemies and fulfil their vengeance so long delayed:

According to their deeds, accordingly he will repay, fury to his adversaries, recompence to his enemies. . . . And the Redeemer shall come to Zion, and unto them that turn from transgression in Jacob, saith the Lord. As for me, this is my covenant with them . . . (Isaiah 59:18-21).

In this period of troubles the expectation of the promised deliverer grew. Many had hailed John the Baptist as the Messiah. From everywhere came reports of miracles and miracle workers.

The claim of Jesus to be the promised deliverer was violently rejected by the Jewish leaders, for he preached no earthly kingdom, no terrestrial delivery, no carnage of the enemies of their people. The resentment against him grew. Vested interests of every sort were offended by him: he threatened the status and temple monopolies of the priests and the social position of the powerful Pharisees. His increasing arrogation of supernatural authority completed his alienation. He was denounced and ended his earthly days by crucifixion, like a common criminal. The handful of Christ's followers, however, continued to believe that he had been the Messiah. That belief seemed indisputable when the apostles were convinced that Christ had risen from the grave. If proof was needed this was proof! It was also to be the cardinal fact of Christianity. Through this triumph over death, Christ became a god, the center of a new religion.

Jesus' peculiar concept of Messiahship, so unacceptable to the Jews, was one of the most essential factors in the independent survival of Christianity. The militant deliverer who would be another David was a Jewish idea attached to the historical experience of Judaism. But the god-man who overcomes death for the sake of his believers was a universal concept in the eastern Mediterranean world; it was the idea of the mystery God. Through this connection the potential scope of Christianity was enlarged and given an appeal no Jewish sect could ever expect to have in the larger gentile world. This messianic idea was to be the bridge from Hebrew to gentile Christianity.

Yet, in the years immediately following the death of Christ there was no gentile Christianity. In spite of the urgent injunction in the Book of Matthew, "Go ye therefore, and teach all nations . . . ," Christianity was a Jewish sect: the kingdom was a spiritual kingdom of Judaism: Christ the Messiah was a Saviour of the Jews. There was no concept of a church and little concept of a new or different dogma.

The Growth of Christianity

It was not the disciples, not even one who had known Jesus, who assumed the work of the missionary commandment. It was Saul, or Paul, of Tarsus who began the transformation of Christianity into a separate religion in the first century. All the world knows the story of his dramatic conversion, the vision on the road to Damascus which turned him from persecutor to advocate of Christ. Armed with his new faith Paul became "the apostle to the Gentiles."

He was not a Palestinian Jew but a citizen of the Hellenistic city of Tarsus. For centuries there had been a steady emigration from Palestine as Jews had fled from the marginal existence of their homeland and had taken up residence in every city of the eastern Mediterranean. With the unification of the Roman Empire Jews migrated to the Roman provinces of Europe, to Rome itself, and to other cities of the western empire. Wherever they went they kept the rituals, the law, and the worship that constituted their identity. Because of their religious exclusiveness in a tolerantly polytheistic world they were a conspicuous minority and from time to time the victims of local persecution and violence. Though often despised, their beliefs also attracted the sympathy of Gentiles. In the moral and religious uncertainty of the Hellenistic world Jewish monotheism, the idea of divine revelation, the austerity of Jewish moral principles, were attractive to many thoughtful and troubled people. But the special requirements of the ritual law—the dietary and ceremonial provisions, and the necessity of circumcision—kept the Jews apart.

On the other hand the Jews of the Diaspora had accepted many of the ways of the Hellenistic world. They were in general more liberal and more cosmopolitan than those who remained in Palestine. They became familiar with the Greek language and culture and their Hellenization progressed so rapidly that in the third century B.C. their sacred writings were translated into Greek for those large numbers for whom ancient Hebrew had become a foreign and difficult language. This definitive work, called the Septuagint (from the "seventy" scholars who were said to have done the selecting and translating), became the basis of the Christian Old Testament. The contact with Hellenism made these Jews of the larger Mediterranean world familiar with the rituals and teachings of the widespread mystery cults. There was thus an overlapping of Hellenism and Judaism. It was in this area that Christianity became a separate religion in the hands of Paul, himself a Hellenized Jew.

Paul traveled widely among the cities of the Greek east living in the Jewish communities that opened their doors to him and making his way by his trade as a tent-maker. He suffered the trials of every missionary of a new and untried faith. In his own bitter words, addressed to his converts at Corinth:

Of the Jews five times received I forty stripes save one. Thrice was I beaten with rods, once was I stoned. Thrice I suffered shipwreck, a night and a day I have been in the deep. In journeyings often, in perils of waters, in perils of robbers, in perils by mine own countrymen, in perils by the heathen, in perils in the city, in perils in the wilderness, in perils in the sea, in perils among false brethren. In weariness and painfulness, in watchings often, in hunger and thirst, in fastings often, in cold and nakedness (II Corinthians 11:24-27).

His faith sustained his frail body and as he traveled he founded the series of churches of which his letters are a catalogue.

Paul drifted more and more into conflict with the Judaic Christians and the apostles. The issue that divided them was precisely the issue of gentile Christianity. The older apostles could not bring themselves to break with the law and the ingrained traditions of Judaism. To them Christ remain primarily a Jewish figure. But Paul saw a new law through the old:

Is he the God of the Jews only? Is he not also of the Gentiles? Yes, of the Gentiles also: Seeing it is one God, which shall justify the circumcision by faith, and uncircumcision through faith. Do we not then make void the law through faith? God forbid: yea, we establish the law (Romans 3:29-31).

The Jews had their commandments from God through Moses. But beyond the Mosaic law was another commandment, "namely, Thou shalt love thy neighbor as thyself. Love worketh no ill to his neighbors: therefore love is the fulfilling of the law" (Romans 13:9-10).

It is to Paul that Christianity owes its basic theology: the doctrine of original sin—the sin flowing down to all subsequent humanity from the disobedience of Adam; the concept of Christ as God; the status of Christianity as a separate religion based on the hope of salvation through faith in Christ; the dualistic view of body and soul, sin and virtue.

The other apostles and Christian missionaries worked as diligently as Paul: new churches sprang up in Palestine; the Apostle John founded a church in Ephesus; there were Christian congregations in the cities of Syria and Asia Minor; Peter traveled widely and it is an almost unshakable tradition that he founded the church at Rome.

Whether these men preached to Jews, Syrians, or Greeks they were driven by the conviction that the end of the world was at hand. Jesus in his own teaching had fostered this notion. It was implicit in the nature of his ethical commandments. Specifically, he often spoke as he did in Matthew, "Verily I say unto you, this generation shall not pass, till all these things be fulfilled" (24:34). Or again, "Verily, I say unto you, there be some standing here, which shall not taste of death, till they see the Son of man coming in his kingdom" (16:28). This sense of imminence passed over to the apostles and the early church and it is almost a certainty that the first generation of Christian preachers and converts looked daily for the coming of Christ again, the millennium, the "day and hour" of which "knoweth no man." This tendency remained prominent in the early church until the second century and even beyond. It was an important wellspring of strength. In the face of such a promise the things of the world—even pain and persecution—were of little importance. It was the source of much of the fanatic zeal that invested early Christianity.

The Roman world was dotted with Christian communities as the cult of Christ grew. Yet its growth was accompanied by great popular hostility. In its early days many people understandably confused Christianity with Judaism—even the Roman government recognized no clear distinction —and the fledgling religion suffered from the widespread antipathy against the Jews. But even as Christianity separated itself from its Judaic background, hostility remained. As similar as Christianity was to the widely accepted mystery religions, its peculiar differences set it apart. The fierce spiritualism of the Christians, their uncompromising monotheism, their disdain of civic or patriotic service, their cult exclusiveness, and their pride of godliness—all made them suspect and hated by most of the pagan world. This popular attitude was the basis of the persecution of the Christians under Nero. Suspected of all sorts of subversive activities, they were punished individually and by local authorities in many areas at various times. But in general, the official Roman attitude was one of contemptuous indifference that passed for toleration.

During the increasing troubles at the close of the second century, persecution became more general and more persistent. The disasters—the plagues, wars, invasion, and sedition—that rocked the state seemed to speak of supernatural displeasure. Men found the source of it in the impiety and atheism of the Christians. Even the philosophic Marcus Aurelius countenanced a severe persecution and Septimius Severus made conversion to Christianity a serious crime. During the military crisis of the third century, the emperor Decius instituted the first widespread and systematic persecution; still the Christians grew in numbers. The Decian persecution passed with his brief reign but the attitudes behind it remained. In the totalitarian state constructed by Diocletian the Christians were a conspicuous, nonconforming minority standing apart from the majority of loyal citizens. They constituted a state within a state. Among other things, they refused to celebrate the divinity of the emperor. The persecutions against them, proclaimed in a series of edicts in 303–304, were severe. But even such edicts were not carried out uniformly. Constantius made no apparent attempt to enforce the most serious of the edicts in his western provinces. Perhaps his son Constantine inherited this policy.

In the confusion of the succession of Caesars and Augusti preceding the rise of Constantine the persecutions continued intermittently, depending upon the disposition of the rulers. It was becoming apparent, even to the most implacable of Christianity's enemies, that persecution had failed to destroy the cult. While many Christians had renounced their faith in the face of threats and torture, the great majority of them had remained firm. Moreover, their fortitude had attracted large numbers of converts and, perhaps even more important, had roused the grudging admiration of still larger numbers of pagans. As Christianity grew, the hostility to it turned to acceptance. The blood of the martyrs was indeed the seed of the church. In 311 Galerius, the most savage enemy of Christianity among the contending emperors, admitted his persecutions to be a failure and extended toleration to the Christians in the form of legal recognition and restoration of property. This became the basis of Constantine's famous Edict of Milan in 313.

The Edict of Milan was, at least for Constantine, more than simply a recognition that Christianity had become too strong to be destroyed. It represented an entente between the emperor and the Christian Church. The Christians were a significant minority in the empire—perhaps ten per cent of the people. In the east, which Constantine came to regard as the most important segment of the empire, the Christians may have numbered twenty-five or even thirty per cent of the population. But more important than their numbers was their spirit. They had generally abandoned their hope of the millennium and had accepted the social obligations of this world. Their concepts of charity and brotherhood made them a stable and healthy force in society. Their certainty of salvation and their general decency gave them a vigor that contrasted sharply with the hopeless lethargy characteristic of dying paganism. Furthermore, Christianity had attracted to its ranks men of great ability and capacity for leadership. In the permissive climate of toleration Christianity became, before the end of Constantine's reign, the pre-eminent religion of the empire. The Roman state had accepted the spiritual state within its borders.

The Strength of Christianity

Though Christianity owed its victory partially to extraneous circumstances, the chief reasons for its triumph were inherent in the Christian faith itself.

It was simple, direct, and appealing. The apostles and other early missionaries preached successfully to the simple, the ignorant, and the hopeless; for they were themselves simple fishermen, laborers, and artisans. But they were imbued with a hope so strong that it could transform those who received it. They spoke in the rough dialects of the common people and the ultimate Greek version of the New Testament was written not in the elegant Greek of the learned but in the *koine,* the common Greek spoken in the streets and market places of every city of the eastern empire. The apostles preached no elaborate theology and propounded no special dogma. They spoke of a new god, of his victory over death, and the hope this held for men as a sinful world neared its end. They had no church in a liturgical sense and no priesthood. They had little or no external machinery of cult administration. Christ had said, "Where two or three are gathered together in my name, there am I in the midst of them" (Matthew 18:20). This was almost literally the shape of the church as it took form in tiny communities of Christians in the towns and cities of the eastern empire. In these communities, the converts obeyed explicitly the often stated commandment to love one another and they expressed their love by sharing the poor goods they had for their common sustenance.

To the early Christians Christ was not some mythical figure who had staged his contest with death in the distant, clouded past. He was a man-god of flesh and blood. When Peter, or John, or James, the brother of Jesus, spoke of him they spoke of a person they had known. They told and retold his parables and his sayings and they told of having seen him after the Crucifixion walking and talking among them.

Christianity, like Judaism, was uncompromising in its insistence upon monotheism, and this set it clearly apart from the mystery religions and from pagan polytheism generally. Most of the hostility, both official and unofficial, toward the Christians during the first two centuries seems to have stemmed from their refusal to worship any god but their own.

From the firmness of Christian conviction flowed an ethical vigor that was one of its most telling advertisements. Much of this was an inheritance from Judaic morality. Some of it was simply the Christian expression of the generalized Stoic morality, which was part of the intellectual climate of late antiquity. But the prime and peculiar source of the moral decency of Christianity lay within Christ's teachings. For he spoke most often not of supernatural things but of behavior. The Sermon on the Mount is typical. This emphasis carried over to the apostles. Paul expressed it in the famous passage in his first letter to the Corinthians, "And now abideth faith, hope, charity, these three; but the greatest of these is charity" (I Corinthians 13:13).

The Challenge from Within

As Christianity gained legal status and general acceptance in the reign of Constantine, it faced a series of dilemmas stemming from its very success. As the religion had grown, the divisive tendencies within it had become increasingly significant. One reason for this was the lack of a regular and authoritative body of Christian doctrine. The construction of ecumenical Christianity was the work of many men working in isolation and often—as Paul and Peter—at cross-purposes. There was little liaison between the cells of individual churches and no central organization to hold them together. In these widely spread congregations there were bits and pieces of holy writings: memoirs, recorded visions, and ritual formulas. The letters of Paul and the other apostles and founders of churches were read to the congregations to which they were addressed. They passed from hand to hand until · the frail writing substance was gone and the words remained only in their hearers' minds. Christ himself had written nothing; but his story, his teachings, the anecdotes and recollections about him, circulated freely in the widening world of early Christianity. The apostles themselves were the primary source of most of the literature of early Christianity. From their words a body of canonical literature began to form. The oldest of the Gospels is that of Mark. Although it was probably not from his hand, it may well have been based upon his account. It was certainly in circulation by the second generation of Christianity and the apostles accepted its authenticity. The Gospels of Matthew and Luke were produced before the end of the first century and both drew heavily upon the material in Mark. The Book of John was probably the last of the gospels to be written down. Thus the basic Christian Scripture came into existence. But the limits of the canon had yet to be established. Works of doubtful authority and pieces of pious fraud existed through the second and third centuries, challenging, damaging, and misdirecting much of the activity of the struggling faith.

Another source of danger to the new church, and one closely related to the problem of an authoritative Scripture, was the continuing operation of prophecy. In part this was a legacy from the prophetic tradition of Judaism. But prophets and visionaries were a familiar phenomenon in late antiquity generally. By its very nature, Christianity itself encouraged direct communication with the supernatural. The most characteristic form of the primitive church meeting was a kind of communal frenzy. Ecstatic members seized by the passion of their faith would speak with the voice of God. Nobody doubted their authority. As Christianity grew away from the direct control of the apostles the authority of continuous prophecy threatened to break its always precarious unity into a thousand different churches each with its own prophet and its own unique connection with guiding providence.

An equally serious danger to Christianity, and one which arose from the same sources of ecstacy and frenzy, was the rapid spread of Christian asceticism. This, like prophecy, was not unique in Christianity. The debasement of the flesh for the exaltation of the spirit had long been practiced in varying degrees in the classical world. With the progressive failure of classicism in the declining centuries of Rome, the ascetic tendency came to dominate many of the mystery religions which swept the empire. It was implicit in such mystical philosophies as Neoplatonism. Quite apart from the general trend, there was an inherent strand of asceticism in Christianity. While Christ had emphasized an ethic springing from the love of God and man, he had set a powerful ascetic example in his own life. He was a homeless, propertyless wanderer. He did not marry and denied himself most of the comforts of ordinary mortals. There was an ascetic tinge to the demands he made upon his disciples and to the commissions he gave them. Matthew records the words, "And he that taketh not his cross and followeth after me, is not worthy of me. He that findeth his life shall lose it; and he that loseth his life for my sake shall find it" (10:38-39). And in the same writing: "Provide neither gold, nor silver, nor brass in your purses, nor scrip for your journey, neither two coats, neither shoes, nor yet staves . . ." (10:9-10). The apostles took up this spirit and it spread to their converts.

The Christian willingness to suffer the most terrible tortures had seen the church through repeated persecution and glorified its martyrs. But even as persecution ceased there still remained in Christianity a compulsion to suffer which was nourished by the wide acceptance of ascetic practice in the pagan world. It was especially prevalent in the eastern

Above: *The Good Shepherd.* c. 350 A.D.
Right: *Colossal Head of the Emperor Constantine.* 306—337 A.D.

OPPOSITE
Above: *Agape or Eucharist of the Early Christians.* 3rd century A.D.
Catacombs of S. Callisto
Below: *Kybele on Processional Car Drawn by Lions.* 2nd century A.D.

19

empire. Many Christians—even whole sects—practiced extremes of maniac mortification: they punished and maimed their bodies, and some even castrated themselves. But the more usual forms of ascetic practice was to embrace the loneliness and discomfort of the hermit's life. St. Simeon Stylites carried his withdrawal to the extreme of sitting on top of a sixty-foot column for thirty years. The most famous of early Christian hermits, however, was St. Anthony who, in the late third century, retired to the Egyptian desert to escape the temptations of the flesh and society and to perfect his soul. The book of his trials, struggles, and visions became a favorite piece of Christian reading and his example was followed by hundreds like him who populated the desert with anchorites. The popularity of asceticism weakened and even threatened to destroy the concept of Christian service. There was danger that in such extreme care for one's own soul the care for one's brother would be forgotten.

At the opposite pole from the ascetics stood the Christian intellectuals, who in their own way were a more serious danger to their faith. Christianity was less prepared to deal with intellectualism than with spiritualism or fanaticism. Revelation, prophecy, even asceticism were not alien to the early spirit of Christianity; intellectualism was. In its early years Christianity may actually be regarded as a "know nothing" movement. Christ himself had turned away from Jewish legalism. Time after time he condemned the scribes and Pharisees, the custodians of the law, in the harshest terms. Yet, he offered no specific substitute for their legalism. He spoke in parables and riddles. He spoke profoundly of basic human problems and relationships. But despite the beauty, profundity, and impact of Christ's teachings they did not constitute a Christian system of philosophy. The "weak and simple apostles" could not supply a philosophy in which to set their religion nor did they see the need for such. Their appeal was emotional and direct, and its results were miraculous. A Christian spirit sufficed for a Christian mind.

Yet, Christianity could not afford to remain intellectually primitive. As it grew in scope, as greater numbers of people embraced it, it climbed the social ladder of imperial society, it had to come to terms with the intellectual heritage of classical antiquity and the problems raised by that impressive tradition. In the course of the second and third centuries Christianity attracted in increasing numbers men who were the products of the schools of rhetoric and philosophy that flourished in every city of the empire. As it fought its way to recognition Christianity had to answer the philosophic questions posed by both its antagonists and its converts. In this inherent conflict between the fanatic spirit of early Christianity and the logical rationalism of the Greek philosophic tradition lay one of the gravest dangers to Christianity. The danger manifested itself in the form of doctrinal disputes so bitter and prolonged that they threatened the very existence of the church. Out of the debates that roiled about these controversies the church gradually and necessarily developed a doctrinal orthodoxy.

The most important of these disputes was the Arian controversy. By the middle of the third century a distinctly "Christian learning" had developed. It was concentrated in the old intellectual centers of the Hellenistic east, Antioch, Nicomedia, Caesarea, but especially in Alexandria. There, early in the fourth century, a priest named Arius raised the fundamental question of the relationship between God and Christ. If God was the perfect, divine, eternal, omnipotent, omnipresent "one"—then where did Christ fit into the pattern of divinity? With destructive logic, Arius concluded that Christ was a creature, made in time, greater than man but less than God, and not sharing God's unique essence. The consistency of the Arian argument won it many adherents. But its implications won it a large and vocal opposition. To the anti-Arians the conclusions of Arius destroyed the very basis of Christianity as a separate religion—i.e., the unquestionable divinity of Christ. The anti-Arians insisted that Christ shared the divinity of God completely and that they were one and the same essence. Within a short time the east was ablaze with this controversy. Not only theologians contended over it; it reached down to the people themselves. Its partisans on either side persecuted and were persecuted. Riots broke out in many places threatening to disrupt civil order. In 325 Constantine intervened and called the first general council of the church to meet at Nicaea to decide the issue. There was bitter debate and, with questionable procedure, the Arian position was finally condemned. But it was not destroyed. The Arian heresy continued to exist for nearly a century in the empire and would have curious political effects of great importance in subsequent history, as we shall see. The emperors who followed Constantine wavered between the Arian and the anti-Arian position. Constantine himself, at his deathbed baptism, received the Arian form of Christianity. Toward the end of the fourth century, however, the orthodox view became more and more widely accepted and the "unitarian" position of Arius was replaced by the concept of the trinity—"one substance in three persons"—a concept which preserved both the saving divinity and the historical humanity of Christ.

Other controversies added to the turmoil of the early church: some came from outside Christianity, some rose specifically from Christianity itself. Gnosticism, one of the most widespread forms of philosophic mysticism, deeply affected Christianity by maintaining that Christ was a spiritual force for light and goodness in opposition to the Hebrew God who, as the Creator of time, space, matter, and flesh, was regarded by the Gnostics as the source of all evil. The Manichaeans, a sect of Persian origin which had become very powerful in the empire, held similar views. Like the Gnostics, the Manichaeans accepted Christ only as a force of light and rejected any human connection for him. Though the church as a whole rejected Manichaeism it, and similar beliefs, remained a latent influence of some importance in Christianity. Among other unorthodox groups originating within Christianity itself were the Monarchians, who held that Christ was "king" and the sole God of Christianity; the Adoptionists, who held that he was a man who, because of the perfection of his life, was adopted as the Son of God; the Nestorians, who preached a radical separation of the divine and human natures of Christ. These factional fights threatened the unity of Christianity even as it became the nearly universal religion of the Mediterranean world. Yet, out of the controversies of the fourth and fifth centuries, the church began to forge its theology. It picked and chose, rejected and accepted, interpreted and clarified. It limited and defined those areas of thought which touched the divine and gave to Christianity an intellectual framework within which it could grow for a thousand years.

The Church Takes Form

This process of definition could not have been carried through without decisive authority and that authority came from the organization of Christianity into an institution. In its beginnings, as we have already seen, the church had little if any organization. Until the destruction of Jerusalem by the Romans in A.D. 70 the Hebrew-Christian center there maintained a vague sort of authority stemming from the apostles. But by and large, Christian churches were independent of each other and of any higher administrative authority. At the local level the Christian churches were modeled upon the organization of the typical Jewish synagogue, the type of religious center developed by the Jews of the Diaspora. The primitive church organization was simple—the congregation and a council of elders, the latter the nucleus of a priesthood.

At an early date a specific office began to emerge in the local churches, that of overseer or bishop. This was to be the key office in the development of an ecclesiastical organization for Christianity. The bishop was the administrative head of the local church and he gradually came to represent it and speak for it. The pressure of persecution and the serious internal problems of the young religion made a more coherent organization necessary. By the second century the bishops were no longer simply the agents of the congregations, they were the masters. There is little doubt that they merited their elevation. They held their churches together under persecution, frequently paying for their devotion with their lives. They regarded themselves as the inheritors of the apostles' mission to carry out the commandments of their Christ. This transfer of the power of the apostles in an unbroken line through the generations of the bishops of the church became known as "apostolic succession." As Christianity was a state within the legal state of the Roman Empire, the bishops became the governors of that state. When the institutions of the empire and paganism failed, the office of the Christian bishop frequently became secular, the bishop often assuming the political power of Roman officials. As a hierarchy developed to support the growing power of the bishop, so the separation between the professional clergy and the laity became more distinct. By the fourth century the episcopal organization of the church was virtually complete and distinctions of rank began to appear—Archbishops, Metropolitans, Patriarchs.

Above even the most distinguished offices of the church stood the idea of the church itself. And this was expressed through councils. When disputes arose which bishops could not resolve, when conflicts occurred among the bishops themselves, then the only recourse was to a council. These were largely regional and provincial before Constantine, in 325, called the first ecumenical or world-wide council (the Council of Nicaea) to deal with the bitter Arian controversy.

Although names and offices would shift with the growth of the church through the centuries, its essential organization was now established. Christianity had become the heir not only of a bankrupt paganism, but of the political authority of a dying empire. The organization of the church reflected that of the empire and profited from the lessons of imperial administration. It was, in some part, this efficient and at the same time adaptable organization that was to make the Christian church the greatest institution of the Middle Ages. It enabled the church to cope with the serious internal dangers that threatened it in the early centuries of its existence, giving it the force, unity, and authority to control the tendencies toward fragmentation.

As early as the second century the church turned its back upon the doctrine of continuing prophecy. It condemned as heretical the most extreme of the several sects which preached the imminent end of the world —a group known as the Montanists. This action marked an epoch in the history of the early church, for it meant that the church was turning from the emphasis upon preparation for the next world to an emphasis upon living properly in this one. The millennial doctrine, of course, remained in the church and cropped up from time to time, as by implication in some of the great heresies of the fourth and fifth centuries, but on the whole the church subscribed from this time on to a wholesome concept of social responsibility. The extremes of individual ascetic practice were moderated by the institution of monasticism, by the substitution of group discipline and rules for the torture of the flesh and soul in isolation. By the end of the fourth century, the rule of St. Basil was widely adopted in the east and monastic foundations were beginning to appear in the western empire as well. By the encouragement of monasticism the church made room within it for those who sought a higher purification than worldly life could give. At the same time it gave to this potent drive the stabilizing influence of external discipline and order.

In the complex matter of doctrine it was the existence of a "church" in an institutional sense that made possible the concept of orthodoxy. By the third century the church had fixed a canon of Scripture among the conflicting claims of a great variety of writings purporting to be sacred. There were still disputed books but the church was in the process of creating the Bible. In the same way the decision-making power of the church arbitrated in that vast doctrinal area outside Scripture. Theology grew from doctrinal controversy and the decisions of bishops, synods, and councils. The church exercised its moderating influence and collective wisdom to pick among the dozens of interpretations and convictions, gradually to evolve that complex structure of belief known as Christian theology.

The organization of Christianity provided a framework of authority in which the most creative minds of late antiquity could work. These are usually grouped under the collective title, the Fathers of the Church. There were many of them—priests, patriarchs, martyrs, theologians, mystics, and saints—and they were intimately connected with the processes of ecclesiastical organization, theological development, and the definition of orthodoxy. But the history of western man was most profoundly influenced by the work of the so-called three great fathers of the Latin church: Jerome, Ambrose, and Augustine.

St. Jerome (346–420) was the archetype of the Christian scholar. He was a learned man whose mind encompassed the vast heritage of classicism. But he was also a passionate Christian with a strong tinge of asceticism. These two aspects of the man were often in painful conflict. But in a larger sense he resolved the conflict and put his learning at the disposal of his faith. He wrote hundreds of tracts and engaged heatedly in many controversies, but his greatest service to the church was his edition and translation of the Bible, both Old and New Testaments, into Latin. It was known as the Vulgate (i.e., for the common reader) and became the standard Bible of the Middle Ages.

As St. Jerome was the ideal of the Christian scholar, St. Ambrose (340–397) was the ideal of the Christian administrator. Jerome brought to the service of Christianity the learning of classical paganism; Ambrose brought to the administration of the church the political wisdom and experience of the Roman state. He was Archbishop of Milan and made it a strong center of the western church. But he was more than an isolated ecclesiastic; he tended to speak for the whole church. He succeeded not only in distinguishing the role of the church from that of the state, but by the vigor of his thought and the power of his personality, compelled even emperors to admit that in matters of faith the church was their superior. It was St. Ambrose who received the confession of Augustine and brought into the church the man who was to be the greatest of the Latin fathers.

St. Augustine (354–430) was the most important theologian of early Christianity. His theology, like that of the church generally, was the result of controversy. He took as his task the work of defending the church against a great variety of divisive opinions and his own theology was created in the heat and passion of argument. He fought the Manichaeans and won on their own ground, demonstrating that Christianity offered a safer and saner refuge for the human spirit. He fought against the Donatists, a dangerous heretical group of religious purists, and defeated them in a contest that agitated all Christendom. In the process he established the important view that the church is superior in sanctity, wisdom, and authority to any of its parts. He argued that the decisions of the church must stand with the Holy Scriptures in their authority. He struggled to resolve for himself and his fellow men the apparent conflict of human will and divine foreknowledge. He did not fully succeed but he established the lines along which the question of predestination would be argued for more than fifteen hundred years. He followed Paul in establishing human sin as a fundamental Christian assumption. His works fill many volumes but the world remembers two especially. His *Confessions,* the story of his search for belief and his ultimate conversion to Christianity, was apologetic in purpose, but it transcended its purpose to become a searching study of the inner conflict of a thinking man. In his *City of God* he laid down the main lines of a Christian history and the fertile idea that history is the revelation of the will of God. In this work history became philosophy (and theology) speaking through both experience and revelation. St. Augustine was not only a writer, thinker, and controversialist, he was also a great church administrator, and for more than thirty years held office as the bishop of the important city of Hippo in his native North Africa.

Rome, Catholicism, and the Western Tradition

As the church developed an ecumenical organization the same stresses began to appear within it that had characterized the earlier world-state of the Roman Empire. The ancient distinction between the Greek east and the Latin west remained in Christianity. The east moved slowly toward the orthodoxy of the Byzantine Empire. In the west, the church moved toward the elevation of Rome as the seat of Christianity and toward the creation of the papacy. It was with this development that medieval Christianity achieved its basic institutional form.

The early stages in the history of the papacy are obscure. It is probable that some of the prestige of the Roman church derived from the traditional reverence for the city of Rome itself. But it was also a large and wealthy church even before the persecutions ceased, and generous in its aid to other western churches. It was, furthermore, the only major church in the western empire which could claim to have been founded by one of the apostles—Peter. Thus, the doctrine of apostolic succession underscored the authority of Rome.

But a related idea was of even greater significance, the Petrine theory. It was based upon the famous words of Christ in Matthew 16:18-19,

And I say also unto thee, That thou art Peter, and upon this rock I will build my church; and the gates of hell shall not prevail against it. And I give unto thee the keys of the kingdom of heaven; and whatsoever thou shalt bind on earth shall be bound in heaven: and whatsoever thou shalt loose on earth shall be loosed in heaven.

This passage contained the seed of Roman supremacy. Since Peter had been chief among the apostles—with authority from the very mouth of Christ—then the church that Peter founded, the church at Rome, must exercise a like authority among the other churches. As early as the second century this impressive claim to supremacy was beginning to be recognized by many western churches. The east, with all its great and wealthy churches claiming apostolic dignity, consistently rejected the Roman claim. But in the west in the late third and early fourth centuries it was established that appeal could be made from provincial councils to the bishop of Rome. Disputes over questions of doctrine and discipline began to be sent to Rome. In the year 455 the emperor Valentinian III ordered the entire western church to render obedience to the pope. The monarchical status of the Roman bishop was clearly established by the end of the fifth century. With the progressive collapse of Roman secular authority in the west, the organization of the church under papal leadership gradually replaced Rome in politics as well as in the things of the spirit.

In summary, the church by the fifth century had grown from a handful of small, persecuted congregations in the midst of a hostile world to a complete and efficient organization which touched most of the aspects of life for millions of people. Yet the triumph of the church was not all gain. In a way the victory of the church was the defeat of its spirit. As the church grew in wealth and ostentation, as it gained the pomp and dignity of monarchy, the humble spirit of Christianity was forced into retreat. In its victory the church became the persecutor of variant opinions among its own members and of those who persisted in disbelief. For the spiritual fervor of early Christianity the church substituted ritual and symbolism. Yet, with all its flaws the institutionalization of the church was the condition for its continued existence. It was Christianity's compromise with historical reality.

THE BARBARIAN TIDE

The Latent Menace

The ultimate transformation of the classical world came about with the penetration of the imperial frontiers by the barbarian Germans from the forests and plains of central and eastern Europe. Centuries before their

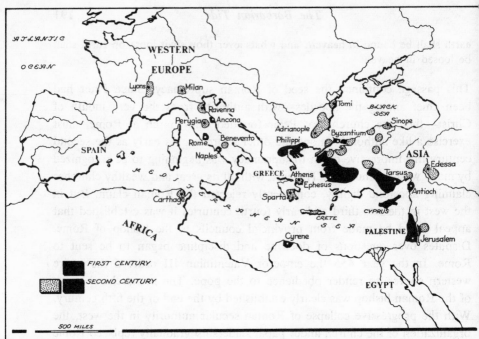

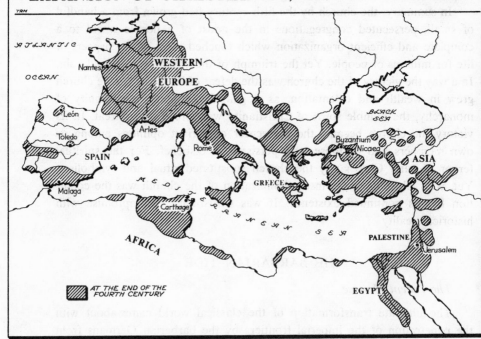

EXPANSION OF CHRISTIANITY, FIRST FOUR CENTURIES

mass invasions into the crumbling empire in the fourth and fifth centuries the Germanic peoples had been known to the Romans. But Caesar's conquest of Gaul and the stabilization of the European frontier along the Rhine and Danube rivers had kept them outside the empire.

About A.D. 100 the historian Tacitus wrote a brief sketch, *Germania,* in which he described the appearance, customs, general culture, and tribal distribution of the Germans. He noted their Nordic cast—the blue eyes, blonde or red hair, large bodies and fair skin; their primitive log and turf houses; their dress of animal skins; their wealth in herds and poverty in soil. He lauded their domestic fidelity and the simple justice of their social ways. He deplored their violence, gambling, and drunkenness. In sum, what Tacitus recorded was the picture of a typical backward people just emerging into a settled agricultural life, retaining their love of war and their simple family-based tribal organization.

But the Germans whom he described did not remain static. Even by the time of Tacitus those living near the frontier had begun to feel the moderating force of civilization: they had begun to exchange their animal skins for cloth; they traded for metal goods and pottery; enterprising merchants supplied their wants and penetrated deep into the interior beyond the frontiers. As Roman goods, tastes, and usages made their way across the frontier they created envy and desire as well as profitable markets. Even more than Roman goods, the rich and peaceful fields of the empire beckoned the Germans across the frontier.

The German tribes were restless and constantly moving. Their limited agricultural techniques rapidly exhausted the soil, and hunger and the growth of population forced tribes to migrate. But a more relentless pressure was that of other peoples from the north and east. The original home of the Germans was the region around the eastern end of the Baltic Sea, and from this heartland new and more savage barbarian tribes continued to come, pushing other groups before them. This drift of population to the south and west brought inexorable pressure against the Roman frontier. From the time of Augustus to the fifth century there was always a "German problem."

As Roman stability declined and the German pressures mounted, the problem of the frontier defenses became critical. German war bands combined into dangerous full-scale armies. The Germans had learned much from Roman tactics and military organization and they threw into the balance seemingly endless hordes of fighters. Roman preoccupation with civil war in the third century gave the barbarian Germans untrammeled opportunity to raid across the frontiers of the Rhine and Danube far into the heart of the empire. With the restoration of central authority under Diocletian the frontiers were recovered, but at a terrible cost. In the century following Diocletian and Constantine the Germanic peoples finally broke over the frontiers in such numbers that they could no longer be turned back.

The Goths and the Eastern Frontier

This ominous breakthrough did not come over the long-pressed western frontier, but across the lower Danube, by the Goths. They were a branch of the eastern Germanic peoples who, originating in the same Baltic lands as their kin, had slowly drifted to the south and east roughly following the line of the Danube. By A.D. 200 they shared the area north of the Black Sea with a polyglot of other German tribes and were a serious threat to the eastern empire.

Yet they were themselves more desperately threatened. Far to the east an obscure set of forces had started the westward migration of the large, loosely related tribe of the Huns. These were typical Asiatic horse nomads, whose whole culture was perfectly formed for war. When the delicate balance of their environment shifted they appeared on the Asiatic threshold of the European continent. Numerous and fierce, they had frightful scarred and twisted faces. Mounted on swift, wiry horses, they seemed to be everywhere at once.

The most easterly branch of the Gothic peoples—called the Ostrogoths for this reason—were defeated by the Huns and their ephemeral kingdom north and east of the Black Sea destroyed. They, along with dozens of other fragmentary Germanic tribes, were absorbed in the Hunnic advance. The western branch, or Visigoths, met the Huns in 372 and were defeated. It was this defeat that drove the remnants of the Visigoths, leaderless and panic-stricken, to the Danube. Facing annihilation by the Huns and with their backs to the river, they asked permission of the Roman government to cross over into the empire. Permission was given and in 376 some eighty thousand Visigoths moved into the province of Moesia.

This was, of course, not a new Roman policy, and it was probably hoped that the Goths would not only occupy this denuded area but would help to defend it. But Valens, the weak co-emperor of the east, could not control his dangerous clients. Within two years, through the emperor's incapacity and the greed and cruelty of his agents among the Goths,

Valens faced a full-scale Gothic rebellion. With a hastily assembled army he met them in battle near Adrianople in 378. His army was destroyed and Valens himself killed. The eastern empire lay open to the Goths. This was not the first time that German forces had won battles over Roman armies. Indeed the "Roman" army itself was largely composed of barbarian contingents. But the Battle of Adrianople came to symbolize a new age, for now the myth of Roman invincibility had been disproved.

The Gothic armies ravaged the Balkans and northern Greece but they could not take cities or strongly fortified places. In 379 Theodosius the Great came to the throne, the last Roman to be able to hold the eastern and western empires together. He achieved by diplomacy with the Goths what war had failed to do, making an alliance with them and granting them the territory they occupied. For a troubled generation the peace was held. Then the death of Theodosius coincided with the rise of Alaric, the greatest of Visigothic tribal kings. Dissatisfied with the status of his people and wanting power and prestige for himself, Alaric marched on Constantinople. Arcadius, the weak and immature son of Theodosius, who was emperor of the east, was powerless to cope with the new Gothic menace. Alaric was opposed instead by Stilicho, a Vandal general who had entered the service and the family of Theodosius. Stilicho maneuvered his armies skillfully enough to force the Goths back and Alaric turned north to skirt the Adriatic and attack Italy. Again the Visigoths met the solid resistance of Stilicho. But this savior of the empire was murdered in 408 on the order of the indecisive and suspicious Honorius, the western emperor and other son of Theodosius. At the same time there was a general massacre of the families of German soldiers in Italy. This pointless barbarity not only removed the one general who might have been able to defend Italy, it brought the wholesale defection of German troops in Italy to swell Alaric's forces. In spite of—or perhaps because of—immense quantities of gold paid by the frightened senators and nobles, Alaric attacked and seized the city of Rome. The eternal city, which had not been taken by a foreign force in eight hundred years, fell! When an attempt to reach the grain riches of North Africa failed and Alaric died, the Visigoths slowly moved north again through the ruined peninsula and into Gaul. There they spread out over an area which extended over the Pyrenees into Spain and as far north as the Loire River. Honorius granted them the sovereignty he could not deny them of their vast, vague, loosely held "Kingdom of Toulouse."

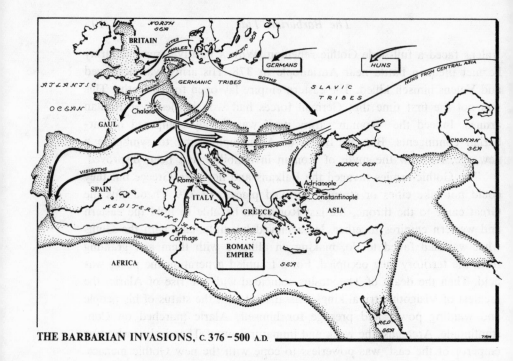

THE BARBARIAN INVASIONS, c. 376 - 500 A.D.

The Dismemberment of the West

With the Visigothic penetration of Italy, the Rhine and upper Danube frontiers had been stripped of Roman forces, and while the Visigoths occupied the peninsula of Italy a horde of west German barbarians streamed across the broken frontiers into Gaul. The Burgundians carved out a kingdom along the course of the Rhone River in southern Gaul. The Vandals and others moved to the west and into Spain. In 429, under Gaiseric, the Vandals crossed over to the rich province of Africa, which was in revolt under a military usurper and former Roman governor. The Vandals swept across North Africa, besieging the city of Hippo in 430. St. Augustine, its bishop, died during the siege. In 439 Carthage fell and became the capital of the Vandal African kingdom. By mid-century the Vandals not only dominated North Africa but had taken to the sea. Their pirate fleets ranged through the western Mediterranean as those of the Goths menaced the Black Sea and the Aegean coasts. In 455 a large Vandal fleet attacked the city of Rome and once more the great city was sacked and looted.[1]

1. It is from this that our word "vandalism" is derived: by a curious twist the careful and systematic looting "technique" of the Vandals has come to mean wanton destruction.

As the western empire was opened to the mass migration of Germanic barbarians, the mongoloid Huns, whose pressures had originally driven the Visigoths to the Danube frontier, continued their westward penetration. In the wake of the Gothic destruction in the Danubian and Balkan lands the Huns raided rampantly across the eastern imperial frontiers. The great resources of wealth taken in loot and bribes from the eastern empire supported a Hunnic force of perhaps half a million men. They were led by a succession of able war chiefs. In the mid-fifth century Attila the Hun (*c. 433–453*) appeared. From a huge semipermanent camp on the plain of Hungary Attila ruled with barbaric splendor. Ambassadors carried his threats and promises to all the nations of the west. His Hun state lived by plunder and ransom, constantly extending the area of its raids and terrorism.

In 451 Attila led a large force into northern Gaul. They were met by a varied army of Gallo-Romans, Goths, and others drawn together by dread of their common enemy. The battle, fought on the plain of Mauriac, and often called the Battle of Chalons, was not a decisive victory for either army, but Attila withdrew. He diverted his attack to Italy and ravaged its northern plain. Venice, by tradition, was founded when people fled to the desolate islands and treacherous marshes that form its site to escape the Huns. The fate of Italy and of Rome seemed sealed once more. A commission under the leadership of Pope Leo the Great went out to meet the Hun king. Attila inexplicably turned back across the Alps. (Later tradition ascribed this "defeat" to the spiritual powers of the pope and the incident did much to confirm papal leadership in the west.) Within another year Attila died and the great empire of the Huns melted away. Its decline had begun well before his time, for the Huns had overextended their territory, and their simple, rigid, nomadic culture had begun to break under the pressure of the changes their conquests brought. Their way of life could not be well accommodated to the forests of central Europe nor the fever-ridden plains of Italy. Within a generation of their greatest power no significant trace of the Huns remained in the western world.

The passing of the Hunnic menace brought another problem. The varied peoples who had been half-allies and half-captives of the Huns settled along the Danube frontier and moved across to occupy large stretches of land devastated by passing armies and Hun raids for more than a century. Of these peoples and remnants of peoples the most important were the Ostrogoths, the easterly branch of those same Goths who had already troubled the empire for a century.

Shortly there appeared among the Ostrogoths another of the strong and able kings whose lives are interwoven with the deeds of the barbarian tribes—Theodoric the Great (474–526). Beginning as king of a small subgroup of the Ostrogoths, he gradually pulled together this scattered and demoralized people into a dangerous force. They began to exert a powerful pressure against Constantinople, the wealthy center of the eastern empire. The wily and frightened eastern emperor, Zeno, took advantage of the chaotic affairs of Italy to rid himself of his new Gothic menace.

The western empire had fallen to pieces under repeated German invasion. A series of nominal emperors had come and gone under the protection of barbarian military leaders. In 476 the last of these shadow emperors, the twelve-year-old Romulus Augustulus, was deposed by the barbarian general Odovacar and the fiction of a western empire died for more than three centuries. This was the pretext that enabled the eastern emperor to direct the pressure of the Ostrogoths under Theodoric away from Constantinople and toward the west. The scheme fell in well with Theodoric's own ambitions and, as the "agent" of the eastern emperor, he began a slow, careful, full-scale invasion of the western empire. At the head of 200,000 Ostrogoths he defeated the army of Odovacar; took Ravenna, which had been the capital-stronghold of Italy for some years; treacherously murdered Odovacar with his own hands and had the troops who had remained loyal to their leader massacred.

Thus by 495—a century after Theodosius and nearly two centuries after Constantine—the western Roman empire had come fully into the hands of the barbarians. The great, rich, peaceful expanse which had been the provinces of the west had become a chequer board of vaguely defined barbarian succession states crowding each other and fighting for the ruined pieces of the western empire. The borders of the empire had ceased to exist.

The province of Britain had been abandoned by the distraught imperial government and a portion of the protective legions was moved to guard more vital areas threatened by the Visigothic invasion of the west. Almost immediately Germanic tribes from the north of Europe—principally Angles, Saxons, and Jutes—began to raid the island. The Romano-Celtic people of Britain retreated to the western extremities of the island and to Ireland. Virtually every trace of Roman influence was destroyed and this most remote of Roman provinces became Anglo-Saxon England—warring, divided, and separated from the major currents of continental influence for

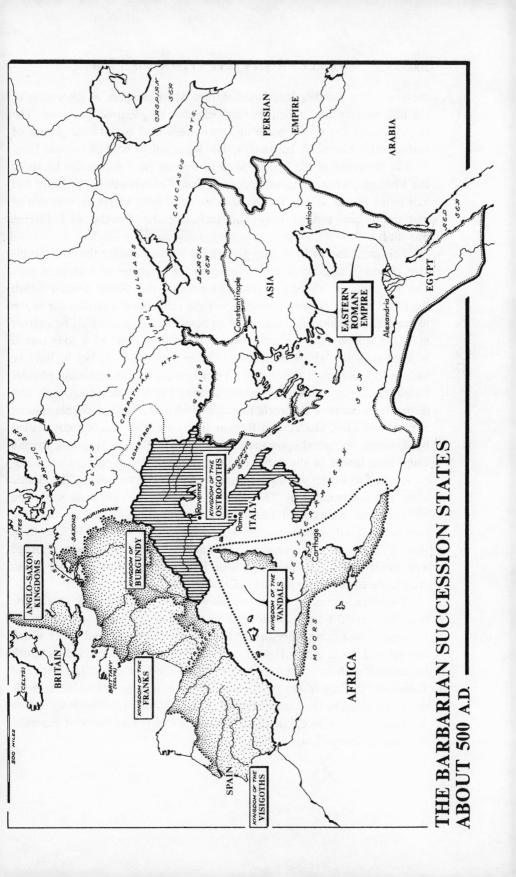

THE BARBARIAN SUCCESSION STATES
ABOUT 500 A.D.

centuries. The Vandals held North Africa. Most of Spain in the course of the fifth century was added to the Visigothic kingdom of Toulouse. The rugged mountains of the north and west were held by tattered groups of various other Germanic barbarians. The Burgundians held on to their kingdom in the valley of the Rhone. Most of Roman Gaul was in the hands of the Visigoths, whose kingdom extended from Spain north to the Loire and east to the Rhone. But by far the most stable of these kingdoms was that of Theodoric, centered in Italy and including the Danube and Illyrian provinces.

This great and ruthless king gave to the western empire the only significant period of stability it was to enjoy in the centuries of barbarian rule. The kingdom of Theodoric gradually became the center toward which the other barbarian powers drifted and the outlines of a new order began to appear. Theodoric was master of an active diplomacy, which he exerted upon the surrounding barbarian states. He held the end of a long thread of legal authority which stretched to the eastern emperor, but in Italy he had, in fact, sovereign rights. With Theodoric the age of barbarian plunder ended. He began to create a system to bring together the antagonistic and disparate elements of the world he ruled. It was essentially a double system; military and civil, Gothic and Roman. The civil state was Roman, staffed by Romans, organized upon the ancient models. Roman laws and Roman coins were issued in the name of the empire. But the military establishment which had been so long German in fact became so legally. The Gothic army was commanded by Theodoric as its chief; the civil state was ruled by Theodoric as its legal head, recognized and sanctioned by the only imperial authority remaining, the eastern emperor. Goth and Roman lived side by side in relative peace, security, and toleration. Prosperity returned with order and the natural wealth of Italy and the western lands began once more to be put to the uses of civilization.

Theodoric's work of reconstitution was, however, the work of a single man; he created no constitution, no system of government apart from his personal authority and prestige. At his death, the peace and order which had reigned for a grateful generation died with him. The kingdom which he seemed to have established so firmly quickly faltered. The death of Theodoric, the last of the great chiefs of the migration, coincided with the rise of Justinian in the eastern empire. The ambition of Justinian to reunite the Mediterranean world involved Theodoric's Italy and the west generally in quixotic destruction.

The New Amalgam

The centuries of the great migrations were a time of cultural fusion, a time which produced the general outlines of the medieval world. Yet, the shock of change was not as great to those who lived through it as it seems to us who can interpret its significance in the perspective of history. The thousands, even hundreds of thousands, of Germanic barbarians who poured into the empire to plunder and settle were a comparatively small number—a dangerous, powerful, and significant number—but still a minority among the millions who lived behind the Roman frontiers. In the meeting of German and Roman there was, on either side, little of the idea of ethnic crusade. The Roman Empire had never consisted of a homogeneous population. Instead, the Romans had imposed upon the diverse peoples of the empire a political, social, economic, and cultural unity based upon the system of Roman government and the vigor of Graeco-Roman civilization. But with the Germanic migrations Rome was no longer able to absorb her new barbarians. Their number and vitality combined to bring about the cumulative failure of the whole classical system, which had been in progress for generations.

The Germans, moreover, despite the violence and plundering which attended their migrations, came into the empire largely to settle and not to destroy. They were almost uniformly impressed with the antiquity and the complexity of imperial civilization. They were quite unwittingly the last collective blow to the system they had come to inherit; for the system was already in the throes of fundamental change. It was a system based upon the city, upon exchange, large free markets, safe transport and easy communications, upon a diversity of labor and products. Long before the age of the migrations, however, the countryside had begun to encroach upon the city. The ruinous policies of the desperate imperial government had already advanced the destruction of the cities of the empire; new centers of life had begun to appear in late classical times—the great, self-sufficient *villas* or country estates; their proprietors, significantly called the *potentiores,* had gained a status virtually independent of government. They had vast and productive lands, abundant labor, even private armies of retainers for the defense of their estates. The Germans simply moved into this system. The initial impact of the invasions destroyed most of the cities that remained and the Germans, by and large, settled down upon the soil. They were a military and proprietary minority. Under Odovacar one-third of the land of Italy was taken for his followers. The same provisions, and the same land, held for the kingdom of the Ostrogoths when Theodoric replaced Odovacar. Similar conditions existed in many other parts of the empire: the turmoil and dislocation were probably not great; the population decline within the empire had forced the abandonment of large tracts of farmland which were appropriated by Germans. Sometimes there were confiscations and outrage. Yet many estates remained in the hands of families which, by the late sixth century, still took pride in their Roman lineage. In all, the sprawling network of nearly self-sufficient estates, held by great proprietors and worked by a depressed peasantry, was interpenetrated by German landholders and the system itself was but little modified.

In other areas of life there was the same sort of amalgamation of Roman and German and a general acceptance of the changed military and political circumstances in the western world. Many Roman nobles willingly entered the service of barbarian kings. Even with the Sack of Rome by the Visigoths and Vandals and the effective political independence of the various German kings in the west, there was no clear or general recognition of any "new" system of government. The Germans themselves largely imagined that they had simply taken over the Roman system as its masters.

Religious Division and Arianism

There remained, of course, many significant areas of antagonism. None of them was of greater importance than religion. In the early years of the Gothic advance through the borderlands of the eastern empire large numbers of them had been converted to Christianity; but, ironically, it was to the Arian form of Christianity, for the Arian heresy had stayed alive in the eastern empire during most of the fourth century.

About the middle of the century Ulfilas (311–381), a Goth educated in the eastern empire, became "the apostle" to the Visigoths. He was an Arian and it was to his faith that he converted his people. It would be absurd to contend that they understood the fine web of theo-philosophic distinctions that separated Arianism from Orthodoxy. What they subscribed to was the religion of Ulfilas. For it was his wisdom and charity, the purity and dedication of his life and not his arguments that converted the Goths. Ulfilas also translated the Bible into a written form of Gothic that he created. This Bible is the earliest linguistic document in any of the Germanic languages.

From the Visigoths Arian Christianity spread to other German peoples with the result that every major barbaric nation that came from the north and east into the western empire was Arian and spread Arianism. The Visigoths took it to Italy, Gaul, and Spain; the Burgundians established it firmly in their kingdom; the Vandals took it to North Africa. It spread across the broad kingdom of the Ostrogoths from the Balkans to the south of France. There was no area of conflict between Roman and German more troublesome than this.

During the same time that the Arian heresy and others like it had developed in the eastern cities, the western empire had been working out the basic principles and distinctions of Catholicism. From such vigorous centers as the Lugdunum (Lyons) of Irenaius, the Milan of St. Ambrose, the Hippo of St. Augustine, and certainly from the great center of Christian authority and organization in Rome, the western empire had been won to Catholicism. Thus, when the barbarians came to impose their political and military dominance upon the western empire, their religion set them apart more clearly than their barbarism from the people among whom they settled. The conflict was obvious everywhere, driving an irritating wedge between the two principal segments of the people of the western world. In North Africa this religious problem was a solid barrier to the creation of a unified Vandal state. In Gaul, orthodox anti-Arianism became the banner of Gallo-Roman "nationalism." Even in Ostrogothic Italy, although Theodoric was scrupulously tolerant as a matter of policy, there was jarring conflict.

The Socio-Cultural Role of the Church

Yet, with all the grim seriousness of the Arian-Catholic division, Christianity and the church remained central to the new culture that was gradually emerging. In the area of politics and administration, the church took a leading role. The gap between the decay and lethargy of Roman government and the German lack of political sophistication was filled by the church. The church was also the predominant intellectual center in the age of the migrations. Secular culture remained, certainly, but it could not compare with the vigor of thought within the church. The classical forms remained but their inner vitality was gone.

The recognition of the failure of classicism may be seen in the figure of Boethius (c. 475–524). He was a noble Roman, traditionally trained in philosophy and rhetoric, who rose to high office in the service of Theodoric. On the suspicion of treason (probably groundless) he was sentenced to death. While he awaited brutal death by torture he wrote *The Consolation of Philosophy,* one of the most popular of all medieval books. In the allegorical framework of a colloquy with Dame Philosophy, Boethius voiced a gentle and Stoic resignation to the turns of fortune. This work was also of a piece with the considerable volume of Boethius' other writings which aimed to recapitulate as much as possible of the classical tradition. He translated and abridged some of the key writings of Greek philosophy and science. His works remained, throughout the Middle Ages, one of the few avenues by which western scholars could maintain any touch with Hellenism.

Cassiodorus (480–573) was a contemporary of Boethius, and like him a scholar. Their early careers were similar; Cassiodorus, however, retired to his estates where he lived in a monastery of his own founding and led his monks in copying manuscripts, an occupation which spread to other monasteries and to which all western civilization owes a tremendous debt. In both Boethius and Cassiodorus there was a conscious attempt to make a cultural transition in a transitional age.

It is significant that the bridge between the classical and the medieval world was the bridge of religion and the church. The church was rapidly assuming the burden of propagation of culture which the state and the secular society of the moribund empire could no longer bear. The vigorous, young, growing institution of the church had vital need of the cultural tradition of antiquity. It had to educate its army of administrators, preachers, and teachers. And, to do this, it turned to the only learned tradition there was, classicism. It picked and chose—sometimes curiously—from the glittering litter of a thousand years of thought and refinement. We have seen the result in such figures as St. Jerome and St. Augustine. The church was committed to the preservation of that large segment of classicism which it could turn to its advantage and that of its people.

One of the most important agencies of this cultural selection and preservation was western monasticism. Along with the scholarly task of collecting and copying manuscripts, the work of the monks was of equal importance in another area. There was a world to be converted; and the monks went out into the pagan fringes of civilization and founded monasteries which became cultural outposts in the barbaric wilderness. These pioneering monks were farmers, like the peasants among whom they lived and worked, and they brought to their flocks not only religion but better methods of construction and farming, better techniques for doing the limited work of their world. They introduced their people to the mysteries of literacy and then to the Scriptures and the liturgy of the church. Much of what they handed on was their legacy from the classical civilization.

In summary, the fourth and fifth centuries, the age of the Germanic migrations, forever separated the western empire from the east—and by more than time and space. In those formative centuries the western world was fixed into the fundamental patterns which were to prevail through the medieval period. The east took another course which we now turn to examine.

SUGGESTIONS FOR FURTHER READING

Primary Sources and Original Works

Many editions of the New Testament, including the now generally accepted Revised Standard Version; the most important source for the early church, especially the Synoptic Gospels, the Acts of the Apostles, and the Letters of St. Paul.

The late-classical and early Christian texts of the historian, Ammianus Marcellinus, and the *Ecclesiastical History* of Eusebius, Bishop of Caesarea.

The *Confessions* of St. Augustine, in many editions, gives a perceptive picture of the late fourth century society of the empire and the *City of God* of St. Augustine, in many editions. There is a good abridgment: **On the Two Cities* (New York: Ungar, 1957).

*Boethius, The Consolation of Philosophy, J. J. Buchanan, ed. (New York: Ungar, 1957).

The Decline of Rome

A. Alfoldi, *The Conversion of Constantine and the Pagan World* (Oxford: Oxford University Press, 1948).

R. F. Arragon, *The Transition from the Ancient to the Medieval World* (New York: Holt, 1936).

*W. C. Bark, *Origins of the Medieval World* (Stanford, Calif.: Stanford University Press, 1958).

A. E. R. Boak, *Manpower Shortage and the Fall of the Roman Empire* (Ann Arbor: University of Michigan Press, 1955).

*Jacob Burchhardt, *The Age of Constantine the Great* (Garden City, N. Y.: Anchor, 1956).

M. Deanesly, *A History of Early Medieval Europe, 476–911* (New York: Barnes and Noble, 1956), perhaps the best modern treatment of this period.

*Samuel Dill, *Roman Society in the Last Century of the Western Empire* (New York: Meridian, 1958).

T. R. Glover, *Life and Letters in the Fourth Century* (New York: Stechert, 1924).

*A. H. M. Jones, *Constantine and the Conversion of Europe* (New York: Collier, 1962).

*Solomon Katz, *The Decline of Rome and the Rise of Medieval Europe* (Ithaca: Cornell University Press, 1955), an excellent brief summary designed specifically for beginning students.

*F. Lot, *The End of the Ancient World and the Beginning of the Middle Ages* (New York: Harper, 1961).

*E. K. Rand, *Founders of the Middle Ages* (New York: Dover, 1957).

*D. A. Saunders, ed., *The Portable Gibbon* (New York: Viking Press, 1952), a one-volume abridgment of Gibbon's massive classic; not the happiest selection perhaps, but it does contain much of the essential Gibbon.

*R. E. Sullivan, *Heirs of the Roman Empire* (Ithaca: Cornell University Press, 1960).

E. A. Thompson, *A History of Attila and the Huns* (Oxford: University Press, 1948).

*F. W. Wallbank, *The Decline of the Roman Empire in the West* (New York: Abelard-Schuman, 1953).

The Rise of Christianity

*Wm. F. Albright, *From the Stone Age to Christianity* (Garden City, N. Y.: Anchor, 1957), especially good for the Judaic context of early Christianity.

*C. N. Cochrane, *Christianity and the Classical Culture* (New York: Oxford University Press, 1957).

*F. Cumont, *The Oriental Religions in Roman Paganism* (New York: Dover, 1957), the classic work on Christianity and the mystery religions.

*E. R. Goodenough, *The Church in the Roman Empire* (New York: Holt, 1931), excellent short account for the beginning student.

M. L. W. Laistner, *Christianity and Pagan Culture in the Later Roman Empire* (Ithaca: Cornell University Press, 1951).

———, *Intellectual Heritage of the Early Middle Ages,* ed. by C. G. Starr (Ithaca: Cornell University Press, 1957).

———, *Thought and Letters in Western Europe,* A.D. *500 to 900* (Ithaca: Cornell University Press, 1957).

A. C. McGiffert, *A History of Christian Thought* (New York: Scribners, 1947), 2 vols., especially Vol. I and the first chapters in Vol. II for the theology, speculation, and controversy of the early church.

*Paperbound edition. In the case of reprint editions, publisher and date of publication given will be that of reprint rather than the original.

❧ 6 ❧

The Byzantine Empire and
the Rise of Islam

THE EASTERN EMPIRE BECOMES BYZANTINE

The fourth and fifth centuries A.D. brought great changes to the eastern Roman Empire, though markedly different from those in the west. The eastern empire, successful in repelling the barbarian invasions, managed both to preserve the major outlines of its classical heritage and to create a distinctive new culture.

Constantine and the Founding of the Byzantine Empire

The key figure in both the preservation and the transformation of the eastern empire was Constantine (*306–337*). After his victory over Licinius, he decided to establish a new imperial center—Constantinople—on the site of the ancient Greek city of Byzantium, which had been founded in the seventh century B.C. as a commercial colony. Constantine chose this site because of its strategic position at the tip of the Golden Horn, the peninsula which juts out into the sea passage commanding the entrance to the Black Sea. From here it would be possible to guard both the Persian frontier to the south and east and the Asiatic frontier across the lower Danube. Moreover, in addition to being in the midst of the most stable part of the empire, Constantinople straddled two of the greatest trade routes of the ancient world: the overland route from Asia to Europe across the narrows of the Bosporus and the water route from the Black Sea to the Mediterranean. The fortifications of Constantinople were begun in 324, and by 332 it had become one of the greatest cities the world had ever known. It was dedicated to the Trinity and the Virgin Mary and called "New Rome which is Constantinople."

This appellation was significant, for Constantine conceived of his city literally as a new capital for the ancient Roman state. The venerable fictions of republican government were preserved: the senate was transferred to the city and regular consular appointments continued; even the practice of pacifying the city mobs with "bread and circuses" was continued, and the beauty and extravagance of Roman buildings, shrines, parks, and mansions re-created.

Yet, from the beginning, the new overshadowed the old elements. The traditions of Roman popular government had no roots in the east; they quickly withered and left imperial autocracy to flourish unopposed and unquestioned. The people who called themselves Romans, the favored population of Constantinople, had no ethnic relationship to the Roman-Italians. They were heavily mixed Hellenistic-Orientals who spoke a babble of dialectic Greek. Their traditions, their habits of mind, their customs and vices, were Hellenistic and almost untouched by Roman influence. Above all, Constantinople was, from its beginning, a Christian city. Perhaps no other feature set it apart so sharply from the old capital in the west, which had its long tradition of paganism.

From this magnificent new stronghold Constantine and his successors beat back the various tribes of Visigoths, Huns, Ostrogoths, and others who crossed the Danube frontier to pillage and loot. Constantinople was too strong to be taken and as long as it stood the greater part of the Roman east was safe.

Constantine died in 337 and his sons fought for their imperial inheritance against foreign dangers, domestic usurpers, and each other. In 360 the last of them died. The empire passed through the hands of a series of emperors of doubtful ability until the shock of the Gothic victory at Adrianople in 378 brought the competent Theodosius to the throne. Shortly after his accession the western imperial line failed and Theodosius held the entire empire. His sons divided it again in the opening years of the fifth century and the dual emperorship continued, often nominally in the west, through the years of mass barbarian invasion deepening the cleavage between east and west. Within a century the broad outlines of the new civilization in the east were apparent. With the reign of Justinian (527–565) the era of transition ended. A new empire had been born in the east; in the west the old had died.

The Succession of Justinian

The dynasty of Theodosius had been followed in the eastern empire by a series of military adventurers ending with Justin I (*518–527*), an ignorant Illyrian soldier of humble origin who had risen to command the imperial bodyguard. It was his nephew Justinian who ruled behind the scenes through much of his uncle's reign and followed him to the throne. The new emperor was the greatest possible contrast to his uncle. Justinian had been raised a "Byzantine"; he was well-educated in both formal and practical learning, and was thoroughly at home in the hothouse atmosphere of

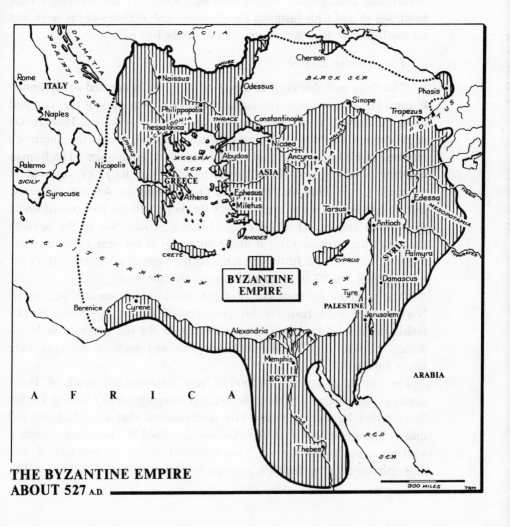

**THE BYZANTINE EMPIRE
ABOUT 527** A.D.

palace intrigue in which he had grown up. Justinian was, however, a man of curious contrasts. He had great strength of will and could carry through long and complicated negotiations without losing sight of his goal. At the same time he was untiring in his attention to the thousand details of imperial administration. Little that went on in the empire escaped Justinian's attention; yet he seldom left the palace. He was morose, wakeful, and inclined to asceticism. Theology was his greatest indulgence and he loved nothing more than to engage in endless debate with the learned bishops and theologians who thronged his court.

Justinian's wife and empress, Theodora, was remarkable in her own right. The daughter of a circus beast-keeper, she was a woman of great beauty and even greater intelligence and nerve. As the emperor's right hand, she shared with Justinian the decisions and anxieties of his reign and no small part of his eminence must be ascribed to her.

The Militant Empire

The reign and the work of Justinian form the watershed of Byzantine history. His dream was to reconquer the Roman provinces of the west and bring the classical world once more under "Roman" authority. This scheme of reconquest was not simply an expensive caprice. It was the emperor's response to his imperial role and to his Christian commitment. The Roman emperor could not permit barbarians to hold "our Italy" or any part of the empire. Nor could the "Chosen of God" permit the defiance of heresy. But he had inherited the conflict with Persia that Rome had passed on to the eastern empire. This had erupted into a serious war in the opening decade of the sixth century: it broke out again in the year Justinian came to the throne. In 532 Justinian sacrificed the hope of complete victory for a "Perpetual Peace" in order to move against the west.

The troubles growing out of the Catholic-Arian conflict in Vandal North Africa gave Justinian his provocation. Within two years Vandal resistance was broken, but along the fringe of the old province in North Africa the war dragged on for fifteen years and parts of this area were never subdued.

The chaotic affairs of Ostrogothic Italy, following the death of Theodoric, gave Justinian a pretext for his next campaign. The resulting Gothic Wars lasted for twenty years. The rehabilitation that Italy had enjoyed under Theodoric was lost. As Tacitus described it, Justinian "made a wilderness and called it peace"; he destroyed all but the memory of Roman greatness in his fruitless attempt to reassert Roman authority. The barest foothold in southeastern Spain was recovered at about the same time. Justinian had doubled his empire; but the cost of his achievement and its implications were greater than any man of his time could have foreseen. The wreck of Vandal power in North Africa, the bitter religious division, the continuing frontier wars, and the oppressive Byzantine system of taxation prepared the way for the Arab conquest which was to sweep across North Africa in little less than a century. Italy was practically laid bare by the Gothic Wars, and throughout medieval times never recovered more than a fraction of its ancient prosperity. More significantly, Justinian's destruction of Ostrogothic power left a vacuum of authority which the Byzantine Empire could not fill in the troubled period that followed. Thus, the conquest of Italy simply opened the door to a new and savage series of barbarian invasions.

The preoccupation of Byzantine arms in the west was, furthermore, too tempting an opportunity for Justinian's eastern enemies. The battered lower Danube frontier was broken again. The masses of people who had been pushed into western Asia and eastern Europe in the course of the fourth and fifth centuries migrated into the Balkans in the wake of the Goths. Bands of Asiatic Huns and related Bulgars raided as far as the

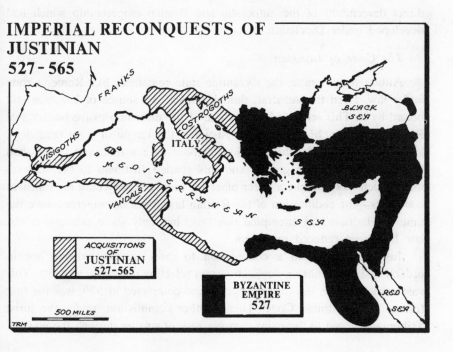

IMPERIAL RECONQUESTS OF JUSTINIAN
527 - 565

FRANKS

OSTROGOTHS

VISIGOTHS

ITALY

BLACK
SEA

MEDITERRANEAN SEA

VANDALS

ACQUISITIONS
OF
JUSTINIAN
527-565

BYZANTINE
EMPIRE
527

RED
SEA

500 MILES

TRM

Peloponnesus. Even Constantinople wàs in danger for a time. In 540 another twenty-year war broke out with Persia. In 562 Justinian bought peace with tribute.

In the interval he had carried on a creditable war on two fronts. Such military vigor and such expansive conquest were worthy of the great days of Rome. Justinian's armies were not a rude and turbulent motley like the barbarian armies: they were orderly forces under military commanders who were the servants, not the masters, of civil authority. The reconquered areas were not turned over to successful generals or semi-independent chieftains; they became units in a "system" of government under the authority of the imperial crown. The Byzantine state, which was clearly differentiated by the time of Justinian, was authoritarian. All aspects of Byzantine civilization, from the most exalted questions of imperial policy to the most absurd and trivial particulars of individual daily life, were the concern of government, which meant, in effect, the emperor. He appointed and relieved all officials; he completely controlled the state's finances and its economic system; he was the sole source of law; he was commander-in-chief of the military establishment; and, not least, he was the head of the eastern church. The emperor's sacred person was clothed in the most awesome sanctity, for the Byzantine government was the direct descendant of the autocratic late Roman emperorship which had developed under Diocletian.

The Code of Justinian

Although autocratic, the Byzantine state remained, like Rome, a state under law. Even the autocrat, though himself the source of law, was still bound by it. This sense of law was one of the most impressive bequests of Rome. However, by the time of Justinian the tangle of legal precedent, legislation, and edict—the tradition of more than a thousand years—had become almost unmanageable, and this goaded Justinian to the achievement which was to make a fairer place for him in history than his transient conquests—the codification of the Roman law. Various emperors since the time of Hadrian had attempted this task, but only some portions of the law had been reduced to system.

Justinian appointed a commission to draw up the existing law in orderly fashion, omitting duplication and selecting among precedents. This vast work, done in less than two years and completed in 529, was the first form of the Justinian Code. Then another commission, under the jurist Tribonian, turned to the more complex task of sorting through the mass of briefs and opinions of Roman lawyers. By 533 the commission had reduced 3,000,000 lines of legal writing to some 150,000 lines, systematically arranged. This work was called the *Digest* (in Greek, *Pandects*). It paralleled the code in outline and was to be its only authoritative interpretation. In the next year the whole code was revised and reissued in its final form. Until the end of Justinian's reign a series of laws were issued to fill in the gaps and complete the construction of a comprehensive legal system. This body of supplementary legislation was called the *Novels*. Finally, the principles of the law were further digested into a student manual, the *Institutes,* for use in the Byzantine schools of law. All together this formed the *Corpus Juris Civilis,* "the body of the civil law," preserved and passed down through the stream of European history.

The immediate result of this great legal achievement was to validate the position of the emperor as autocrat and to spell out in clear, legal terms the elaborate system of Byzantine government and society which formed a massive pyramid with the emperor at its peak.

The Eastern Church

The church, like the law, formed an integral part of the Byzantine state system. From the imperial court and the person of the emperor the line of authority ran to the Patriarch of Constantinople, to the metropolitans and archbishops, to the bishops, and finally down to the village parochial priests and the monks in their cloisters. Although church organization closely paralleled the hierarchical structure of the state, it remained clearly subservient to the state. Yet it remained an exalted institution which worked smoothly with the secular authority. The eastern church never took the separatist direction of the western church, and no independent and authoritative center such as papal Rome was ever allowed to establish itself outside the state's authority. Almost from the moment of the legal recognition of Christianity, the eastern church was under imperial control. The authority that convened the Council of Nicaea was the authority of Constantine and his motives were fully as much secular and political as religious and doctrinal. It was clear that the church was a state church with the emperor as its head. Caesaropapism (the control of religion by the emperor) remained the rule in the eastern church for more than a thousand years.

Both church and state were concerned with the promotion of orthodoxy. All the powers of the state which in Rome had been turned to the destruction of Christianity were in Byzantium turned to its preservation and to the destruction of paganism. There was, to be sure, a brief and abortive pagan revival under the emperor Julian (*361–363*), called "The Apostate," but all subsequent emperors were Christian. In 438 Theodosius II could claim somewhat extravagantly that no pagans remained in the empire. In 529 Justinian closed the philosophic schools of Athens. This religious zeal of the emperors was not a vulgar hypocrisy; the idea of religious self-determination was alien to every tradition from which Byzantine civilization sprang. The Byzantine emperors were the descendants of those late Roman emperors who made the cult of the emperor a test of imperial loyalty. They were, furthermore, the rightful heirs of those priest-kings, the agents of heaven who had ruled in the east for thousands of years. Thus it is not surprising that the church should have been a department of the state.

Nor was the emperor merely concerned with church organization. As Guardian of the Keys, Chief of the Apostles, and Pastor of the Flock, he claimed the same spiritual powers that the popes were beginning to claim in the western church, and was actively concerned with the cure of souls and the delineation of orthodoxy. In his own eyes and in those of his subjects his position as emperor was inseparable from his role as the head of the eastern church.

His subjects also took their theology seriously. Before the end of the fourth century, Gregory of Nyssa complained of Constantinople,

This city is full of mechanics and slaves who are all of them profound theologians and preach in the shops and the streets. If you want a man to change a piece of silver, he tells you in what way the Son differs from the Father; if you ask the price of a loaf of bread, you are told by way of reply that the Son is inferior to the Father; and if you inquire whether the bath is ready, the answer is that the Son was made of nothing.[1]

This theological temper was part of the deep-seated religious tradition of the Ancient Near East, translated into Christian terms and heightened in intensity.

We have already seen how the empire was divided by the Arian controversy of the fourth century. In the following century the passionate debate over the nature of Christ continued. The Nestorians, who held that the two natures of Christ, the human and the divine, were completely separate, were condemned in 432 at the Council of Ephesus. Subsequently the reaction against Nestorianism went so far that it too, claiming that

1. Quoted in James W. Thompson and Edgar N. Johnson, *An Introduction to Medieval Europe, 300–1500* (New York: Norton, 1937), p. 41.

Christ had only a divine nature, became heretical. For this reason it was called the Monophysite heresy (one-nature), and was condemned at Chalcedon in 451. These were but two of the most important in a long string of heresies propounded and defended in the religio-intellectual centers of the eastern empire—at Alexandria, Ephesus, Antioch, and Constantinople itself. In every instance, however, such religious controversy had political overtones. The Monophysite heresy was particularly popular in the Egyptian and Syrian churches, which retained many of the tenets in opposition to the councils. Their heresy became a badge of rebellion against the empire and, despite the most severe governmental measures, this regional tendency was never entirely stamped out. On the contrary, the advance of Islam in these areas was greatly facilitated by such religious and political dissension. Even in Constantinople the Monophysite heresy became identified with popular factionalism opposed to aristocratic preferment and religious orthodoxy. This was at least a partial reason for the so-called Nika riots of 532 that started in the Hippodrome, the lavish public race-course of the city. Fires were set throughout the city and Justinian himself was almost killed before the army arrived to quell the riots.

In spite of the turbulence of Byzantine popular religion the most fundamental manifestation of eastern Christianity was mysticism. We have already seen that the vigorous mystery religions which overwhelmed Roman paganism in the third century flowed into the Mediterranean world from the east. Indeed, Syria, Anatolia, and the hinterland of western Asia had been the home of religious mystery and fanatic ecstasy in one form or another since prehistory. In the early history of Christianity the great mystic and spiritualist heresies grew in the churches of the east and this current flowed directly into Byzantine Christianity, pervading it with a literal belief in miracles, saints, relics, and sanctity. The besetting purpose of the eastern Christian was to achieve the state of grace, the mystic union with God through Christ. For this reason the question of the nature of Christ and his incarnation were crucial to eastern Christianity.

Monasticism was its most revered expression. The Byzantine Empire was dotted with monasteries and their priors and abbots were frequently the most important religious personages in the eastern church; the Patriarch of Constantinople was regularly appointed from the monastic clergy. On the whole, however, the monastery was a refuge in which the practice of holiness was ardently pursued and an atmosphere of tranquillity tended to prevail.

Just as the western church had become the custodian of the Latin tradition, so the eastern church was the principal custodian of Greek learning, and for much the same reason. But it was much less exclusively so because a strong tradition of secular learning continued in the eastern empire. Schools of rhetoric flourished along with professional schools of all sorts. Indeed, the basic form of the classical educational system was retained. Byzantium continued to produce men of learning in virtually every discipline during the centuries of comparative intellectual darkness in the west. Byzantine courtiers and gentlemen ornamented their speech with classical allusions and quotations from the Greek poets. Yet, in all, the intellectual contribution of Byzantium was more one of transmission than of creativity, for novelty and vigor tended to be crushed by the weight of the Greek tradition.

Byzantine Art

It was to Byzantium that Christianity owed its first significant art. Early Christianity had retained the Judaic fear of idolatory and the consequent suspicion of artistic representation. Moreover, Christian worship had required neither special religious buildings nor artistic symbols. Christianity made its peace with art slowly and unevenly; and when it began to do so it was in the eastern empire, where the artistic tradition of Graeco-Roman classicism survived at a time when the barbarian invasions had destroyed it in the west.

The key to Byzantine art was its religious purpose; and the purpose determined the form. Although it used the techniques of the classical tradition, it deliberately rejected much of the classical naturalism; for this new Christian art was dedicated not to the glorification of man but to the glory of God. The chief aim was to evoke the awe and intensify the religious experience of the beholder, to give him the impression of overwhelming majesty. The most characteristic form was the *ikon,* representing a sacred image. As objects of reverence, ikons quickly appeared both in the churches and on the devotional altars in individual homes.

The ikon figures soon became highly stylized and eventually synonymous with Byzantine art. The figure is typically flat and angular; it stands stiffly, face stricken as with some supernatural vision, eyes wide and staring. It is set against a patterned background in which the symbols of its identity mix with the lines and angles of the central figures to give a geometric effect to the whole. These figures embellished the domes of cathedrals, staring down on the worshipers below; they marched in orderly rows above the colonnades of church naves; they decorated the altars of the rich and the humble.

The use of *mosaic*—"painting" by setting chips of stone or colored glass on a binding surface to form a picture—was as typical of Byzantine art as the ikon figure. The stiffness and formality produced by this technique was highly appropriate to the religious function of Byzantine art, and the result was a near-perfect blending of purpose and form. Because it required a rigid surface for support, mosaic was best adapted to the decoration of architecture, indeed, its chief employment was in church architecture. The Byzantine artists raised the mosaic from the floor, where the Romans had used it, to the walls and ceilings of churches and gave it a new and more exalted purpose.

These churches, glowing with mosaic beauty, were themselves the crowning achievement of Byzantine art. They gave to Christianity its first truly distinctive places of worship. In the transitional period of late antiquity, as the Christian cult grew into a world religion, it found need for an architecture. But in this, as in other arts, Christianity had no tradition. Some of the old temples of pagan gods were converted to Christian use, but they were generally unsatisfactory. The Christians turned to the great Roman public buildings that had been designed to accommodate large numbers of people. These were used and then gradually adapted as Churches. The "basilican" churches—so-called from the parent form of the Roman *basilica* or law court—were gradually adapted and widely used in both east and west in the fourth century. In the west they remained the basic form of church architecture for many centuries. But as the east moved toward a peculiar ritual and tone of worship a new architecture evolved.

This was perfectly exemplified in the greatest of all Byzantine structures, Saint Sophia or the Church of Holy Wisdom, built by the emperor Justinian. In art, as in law, war, and administration, Justinian was a pivotal figure. He loved to build almost as much as to conquer or speculate. When large sections of Constantinople were burnt during the Nika riots, Justinian had an unparalleled opportunity for rebuilding. He resolved that the crown of the city should be Saint Sophia. The combination of Justinian's lavish outlay of wealth—320,000 pounds of gold—and the talents of his chief architects, Anthemius of Tralles and Isidore of Miletus, produced one of the truly great buildings in the history of civilization.

In its construction and massiveness Saint Sophia recalls the architecture of the Romans; in its arrangement and design it is reminiscent of the earlier Christian basilica. But in the sum of its effects it transcends both of these earlier traditions and emerges as an architectural masterpiece distinctly Byzantine. Its central feature is an enormous dome 46 feet deep, more than 100 feet across and suspended nearly 180 feet above the ground. The method of construction is called "spherical pendentive," since the support comes from both the piers and the sections of a cutaway dome. It is further strengthened by a smaller series of half-domes thrusting against the central dome. The technique was a refinement of Roman practice and may well have owed something to oriental, especially Persian, influence, but it surpassed any domed structure built before it. Outwardly Saint Sophia is a huge and impressive mountain of masonry; from within it becomes even more impressive. Through the ring of forty windows that surround the central dome light filters down into the cavernous interior, and the enormous dome seems to float suspended upon a crown of light. Every surface was richly decorated in mosaics and gold leaf to pick up each ray of light and reflect it in a myriad of colors to every corner of the building.[2] A hundred heavy chandeliers hung by silver chains as thick as ship hawsers. None of the buttressing domes which break the external unity of the building are obvious from within; they disappear in the vastness of the ceiling, which spans nearly 60,000 square feet of tiled floor.

A contemporary of Justinian, the historian Procopius, thus described the effect of this church upon the beholder:

His mind rises sublime to commune with God, feeling that He cannot be far off, but must especially love to dwell in the place which He has chosen. And this takes place not only when a man sees it for the first time; but it always makes the same impression upon him, as though he had never beheld it before.[3]

This effect was not accidental. The church had been designed to enhance the mystic union with God, which was the chief aim of religious worship. It was designed—with its dependence upon the dome, the circle, the sphere —to reflect the passive adoration characteristic of the Byzantine service. It was designed in its overpowering magnitude to impress upon the wor-

2. When the Moslems took the city of Constantinople in the fifteenth century, the great church of Justinian was turned into a mosque. Practically all the naturalistic representations were painted over. Only recently has the Turkish government permitted scholars to begin a restoration of the interior.

3. Quoted in Lynn Thorndike, The History of Medieval Europe, 3rd ed. (Boston: Houghton Mifflin Co., 1949), p. 101.

shiper the majesty of God and, no less, the majesty of the church, the state, and the emperor.

The impressive remains of fortifications, public buildings, and churches dot the lands of Justinian's western conquest so that some of the best examples of Byzantine art may be found in the cities of Sicily and in Ravenna in northern Italy.

The State as a Machine

As important as any of his achievements was Justinian's reorganization of the military and administrative system of the empire, which in its effect persisted to the end of Byzantine history. Long before Justinian the eastern and the western empires had begun to go their separate ways. As we have seen, one of the critical factors in the collapse of imperial security in the fourth and fifth centuries was the practice of entrusting defense to barbarian troops under barbarian commanders. The ruin of the empire was completed when these commanders began to use their strength against the feeble rule of the Roman state. We have noted the progressive fragmentation of the west under the impact of a succession of such ambitious barbarians. The eastern empire had started along the same ruinous path with Stilicho and others in control, but this tendency was checked in the last half of the fifth century.

The eastern emperors discovered a counterbalance to the German barbarians in the Isaurians and Armenians from the hills of Asia Minor and southwest Asia. These sturdy tribesmen gave the eastern empire its most reliable soldiery; and the emperors managed to instill in them a sense of imperial loyalty and service which was one of the prime factors in the longevity of Byzantium. These men played the same role for the Byzantine Empire that the Italian peasantry had played for Rome in the first expansion of her empire, and the Illyrian peasantry in the time of Diocletian and Constantine. To be sure, German barbarians continued to be used by Byzantium in direct service and as allies, but the core of the Byzantine army was the Asiatic force. It won Justinian's principal victories and maintained an effective imperial defense system for centuries after him.

The ancient Roman military establishment had been progressively modified so that the Byzantine army bore little resemblance to it. Contact with the horse-riding nomads of Asia and with Gothic and Persian cavalry had finally proved that infantry was no longer effective. The Byzantine Empire had to fight highly mobile enemies along unstable frontiers. It could not afford a far-reaching net of garrison forces. Thus the basic force of the Byzantine army was heavy-armed cavalry. The army was a highly disciplined and compact striking force. The routine tasks of defense were left in the hands of local people in frontier areas who served as irregular militia, compelled by the oldest of motives to protect their own lands and thus the empire. Vulnerable links in coastal routes were fortified and held by garrisons, and massive fortifications were built at a few points along the frontier.

Naval defense was in the hands of a small but effective fleet. It was not designed for major aggression but for key defense. Both the army and navy had an awesome weapon in the so-called "Greek fire." This was one of the most closely guarded secrets in history; part of the emperor's coronation oath was never to reveal the process of its manufacture. Greek fire was a highly combustible liquid or semisolid substance which could be thrown in flaming gobbets into troop formations, but especially into the rigging of ships.

Not only did the Byzantines maintain a reliable military establishment, they had a reasoned and consistent military policy. War was not a matter of honor or bravado; it was the means for achieving specific state goals. The empire kept a careful log of its enemies, finding out as much as possible about them. War was tailored to the weakness of the enemy—and with considerable success. Warfare was regularly supplemented by diplomacy and the Byzantine Empire clearly regarded its diplomatic policy as "war by other means." It was a matter of principle to foment trouble among enemies and potential enemies, to enliven their feuds, and to feed their mutual mistrusts. Thus Byzantine subtlety and Byzantine gold were important instruments of survival.

The elaborate diplomatic network of agents, spies, and representatives was part of an even more elaborate system of civil administration which reached literally into the life and home of every citizen of the Byzantine Empire. In this, Byzantium was the heir of the bureaucratic Roman state forged by Diocletian and Constantine. From the imperial court to the most remote customs house, the servants of the state regulated the life of its people and reported on each other. Lines of administration crossed to provide checks and balances. There were territorial divisions, prefectures, provinces, dioceses. There were legal, military, and financial responsibilities that cut across territorial jurisdictions. There were thousands of officials in a hierarchy of grandiose titles which must have taxed even the Byzantine imagination. But in spite of all these precautions, corruption and inefficiency flourished. Justinian tightened the system; he joined rich provinces to poor ones to equalize their taxes. Special officials in each province were appointed to protect the people against their government. Justinian's successors further refined the system and the continued operation of its bureaucracy became an important factor in the order and stability of Byzantine civilization.

The Economic Foundations of Byzantium

The basic reason for the survival and transformation of the eastern empire was the success of its economic system, just as economic failure had been fundamental in the decline of Rome. The Byzantine Empire had certain advantages that the late Roman Empire had lacked, advantages which enabled it to use successfully a controlled economic system not unlike that which had failed Rome. To begin with, Rome had never been able to arrest the unproductive concentration of land in the hands of the powerful and wealthy; Diocletian's economic reforms had failed because he could not stabilize the monetary system; and the later Roman Empire had been unable to stop the disastrous inflation which destroyed the taxpaying capacity of its most productive classes and thus doomed any schemes of wage-, price- and job-fixing. Above all, Rome had been unable to preserve the productive capacity at the center of the empire or to prevent the collapse of commerce on an empire-wide scale.

Byzantium, by contrast, managed to arrest economic decline in a number of ways. Highly significant in this was a sound monetary policy initiated by Constantine; he swept away the debris of Roman coinage and created a new base for imperial exchange, the gold *solidus*. The value of this currency was maintained with remarkable consistency and it was honored throughout the medieval world of the west as well for eight hundred years.

Equally important was the inherent recuperative power of the eastern empire. Long before the existence of the Roman Empire, this area had contained the greatest financial centers and the major industrial plants of the Mediterranean world. Its productive capacity had recovered from the wars of the Hellenistic kings and from the destruction and indemnities of Roman conquerors. It had enjoyed unparalleled prosperity under the Pax Romana. And it weathered, though precariously, the general ruin of the empire in the third century. Thus, the Byzantine Empire inherited a fundamentally sound economy which it was able to revitalize and maintain.

This economy depended upon three closely related sources: agriculture, trade, and industrial production. Byzantine government was more or less continuously watchful of these sources and bent its policies to their preservation.

The great urban centers of the eastern empire demanded food. By the fifth century Constantinople alone had more than a million people. There were in addition dozens of other cities to be fed and the principal trade of the empire was in agricultural produce. This flowed principally from thousands of small family farms which were peasant holdings and the government supervised the maintenance of their productivity. In the first place, every mouthful of food in the empire was carefully calculated. If a peasant left his plot, if it became range land, or if it were gobbled up by a great estate, the food supply of the empire was reduced by that much. Further, the peasant class was the social base upon which the empire rested, its members the fundamental producers and consumers of the empire. It was part of Byzantine state paternalism to see to it that the peasant stayed on the land—his own land and in a particular place. Finally, the peasant was the concern of government because he was essential to the military system and to the system of taxation. Asia Minor was both the breadbasket and the principal recruiting ground of Byzantium. It was the loyalty and hardihood of the peasantry there that freed the empire from the mercenary incubus of barbarian troops. Those who fought for the state were rewarded with plots of land. This relieved the state of the crushing burden of supporting an idle garrison force and at the same time increased the production of food for the empire. The government's "farm policy" also provided cultivated land against which the state could charge its most important duty, the land tax. Thus Byzantium had the basis for a comprehensive, regular, and efficient system of taxation which defrayed the costs of government and was a principal source of its continuing strength. The emperor was able to maintain his army and its companion civil bureaucracy. These in turn enabled him to keep the peace and protect the empire's productivity, police the frontiers, and collect the taxes. It was, in short, a self-perpetuating, well-oiled governmental machine which did not begin to falter seriously until well into the twelfth century—seven hundred years after the "fall" of Rome. The domestic agricultural economy of the empire was constantly bolstered by vigorous trade: the products of the Black Sea flowed out into the Mediterranean; the products of Asia Minor and the Near East flowed across the narrow Bosporus to Europe. Constantinople, from her superb position at the juncture of these routes, became an imperial toll station and the 10 per cent duty on imports and exports was a rich source of revenue.

Many of the goods which poured into the trade funnel of the "Golden City" were the products of the distant Orient. Indeed, the Oriental trade was one of the important sources of Byzantine prosperity. It was for Byzantium, as it had been for Rome, principally a trade in luxuries. The routes were uncertain and the distances immense. One route went far to the north around the end of the Caspian Sea and through the territory of the turbulent nomadic peoples of the *steppe,* to the Black Sea ports. A middle route passed through Persia, but its reliability depended upon the always unstable relations between Persia and Byzantium. The sea routes of the south, through the Persian Gulf and the Red Sea, were also vulnerable at many points. But the trade continued because the demand continued.

At times, the hazards and profits of this trade with the Orient inspired Byzantine domestic industry to supply its own demands. The classic example is silk, which was the principal item of the eastern trade. About the middle of the sixth century the closely guarded secret of its production in distant China was discovered. According to Justinian's historian, Procopius, a party of Nestorian monks from Asia smuggled into Constantinople (allegedly in hollow bamboo staves) some silkworms and mulberry seeds or seedlings. Justinian apparently questioned neither their motives nor their theology but threw his whole support behind the industry that grew from this enterprising larceny. Before the end of his reign silk was a major product of the eastern empire. The silk fabrics which denoted the varied ranks of nobility, which were taken by ambassadors to dazzle foreign kings, and which were sold in the open markets of Constantinople, were the products of an industry owned and operated by the state.

This was true not only of silk; the state owned the bakeries which made bread for the public dole, while work in the bakeries provided a form of public relief. The state also maintained a close rein on the manufacture of military supplies and weapons. The line between state monopoly and private production was, in every instance, difficult to discern, for what the state did not own it controlled. The guild system, which had come from the Romans in a somewhat unsystematic form, was expanded to contain every business and form of industrial production in the Byzantine Empire. And the guilds were controlled by the state. Interest rates were fixed, trade practices dictated, markets set—all by the state. The state further controlled the workers and businessmen themselves; they were as subject to regulation as the peasant farmers.

Yet, with all the restrictions and controls, the social classes of Byzantium were not closed orders. Membership in the upper classes was based upon wealth, enterprise, and fortune, not heredity. The considerable rewards for service to the state could elevate a comparatively humble family to the highest nobility. This social mobility in a controlled society was part of the paradox of Byzantium.

The Empire Survives

Justinian's conquests and reforms had been spectacular—many of them were to be lasting in their influence—but within the generation following his reign a reaction set in. Not only had the empire overextended itself in finance and arms, but the pressure of its many enemies ominously increased. It became clear that the west could not be held. In the destructive wake of the Gothic Wars in Italy a new barbarian people, the Lombards, streamed across the Alps to become the heirs of both Theodoric and Justinian. For another century Ravenna and a narrow foothold of territory around it remained in Byzantine hands to remind the east of its glorious conquest. Spain slipped back into the hands of the Visigoths. In the east the Persian problem flared again into full-scale war that consumed Byzantine energy for more than half a century with only intermittent peace. By 615 the Persians had taken Damascus, sacked Jerusalem and its holy places, and held Chalcedon across the straits from Constantinople. From the north a steadily growing stream of peoples from the steppe poured into the Balkans. These migrations were as significant for central and eastern Europe as were the Germanic migrations for the west. On the edge of eastern Europe were the fierce nomads of Asia. During the time of Justinian and after, one of these peoples, the Avars, spread out along the Danube valley and established a powerful kingdom on the northern flank of Byzantium. At the opening of the seventh century the Byzantine Empire faced a struggle for its very existence.

To the challenge of this crisis rose a new dynasty, that of Heraclius (610–641). Under Heraclius the empire once more assumed the offensive. The Avars pressed toward Constantinople and reached its outer defenses. But the fortifications of the great city held. Heraclius could then turn his attention to the more serious problem of the Persian penetration into the productive heart of the empire. This last phase of the historic contest with Persia was a desperate back-and-forth struggle that lasted nearly twenty years and unsettled the whole Near East. But by 628 Persia was beaten, and a pressure which had been almost constant for centuries was removed. The Avars, meanwhile, mounted their greatest attack upon Constantinople in 626, but again the city withstood them. From this point Avar power declined. Their huge empire, which stretched from the Polish plains to the Gulf of Corinth and from Bavaria to the Russian steppe, melted away as quickly as that of the Huns. The Byzantine Empire was temporarily safe from the barbarian menace to the north. Late in the seventh century, however, the Bulgars streamed into the Balkans, presenting Byzantium with still another threat. But even more significant was the threat building up to the south and east of the empire.

Before the death of Heraclius, the Arabs, a new conquering people armed with a new and invincible religion, had begun their expansion. Damascus fell to them in 635. By the next year all Syria and Mesopotamia were in their hands. In 637 much-conquered Jerusalem was taken again and in 641 the Arab conquest of Egypt was under way. Islam and Byzantium were to face each other in the Near East, across a shifting cultural and political frontier, for the remainder of the Middle Ages. In those centuries Islam grew in power and the Byzantine Empire slowly settled into its long pattern of decline.

It was in contemplating the history of Byzantium from Heraclius to the fall of Constantinople that Gibbon placed his deadly stigma upon the character of the Byzantine Empire: "At every step, as we sink deeper in the decline and fall of the Eastern Empire, the annals of each succeeding reign would impose a more ungrateful and melancholy task. These annals must continue to repeat a tedious and uniform tale of weakness and misery."[4] Fortunately this questionable judgment is the measure neither of the greatness of Gibbon nor the significance of the remaining eight centuries of Byzantine history. It is true that the dynastic history of the imperial house presents a varied picture of murder, torture, insanity, and palace revolution. But it is equally true that the well-founded system of Byzantine civilization continued to function and quite unintentionally to share in the shaping of western civilization. Even in decline, the Byzantine Empire was a bulwark in the east protecting the inchoate civilization of the western world. Constantinople was a center of wealth, trade, and urban sophistication; it was the greatest city of Christendom. It was from this great center that the west was to derive an important impulse to the even-

---

4. *Decline and Fall of the Roman Empire,* XLVIII, 1.

tual revival of urban life and trade in the high Middle Ages. Constantinople and the Byzantine Empire continued to preserve an important part of the classical heritage of western man until the west was ready to accept it once more. Byzantium was, finally, the center from which that same heritage went forth to civilize and Christianize the Slavic world and to draw a significant line of force between the Teutonic-Latin west and the Greek-Byzantine-Slavic east.

THE PROPHET, THE CRESCENT, AND THE SWORD

During the reign of Heraclius I the Byzantine Empire seemed on the verge of a new golden age. By 630 the Persians had been decisively defeated and pushed out of Asia Minor and Syria, and the Holy Cross solemnly returned to Jerusalem. The rich spoils of Persia poured into Constantinople. The Avars, after making a last unsuccessful attempt to storm that fortress city had turned back north, their power and their empire melting away. But at this moment of triumph Byzantium was confronted by a new enemy. In 634 Arab armies captured Palestine and went on to rout both Persian and Byzantine forces, and by the death of Heraclius Syria, Persia, and Egypt were in Arab hands.

The Matrix of Islam

From prehistoric times Arabia, like the Iranian highlands and the steppe of central Asia, had been the cradle of numerous peoples; and, as in those regions, a delicate balance between population and food supply had meant a constant forcing out of those peoples in search of more fertile land along the northwestern borderlands. Those who remained (known as *bedouins*) were molded by the demands of their harsh and precarious environment. They were fierce, hardy nomads who wandered over more than a million square miles of the barren Arabian peninsula driving their sheep and goats from one meager pasture to another, depending on their horses and camels, by whose number they measured their wealth. They lived in strongly patriarchal tribes, whose law was ancient custom; since they were warriors by preference and bandits by necessity, it is not surprising that their custom sanctioned both war and theft. Although the bedouins numbered many tribes whose only political connection was an occasional alliance for purposes of war or defense, they shared a common way of life.

Interior, Saint Sophia. 532—537 A.D. Istanbul.

Above: *Emperor Justinian
and Attendants.* c. 547 A
Original in S. Vitale,
Ravenna.
Left: Miniature from
Muhammad's *Treasury
of Secrets.*

The one fertile part of Arabia is Yemen at the southern tip of the peninsula, marked off from the sandy desert of the interior by a range of mountains, the Hijaz, meaning "barrier." From Yemen, north and west toward Sinai, sheltered by mountains, another way of life—that of the townsman and the merchant—developed. The ancient world had long offered a market for the agricultural products of the southern coast—the fabled "perfumes of Arabia" and such aromatics as myrrh and frankincense. Principal arteries were the coastal route that went overland to Syria and Egypt and the Red Sea route for the more distant trade of the Far East from Japan, China, and the Spice Islands by way of Ceylon and India. This trade had increased in importance as the wars between Persia and the Byzantine Empire made trade precarious over the "middle route" and the savage, nomad kingdoms of the Russian steppe harried the caravan routes north of the Caspian Sea.

As a result a number of trading communities had sprung up along the Arabian shore of the Red Sea, the most important of which was Mecca. It was located, like most trading cities, at a commercial crossroads. North from Mecca ran the main caravan route to Syria and the Mediterranean, so that goods from the Mediterranean world flowed through Mecca bound for the east while eastern goods passed through the same markets on their way to Byzantium, Egypt, and Syria. Meccan merchants had trade agreements with the Byzantine Empire, Persia, and Abyssinia and commerce was more or less constant. It reached its peak twice a year when mile-long caravans transported goods in bulk north and south. As in many trading cities, the merchant aristocracy constituted the ruling class. It was in this hot and dusty town that Mohammed (*c.* A.D. 570–632) was born.

Mohammed and the Founding of Islam

The prophet who was to found one of the world's most widespread religions was the son of a modest Meccan family, most likely involved in commerce but not of the "inner" merchant aristocracy. Little is known of his early life except that he was orphaned and probably raised by his grandfather in very poor circumstances. It is assumed that he engaged in some form of commerce—though again, this is supposition. As in the case of every great religious leader, the figure of Mohammed has been surrounded and obscured by a mass of pious tradition. We know that he married a rich widow, Khadija, some years older than himself. Says the Koran, "did he [God] not find you . . . in want and make you to be free

from want" (93:6-8). Having been thus made "free from want," Mohammed assumed the management of his considerable estate and probably lived
much like any other Meccan merchant.

It was not until he was about forty that Mohammed received the first
of a series of divine revelations upon which he based his religious teachings. There is no record of whether it came as the result of a long spiritual
search or as a sudden insight. At first he confined his teaching to his
family, and then friends. Eventually he began to preach more widely, seeking converts. In contrast to the polytheism practiced by both the bedouins
and townspeople, Mohammed recognized only one God, Allah, and spoke
of himself as God's prophet. And like the Hebrew prophets he condemned
polytheism and idolatry.

His success was modest, but sufficient to alarm the merchant aristocracy of Mecca. In a society in which religion and politics were inseparable,
the revolutionary nature of Mohammed's religious teachings implied the
possibility of political unrest. And political unrest is a threat to commerce.
Moreover, Mecca was not only an economic center but also a religious
shrine for the various gods of the desert people who came to trade there.
In the shrine called the Kaaba were housed the sacred stones representing
the primitive gods of the Arabic pantheon, and this, as well as other
shrines, attracted pilgrims, and hence, business to Mecca. It is not surprising then that public opinion mobilized against this dangerous radical
who, by his general teaching and his attack on idolatry, threatened both the
prosperity and religious status of his city.

As the persecution against Mohammed mounted, he received an op-
portune invitation to the city of Medina, about three hundred miles to the
north of Mecca. Politically more primitive than Mecca, Medina lacked
a central government to command the loyalty of its population and was
beset by continual strife among numerous clans and families pushing their
own interests. In addition, there was a deep cleavage between the native
Arabs and a large Jewish settlement. Having heard of Mohammed and his
teaching from the traveling caravans, representatives of Medina decided
to invite him to come and bring peace and order to their city. To the Jews
his religious teaching, with its emphasis on monotheism, seemed not unlike
their own; to the Arabs he appeared as one marked by supernatural power.
And so Mohammed "fled" from Mecca to Medina.

This flight, *hegira,* marks the formal beginning of the scoio-politico-
religious system of Mohammedanism. The year was 622, the first date in
the history of the new religion. In Medina, Mohammed became the political

and religious head of a theocratic community. Like most successful religious leaders he was a skillful administrator and politically adept. To the Jews of Medina he extended a temporary toleration rare in their history. He drew together the native population and the converts who had followed him from Mecca and overcame the hostility to "outsiders" characteristic of Arab parochialism. The tie that bound Mohammed to his people and his people to each other was religious. He was both ruler and prophet under the awesome sanction of God. The city of Medina was Islam—the community of believers. In 622 this community was a single city; within a century it was a significant part of the world.

The fame of Mohammed and his city spread. The desert tribes drifted toward Medina and Mohammed found himself the head of a growing political movement. He turned its force against Mecca. His converts preyed upon the fat commerce of that city. Raids and banditry grew into war. In 628 Mohammed negotiated a ten-year truce on equal terms with Mecca. Two years later he was its master and made it the permanent center of Mohammedanism and its ancient Kaaba—cleansed of idolatry—his central shrine. Mohammed's success made him the most formidable political force in Arabia. The distant bedouin tribes sent delegations to Mecca to put themselves under his authority. Their political submission was, at the same time, a religious act. Shortly after his Meccan triumph Mohammed died. He had formed the scattered polyglot of Arab tribes into an Arab nation and armed it with a new and powerful religion.

The Religion of Mohammed

Mohammedanism was the product of the series of revelations beginning with the first Meccan revelation of 610 and continuing throughout Mohammed's life. He passed these revelations on to his followers, many of whom knew them by heart. Some of the revelations were dictated and written down. But at the death of the prophet there was no "gospel," no one authentic and complete text. In the following generation Mohammed's people and their faith exploded into conquests which carried them far beyond Arabia. A body of essential doctrine became increasingly necessary and Mohammed's successors commanded that the revelations be collected ". . . from palm branches and tablets of stone and the hearts of men." This was done by the chief secretary of the prophet, and by 651 the collection was completed. Islam had its sacred scripture, called the *Koran,* "the Reading."

It differs from the scripture of the Hebrews or the Christians in that it was neither the work of many hands nor of many centuries; but of one man. Like the Hebrew and Christian scriptures, however, the Koran claimed divine inspiration for its every word. Like them also it touched on many things. As Mohammed forged Islam he was the head of a government as well as a religious leader. He drew his authority for decisions about war, justice, administration from the same source as his decisions about sin, prayer, or worship. The Koran thus comprises not only the highly poetic transcendent but the highly prosaic mundane as well. Yet, while it may be regarded as a political constitution and an economic gospel, the Koran is primarily a religious document, in the most exalted sense of that term, and one, furthermore, of great profundity and enormous historical significance. Since no one knew in what order of time the revelations had come, and since no one could presume to pass judgments of value upon the word of God, the Koran was arranged in neither a historical nor a topical order, but by length, the 114 suras, or verses, following each other from the longest to the shortest. All were equally the word of God and all were equally binding upon the true believer. Through the centuries following its compilation the Koran was kept scrupulously unaltered. A considerable body of commentary grew up about it and a theology sprouted from it, but the Koran itself remained the core of Mohammed's religion. "This day I have perfected for you your religion and completed My favour on you, and chosen for you Islam as a religion" (5:3).

Despite his claims of divine inspiration, Mohammed's teaching clearly owed much to outside influences, especially to Judaism and Christianity. Both religions had existed for centuries in the lands bordering Arabia. Persecution, zeal, opportunity, commerce, and a hundred other motives had brought both Christians and Jews to every center in Arabia and their ideas were a part of Mohammed's intellectual environment. It is impossible to say precisely when or where, or through what specific contacts, if any, Mohammed came to know these older religions. Probably the Christian influence stemmed from the various heretical doctrines which were forced out of the main centers of orthodoxy in the eastern empire, notably Nestorianism. Mohammed accepted the divine inspiration of Christ but not his divinity. He accepted the Christian millennial teaching and his fervent call to repentance is based upon a belief in the last judgment. He respected the holy book of the Christians as a true revelation, if only a partial one and inferior to his own. But to the Jews and their beliefs Mohammed owed his principal debt. Indeed, the leading idea of Islam

—that there is but one god—is probably Judaic. Certainly Mohammed's Allah is very like the God of the Old Testament, in his wrath and sternness as well as in his compassion for his chosen people. As Mohammed accepted the divine inspiration of Christ, he accepted the patriarchs and prophets of the Old Testament. Adam, Noah, Moses, as well as Christ, had received the revelation of God; but again only partially and imperfectly. Mohammed was the last of the prophets, the fulfillment of God's will for man. The others had prepared the way for him. Mohammed regarded both Christians and Jews as "people of the book," near in sanctity to Islam. It was only for their stubborn refusal to accept the completion of their religion in Islam that they came to be persecuted.

It does not diminish the greatness of Mohammed that his religion was eclectic. Most products of civilization are. While he borrowed substantially from other religions he put his own stamp upon them, changing and molding them until they achieved a form essentially new and vitally different.

The central conviction of Islam is monotheism. "Allah! There is no God save Him, the living, the eternal." He is the creator and preserver of the universe. He is a god of power, like the Jahweh who spoke to Job out of the whirlwind. But like the God of the prophets, Allah is a god of mercy. In the infinity of God there is no thought or deed unknown to Him; and to know is to will, in the mind of God. This resolute consistency led Mohammed to one of the most significant beliefs of Islam, predestination and its consequent fatalism. The devout believer was convinced that God knew and willed every breath and every moment of his life. This conviction made him reckless in battle and patient in adversity. It cloaked the absurdities of this imperfect world in the inscrutable will of God. "Allah is He besides whom there is no god, the Everliving, the Self-subsisting by whom all subsist; slumber does not overtake Him nor sleep; whatever is in the heavens and whatever is in the earth is His; who is he that can intercede with Him but by His permission? He knows what is before them and what is behind them. . . . He is the Most High, the Great" (2:255).

In Islam, as in Christianity and Judaism, theology and ethic are closely bound together; in spite of predestinarian inconsistency. Man's love of God and his obedience to Him are the requisites of salvation. And salvation is the end and purpose of human life. At some time known only to God, the world will end in fire and destruction; and the dead of all time will rise from their graves to face heavenly judgment for their earthly lives. A hell of livid flame and excruiating torture awaits the wicked. For the virtuous, the reward of their virtue is a heaven of sensual delights—the blessings of wine without its customary penalties, the company of beautiful women (Islam is a masculine revelation), and the blessed rejuvenation of appetite.

Salvation and damnation were both contingent upon behavior. Mohammed created for his faithful the most simple and realistic code of behavior ever sanctioned by a great religion and he placed behavior in the forefront of his doctrine. There are "five pillars of faith": belief in God, prayer, alms, fasting, pilgrimage. God is one, the curator of the universe, and his relationship to man is revealed through his prophet Mohammed and the book of his prophecy. The Mohammedan prays five times daily at appointed hours, with ritual exactness. He prepares for prayer by washing, usually more ritualistic than hygienic, and prostrates himself toward Mecca. He thus reminds himself of man's duty to adore God. The Mohammedan is obliged to be as merciful to his fellow men as his God is to him and he incurs, with his belief, the duty of giving material aid to the unfortunate. Mohammed echoed St. Paul's belief in the perfection of charity and every Moslem nation swarms with beggars so that no opportunity will be denied the rich to gain favor in the eyes of heaven. Fasting was enjoined generally but a special period of fast was set aside—the Month of Ramadan. This was a pre-Islamic time of fasting, celebrated especially at Mecca. Both the month and the practice were retained by Mohammed.[5] Finally, in order that men might profit from the residual holiness of the prophet, his city of Mecca became the goal of Moslem pilgrimage and each believer hoped to make the journey at least once in his life. As Islam became a world religion this duty became for most people impossible and, for many, an incredible expense and hardship. Yet they continue to come by the millions each year to drink the brackish water of the holy well, to walk in the steps of the prophet, and to pass seven times around the shrine of the Kaaba.

Seldom have men been so zealous in the performance of the letter of religious law as are the people of Islam. Around the five cardinal principles of faith there are a multitude of injunctions, beliefs, practices, which give Mohammedanism its characteristic shape. It is a man's religion for a man's

5. The apparent severity of this long fast was moderated by the fact that it pertained only to the hours of daylight. During the twenty-nine days of Ramadan the business of day and night was virtually reversed, with stores and places of entertainment open from dusk till dawn. The last ten days of the fast, however, were customarily observed with more rigor.

society. Polygamy is sanctioned. Women are secluded even in worship. But the status of women has nothing to do with asceticism. Islam holds no brief for celibacy and encourages even as it controls the sexual impulse. The Moslem is expected to marry, to beget children, and he is not discouraged from participation in the world. Wealth is not normally equated with sin nor pusillanimity with virtue. The believer is, by and large, the judge of his own orthodoxy. Islam is an open religion. It has no priesthood, no impenetrable mysteries, no sacraments.

The Moslem Conquests

At the death of Mohammed, Islam had united Arabia into a religious state. The new faith had a vitalizing effect upon its adherents and it combined with a host of more wordly energies to make the Arabs a telling force in history. They were a "have not" people with a pardonable urge to change that status. It was the achievement of Mohammed to give them a group identity their jealous tribes had never been able to achieve; to arm them with a faith in which it was possible to gain heaven through death or riches through conquest; and to make them aware of their strength and unity.

Yet everything was threatened by the death of the prophet. His unique status could not be inherited, even had there been a son to succeed him. The only tradition of succession was that of tribal election, but Mohammed's religious state had already so far surpassed the tribe that the tradition was no longer applicable. A handful of his closest associates seized the initiative. One of them, Abu Bakr, an early Meccan convert and a respected elder, was imposed upon Islam with the title of Caliph, or successor of the prophet and head of the state. But this bold stroke was not universally accepted and Islam began to falter. The tribes close to Mecca and Medina remained loyal. The more distant ones broke away and the wars of reconquest began. Within a year Arabia had been won again more strongly than before and the victorious armies of the caliph had spilled over into the northern and western borderlands.

The new head of Islam grew powerful, feeding upon war and loot. The hardihood of the desert Arabs proved itself in battle after battle. From the armies sprang capable generals. To Arab strength was added the weakness of their enemies. The long wars between the Persian and the Byzantine empires had exhausted them both. The subject peoples on the fringes of either empire had suffered from and paid for the interminable wars. In Syria-Palestine Byzantine military occupation, heavy taxation, and the effect of the Monophysite heresy in bolstering Syrian "nationalism" prepared the way for Mohammedan conquest. Several minor Byzantine forces were defeated by the Arabs. In 636 a full-scale army was crushed and all Syria fell into Arab hands. A similar penetration had been going on in Mesopotamia, the restless southern border of Persia. In 637 a decisive battle was won by Arab forces on this "eastern front," and the key Persian city of Ctesiphon was taken. The forces of Islam were solidly in possession of the Fertile Crescent, the control point of near eastern economy and a strategic position for the conquest of both east and west.

Egypt proved as vulnerable as Syria, and for the same reasons. By the year 641 all of Egypt except Alexandria had been won by Arab armies and the Egyptians welcomed them as liberators. Within another year Alexandria had fallen. At the same time the Arab armies of the east were pushing their way into the heart of the old Persian Empire and by 650 they held much of the Iranian plateau.

With the spectacular success of Arab expansion the new empire faced a series of serious internal problems. The conquests had been so rapid that only the most perfunctory system of administration could be devised. By and large, Persian and Byzantine practices were retained by the Arabs. The new masters confiscated state lands and parceled them out as rewards to their faithful soldiery. Thus, the Arabs formed a military aristocracy in their conquered lands. They generally did not interfere with established civil administration and were content to extend toleration to the religions of the conquered. A simple tax system was imposed upon the subject peoples but taxes were still not as burdensome as those of either the Persians or the Byzantines. Arab toleration of religion brought to many peoples a spiritual and intellectual freedom unknown for centuries. The new regime flourished.

But it had its weaknesses. The Arab assumption that Islam was peculiarly their religion made for a deep cleavage between conqueror and conquered. Moreover, under the pressure of conquest, the Arabs began to have serious differences among themselves, which pushed them rapidly toward civil war. The two strongest forces of dissension were the inherent separatism of the nomad Arab group and the dynastic ambition of the powerful generals and governors who had led the conquest. A strong caliphate was needed to restore unity, but the caliphs who followed Abu Bakr were unable to maintain control of their explosive empire or to restrain the factionalism which made and unmade them with murderous regularity. Finally, in 661, Mo'awiya the governor of Syria, proved strong and shrewd enough to impose himself upon all of Islam. Mo'awiya founded the Omayyad dynasty, named for the Meccan tribe to which he belonged. The new dynasty based its success upon another surge of expansion. Arab forces penetrated Anatolia to the Black Sea and took Chalcedon across the straits from Constantinople. Having reached the coast in Syria and North Africa the desert Arabs became seafarers, and with momentous success. An Arab fleet, cooperating with the land forces in Asia Minor, blockaded and besieged Constantinople itself. The city held but the Arabs extracted a favorable truce in 678. At the same time an Arab army swept from Egypt across North Africa, scattering the remnants of Byzantine authority. In the east other Arab armies pushed on to the limits of Alexander's empire on the Indus River and beyond to the north and east. The wealth and power derived from these conquests enabled the Omayyads to move in the direction of a traditional monarchy based upon Persian and Byzantine models. But they did not succeed in completing the pattern. They established the practice of dynastic succession but failed to establish the principle; and succession through the following century was as often by assassination as by bequest.

The vast conquests once again spawned separatist movements under disaffected generals and rebel leaders. Often these political or economic revolts were joined with bizarre religious movements and Islam, like Christianity, was torn by schism. Yet its internal divisions did not diminish Islam's vitality, and expansion continued. In the east, Arab forces may have reached China and certainly established themselves on the high plateau of central Asia and to the south in the Indian Punjab.

Mohammedan pressure against the Byzantine Empire mounted, by land and sea. In 717–718 the capital was again besieged and Asia Minor invaded. Byzantium was saved only by one of those periodic political miracles which mark her history. The critical struggle with Islam brought forward the great soldier-emperor Leo III (*717–741*), "the Isaurian," who saved his state from Islam as Heraclius a century before had saved it from the Persians. The Moslem siege was broken and Asia Minor recovered to the Taurus mountains. The Byzantine Empire stood once more as the eastern bastion of Christianity. Through the Byzantine wars Christianity and Islam were committed to an enmity which was to persist for centuries and finally involve the west in the crusades.

As if to compensate for the failure against Byzantium, Islam pushed on to the Atlantic coast of North Africa. Then, with arrogant disregard for continental divisions, an ex-slave began the conquest of Spain. His name is still preserved in Gibraltar, Gebel al- Tariq, "the mountain of Tariq." Under Tariq and others the conquest of Spain was as rapid and decisive as Moslem conquests at the other end of the world. The weak and decadent Visigothic kingdom offered scant resistance. The remnants of Spanish Christendom were lodged in the impenetrable and unprofitable mountains of the north and west of the peninsula; and the force of Moslem expansion bypassed them to gain the Pyrenees; then down the slopes and passes into southern Gaul. Mohammedan armies surged north to the vicinity of the Loire River. There they were finally defeated in 732 by a force of Franks under Charles Martel near Poitiers (called the Battle of Tours by a time-honored error). The western limit of Islam had been set and even the men who participated in that momentous battle could have had only the vaguest notion of its significance. The Moslems withdrew behind the Pyrenees to continue their occupation of Spain, or parts of it, for the next seven and a half centuries.

The Abbasid Caliphate and the Height of Moslem Power

Within a generation after Tours the tangled internal problems of the Arab empire destroyed the last of the Omayyad caliphs. This dynasty was replaced in 750 by another, the Abbasid, claiming doubtful descent from Abbas, the uncle of Mohammed. The prophet had given his people a religion; the Omayyads had given them a world empire. The Abbasids were to give them a civilization and a golden age. The new dynasty represented a fundamental change of direction in the world of Islam. The wars of conquest had ended. The Arab warrior aristocracy that had been the driving force of conquest was unequal to the tasks of peace and unable to exploit indefinitely the peoples of higher and older cultures whom they had conquered. The movement behind the Abbasid caliphate was cloaked in religious terms and obscured by factional slogans, but its substance was the social and political protest of the non-Arab people of an Arab-subject empire. This protest found expression in the towns and cities, particularly in the central and eastern portions of the empire, in those sections which for centuries had been the center of Persian influence.

It is significant of these forces that Mansur (754–775), the second Abbasid caliph and real founder of Abbasid power, established his capital at the new city of Baghdad on the Tigris River, in the very heart of the old Persian Empire. The choice of site was governed by economic rather than military or political considerations. It was in the traditionally river-rich land of Mesopotamia; and it was in a strategic position to control the

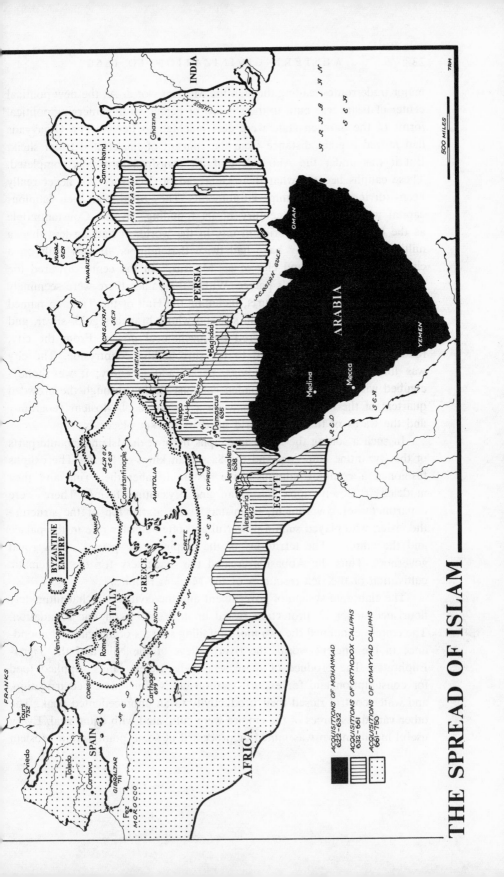

THE SPREAD OF ISLAM

ACQUISITIONS OF MOHAMMAD
622-632

ACQUISITIONS OF ORTHODOX CALIPHS
632-661

ACQUISITIONS OF OMAYYAD CALIPHS
661-750

major trade routes leading through the Moslem world. As the new political center of Islam was built in the shadow of Persia, so the emerging political forms of the Saracen state were also indebted to Persia. The Omayyads had moved a great distance from the concept of the elected tribal sheik. But it was under the Abbasids that the transformation was completed. These caliphs became what their Omayyad predecessors had never really been—divine, absolute, imperial autocrats. They ruled from their fabulous capital which, within a century of its founding, rivaled Constantinople as the largest and most brilliant city in the world. It had no less than a million people and may have had twice that number. It was built on a circular plan, the "round city of al- Mansur." In the center towered the green dome of the caliph's palace. Within the palace there were seemingly endless rooms, corridors, courts, including the Hall of the Tree, so named for a gold and silver tree, of full size, on whose branches gold, silver, and jeweled birds sang and twittered by mechanical power. From the city, roads and waterways radiated to the surrounding countryside. The city was filled with glittering buildings, parks, and greenery; it was honey-combed with narrow alleys, shaded canyons cutting through the crowded quarters of the city. Its quarters were a catalogue of Moslem geography and the wares of the entire world filled its market places.

In such a setting the Abbasid caliphs became the Islamic counterparts of the Byzantine emperors and the Sassanian kings of Persia. The caliphs fashioned a complex administrative system to abet their rule and they modeled it closely upon Sassanian and Byzantine forms. There were departments of government, "ministers," and at the top of the structure the vizier, who played such a powerful and often sinister role in the palace and the empire. The territories of the empire were placed under royal governors. Thus the Abbasids created the machinery for the systematic cultivation of the rich resources of the Moslem Empire.

The elaborate system of government and the civilization that ultimately flourished under its protection rested upon a solid economic foundation. The empire contained the two most unfailing sources of agricultural abundance in the ancient world, the river valleys of the Nile and the Tigris-Euphrates. The produce of these seemingly tireless lands supplied food for consumption and for export. Careful cultivation, increased irrigation, and water control raised their productivity to an unprecedented peak. The other varied resources of the empire were cultivated with equal zeal. Every useful metal known was mined or processed at some point within Moslem lands. Textiles of every sort were produced in such quantities as to become a primary industry. The rich resources of the Moslem world became the burden of an extensive trade that crossed the empire from Spain to Persia, then on to the east to India and China. The orderly and systematic government which the Abbasids brought to the empire greatly facilitated this profitable commerce. Spices, drugs, silk, precious metals and jewels, paper, exotic animals, felt, slaves, and a thousand other commodities flowed along the routes of trade. The empire developed a stable coinage of its own to rival Persian and Byzantine models. Wealth was concentrated in the key commercial cities along the routes of trade. These became important centers of exchange and their merchants became the economic and then the social elite of Islam. The proud, old Arab aristocracy merged with the merchant oligarchy of non-Arab origin. The distinctions of conqueror and conquered tended to disappear and be replaced by a broad sense of community based upon the faith of Islam and the Arabic language. Many unconverted peoples remained under Abbasid authority. They were taxed and tolerated and they remained unconverted largely because they chose to. But, by and large, Islam was becoming the universal religion of all who lived in the Moslem Empire.

Abbasid power reached its height in the reign of Harun al-Raschid (*786–809*), the brilliance of whose court is reflected in the rich tapestry of the *Thousand and One Nights.* Yet even before the end of Harun's reign cracks began to appear in the unity of his empire. The power of the Abbasids was concentrated in the Near East, but away from Baghdad their power was weaker. Western North Africa and Spain had tended to independence for a decade before Harun and local dynasties had set themselves up there. In the generation after Harun this tendency to local and regional independence continued and, as usual, every local revolution had its own religious heresy. In little more than a century Egypt was the center of a new and powerful absolutist dynasty. By the middle of the tenth century a subgroup of the Turks, called the Seljuks, were a dangerous force in eastern Islam. Within a century these tough Asiatic nomads had swept away the scattering of petty dynasties and by the end of the eleventh century had taken Baghdad. The political unity of the Moslem world was broken but its economic and cultural unity remained.

In time nearly every significant port city and maritime district of the Mediterranean fell into the hands of Moslems of one factional persuasion or another: Crete was a Moslem pirate den from 826 to 961 and the base of lucrative operations against the Byzantine Empire; before the middle of the seventh century Cyprus was a Moslem stronghold; Moslem forces from North Africa took rich and strategic Sicily from Byzantium in the course of the ninth century; even in Italy, Bari and Taranto were Moslem-held; Naples and Rome were threatened, besieged, and ransomed. The Mediterranean became the western seaway of Moslem international commerce.

Baghdad remained a fabulous city and titular capital of the Moslem world. But it was rivaled by Damascus in Syria, Cairo in Egypt, and Cordova in Spain. Each was a notable economic center from which a net of prosperity spread out. Each was the center also of a comparably rich cultural life that flourished under the protection and patronage of the great and wealthy and with the blessing of government. The political division following the height of Abbasid power was a crucial factor in allowing regional styles of culture to develop within Islam. At the extremes of the Saracen world Spain created its own rich medieval culture and in Persia there was an equally important revival of the old, sophisticated, Persian culture in new Moslem dress. Indeed, some of the most enduring of Islamic writing, especially poetry, is written not in Arabic but in Persian.

The Arabic Culture

In the age of conquest the cultural baggage of Islam consisted almost entirely of its religion and its religion almost entirely of one book. There is a story that, after the fall of Alexandria, the Caliph Omar ordered its library destroyed, saying, "If these writings of the Greeks agree with the word of God, they are useless, and need not be preserved; if they disagree they are pernicious, and should be destroyed." The story is almost certainly false. The library had been damaged by Roman siege in the time of Caesar and virtually destroyed by Christian fanaticism in the fourth century. Yet the statement attributed to the conquering caliph was typical of the attitude of the Arab military aristocracy. But it was moderated at each step in the conquest. The religion of Islam and the Arabic language were, as we have seen, rapidly extended to the other peoples of the Arab empire. The religion of Islam was not merely a single facet of life. It was a culture pattern touching society, government, and every aspect of Moslem life. To a certain extent Arabic became Islam's international language because of its connection with religion. It was the language in which God had spoken to the prophet, and it was soon established that the Koran was never to be translated. Thus, as Islam spread, Arabic followed and became the tongue of millions of non-Arab converts. It proved to be not only a canonical language but one possessing the potentialities of a great literary language as well.

In the Abbasid era Arabic literature was highly developed in a dozen forms of poetry and prose. The Arabic language had absorbed the influences and the literary forms of older civilizations. The rich literature of Islam is almost closed to western eyes and minds because of the barrier of translation. We catch only an occasional glimpse into Islamic fable in the *Thousand and One Nights;* of epic in Matthew Arnold's *Sohrab and Rustam,* based on Arabic sources; of lyric epigram in the *Rubáiyát,* the casual poetry of Omar Khayyám, a great Persian mathematician of the eleventh and twelfth centuries. While we are richer by such glimpses they give us no real idea of the magnitude and scope of Islamic literature. For example, the *Book of Songs,* a collection of Arabic poetry made in the tenth century, runs to twenty substantial volumes. Literature, especially poetry, was the most honored form of Moslem intellectual activity. Royal courts were awed into tears by the concentrated beauty and wisdom of a single, polished verse. Every court maintained its retinue of poets; some, we are told, numbered into the hundreds. Caliphs, sultans, and emirs paid fantastic sums to poets who pleased them. Nor was there a lack of popular response: whole villages would squat in the dust to hear the wandering poet chant an interminable epic. All Arabic literature of whatever form was deeply responsive to poetry; even theology and law were permeated by poetic expression.

Poetry was connected with scholarship through the complex precision of its formal structure and the metaphysical quality of much of its expression. Thus, the poet was as often as not a man of learning. Islamic scholarship and learning are as old as Islam itself. Every Moslem had to know the Koran, and as a result it became the staple of education. The first words of a child were, "There is no God but Allah and Mohammed is His prophet." From this beginning the goal was to memorize the entire Koran, and special deference was paid to those young scholars who accomplished this feat. The customary ancillary disciplines of grammar, logic, and mathematics were taught under the impressive shadow of the Koran.

Every mosque became a school, and a university. The complexity, contradictions, and difficulty of the Koran gave a province to sacred scholarship. Schools and libraries flourished. The universality of Arabic made it possible for scholars to work and travel anywhere: and everywhere they were welcome. The state encouraged and subsidized them; the young sought their instruction; society honored them.

As Islam conquered a world, Islamic scholarship was subjected to a variety of influences—Byzantine legalism and administration; Hebrew, Christian, Aramaic, and Zoroastrian theology, mysticism, revelation; and, most important of all, the powerful general influence of Hellenism. In Syria, Egypt, and the Near East the Greek tradition continued to flourish, passed down through many hands since Alexander and the Hellenistic monarchs. It was through the Byzantine Christians and heretics, and the Hellenized Jews of these areas, that Hellenism came to Islam. Greek works were translated and widely disseminated. Strange to say, the imaginative literature of the Greeks—their poetry, drama, and romance—had only the slightest effect upon Islam; perhaps because it already possessed such a rich literature of its own. But Greek science and philosophy made a tremendous impact. Editions of Euclid, Galen, Hippocrates, Dioscorides, and Ptolemy, parts of Plato and Aristotle, and many other Greek philosophic and scientific works were translated and studied at various places in Islam. To this rich inheritance the Moslems added other influences, notably Hindu science and mathematics. The ancient and substantial Indian works on astronomy were translated, and the "Arabic" numerals and the concept of zero, among other things, were introduced into Moslem science in this way. The background of Moslem science and philosophy was eclectic, but its vitality was native, and its products distinctly Moslem.

By the ninth century Moslem mathematics included the principles of advanced algebra (itself an Arabic term), trigonometry, and geometry. There were major works of astronomy, scientific geography, and chronology. From halting beginnings in other cultures Moslem scholars virtually created the science of chemistry. Like their fellow-workers in the medieval west, Moslem chemists were often alchemists first, preoccupied with the search for the "philosopher's stone." But in their fruitless search they developed an important procedure and methodology, the idea of careful and precise experimental notes on which the "scientific method" is based. Their most important work, however, was in the identification and preparation of drugs and their most important connection, consequently, was with the science of medicine.

It was in the theory and practice of medicine that Moslem science achieved its greatest distinction. Moslem medicine was built upon the already distinguished achievements of Greece and India. A lively trade in drugs and medicines had poured through Arabia long before Islam. With the increase of Moslem wealth and the dictates of Moslem charity medicine flourished. There were numerous medical schools and every city had its hospitals which provided physicians and students with their living texts in the diseased and the suffering. Moslem medicine was more "scientific," reasonable, and humane than western medicine would be for more than a thousand years. It was solidly based upon observation, experimentation, and records. It relied more heavily on drugs, medicines, hygiene, diagnosis, and treatment than upon surgery. This was probably because of religious prohibitions, but the sick reaped the benefits and were spared the agonies of unanesthetized butchery. Islam's greatest science produced a long list of distinguished physicians and medical scientists. The two most eminent were Muhammed al-Rāzi (*c.* 844–926) and Abu ibn-Sina (980–1037). These men are best known by their Latinized names, Rhazes and Avicenna. Their medical works found their way into Latin translations and were undisputed authorities in European medicine until the eve of modern times.

Moslem philosophy was almost as impressive as Moslem medicine; its debt to Hellenism much greater. In the earlier, more puritanical days of Islam there was little place for speculation. The Koran was enough. But skepticism and curiosity came with wealth and conquest and followed the contact with higher cultures. Nevertheless, it was the Koran and its religious thought which provided the starting points for Moslem philosophy, when the semireligious and mystical thought of late Hellenism was brought to bear upon this central core of Mohammedanism. Islamic scholars began to subject the Koran to interpretation, to attempt to bring it into conformity with the conclusions of Greek thought. This attempt spawned a great variety of "heresies" and contributed its arguments to others. In time philosophy even called the Koran itself into question. But Moslem philosophy continued to grow. It came to deal with politics, logic, natural philosophy and natural science, and finally with metaphysics. In all these areas the influence of Aristotle was paramount.

Moslem philosophy had a long life and its greatest philosopher and Aristotelian did not appear until the twelfth century. He was Muhammed ibn-Rushd (1126–1198), known in western philosophy as Averroës. In the best philosophic tradition he was a practical and many-faceted expert; jurist, physician, counsellor, theologian, philosopher. He was the ornament of Moslem Spain and his writings, on a staggering list of subjects, are a philosophic and scientific library. In a sense, he was the Aquinas of Islam in that he attempted, in his most important works, to superimpose the religious tradition of Islam on the rationalist tradition of Aristotle. He followed Aristotle in holding that God is mind and the source of energy in an otherwise mechanistic world and borrowed a Neoplatonic theory of divine emanation falsely attributed to Aristotle. In his concept of the nature of man he followed Aristole's ideas of active and passive elements, potency and actuality. He doubted personal immortality. Where possible, he reconciled philosophy and religion; where this was not possible, he chose philosophy. He was manifestly guilty of the charge so often to be made against western medieval scholars that they preferred Aristotle to orthodoxy. Because of his questionable position on religion the greatest of Moslem philosophers has been virtually ignored by his own people and his main influence was in the west.

A rich and cultured society cannot live without art. When the Arabs swept out of the desert they had no plastic arts except handicraft and their religion was as stern as Judaism in prohibiting idolatry. What art they needed they borrowed and their principal borrowing was in architecture. At first they built forts or places of worship in the towns they founded at strategic points along their routes of conquest. They either had them built by local artists or clumsily adopted local styles. Yet, obvious as these borrowings from Byzantine, Syrian, Persian, or Mesopotamian forms were, the rudiments of a purely Islamic art began to develop even in this early period. As the empire grew, the process of artistic borrowing and assimilation continued. India and even China made their contributions. These varied artistic forms and styles moved as freely through the vast Moslem Empire as did trade. Artists and patrons traveled and returned home with impressions of beauty which they then adapted for themselves. Seldom has art been so fluid over so great a territory. By the time of Harun al-Raschid Islamic architecture had achieved a rich and distinctive style.

Since Islam was a religious community it lavished great care upon the conception and decoration of its mosques. In Islam, as in the medieval west, the sacred building was the center of art. While the style of mosque architecture was controlled by the cooperation of borrowed artistic elements, its form was controlled by religious function. The typical mosque has a court with a basin and fountain for washing before prayers or service. The court is surrounded by a gallery or sheltered portico for study and contemplation. The interior is attached to the side of the court facing Mecca and is a rectangle. To these essentials Moslem art added details; a Byzantine dome, Mesopotamian glazed brick, Persian columns and horseshoe and pointed arches. The outside of the mosque is frequently plain and undistinguished except for its minarets, the corner spires from which the call to prayer is droned at the canonical hours. But inside every surface flames with the color from tile, mosaic, inlay, colored glass, variegated stone, and intricate rug designs. Everything was gracefully abstract to avoid the charge of idolatry. This nonobjective patterning carried over into every other art form; pottery, book illumination, metal chasing, and above all the textiles and carpets which were the staple luxuries of the Moslem world. Eventually, just as philosophy challenged religion, art broke away from abstraction. But even the representational art of mature Islam was dominated by the conventional forms and surface decoration of the earlier style.

Islam and the West

Islamic civilization reached across the barrier of religious and political differences to affect the development of the Christian west. Like the Byzantine, the Saracen civilization was vastly superior to the early medieval civilization of western Europe. But while Byzantium was separated from the west by a hostile sea and the Slavic Balkans, the Islamic Empire abutted Christian lands all through the western Mediterranean. Until the high Middle Ages, Moorish Spain poured its influences across the Pyrenees to contribute to the civilization of southern France. The Moslem holdings in Sicily and southern Italy became centers of cultural exchange. Even after the Norman conquest of these areas in the eleventh century, Islamic influence remained strong and was bequeathed to the German kings and emperors of the twelfth and thirteenth centuries.

It was from the hands of Moslem translators and scholars that the west received the texts of Aristotle and the Moslemized Aristotelianism which were to form the basis of the twelfth-century Renaissance.[6] Much of the popular literature of the western Middle Ages derived from Islam and the east. The fantastic Oriental cycles of medieval romance came from this source. Tales from the *Arabian Nights* and other Moslem, Syrian, Persian, and even Chinese stories filtered into western literature and lived not uncomfortably with the romantic vestiges of classical antiquity and the folk tradition of Germanic barbarism. The songs of the troubadors derived much from Moslem influence, especially in theme and possibly also in form. Moslem architecture had many suggestive anticipations of western Gothic and that impressive style may well owe such features as its pointed

6. See p. 421.

arch, cusped windows, and open-cut stone tracery to Islamic models. Certainly the castle-fortresses of the medieval western barons suggest Islamic influences. Thousands of eastern products and their Arabic names found their way into western hands, for commerce has high disregard for creeds and boundaries. Such commercial terms as tariff, traffic, and check; such commodities as gauze, cotton, satin, and damask; and the names of many drugs and medicines are Arabic.

Yet important as all these influences were in the development of various aspects of western civilization, the chief impact of the Moslem world upon the west was negative. Islam controlled the Mediterranean during most of the formative period of the western Middle Ages. As a consequence, medieval civilization was continental rather than sea-based. Its principal centers were deep in the interior of Europe instead of on the shores of the Mediterranean. Because of this, at least in part, medieval civilization was forced out of the mold of classicism because it was denied access to those areas in which the classical empire had flourished and those conditions which had so much determined the shape of classicism. Moslem power dominated the principal trade routes of the world, which ran from the east through the Mediterranean to Moorish Spain. As a result of this partial economic domination, the west was forced into a fundamentally rural instead of urban pattern. The profound consequences of this economic fact need not be labored. Finally, the very existence of Islam provided Christendom with a cultural, political, and religious opponent of such strength that the western world could not forego the challenge. The conflict between Christian and Saracen became one of the determining factors in the slow development of European supremacy in modern times.

SUGGESTIONS FOR FURTHER READING

☙❧

The Byzantine Empire

N. H. Baynes, *The Byzantine Empire* (Oxford: Oxford University Press, 1925).
Charles Diehl, *Byzantium: Greatness and Decline,* tr. by N. Walford (New Brunswick, N. J.: Rutgers University Press, 1957).
*J. M. Hussey, *The Byzantine World* (New York: Torchbooks, 1961).
Harold Lamb, *Theodora and The Emperor: The Drama of Justinian* (Garden

City, N. Y.: Doubleday, 1952), somewhat fictionalized and highly readable account.

C. R. Morey, *Early Christian Art* (Princeton: Princeton University Press, 1942); see the appropriate chapters for Byzantine art.

Procopius, *The Persian Wars, The Vandalic War,* and *The Gothic Wars* (New York: Macmillan, 1914), 6 vols.; the chief historian of Justinian's court in the standard Loeb Edition.

————, *Of the Buildings of Justinian,* tr. by A. Stewart (London: Palestine Pilgrims' Text Society, 1896).

————, *The Secret History,* tr. and intro. by R. Atwater (Chicago: P. Covici, 1927), the most fascinating of his writings, an intimate attack upon the court, especially the Empress Theodora.

*D. T. Rice, *Byzantine Art* (Baltimore: Penguin, 1954).

*S. Runciman, *Byzantine Civilization* (New York: Meridian, 1956).

*P. N. Ure, *Justinian and his Age* (Baltimore: Penguin, 1951).

*A. A. Vasiliev, *History of the Byzantine Empire (324–1453)* (Madison: University of Wisconsin Press, 1952), massive and authoritative.

The Islamic World

The Koran is available in any of several translations.

The Thousand and One Nights, probably the best known of all examples of Arabic literature, available in almost countless editions.

T. W. Arnold, *The Caliphate* (Oxford: Clarendon Press, 1924).

T. Arnold and A. Guillaume, eds., *The Legacy of Islam* (Oxford: Clarendon Press, 1931), a series of essays by various authorities.

A. J. Asberry, *Omar Khayyám, A New Version based upon Recent Discoveries* (New Haven: Yale University Press, 1952), a scholarly if not a literary improvement upon the traditional translation of Edward Fitzgerald.

C. Brockelmann, *History of the Islamic People* (New York: Putnam, 1947).

*E. Dermenghem, *Muhammad and the Islamic Tradition* (New York: Harper, 1958).

M. S. Dimand, *A Handbook of Muhammadan Art* (New York: Metropolitan Museum of Art, 1958), standard and compact, but somewhat prosaic.

G. E. von Grunebaum, *Medieval Islam: A Study in Cultural Orientation* (Chicago: University of Chicago Press, 1954).

*A. Guillaume, *Islam* (Baltimore: Penguin, 1956).

P. K. Hitti, *History of the Arabs* (New York: Macmillan, 1951).

G. LeStrange, *Baghdad during the Abbasid Caliphate* (Oxford: Clarendon Press, 1900).

B. Lewis, *The Arabs in History* (London: Home University Library, 1950).

S. W. Muir, *The Life of Mohammed* (Edinburgh: J. Grant, 1912).

D. O'Leary, *Arabic Thought and Its Place in History* (New York: Dutton, 1939).

————, *How Greek Science Passed to the Arabs* (London: Routledge, 1949).

*Henri Pirenne, *Mohammed and Charlemagne* (New York: Meridian, 1957), a famous book by a great medievalist, a look at Islam as a negative influence upon the west.

The Rose Garden of Sa'di, tr. and ed. by L. Cranmer-Byng (London: Murray, 1919).

E. I. J. Rosenthal, *Political Thought in Medieval Islam* (New York: Cambridge University Press, 1958), a fine study of Arabic intellectual history as well.

Sa'di's Scroll of Wisdom (New York: Dutton, 1909).

G. Sarton, *Introduction to the History of Science* (Baltimore: Carnegie Institution of Washington, 1927); see appropriate section of Vols. I and II of this classic work.

L. Thorndike, *A History of Magic and Experimental Science* (New York: Macmillan, 1923), Vols. I and II; chief emphasis on western medieval science, but does touch Arabic contributions.

*Paperbound edition. In the case of reprint editions, publisher and date of publication given will be that of reprint rather than the original.

7

The Rise of the Frankish Empire and the Recovery of Europe

FROM CLOVIS TO PEPIN: AN EMPIRE WON

The impact of the mass Germanic invasions toppled the already feeble Roman authority in the western empire. Nor were the various barbarian states that rose on its ruins able to achieve political stability: they fell with bloody regularity as wave after wave of peoples swept over each other. Even the most stable and productive of the succession states, Theodoric's Ostrogothic kingdom, did not long survive the death of its great chief. But not only did the barbarian migrations complete the political dismemberment of the western empire, they also shattered the economic network that had held Roman Europe together. This was perhaps even more significant than the political consequences of the migrations.

Clovis and the Winning of the Frankish Empire

Among the largely transitory kingdoms, only one, that of the Franks, survived to provide the basis for a new European power system.

For more than a century the Franks had dwelled in a large region centered in the lower Rhine valley. They comprised two loose and indistinct tribal groups: the Salian Franks, who lived along the seacoast, and the Ripuarians, who lived along the banks of the Rhine. They had fought against the Romans and had also served them as allies or mercenaries against Huns and Visigoths, Saxons and Frisians. In time they had drifted across the broken northern frontier to settle as far into Gaul as the river Somme.

In 481 a young chief named Chlodoveg, more familiarly Clovis (*481–511*), succeeded to the headship of a petty subgroup of the Salian Franks. Before the end of his life he had become king of most of the Frankish people and of a large and wealthy kingdom. Clovis was not unlike the shrewd and able leaders who had appeared before him in the histories of the other German nations. He possessed the same savage vitality that had set Theodoric and Alaric at the head of their peoples, and he did not flinch from treachery and cruelty. Moreover, he was fortunate in his time. For more than a century the western empire had been battered by invading tribes and Rome had shrunk away from her barbarian frontiers. This was especially true in northern Gaul, which was separated from the south by the Visigothic kingdom of Toulouse and the kingdom of Burgundy. It was into northern Gaul that Clovis led his war band in 486 against Syagrius, a renegade Roman governor who ruled this isolated fragment of a province called the "Kingdom of Soissons." Clovis won; Syagrius was treacherously murdered; and the Frankish Empire had its base.

There was apparently little shock and dislocation. Clovis was shrewd enough not to alienate his subject people unnecessarily. There was plenty of military booty and abundant public lands with which to reward his warriors. The wealth of taxes in coin and kind which had supported the skeleton of Roman order was taken over by Clovis. In this region of Gaul, as nearly everywhere along the old frontier, vast stretches of land lay untilled and unclaimed. Clovis' Franks slowly expanded from their own lands into the fringes of the conquered area. In this important respect the Franks differed from the earlier Germanic invaders. Their movement was an expansion rather than an invasion, for they retained their own lands while occupying those that they had conquered. Thus they were not cut off from their own people and their native resources, to be lost in an alien population. This continued to be the case as the Frankish conquests mounted. The Rhine valley remained the center of their growing empire. In 496 the kindred Ripuarian Franks appealed to Clovis for aid against the Alemanni, who had long held the upper Rhine valley. Clovis defeated the Alemanni and gained the kingship of the Ripuarians as well. These conquests further strengthened the essentially German and barbarian character of the Frankish state. It was growing from its Rhenish center to include not only the Gallo-Romans to the south and west but the backward Germans to the south and east.

During the campaign against the Alemanni Clovis made what was to be perhaps his most crucial decision. He allowed himself to be converted to Christianity: and, what is more significant, to orthodox, Catholic Christianity. Thus the Franks became the only major Germanic people of the west who were not Arians. This decision was not accidental. From the beginning of his Gallic conquests Clovis had been careful not to offend the powerful Catholic clergy. They in turn had seen in Clovis a potential ally against the Arians, for whom they cherished fanatic hatred. Clovis had artfully cultivated their hopes by marrying a Catholic Burgundian princess, and allowing his children to be baptized in their mother's faith. Finally, at Rheims, traditionally in 496, Clovis and three thousand of his warriors received baptism. Eager piety contrived the legend that he had sworn an oath in the heat of the Alemannic war to become a Christian if the Christian God gave him a victory. Perhaps a truer picture of his motives can be gained from the statement attributed to him (by Gregory of Tours in his *History of the Franks*) on the eve of his war against the Visigoths: "It causes me great grief that these Arians should hold a part of Gaul. Let us go with the aid of God and reduce them to subjection."[1] But whatever his motives, Clovis had made a powerful ally. His conversion established a bridge between German conquerors and Latin-Roman conquered such as existed in no other German state. The clergy, especially the bishops, who were the most important socio-political group in Gaul, became his ardent supporters. They sanctioned his conquests and glossed his barbarities. Says the bishop and historian Gregory of Tours after a frightful recital of atrocity and double-dealing, "For God daily overwhelmed his enemies and increased his kingdom because he walked uprightly before him and did that which was pleasing in his sight."[2] His religion paved the way for further conquests. It invested his simple followers with a sense of special destiny. Their cry was, "Long live Christ, who loves the Franks; may he protect the army." In no other way could they explain the remarkable success of their arms except in the mysterious alliance of their own strength, the craft of their king, and the blessing of God.

In the Arian kingdoms of the Burgundians and the Visigoths, the clergy and the orthodox welcomed Clovis and withdrew support from their hated Arian masters. He secured the alliance of the Burgundians and with their aid moved against the Visigoths in western and southern Gaul. This

1. Quoted in O. J. Thatcher and E. N. McNeal, *A Source Book for Mediaeval History* (New York: Scribner's, 1905), p. 30.
2. *Ibid.*, p. 32.

king who "walked uprightly" killed the king of the Visigoths with his own hand to remove any doubt about the legitimacy of his succession. He forced the Visigoths to vacate all their Gallic lands except the Mediterranean coast and pushed them into Spain. At the conclusion of his Visigothic war Clovis' realm stretched from Bordeaux on the Garonne to the borders of heathen Bavaria and the Slavic lands of the Elbe; from the Frisian marches of Holland to the Riviera. In the year 511 he died at his new capital of Paris at the age of forty-five, worn out with his achievements, his brutalities, and his lecheries.

The Merovingian Succession

Shortly before his death Clovis partitioned the kingdom among his four sons, following the Frankish custom of treating the state of a king like the personal property of an individual, a policy that was to result in frequent civil war among the Franks. The successors were truly the sons of their father. In the fifty years that followed they pushed the Frankish realm through Provence to the sea; they reduced Burgundy from an allied to a subject state; they increased the Frankish-German holdings in the east by the conquest of the Ostrogothic lands north of the Alps and the tribal lands of the Bavarians and Thuringians. They had time and energy left over to fight savagely among themselves. The victor, Chlotar, triumphed by outliving his brothers. For a brief time, 558 to 561, Frankland was once more a kingdom, only to be redivided among the four sons of Chlotar in 561. This partition was of great historic importance because it defined the regional divisions which would persist through the history of the Frankish Empire. Austrasia, the "Eastland," contained the old Frankish homeland of the lower Rhine and northeastern Gaul and extended to include the more purely German lands to the east. Neustria, the "Newland," contained most of northern Gaul, roughly the lands of the "Kingdom of Soissons" which Clovis had conquered in the initial Frankish expansion. To the south the kingdom of Burgundy formed another unit. The fourth was Aquitaine, the broad, rich plain of southwestern Gaul which had been won from the Visigoths. The state, thus generally comprised in these regional kingdoms, remained largely unaltered for the following two centuries. It was ruled during that time, in whole and in part, by the descendants of Clovis. That complex dynasty is called Merovingian, taking its name from Merovech, a shadowy ancestor of Clovis.

The strong blood of Clovis and his warlike sons weakened as it passed to their Merovingian successors. The degeneration of the royal house was a leading characteristic of this middle passage of Frankish history. The Merovingian kings were weak and timid, diseased and short-lived. Distrustful of everyone, they were, nevertheless, the pawns of their queens and the instruments of their nobility. For more than a century one Merovingian after another was elevated to the meaningless dignity of rule, while the decisive powers of the state were divided among the greedy and irresponsible nobility.

Yet this fragmentation was not exclusively due to the weakness of the royal house; it was inherent in the nature of the Frankish state. Nearly everything in its history militated against centralism: the empire that the Franks won in Roman Gaul was already barbarized by generations of German occupation; the lands they added to the empire across the Rhine had scarcely felt the civilizing influence of Rome; commerce and exchange had almost ceased; cities had already been turned into villages and the economic focus of society was the country villa. With the decline of the classical empire the villa system had become widespread in Gaul. The Franks simply moved into the system. It was most congenial to them—simple, effective, workable. When they did not find it, as in the more German lands of the east, they imposed it. Thus the Frankish state was essentially a patchwork of agricultural holdings; and by its very nature it tended to localism.

The Frankish kings could not prevail against this localism. They were absolute in theory and in pretense, but in fact their powers—even under the best circumstances—were severely limited. The sources of taxation which had been the basis of Roman government had dried up, the wealth of the king was land. In this economic sense he was no different from his nobles, but simply the first among equals. The king and his court moved from one royal estate to another, for it was easier to go to the food supplies than to bring them to the court. The difficulty of transportation and communications aggravated the problems of government. There was no tradition except that of the tribal monarchy, and the rights of the Frankish king were those of the chief of a primitive war band. Whatever the band won was in the name of their chief and was his to dispose of as largess. The same rule applied to the relationship between the Frankish king and his nation. There were no political institutions in the Frankish state: the state was the king and the powers of the state were simply the extension of the king's power. Frankish law, even after many centuries, remained a painfully literal body of static custom—it failed to develop any theoretical basis for judicial principles. The king delegated his august powers to royal agents, called counts and dukes, who exercised them in vaguely defined districts. These tended to be coterminous with the older Roman subprovincial units and border provinces. Since the kings had little or no money with which to reward their officials, they paid them in land and power— diminishing their own power in the process. The king's authority was a personal authority and when he was strong he could govern. When he was not, which was more often the case, he was the tool of his nobles. Wealth and power concentrated in their hands and the progressive failure of royal government hastened the process.

Men who could neither protect themselves nor look to government to do so "commended" themselves to some strong local magnate. This process of commendation put the manpower resources of the Frankish state not at the unique disposal of the state, that is, the king, but in the hands of the nobility. The same fears and insecurities that led men to surrender their freedom made them surrender their lands. If a man were pressed by debts and poverty or harried by those stronger than himself he might grant his land to another powerful enough to protect it. He gave up the ownership of his land but he received the land itself from the new owner to use as a *benefice*. This occurred at every level, from the peasant to the king. A great lord might grant additional land of his own as a benefice in order to secure its cultivation. The king often granted benefices in return for military service. The weakness and discontinuity of government which permitted such concentration of land and power tended to surrender legally what it had lost by default. Great lords demanded and received from their feeble kings the rights of private jurisdiction, such extensive immunities that sovereignty, the most definitive power of government, became vested in the same hands that held the land of the Frankish realm. This general situation —the control of men and land by private individuals and the exercise of sovereign power by local authority—represents the substance of feudalism. Its final realization was only temporarily postponed by the rise of another Frankish dynasty, the Carolingian.

The Mayors of the Palace

The Carolingian[3] dynasty had its origins, curiously, in the same localist tendencies that destroyed the descendants of Clovis. Long before the Carolingians became a royal family they were powerful landed lords. The first

---

3. The name Carolingian is actually an anachronism, for it comes from the name of the greatest king of the dynasty, Charlemagne (Carolus Magnus in Latin) rather than from the name of the founder of the dynasty.

of many Carolingians to bear the name of Pepin held personal lands comprising roughly the modern state of Belgium, in the heart of the old Frankish-Germanic territory of the north. This powerful lord, Pepin I, was chosen by the Merovingian King Dagobert (*628–638*) as his Mayor of the Palace. This office had begun humbly in the royal household where the mayor was the superintendent of the royal estates and menage. As the royal estates began to comprise a kingdom and the household a government, the mayor of the palace became a sort of prime minister and the "second man" of the realm. Offices and honors, like land, tended to become hereditary and the office of mayor of the palace became the prerogative of the family of Pepin.

The weakness of the later Merovingian kings encouraged chronic rebellion within the Frankish state and placed the remaining royal land and power in jeopardy. At this stage the Carolingian mayors stepped forward to assume the responsibility for preserving royal authority, motivated less by selfless devotion than by their own family ambitions. In 678, at Tetry in Picardy, Pepin of Herstal (*687–714*), the grandson of Pepin I, defeated the Neustrian nobility and captured their puppet king. With this victory he could claim to be mayor of the entire Frankish Empire. But great sections of the empire still remained to be wrested from the nobles and returned to royal authority. Wide and wealthy Aquitaine had been nearly separated from the empire. Brittany, Gascony, and Burgundy were in full revolt. The old German tribal areas, which the sons of Clovis had conquered, were drifting away from Frankish control in the direction of regional independence. Pepin of Herstal took the field and fought fiercely and almost constantly to repair the Frankish state. He could do no more than establish a tradition and make a beginning.

Both were passed on to his illegitimate son Charles (*714–741*), soon to be called Martel, "the Hammer," for the blows with which he stopped the Saracen advance in Europe. Much of Charles' success stemmed from his own impressive personality. Government in his time was not a distant impersonal force, but a present power in the hands of a flesh-and-blood individual. Charles was a commanding figure—vigorous and decisive, a king in all but name. He lorded it over his baronage because he was a better man than any of them. But Charles brought to his office more than personal forcefulness. He drew support from the vast lands of his own family which high office had enlarged for more than three generations. He also treated the remaining crown lands as his own, and used them to support his policies and bribe his enemies. Charles turned his attention and resources to fighting the same problem of decentralization against which Pepin of Herstal had made a start. With the support of the Austrasian nobility he completed the subjugation of the Burgundians and the Bavarians. Aquitaine was forced back to allegiance and the Frankish state resumed its ancient boundaries. In each of these areas he followed victory in the field by a policy of uprooting local authorities and established Austrasian counts and dukes in their place. Each conquest strengthened Charles and the state and put new resources into his hands. With consolidation progressing rapidly he turned to the troublesome borderlands of the north, the lands occupied by the heathen Frisians, inland from the North Sea coast, and the Saxons on the northeast frontier. His success in these campaigns brought him new land and increased power.

Both Charles' wars of reconquest and his wars of expansion were carried on in the face of a new and serious menace to the Franks—the Saracen threat in the south. When Charles Martel succeeded Pepin as mayor of the palace, the Berbers of North Africa and a motley army of Arabs and Syrians had virtually completed the conquest of Spain. By 725 they had pushed across the Pyrenees and into Gaul in the wake of Charles' wars there. As the tide of Moslem advance moved toward the north Charles Martel marshalled his forces. His own Austrasian nobility backed him. He gained alliances where he could—one with the king of the Lombards in northern Italy. Much of the reconquered territory was too raw to be trusted and a good bit of it was already in Moslem hands. He turned to the church, first with requests, then with demands, and finally with confiscations. This confiscated land he divided into benefices and parceled out to trusted men in return for their military service, thus purchasing their loyalty and rewarding their courage. The church and the clergy condemned him even as they survived under his protection. The Saracens and Franks met near Tours or Poitiers (the exact site is unknown) and the heavy Frankish cavalry won the day. The Battle of Tours was not decisive in itself. It was rather the first in a long series of battles and skirmishes which lasted for more than twenty-five years. Ultimately the internal troubles of Moslem Spain and the unrelenting pressure of Charles' Franks forced Islam back into Spain.

The aid of the church, though exacted at sword's point, had been a vital factor in the long campaign against the Saracens. In another area, cooperation between Charles and the church came more easily. Charles gave valuable help to the missionaries working in the German and Frisian lands on his northern frontier, and no less a personage than St. Boniface,

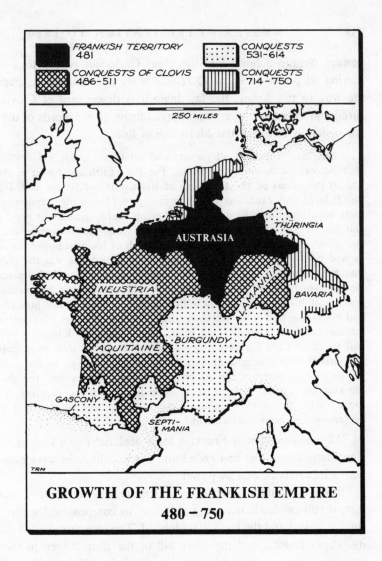

AUSTRASIA

THÜRINGIA

NEUSTRIA

ALAMANNIA

BAVARIA

AQUITAINE

BURGUNDY

GASCONY

SEPTI-
MANIA

TRM

GROWTH OF THE FRANKISH EMPIRE
480 – 750

the famous "Apostle to the Germans," secured his active support. Christian zeal may have had some part in Charles' policy, but his chief motives were military and political. The missionary clergy formed—probably quite unwittingly—a civilizing and Christianizing fifth column, preparing the way for Charles' armies.

From Mayor to King: The Founding of the Carolingian Monarchy

Backed by his successes, Charles adopted a princely title during the last years of his life, and no one dared challenge his right to it. At his death in 741, his sons Carloman and Pepin the Short inherited his vast powers. Within a few years the pious Carloman retired to a monastery, leaving all power to Pepin (751–768). By the end of 751, Pepin cleared the way to the throne, the last inglorious descendant of Clovis was tonsured and thrust into monastic imprisonment. In the words of the Carolingian historian Einhard, the Merovingian line

. . . had long since lost all power, and no longer possessed anything of importance except the empty royal title. For the wealth and power of the kingdom was in the hands of the Praefects of the Court, who were called Mayors of the Palace, and exercised entire sovereignty. The King, contented with the mere royal title, with long hair and flowing beard, used to sit upon the throne and act the part of a ruler, listening to ambassadors, whencesoever they came, and giving them at their departure, as though of his own power, answers which he had been instructed or commanded to give. But this was the only function that he performed, for besides the empty royal title and the precarious life income which the Praefect of the Court allowed him at his pleasure he had nothing of his own except one estate with a very small revenue, on which he had his house, and from which he drew the few servants who performed such services as were necessary and made him a show of deference. Wherever he had to go he travelled in a waggon, drawn in rustic style by a pair of oxen, and driven by a cowherd. In this fashion he used to go to the palace and to the general meetings of the people, which were held yearly for the affairs of the kingdom; in this fashion he returned home. But the Praefect of the Court looked after the administration of the kingdom and all that had to be done or arranged at home and abroad.[4]

In 752 a convocation of Frankish lords declared Pepin king of the Franks. The Merovingian line had ended and the Carolingians were now the royal house in name as well as power.

Strongly grounded as the new dynasty was in military and political fact, it still needed sanctioning authority to compensate for the hereditary right it lacked and the legality it violated. The church provided that authority. Pepin had courted the good will of the church even to the extent of returning some of the lands seized by his father. The Gallic clergy tended to support the new monarchy and St. Boniface may have been present at Pepin's coronation to anoint him. It remained, however, for the next few years to confirm a working relationship between the church and the Carolingian dynasty. That important relationship was the direct result of a series of troubles which desperately pressed the papacy at this time.

In the wake of the Gothic Wars of Justinian in the mid-sixth century, the savage Germanic Lombards had crossed the Alps to occupy the Po

4. Quoted in A. J. Grant (trans. and ed.), *Early Lives of Charlemagne by Eginhard and the Monk of St. Gall* (London: Chatto and Windus, 1922), pp. 8-9.

valley and much of northern Italy. With the collapse of every civil power in Italy the Lombard kingdom was firmly established. In the next two centuries the Lombards became civilized, Christianized, and ambitious for more extensive lands. They aimed at nothing less than a Lombard kingdom of Italy; and only two powers opposed them—the spiritual and temporal power of the papacy and the temporal and legal power of the Byzantine Empire, which still retained a foothold in Italy. The papacy was closely allied with Ravenna, the administrative center of Byzantine authority in Italy. Liutprand (*712–744*), the great king of the Lombards, began to press hard against the weak Byzantine forces centered at Ravenna to bid for the domination of Italy.

In 726 the iconoclastic controversy broke out far away in Byzantium. The austere emperor Leo the Isaurian (*717–741*), long a religious purist, took a strong stand against what he considered the idolatry and superstition of image worship in the eastern church. The position of the emperor split the church and state into bitter, warring camps and the bitterness spread to every part of the empire—Italy included. The pope disagreed violently with the emperor on the issue of iconoclasm. At the same time popular revolts in Ravenna over the same issue paralyzed the Byzantine forces and the Lombards quickly took most of the exarchate.

Faced by the Lombard advance, the papacy found itself with no secular protection. A brief attempt at cooperation with the Lombards was soon abandoned as too risky. Pope Gregory III (*731–741*) then turned to the only substantial power left in the west, Charles Martel. But Charles needed the military support of the Lombards more than the spiritual support of the papacy. By the reign of his son, Pepin the Short, this was no longer the case. The Lombards defeated the last remnants of Byzantine authority in Italy and invested Ravenna in the same year that Pepin's coup made him king of the Franks. The Lombard advance moved on toward Rome. The pope, Stephen II (*752–757*) reopened desperate negotiations with Pepin. He approved the dynastic change and in 754 fled to Pepin's court. He assured Pepin of his powerful spiritual support, symbolized in his personal anointment of the new king. Pepin was prepared to repay this valuable favor and took the field against the Lombards. Within two years he had defeated them and in 756, with a dramatic gesture, his representatives laid on the tomb of St. Peter the keys to the conquered cities of Italy and a deed of property known to later history as the Donation of Pepin. It was a grant to the pope of sovereignty over all the lands formerly belonging to the exarchate of Ravenna. This broad strip of territory, stretching from Rome diagonally across the peninsula to Ravenna, became the Papal States which, for a thousand years, were destined to play such an important and equivocal role in the chaotic affairs of Italy. By this grant of the Frankish king the papacy became a significant secular state in Italy and the alliance of the Frankish Empire with the Roman papacy, which had begun with the conversion of Clovis, was renewed more strongly than ever.

THE CHURCH, THE PAPACY, AND THE FRANKISH EMPIRE

The Church in the Dark Age

During the troubled centuries of the decline of Roman power in the west the church had assumed many social and political functions which the state could no longer exercise. But, although it continued to grow within the barbarian succession states, it suffered from the general instability of government characteristic of this period. The forces of separatism were strong and the breakdown of the Roman communications system favored this tendency. The inchoate structure of papal command was simply not powerful enough to enforce unity, and local bishops tended to go their own way. Many times they did what they had to do; often they did merely what they wished to do. In many areas bishops ruled virtually as little kings. By default of government or by grant of barbarian masters they taxed, rendered justice, and enforced what law there was. They were often good and conscientious men who gave their people the best government to be had and who managed their diocesan affairs with integrity and skill. But perhaps even more often, the wealth and prestige of the office attracted the unscrupulous men against whom the pious records of the time inveigh so bitterly. But whether good or bad, the clergy of the western church constituted an important social class, a class with increasing secular concerns and individually almost independent of higher ecclesiastical authority.

The church was plagued not only by localism and the rough barbarism of the age, but by serious doctrinal division. We have dealt in an earlier chapter with the spiritual, intellectual, and doctrinal substance of heresy. The barbarian west was not divided so much by the differences of doctrine as by the extension of those differences into political action. As the barbarian kingdoms took form, the Arian religion that prevailed among them created another serious division. Orthodoxy and heresy battled in every region of western Europe and their animosities are reflected in a thousand curses and condemnations which survive among the tattered documents of this dark age.

In such trying circumstances—divided and warring within itself—the church nonetheless continued its function as an agency of civilization. But these efforts too were hampered by the almost complete disappearance of secular learning. In a few villas and cities men still played at the game of learning but, increasingly, secular society was dominated by barbarians. Scholarship, even rudimentary literacy, was scarcely to be found outside the church; and within the church, the literary culture that remained was little more than a mockery of the great tradition from which it came. Everything was simplified for a more simple and backward society. Such learning as remained was not broad and humane, but narrow and practical—the rudimentary bookkeeping or uninspiring annals of local monastic chapters. Superstition and ignorance triumphed over the rational humanism which had been the glory of Graeco-Roman classicism. The weight of barbarism was too great; and the church had too much to do.

Latin had long since been confirmed as the language of the church. Its continued use preserved some of its classical masterpieces for the sake of instruction if for no other reason. But the corpus of classical literature was more depleted with each generation. Monks such as those so carefully trained by Cassiodorus made copies of standard works, but these tended to be sterile museum pieces having little general cultural impact in their own time. Those who were literate turned to *epitomes,* brief and often scandalously incorrect abridgments of the classical authors. The schools—and they were wholly church schools—restricted their pupils to a few such works and a handful of textbooks. The most popular of these was the grammar of Donatus, a fourth-century schoolmaster and writer whose book became the standard work on language throughout the Middle Ages. The intellectual poverty of the age can nowhere be better seen than in the enormous reputation gained by such a modest attainment as this. Even the Latin language, the very vehicle of thought and expression, rapidly degenerated. Its slow decline from the excellencies of Cicero, Vergil, Horace, and even the great literary figures of the Silver Age, was accelerated in the chaotic centuries of barbarism at the end of the classical era. As the church spread Latin to those who had never used it, as the service of the church put the old pagan tongue to new purposes, its subtleties were lost, its forms broken down, its structure simplified, its vocabulary abridged.

The roster of literature is neither long nor brilliant in these times. In the early seventh century Isidore, Bishop of Seville (*c.* 560–638) was one of the most learned men of the western world. He expended a considerable amount of his learning on an encyclopedic work of etymology. It was a great compendium of knowledge; literally, a book about a thousand things that were often explained by the derivation of their names. More often than not these etymologies or derivations were wrong. Isidore, for all his labor, had little or no sense of discrimination between important and unimportant things. He was as credulous as a child and soberly retold once more the monster stories, fabulous accounts of strange places and exotic beasts that were hoary before Herodotus. But with all its inadequacies and absurdities, the *Etymologies* of Isidore was one of the most authoritative books of the Middle Ages—again a commentary upon the condition of learning.

A younger contemporary of Isidore was the Italian poet Venantius Fortunatus (*c.* 580–610), who spent most of his life in Gaul as one of the ornaments of the corrupt Merovingian court. Like Isidore, Fortunatus was also a churchman, Bishop of Poitiers, and his most important works were hymns. Despite, or perhaps because of, the simplicity of their language, they have a childlike eloquence and moving imagery far removed from the sophistication of the classical tradition. They belong not only in meter and form but in spirit to the Middle Ages.

Gregory, Bishop of Tours (*c.* 538–593), was a friend of Fortunatus and one of the most important prose writers of the early Middle Ages. His *History of the Franks* is almost the sole source of our knowledge about them during the crucial sixth century. This fact, rather than the inherent merit of the book, accounts for Gregory's literary renown. Both the book and the man shared the faults of Isidore of Seville. Gregory was naive in the extreme; his historical judgments were frequently swayed by partisanship of the most obvious sort. But with all its faults of judgment and flaws of grammar, the *History of the Franks* is a vigorous and lively work, illuminating an age about which we would otherwise know almost nothing.

Nevertheless, the poverty of literature and learning in western Europe in the age of Gregory of Tours, Fortunatus, and Isidore of Seville is symptomatic of the general decline of culture in the wake of barbarian conquest.

The Rise of the Papacy

The one institution that remained to contest the dismemberment of Europe was the papacy. By the time of the Frankish Empire the pope stood at the head of western Christendom, and the papacy was the one ecumenical organization in the western world. It clung tenaciously to the ideal of unity and bent its considerable powers to achieve it. We have already re-hearsed the list of forces which militated against the unity and organization for which the papacy fought—the monarchical independence of bishops and the failure of papal control over them, as well as heresy, corruption, secularization, and the encroachment of barbaric ignorance.

The key to the problem of papal control, or the lack of it, was the barbarian kingdoms. These rude states were the units of meaningful politi-cal power and the church had to come to terms with them. Thus, before it could demand ecclesiastical reform and spiritual regeneration, the papacy had to become a political power. The man who most clearly realized this necessity was Pope Gregory, justly called the Great (*590–604*). Gregory was born into an old and wealthy Roman senatorial family. Nurtured in the classical-imperial tradition of social responsibility, he entered public life and at thirty was praefect of the city. Rich, talented, and dedicated, he rejected the brilliant secular career which was assured him. Instead, he founded a number of monasteries, gave what remained of his fortune to charity, and retired to one of his own monasteries to become its humblest monk. But the church had too compelling a need for men of Gregory's caliber and he was returned to the world and ultimately in 590 elevated to the papacy—by acclamation.

The monk had become the pope but the politically astute Roman aristocrat shared the papal throne. At stake was nothing less than the survival of the papacy. Its enemies were many: the church itself was divided and permeated with ignorance and corruption; its powers and prestige had been diminished by the barbarian kingdoms which every-where subordinated the clergy to the state. The Lombard kingdom, well-established in northern Italy, constituted a prime danger. To combat it, Gregory organized the resources of the papal household into a smoothly operating system that was to serve the papacy for centuries. He poured this wealth into efforts against the Lombards and support for the exarchate of Ravenna. It was largely to the credit of Gregory—not to the sorry efforts of the Byzantine authority in Italy—that the line was held against the Lombards.

Serious as the Lombard menace was, Gregory's assault upon it was part of a much larger and grander conception—exclusive papal direction of a church and a religion that would dominate the world. This aspiration had been implicit in the papacy almost from its foundation, but Gregory voiced it explicitly for the first time and began to implement the grand design. Combining historical precedent with current political exigencies,

Gregory forged the arguments for papal supremacy. He spurned the claims of the Byzantine emperor and his captive patriarch: the Roman church, not the church of Constantinople or any other, was the "head of all the churches." In Gregory's unshakable view there was but one church and no salvation except through it—no good work, no forgiveness of sin, no saving truth. He was indeed the architect of papal Roman-Catholic supremacy.

There was no cleric great or small over whom Gregory did not claim jurisdiction. To bishops—Arian and orthodox, Goth or Frank or Gallo-Roman—he wrote imperious directives and fiery censures for their manifold transgressions, even when he could not reach them with his authority. To the great and the ordinary he wrote almost a thousand letters. They were friendly and simple or stern and commanding. He wrote commentaries on Scripture, works of theology and speculation, pious reports of miracles and saints. The volume and effect of his writings rank him as one of the great Latin fathers of the church. At the same time these writings reveal —as do those of his literary contemporaries—the decline of classicism and the emergence of a new mode of learning. It was Gregory who made the famous and naive protestation that he would not fetter the words of God "to the rules of Donatus." But through the pedestrian prose and bad grammar of his writings shines the devotion, strength, and ability of this great papal administrator and apologist.

Nowhere was Gregory's success in reasserting papal leadership more evident than in the missionary work which he so vigorously sponsored. According to the Venerable Bede, before Gregory became pope he was impressed by the sturdiness and beauty of some captives offered for sale in the slave market of Rome. He asked if they were Christians and was told, no. "Alas," quoth he, "it is a piteous case that the author of darkness possesseth such bright beautied people, and that men of such gracious outward sheen do bear a mind void of inward grace." He asked what they were called and was told "Angles," to which he replied in a classic pun, "Well are they so called, for they have an angel's face, and it is meet that such men were inheritors with the angels of heaven."[5] The wish expressed in this charming, and doubtful, story was fulfilled in 597 when Gregory sent a mission to Britain to convert the Anglo-Saxons. The mission was led by St. Augustine (d. 604)—later the first Archbishop of Canterbury— who was strikingly successful in gaining the confidence of several petty

5. *Ecclesiastical History of England,* II, 1.

Anglo-Saxon kings. Within two generations England was brought within the fold of the western church. This was an extremely important victory for the papacy. But no less important was the agency which brought it about. That agency was Benedictine monasticism, and the conversion of Britain was the result of an alliance between the pope and the Benedictines which was destined to have far-reaching results.

The Benedictine order had been founded about a century before Gregory became pope by a young man remarkably like Gregory, St. Benedict of Nursia (*c.* 480–543). Benedict came from the same wealthy, aristocratic Italian stock as Gregory. He also was marked out for a secular career but, while still a schoolboy, bolted the wickedness of the world and fled to the wilderness to lead a hermit's life. He practiced the traditional austerities with zeal and attracted a following. For more than a century asceticism had been a fixture of the eastern church. It had been transferred to the west and was gaining enormous popularity by the time of St. Benedict. It had already provided the western church with a number of saints, and eremite groups were established in many places. But the ascetic expression was a frenzy rather than a movement, dangerous to orthodoxy because it was uncontrolled. St. Benedict, recognizing this danger, founded a monastery at the site of Monte Cassino, and provided it with a code, the Rule of St. Benedict, about 529. This was the rule upon which all later western monasticism would be based. Its primary characteristic was moderation; its primary aim, to control the perilous fever of self-sacrifice. The rule was strictly authoritarian. The abbot was to have complete power over the individual monk and the monk was to learn the duty of obedience. The rule regulated with equal strictness every moment of the monastic day—the hours of sleep, work, prayer; indeed, *what* work and *what* prayer. The monks were a community; they were to have no possessions of their own and they were to be fixed within their monastic walls, insulated from the world, directing their wills to the salvation of their souls.

By the time of Gregory the Great the Benedictine order was both well-established and popular. The encroaching menace of the Lombards drove the monks of Monte Cassino to the protection of the papacy at Rome. There was great spiritual affinity between the personal ideals of Gregory and the Benedictine way of life. (He may even have formally joined the order.) Further, Gregory realized that this order held enormous potential for the church and for his grandiose schemes of reform and papal leadership. In that realization was founded an alliance between the monks and the pope as fruitful as that between the Franks and the church. By the purity and dedication of their lives the monks were a natural agency for the moral reform so desperately needed in the church. Closely related to the need for moral reform was the need for preserving and disseminating learning. Originally the Benedictine order had concentrated its energies on prayer and manual labor, but under the influence of Gregory it began to change its emphasis and undertook the work—already begun by isolated monastic groups—of spreading such knowledge as was available at the time. Thus the alliance between Gregory and the Benedictine order opened up a new course—a great missionary undertaking that was to bring Christianity and civilization to the pagan fringes of the world and converts to the foot of the papal throne.

It was within this context that Gregory's mission to Britain was conceived. St. Augustine was a trusted Benedictine monk, and his basic foundation in England—Christ's Church at Canterbury—was dominated by a Benedictine chapter. Gregory's confidence was more than repaid. His faithful missionary monks carried their religion and their rule rapidly throughout the barbaric and divided island. Through the zeal of the Benedictines a new realm was added to Christendom and to the obedience of Rome. Within a century the English church was organized, and an episcopal organization imposed upon the monastic foundation laid by the Benedictines. Local British kings cooperated with their churchmen and out of many warring kingdoms a nation began to evolve, political unity growing out of the unity of religion.

Celtic Christianity

Moving northward from the Saxon kingdoms of the south, the papal missionary movement met the vigorous thrust of a countermovement, which had its origin in Ireland. Celtic Christianity, rooted in the last days of classic Gaul and Roman Britain, was one of the most fascinating and exotic developments in the varied history of the Christian Church. It stemmed largely from the personality and work of one extraordinary individual—St. Patrick (c. 389–461).

This patron saint of Ireland was not an Irishman at all, but a Briton. As a young man, about the year 400, he was captured in an Irish pirate raid on the British coast. He was taken to pagan Ireland and, after several years escaped, not to his native Britain but to Gaul. There he received both his education and his Latin name of Patricius from the Gallic churchmen. In mid-fifth century Gaul, Christianity was making rapid strides, combining two traditions, which had a formative effect on the young

Briton. In the first place Gallo-Roman Christianity, more than any other Christian movement in the west, had appropriated the poetic, scholarly tradition of late Latin classicism. Almost everywhere else external pressures were destroying the remnants of the classical tradition: the North Africa of Cyprian and Augustine had fallen to the Vandals; the Danube and Rhine provinces had been overwhelmed by barbarians; even Italy was under attack. Only in Gaul was the classical tradition kept alive by the church. In the second place the extreme forms of asceticism, which had gained such popularity in Syria and Egypt, had been transferred to the west and had taken root most firmly in Gaul. The Egyptian forms and rules of monasticism were practiced in Gaul almost a century before St. Benedict. At the time of St. Patrick the eastern form of ascetic life predominated in Gaul, and was adopted by him.

Probably it was in search of martyrdom, or at least hardship, that Patrick resolved to return to his Irish captors as a missionary. He took with him his fanatic courage and the two intertwined traditions of classical scholarship and Oriental asceticism. With his missionary success these became the principal ingredients in the unique movement that grew out of his work. The deeds and miracles of the saint are too numerous to mention; few figures are more encrusted with pious hyperbole. Within a short time St. Patrick's faith had conquered Ireland: clan after clan adopted his religion and abandoned their venerable druidism.

The organization of Irish Christianity was, understandably, a network of monasteries. These became the central, vivifying influences in the creation of a Celtic-Christian culture of great richness and vitality. The influences that St. Patrick had introduced quickly took root and grew, with and beside the native pagan Celtic-Irish traditions. For two centuries after St. Patrick, Irish Christianity flourished in isolation from the rest of the Christian world. While the papacy grew and extended its influence over continental Christianity, while the barbarian kingdoms conquered western Europe, Irish monasticism continued on its unique course divergent from the mainstream of the Latin Church. Irish asceticism was famous: the monks often slept in brooks and streams even in the cruelest cold; they prayed for hours with arms outstretched in the sign of the cross; many courted a living death, walled up in their cells or sleeping in graves dug by their own hands they devoted themselves to prayer and self-imposed penance on meager fare pushed through a small opening, finally dying silent and alone. But the Irish monks honored equally the tradition of ancient scholarship. There were men of learning among them at a time when continental classicism was virtually nonexistent. They knew Greek when it was scarcely known anywhere else in the western world. They were fine scribes and their illuminated manuscripts—like the Book of Kells inscribed in the monastery of that name—were the most beautiful and intricate ever produced. The Irish monks were imbued with the same missionary zeal that had brought their religion to them. From Ireland they spread their beliefs and a chain of monasteries to Scotland (whose very name means "the land of the Irish," from the Latin, Scotus), and then to England.

In the last decade of the sixth century, at the same time that Augustine was establishing the Benedictine order and Latin Christianity in the southern kingdoms of England, the vigorous influence of Irish Christianity was civilizing the north. From a number of monastic foundations this influence poured down through the island to meet Catholic orthodoxy. Between them they shared the work of Christianizing Anglo-Saxon England, though their cooperation was not always harmonious. In the end Roman orthodoxy won the day. The last major dispute was settled at the Council of Whitby in 664; and Irish Christianity returned to the central line of western Christian development.

Fortunately, the vitality so characteristic of the Irish monks was not suppressed but merely redirected by this return to the fold. The church had found in the remote western extremity of the world a source of new strength. With the blending of Irish and Benedictine monasticism, each enhancing the strength of the other, England became the shining ornament of the Christian world. The English clergy, from top to bottom, included men of awesome learning and refreshing piety. Under their able rule the fledgling English church grew in strength and prestige. The tradition of monastic scholarship, strong in both the Irish and Benedictines, reached its apex in the work of the Venerable Bede (c. 672–735), a monk of the monastery of Wearmouth-Jarrow in northern England. Though he lived scarcely a century after Isidore of Seville and Gregory of Tours, his learning and scholarship set him a world apart from them. His *Ecclesiastical History of England* is unquestionably the finest piece of historical writing of the early Middle Ages. A prodigiously learned theologian, he was also a superb stylist who knew Greek as well as Latin.

Apostles to the Germans

Even before its accord with Catholicism in England the Irish monastic movement, in its insatiable missionary zeal, had pressed on to the continent.

The heroic and devoted monks scattered their monasteries throughout Frankish Gaul, Lombard Italy, and the kingdom of Burgundy. But perhaps their most important work was done in the wild German frontier lands to the east. Their monasteries—such as St. Gall in Switzerland and Bobbio in northern Italy—became centers from which missionaries went forth to do the work of civilization. Frontier monasteries became centers of learning like their parent foundations in Ireland and England. The monks, by the austerity of their lives and the purity of their faith, set a high example for the simple pagans among whom they worked. At the same time they were a disturbing contrast to the crude, ignorant, and licentious Gallic clergy. On the continent, as in England, the Irish monastic movement finally joined hands with the larger movement of clerical reform under papal leadership. By 700 most of the Irish foundations in western Europe had abandoned their independent rule and become Benedictine. The fruitful alliance between the papacy and the Benedictines continued. At the same time, the missionary tradition that Irish monasticism had established on the continent was strengthened by the tie with Rome, and another wave of Anglo-Irish monks surged across the narrow seas to continue the work of their predecessors.

The greatest of all Anglo-Saxon missionaries was Winifrith, better known as St. Boniface (*c.* 680–755). A man of tremendous spiritual and intellectual audacity, his long life represents the culmination of the varied movements which formed his background. He was an Anglo-Irish Benedictine, confirmed in the tradition that had quickened Christianity in the north for centuries. He was dedicated to the dual task of converting the pagans and reforming the almost equally pagan Christianity of the Franks. From the other end of the world, he took up the work which Gregory the Great had begun in Rome a century before.

Following the trail of his earlier countrymen, Boniface turned to the eastern German frontier of the Frankish Empire. The grateful church rewarded his efforts and acknowledged his success by making him the bishop of all the lands and peoples whom he converted. With every spiritual conquest his power and prestige grew. Not only did he receive the blessing of Rome, he also received the support of the Carolingian mayors of the palace. Long since, these astute warrior-rulers had realized the value of the missionary work done by the Irish and Anglo-Saxon Benedictines, and both Charles Martel and Pepin the Short actively supported Boniface in his work. They saw that the conquest and control of their dangerous border peoples would be greatly facilitated by the moderating influence of Christianity. Their hopes were not misplaced. Missionary penetration in Germany had much the same effect as it had had in England in the previous century. The monasteries provided centers of civilization and, as more were founded, they came to constitute a tough-tissued network binding the German lands together and giving them a unity that their warring tribes had never been able to achieve.

The general reverence in which the saintly Boniface was held and his close relations with the Frankish rulers made him the natural spokesman for the papal cause in northern Europe. Again the work of Gregory the Great was taken in hand. In addition to his exalted dignity, first as bishop and then as archbishop of the whole German frontier, he was made papal legate for the supervision and reform of the Frankish church. In this work too, Boniface's efforts capped a long development. He added to his legatine authority the force of his personality and the weight of his deeds. The Frankish church responded. He was unrelenting in his attack upon the abuses of the clergy, enforcing his commands with visitations and councils. In this work, as elsewhere, he received the active support of the Carolingians—but again, not from entirely pious motives. The Frankish clergy, like the nobility, were the enemies of the type of strong central government the Carolingians represented. Thus, the efforts of Boniface to reduce their independence played into the hands of the Carolingians. Furthermore, as we have seen, Pepin the Short, in his scheme to replace the effete Merovingian line, looked to the church for support and encouraged it by encouraging reform.

In the coronation of Pepin as king of the Franks and in the church's sanction of that dynastic revolution, the dominant currents of several centuries of secular and ecclesiastical history met. The Franks had passed through the formative period of their history and were approaching the height of their power. The church had struggled back from decay and disunity to a more vigorous and unified position than it had ever had in the west. The solemn ceremony in which Pepin became king of the Franks "by the grace of God," marked the first "official" step in the binding together of the destinies of the Frankish state and the papacy—a union that was to have great significance for medieval Europe.

CHARLEMAGNE

Each Carolingian ruler, whether mayor or king, had added to the achievements of his predecessors. But the crowning achievement of this dynasty was the work of Charles the Great, son of Pepin, known as Charlemagne (*768–814*).

The Military Consolidation of the Empire

In 768 the Frankish nobility raised Charles on their shields to signify the successor to Pepin the Short. But again it was a double succession, for Pepin had divided his realm between Charles and his brother, Carloman. The double reign began inauspiciously. The two brothers disliked and distrusted each other and the chronicle of the next generation might well have been a repetition of the disastrous fratricidal wars of the Frankish past. But, after three years, the weaker Carloman died and Charles ruled alone.

Both the successes and failures of Charles' reign were determined largely by war. There was scarcely a year in which the king did not take to the field. War was an integral part of the Carolingian system both for economic and socio-political reasons. Every Carolingian monarch, even

---

CAROLINGIAN MAYORS AND KINGS

PEPIN I
d. 639
Mayor of Austrasia

PEPIN OF HERSTAL
(687-714)
Mayor of Austrasia and Neustria

CHARLES MARTEL
(714-741)
Mayor of Austrasia and Neustria

PEPIN III (the Short)
(741-768)
Mayor of Neustria
King of the Franks (752)

CHARLEMAGNE
(768-814)
King of the Franks
Emperor (800)

LOUIS THE PIOUS
(814-840)
King and Emperor

Charles, was first of all a war chief. Even before he became king, Charles had a military reputation and was known as "Iron Charles." In the course of his long reign he was to gain the more famous epithet "the great," and rank with such military figures as Alexander, Hannibal, Caesar, and his own grandfather, Charles Martel.

Within a few months of the double coronation of Charles and Carloman, Aquitaine broke into revolt, as if to test the untried kings. This most wealthy and civilized portion of the Frankish Empire had been joined uncomfortably to the Frankish state since the days of Clovis, and hardly a generation had passed without a rebellion. Charles struck hard, swiftly, and without the cooperation of his brother, who refused to commit his troops. Charles had only a small force, but speed and audacity tumbled his opposition. Within two months the first of his domestic revolts was successfully crushed and his personal prestige was in the ascendant.

With Carloman's death, the eastern segment of the empire also fell to Charles. In this area the young king faced a complex set of problems. The nobility of his brother's kingdom had no reason to trust their new king. Across the Alps to the south the Lombards again threatened to extend their power over the entire peninsula of Italy at the expense of the papacy. To the east Bavaria was practically independent under an able and wily duke eager to exploit every chance to strengthen himself. To the northeast lay the numerous Saxons, the continental branch of the peoples who had invaded Britain three centuries before; they were a constant threat to the entire northeastern section of the Frankish empire.

It was against the Saxons that Charles turned his forces first. This campaign was essentially a tactical maneuver: if he succeeded in a Saxon war, he could bind Carloman's men to him in success and booty at the expense of a common foe; he could isolate potentially hostile Bavaria and confound a possible Saxon-Bavarian alliance; and he could free his hands for an Italian campaign. But at the same time, a Saxon war was dictated on even more basic grounds. The Saxons were numerous, fierce, and barbarian; hungry and expansive. They represented to Charles and the Frankish Empire precisely the same sort of threat that the Franks themselves had been to the Romans in an earlier age. This historic analogy was not lost upon Charles. Furthermore, the Saxons were beginning to move toward a larger unity in their hostility to the Franks. Charles also had a religious concern that cannot be ignored: the Saxons were pagan and their rites, which involved nature magic and human sacrifice, were horrifying to the Franks. Moreover, their religion acted as a cohesive force adding to their strength and unity. Charles decided that if he could undermine their religious unity he would pave the way for a political victory. Moving with the speed that was already becoming legend, he led his army into Saxony, leaving the enemy no time to form a front. He struck directly at one of their principal religious centers. Having captured it, he ordered the sacred trees cut down, burned the buildings, and seized the considerable treasure of this sacred place to distribute among his nobles and soldiers. Then he marched straight through the heart of Saxony devastating the countryside, until the Saxons sued for peace. Charles had accomplished his purpose: he had paid back Saxon raids in kind. He demanded an end to further raids and the Saxons accepted his terms. He could not know that this was only the beginning of thirty years of strife with them.

Then he turned to Italy. The threat of the Lombards against the papacy provided a convenient pretext for Charles to move against a power which was also a potent menace to him. Although Pepin had defeated the Lombards, he had left them as independent allies of the Franks. The next step was annexation. Charles' plan for European expansion left no room for a strong Lombard state that would intrude into the heart of the growing Frankish Empire. With masterful strategy Charles forced the Lombard king, Desiderius, to wager his kingdom on one key fortress, Pavia. This citadel was besieged and taken after nine months of resistance. Charles assumed the Iron Crown of Lombardy and extended the Frankish realm to Italy. He was gradually encroaching upon the barbaric borderland that separated him from the sphere of the eastern empire. (Emperor Constantine V must have pondered the Greek proverb, "The Frank makes a good friend, but a poor neighbor.")

Events now turned Charles' attention to the western extremity of his growing empire. At the annual encampment of the Frankish nobility in 777, Charles entertained an exotic embassy. The Moslem governor of Barcelona was planning a rebellion against the caliph of Cordova and sought the aid of the Franks. Charles pledged his support. His motives are not quite clear. Perhaps Charles saw in this an opportunity to divide and destroy an ancient enemy. He may even have thought he could conquer Spain completely—for in those triumphant years of expansion there seemed no reason to set limits to his ambition. Moorish Spain was not only a dangerous enemy but a rich prize. On the other hand, he may merely have wanted to establish a buffer between Spain and west Frankland. Whatever his hopes, however, Charles had to settle for less. He led his Franks over the Pyrenees and took a few northern strongholds. But the planned revolt did not take place. Frankish advance stopped at the fortress of Saragossa. Without time and support Charles could not take it; and he had neither. Word came that the Saxons had rebelled again and were streaming across the eastern frontier. Charles withdrew from Spain. No lands had been taken; there was no booty to distribute; and the ill-starred campaign was capped by a final disaster. As the Frankish army moved in column through the deep passes of the Pyrenees the wild Basque tribesmen fell suddenly on the rearguard, killing practically every member of it, and then melted away. Among the dead at the Pass of Roncesvalles was one whom the historian Einhard calls Hruodlandus, praefect of the Breton frontier. He was to reappear as the hero of the *Song of Roland,* the most famous medieval *chanson de geste* ("song of heroic deeds"), inspired by the events at Roncesvalles.

Charles turned savagely to the Saxon frontier and the Saxon wars assumed the stature of a crusade. Year after year Frankish armies penetrated Saxon lands, burned their crops and villages and looted their shrines. With each Frankish victory came Saxon submission and solemn guarantees of peace. With each Frankish withdrawal there were Saxon uprisings. The most fearful atrocities marked these years of bitter fighting. After one campaign Charles uprooted some ten thousand of the defeated Saxons and scattered them over other parts of his empire, hoping to break resistance by resettlement. The policy had no noticeable effect. On another occasion he ordered forty-five hundred Saxon prisoners beheaded, personally supervising the grim task. Such acts of terror only stiffened the opposition. In the long run, however, Saxon savagery and independence could not withstand Frankish organization and stubbornness. Inch by inch Saxony was conquered. It took eighteen campaigns and almost thirty years in all. Charles consolidated each gain by building forts and stationing garrisons. Persuasion was joined to force. In 781 the bishopric of Bremen was formed and the church moved in behind the armies. A network of missionary churches and abbeys grew out of the military posts. Saxony was slowly drawn into the orbit of the western, Christian world and Charlemagne had taken one more stride toward a united northern Europe.

To the south of Saxony lay Bavaria, held by Duke Tassilo, a cousin of Charlemagne. For more than twenty years these two men had eyed each other with suspicion. Tassilo was able and shrewd; no match for Charles in power and resources, he was his equal in ambition. In everything but name Bavaria was already independent; yet Tassilo resented the fact that his independence hung upon the will of Charles. As the exhausting

Saxon war at last came to a close, Tassilo made his long-delayed move into open rebellion and allied himself with the Avars, whose lands abutted his on the east. The potential danger of such an alliance to the Franks was enormous. But the potential was never realized. Charles moved with his customary speed against Bavaria. At this show of force Tassilo capitulated and made submission to Charles. Bavaria was put directly under Carolingian counts and, within a year, Tassilo was deposed, tonsured and removed to a monastery. Even with the Bavarian rebellion broken the Avars remained. Charles prepared carefully for the Avar wars. Einhard calls them the most important of Charles' reign save only the long conflict with the Saxons. The Avar empire had been in decline for over a century, but it was still a formidable power. The wars took eight years to conclude but, in the end, Charles' victory was complete. Pannonia was devastated and became a barren protective belt on the eastern flank of the Carolingian Empire. Because the wars were profitable they were popular. Victory gave the Franks the store of wealth that generations of Avar loot and tribute had piled up.

The Imperial Coronation

Through more than thirty years of war Charles had finally completed the work begun more than three centuries before by Clovis. The kingdom of the Franks had been turned into an empire. It remained only to turn its king into an emperor. On Christmas day of 800, in the Church of St. Peter in Rome, the king of the Franks was crowned "Emperor of the Romans." As Charles rose from prayer Pope Leo III stepped forward and placed a crown upon his head, while the crowds shouted, "To Charles Augustus, crowned of God, great and pacific Emperor of the Romans, life and victory!"[6]

Charles' coronation marked the culmination of that combination of accidents and choices that had enabled the Franks to survive their fellow barbarians and to extend their power over most of western Europe. Charles' realm was not the old Roman Empire—that had been dismembered centuries before—but the magic of the imperial ideal and of the imperial title had survived and remained powerful enough to transcend historical fact. It suited men to believe that the empire had never died and that Charles' assumption of the imperial title was simply the *translatio imperii,* the "succession of imperial power" to yet another hand and another

6. Thatcher and McNeal, *A Source Book for Mediaeval History,* p. 48.

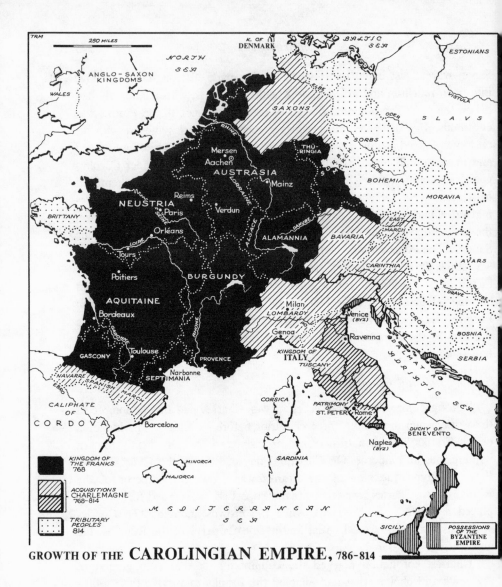

GROWTH OF THE **CAROLINGIAN EMPIRE,** 786-814

dynasty. The coronation, moreover, celebrated the fusion of what had been in times past discordant and opposing strains: the Roman, the German, and the Christian.

A Picture of the Emperor

Curiously, Einhard, Charlemagne's biographer, noted that the coronation came as a surprise to Charles and that he was somewhat troubled by it. Charles may have disliked the implication that his imperial power was the gift of the church. Or he may have feared an unfavorable reaction from

Constantinople. Perhaps, too, he felt that his new position might alienate him from his own Frankish people, the source of his strength. But in the end the attraction of the imperial tradition outweighed all other considerations and he accepted the dignity which no German king had taken before.

Einhard's account of Charlemagne at the time of his coronation is the more pertinent because the biographer was a close friend of the emperor —and at times his secretary and adviser. His short and straightforward portrait of Charles is surprisingly candid: Charles was an impressive figure, over six feet tall, heavy, and prodigiously strong (he could bend a sword blade double in his hands). He had a round head, commanding eyes, and a large nose over a drooping mustache. Oddly enough, for a man of his size, his voice was thin and high-pitched. But there was no doubt about the power of his presence. His every movement carried the authority of a lifetime of rule.

In many ways, Charles was still a typical German tribal king. Each year he called an assembly of Frankish landowners to sanction his acts and approve military levies. At these meetings Charles singled out the most notable men and honored them. He solicited the advice of respected elders. He joined the roughhouse of the vigorous young warriors. On these occasions he was the king of his people in a uniquely personal way. He wore the simple dress of the Franks, the tunic cinched with the ever-present sword belt; the close fitting "barbarian" pants, bound with crisscross bands. He was always readily available to any of his subjects and generous with the legion friends who constantly crowded around him—his "table companions" in peace, his command staff in war. He loved the barbarous old "Songs of Deeds," sung in his own Germanic dialects; and the rough jibes and crude jokes of the mimes who flocked to his court. He hated loneliness and temperance. He was a man of lusty appetite, be it for food, drink or women. A succession of wives and concubines gave him no fewer than eighteen children. He was fond of his children's company and denied them nothing. The picture of the great king playing, relaxing, dining, swimming, hunting with his court and family is most ingratiating. Perhaps the most striking impression we get of Charles is of one whose activity was ceaseless. He was constantly on the move, taking his court with him. The empire could scarcely be said to have had a capital; wherever the king was, there was his capital. He saw every corner of the realm—making decisions, holding court, redressing grievances, leading the hunt he loved so well. This peripatetic court was essentially the government of the Frankish Empire. The center and focus of it was Charles himself.

Charles and the State

In the years following his imperial coronation, Charlemagne turned increasingly to the work of peace. In addition to the constant job of policing the realm, there was still a need for considerable military consolidation. The Spanish war was resumed and Charles gradually brought a piece of northern Spain under his control. This was established as a Spanish march, a protective barrier between the Franks and the Moors. On the other menaced frontiers Charles had already begun to establish similar protective barriers in depth. During the Saxon wars the "Dane-mark" had been founded, in the peninsula that still bears its name, in order to frustrate a coalition between the Saxons and the Danes. Once Saxony was fully conquered Charles established a march against the Slavs just beyond the Saxon border to the east. After the Avar wars two more such marches were set up along the Bavarian-Bohemian frontier. Altogether these formed the defensive bulwarks of Charles' empire. He incorporated the marches into his governmental system. Each was administered by a royal *mark-graf,* "count of the march" (the later titles of margrave and marquis are derivatives) with extensive military power and discretionary authority. These marches, especially the ones on the eastern frontier, became important outposts of civilization. They were areas of colonization and, of course, Christianization. An episcopal organization was set over the marches and the church continued to work with the state against barbarism and paganism.

Within the vast area of the Carolingian Empire the reign of Charlemagne brought an order and stability which had never before existed. In general outline the old Merovingian system of government was maintained. But as Charles' conquests more than doubled his empire, the system was radically extended and a number of modifications introduced. The most serious weakness of Merovingian government had been the inability of the crown to control its powerful subordinates and the consequent alienation of land and authority. Under Charlemagne the management of local affairs was still in the hands of royal counts. But Charles saw to it that they were closely controlled. They were his agents. They derived their powers from him and, while they were normally appointed for life, he could and did sometimes remove them from office. The counts were usually powerful magnates whose lands lay in the regions they administered. The control of their tendency to seize and abuse power was as difficult as it was necessary. In order to effect this control Charles created the office of *missus dominicus,* "the king's agent." The empire was divided into large districts and these officials, traveling in pairs, made periodic tours. They were invested with great powers and yet hedged in by royal restrictions. The *missi,* usually a lay lord and an ecclesiastic, provided a check upon each other. They never traveled the same circuit in two successive years, thus preventing collusion with local authorities, and they were never assigned to areas where they had holdings of their own. They were compelled to render regular and careful reports and they were empowered to check abuses wherever they found them. They brought the impartiality of royal justice to every village and estate. They could even remove local officials from office. The effectiveness of the *missi* depended not only upon their own integrity and ability, but ultimately upon the personal force of Charles himself.

As the great king extended the range of government he rapidly passed beyond the limits of tradition and customary law. To express his will in areas not covered by existing law, he issued throughout his reign a series of edicts often called *capitularies,* chapters or, more correctly "headings" under which orders were issued. The scope of this legislation by decree is almost as broad as the province of government itself. Some of the capitularies are simple, summary orders; others are detailed administrative directives such as the so-called *Capitulare de Villis,* on the management of royal estates. The very scope and variety of the capitularies make them a rich source of information about the age of Charlemagne. They are, at the same time, clearly indicative of the personal force of Charles the Great.

Indeed, all the reforms which flourished in his reign flourished because of that same personal force. The government of Charles was strong because he was strong. In the last analysis it was a royal paternalism; and it was based upon the military-political-economic power of the king. The family wealth of the Carolingian mayors had been added to the crown lands of the royal house in the generation before Charlemagne. With each conquest the royal estates grew. Charles drew substantial support from these personal holdings which, quite apart from any other consideration, made him the most powerful person in the realm. Every Frankish warrior owed him the military service which had been a royal right since the days of Clovis. In military organization he was a worthy successor to his grandfather, Charles Martel. His constant campaigns, ranging over half a continent, transformed what might have been a "feudal levy" or unkempt militia into a regular military establishment. For a generation Charles was able to stop the growth of military feudalism and command the loyalty of a great body of troops. In the military, as in the civil administration, the decisive power was the king's, and his personal leadership was a significant factor in his military success.

The same autocratic power that Charles wielded so impressively elsewhere, he wielded over the church. He regarded it as "his" church. In this attitude he followed the tradition not only of his own family but of the earlier Merovingians, who had subordinated the church to the state. But to the arguments of tradition and expediency Charles added another, the argument of divine right. This was certainly traditional in part. The ancient Merovingian kings, even when superficially Christian, had still been surrounded with an aura of pagan divinity. The late classical kingship of the Roman Empire was a concept which flowed into the barbarian tribal monarchies, and which continued to exist in the Byzantine Empire. Charlemagne was convinced that he was the agent of God. From this lofty position it was perfectly natural for him to treat the church as simply another of those many provinces which lay within the scope of his responsibility.

This conception made it thoroughly plausible, indeed proper, that he be not only king but emperor. If anything dampened his enthusiasm, as Einhard intimates, on the occasion of his imperial coronation, it was the implication that he owed his elevation to the pope. In fact, this was to be one of the precedents cited some centuries later in the bitter struggle between the papacy and the empire. But in his time, Charles clearly stood above the papacy. It existed at his sufferance. He usually cooperated with papal designs and treated the pope with great deference for his sacred office, but there was no question of equality, dual monarchy, or the "two swords." Charles regarded the pope as he regarded his Frankish bishops, as subordinates, to be chosen, directed, chastised if necessary.

His legislation touched matters of religion and ecclesiastical policy as freely as it touched the secular. He dealt with church property, he dispensed church offices when he needed to use them, and went so far as to set up bishoprics whose holders he then appointed. He was not above preaching to his clergy on discipline, piety, and learning. And he was a regular pedant in his insistence on liturgical purity.

Charles was, nevertheless, very generous to the church. Like his predecessors he realized the invaluable service organized religion rendered to the state. He fostered the civilizing work of the church; he made no attempt to curtail its temporal role. The church could not complain of his material support for he gave a great part of the booty from the Avar wars to the papacy, and he gave land to the church everywhere. At his death he was to give two thirds of his vast estates to his bishops.

The Carolingian Renaissance

It was in cooperation with the church that Charlemagne affected that momentary intellectual revival which is often called the Carolingian Renaissance. The stimulus was the interest of the king, but the response necessarily had to come from the clergy. The concept of lay learning was almost dead by the ninth century and intellectual skills were largely those of the clergy. This fact determined both the excellencies and the limitations of the Carolingian revival. The emperor himself was a zealous scholar. He had managed to pack into his crowded and active life at least the rudiments of learning. In addition to his own Frankish dialect and those of related German peoples, he could speak Latin with native fluency and even some Greek. His speech was cultivated, "fluent and ready, and [he] could express with the greatest clearness whatever he wished." Charlemagne's taste and interest in learning led him to encourage it. But there was a more basic motive. He was not content with the simple monarchical system of the Merovingians. Wherever he looked he saw the need for reform: he wanted a more stable and systematic government and a more efficient economic organization for his empire. And he realized that only with the help of educated administrators could he achieve these aims. To this end he established the famous palace school at Aachen. Its moving spirit was the English scholar Alcuin (735–804). He had studied in the cathedral school at York in Northumbria and his erudition flowed from the same sources of Anglo-Irish religion and learning that had already enriched the continent for a century. Charles had met Alcuin in Italy and persuaded him to return to Frankland, where he remained for the rest of his life. Like Bede, of the previous generation, Alcuin was a thoroughly competent scholar and dedicated teacher. He was not only the master of Charlemagne's school, but the author of most of its textbooks, ranging from spelling to dialectic.

The fame of Alcuin and the patronage of the emperor attracted a brilliant group of men to Aachen. Paul the Deacon, a Lombard scholar and historian of his people, came from Italy. Also from Italy came Peter of Pisa, a noted grammarian. From Visigothic Spain came the poet Theodulf. Only a few Franks graced this learned circle, among them, Einhard. The court and the school flowed easily together and Charles himself was as eager a pupil as any young scholar at the benches. The distinguished men of learning were regular members of the court circle surrounding Charles and his family. The members of the court took their meals together and the table was turned into a colloquium over which the king himself presided. The palace school was attended by the children of the nobility and officialdom; but any child who showed intellectual promise might find his way to the school. One of the most warmly human pictures we have of Charlemagne is his visiting the school, questioning the wide-eyed children with mock seriousness; rewarding learning with a pat, or punishing laziness or carelessness with a royal scolding. The school had already begun to accomplish Charles' purpose before the end of his reign. Its graduates were finding places in every department of government and the next generation of abbots and bishops was deeply impressed by the training of Alcuin and the palace school. With encouragement from Charles, the influence of the palace school extended to monastic and cathedral schools throughout the empire.

One of the important consequences of the Carolingian scholastic revival was a serious interest in classical studies. Under the leadership of Alcuin and his circle, and with the cooperation of other schools and scholars, classical texts began to be systematically collected and preserved. Practically all the classical texts we now have we owe to Carolingian manuscripts. Many monasteries had libraries which were not to be rivaled in size or quality until the great collections of the Renaissance. In connection with the classical revival and the collection and copying of manuscripts, Alcuin introduced an important writing reform, a new "book hand" called Carolingian *minuscule*. With its beautifully rounded and shaded characters it produced fine manuscripts and rapidly became the standard form, replacing the spidery, difficult, and illegible hand that had been the vogue before. Charlemagne was interested in this calligraphic reform and used to keep writing materials under his pillow so that "he might in his spare moments accustom himself to the formation of letters. But he made little advance in this strange task, which was begun too late in life."

In addition to an interest in the ancient classics, Carolingian scholars were interested in the basic texts of the Christian tradition. This too reflects the interest of the king, for Charlemagne was convinced of the pseudo-priestly character of his monarchy and thought of himself as a pre-eminently Christian king and emperor. A standard, authoritative reading of St. Jerome's fourth-century Vulgate was established; the Roman liturgy was adopted and made uniform in the Frankish Church; a standard Benedictine rule was imposed upon all monasteries; and a standard edition of the works of Gregory the Great was carefully prepared. There were dozens of commentaries upon Scripture and quotation books collected from the writings of the church fathers.

With all the support of Charles and with all the initial vigor that it displayed, the Carolingian Renaissance never became a general movement. In spite of royal encouragement the secular nobility and the laity generally were little affected by educational reform and took only the most passing interest in literacy. For the most part, the Carolingian Renaissance was narrowly clerical and had little impact upon the great mass of society; furthermore, it produced little original work of high quality. Its efforts were extremely tentative. Much of it has the formal quality of a school exercise and the naiveté that such exercises imply. The age produced no first-rate author and no single literary classic. Einhard's *Life of Charles the Great,* for all its historical value, is not great literature. Even the Carolingian scholarship, to which western literature is so greatly indebted, was more mechanical than creative. With only a few exceptions, there was a singular lack of the critical spirit so essential to sound scholarship. Alcuin, who tended to set the tone of this learned revival, was neither original nor creative. He was a scholastic pedant with a prodigious and undiscriminating memory for quotation.

Charlemagne's brave attempt to build a cultural monument to himself and for his people lasted only through the generation of his grandsons. Einhard survived Charles and continued his literary work. His younger contemporary Lupus, Abbot of Ferrières, was one of the most astute and learned men of his time, a great Latinist and manuscript collector. The learned Abbot of Fulda, Rabanus Maurus, wrote an encyclopedia more popular than that of Isidore of Seville—and almost as naive. The age abounds in monastic chronicles which are a fascinating source of historical anecdotes. Joannes Scotus Erigena (*c.* 815–877), the most original and creative philosophic mind in a span of seven centuries, was the ornament of the court of Charles the Bald, one of the grandsons of Charlemagne. He was respected as a famous scholar and teacher, but his lofty speculation —perhaps the first mature philosophic system of the Middle Ages—was not really understood and had no significant influence until the twelfth century. He left no disciples in his own time and was himself the last great figure of the Carolingian Renaissance. The narrow base on which it rested was violently shaken by the political and military disasters of the century after Charlemagne.

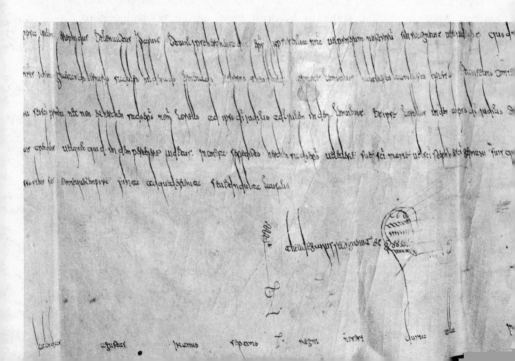

Interior, Chapel of Charlemagne. Consecrated 805 A.D. Aachen (Aix-la-Chappelle).

OPPOSITE
Above: *Charlemagne?* 9th century A.D.
Below: *The Judgment of Charlemagne for the Abbey of St. Denis*
(detail). 22 July 775 A.D.

The Weaknesses of the Carolingian Empire

Charlemagne's renown grew as the years of his reign stretched into decades. Legend had already begun to encrust his name. The barbarian peoples beyond the marches held him in awe. In 812 the eastern emperor, after a decade of diplomatic maneuvering, finally recognized Charles as emperor of the west. His name carried even to distant Baghdad and the caliph Harun al-Raschid sought an alliance with Charles to harry Byzantium on its European flank. To signify his goodwill Harun sent Charles an elaborate water clock and an elephant, which was one of the wonders of the Frankish court.

The legendary reputation of the emperor Charles masked the effects of age but, beneath the mask, the forces of disintegration worked with increasing rapidity, not only upon the weakening body of Charles but upon the empire which depended so directly on him.

Even the vigor of Charlemagne's youth might not have sufficed to reverse the tendencies which had now become apparent, for these stemmed from fundamental weaknesses in the structure of the Carolingian Empire.

The empire did not rest upon an adequate economic base; the state of Charles the Great was fundamentally agrarian. There were cities, of course, and there was some trade, perhaps more extensive than we now suspect. But the greater number of people lived upon the soil and counted their substance in acreage, flocks, and produce. This was true even of the king. The Carolingian agricultural economy, furthermore, could seldom boast a surplus. In fact, it usually tended to the level of subsistence—not above. In good years, the people could feed themselves.

As long as the Franks were expansive they supplemented their imperial income by conquest; they did not raise the level of productivity but simply brought more land into their hands. The wars of Charlemagne had been, by and large, extremely profitable, not only in conquered land but in booty, coin, plate, and treasure. The military loot sufficed to give the crown an enormous surplus in the simple economic system of the Franks. It was this wealth, created by war, that enabled Charlemagne to implement his administrative reforms, support the cultural activity of the Carolingian Renaissance, and purchase the doubtful loyalty of some possible enemies at home and beyond his frontiers.

Charlemagne's empire, however, was largely self-limiting; and its limits were reached in his time. To the east lay the Slavic corridor, which offered no profit to match the cost of its conquest. To the west lay the ocean. To the north beyond the "Danish mark" was the land of the fierce Vikings, who were becoming restless before the end of Charles' reign. Spain, southern Italy and the Mediterranean were securely held by the Saracens. This latter represented the most severe limitation to the economic growth of the Carolingian Empire. The potentiality of trade and industry that would, in time, make the barbaric north Atlantic coasts the market place of the world was not to be realized for centuries. The sunny Mediterranean, which had been the broad highway of western commerce since the beginning of civilization, remained so—and Charles had no access to it. The Arab historian, Ibn-Khaldun, was not far wrong when he wrote that the Christians could not float a plank upon that sea. Thus, its natural limits of expansion reached, the empire of Charles the Great began to regress, to run down in prosperity as the old king neared the end of his long reign.

This process of economic decline bred an increasing restiveness among the natural enemies of royal stability both within and beyond the borders. The incipient regionalism which Charles and his ancestors had fought so constantly in Aquitaine, Bavaria, Saxony, and elsewhere began to reassert itself. The widening cracks of modern national division were beginning to spread across the artificial unity of the Carolingian Empire. The selfish desires of the nobility, each to be king of his own estates, added to the problem of internal control. Civil disobedience was on the upswing everywhere: the *missi dominici* were resisted by armed bands; formidable rebellious lords went unpunished; the military discipline that had once marked Charles' army was weakened by desertion. Men refused their obligatory military service and hid their wealth.

All these incidents testified to the increasing arrogance, power, and independence of the nobility, and the weakening of the control that the strong Carolingians had managed to exercise. In the vigor of his youthful rule, Charles had unwittingly contributed to the problems of his old age. A lifetime of war had been profitable for the nobility but costly for the mass of the people. The backbone of Charles' conquering army had been the Frankish peasantry, the loyal, sturdy freeholders sworn to render military service to their king. As the wars carried them farther from home and kept them beyond the time of planting or harvest on some burned-over frontier, their own modest estates suffered. Charles had been aware of this cost and its consequences and had tried to distribute the burden of service, but with no great success. The simple, inflexible economic system of the Frankish Empire gave him no real alternative. In the distribution of lands and booty the lion's share had gone to the greater nobility, the regional lords who led the contingents of the army. The loyalty of these men was kept by grants of land and with each campaign they grew stronger. And with every victory Charles fed his secret enemies. As they grew strong the lesser men around them diminished, losing first their lands and then their freedom until the whole lower segment of Frankish society was dragged down toward the hopeless immobility of serfdom.

As these complex and inevitable internal problems broke the surface serenity of Charles' last years, he turned to prayers that were not answered and laws that could not be enforced. Troubles spread across the marches; raids came, and went unpunished. Moslem power in Spain was on the upsurge again, striking at the Mediterranean coasts of the empire and the Rhone valley. The savage Danes on the northeast frontier had cut through the frontier to menace Saxony and their seafaring cousins were harassing the Frankish coasts with pirate raids. The Vikings were gathering. One of the later biographies of Charlemagne, written by a monk of St. Gall, tells a grimly prophetic story. Charles was visiting one of his western port cities of Gaul when Vikings raided the city. The great king looked on helplessly and wept. "Do you know why I weep so bitterly, my true servants? I have no fear of these worthless rascals doing any harm to me; but I am sad at heart to think that even during my lifetime they have dared to touch this shore; and I am torn by a great sorrow because I foresee what evil things they will do to my descendants and their subjects."[7]

The tragedy of Charlemagne was that, like Augustus, he outlived those he wished to succeed him. In 810 Pepin, his favorite son and chosen successor, died; and in the next year his son Charles followed. Only one remained, the least able and least warlike of the three, Louis, already called "the Pious." Charlemagne raised Louis beside himself to the throne of the empire and its exalted title. He disposed of his vast personal treasury and lands and made his peace with God. In January, 814, Charles the Great died, "in the seventy-second year of his life and in the forty-seventh year of his reign."

7. Quoted in A. J. Grant, *Early Lives of Charlemagne* . . . , pp. 138-39.

SUGGESTIONS FOR FURTHER READING

᠁

General Works

The Cambridge Economic History (Cambridge University Press, 1941-52), Vol. I, ed. by J. H. Clapham and E. Power, deals almost entirely with medieval agrarian economy; Vol. II, ed. by M. Postan and E. E. Rich, deals largely with medieval trade and industry.

The Shorter Cambridge Medieval History, ed. by C. W. Previté-Orton (Cambridge: Cambridge University Press, 1952), tends to correct if not replace the older multivolume *Cambridge Medieval History* which, however, may still be read with considerable value; see especially Vols. I and II.

J. W. Thompson and E. N. Johnson, *An Introduction to Medieval Europe, 300–1500* (New York: Norton, 1937), probably the best and certainly one of the most comprehensive of medieval textbooks.

J. M. Wallace-Hadrill, *The Barbarian West, 400–1000* (New York: Rinehart, 1957).

Primary Sources and Original Works

The historical work of the Venerable Bede. A standard text is the Loeb Edition, but there is a good abridgment entitled **History of the English Church and People,* tr. by J. Sherley-Price (Baltimore: Penguin, 1961).

The works of Gregory the Great; there are many editions and selections.

The Rule of St. Benedict (London: Newman Press, 1952).

Gregory of Tours, *History of the Franks,* tr. by O. M. Dalton (Oxford: Clarendon Press, 1927).

Early Lives of Charlemagne by Eginhard and the Monk of St. Gall, tr. and ed. by A. J. Grant (London: Chatto and Windus, 1922).

Special Topics

S. Dill, *Roman Society in Gaul in the Merovingian Age* (London: Macmillan, 1926).

A. Dopsch, *The Economic and Social Foundations of European Civilization* (London: Kegan Paul, 1937), a famous "thesis" book on the question of the continuity of classical culture into the Middle Ages.

E. S. Duckett, *Alcuin, Friend of Charlemagne* (New York: Macmillan, 1951).

———, *Anglo-Saxon Saints and Scholars* (New York: Macmillan, 1947).

———, *The Gateway to the Middle Ages* (New York: Macmillan, 1938).

H. Fichtenau, *The Carolingian Empire,* tr. by P. Munz (Oxford: Blackwell, 1957), a series of essays on several leading topics of Carolingian scholarship.

T. Hodgkin, *Charles the Great* (London: Macmillan, 1897).

*W. P. Ker, *The Dark Ages* (New York: Mentor, 1958), a distinguished literary history, but somewhat demanding.

M. L. W. Laistner, *Thought and Letters in Western Europe,* A.D. *500–900* (New York: Dial Press, 1931).

W. Levison, *England and the Continent in the Eighth Century* (Oxford: Clarendon Press, 1946).

*H. Pirenne, *Mohammed and Charlemagne,* cited for Chap. 6 (an opposing view to Dopsch's, *q.v.*).

*E. Power, *Medieval People* (London: Methuen, 1950), contains a reconstruction of the life of a Carolingian peasant.

*R. Winston, *Charlemagne: From the Hammer to the Cross* (Indianapolis: Bobbs-Merrill, 1954), best biography of Charles.

H. Zimmer, *The Irish Element in Medieval Culture* (New York: Putnam, 1891).

*Paperbound edition. In the case of reprint editions, publisher and date of publication given will be that of reprint rather than the original.

➣ 8 ➢

Chaos and Feudalism

NEW STATES FOR OLD:
THE TRANSFORMATION OF THE CAROLINGIAN EMPIRE

The Carolingian Succession

Louis the Pious succeeded to an inheritance of troubles that would have taxed even the strength of his father, Charlemagne: it overwhelmed him. Louis was by now middle aged and had already fathered a wolf pack of sons who began almost immediately to clamor for their shares of the empire. Like Lear, Louis initiated a series of divisions which only partially satisfied any of the rapacious brothers. Then, in 823, by a second wife, Louis sired "a son of his old age" who immediately became his favorite. The doting Louis made another division of the empire in 829 to accommodate the child, Charles. This act drove the older brothers into open revolt. Louis lacked the strength and prestige to hold the loyalty of his army and the troops scattered to serve the sons against the father. The magnates, who had already begun to escape the close rein of Charlemagne, hastened to claim their independence. Each man served his own interests; parties formed overnight around the standards of father and sons and civil war raged from one end of the Carolingian Empire to the other.

Neither the death of his son Pepin in 838 nor that of the Emperor Louis in 840 solved the problem of succession that had already boiled for almost a generation. Three brothers remained: Lothair, the eldest; Louis,

289

who was to be called "the German"; and the half-brother Charles, now almost grown and soon to be known as Charles "the Bald." The two younger brothers allied against Lothair, who claimed the imperial title, and another round of civil war reached a bloody climax in the pitched Battle of Fontenay in 841. Louis and Charles gained a inconclusive victory, for neither faction was strong enough to press for a further decision. Out of the impasse came a formal treaty of partition in 843, called the Treaty of Verdun. By its terms the empire was divided into three realms: Lothair held on to the imperial title and the ancient Frankish heartland of the lower Rhine. To this area was added a long corridor of land stretching south across the Alps to include northern Italy. This ill-contrived "Middle Kingdom" was known as Lothairingia, the land of Lothair (the French province of Lorraine still preserves the name), and it was destined to be the bloodiest battleground in the history of continental Europe. Charles the Bald had always drawn his chief support from the south and west (his mother had been a princess of Aquitaine) and the general area of West Frankland—mainly Romance in speech—went to him. Louis, who

TREATY OF VERDUN, 843

had been given the subkingdom of Bavaria twenty-five years before and who had identified his interests with the German lands, took the eastern empire—mainly Teutonic in blood and speech.

A significant document survives from the preliminary negotiations of the Treaty of Verdun. The two suspicious brothers, Charles and Louis, exchanged oaths before their assembled armies at Strassburg. Each swore his loyalty to the other, before the troops of the other, and in the language that the troops understood. The oath that Charles took was, as one would expect, in Old German. But that which Louis spoke to the men of West Frankland was in a Romance dialect from which modern French stems. These Strassburg Oaths are a subtle indication that at least two of the most basic divisions of modern Europe were beginning to form: the West Frankland of Charles the Bald was assuming the shadowy outlines of historic France; the East Frankland of Louis, those of Germany.

The pernicious divisions of the realm continued. At Lothair's death, in 855, his unstable state was divided among his three sons. In 876 the lands of Louis were similarly divided. With each shift of territories, the greed and pride of uncles and nephews flared into war. In other parts of the empire—the south of France, Burgundy, central Italy—local strong men declared themselves kings with no one to deny them. The weak central government, the fragmentation of authority, allowed those who dared seize power to do so. Everywhere offices and lands became hereditary. As internal dissolution followed partition and civil war, the external enemies who had been held at bay by Charlemagne's power seized their opportunities. Moslem pirates, striking from North Africa, Sicily, and Spain, ravaged the Mediterranean coasts of Europe time after time. They even endangered Rome and penetrated the suburbs of the city before they were beaten back. Commerce of all kinds came to a standstill in the western gulf of the Mediterranean. Far to the east another menace emerged from yet one more of those seemingly endless nomadic peoples of central Asia; this time it was the Magyars. With Charlemagne's destruction of the Avar kingdom, the way had been opened to them, and once more Europe knew the terror of "the Huns," as the Magyars were called. They spread out of the Danube valley to strike at Italy, Burgundy, the whole German frontier, and even into West Frankland.

The Vikings

The most serious external threat to the faltering empire came, however, neither from Saracen pirates nor Magyar horsemen, but from the raids

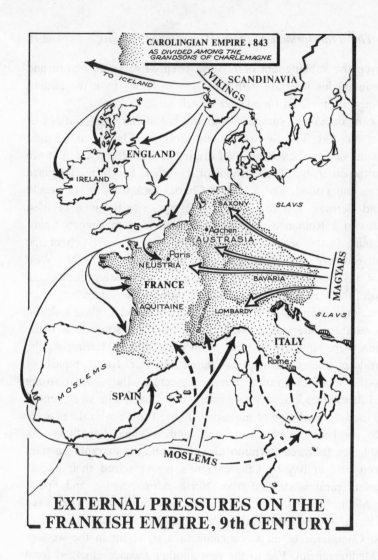

EXTERNAL PRESSURES ON THE FRANKISH EMPIRE, 9th CENTURY

Caption/labels within map:
CAROLINGIAN EMPIRE, 843 — AS DIVIDED AMONG THE GRANDSONS OF CHARLEMAGNE

TO ICELAND — VIKINGS — SCANDINAVIA
ENGLAND
IRELAND
SAXONY — SLAVS
Aachen — AUSTRASIA
Paris — NEUSTRIA
FRANCE — BAVARIA — MAGYARS
AQUITAINE — BURGUNDY — LOMBARDY — SLAVS
ITALY — Rome
MOSLEMS
SPAIN
MOSLEMS

and migrations of the savage Norsemen, or Vikings, pouring out of the wastes of Scandinavia. This indeed was the age of the Vikings. For centuries the Norsemen had inhabited Scandinavia, surviving its cold and hardships. The poverty of the land and rigor of the seasons had turned them to the sea from early times and made them shipbuilders, fishermen, and pirates. Their way of life was simple and hard, their economy rudimentary, their religion a vigorous and realistic paganism. They resembled other branches of the great family of Germanic peoples whose migrations in earlier centuries had changed the political and ethnic map of Europe. But the new barbarians were completely untouched by the moderating influence of the older civilizations.

Their migrations were set in motion in the ninth and tenth centuries by a combination of forces. The gradual increase of population was pressing against the limit of their land's productivity. There was the lure and profit of sea adventure wedded to ambition, daring, and curiosity. Furthermore, in the second half of the ninth century a larger political pattern began to be imposed upon them. In Norway, a chieftain named Harold the Fairhaired (*860–930*) formed the first Scandinavian kingdom. Similar states were soon formed in Denmark and Sweden. The move toward central authority was bitterly fought by the many village and sea "kings" and, as monarchy won out, many lesser chieftains still refusing to submit, combined into raiding bands to move out across the narrow seas. These rebellious adventurers were the spearhead of the great Viking migrations which were to have such far-reaching effect upon the civilization of the Middle Ages. The success of their raids along the coasts of northern Europe revealed the weakness and division of their enemies: more adventurers followed. From their homelands the Norsemen moved out along three general routes.

The "eastern route" was largely dominated by the Swedes. They followed the long bend of the eastern Baltic, penetrating the Gulf of Finland and the rivers leading into the plains of Russia. At Novgorod they established a permanent base from which they moved south to the Dnieper River and thence to the Black Sea. Their relations with the varied Slavic peoples must be reconstructed from the most sketchy pieces of evidence. There was no Russia in a large political sense, but from time to time one local prince or another could gain a temporary hegemony. Byzantine history has scattered references to such ephemeral "kings" of the Russians. Those same references occasionally refer to "Varangians" among the motley forces of the Russian armies. This was one of the names by which the Slavs knew the Swedes, who were appearing among them in the ninth and tenth centuries in increasing numbers. From a beginning as adventurers, pirates, traders, and mercenaries, the Swedes soon gained the upper hand along the river routes leading to the Black Sea. They took advantage of the endemic localism of the Slavs to impose their harsh protection upon them.

In the mid-ninth century a Swedish chieftain named Rurik established himself at Novgorod and in the next generation his successors took the important southern fortress of Kiev. The duchy that grew from Varangian Kiev was the nucleus of the first Russian state. (Even the names Russia and Russian seem to have derived from *Rus,* another name by which the Slavs knew their masters.) The restless adventuring of the Swedes eventually brought them to Constantinople. Half-pirate, half-merchant, they dominated the rich trade in heavy goods and raw materials that flowed out of the vast hinterland of Russia into the Golden City. A Moslem representative of the caliph of Baghdad wrote of these adventurers from another world:

I saw how the Northmen [Norsemen] had arrived with their wares, and pitched their camp besides the Volga. Never did I see people so gigantic; they are as tall as palm trees; and florid and ruddy of complexion. . . . The men among them wear a garment of rough cloth, which is thrown over one side, so that one hand remains free. Every one carries an ax, a dagger, and a sword, and without these weapons they are never seen. Their swords are broad, with wavy lines, and of Frankish make. From the tip of the finger-nails to the neck, each man of them is tattooed with pictures of trees, living beings, and other things.[1]

The Varangian route became an important artery of trade, bringing the half-civilized Swedes in direct contact with the fabulous Byzantine east that most of the more civilized peoples of the west knew only in fables. The lively trade brought from Constantinople vast quantities of precious metal and coin, trade goods and trinkets which have been found in the burial treasures of Swedish Viking kings. For almost two centuries, until the eve of the Crusades, the Byzantine emperors recruited their personal bodyguards from the Varangians.

On the other side of the world, the Norwegian cousins of the Varangians were opening the "western passage." Before the end of the eighth century they had skirted the northern point of Scotland and raided the Irish coast. By the middle of the ninth century their ramshackle, fortified villages dominated the bays and inlets of the Irish coast. They raided inland almost at will and the native clans, hating each other as much as the invaders, could make no common cause against them. The rich monasteries which had been the western outposts of civilization for centuries were the targets of these Norse raids; Danes followed Norwegians to complete the ruin of medieval Ireland and Celtic Christianity never recovered.

Using Ireland and the northern islands as steppingstones the Norse sailors pushed on to the west across the open sea. Some time after the middle of the ninth century they discovered Iceland and began to settle there. Word came back from a ship, storm-blown far to the west, that there were lands to be had there. A chieftain named Erik, "the Red," set

1. In Norton Downs (ed.), *Basic Documents in Medieval History* (Princeton: D. Van Nostrand Co., 1959), p. 38.

a colony on the tip of Greenland. Leif, the son of Erik, pushed on to the coast of North America. Thus, more than five centuries before the Age of Discovery the Vikings had "discovered" North America and made it the western anchor of a flourishing Atlantic empire.

Iceland remained the center of this Viking land and continued to attract streams of colonists. It supplied, in turn, most of those who migrated to the more westerly colonies. The colonists brought to Iceland both the political institutions which had begun to shape Norse society in Scandinavia and the traditional folklore of their homeland. In this isolated and desolate corner of the world this cultural heritage was elaborated into what was to be the richest, purest, and most perfectly preserved of Teutonic literary forms: the myths and hero stories collected into the Eddas and Epic sagas. Embodying a great variety of forms and subjects, this literature brings to life the Norse gods: Odin, the wise friend of man; Thor, the protector of Midgard (the inhabitable earth) against the Frost-Giants; Loki, the mischievous negator. Equally impressive are the traditional heroes, partly mythical, partly historical figures. We shall return to consider them in Chapter 10.

Important as were the effects of the Viking migrations to the extremities of the world, the greatest impact upon western civilization was made by those who took the "middle passage" that led them to the shores of Anglo-Saxon England and the seaboard of the Carolingian Empire.

The division of England among its petty kings invited attack and, by the middle of the ninth century, the Danes had gained a firm foothold on the northeastern shore and were raiding and settling all along the North Sea coast. What might well have been another complete Teutonic conquest of England was halted by Alfred the Great (*871–900*), king of Wessex, who mobilized what resistance was left in England. The best he could do was to hold the line that Danish conquest had defined. By the Peace of Wedmore (878) the island was divided. The area of Danish occupation, called the Danelaw, comprised eastern and northeastern England; it was separated from the Saxon holdings by a line from London northwest to Chester. Indeed, most of England was in Danish hands; but in the portion of the island that he held Alfred began the work of national unification. He strengthened London as the base of a line of fortifications that traced the frontier. He organized a naval force and set up a military system, basing service upon wealth. Out of the grim necessity of survival Anglo-Saxon England was finally achieving unity.

Alfred, like Charlemagne, attached great importance to learning and

made his court the center of a renaissance. Himself a scholar of considerable accomplishment, he translated from Latin into Anglo-Saxon Boethius'
Consolation of Philosophy, the *Pastoral Care* of Gregory the Great, and
possibly the *Ecclesiastical History* of Bede, in addition to other works. He
also had a hand in starting the *Anglo-Saxon Chronicle,* the most valuable
source for English history up to the consolidation of the Norman Conquest
in the eleventh century.

The task of retaking the Danelaw was left to the sons and descendants
of Alfred. Although the Danes continued to migrate to England, the united
opposition created by Alfred's work gradually reduced the Danelaw and
integrated it with the organization of the growing state. At the same time

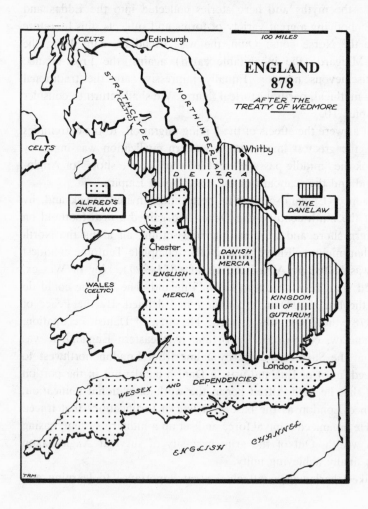

the English Danes were slowly losing their alien character by merging with the native, predominantly Anglo-Saxon population.

On the continental side of the Channel, the same pattern of raid, settlement, and conquest was taking place at the expense of the Carolingian Empire. The disunity of the heirs of Charlemagne and the incipient feudalism of the coastal regions invited the Vikings: the river valleys opened up the interior to them. The towns of the Rhine and Scheldt were devastated; Rouen and Paris, on the Seine, were attacked in 843, 845, 851, and 861; the lands, cities, churches, and monasteries of the Loire valley were devastated in 853—their spires and holy crosses proclaiming their wealth and defenselessness; the Vikings also penetrated deep into the south of France along the Garonne. Even Moorish Spain and the Mediterranean were not free of them. The records of the age are filled with sorrows, prayers, and curses.

With the second half of the ninth century, in West Frankland, in Russia, and in the distant western world, Norse raids grew from the pirate attacks of a few dozen marauders into migrations intent upon conquest and settlement. In 882 the whole of Frisia came into the hands of one Viking chieftain. In 885 forty thousand Norsemen and seven hundred ships moved up the Seine and laid siege to Paris, the key fortress whose control meant the domination of northeastern France. Paris was saved by the sturdy resistance of its people and the leadership of its count and bishop through a harrowing siege of almost a year. In unmistakable contrast to the courage of his Parisian subjects, the weak and indecisive Carolingian king Charles the Fat (*881–887*) bribed the same Viking army that Paris had resisted. Paris stood, but downriver toward the sea Viking settlements took root, with Rouen becoming a Viking capital of sorts. In the next generation, the West Frankish king, known to history by the devastating name of Charles the Simple (*893–923*), granted to the Viking leader, Hrolf the Walker, the land of the lower Seine valley. By the terms of their treaty, this land became the Duchy of Normandy; the uncouth barbarian adventurer became its duke, Christian lord, and vassal of the king. Of all the Norse settlements from Russia to Greenland, none was to affect western civilization and European history more profoundly.

The Founding of Capetian France

The Viking seizure of Normandy was simply one instance of what had become a universal trend in western Europe. On every frontier, in every province, local power was firmly gathered into the hands of either invaders or native magnates. In 887 the lords of the north of France met at the assembly of Tribur and deposed the cowardly and incompetent Charles the Fat, a descendant of Charlemagne, electing in his stead Count Odo of Paris, the hero of the Viking siege. For a century the constantly diminishing dignity of the kingship was wrested from one hand to another. There were still Carolingians; the claim of Charlemagne's blood was strong, and the church lent its powerful support to tradition. Twice the descendants of Odo (they are often called Robertians after Odo's father, Count Robert the Strong) held the throne briefly. Then in 987 the last West Frankish Carolingian died and the shadowy claim of the Robertians resulted in the election of Hugh Capet by the nobility.

Hugh was the heir of Count Odo and Robert the Strong, and with him began the first completely French dynasty, that of the Capetians. But in 987, neither fame nor power commended the house of Hugh. On the contrary, the most compelling reason for his election was his weakness. The title of king brought with it the meaningless claim to "crown lands." Most of these had long since been alienated, and what few remained were widely scattered and of little consequence. What practical power Hugh Capet had, he had as a result of his own family lands, the holdings of the counts of Paris. As he became king, these lands became the new royal domain. Called the Île-de-France, it constituted a narrow corridor between Paris on the north and Orléans on the south, seventy miles distant. This scant holding was dwarfed by the vast domains that boxed it in on every side—the lands of the Count of Champagne to the east, Flanders to the north, Blois to the west; and, more distantly, the powerful and extensive duchies of Normandy, Burgundy, and Anjou. In terms of any actual military strength, Hugh Capet was not even the first among equals.

In the time of Hugh Capet, then, the kingship was more a tradition than a political, economic, or military reality; yet a tradition so deeply rooted that not even the most powerful and ambitious of territorial lords seriously attacked it. Its roots went back through the Carolingians to the pagan sanctity of the German tribal kings, on the one hand, and to the classical divinity of the Roman emperors, on the other. The king's office was a holy office; Charlemagne had not doubted this, nor did Hugh Capet nor did the nobility who elected him. Divine right and supernatural sanction were part of the tradition and of cardinal importance. The church consistently supported the monarchy. Closely related to the sacred position accorded the king was the theory of his moral supremacy. He was the keeper of the peace, the ultimate judicial authority, the champion of right.

The great lords who towered above him in actual power were, in theory, his dependents. The elaborate network of feudal law was evolving to spell out the details of that dependency.

Interested as the Capetians were in laying claim to the theoretical rights of kingship, their most pressing concern was practical survival and the enlargement of the small powers which they actually held. The early Capetians worked unceasingly to assert their authority in their own lands. In this they differed not at all from the counts and dukes who were their neighbors. Everywhere local lords fought for their independence against any tendency to centralization. Every fortified country house was a pro tem palace and every tattered robber-baron a sovereign in his own eyes. Year after year the Capetian kings took the field to reduce the bandit nests that infested the countryside. Rebellious petty vassals were frequently as powerful as the king. It was not until the reign of Louis the Fat (*1108–1137*), over a century after the death of Hugh Capet, that this work was completed and the Capetian kings were truly kings even in the Île-de-France. Much of the credit must go to that warrior-king. His energy equalled his bulk and though, in his later years, he had to be hoisted into the saddle, he was a formidable champion. The weight of his sword earned respect for his crown. He was able to pass on to his son, Louis VII (*1137–1180*) a pacified and reasonably orderly state.

In the work of asserting feudal authority, the Capetian kings were actually no more successful than the great dukes and counts. But the kingship which the Capetians held added another dimension to their work. As they made good their claims to authority in their own lands, they received appeals for help from beyond the borders of the Île-de-France. In their royal capacity they heard these appeals and wherever possible answered them with effective force. This not only enhanced the prestige of the monarchy but gradually enlarged the royal domain. By the time of Louis VII in the later twelfth century, the king of France was a force no longer to be ignored. He was still surrounded by great and powerful lords, but the time was at hand when he could stand equal to them. He still ruled only a fragment of the land vaguely known as France. It was criss-crossed with lines of political and ethnic division; but the king held a royal realm of some extent, loyal to him, and strategically located in the heart of what was to be the France of modern Europe.

The growing power of the Capetian kings was in no small part due to their successful insistence upon hereditary royal succession. Since the early Merovingians there had always been a deep, though often unrecognized, split between the concepts of royal election and hereditary succession. In practice, in both Merovingian and Carolingian times, the two concepts had been combined. The crown tended to stay in a royal line, with each successor being commended by election of the army or some ad hoc assembly of notables. At the end of a dynasty, or in the case of a weak or incompetent king, the right of election bridged the dynastic gap. Hugh Capet was elected king, but a positive factor in his election was the hereditary claim of his family. To confirm that claim, within a year after his election, Hugh had his son Robert elevated beside him as coruler. When the father died in 996, the son was already king. Indeed, the Capetians managed to provide an unbroken line of male heirs for more than three centuries, so that there was no need for the elective principle to be invoked. As the centuries passed, France, the crown, and the family of Hugh Capet became one and the same thing; the dynastic principle was established.

The Emergence of the German Empire

While Carolingian West Frankland was becoming Capetian France, a similar transformation was taking place in the German lands to the east. The same combination of internal weakness, external pressure, and feeble or unfortunate kings quickly broke down whatever unity Charlemagne had been able to impose upon these parts of his empire. Even under so great a ruler as Charlemagne the eastern empire had never been thoroughly integrated into the Carolingian state system. Rebellion was always just below the surface. Under his successors and in the disorder of the ninth century, power and authority passed into the hands of local magnates. In the German lands this process of fragmentation was more clearly patterned than in the west.

The Frankish kings had never been able to destroy the basic tribalism of Germany and had in many ways simply accepted it. When the time of troubles came, the eastern empire broke along lines already long established. The large areas of common tribal settlement became the units of decentralization—Saxony, Bavaria, Swabia, Thuringia, Franconia. In each of these the initiative was taken by some great family which became identified with the regional interest. The heads of such families became the tribal dukes or "stem dukes" (*Stamm* means stock, race, tribe, and family in the largest sense). Charlemagne had fought bitterly against these regional dynasties. He had succeeded in destroying or replacing some of them, but the circumstances of the century following his death brought them back or others to succeed them. The real political power in the German lands of the empire rested in the hands of these tribal dukes; there was no larger substitute for their intense tribal patriotism and sense of regional identity.

The last pale eastern Carolingian, Louis the Child, died in 911. He had been unable to defend the realm and his brief reign had been punctuated by Norse and Magyar raids. The great dukes had organized their regional defenses and whatever victory there was, was theirs. The government had already passed into their hands and with it the right of royal election. They chose one of their own number, Duke Conrad of Franconia (*911–918*), with whom German medieval history began; with him also was joined the great issue of German medieval history—the issue of regionalism or unity. Conrad was not content to be a "chairman of the board." He aspired to the realities of his kingship; he fought untiringly, but unsuccessfully, against his fellow dukes. His final act was a curious reversal. The most powerful of the dukes, and Conrad's most implacable enemy, was Henry, Duke of Saxony. From his deathbed Conrad sent to Henry the symbols of kingship, designating him as his successor. Perhaps this was a bitter gesture of capitulation; perhaps it represented the hope that the magic touch of kingship would quicken a sense of larger purpose in Duke Henry.

The other great dukes were neither united nor powerful enough to dispute the right of his succession, and they sullenly elected and accepted their new king. Whatever Henry the Fowler (*919–936*) may have thought of his royal dignity, he was realistic enough to know that the base of any real power lay in the resources and warriors of his own duchy. His powers were already considerable and, as Conrad's successor, he commanded the loyalty of most of the Franconian nobles as well as his own. He turned, like his Carolingian predecessors, to the unprotected eastern frontier. In a series of campaigns he set up marches against the Slavs and reconquered Charlemagne's "Dane-mark." The southeastern flank of Saxony lay open to the fierce Magyars. Henry bought a truce with them in tribute and prepared to move against them. All along the frontier he scattered a line of fortifications (*burgs*) which became nuclei of later cities and the focal points of resistance to Magyar attack. His solid preparations and growing strength enabled him to defy, and then defeat, the Magyars in 933. To the west Henry was able to extend his ducal and royal powers by interfering in the chaotic affairs of Lothairingia. At his death in 936 Henry the Fowler had aggrandized his duchy into a truly royal realm and established the foundations for the Saxon dynasty. His son, who would be known as Otto the Great (*936–973*), inherited the ducal powers of his father and the royal title followed without serious opposition.

Otto was only twenty-four years old at the time of his succession, but already a seasoned warrior and such a promising administrator that Henry had chosen him over his older sons. Highly ambitious, Otto already entertained a grander notion of monarchy than his father's: the re-creation of Charlemagne's state. The tribal duchies, fighting for independence from royal control, found allies in Otto's devil's-brood of relatives, brothers, half-brothers, and sons who resented his preferment. Otto tried to use them to control tribal fragmentation in the interest of the monarchy. But they allied with the dukes against him or identified with tribal interests. Time after time, for twenty years, they rebelled.

Even as Otto failed to create a working administration based upon his own family, he had already begun to turn his hopes in another direction, toward the church, especially the bishops. In Ottonian Germany—as everywhere else the church favored monarchy against sectionalism, and threw its considerable support behind those forces in society which seemed to favor order, stability, and tradition. More than the moral support of the church as an institution, Otto sought the practical political support of the bishops. The aims and purposes of the bishops were not always the same as those of the church. Indeed, in the disorder of the ninth and tenth centuries the centralized administrative system of the church declined even more rapidly than the secular state system. The church increasingly lost control, particularly of its bishops, as feudalism touched its vast territorial holdings. By the time of Otto the Great the bishops and archbishops of Germany—and this was not peculiar to Germany but common to all western Europe—were scarcely distinguishable from the secular nobility. To begin with, they were of the same class, for there had long been a tendency to draw the upper clergy from the nobility. Possessed of abilities and ambitions similar to those of the secular nobility, the clergy were often more effective as administrators than their secular counterparts. They were, as a rule, more educated, and even the most worldly of them could not entirely escape a sense of community with the historic, unitary tradition of the church. The episcopal clergy in Germany were drawn to the monarchy because the domination of the tribal dukes was as much a threat to them as it was to the crown. Otto the Great recognized the enormous value of his bishops and made them the basis of his system of government. The key to their value, however, was not only their ability and strength; it was basically that their offices could not become hereditary and that their appointment was controlled by the king. Otto could entrust them with lands and powers without fearing that, in the next generation, he would have to fight the claim of a son. For, however secular the bishops were in their ambitions and personal lives, they were legally bound by clerical celibacy. Further, the king continued to exercise the same rights of appointment and control of bishops that the Merovingian and Carolingian kings had enjoyed. The church had never been able to contest this right successfully and Otto ruled his church as he ruled his household and his kingdom. Thus Otto was able to construct a web of administrative control over the lands of Germany: his bishops were his governors, agents, and frequently his military commanders; these men made possible the Ottonian Empire and were a powerful reason why Otto was the most effective ruler of the tenth century.

By mid-century Otto had imposed upon the inherent separatism of the German states a unity they had not known since the days of Charlemagne. At mid-century the Magyars again surged across the East-mark and up the Danube valley in force. They found allies among many of Otto's nobility, ready as always to destroy a kingdom or a continent for the sake of a few square miles of sovereign land. This time the Magyar horde was not met by a Saxon king-duke but by a German king, commanding a great pan-German army. Otto met the Magyars in 955 on the Lech River near Augsburg; he defeated them completely in one of the great massacre-battles of medieval history. They withdrew to the plain of Hungary to become the Magyar-Hungarians of European history, never again to be a serious threat to the security of the west. The defeat of the Magyars signaled Otto's triumph on every frontier. He had continued his father's policy of building a solid rampart against the Slavs, and his Christianizing, colonizing work was already carrying German influence deep into eastern Europe. He had established himself as a power along the western frontier in Lothairingia. He had brought the tribal dukes to heel on more than one occasion and had successfully disputed any right to independence from the crown they might have claimed. He had revitalized the concept of monarchy and attached himself firmly to the tradition of Charlemagne. His decisive victory over the Magyars had, in a sense, been the proof offered to all the people of Germany of his right to moral and political sway over them.

The Formation of the Holy Roman Empire

Even before his defeat of the Magyars, Otto had begun to turn his attention in another direction and toward another goal. The history of Italy and of the papacy was already bound up with the history of Germany.

As Otto became more king than Saxon duke he was inevitably drawn into this historic connection. Italy had shared the general chaos of Europe during the breakup of the Carolingian Empire. In the south, Moslem fleets had seized Sicily in 917; for the past thirty years they had harried the coast of Italy from the maritime Alps to the straits of Messina, establishing strongholds at strategic points on the mainland. The Magyars had raided the plain of Lombardy at the turn of the century. The descendants of Lothair had tried to hang on to the Italian portion of their inheritance. As the family grew with the generations the claims diffused and each claim produced an "emperor." All of them were strong enough to exploit, none was strong enough to protect. The kings of Burgundy, counts of Provence, dukes of Bavaria and Swabia—all vied for the pieces of Italy. Lesser lords in every district seized what they could in the general confusion and a hundred petty noble families reared castles which were often little more than bandit lairs. The papacy, stripped of the support of a powerful secular arm, was the captive of whatever self-seeking faction of Rome happened to gain a momentary triumph over its myriad rivals. The popes who were the creatures of these local factions were men—sometimes boys— whose profligacy was matched only by their incompetence. The papacy lost completely not only what temporal authority it had had, but also the spiritual leadership of western Europe.

In 951, in order to prevent the magnates of southern Germany and Burgundy from seizing the Lombard plain, Otto the Great marched into northern Italy and declared himself king of the Lombards. Ten years later the pope called upon Otto to protect the lands of the church from his greedy Lombard vassals. Otto's price was the imperial title, which no one had effectively held for almost forty years. In February of 962, Otto the Great was crowned emperor. His youthful ambition to emulate Charlemagne had been fulfilled. As if to admit his debt, he renewed the grants, titles, and immunities that the papacy had enjoyed under Charlemagne; but Otto made it as clear as Charles had done that the church of the new empire was to be an imperial church and the pope subordinate to the emperor. The so-called Ottonian Privilege stated clearly that while the emperor guaranteed the integrity of papal lands and powers, he also was to receive the fealty of any future pope.

It took almost five years for Otto to bring the chaotic situation in Rome and the papacy under control, but by 966 he had created the state which was to be known as the Holy Roman Empire. It was holy only in the sacred claim of the emperors; it was Roman only in the vague classical precedents which its German rulers invoked and in its inclusion of the *Roman* papacy; it was an empire not at all—but an unfortunate and awkward combination of Germany and Italy. It was, in short, a most improbable state. Yet it was one of the constant realities of medieval politics and an important factor in the destinies of both Germany and Italy.

The power of Otto the Great passed undiminished to his capable son, Otto II (*973–983*), who continued through his short reign to burnish the fame of his dynasty. Otto II left an infant to succeed him, and all the troubles which three generations of Saxon rulers had managed to hold in check broke loose. The child-emperor, Otto III (*983–1002*), was reared by priests and women rather than warriors, and in an alien tradition. His mother was a Byzantine princess who imbued her son with the ancient Graeco-Roman-Oriental formalism of Byzantium until he was lured into mistaking the pompous forms of royalty for its substance. He failed to realize that to be a Roman emperor he had first to be a German king. On his death, at the age of twenty-two, the imperial title passed to a cousin, Henry II (*1002–1024*), Duke of Bavaria, who was the last king of the Saxon dynasty. Henry managed in part to repair the powers of the imperial house.

Following Henry's death, an election brought a new dynasty, the Salian, to the empire in the person of Conrad II (*1024–1039*). Both Conrad and his son, Henry III (*1034–1056*), were able and strong-minded rulers. They continued to do the work of Otto the Great, ruling effectively in Germany and imposing themselves upon the papacy in Rome. The apex of the German medieval empire was reached in the reign of Henry III. Germany was as united as it was to be for centuries. Royal power was vested strongly in the crown, which was virtually undisputed from ducal castles to crossroads market towns. Both Conrad II and Henry III worked to secure their hold upon a central area of crown land in Franconia and Swabia, where their ducal power was strongest, and to extend their authority into Thuringia and southern Saxony. To this end they scattered strong castles at strategic points all through these lands and garrisoned them with a new kind of feudal retainer, called *ministerials*. These were trained warriors but not nobles, and though they held land to support themselves, it was not in the form of *fiefs*. Dependent on the crown, they remained loyal to it, and were used to great effect by later emperors. The long struggle with the tribal dukes seemed won. Henry took his sacred imperial duties as seriously as his royal responsibilities. He was personally dedicated to ecclesiastical reform and interfered repeatedly to strengthen the spiritual fiber of the church. He deposed three unworthy popes and elevated a succession of able and pious German reformers to the papal throne. This serious dedication to reform was one important consequence of a cultural and intellectual revival often called the Ottonian Renaissance.

As the court of Otto the Great became the center of a royal administration, it also became one of the principal centers of learning in northern Europe. In part, at least, this came about through Otto's own intellectual interests. In part, it was the natural result of the concentration of royal wealth and power that attracted scholars and men of learning, as well as adventurers and fortune hunters. From Otto's brilliant and cosmopolitan court inevitable influences radiated out to the provincial centers of the empire. The Ottonian Renaissance was, like the Carolingian, essentially clerical in character. It was dominated almost entirely by high-ranking ecclesiastics and thus was naturally related to the important role of the church in Otto's political system. The court and the chancery were the schools for the men who would fill the key bishoprics of Germany and Italy. The talented younger brother of Otto, Bruno, Archbishop of Cologne, is a striking case in point—an able administrator and soldier, a scholar and patron of learning. Many other episcopal and monastic centers became, like Cologne, centers of learning, art, and literature. The Ottonian Renaissance produced histories and chronicles of some importance: a revival of interest in legendary materials, draped in the uncomfortable gear of Christianity, and Christian themes treated in the hearty manner of the traditional epics and lays. The leading figures in this renaissance were vigorous personalities, often capable in several fields. Lieutprand of Cremona, a historian with considerable literary talent and broad learning, was also a man of affairs; Widukind of Corbey was a Saxon monk and historian who wrote with resounding chauvinism and some historical understanding of the deeds of the Saxon kings, Henry I and Otto; Ekkehart of St. Gall wrote one of the most warm and charming of monastic chronicles. But the most remarkable figure of the Ottonian revival was a woman, Hroswitha, the nun of Gandersheim. A protégée of the royal family, she was dedicated to the court, and wrote a verse-history of the reign of Otto as well as poetic versions of pious legends. Her most curious and original work was a series of plays in the manner of the Roman dramatist Terence, to counteract the popularity of that attractive pagan. She drew her themes from saintly matter but her spirit from Terence himself.

In the generations of Otto's successors the effect of this renaissance spread and was joined by a number of other streams of influence. Theophano, the sophisticated Byzantine wife of Otto II, brought Greek scholars and Byzantine art forms to her German court. The impressionable Otto III was deeply influenced by Gerbert of Aurillac, a French monk whom he made Pope Sylvester II. Gerbert was a man of great learning and interest in the classics, especially in Aristotle, and so skilled in mathematics and mechanics that he gained a reputation for sorcery. But Gerbert's learning was overshadowed by his dedication to the cause of general reform in the church. His concern for this, as well as that of other churchmen, was soon to be joined with the major reform movement led by the Abbey of Cluny; it brought about the first great reformation within the church during the medieval period.

At his death in 1056, Henry III ruled the strongest state in Europe, but a state which the next generation was to embroil in one of the most serious conflicts of medieval history.

The Establishment of Norman England

As the Salian emperors created a powerful, centralized monarchy in Germany, as the Capetian kings of France set themselves the task of expanding their holdings about the fortress of Paris into a royal realm, the third great medieval state of western Europe came into existence—Norman England.

The work of Alfred the Great had created the basic outline of an Anglo-Saxon state on the eve of the tenth century. His successors continued his work until 1016, when the precarious independence of England was swamped in a second Danish invasion. In the last years of the tenth century Denmark came into the hands of an able and ambitious king, Sven "the Fork-Bearded" (*c. 985–1014*). He was able to overturn the struggling monarchies of Norway and Sweden and put together a great northern empire centered in the Baltic. It was Knut (English Canute), the son of Sven, whose mighty fleet landed on the shores of England in 1016. His conquest and the timely death of the reigning Saxon king made Knut king of England as England became the western portion of the Danish empire. His invasion did little to disrupt the pattern of English life, but it was the beginning of a tangled skein of dynastic claims and counterclaims that led to the most important invasion in the history of England.

At the death of Knut, his wrangling sons fought for the Danish throne and allowed England to drift away. The *witan,* the ancient Anglo-Saxon assembly of notables, was able again to elect a king of the house of Alfred —Edward the Confessor (*1042–1066*). Edward had spent most of his

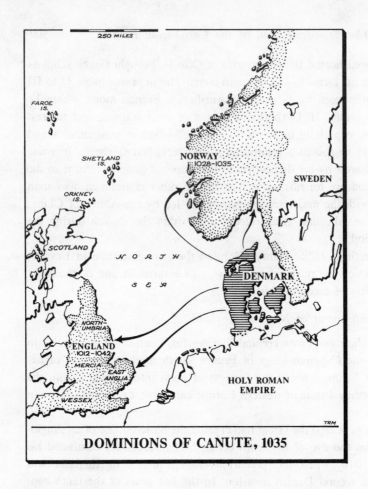

DOMINIONS OF CANUTE, 1035

The map shows: FAROE IS., SHETLAND IS., ORKNEY IS., SCOTLAND, NORTH SEA, NORTH-UMBRIA, ENGLAND 1012-1042, MERCIA, EAST ANGLIA, WESSEX, NORWAY 1028-1035, SWEDEN, DENMARK, HOLY ROMAN EMPIRE. Scale: 250 MILES.

life in exile on the continent at the court of the Duke of Normandy, to whose family he was related. As the new English king, his strange accent, foreign ways, and Norman friends quickly alienated a powerful Saxon faction. This faction was led by Earl Godwin of Wessex, the real power behind the throne. He hoped confidently that his family would succeed the childless Edward. The same hope was as confidently cherished by William, Duke of Normandy. A piece of luck brought these two expectations together. Harold, the son and heir of Godwin, was shipwrecked on the Norman coast and fell into William's hands. His host-captor gave him his freedom only upon Harold's promise to support William's claim on the death of Edward. The stage was set. When Edward died, the witan chose Harold, the most logical native claimant, as king. This provided the pretext for the Norman invasion.

A sequence of able rulers had made Normandy one of the most powerful duchies of the French mainland. None of its dukes had been more able, vigorous, or greedy than William. His shadowy claim to England, based upon promises extracted by threat, gained solid backing from the church. The same invigorated and reformed papacy that the Emperor Henry III had created came to the aid of William's enterprise, in return for his promise to reform the English church and to attach it firmly to Roman obedience once more. With papal blessing, William and a great host sailed for England. Fair winds and good fortune allowed the invading army to land without opposition on the Channel coast. While William's forces had been preparing to sail, the Saxon king, Harold, had been forced to take his army to the north to fight off a Norse invasion coupled with a local rebellion. The combined Norse and rebel force was defeated and Harold's exhausted troops marched back to the south to meet the Normans, who had already landed. On October 14, 1066, near Hastings, Harold's army was cut to pieces and he was killed. William, Duke of Normandy, became William the Conqueror (*1066–1087*).

He was well-named, for the fact of conquest easily overshadowed his mendacious claims to legitimate succession; and the fact of conquest enabled William to make certain important modifications in the political system of his new realm. The men who flocked to his standard for the invasion were not a feudal army. William had been generally unable to induce his vassal landholders in Normandy to leave their own lands unprotected and follow him on such a distant and uncertain adventure. Consequently, his army was composed mainly of adventurers, mercenaries, professional soldiers, younger sons of noble families from Normandy and, indeed, from all over western France. At the core of the invading host were a handful of William's most trusted Norman friends. This army fought not to discharge feudal obligations, but to win land and booty, and it looked to William to divide the spoils. Thus, William immediately began to parcel out portions of England to reward his followers.

But outweighing William's obligation to his followers was the necessity of protecting his own position. He had conquered a foreign land swarming with enemies. There were still powerful Saxon lords who might rise against him at any time. The wild tribes of Wales and the Scottish highlands could sweep across the borders almost at will. A substantial invasion attempt from Norway had been broken on the very eve of his own success; another might come at any time from either Norway or Denmark. His position as lord of Normandy was in jeopardy for every moment and every mile he was away. His only solution was to divide England into feudal fiefs in the hands of able warriors, trusting them to defend for him lands which they could regard as their own. Great fiefs were given at every strategic point in England—along the Welsh and Scottish borders, in Northumbria, and all along the eastern coast. Every promontory where a holding action might be necessary or effective was quickly filled with a castle. Three years after his invasion William conducted a "harrowing of the north," creating a zone of devastation as a barrier to further Norse raids. An intricate line of fortifications was established leading to a marshaling point on the Channel coast, to secure a possible retreat. The lands of Saxon lords who had resisted the invasion were confiscated by the crown and enfiefed to loyal Normans. Gradually the distinction between loyal and disloyal Saxons blurred and England became a patchwork of Norman-French holdings.

By the generation of William's sons there were over a thousand castles scattered through England, each grim, stone tower marking a Norman stronghold.

The feudalization of his conquered kingdom was forced upon William by the lack of an alternative. As Duke of Normandy he had fought the same battle with his landed lords as the other French dukes and the Capetian kings. He determined to build safeguards into his English system. In the first place, the entire realm of England was his by right of conquest. There were no prior claims, no tribal rights, no residual privileges. While hundreds of fiefs lay across the island—some of them immense in size—William retained the basic Anglo-Saxon territorial divisions of the "shires." In each such local district he retained crown land—almost one-sixth of the land of England—and in each shire he claimed the rights of sovereign. Those rights were enforced by a *shire-reeve* (sheriff), normally a powerful lord and, at the same time, agent of the king, judge of his local court, commander of the local military levy, and overseer of royal estates in the region. William made sure that he created no vassal powerful enough to defy him and was most cautious in granting the immunities which had made "kinglets" of so many lords on the continent. The dangerous concentration of private forces was checked. William demanded a quota of knights from each of his vassals and held them to it. In this way he had the service of some five thousand knights, a truly formidable host by feudal standards. Further he demanded the personal loyalty of every fighting man so that there was no substructure of secondary allegiance between the king and his soldiery. This was confirmed in 1086 in the so-called Oath of Salisbury, by which every knight of the realm swore primary vassalage to the crown.

Now and again, in England as in Normandy, ambition, grievance, or greed would impel a local revolt. But in each case William quelled it without serious trouble. His success was, however, fully as much the success of the man as of the system; for the system depended upon the personal qualities of the ruler. The Norman-French aristocracy of England were as eager as the Norman lords had been to be kings in their own fiefs and rid themselves of royal control. But between them and their independence stood the solid figure of William, one of the great, commanding personalities of medieval history. William was a personal champion of immense strength: he was large and heavy-framed, and as he grew older he became enormously fat; he had a grim and brutal sense of humor which could flash momentarily to be followed by a black mood or terrible burst of temper. He took a kind of cynical pride in his illegitimate birth; but, on one occasion, he sacked a town whose people had the effrontery to flaunt it. On another, he beat his queen so unmercifully that he was constrained to build a church in penance, the famous Abbé aux Hommes in Caen.

William was confident in his strength because he never lost sight of the political realities that surrounded him. By the end of his reign he had established himself and his socio-governmental system so firmly in England that there was no longer any serious question of a Saxon reversion. A symbol of his solid control was the *Domesday Book*. This invaluable document was a detailed survey of the lands and resources of England begun in 1085 by William's order, hence the term *doom,* signifying order or decree. Every foot of English land was entered by counties or shires, baronies and subholdings, with the names of the lords who held them.

THE FEUDAL MONARCHIES

ENGLAND	FRANCE	GERMANY
		End of *Carolingian Dynasty* 911
		CONRAD I (*911-918*)
		Saxon Dynasty
		HENRY I (*919-936*)
		OTTO I (*936-973*)
	End of *Carolingian*	OTTO II (*973-983*)
	Dynasty 987	OTTO III (*983-1002*)
	HUGH CAPET (*987-996*)	
	ROBERT I (*996-1031*)	HENRY II (*1002-1024*)
		Salian Dynasty
	HENRY I (*1031-1060*)	CONRAD II (*1024-1039*)
		HENRY III (*1039-1056*)
Norman Dynasty		
WM. I (*1066-1087*)	PHILIP I (*1060-1108*)	HENRY IV (*1056-1106*)
WM. II (*1087-1100*)		
HENRY I (*1100-1135*)	LOUIS VI (*1108-1137*)	HENRY V (*1106-1125*)

Every estate was listed with its basic productivity, its peasants, its stock, its woods and pastures. The *Domesday Book* was a tax roll to inform the king of the resources of his realm and enable him to mine those resources more effectively. There were few kings or lords of William's time who could boast such personal control over the lands they claimed.

In 1087 William the Conqueror died of an injury. Normandy and its ducal powers passed to the eldest son, Robert; England to William II, called Rufus "the Red" (*1087–1100*). The brothers fought bitterly and both realms suffered. But William Rufus was more effective than Robert and eventually succeeded in gaining a claim to Normandy as well as England. He inherited his father's ruthlessness, brutality, and greed; he pressed every feudal and sovereign right to the utmost. His barons revolted several times and were put down. Rufus was killed in a hunting accident, under highly suspicious circumstances, and his younger brother, Henry, third son of the Conqueror, prudently seized the treasury and then easily assumed the crown.

Henry I (*1100–1135*) was the most able and attractive of William's sons. His brother Robert constantly intrigued against him and he was compelled to crush a number of baronial uprisings. Finally he invaded Normandy, captured Robert, and united the two pieces of the Norman inheritance in his own hands. He continued to rule in the spirit and with the devices of his father and brother William Rufus. His rule was harsh but effective and, by his death in 1135, his English realm at least enjoyed an unprecedented degree of peace and order. With Henry I the Norman dynasty reached its climax and its end.

In the three centuries since the death of Charlemagne, the Carolingian Empire had been dismembered and the map of western Europe rearranged around the core of three great monarchies—Capetian France, Saxon-Salian Germany, and the Anglo-Norman state of William the Conqueror. It was within the area of these three states that the major developments of European medieval civilization were to take their most important and characteristic forms. On their periphery dozens of lesser states, which would add their varying portions to the amalgam of western civilization were beginning to form.

The Borderlands of Feudal Europe

Shortly before William's conquest of England, another band of land-hungry Norman adventurers had begun to carve out lands for themselves in southern Italy. For more than half a century this troubled region had been the scene of continuous and destructive petty war. It was the last substantial outpost of the Byzantine Empire in the west, but the imperial government, under weak leadership and perilously pressed by barbarians nearer home, could make only a feeble and fitful defense of southern Italy. With the end of Carolingian authority in Italy, the Lombard nobility began to push old claims to lands in the south. The Saracen pirates made destructive raids along the coasts. In these circumstances the Normans were able to infiltrate and establish themselves at many points. In 1053 a Norman host under the strong leadership of Robert Guiscard seized Apulia and

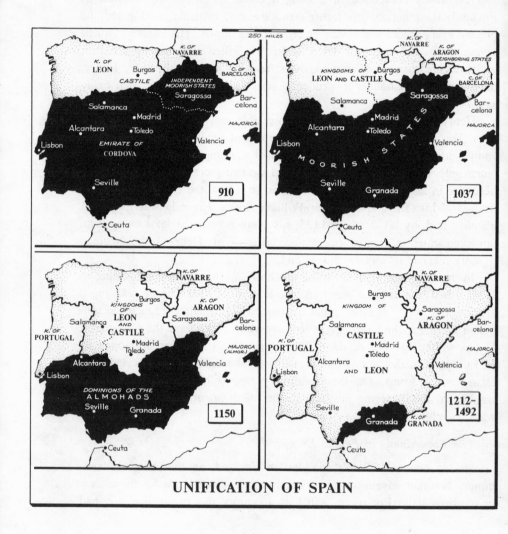

UNIFICATION OF SPAIN

Calabria. The papacy, making a virtue of necessity, recognized the conquest, and the conquerors were content to call their lands papal fiefs. Thus was established another Norman state which was to play a significant role in the affairs of feudal Europe.

The unity of Moslem Spain had fallen into more than twenty petty kingdoms by the middle of the eleventh century, and the minuscule Christian states of the northern mountains began their slow work of reconquest and expansion. Alfonso VI of Castile captured the citadel of Toledo from the Moors in 1085, and it became the southernmost point of an extensive state. With the aid of the legendary hero Ruy Díaz de Bivar, el Cid, he doggedly maintained his position and Castile became a permanent fixture in the emerging state system of Christian Spain. The lure of adventure, the hope of gain, and family connections attracted many southern French nobles to Spain. The Spanish march that Charlemagne had founded broke away from the failing empire in the late ninth century. By the opening of the twelfth century, several pieces of territory had been added to it to create another Spanish state centered on the port city of Barcelona. Navarre and Aragon, beginning also as parts of the Carolingian Spanish march, took part in the expansion to the south; their fortunes and dynasties intermixed in the eleventh and twelfth centuries. But the differences between the several emerging Spanish states were all dwarfed by the common enterprise of reconquest, which assumed the aspect of a crusade and left its stamp upon the character of Spain.

On the fringes of Norman England the Welsh, the Irish, and the Scots stubbornly resisted efforts to penetrate their marginal lands and committed themselves to a domestic enmity which would trouble the affairs of the British Isles for centuries.

In Scandinavia the death of Knut in 1035 not only freed England from the Danish empire, but enabled its other components to break away. Most of the fierce energy which had made the Danes such formidable conquerors in earlier centuries was turned to the reconquest of the empire and western Europe was spared. Norway and Sweden played a less expansive role in the eleventh and twelfth centuries and were absorbed in parallel struggles to establish monarchical government. In the whole of Scandinavia in these centuries the spread of Christianity and the growth of the church proved of some importance.

Similarly, in eastern Europe the spread of Christianity had important consequences for the Slavs. More frequently than not the church was identified with the German expansion to the east. Indeed, the Christian-

German pressure became the decisive factor in the development of eastern Europe in the medieval period. After several centuries of transient and stormy independence, the Slavic kingdom of Bohemia was finally reduced to German obedience by Emperor Henry III.

In the late tenth century, as the eastward expansion of Otto the Great reached the Polish steppe, the tribal peoples of that vast area crystallized into a nation. From the beginning, German influence was the most important external determinant. As Christianity penetrated Poland, it was Bohemian-German-Latin in form. In the opening years of the eleventh century, a monarchical organization took shape in Poland, following the pattern of Ottonian Germany. The weakness of Germany under Otto III and the troubles of the later eleventh century coincided with the reigns of a number of able Polish kings; and Poland became one of the great territorial powers of medieval Europe. Boleslav the Bold (*1058–1079*) ruled a huge territory and was able to dictate his wishes to Russian Kiev. Boleslav III (*1102–1138*) defeated the Danes in Pomerania, the Germans in Silesia, and the Hungarians on his southern border. This was the great age of medieval Poland but its historic destiny was—like the rest of the western Slavic states—to fight a losing battle against German pressure.

In Hungary, Stephen I (*997–1038*) amalgamated the Magyar tribes effectively. Stephen also brought his state decidedly into the German-Latin-Christian orbit of the west. For the next century the fortunes of Hungary swayed back and forth with the pendulum of German politics.

The southern and eastern Slavs continued to be drawn to the great cultural and political lodestone of Constantinople.

We now return to consider the central states of western Europe, the form of their government, and the pattern of their social order.

FEUDALISM

The states which took form at the core of western Europe in the centuries following the breakup of the Carolingian Empire—and to a lesser degree those in the borderlands of western Europe—were feudal monarchies. Their political structure, their social order, and the organization of their economies constituted a way of life generally known as feudalism. For almost five hundred years, European civilization developed within the framework of the feudal system.

The Origins of Feudalism

Medieval feudalism crystallized in the ninth century as a consequence of civil wars, the collapse of orderly central government, and the constant danger of savage invasion. Such total crisis brought men face to face with the elementary problem of self-preservation. The protective power of government was either far away or nonexistent. The poor and the weak turned to the rich and powerful for protection, paying for it with their lands and services. Freeholding peasants surrendered their lands to neighboring strong men and then worked them as share croppers. Great landholders subdivided their estates, granting portions to men who, in return, would ride with them as soldiers. Public officials such as the Carolingian counts broke away from the feeble restraints of royal authority and assumed whatever sovereign powers they were able to exercise. Out of this flux the patchwork of territorial feudalism gradually emerged, and the holding of land became the basis of the great pyramid of feudal society.

At the bottom were the thousands of mounted warriors whom we may now begin to call knights. In general they held enough land to support themselves, their families, and their horses—often barely enough. They held their estates from some lord and in return were obliged to render him military service. Such a lord might command a few dozen, rarely a hundred knights. The knight's lord, in his turn, held his lands from someone else, another and still more powerful lord, a count or duke, and owed him his own service as well as that of his knights. At the top of the pyramid was the king who, in theory at least, commanded the service of his great lords, who commanded the service of their dependents; and so on down the scale. We have seen that William the Conqueror had the service of some five thousand knights. But such extensive power was most unusual, for in operation feudalism was never as orderly as its theory. In reality, each lord strove to be as independent of higher authority as possible. More often than not feudal service was no more than the service that an overlord could compel. In the times that bred feudalism any man's rights—even the most powerful—reached only to the end of his lance. The strong tradition of royalty was attenuated; the powers of government that made a king sovereign fell from his hands into those of local lords. The king, in the feudal world, was transformed into a suzerain, that is "the lord of a lord," the chief figure in feudalism; but his powers were only over his own vassals and those closely circumscribed by law and practice.

The origins of feudalism are most obscure. The ninth century was hardly a time conducive to the keeping of elaborate records and the men who forged the rudiments of the feudal system were probably not aware that their efforts to survive could be described as a "system" at all. What they did was to take existing institutions and practices that seemed useful and modify them to suit necessity. In this sense the feudal system had roots farther back than the ninth century.

The great Carolingian mayors and kings had made a practice of granting land in exchange for military service. The *vassi dominici,* "royal vassals," as the recipients of these grants were called, were the backbone of the Carolingian military system and their "vassal" lands were scattered all over western Europe. Behind this practice lay a tangle of traditions and precedents. The reward of warriors and the selfless service they were expected to render go back to the primitive Germanic institution of the war band, which was not far separated either in time or spirit from the age of Charles Martel or Pepin the Short.

The relationship between land and service also goes back to a number of late Roman practices which were absorbed and adapted by the invading Germans. In the centuries of Roman decline the reciprocal practices of *clientage* and *patronage* had been vastly extended and applied to the villa economy of the countryside. Landless men or small proprietors who could no longer protect themselves sought the protection of powerful landholders. In return for protection they served their protectors, mostly as agricultural laborers, and received a portion of the goods their labor created. This arrangement was called *patrocinium.* A similar institution was *precarium,* also dating from late Roman times. In this form of tenure a landowner granted a piece of land to another upon petition or "prayer," *precarium.* Such land freely granted could be summarily taken back, hence the implication of "precarious tenure." In actual practice this was simply another way of relating landholding to agricultural production, and the peasant paid for the use of the land with a part of his crops. The *precarium* was not always a peasant holding. Often a great landowner would grant to a subordinate a sizable tract of land in order to assure its cultivation. The church found this especially expedient as it became the proprietor of extensive lands.

There were many other ways in which land was held, in varying degrees of dependency, but it would be absurd to insist that sharp legal distinctions were recognized. What late Roman antiquity produced and what the barbarians took over in the early Middle Ages was an agricultural system characterized by large estates worked by peasants, generally unfree, in fact if not at law. Roman institutions, German institutions, and simple necessity blended inextricably together.

In the course of the eighth century other terms to designate land held from another were gradually replaced by the term *beneficium* or *benefice*. In fact again, if not at law, the benefice was another step toward military-territorial feudalism for, in general, the holder of a benefice held it on condition of military service. The Merovingian kings—often because they had to and not because they wanted to—rewarded their retainers, their troop commanders, and soldiers, and paid their counts and dukes by granting them benefices. The strong Carolingians continued the practice and were able to control the inherent tendency to decentralization of power that went with it. The almost constant wars that culminated in Charlemagne's empire made it necessary to extend the practice of granting benefices. Yet even Charlemagne found it difficult to enforce the service due for benefices, and equally difficult to keep land and prerogatives from drifting across the narrow line separating the dependent benefice from the independent *appanage*. Long before Charlemagne benefices had begun to clump together into vast domains held by men who were rapidly being transformed by their power and riches into a privileged class—the feudal aristocracy.

In a broad sense, feudalism had been developing for centuries. It was not some radical departure from tradition suddenly created in the confusion and danger of the ninth century. Men were already accustomed to thinking in feudal terms about landholding, military service, and social relationships. One step remained: to transform the benefice into a hereditary estate. By the tenth century, in so far as the records are clear, the benefice had become hereditary and was commonly called *feudum* or *fief*.

Vassal and Lord: The Operation of Feudalism

Most of the land of western Europe was cut up into fiefs ranging in size and importance from a poor knight's fief of a few square miles to the great feudal counties and duchies. All the holders of fiefs were *vassals* (this term, which had signified simply a soldier in Carolingian usage, had come to apply exclusively to the nobility, and embraced the whole range of grandiose feudal titles—duke, count, earl, viscount, lord, baron, castellan, marquis). Even the Norman kings of England were vassals to the French crown for the duchy of Normandy. There was no implication of a menial relationship in the concept of vassalage. The ancient connection between land tenure and the obligation of service remained, but the connection took the form of a feudal contract which was, in essence, mutual obligation between vassal and lord. This obligation was fundamentally military in nature. The very reason for the existence of feudalism at all was the overt necessity of defense and self-protection in the face of the failure of government, the hazard of invasion, and civil war. Yet it is difficult and misleading to generalize too freely about the nature of feudal contracts and obligations. The very forces which made feudalism necessary made it a local system; even the term "system," when applied to feudalism, is rather misleading. In the details of feudal relationships there were literally as many "feudalisms" as there were fiefs, for local contractural arrangements were made in terms of peculiar local conditions and tended to freeze into customary law on the same basis. Certain limited generalizations, however, can be made to define the broad outlines of this complex, varied, significant phenomenon.

The vassal held his fief in return for military service in the forces of his lord. In the case of a small fief, he might owe only his personal service, or that of a handful of men. If his fief was large, he was obliged to furnish a considerable host (the Count of Flanders owed the service of a thousand knights to the English king). Such an obligation usually meant that the vassal subdivided his fief to vassals of his own, whom he held to the same sort of service as he was held by his overlord. This process was called subinfeudation and was frequently carried down to several levels. But its purpose at every level was initially military; to put land into the hands of those who could protect it, for the constant of feudal society was war. Every feudal lord strove to defend his lands and it was the solemn obligation of his vassals to aid him in this. But every feudal lord strove also to extend his lands at the expense of his neighbors; in this his vassals generally set a limit to their service, often forty days a year.

While the most basic obligation of the vassal was military service, he also had a civil obligation of great importance in court service. At the summons of his lord—often at regular intervals—he had to appear at the lord's court in assembly with his fellow vassals. It was in these sessions that the business of the fief was carried on. The basic reason for court service was simply that no feudal lord was sovereign. Whatever decisions had to be made about land, services, or feudal relationships were decisions necessitating the concurrence of all participants. Even such seemingly personal matters as the lord's choice of a wife or his decision upon a husband for his daughter were matters in which the assembly of vassals was concerned, for such matters touched the fortunes of the fief.

The almost interminable disputes between vassals were settled at the lord's court by deliberation. Disputes between lord and vassal were likewise settled, and the other vassals had to concur with the lord before he could declare that a feudal contract had been broken and a vassal was consequently to forfeit his estates. The practice of deliberation goes back through Carolingian usage to the Germanic tribal council, but it also points forward to the royal courts of the High Middle Ages and the deliberative functions of the French Estates, the German Diet, and the English Parliament. It was the court service of the feudal vassals that created the precedents of feudal law.

Below the two primary vassal duties of military and court service were a number of lesser obligations more or less common throughout the feudal system. The most important of these was *relief*. In operation it was an inheritance tax. When a vassal died, his heir had to pay relief in order to inherit the fief. Originally it may have been a simple token payment but, by the twelfth century, it was a valuable source of income to lords powerful enough to enforce it. It could be as much as the total revenue of the fief for a year (the relief for the rich county of Flanders in 1212 was the enormous sum of £50,000). Closely related to relief was *escheat,* the reversion of the fief to the overlord if its holder died without an heir. The logic of escheat was simple enough. The whole feudal system rested upon the assumption that land had to be protected by a strong hand. If a piece of land had no master, it was the duty of the lord and his assembly to provide one.

Another obligation of the feudal vassal was *aid*. In particular cases and fiefs it might include many things, even helping an heir pay the relief for his estates or raising money for a variety of reasons. But in general there were three customary aids: the ransom of the lord if he were captured, the knighting of his eldest son, and the marriage of his eldest daughter. All three of these occasioned exceptional expense and all three were directly related to the common business of the fief, which was the concern both of lord and vassal. Even hospitality was regulated by feudal law. The number of times in a year that the lord could visit his vassals was set, along with the duration of his stay and the number of retainers and horses he could bring with him.

On the lord's side of the feudal contract his principal obligation was to protect the lands and interests of his vassal, just as it was the principal duty of the vassal to render the military service on which such protection depended. If, as we have seen, a piece of land lost its master, it was the obligation of the overlord to provide another, for the security and protection of his entire fief. The practice of *wardship* grew from this necessity. The widow of a vassal and his minor children fell under the protection and control of the lord, and it was his obligation to provide a husband for the widow. Romantic considerations played little or no role in such a choice; the lord was concerned with providing an able man to assume the military obligations of the fief. Similarly, it was his duty to hold and protect a fief which would, in time, be the inheritance of a minor son, and to provide a suitable husband for the minor daughter of a deceased vassal.

Every facet of this elaborate interdependence was related to honor and duty: when the vassal received his fief he knelt before his lord, placed his hands between the lord's hands, and swore a solemn oath of faithfulness. This double ceremony was commonly called *homage*—the vassal became the "man" (in French, *homme*) of his lord—and *fealty,* the oath of faithfulness. The lord then handed his new vassal some symbolic representation of his fief, a hank of grass or a clod, and they exchanged a ritual kiss. These were serious obligations in a society which depended upon them for survival. But serious as they were they were often ignored or abused. While the sanctity of feudal duty represented a value-system to which all men made sòme deference, the very nature of feudal society made the uniform enforcement of obligations almost impossible. Basically, every lord wished to increase his hold upon his vassals and every vassal wanted to be free of the demands of his lord. This deep-seated conflict underlay the bloody turbulence of the feudal centuries. Vassals who were powerful enough regularly defied their lords and could usually find sufficient pretext in some slight or injury. Warring lords made attractive offers to strategically located vassals to change allegiance. Lords exacted every penny of feudal obligation from vassals they could dominate. They exploited the revenues from the fiefs of minor heirs and used their wards as pawns for their own advantage.

The Spread of Feudalism

As a territorial system feudalism developed unevenly and sporadically. In north central France, where the collapse of Carolingian government was most complete and Viking raids most destructive, the development of feudalism was early and general. German feudalism followed French forms. Norman feudalism was almost as complete, but the power and prestige of the Norman dukes—and later Norman kings of England—was never as seriously circumscribed as that of the French feudal kings. The borderlands of western Europe could not, of course, escape entirely the impact of feudalism. German conquerors took its practices and concepts with them into Slavic eastern Europe and Italy. The Normans took it to Sicily and to England. Even in Scandinavia feudalism was not unknown. By and large, however, the most characteristic features of feudalism were to be found in northern France, Germany, and Norman England. As feudalism matured in this broad area, its complexities became almost endless. A typical example is supplied by the powerful Count of Champagne. His lands lay scattered across central France around and among the Capetian crown holdings of the Île-de-France. They touched Normandy on the west, Burgundy and the empire on the east. He was vassal for parts of these lands to no less than nine overlords—including the king of France and the German emperor and several lords considerably less powerful than he. Not a year passed without a serious dispute arising from such a tangle of claims, rights, obligations, and jurisdictions. The concept of *liege* vassalage developed. The man who held fiefs from several lords designated one as his "liege" or chief lord, to whom he owed service above all others. This device worked only imperfectly. The process of subinfeudation complicated the exercise of authority, for lords tended to lose control of rear vassals who held fiefs from their tenants-in-chief. In general, it was not until the late twelfth and thirteenth centuries that growing royal power was able to impose upon the feudal system anything like the order implied in feudal theory.

It remains to note the important place of the church in the feudal system. Since the fourth century, and even before, the church had been acquiring land through purchase, settlement, and pious bequest. By the ninth century a single monastery, Fulda, owned fifteen thousand manorial estates; and the lands of St. Denis lay scattered all over France. In the lawlessness and disorder of the ninth century these extensive church lands were in the same danger as secular lands and had to be protected. In many cases the church sought lay protectors to whom ecclesiastical lands were granted in fief. There was ample precedent for this from Carolingian times when the great mayors and kings regularly seized church lands to divide among their *vassi*. Without the restraint of responsible government, however, the protectors of the church lands often became their oppressors. Thus, bit by bit, church officials themselves assumed the feudal role of protection. Principally these men were bishops and archbishops, the officials who, from the early history of the church, had borne the responsibility for its worldly affairs.

Especially in the prolonged crisis of the ninth and tenth centuries, the fighting bishop was a familiar figure. He wore the armor and used the weapons of the lay nobility. Some bishops—with laudable nicety—preferred to use the skull-crushing mace, thus avoiding the scriptural injunction against taking up the sword. We have seen the good use to which Otto the Great put his German bishops. By and large, the ecclesiastics who served Otto and other kings and princes were fighting men rather than spirituals. They took little interest in the purely clerical affairs of their offices. There are records of men being passed unceremoniously through the clerical hierarchy in a matter of days or weeks in order to hold a bishopric. Many able ecclesiastics like Otto's brother, Bruno of Cologne, were shuffled back and forth between secular and church appointments as need arose. In such hands and such circumstances abuses were inevitable. The weakness of the papacy in the ninth and tenth centuries did little to moderate them. Yet by no means were all feudal bishops spiritually unworthy. Many managed to bridge the enormous gap between the two aspects of their vocation to become both effective lords and effective shepherds. In the course of the eleventh century the reforms which emanated from the rejuvenated papacy and the beginnings of the recovery of secular order had their effect upon the feudal episcopacy. Yet, as late as the sixteenth century, the armed bishop was not an unfamiliar figure. And whether armed or robed the bishop was always a key figure in medieval society.

The Feudal Nobility and Knighthood

Perhaps more than any other system of government or society the feudal system was dependent upon men rather than forms or laws. The personal relationship of one man to another was its essence: and the men who entered into these relationships were the feudal nobility. Numerically they were a small class in comparison to the total population. But this very fact made for a remarkable degree of cohesiveness. They were further knit together by dynasty. In the very centuries when nationalism was beginning to divide Europe into its component states, the nobility that dominated its affairs was a singularly international group. Family alliances cut across and complicated the pattern of feudal tenure. A single lord might hold territories which violated the vague boundaries of two or even three later countries. The appeal of advantageous marriage could connect distant families. The adventuring spirit of landless younger sons often extended a web of family connection over many miles.

In terms of feudal law there were three estates: the first estate was the clergy, serving society through prayer; the second was the nobility, serving society with arms and office; everyone else was a member of the third estate, whose duty was labor in support of their betters. But this tripartite division was somewhat unreal, for the deeper distinction was simply noble and non-noble. Even the church was compelled to accept what became in medieval eyes a "natural" division of society. With the feudalization of the church the upper clergy were drawn from the secular nobility while the parish clergy were normally of non-noble origin. It was almost impossible, even in the church, to cross the line between noble and non-noble.

Above everything else, the nobility was a military class. From the poorest knight to the most exalted king, the feudal lord, whether lay or ecclesiastical, was a professional warrior. This fact dominated his life. The training for the exacting profession of arms began at a tender age; at seven or eight the young noble was taken from his home and put under the guidance of another lord, sometimes his father's overlord, often his maternal uncle. For the first few years of his training he was a page serving in the household under the tutelage of the lady of the castle. It was in this connection that the beginnings of chivalry are to be found. In time, this became the elaborate code of knightly behavior with its religious overtones, its painfully sharpened sense of *noblesse,* and its adoration of women. Even in the crudest courts of the tenth century, the young page became acquainted with the language, the etiquette, and the attitudes of courtly life. He might even have learned to play the lute. But customarily the page, like his lord, was innocent of literacy: book learning had little to do with survival.

At the age of fourteen or fifteen the page became a squire, literally a "shield-bearer," and gave up the company of his lady for that of his lord. At this point his training began as an apprentice to his master in the profession of arms. As a squire, he cared for the horses and learned to live with them. He took care of weapons and armor and accustomed himself to their use, under the watchful eye of the lord, or experienced men-at-arms. It was hard training, relying more upon example than precept, and the young man dragged himself to his bed after a day of blunted swords with every bone bruised. When the lord went to war the squire accompanied him, eager for a chance to parade his fledgling prowess. It was not uncommon for a squire to win his knight's spurs in battle. It is probable that more often he won a broken head, but history leaves little record of such inglorious failure. The constancy of feudal war made it almost a certainty that the young squire would have actual military experience before his training was done. The end of his training was knighthood. At about eighteen or twenty he was given arms and a mount of his own and received the *accolade,* usually from the lord who had trained him. This consisted of a primitive test of strength, a mighty blow across the back with the flat of a sword. If it did not send him sprawling, it was the last blow he would have to endure without vengeance. In later centuries the ceremony of knighthood was caught in the tendrils of chivalry. The church entered the picture to give the ceremony religious significance; the knightly ideal was spiritualized in the terms that the world knows from Parzival (Parsifal), the Knights of the Round Table, and the legend of the Holy Grail.

Equipped with the tools of knightly honor and half a lifetime of rigorous training, the young man took his place in feudal society. If he was fortunate enough to be an elder son, he looked forward to his father's fief. If he was not, he looked for service with some other lord and the chance to make his fortune. He might win a fief of his own; he might be able to marry well; he might become the lay champion of a religious foundation and acquire lands in return for protection; or he might simply become a bandit. But whatever he won, he won through his military skills.

The formidable figure of the knight dominated medieval warfare. War had become a highly specialized business. From Carolingian times on, the mounted warrior gradually replaced the foot soldier. The core of Charlemagne's army was a special group of horsemen who rendered military service in exchange for land to support them. They were the earliest vassals. The increasing use of the horse in medieval warfare prepared the way for the knight and the feudal lord. Irregular infantry service could be rendered by any able-bodied man; but mounted service was another matter. A horse was an expensive animal, requiring special care and special food beyond the means of the average peasant. According to eighth-century Frankish records, a horse was valued at more than twenty oxen. Cavalry service was thus associated, almost from the beginning, with special wealth and consequently with privilege. The fief had at least part of its origin in the necessity of supporting its mounted master. But the mounted warrior was so much more effective than infantry. He had mobility in the face of Viking, Saracen, or Magyar raids. Standing in the stirrups he could swing a sword or ax with devastating leverage. Even the dreaded Vikings could not stand against the weight of heavy cavalry in pitched battle.

Throughout the course of the Middle Ages the armor and weapons of the knight became more elaborate. In late Carolingian times he dressed in a knee-length leather coat and quilted breeches. He carried a lance, sword, and Frankish ax. A man of some substance might have had a metal head-piece. By the middle of the eleventh century the leather coat was reinforced by metal rings or scales and shortly gave way to chain mail. This highly effective armor was worn in a long shirt, or *hauberk,* which reached to the knees. Often the legs were also armored and the head protected by a simple, conical helmet with a nosepiece. The Carolingian handsword had grown into the great, straight-bladed, two-handed cavalry broadsword, almost as tall as a man. The knight carried a long lance for initial attack. He might also use a battle-ax, mace, or a fearsome variation called the Morning Star, a spiked steel ball attached to a handle by a short length of chain. He carried, finally, a body-length shield. As the knight's equipment and armor grew heavier, special breeds of horses—Percherons, Belgians, and the like —were developed to bear the added weight. From helmet to horse the knight's equipment was as expensive as it was formidable. The skilled armorer was the most valued of medieval craftsmen. His materials were costly and his art laborious. The rustic skill of the castle or village black-smith was not equal to such work. It is understandable why the expense of knighting a lord's son became one of the customary *aids* and why the armor of a fallen knight was a rich prize for his assailant. In the course of the twelfth and thirteenth centuries armor, like the art of war, continued to be refined and elaborated until the link chain was completely replaced by the polished, embossed, intricately articulated plate armor of the later Middle Ages.

Despite the prevalence of war, feudal armies were small and most engagements limited. Feudalism tended to be a local system and the disputes that led to war were generally local too. Such a mass effort as Otto the Great's battle on the Lech or Duke William's invasion of England were unusual. Normally a few hundred knights made up a considerable army. Until very late in the Middle Ages tactics were virtually unknown and a battle was a melee in which individual knights fought each other, frequently stopping to take a prisoner or strip a fallen enemy, with complete disregard for unit discipline. The knights were usually backed by a motley of retainers, squires, and men-at-arms; but these took only a secondary part in combat. The knight was prince of the field.

In the intervals of peace the knightly lord planned and prepared for war. His training and occupation governed everything else he did or was. Hunting was an obsession second only to war. The wild forests which covered northern Europe were filled with game—wolves, wild boar, deer, and sporting birds. The noble cherished his hunting dogs and falcons almost as much as his horses and they, as well as the art they served, were symbols of noble privilege; hunting became a cult.

The business of the fief consumed considerable time. The lord had to maintain his court and "do justice" to his vassals. If the fief was large there was the necessity of visitation to keep him almost constantly on the move. If it was small, he had to tend personally to many of the details of agricultural management.

Life in the noble household centered in the castle. It was more a fortress than a home and its primary purpose was military, not domestic. The haphazard forms of earlier fortification had given way, by the tenth century, to a fairly definite castle form. It consisted usually of a deep ditch encircling a mound of earth. On the mound was a fortified tower called a *motte,* or keep. The protective ditch was rimmed with a palisade of upright logs. In time, the keep tended to be made of stone. Much later—not before the twelfth century—the outer walls were made of stone too. Every fief had its castle strategically located for defense and attack; a great fief might have several. These grim structures were the center of feudal life. The castle keep was the residence of the lord. Its windows were narrow and unglazed; the great hall was dark and drafty; the sophistication of the chimney did not appear until the twelfth century and the smoke from the hearth and illuminating torches added to the castle's gloom and discomfort. Furniture was sparse and uncomfortable; and privacy, even for the most personal activities, was nearly nonexistent. The lord's wife was the mistress of the household and supervised the thousand tasks necessary for the self-sufficiency of the castle community.

Entertainment was scarce; the court attendance of the lord's vassals was an occasion. Religious holidays, local fairs, a wandering minstrel with a dancing bear, or a band of jugglers might break the monotony. Meals consisted almost entirely of meat with bread and a few vegetables. They were served in the great hall on plank tables put up and taken down for every meal. Food was accompanied, preceded, and followed by incredible quantities of wine, beer, or ale. Drunkenness was a normal vice, vying with obesity and violence for the life of the feudal lord. The social life and attitudes of the nobility tended always to be brutalized by the constant exposure to war and violence and the lack of any secular tradition of gentility. Customary law and the primitive forms of chivalry governed the relations of noble peers and fellow vassals. But the lord was a law unto himself with regard to other people. He often beat his wife, who was completely under his control, having no rights at all under feudal law. He might slay his servants; the peasants on his estates were almost completely at his mercy. If he possessed the right of "high justice" his prestige was enhanced by a gallows at the gate of his castle; and it was usually decorated with the broken corpse of some poor wretch caught in theft or trespass.

Despite the universality of the church, religion did little to moderate the brutalities of feudal life. The noble observed the habitual forms of religious worship—he might even have a chapel with attending priests. But the church had no noticeable effect upon his behavior. At the local level, the church itself was involved in the feudal system; the village priest was usually an ignorant peasant and the local bishop was frequently as greedy and brutal as any secular lord. At times, in certain parts of Europe, the church made heroic efforts to restrain the ferocity of feudalism. In the tenth century the church proclaimed the Peace of God; in the eleventh, the Truce of God—but with no lasting effect. The lord in his castle was a sovereign of his church as he was of his king. At the best, the feudal lord and knight was a brave warrior, a conscientious proprietor, and a gentleman farmer; at the worst, he was a bloody-handed bandit.

The Manor and the Peasant: The Economic Basis of Feudalism

The way of life of the feudal lord, the whole system in which he was involved, rested ultimately upon the back of the peasant—the lowest, the least-esteemed, and the most useful member of medieval society. The significance of the peasant derived from the fact that feudal Europe depended almost entirely upon agriculture, and agriculture depended upon the work of the peasant. The invasions and disorder of late Carolingian times had virtually finished whatever urban life had survived in most of Christian Europe. Security, communications, and money had almost disappeared and, with them, the trade on which the existence of cities depended. Communities remained—around the walls of castles, in episcopal or monastic centers—but they were small and generally self-sufficient. Since late Roman times the gradual disappearance of cities had thrown the economic burden of society increasingly upon the countryside. With each step the peasant was bound more securely to the soil, his life bounded by the confines of the feudal manor.

As the fief was the unit of feudal political life, so the manor was its economic unit. The great fiefs that divided Europe were all subdivided, in turn, into manors. The manor was, most simply, an estate. A simple knight might have only one manor, or two or three. The lands of a great lord might contain hundreds, even thousands of manorial units.

The center of the manor was the manor house, in which the lord, or his deputy, steward, or bailiff lived. The manor house was almost always fortified and might even be a castle. Nearby was the village in which the manorial peasantry lived. Round about the manor house and village were the lands of the manor. They consisted usually of a common pasture in which the stock of the village grazed; a woodland that supplied the lumber, the chief technological material of feudal life, and that also supported the half-wild swine of the village drove; and, most important of all, the arable land which provided the crops. This consisted of two parts, the lord's portion, or *demesne*—as much as one-third, as little as one-sixth—and the portion of the peasantry. All of it was divided into two fields in the poorer parts of Europe, three fields where the soil was richer. In north central Europe the three-field system was general: each year one of the fields was allowed to lie fallow, one was planted in spring grain, one in winter grain. They were rotated from year to year. Within each field the land was further divided, usually into strips the length of the field. Each was separated from the other by a narrow ridge, or *balk*. Every peasant family had strips in each of the fields. The demesne land of the manor's lord usually consisted of strips alongside those of his peasants. The whole estate was cultivated in common, largely from necessity. The soil was heavy, tools poor, and oxen scarce. It sometimes took as many as ten oxen to pull the crude, clumsy plow and many entire villages possessed no more beasts than this. At planting and harvest all the men, women, and children of the village turned out. After harvest the yield was divided according to the holdings of individual families.

There was an almost endless variation in the form and size of peasant holdings, ranging from manorial strips to individual farms. And the conditions under which these were held similarly ranged from legal slavery to the considerable personal freedom associated with individual ownership. But, in general, the same necessities which had caused the spread of feudalism operated to spread the institution of manorialism. The manor economy radiated from the feudal core lands of northwestern Europe in every direction to become the typical pattern of local agriculture—and to remain so for most of the Middle Ages. Local variations in land tenure and in the personal relations between the lord of the manor and his peasantry continued to exist, but by far the greatest number of the peasants were serfs— indeed, the terms "serf" and "peasant" tended to become synonymous in feudal society.

In a strict sense, the serf was not a slave, for he legally retained his

West Façade, St. Etienne. Begun c. 1050. Caen.

Left: Philip II, King of France.
Below: *Statues of the Saints.*
Façade, St. Trophime. 12th
century. Arles.
Opposite: Cloister at Monreale.

Cathedral at Worms.

freedom. But his condition was no conspicuous improvement upon slavery. He was bound to the soil, to the manor, and to the lord. His labor, if not his body, was the possession of the lord of the manor. The relationship between the lord and his serfs was a menial equivalent of the relationship between lord and vassal. Like vassalage, serfdom was based upon the use of land rather than its ownership, upon customary law, and upon mutual contractual obligations. The most pressing obligation of the peasant was labor on his lord's land. He normally owed three days' labor in each week, called "week work"; special work, called "boon work," which the lord could demand at any time; and a host of specific tasks such as work on roads, forest or swamp land, fortification, and others. In all, the lord claimed well over half the labor of his serfs.

In addition to the obligation of labor, the peasant was weighed down with rents and fees of a dozen sorts. He had to grind his grain at the lord's mill; brew his beer or press his wine at the lord's brewery or winepress; bake his bread in the lord's oven—and for each service he paid a fee. He paid a fee at death (the peasant equivalent of relief). He paid a fee upon marriage. If a young peasant wished to marry outside the manor community his family paid a ruinous compensation to the lord for the labor taken from him. The same was true if the peasant's son entered the church.

To rents, fees, and taxes were added fines and punishments set by custom and judged in the lord's local courts. The records of manorial law bristle with hideous and bizarre punishments reserved for poaching in the lord's close, fishing in his pond, or gathering live wood in his forest. The lord could usually kill, maim, or abuse his peasants at will. Economic considerations and the iron restrictions of custom probably modified this right. But the gulf between lord and peasant was as broad as society. As late as the eleventh century the nobility disputed with the church that the peasant was not even a human being and did not possess a soul. Yet the mutual nature of manorial life reached across the gulf. The paternalism of the lord could be benevolent. In time of danger his castle or manor house protected the peasants of the village. In time of famine he might open his barns to them. He put his breeding stock at their disposal to improve the wretched quality of their work animals. There are even a few instances of the remission of fees and taxes.

The life of the manorial village was hard and monotonous. Agricultural methods were primitive and crop-yield was low. There was seldom enough fodder to winter the animals and all but the few best and strongest were slaughtered in the fall. Those that were kept often had to be carried bodily out to pasture in the spring. The peasant's diet consisted primarily of dark bread, gruel, and ale or beer—all products of the grain which was the manor's principal crop. These staples were supplemented by fresh vegetables in season, butter and cheese. Meat was a luxury. At the time of fall slaughter there was some fresh meat, but usually it was smoked or salted, and always meagre. Salt pork, the stringy and unpalatable meat of the half-wild village swine, and salt fish, often spoiled, were as close to meat staples as the peasant came. His hut was squat, heavy-walled, thatch-roofed, and dark. It sheltered both his family and his livestock; the manure heap before his door measured his status in the village. A hole in the roof served as a chimney and let in as much rain and cold as it let out smoke.

Near the huddle of peasant cottages was the village church and parsonage. Both the church and its priest were supported by the community. A special portion of manor land was set aside as "God's acre." This was farmed by the peasants, like the lord's demesne, as a manorial obligation. In addition, peasants owed the church an annual tithe and a handful of other payments. The priest himself was normally one of the local peasantry. Appointed by the lord of the manor, he was instructed and examined by the local bishop, but it was rare for him to know more than a few words of the Latin service. His ignorance was only exceeded by that of his parishioners. Yet the very existence of a village church and the celebration of its ancient forms, no matter how ineptly, was a source of spiritual comfort. And the village parson, we must imagine, was often a man of rustic virtue.

With all its burdens of labor, poverty, taxes, fines, and fees the life of the peasant had its compensations. The authority of village custom, to which even the lord was forced to bow, gave to the peasant a satisfying predictability about his world. The static life of the village provided him with a social universe in which to take his place. The affairs and gossip and day-to-day alarms of the village made his topics of conversation. The celebration of church festivals, saints' days, and Sundays gave him amusements. The pleasures of singing, dancing, drinking, and making love have never been entirely usurped by the privileged.

Like the late Roman villa and the primitive German village, which were its ancestors, the medieval manor was an almost entirely self-sufficient socio-economic unit. Most of the necessities of the community were produced by its members. Men and beasts produced the labor; the fields and gardens, pastures and streams provided the food; hides and wool and flax were turned into clothing. Each village had its artisans—blacksmith, wheelwright, carpenter, cellarer, and midwife. Only a handful of necessities, such as iron, pitch, and sometimes salt, had to be imported. Occasionally the manor produced a surplus; it might possess some unique product, such as salt. Local fairs grew up for exchange. Static as the manorial system was —and it certainly was one of the most stable patterns of existence in human history—still the slow effects of change worked over the centuries.

The same forces which had already begun to modify the structure of feudalism by the eleventh and twelfth centuries touched the manorial system, too. The bedlam of constant local war abated somewhat as the kings began to make headway against feudal separatism. The beginnings of commerce and the revival of town life created markets for the peasant's agricultural goods and extended the boundaries of his world. Increased demands for goods and the pressure of increasing population extended manorial agriculture into the unclaimed swamps and forest lands of much of Europe. This pioneering work was undertaken by great kings and little lords and in the reclaimed lands peasants demanded and got more freedom as the price of their labor. The feudal and manorial systems were moving toward the great changes of the High Middle Ages, leaving behind the conditions and necessities which had created them.

THE CRUSADES

In the two centuries following 1095, thousands of people—from kings, emperors, and bishops to runaway serfs and freebooting adventurers—left western Europe for the Near East. Their purpose was to recover the Holy Land and the sacred places of Christianity from the hands of the Mohammedans. They usually sewed on their clothing the sign of the cross, symbol of their Christian purpose, and were thus called Crusaders, "wearers of the cross." There were seven distinct Crusades and a number of lesser movements of crusading temper. Two of them had momentary success: the others were inglorious failures. Yet the Crusades were perhaps the grandest enterprise of medieval feudalism; in many ways certainly the most characteristic. In their blending of Christian idealism and savage warfare, they are perfect illustrations of the fusion of widely disparate elements so characteristic of the Middle Ages.

The Causes of the Crusades

The ultimate causes of the Crusades lay far from western Europe on the eastern fringes of the Moslem Empire and in the councils of Byzantium. Early in the eleventh century another wave of horse nomads from western

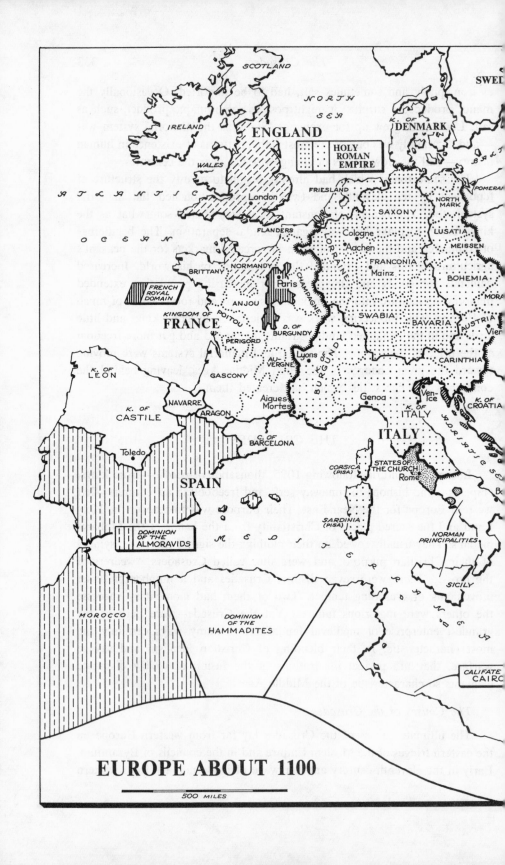

EUROPE ABOUT 1100

500 MILES

THE
LATIN STATES
IN SYRIA
1140

150 MILES

Asia, the Seljuk Turks, poured across the eastern borders of Persia, to become by mid-century, the dominant people in that rich and cultured heart of the Moslem east. The Caliph of Baghdad was the helpless tool of the Seljuk Sultan. The new conquerors embraced Islam and Islam's historic hostility to the Byzantine Empire. Seljuk expansion pushed on to the west to take the Syrian coast and across the Taurus mountains into Asia Minor. The Byzantines fought desperately for this essential portion of the empire but, at Manzikert in 1071, virtually the entire Byzantine military—some one hundred thousand men—was annihilated. Within a matter of years the whole subcontinent of Asia Minor and the Syrian coast almost to the Egyptian frontier were in Seljuk hands.

As the Seljuk invasion brought Islam face to face with Constantinople across the Bosporus, a kindred host of nomads, the Patzinaks, followed the Huns, the Bulgars, the Magyars up the broad corridor of the Danube valley into the Balkans. Byzantium was encircled. Moreover, the whole economic structure which, more than anything else, had enabled Byzantium to survive the crises of centuries, was desperately threatened. Asia Minor was the recruiting ground for her soldiery and the granary of the empire. The cities of Asia Minor and Syria were important producers and consumers of Byzantine goods and the Balkans were an area of raw materials and markets. The great city of Constantinople could not long survive in economic isolation.

In these desperate times Alexius Comnenus (*1081–1118*) came to the throne of the eastern empire. He appealed to the west—to individual lords and finally to the pope—to save the eastern Christian empire and, incidentally, to recover the Holy Land. The appeal to the pope came at a propitious moment. The papacy had recovered from the apathy and abuse which had immobilized it in the two previous centuries. The reform program which had begun at the French monastery of Cluny had grown through the tenth century into a powerful surge of reforming vitality which had charged all of western Christendom. By the middle of the eleventh century the Cluniac[1] movement had touched the papacy. The ascetic ideal of St. Benedict and the theocratic program of Gregory the Great were once more taken up by a series of militant popes. The ecclesiastico-political aims of the reformed papacy had clashed with the German emperors over the question of the investiture of bishops. Gregory VII (*1073–1085*) had defended successfully the most extravagant claims to papal supremacy ever put forward.

1. See pp. 350-51.

The pope who received the urgent embassy of Alexius Comnenus was Urban II (*1088–1099*). He was an ascetic, a Cluniac monk like his friend Gregory VII; and, like Gregory, he set no limit to his ambition for the advancement of papal claims. In the appeal of the eastern emperor he saw an ideal opportunity for furthering these. He had already preached a holy war against Islam in Spain and had seen knights and barons respond to his call. Not half a century had passed since the eastern orthodox church, after a long history of doctrinal dispute, had split away from the Catholic west. As the head of a great, armed host moving to the east, could Urban not reunite the Christian world under his hand? It was an ambition thoroughly consistent with the aims of the reformed papacy. Further, as the head of that same host, would there be a power in the world to stand against him and his church? In the appeal of the eastern emperor Urban II saw the means of elevating the papacy above the warring factions of feudal Europe, the means of implementing a policy which had been more dream than reality even for Gregory VII.

Another set of circumstances served papal policy. Each year, from every corner of western Europe, people set out to visit the holy places of their faith—scenes of miracles and martyrdom. They went to be healed, to do penance, and simply to see. They might journey to some local or regional shrine a few days distant; they might visit the great shrine of Compostella in northwestern Spain, where a strong but spurious tradition placed the tomb of the Apostle James; they might journey to Rome with its hundreds of sacred places. But the greatest and most arduous of pilgrimages was that to the Holy Land. In spite of the Moslem occupation of Palestine, the pilgrimage traffic continued and was tolerated by Islam to which Palestine and Jerusalem were also sacred. There were over a hundred mass pilgrimages there in the eleventh century alone.

With the Seljuk conquest of Palestine and coastal Syria, Moslem policy changed. Stories began to drift back to the west of atrocities committed against peaceful pilgrims, of offenses to the holy places themselves. In the light of ancient hostility these stories were believed, repeated, and magnified. The stories of the men who had fought the *paynim* ("pagans") in Spain and southern Italy confirmed the worst rumors. As Urban II warmed to the idea of a great crusade, popular preachers, wild-eyed fanatics, like Peter the Hermit, were already spreading the idea of an armed pilgrimage along with propaganda stories of Christian martyrdom and Turkish outrage.

When Urban II decided to preach his crusade at the southern French city of Clermont in 1095, the scene was set. Thousands had gathered there and Urban spoke from an elevated platform in the midst of a swirling throng. He spoke of Moslem blasphemy and the hideous torture of Christians in the very land of Christian origins. He spoke of the glorious western tradition of unrelenting enmity against the "kingdoms of the pagans" in the name of the "Holy Church." As a Frenchman, he skillfully manipulated his predominantly French audience. He reminded them of their Frankish heritage, their freedom, their valor, and their historic connection with the church. He went on to paint a picture of the opportunities for ambition in the east, that paradise which the Bible itself says "floweth with milk and honey." He shamed, he coaxed, he promised, he threatened. As he ended, a spontaneous cry rose from the throng around him, *"Dieu li volt!"* God wills it. The crowd surged forward to take the cross. The first crusade was thus kindled.

The First Crusade: Jerusalem Delivered

During the winter of 1095, as Urban and his agents solicited support for the crusade, popular preachers like Peter the Hermit spoke at a thousand crossroads, towns, and villages. From Germany and France great throngs of peasants and petty townsmen responded in a burst of fanatic enthusiasm. Like a devouring pestilence the Peasants' Crusade swept up the Rhine valley and down the Danube. It was a conglomerate of undisciplined mobs without military experience, food, or even a sure knowledge of where Jerusalem was. Their progress was marked by murder, rape, and pillage. Finally they reached Constantinople. The eastern emperor, shocked at the sight of this motley and rapacious mob, hastily provided ships to take them to Asia Minor. There they met a Turkish force and were cut to pieces. In the meantime the First Crusade was beginning to form.

It is often called the Barons' Crusade, for not one of the kings of western Europe took part in it. Ironically, Philip I of France, William Rufus of England, and Henry IV of Germany were all under papal excommunication at the time, for one offense or another. The First Crusade was composed largely of feudal lords, the majority of them French. It began to form in four large contingents, numbering more than thirty thousand men, not counting the straggling bands of camp followers, traders, prostitutes, and hangers-on. Leadership fell to a group of nobles including Godfrey of Bouillon, a northern French baron; Raymond, Count of Toulouse; Bohemond and Tancred, Norman lords of southern Italy; and Ademar, the papal legate and Bishop of Puy. Godfrey, strong, courageous, and almost fanatic in his religious zeal, was probably the purest crusader among them. Raymond, who had fought the Saracens in Spain, had long since lost whatever zeal he might once have had; he calculated the risk against the booty and took the cross. Bohemond and Tancred made no effort to disguise their aims; there were lands to be seized in the east, so why not a Norman kingdom there as in England and Italy? Indeed, for a generation they had been attempting to win the Balkans from Byzantium.

The motives of the leaders were no different than those of their host. The hope of gain was a powerful stimulus. Still other inducements were added to simple avarice. Urban II proclaimed that a crusader's family and property were under the protection of the church. Burdensome feudal dues and obligations were lifted. Full penance was to be gained by any man who took the cross. The very idea of a soldier for Christ is a paradox. But although it is easier to see hypocrisy and crass motives than genuine Christian devotion here, it would be wrong to assume that true zeal was absent. The crusaders were blunt and unlettered warriors, not monks, but many of them were moved by honest religious motives. To overlook this is to misunderstand an important aspect of medieval civilization.

The main divisions of the crusading army made their way to Constantinople, most of them overland through the same blighted lands that had suffered the scourge of the previous year. Settlements closed their gates and armed their walls. Privation and hostility met them at every step. Reaching Constantinople, their tempers already raw, the Crusaders were dazzled by its riches. It was proposed to take that city and forget the Turks. The rough crusaders had nothing but contempt for the Byzantines— contempt mixed with suspicion and envy. The Byzantines and Alexius Comnenus were equally suspicious and fearful of their deliverers. With subsidies and promises of lavish aid, the emperor extracted an oath of fealty from the leaders of the Crusade. As a matter of expediency they complied—knowing it would be hard enough for him to hold them to it.

They crossed to Asia Minor and reached Nicaea, where the picked bones of their peasant predecessors had been left as a warning. The city surrendered in the face of hopeless odds. Inland a few miles, the crusaders met their first Turkish army and defeated it. Asia Minor lay open to them and they set out across its bleak interior for Antioch in northern Syria. After a harrowing march they invested Antioch in an equally harrowing siege. Climate and disease were more fearful enemies than the Turks but after eight months Antioch surrendered. The crusaders defeated a relieving army which the governor of Mosul brought only days too late to save the city. A curious and typical incident played no small part in the victory.

A priest named Peter Bartholomew, guided by a vision, found the holy lance which had pierced the side of Jesus at his Crucifixion. Armed with this invincible symbol, the Crusaders were convinced that victory was certain.

From Antioch the Crusaders pressed on down the coast to Jerusalem and, in June of 1099—their numbers reduced to less than twelve thousand men—they stood under the walls of the Holy City. The governor of Jerusalem offered reasonable terms; they were refused. The small Moslem garrison held out for more than a month before the crusaders broke over the walls and into the city. None was spared in the carnage. All the fanatic hatred and religious zeal, all the frustrations, injuries, and appetites of the crusaders found a focus in the slaughter of unbelievers. More than seventy thousand Moslems were slain. The streets were piled high with dismembered corpses and the crusaders rode through torrents of blood. Amid the almost unbearable stench in the hot summer sun, they celebrated their accomplishment in a city of the dead. They crowded, weeping and fainting, into and around the Church of the Holy Sepulcher to worship the Christ whom their arms had glorified. The First Crusade was a success.

But it owed as much to Moslem-Turkish division as to the strength of the crusaders. The Seljuk wave began to lose its force even as it reached its height. Before the crusaders left Europe the Seljuk empire was convulsed by civil war. A dozen local powers rose in its backwash and no united effort against the crusaders was possible.

By 1099 a considerable territory in Asia Minor, Syria, and Palestine was in the hands of the crusaders. The victors turned to the spoils. But the division had already begun. Baldwin, the brother of Godfrey of Bouillon, had turned aside a full year before to seize the city of Edessa inside the great bend of the Euphrates. It became the seat of the County of Edessa, the first of the crusading states of the Near East. The land and cities around Antioch were similarly taken and Antioch itself was reluctantly granted to Bohemond. After its conquest, Jerusalem was established as a kingdom with Godfrey as "defender." In none of these states was the claim of the eastern empire recognized. They belonged to the crusaders by right of conquest. The caution of Alexius Comnenus they preferred to regard as cowardice and desertion; they declared their oaths to him broken. From Antioch, Bohemond campaigned more vigorously for Byzantine lands in southern Asia Minor than he had ever done against the Turks. He renewed the plans of his family for a Norman conquest of the Balkans. The coastal trade of Syria and Asia Minor, which had been a Byzantine claim for centuries, was surrendered to the enterprising seamen of such Italian city-states as Venice, Genoa, and Pisa. They had supported and supplied the crusaders from the sea and in the years following the First Crusade they held virtually every coastal town from Jaffa to Rhodes. The king of Jerusalem—Baldwin succeeded Godfrey, who died in 1100—was the feudal overlord of the Latin states of the east. The great fiefs, Baldwin's Edessa, Bohemond's Norman Antioch, and Tripolis, conquered by Raymond of Toulouse, were as jealously independent as their European counterparts. The Greek Church was uprooted in the conquered lands and replaced by Latin Catholic service and papal discipline.

The Loss of the Latin East

As the Latin states took form, most of the crusaders returned home. The stream of pilgrims began once more. But the peace which had been bought with Moslem blood could not long remain and the masters of the Syrian fiefs knew it. They built magnificent stone castles to defend strategic points, the first such structures in feudal history. They had greatly advanced their knowledge of fortification with the aid of Byzantine-Greek architects, and the Syrian castles still stand as some of the world's most impressive ruins. But men were essential to defense and, even if feudal obligations could be enforced, no more than six thousand fighting men could be mustered from all the Syrian-Latin states. This crisis of defense was met by the formation of a number of strange, semimonastic, crusading orders: the Knights Templars, the Hospitalers, and the Teutonic Knights. There was no truer expression of the crusading spirit than these orders. The Templars, so-called from their headquarters near the site of Solomon's Temple, were an organization of French knights dedicated to the protection of pilgrims and the defense of the Holy Land. Their strict rule was drawn up by the great St. Bernard himself; they lived like monks in piety, silence, and filth. To the normal monastic virtues they added the virtues of the warrior, the rigorous practice of arms, and the efficient dispatch of assassins. The Hospitalers were a similar order. They had been founded somewhat earlier to care for pilgrims but, along with the Templars, they also became a military order. The Teutonic order was of the same sort but composed of German knights. They all wore distinctive costume, principally a robe with an identifying cross. These orders quickly spread from the Holy Land back to western Europe. Their purpose caught the imagination of many people, who showered them with gifts until they became rich and powerful.

At its best the kingdom of Jerusalem was an unstable state. The castles which should have defended it were the strongholds of an arrogant feudality. The military orders, acknowledging only the distant headship of the pope, hated each other as bitterly as they did the Moslems. And the Moslems themselves were gradually recovering a measure of unity. In 1144 they captured Edessa, threatening the whole Latin kingdom. Another crusade was needed.

On the request of Pope Eugenius III (*1145–1153*), St. Bernard, the most imposing figure of his generation, was to stir Christian effort. By threats, and pleas, promises and eloquence, Bernard enlisted Louis VII of France and Conrad III of Germany. The Second Crusade set out in 1147, the German contingent first, followed by the French. They took the now infamous land route and repeated in detail the rapine and devastation of their predecessors. Again the Greek emperor transported his dangerous guests across the straits and promised his aid. At the site of the first great victory of the First Crusade, not far from Nicaea, the German army met the Moslems and was disastrously defeated. The French followed them into disaster. With little more than a remnant of their forces, the two kings finally reached Jerusalem. The Christian holders of the Holy Land were suspicious of the newly arrived crusaders. An ill-contrived attack on Damascus failed, as did one on the Moslem stronghold of Ascalon. Conrad III returned to Germany and Louis VII to France. The Second Crusade was over. Its only profit went to Roger, the Norman king of Sicily, who used the distraction of the crusade to mask a crusade of his own against the Byzantine Balkans and Greece.

At this crucial moment in the affairs of the Near East, one of the most dramatic figures of the crusades, the great Moslem leader Saladin (*1174–1193*) succeeded his uncle as the strong man of Egypt. He was a Turk and a soldier, but he was also a statesman. In time he added Moslem Syria to his rich holdings in Egypt and gained the orthodox support of Baghdad. While Saladin created a united Moslem federation, his Christian neighbors continued to court disaster by their division. The inevitable inflammatory incidents occurred and full-scale war followed. Saladin met the hastily assembled Latin forces in the desert not far from the Sea of Galilee and destroyed them. He pressed on to Jerusalem. Under its walls he offered generous terms in place of a siege of the Holy City. He was refused, and after a twelve-day siege the city fell. But there were no scenes of carnage and outrage. Saladin charged a heavy ransom for those captives who could pay and released thousands of the poor who could not. He allowed peaceful Christian pilgrimage to continue under his protection.

The Third Crusade and the Decline of the Crusading Spirit

No matter how courtly a victor Saladin was, the Holy City was again in Moslem hands. Western Europe once more heard the call to a crusade. Among the first to respond was the aged German emperor, Frederick Barbarossa who, as a boy, had accompanied the abortive crusade of Conrad III. He led his army over the land route and reached Asia Minor only to be drowned while crossing a stream. Without him, his army fell to pieces and only a fraction of it reached Acre to join the French and English contingents, which had come by sea.

With Barbarossa dead leadership of the Third Crusade fell to Richard I of England (*1189–1199*), soon to be called *Coeur de Lion,* the Lion-Hearted. He was young and strong and eager to try his powers. Saladin and the Moslems seemed worthy of his mettle and he took the cross. But he had one indispensable condition. If he went, Philip Augustus, the king of France, had to go too. He wanted no such enemy at his back. They took their oaths together and started for the Holy Land. Philip reached it first; Richard had stopped along the way to make several lucrative conquests. The object of their attack was the port-city of Acre. The weight of Richard's reinforcements forced the long-besieged city to surrender. Philip Augustus, pleading illness, returned to France and an interest more consuming than the Crusade—Richard's French fiefs. Only Richard remained to lead the "Crusade of the Kings." He was a splendid soldier, a fine general, and a great military engineer. He deserved a better army. It was a typical feudal host: the German survivors of Barbarossa's contingent melted away; the French baronage refused to take orders from Richard, and his own Norman-French knights were almost as scheming and unreliable.

Richard and Saladin were worthy foes. They met time and again in battles and sieges that carried them up and down the coast. In time they came to admire each other. Richard even proposed, at one time, a marriage alliance between his sister and Saladin's brother, but the scandalized pope, Clement III, would have none of it. In a battle before Jaffa, Richard's horse was killed and Saladin sent him a splendid mount from his own stables. As Richard lay sick with fever, Saladin sent his own physician to attend him. But neither could budge the other. Saladin held the hinterland; Richard, the coast. In 1192 they signed a peace treaty. Richard was to keep the coastal cities that were then in Christian hands. The city of Jerusalem was to be free, as before, to Christian pilgrimage, but was to remain Moslem. The result of Richard's Crusade was the capture of three inconsequential cities—Acre, Jaffa, and Ascalon—and the return to the staius quo in Jerusalem which had originally provoked the Crusade. He sailed for home only to be captured and held for ransom by the German emperor, Henry VI. He found his fellow Christian lords, his own brother John included, to be more faithless and less gentle than the gallant foe he had left in Palestine.

In 1199, the year of Richard's death, Pope Innocent III preached a Fourth Crusade to expel the Saracens from Egypt. His call was answered by the land-hungry Normans of Sicily and the north and by the predatory lesser baronage of France. The crusaders called upon Venice to transport them. They were penniless, as usual, and the shrewd Venetians negotiated. They demanded 85,000 silver marks and one-half of all conquests. The money could not be raised, as the Venetians had foreseen, whereupon they assumed the lion's share in the direction of the Crusade. The Venetian leaders, including the Doge, Enrico Dondolo, solemnly took the cross in a magnificent ceremony at St. Mark's, and the expedition against Egypt was set on foot. At the very moment when they were pledging themselves to the holy conquest of Egypt, their ambassadors in Cairo were signing a trade treaty with the sultan.

The Venetians directed the Crusade first to Zara, a city on the coast of Dalmatia, and a strong point that Venice had long desired to secure her position in the Adriatic. That it was also a Christian city upon which the fury of the crusaders was turned, seems to have been of little concern to the Venetians, or to the crusaders. Zara was sacked and burned. This pious work completed, they turned next, not to Saracen Egypt, but to Christian Constantinople. After a nervous truce, during which the Venetians and crusaders interfered in the complex domestic politics of the city, their ferocity was unleashed again. The great city of Constantinople, ancient citadel of culture and center of eastern orthodoxy, fell to the crusaders who, with unparalleled horrors, ravaged its churches, its mansions and palaces, its markets, schools, and brothels. By this time, Innocent III had excommunicated the whole Crusade, but the economic purpose of Venice had been served. Venetian hands held undisputed possession of the routes to Constantinople and the east.

Long before the moral disaster of the Fourth Crusade, the crusading spirit had begun to wane. Indeed, the failure of the Second Crusade had raised many doubts, which fell in with the questioning spirit and anticlericalism that were beginning to stir in the twelfth century. Yet the crusading ideal retained some vigor. About 1212 a spiritual fever, reminiscent of that carried so long before by Peter the Hermit, raged through western

Europe once more. Thousands of children from France and Germany took the cross and started for the Holy Land, convinced that innocence could be a more effective instrument of God's will than arms. It was a magnificent and pitiable gesture. Many were sent back home by responsible officials. Thousands perished of hunger and exposure. Thousands more glutted Moslem slave markets, whence enterprising Christian merchants took them. The great pope, Innocent III, attempted to revive the lagging spirit of the Crusades. The response was a Fifth Crusade against Egypt, the key point of Moslem power. Its momentary success was squandered by the greed of the crusaders.

The Sixth Crusade was, in many ways, the most extraordinary for its prosecution, its personnel, and its success. The brilliant young German-Sicilian emperor, Frederick II (*1220–1250*), had vowed a Crusade. When illness made it impossible for him to go, Pope Gregory IX placed him under excommunication. The excommunicated emperor then entered negotiations with the Moslem sultan of Egypt in 1229 and succeeded— without the expenditure of a single soldier—in gaining the most favorable peace in the Near East since 1099. In effect, he once more gained Christian possession of Jerusalem and its surrounding territory. This striking success was rewarded by a papal crusade preached against Frederick's lands in Europe and by an interdict laid upon the restored kingdom of Jerusalem. Nonetheless, Jerusalem remained in Christian hands until 1244, when it was taken once more by the Moslems to remain Moslem for almost seven centuries.

The fall of the Holy City caused the feeble crusading spirit to rise once more. It was appropriately reserved for the saintly Louis IX of France to lead the last Crusade to the Near East. Its target was again Egypt; and it succeeded only in failure. The Christian knights who were not killed were captured. Louis himself was among the prisoners and the sultan graciously released him, upon the payment of an enormous ransom. In his old age Louis mounted another expedition, this time to North Africa, where he died before anything could be accomplished.

The Consequences of the Crusades

The Crusades had stretched over nearly two centuries. Their success, measured in terms of their specific purpose, was almost negligible. In 1095 the Holy Land was in Moslem hands. In 1270 it was again in Moslem hands (to remain so until the First World War seven hundred years later). The hope of the Byzantine emperors, that they might use the military strength of the Crusades to recover their lands in Asia, had come to nothing. Indeed, they had lost still more land to the crusaders and finally suffered the sack of Constantinople at the hands of their supposed champions. The hope of the papacy, to turn the force of the Crusades to its political and spiritual ends, and to restore the obedience of the eastern church to Rome, had also failed.

Yet in a dozen subtle and important ways the Crusades opened doors to the developing culture of western Europe. The experience of the Crusades had the effect of battering down the walls of narrow parochialism with which the isolated units of western Europe had surrounded themselves. The ignorant barons of France, Germany, and England were introduced to a larger and more cosmopolitan world than they had ever known. The thousands of westerners, "the Franks," who stayed for generations in the Latin kingdom of the Near East, were thoroughly transformed by prolonged contact with a civilization they quickly acknowledged as superior to their own. Even to the transient adventurer, the Crusades revealed not only strange sights and exotic customs but, more important, the knowledge that there were other cultures and other faiths than his own. Not even the most benighted Christian could fail to be impressed with some aspect of Islam.

Most of all, the Crusades affected European economic development. The demand for eastern goods—everything from fabrics such as cotton, muslin, and damask to drugs, condiments, and spices such as alum, incense, indigo, pepper, ginger, cloves, cinnamon, and the strange new sweetening agent called *zucra,* which came from cane reeds—created a lucrative market in western Europe. The Italian cities of Venice, Genoa, Pisa, Amalfi, and other Mediterranean ports had played an important role in the Crusades and had received trade concessions all through the Near East. They were thus in a position to serve the expanding markets of the west, and, through their enterprise, to create new ones. Their example and the broad nexus of their trade were factors in stimulating the growth of towns everywhere in western Europe: larger and better ships were developed; coinage was stabilized; banking services and commercial paper began to be used.

These economic changes in turn affected the social and political structure of western Europe, and in the long run served to undermine and finally destroy feudalism. The Crusades were by no means solely responsible for these wide-ranging developments, but they played a significant role in them.

SUGGESTIONS FOR FURTHER READING

G. Barraclough, *Origins of Modern Germany* (Oxford: Blackwell, 1946), probably the best short history of medieval Germany.

P. Boissonade, *Life and Work in Medieval Europe,* tr. by E. Power (New York: Knopf, 1927).

*J. Bronsted, *The Vikings* (Baltimore: Penguin, 1962).

Cambridge Medieval History and *The Shorter Cambridge Medieval History,* Vol. I, cited for Chap. 7.

G. G. Coulton, ed., *Life in the Middle Ages* (Cambridge: Cambridge University Press, 1928-30), 4 vols.; readings in religion and popular thought, manners, morals, and the way of life in the Middle Ages.

————, *The Medieval Village* (Cambridge: Cambridge University Press, 1925), a standard work by a great authority.

*E. S. Duckett, *Alfred the Great: The King and His England* (Chicago: Phoenix, 1958), the standard biography of Alfred.

J. Evans, *Life in Medieval France* (London: Phaidon, 1957).

*F. L. Ganshof, *Feudalism* (New York: Harper, 1961).

M. Gibbs, *Feudal Order, A Study of the Origins and Development of English Feudal Society* (New York: Abelard-Schuman, 1953).

C. H. Haskins, *The Normans in European History* (Boston: Houghton Mifflin, 1915), a classic work.

U. T. Holmes, *Daily Living in the Twelfth Century* (Madison: University of Wisconsin Press, 1952).

T. D. Kendrick, *A History of the Vikings* (New York: Scribners, 1930).

*H. Lamb, *The Crusades, Iron Men and Saints* (New York: Bantam, 1962), exciting account, somewhat fictionalized.

Medieval Germany 911–1250, Essays by German Historians, Vol. I tr. and ed. by G. Barraclough (Oxford: Blackwell, 1948).

Memoirs of the Crusades (New York: Dutton, 1933), Joinville's account of the Crusade of Louis IX and Villehardouin's of the Fourth Crusade.

R. B. Merriman, *The Rise of the Spanish Empire* (New York: Macmillan, 1918), a standard multivolume history of Spain; see Vol. I

N. Neilson, *Medieval Agrarian Economy* (New York: Holt, 1936).

*C. Oman, *The Art of War in the Middle Ages* (Ithaca: Cornell University Press, 1960).

*S. Painter, *The Rise of the Feudal Monarchies* (Ithaca: Cornell University Press, 1951).

C. Petit-Dutaillis, *Feudal Monarchy in France and England from the Tenth to the Thirteenth Century* (London: Kegan Paul, 1936).

A. L. Poole, *From Domesday Book to Magna Carta* (Oxford: Clarendon Press, 1951).

S. Runciman, *A History of the Crusades,* 3 vols. (Cambridge: Cambridge University Press, 1951-54), the best modern account.

R. C. Smail, *Crusading Warfare* (Cambridge: Cambridge University Press, 1956).

*C. Stephenson, *Medieval Feudalism* (Ithaca: Cornell University Press, 1942), probably the best general treatment of the subject, readable and sensible.

J. W. Thompson, *Feudal Germany* (Chicago: University of Chicago Press, 1928), authoritative but rather ponderous; a series of essays on topics in German feudalism.

P. Vinogradoff, *The Growth of the Manor* (New York: Macmillan, 1905), a pioneering classic of the subject.

William, Archbishop of Tyre, *A History of Deeds Done Beyond the Sea,* tr. and ed. by E. A. Babcock and A. C. Krey, 2 vols. (New York: Columbia University Press, 1943), one of the standard contemporary accounts of the Crusades in a fine modern edition.

*Paperbound edition. In the case of reprint editions, publisher and date of publication given will be that of reprint rather than the original.

∝ 9 ∝

The National Monarchies and
the Economic Revolution

GERMANY AND ITALY: EMPIRE AND PAPACY

The crusades were a counterpoint to events that were happening in Europe. We turn now to examine those events so closely related to the limited successes, the abundant failures, and the eventual abandonment of the Crusades.

The Investiture Struggle

In Germany, the feudal nobility took advantage of Henry IV's minority to seize rights and lands wherever possible. By the time he reached his majority, Henry was almost fanatically resolved to break the power of the feudality. He turned first to the ancestral crown lands of Saxony and Thuringia, planning to make this the base of royal power from which to recover control of the rest of Germany. Here, as elsewhere, he aroused hostility as he encroached on vested privilege. He turned to the church for resources, confiscating and seizing control of lands and selling church offices on an unprecedented scale. This policy was ill-timed, for the church had been gathering new strength as a consequence of internal reform. It was inevitable that his enemies should find each other, and Henry IV's entire reign was to be spent in fighting either singly or together the entrenched German nobility and a newly vigorous and reformed church.

Ecclesiastical reform had spread steadily during the previous generation, aided, ironically enough, by the pious dedication of Henry III. Though not initiated by the papacy—having begun far from Rome— it reached the papal throne in the reign of Henry IV (*1056–1106*) and contributed to the strengthening of papal power. The reform movement stemmed by and large from a single source, the monastery of Cluny in the rugged hills of southeastern France. The congregation of Cluny had been founded in 910—in the darkest days of the church's history—weak in the face of feudal anarchy and barbarian invasion, unable to combat the avarice or mitigate the ignorance of its own officials. Church lands were seized by lay lords and "protectors" or sold by unscrupulous bishops and abbots. Financial abuses flourished everywhere and clerical rights were virtually nonexistent. Monastic discipline was in ruins; the life of the spirit was neglected from the papacy down to the local parishes; and the inherent paganism of popular religion surged up to threaten the hold of Christianity upon the minds of European men. Some attempts at re- form had been made, but with little success. Nevertheless, a few dedicated souls, both churchmen and laymen, persisted in these efforts. One was the Duke of Aquitaine, who had originally granted the lands to the monks of Cluny. From their remote and desolate outpost, these monks started the most important reform movement of the medieval church.

The success of Cluny lay in a number of significant departures from conventional monastic practice. From the first, the Cluniac movement had a unique principle of organization. (One of the weaknesses of the older monasticism had been the local independence of individual houses, each under its own abbot. At times there had been common purpose and even limited cooperation, but in general monasteries had been controlled by local bishops or secular lords. This had led inevitably to a decline of the monastic spirit, to corruption, and secularization.) The Cluniacs insisted on freedom from lay control and from the interference of the secular clergy. The founder renounced any claim on the land he had given and Cluny recognized no lord but the pope. From its single house the Cluniac movement grew to embrace other nearby monasteries; but each came under the supervision of the Abbot of Cluny; each was administered by a prior appointed from Cluny, and the Abbot controlled his priors closely. Thus, as the Cluniac movement expanded, it was moved by a single pur- pose and a single will. By the twelfth century the Cluniac organization controlled three hundred priories, from Spain to Germany, and from Italy to England.

Within the monasteries the reformed Benedictine rule of the Cluniacs insisted upon a return to personal holiness and obedience. As was typical of medieval religious movements, the very rigor of Cluniac rule attracted great numbers of men and, even more important, men of talent and ability. The fame and influence of Cluny spread; its monks were sought as bishops and the movement began to have its effect upon the secular clergy. Wherever they went and whatever offices they assumed, the Cluniacs held to their exalted standards. They attacked the widespread practice of priestly marriage among the parish clergy. They attacked the equally widespread practice of lay control of church foundations. It was their goal to re-create the church as the instrument of God's will, free of every worldly taint. This was a revolutionary ambition in feudal society. Cluniac reform was vigorously opposed on every hand by outraged parish clergy and threatened feudal bishops. Yet it persevered and thrived upon opposition. Cluniacs sought and found martyrdom in a hundred grisly ways; they also found their way to Rome and the papacy.

Papal adoption of Cluniac reform is identified with one outstanding personality, "the monk Hildebrand," who was the moving force behind papal policy for a quarter of a century and who finally became Pope Gregory VII (*1073–1085*). Never has the doctrine of papal supremacy had a more vigorous champion. Gregory's aims were essentially those of the temporal monarchs of his time—the Capetian Philip I, William the Conqueror, and the emperor Henry IV—sovereign monarchical power. Yet the ambition of the Gregorian papacy brought it into direct conflict with the temporal monarchies. Gregory visualized the world in arch-Augustinian terms: God is the sovereign of the world, the human agent of His will is the pope; therefore, the greatest of the world's powers are directly subordinate to the pope just as their vassal tenants-in-chiefs are subordinate to them. Gregory seized the feudal system and imposed himself at its apex. Every temporal power that denied him obedience was not only his enemy, but also the enemy of God.

The focus of the struggle for the recognition of his claims was Germany. In the first place, the control of the state over the church was most flagrant there. We have already noted the importance of the control of bishops to the German monarchy. In addition, the German emperors had assumed the right to dictate policy to the popes and even to depose and appoint them. The contest for theoretical and practical supremacy, between pope and emperor could no longer be postponed. Finally, the direct involvement of German kings in the affairs of Italy was an intolerable restriction upon the freedom of action that Gregory's bold plans demanded.

Long before he became pope, Gregory (Hildebrand) had begun to move against the power of the German empire. The Norman seizure of Sicily and southern Italy had thus been turned to advantage when Gregory advised Pope Nicholas II to ally himself with the Normans, persuading them to designate their conquests as papal fiefs. Although this precipitated the long-threatened break with the eastern church and the Byzantine Empire, the Norman alliance promised to be a useful instrument in coping with the more pressing challenge to papal authority posed by Germany. In 1059, Gregory's aims were further served by the promulgation of a new papal electoral law—also at his urging. By it, the election of a pope was declared to be the prerogative of the cardinal clergy of Rome, a body composed of the ranking officials of certain churches in Rome, to be known as the College of Cardinals. Thus the pope, as Bishop of Rome, would be regularly elected by his own clergy as prescribed by Canon Law, and the pernicious interference of German emperors stopped. The reformed papacy soon began to assert its authority against the German bishops who had been enfiefed with the strategic lands of northern Italy, controlling Lombardy and the passes into Germany. In yearly synods the pope heard charges against these feudal lords and moved to censure them and even to remove them from office. Thus Gregory had helped pave the way for a contest with German imperial power even before he became pope.

Within two years of his accession to the papal throne, Gregory joined battle more directly, choosing the crucial issue of lay investiture. Investiture was the highly symbolic ceremony in which a bishop received the tokens of his power. This power had originally been purely spiritual, symbolized by the crozier, representing his pastoral care, and the ring, representing his spiritual union with the church. As the bishops became key feudal figures, holding their lands as fiefs, the ceremony was expanded to include the bestowal of such secular symbols as the scepter, and the whole proceeding was usurped and dominated by the temporal lords, especially the kings, who increasingly depended on the loyalty and talent of their bishops. This intrusion of the secular overlords into the investiture ceremony was called lay investiture; to both the church and the state it represented actual control of the appointment of bishops. The contest that raged over the next half century is often called the Investiture Controversy.

Early in 1075 Gregory, through a Roman synod, issued decrees against a number of abuses, including lay investiture. Almost immediately he followed these decrees by excommunicating, suspending, or deposing a number of the most powerful German clergy on a variety of charges. Most of these men were close to the emperor, some attached to his court. Henry IV replied by appointing bishops to several vacant sees and pointedly investing them with the episcopal ring and staff: the battle was clearly joined. Gregory threatened the emperor with excommunication. Henry summoned a council of his own German bishops who voted to depose the pope, "not Pope but false monk, Hildebrand!" Gregory, supported by a great assemblage of Italian clergy, solemnly excommunicated the emperor, placed the papal curse upon him, deposed him, and released his subjects from all obedience to him.

This was a priceless opportunity for the German nobility, and revolt flamed everywhere. At a diet assembled at Tribur in October of 1076, the feudal nobility acknowledged the excommunication of the emperor. They told him that if he had not received absolution at the hands of the pope by February 22, 1077, they would choose another emperor. They invited Gregory himself to Germany as president of a diet to confirm the deposition of the emperor and to anoint a successor. Henry IV, already badly defeated, realized that everything would be lost if Gregory were allowed to appear in Germany as the judge of an emperor before the emperor's own people. Resolved to meet the pope in Italy, in the bitter cold of winter, Henry crossed the Alps with a small party. At the castle of Canossa, in northern Italy, the party encountered the pope, already on his way north. Assuming the sackcloth of penance, the young emperor stood in the snow before the castle gate for three days, while Gregory struggled with his conscience. By his penitential submission Henry had placed the pope in an impossible position. As a sincere and dedicated reformer he could not refuse to absolve a contrite sinner, emperor or not. Yet to absolve him was to lose a political advantage which promised to lay imperial Germany in ruins at his feet. In Gregory, the politician struggled with the priest: The priest won out; Gregory absolved his rival. This dramatic face-to-face meeting of pope and emperor was scarcely noted by contemporaries, but modern scholars have come to see it as symbolic of one of the crucial contests of the Middle Ages.

Henry returned to Germany after making a number of empty promises to the pope. Though he had prevented the coalition of his enemies, his victory was short-lived. The nobles continued their revolts, "electing" an antiking who was little more than a straw man; but Gregory again saw his opportunity and declared Henry IV excommunicated and deposed a second time in favor of his more manageable rival. Henry countered as before by summoning a friendly council of German bishops to depose Gregory. But this second impasse of depositions was resolved in a different way. The arrogance as well as the success of Gregory had won him many enemies. A substantial number of the German ecclesiastical lords resented his reforming interference; many more held him responsible for unleashing again the destructive forces of civil war. The long connection between the German church and the empire was not easily broken; the German bishops turned more naturally to the emperor than to the pope. The same uncompromising rigor that Gregory VII had exhibited against Henry IV had alienated secular lords everywhere. In 1081 Henry once more crossed the Alps but this time with an army at his back, ready to enforce his deposition of the pope. He seized Rome, besieged Gregory in the Castel Sant' Angelo and, with the aid of a submissive synod, elevated a pope of his own choosing, Clement III.

From his fortress Gregory called upon the Norman allies he had courted thirty years before. They arrived too late to battle the Germans; Henry had already left. Having no other enemy, they turned upon the city of Rome. They sacked and plundered it unmercifully, leaving more than a third of it in ashes. When they left, Gregory left with them, not daring to remain in the ruins of the city whose destruction he had wrought. Gregory was broken; he died within a year at Salerno, supposedly with the words, "I have loved justice and hated iniquity, therefore, I die an exile." He had failed by virtue of the very height of his ambition. But he had made a most notable beginning. Another pope in little more than a century would be able to exercise the powers that Gregory had only been able to claim. Yet the victory was his; the popes who followed him—after the interval of Henry's antipope—were dedicated reformers. They lacked his furious passions but they followed the line he had drawn so firmly.

The fortunes of Henry IV and the German empire declined. The great lords were content with a helpless king. His sons, one after another, rose in factional revolt against him. He was captured and imprisoned by his son, the future Henry V, and died in 1106, the church forbidding his burial in consecrated ground. In 1122, by the Concordat of Worms, the issue of investiture was finally settled by compromise. Henry V (*1106-1125*) was too strong for the papacy to destroy, and the growing reform movement had strengthened the papacy and made it once more a force which the secular lords could not ignore. The investiture contest had already been settled in both France and England on the basis of the same compromise as the Concordat of Worms. By the terms of the concordat, episcopal election was to be by cathedral chapters. In Germany, the bishop was to receive first the symbols of his temporal authority from the emperor, then the spiritual symbols at the hands of his archbishop. In Italy and Burgundy, the temporal investiture was to follow the spiritual by six months. The emperor retained the right of decision in disputed elections. Thus, the compromise clearly recognized the dual nature of the medieval bishop. He remained, by its terms, both a knighted lord and the servant of the lowly. The church, rising in prestige and political independence, had actually won a considerable victory over the empire; for the emperor had been forced to renounce a basic power of the state over the church.

The Imperial Revival: The Reign of Frederick Barbarossa

Henry IV's brutal and aggressive son ruled as Henry V and died without issue in 1125. The contest for the emperorship brought anarchy and civil war once more, the strongest contenders being the Hohenstaufen lords of Swabia and the Welf house of Bavaria. The other princes[1] of Germany welcomed their struggle, for in civil war lay their opportunity to entrench themselves. By 1152 the exhausted factions were ready for peace. Even the princes were ready to capitulate to a king with sufficient power to restore order. The last of the interim kings had been the ineffectual Conrad III, a member of the junior line of the Hohenstaufens. At his death the princes turned to the head of that house which had claimed the throne for a quarter of a century. Frederick of Hohenstaufen—Barbarossa, for his red beard—became Frederick I (*1152–1190*) and a new dynasty came to the imperial throne.

Frederick's first task was to reestablish the monarchy. The princes were virtually independent in their fiefs; the crown lands which had once supported the strength of Saxon and Salian emperors had been alienated and usurped until little remained; only in Swabia—of which he was the duke—was Frederick sure of his powers. To attempt a reconquest of the old crown lands in central Germany was to court civil war once more, since these were firmly held by the respective princes. The largest portion

---

1. The term "princes" is customary in reference to the German lords because of their traditionally strong independence.

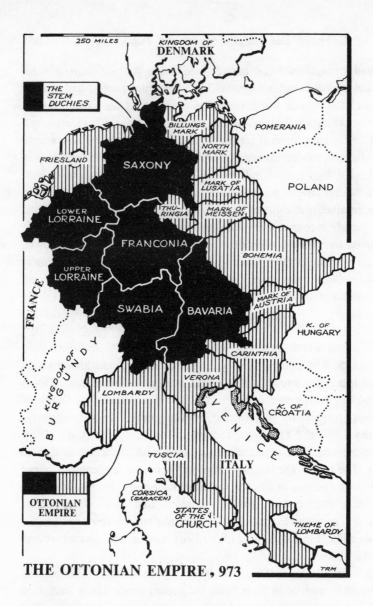

THE OTTONIAN EMPIRE, 973

of the old crown lands was in the hands of Henry the Lion, duke both of Bavaria and Saxony and whose family claimed Frederick's throne—a lord more powerful than the king.

Since the days of Charlemagne the dukes of Swabia had looked covetously toward Burgundy on their western border and to the plain of Lombardy across the neighboring Alps. Frederick decided to try once more in his hope of building a base for a new German monarchy. He surrendered the ancient lands of the north and center of Germany to their feudality, built what safeguards to order he could, and turned toward Burgundy. In 1156 he acquired Burgundy by a fortunate marriage and assumed its rule. Under Frederick's capable hand it was quickly pacified.

As Frederick turned from Burgundy to northern Italy he faced a new threat to his authority in the towns of Lombardy, one that had been slowly growing for nearly half a century. The Salian emperors, as we have seen, had controlled their Italian lands through their bishops. But the Concordat of Worms had weakened imperial rights in this area. A generation of civil war and weak, hard-pressed German kings had allowed Lombardy to slip away from imperial control. Merchant communities had grown up around the centers of episcopal administration and the spirit of town life was beginning to stir. Under the stimulus of the Crusades trade increased and the merchants of the Lombard towns were its chief beneficiaries. As they grew in wealth they chafed under the generally unsympathetic rule of their foreign bishop-lords. Encouraged by the troubles occupying the German kings elsewhere earlier in the century, they seized their opportunity. In town after town the bishops were expelled and self-governing communes established, their affairs controlled by their own citizens. However, these communes loved each other as little as they loved their German masters, and their intercity rivalries and merchant greed had kept Lombardy in constant turmoil.

The arrogance of the Lombard communes could not be tolerated by Frederick if his plans were to succeed. But as he prepared to move against them he found his designs enmeshed in the complex net of Italian politics. Frederick's ambition had already alarmed the papacy. His views on imperial supremacy were no secret; he regarded himself not only as the heir of Charlemagne and Otto the Great, but of Constantine and Justinian. When he moved to reestablish his imperial authority in northern Italy, the pope once again allied himself with the Normans of Sicily. In 1158 Frederick, with a large and competent army, invaded Italy and laid siege to Milan, the strongest and most obstreperous of the Lombard towns. The pope and the king of Sicily countered by supporting Milan. But since this alliance was more nominal than real, Frederick succeeded in taking the city. From his now strengthened position the emperor demanded every vestige of his legal rights in Lombardy. Compliance meant ruin for the Lombard towns, and the obvious direction of imperial policy pointed clearly to trouble for the pope and the Norman-Sicilians. Thus Italy united against Frederick.

For the next fifteen years a savage war ravaged the Lombard plain. Frederick repeatedly defeated the ragged armies of townsmen. Milan was taken again, burned to the ground, and its proud citizens reduced to agricultural serfs. But each time the stubborn townsmen came back, stronger than before. In the face of stark destruction, the towns banded together into the Lombard League. More than twenty cities made common cause against Frederick. At every turn the papacy supported the cities. Frederick marched on Rome. He made and unmade popes; he was excommunicated; he elected antipopes. In 1174—for the fifth time—Frederick invaded Italy, besieged the League's strong point without success, and finally offered to negotiate. His offer was refused. In the battle that followed, at Legnano in 1176, Frederick's feudal army was destroyed by the Lombard militia, the first clear presage of a new day in the history of medieval warfare. Frederick was ready to compromise as his great design for the conquest of Italy lay in ruins. He made a six-year truce with the Lombard cities and left them to fight among themselves, made a similar arrangement with William II of Sicily, and recognized the papal rights of his redoubtable opponent, Alexander III, who had been the evil genius of Italian resistance for nearly twenty years. Frederick was still a power to be reckoned with in Italy, but now he turned back to the affairs of Germany.

The disaster at Legnano had resulted from, at least in part, the refusal of his German lords to support Frederick and deliver their feudal levies. The chief among the refractory vassals was Henry the Lion. For the twenty years that Frederick had been immersed in the troubles of Italy, his great Saxon-Bavarian rival had been building a principality in the north. From his German fiefs he had pushed into the Slavic lands of the east and conquered vast territories there that he ruled in sovereign right. He had fought his German peers as ruthlessly as he had the Slavs; he had arrogantly interfered in the rights of the church and seized its lands. Henry's power made him the natural leader of the German feudality, but it also earned him a dangerous host of enemies. When Frederick returned to his German court the enemies whom Henry the Lion had made in such generous numbers came to lodge their charges against him. Many who had no personal grievance saw in his strength a greater menace than the crown posed. Frederick Barbarossa added these charges to his own and summoned Henry to defend himself before the court. He did not appear and Frederick condemned him as a contumacious vassal and stripped him of his fiefs. Henry's support melted away and Frederick's prestige soared. In 1189, when Frederick came to Saxony to enforce his decree, he was met by Henry on bended knee, surrounded by a host of lords who hailed their emperor.

In the meantime Frederick had turned his ambitions once more toward Italy. Half a lifetime of war had brought his Italian schemes to nothing. Where war had failed, diplomacy finally succeeded. He made peace with the Lombard League. Its cities recognized his overlordship; their officials held office as his agents; they paid a handsome annual tribute for the privilege of imperial rule and Frederick's recognition of their legal existence. Frederick concluded a marriage alliance with Norman Sicily, betrothing his son and heir to Constance, the daughter of William II. At the marriage feast the ageing emperor elevated his son beside him on the throne as co-emperor. Frederick Barbarossa was at the height of his power and fame. Poets sang of his deeds and historians solemnly chronicled them. At the age of sixty he still entered the lists and acquitted himself as solidly as he had in the battles of his youth. He was the perfect knight and the epitome of the feudal monarch. He had made good once more the imperial claims of the German kings. Calling his realm the Holy Roman Empire, he considered himself its sacred and secular head and supported his claims with the weight of authority, German tradition, and Roman law. The weak and fearful popes who had succeeded Alexander III were no match for him.

His last great enterprise was the Third Crusade, whose leadership he seized. He was killed in its course in 1190. His name passed quickly into legend, which held that the old emperor slept in the cavernous heart of a mountain, waiting the call once more to bring peace, prosperity, and honor to his people.

The Failure of the German Empire

Henry VI succeeded to the throne and policies of his father. The claims of his Norman wife gave him a leverage in southern Italy and before long he was solidly in control of that rich and well-ordered kingdom. The pope quaked at the thought of his German enemies both to the north and south of the papal states. In Germany Henry's reign was troubled by the renewed hostility of the Welfs and Henry the Lion. The German feudality shared the alarm of the pope at the growth of royal power, an alarm which increased when Henry forced the German magnates to crown his infant son, Frederick II.

Then suddenly, in 1197, Henry VI died and his empire fell to pieces.

**THE GERMAN-NORMAN EMPIRE
ABOUT 1200**

Central and northern Italy were already in revolt against German rule. The grumbling feudality of Germany was ready as always to rebel. An uncle of the new boy-king tried to preserve the Hohenstaufen crown first as regent, then as emperor. Otto of Brunswick, the son of Henry the Lion, seized this opportunity. The Welf-Hohenstaufen quarrel had already spread beyond Germany and Italy. Otto had the support of his English royal relatives, since his father, Henry the Lion, had been the son-in-law of England's Henry II. The Hohenstaufen Henry VI had been the jailor of Richard the Lion-Hearted and the recipient of his enormous ransom. The exiled Welfs had long gained sanctuary and money at the English court. Otto had little difficulty gathering support among the easily corrupted German princes and was shortly elected king. The rival kings and parties launched Germany into another spasm of civil wars. The reversal of imperial fortune was completed in 1198 when Innocent III (*1198–1216*) came to the papal throne, the greatest of medieval popes and the man who would reap the harvest of Gregory VII and Alexander III.

Innocent's "German policy" grew from the necessity of keeping German Sicily separated from the empire. For thirteen years he played upon every turn of fortune in the turbulent affairs of the empire. He supported the Welf Otto, even crowning him emperor, only to find in him another menace to papal independence. As Otto threatened to unite Sicily and Germany in his own name Innocent excommunicated him and reluctantly endorsed the seventeen-year-old Hohenstaufen heir, Frederick II (*1215–1250*). In this peculiar way the papacy was forced not only to accept but to sanction the return of its traditional enemies.

Frederick II had been snatched from disaster by the papal blessing and a faction of German princes was found to confirm his coronation with reelection to the German kingship. The ground was quickly cut from beneath the claims of Otto of Brunswick. Within two years his cause was destroyed at the Battle of Bouvines in Flanders, far from either Sicily or Germany. Immediately upon his election Frederick II went to Germany, where he was generously welcomed by the princes and loaded with empty honors. But there was little he could do to reverse the course into which imperial history had long been turned. The tribal duchies, since the days of Otto the Great, had been slowly dismembered by the persistent efforts of three imperial dynasties and by the attrition of periodic civil war. They had been replaced by a patchwork of princely holdings which divided Germany into literally hundreds of petty states; the process of feudalization had been encouraged by the early Hohenstaufens. Frederick II could do little but accept it in its completed form. Germany belonged to the princes; not the emperor. Frederick made the princely fiefs fully hereditary, granted the princes full jurisdictional sovereignty, and gave over to them the towns which were beginning to spring up in Germany as they had earlier in Italy. It was but one further step to the feudal chaos which was to reign in Germany for the entire later Middle Ages.

In the year 1220, his arrangements and concessions made, Frederick returned to the more congenial climate and the more rewarding rule of his native Sicily. In this land he was the heir of a far different tradition. By the beginning of the twelfth century the Normans had succeeded in conquering the entire island of Sicily and uniting it with practically all of Italy south of the papal states. This conglomerate state was comprised of varied elements. The many conquests which had rolled across it in the centuries since the fall of Rome had all left their marks and their cultural residue. The Norman kingdom of the Two Sicilies, as it came to be called, contained Latins, Lombards, Greeks, Saracens, Jews, Germans, and, of course, Normans. The Norman rulers had had the good sense not to try to press their diverse subjects into a common mold. Instead, they had made diversity a source of strength, drawing upon traditions and skills much older and more sophisticated than their own: all public documents were issued in Greek and Arabic as well as Latin; most high officials of the government were Greeks; the financial administration was largely staffed by Saracens; Norman feudal knights served side by side with Moslem cavalry. The Norman kings of Sicily ruled with the aid of a skillful, literate, and responsible bureaucracy. The king was lord, not feudal overlord. His council was a body of "department heads," not an assemblage of semi-independent barons. The income of the crown was larger than that of any other western state, flowing not from manorial rents but from taxes upon trade and industry, tariffs and tolls, and from nonfeudal royal land; and it was a money income.

Frederick II, though half German, was in taste, spirit, and sympathy a Sicilian. The animosities which had troubled the Hohenstaufen succession to Sicily faded away with Frederick, and he succeeded without opposition to this remarkable kingdom, becoming its most remarkable king. Personable and wise, his many accomplishments earned him the title of *Stupor Mundi,* "The Wonder of the World." He was a virtuoso of languages, a dilettante in science and mathematics, a lover of art and collector of manuscripts. At the sumptuous palace that he built he surrounded himself with scholars, poets, and men trained in the Roman law. Corresponding learnedly with Moslem and Jewish philosophers, mathematicians and scientists, he brought many of them to his court, which became the most brilliant in Europe. He maintained a collection of domestic and exotic animals that he studied with scientific care and on which he performed a series of experiments. As an encouragement to the spread of learning he founded the University of Naples.

In an age when religion and the church dominated the universe of thought, Frederick II stood apart and was duly called atheist, blasphemer, and infidel. From his court issued the most humane, rational, tolerant policies of his time. His *Liber Augustalis* rivaled Justinian's code or the Canon Law as a legal system: it took the powers of the state out of the hands of the feudality and redefined the state itself as a legal entity; it abolished the pious absurdity of trial by combat and ordeal. Frederick emulated the state-monopoly economic pattern of the Byzantine Empire and was the master of the most advanced economy in Europe. He had a well-trained, well-paid, and loyal professional army—largely Saracen, to the outrage of the orthodox. In the catholicity of his interests and the scope of his intelligence and vitality he was a fair precursor of the brilliant figures of the Renaissance.

Frederick II was heir not only to the culture of Sicily; he was heir to the political policies of his Norman and German ancestors. These dictated the establishment and maintenance of a strong, secular state in Italy, a course which must inevitably lead to conflict with the papacy. In an age when papal power was at its height, Frederick had the additional disadvantage of confronting a series of extremely able and dedicated popes. As the price of his coronation he had been forced to make great concessions to the wily Innocent III, in effect ceding control of the German and Sicilian church to the pope. We have already noted the consequences of his crusading efforts,[1] his success against Saracens, his failure against Christians. In any case, his natural enemies combined with the hostile papacy against him. The north Italian towns wanted a strong emperor as little as did the pope. Frederick's German vassals ignored their feudal obligations. The pope struck with his spiritual weapons and wholesale propaganda against "this king of pestilence." Frederick appealed for a reform council and called upon his fellow secular monarchs not to desert him in the face of their common enemy. The contest swayed back and forth. Frederick was excommunicated, deposed, and a crusade was preached against him. At one time Frederick besieged and almost captured the city of Rome. In the

2. See p. 345.

midst of this battle for supremacy or destruction, Frederick II died, in 1250. The papacy pressed on to destroy every vestige of the Hohenstaufens.

Frederick's son, Conrad, followed him to the throne. In 1254 he was succeeded by his illegitimate half-brother, Manfred. Papal hostility was unrelenting. Hoping to trade still upon the old Hohenstaufen-Angevin enmity, the pope offered to support Henry III of England if he would seize Sicily for his son. Henry could not afford the campaign. The pope then turned to the French royal house and Charles of Anjou, brother of Louis IX. In 1266 Charles invaded Sicily and Manfred was killed in battle. Two years later the last heir of the Hohenstaufens, the fifteen-year-old grandson of Frederick II, was captured and beheaded in the market place of Naples.

In Germany, the death of Frederick's son Conrad in 1254 was the signal for renewed civil war, bringing about the anarchy of the Great Interregnum, which lasted until 1273. In this interval the last hope of German unity faded. At long last the princes gained the petty sovereignty which had been their goal for centuries. The great hope and the great age of the medieval German Empire died together.

ENGLAND AND FRANCE: THE GREAT DEBATE

The Angevin Empire, Won and Lost

The conquest of England by the Norman Duke William in 1066 and the establishment there of a Norman-French dynasty whose rulers were vassals of the French kings, linked the fortunes of France and England and embroiled both in one of the great contests of medieval political history.

From the time of Hugh Capet, the French kings had fought to establish a centralized monarchy against the forces of feudal particularism. The great vassals of the crown were equally determined to retain their independence, none more than the dukes of Normandy. Throughout the reigns of William the Conqueror and his sons the hostility between the Capetians and their Norman vassals grew. Then, in the middle of the twelfth century, a string of circumstances began to unravel which further entangled the affairs of England and France.

The string began far from either Paris or London in the lands of Duke William X of Aquitaine. Although his lands were extensive, the duke's actual powers were slight and constantly being challenged by his barons. A strong son might have helped William control the barons, but he had no son. He had instead a daughter, Eleanor, young, beautiful, and passionate, raised in her father's cultivated and urbane court, and knowledgeable beyond her years. She was as rich a prize as the lands of her duchy. As the time of his death neared, Duke William made provision for his daughter. For almost thirty years his energetic and popular contemporary, Louis VI, the Fat, had been building the prestige of the Capetian monarchy, and on several occasions had taken up a distant cause in the name of his royal authority. It was his friend Louis VI whom William now asked to arrange a suitable marriage for his daughter. Louis promptly betrothed Eleanor to his own son, who succeeded as Louis VII when his father died shortly after.

Louis VII was gentle and devout. He made little headway in enforcing the royal will in his wife's turbulent lands and almost as little in enforcing his will upon her. She hated his court and despised him. She once said that she thought she had married a king, but found she had married a monk. In 1147 Louis VII left for the Second Crusade and Eleanor went with him. The entire misadventure was spiced by the rumors of her love affairs, scandalous enough at best, but unbearable in the holy atmosphere of religious war. She flaunted her infidelity. The king charged her with barrenness; she had produced two daughters but no son for the succession. In 1152 a French clerical council, at the insistence of the king, declared them divorced on the pretext of consanguinity. The inheritance of Aquitaine was a high price to pay for royal spite.

Eleanor was immediately besieged by suitors and in less than two months was married to Henry Plantagenet, Count of Anjou. He was squat, ugly, freckled, demonically vigorous, and ill-tempered. He was also the greatest feudatory of France; in addition to Anjou on the Loire River, he held Touraine and Maine, to form a solid block of land to the west of the royal Île-de-France. His father had taken advantage of the failure of the line of William the Conqueror to seize Normandy and Henry ruled as its duke. His marriage to Eleanor brought him Aquitaine, with its claims to Poitou and Gascony.

In 1154 Henry Plantagenet became Henry II (*1154–1189*), King of England. But for the twenty years before this epochal accession, England had endured a time of troubles and anarchy. The strong rule of the Norman kings had ended with the death of Henry I, the last son of the Conqueror, in 1135. There being no legitimate son to succeed him, the throne was seized by a nephew, Stephen of Blois, who was opposed by the daughter of Henry I, Matilda. Neither was strong enough to win conclusively and the baronage eagerly took advantage of the paralysis of royal power. For a generation England was at the mercy of rampant feudalism. Henry I had chosen Geoffrey of Anjou as a husband for Matilda in the hope of finding a protector for her and her realm in that rough-neck baron. But Geoffrey had done little more than take what English crown lands he could on the continent and sire the son who would bear the royal claims of his mother.

As Stephen's disastrous reign drew to a close he came to terms with Matilda's son, now the heir to his family's lands, his father's conquests, and the dowry of Aquitaine—Henry of Anjou. With little more than a show of force, Henry succeeded Stephen in 1154. He was the master of an impressive "empire" that stretched from the Scottish border through England and western France to the Pyrenees. The center of these vast domains lay in its French lands and the French King, Louis VII, faced a vassal who held two-thirds of France while his own lands were but a fraction of the rest of France. The Capetians' implacable determination to be supreme in France now ran squarely into the equally implacable determination of the Angevins to hold and rule their empire.

To a remarkable degree the next half-century of this struggle was determined by the contrasting personalities of its chief figures. While the timid and indecisive Louis VII was no match for Henry II, he was able to attack him indirectly with some effect. By a series of marriage alliances Louis attached to himself the powerful vassal family of Blois to balance the scale against the Angevins. But such friends and relatives were almost as dangerous to Louis as to Henry. Whenever possible Louis supported the enemies of his great rival. Henry battled to break the independence of his French barons and behind each baronial revolt was the hand of Louis VII. Louis took what advantage he could of Henry's troubles with the church and actively suported Thomas à Becket in his long and bitter contest with the crown. When Henry's "faithless brood" of sons revolted against him they did so with Louis' aid. He played a conspicuous part in the great rebellion of 1173, led by those same sons and swelled by the baronage on both sides of the Channel. Henry weathered it and restored order to "every house but his own."

Louis VII, who had never really been young, was quickly old; and an able son replaced a senile father—but not his policy. In his last years, Henry II had to face Philip II, called Augustus, one of the most effective of Capetian kings. The rapacity of Henry's sons again made cause with the French king against their father. In the summer of 1189 this combination defeated Henry in battle and humiliated him in conference. He never recovered and before the end of the year he died, turning his face to the wall with the bitter words, "Shame! shame on a beaten king."

He was succeeded by his oldest surviving son, Richard I, the Lion-Hearted, who inherited with his throne the enmity of his Capetian cousin and former ally, Philip II (Augustus). From the moment of Richard's accession, the Capetian-Angevin contest began to swing in favor of the Capetians. They had the advantage of producing during the following century and a half three outstanding kings—Philip Augustus, Louis IX, and Philip IV—while their Angevin counterparts—Richard I, John, and Henry

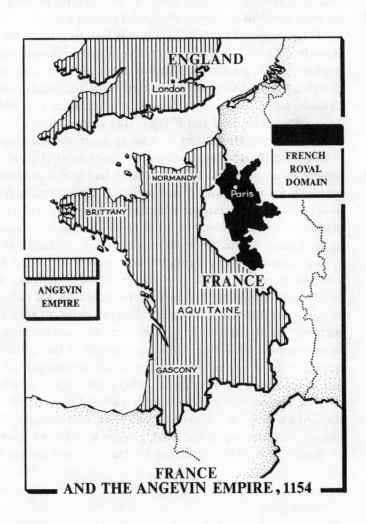

**FRANCE
AND THE ANGEVIN EMPIRE, 1154**

III—were among the most unfortunate and incapable of English medieval rulers. The Capetians were further served by economic and social developments, some of which they themselves helped initiate, others of which they were shrewd enough to exploit. These changes, discussed later in this chapter and in the next, were undermining the basis of feudalism and, harnessed by the ambitions of the Capetian kings, they were to help in the realization of a centralized, national state in France and in the disappointment of the irresponsible feudal ambitions of the Angevin kings of England. By the end of the thirteenth century, the Angevin continental possessions had been reduced to a coastal redoubt around Calais and a precarious hold on Aquitaine and Gascony. France, however, was well on her way to becoming the most powerful and highly centralized state in Europe.

Philip Augustus (*1180–1223*) had as little taste for battle as his father. But where Louis VII had been capable of only fortuitous intrigue, Philip was one of the greatest of medieval diplomats. The Angevin Richard I, though a great military commander, was rash and inconsistent. The Third Crusade, for all its pretence, was no more than an interlude of specious amity between Richard and Philip.[2] After scarcely four months Philip returned from the Holy Land to take up again the main concern of his dynasty. He played shrewdly on the ambitions of Richard's regent, his brother John, as faithless to Richard as he had been to his father. John was no match for Philip, who gained territorial concessions in Angevin lands, invaded Normandy, entrenched himself in Flanders, and set up a Danish marriage alliance by which he could revive the claims of Sven and Canute to the English throne. Luck fell in with policy: Richard was captured on his way home from the Crusades, and imprisoned by the Hohenstaufen emperor, Henry VI, whose own family enemies, the Welfs, had long enjoyed Angevin support. The emperor bargained for his prize. But instead of ransoming Richard, Philip and John paid Henry to keep him prisoner. Richard's partisans, including his mother, the aged queen Eleanor, paid more to ransom him—twice the annual revenue of the crown—and he was freed. For the remaining five years of his life Richard carried on a furious war of vengeance and reconquest. Philip's advantage was tottering; at one point he himself barely escaped being captured by Richard. But in 1199 Richard was killed in a petty battle and Philip could resume his spider's net around John, whom men had already begun to call John "Softsword."

John (*1199–1216*), inheriting his family's cause against his sometime

2. See pp. 343-44.

Capetian ally, also faced domestic troubles that played directly into Philip's hands. John's claim to the English throne was disputed by a nephew, Prince Arthur, the son of John's long-dead elder brother Geoffrey. Arthur raised rebellion among John's French vassals and was immediately recognized by Philip. With this leverage Philip was able to force John to make submission for his French fiefs. John's incredibly bad political sense, his perfidy, and general unpopularity rapidly increased the number of his enemies. Philip chose his time and, in 1202, in a solemn feudal court, Philip had John condemned by his willing peers. John was so overwhelmed with troubles in England that he could not fight back. His cold-blooded murder of Prince Arthur alienated his English barons completely. Philip, having established the Angevin lands as French fiefs, and having declared them forfeit from John, now proceeded to overrun them. Within two years he was master of the largest part of the Angevin "empire," including the old duchy of Normandy.

On the other hand, the growing power of the French crown enabled even John to find friends among the anxious French feudality. He found another friend in the Welf claimant to the imperial throne, Otto of Brunswick. Philip II hastened to counter this dangerous alliance by an agreement with the young Hohenstaufen, Frederick II. As a consequence of these wide-ranging alliances, open war threatened to engulf all of northern Europe. Otto of Brunswick marched into France from the north and east. John's forces invaded from the Angevin lands to the south and west. Philip, who had been wise enough to prepare for a war he had hoped to avoid, quickly sought battle with Otto before the two forces could join against him. They met at Bouvines in Flanders in 1214. In the pitched battle that followed, Philip's smaller but more effective force swept the field. Otto himself narrowly missed being killed. John left for England. Philip's victory was a decisive blow to the Angevin empire. Enough of it remained to be the seeds of the Hundred Years' War and to ensure intermittent hostility for the next two centuries. But no Angevin ruler could again seriously claim to be the effective ruler of the French lands his family had held so long.

The Growth of the National Monarchy in France

The Battle of Bouvines marked more than Philip's triumph over John; it also marked the victory of central authority over feudalism. For now the Capetians held a significant portion of France to support their royal claims.

The transition from a feudal suzerainty to a monarchical sovereignty was accompanied by economic and social as well as political changes—

changes that were reflected at the king's court. The feudal household offices were gradually replaced by departments staffed with trusted, salaried men, appointed by the king. Many of them were clergy; some were poor knights whose poverty made them trustworthy. The feudal *curia*—vassals in attendance upon their overlord—was expanded to correspond to the increased holdings of the crown; the power of the king dominated it and its intermittent sessions gave "advice and consent" to royal policy. The increasing judicial business of the crown necessitated a more or less permanent court of justice, split off from the royal household and the *curia regis* and filled with trained legalists. Perhaps more than anything else, the increased revenues of the crown marked a transition in the nature of royal government. The vastly expanded royal lands poured their wealth into Paris in the form of feudal and manorial rents, fees, and fines. Many feudal services were being commuted to money payments that began to take on the regularity of taxes. The complex financial business of the crown tended to split off another "committee" from the *curia regis* to handle it; it was the beginning of a regular treasury, the *Chambre des Comptes* ("Chamber of Accounts"). The cash revenue of the king gave him a freedom and power that a purely feudal lord could never have. In diplomacy Philip sealed his alliance with Frederick II with a gift of 20,000 *livres* (silver pounds). He was no longer dependent entirely upon feudal military service and could hire mercenaries. They and contingents of foot soldiers supplied by the towns played a significant role, for example, in the victory at Bouvines.

The reform of royal government filtered out to the countryside. The king used his strengthened position as feudal overlord to enforce his will upon wayward petty vassals. He began to replace the older, local crown officials—they were paid in fiefs and, of course, tended to heredity and independence—with "new model" administrators, salaried, nonfeudal men, appointed and removed by the king. Their functions were still generalized and they resembled Charlemagne's *missi dominici* rather than more modern bureaucrats, but in one form or another royal administration, royal justice, royal protection, and royal taxes were beginning to reach to every corner of the growing realm of France.

The growth of royal authority was especially welcomed by the towns, which had begun to revive in France as they had all over western Europe. They tended, as we shall see, to make common cause with the crown against the feudality. Philip Augustus recognized the value of their support and, during his reign, began the flow of royal charters to towns in return for the service of their militias and the taxes upon their growing wealth.

On the eve of his death Philip Augustus made his last great territorial coup. The south of France had always been alien in spirit and tradition from the lands of the north, and the king's authority had never penetrated deeply there. In the closing years of Philip's reign this whole region had been shaken by one of the most extensive of medieval heresies, the so-called Albigensian movement.[3] At the call of Pope Innocent III, a rapacious horde of "crusaders" had descended upon the south to stamp out the heresy and appropriate fiefs for themselves. Philip had watched carefully the destruction of the old county and ducal powers there and the division of the land among the snarling, quarrelsome, and petty crusading lords. Then he sent an expedition under his son, which was able to demand the feudal submission of virtually the whole territory. During the next century, royal power was consolidated in the south of France and this region slowly brought within the scope of the expanding realm.

By the time of his death in 1223, Philip Augustus had established the broad outlines of a new nation. The reign of his bellicose, rash, and incompetent son was mercifully brief. The next successor, Louis IX (*1226–1270*), was a boy of twelve when his father died. His regent was his beautiful, able, and strong-willed mother, Blanche of Castile, a granddaughter of Eleanor of Aquitaine and worthy of her lineage. She held the realm together, retained the support of the church and the towns, and dealt with baronial revolts. She was known as "good Queen Blanche" to everyone but the recalcitrant nobility. In 1236 Louis IX began his personal rule. He is best known to history as St. Louis, yet his saintliness was not confounded with weakness and his reign was equal to that of Philip Augustus. Louis was the epitome of the Christian knight; he lived piously and simply and without display. The people of Paris loved him and called him Brother Louis. A man of justice and principle, he carried these ideals into public policy. He equated the peace and order of his realm with obedience to royal law and was zealous in "doing justice." Louis reaped the benefits of half a century of centralization. He tightened the system of royal administration and was stern in his punishment of villainy and peculation among his officials. He was able to initiate and enforce legislation without the consent of his vassals and to demand the universal acceptance of royal

3. See pp. 413-14.

coins. He tried, without success, to abolish the curse of private war. Like his rationalist contemporary, Frederick II of Sicily, he opposed trial by combat and ordeal. Devoted to peace, religion, and the church, he gave his life for his principles as the last great crusading king. The personal qualities and enlightened policies of Louis IX popularized the monarchy as never before. Philip Augustus had created a centralized monarchy; Louis IX, a national monarchy.

After another transitional reign, that of Louis' inconsequential son, Philip III, the last of the great Capetian kings of the High Middle Ages, Philip IV (*1285–1314*), called "the Fair," came to the French Throne. It remained for him to complete the work of Philip Augustus and Louis IX, to transform the French monarchy into a royal absolutism. There is a distinctly modern flavor to everything about Philip IV. He was not interested in chivalry, honor, or religion; he was interested in money. His financial policies are the key to his reign and to its modernity. Louis IX had come halfway to a regular, national taxation; Philip IV completed the transition. He exacted all feudal payments due the crown with such ruthless regularity as to reduce them to the status of taxes. He taxed the church, the towns, commerce, income—on a dozen ingenious pretexts: he confiscated the wealth of the Jews and the Italian bankers resident in France; he systematically ruined the great crusading order of the Knights Templars, which had lost its crusading purpose but retained its wealth; he forbade the export of precious metal and debased the currency to meet royal debts.

In his financial innovations as in everything else Philip IV sought the advice of a new group of crown counsellors—clever, "bourgeois" lawyers, the products of the growing universities. The French monarchy took another step toward the modern world by choosing these men to replace the baronial and clerical advisers who had for so long stood behind the throne.

Another important innovation of Philip's reign was the calling of the first Estates-General, a representative national assembly. But his motives were neither constitutional nor egalitarian. He needed a broader basis of consent than the old feudal assembly of notables gave him. There were people, classes, and money no longer represented by these peers. Thus, in 1302 Philip summoned to his court not only his great vassals, but the rear vassals of the crown, both lay and ecclesiastical; and, significantly, representatives of the chartered towns. In 1308 and in 1314 he called similar assemblies, but in each case they were "called" by the king and, furthermore, called to give their consent to royal policy—not to share in its formulation, not to deliberate, and not to protest. The Estates-General began as a body subordinate to a powerful king. It took nearly five hundred years and a bloody revolution before it became more than that.

The specific policies which the Estates were asked to sanction provide a summary of the chief issues of Philip IV's reign. The assembly of 1302 was called to consider the king's quarrel with the papacy. The pompous claims of Boniface VIII to papal supremacy had collided with the national aims of Philip IV. The king, in his ever-present need for money (this time to help finance a further war against the remaining English lands in France) had levied a war tax on the clergy. Pope Boniface retaliated by forbidding clergy to pay any tax to lay authorities without papal permission. Philip tried and jailed a papal legate; the pope denied his right to do so, claimed papal sovereignty over all secular monarchs, and threatened Philip with the condemnation of a council. It was in the face of this threat that Philip called the Estates-General. He backed his case against the pope with an elaborate propaganda campaign that was helped along by Boniface's profligacy and arrogance. The Estates each sent a separate letter of protest to the pope upholding their king and their state. On the crest of a popular anticlerical wave, Philip was able not only to humiliate Boniface VIII, but to force the election of a French successor to begin that period of French dominated papal history known as the Babylonian Captivity. The papacy had defeated the empire only to become the captive of France.

An almost identical pattern was followed in Philip's attack upon the Templars. Disbanded in the Holy Land, they centered their order in France. Their great wealth in lands and money, their tax-free status, their banking and lending operations, made them a fat prize; their arms and their military organization, added to their wealth, made them a potential danger to the state; their pride, display, and hypocrisy made them generally hated. In 1308, another Estates-General loyally supported the king in condemning the Templars. Their goods were confiscated and the Templars themselves hounded out of existence with carefully prepared charges of every imaginable crime and perversion for which they were tortured, hanged, and burned.

Finally, in 1314 Philip called the Estates again to grant him money to press a long-smoldering war in Flanders. In the same year he died. He was followed in rapid succession by three sons who ended more than three centuries of Capetian rule. The tiny territory in the vicinity of Paris

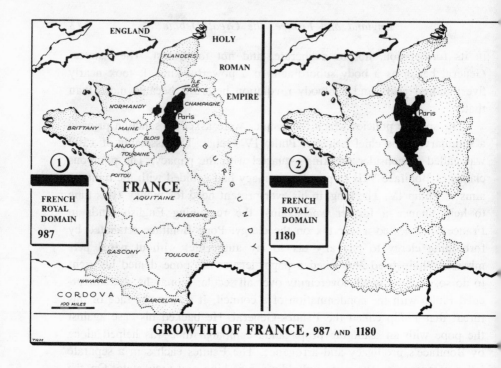

ENGLAND
HOLY
FLANDERS
ROMAN
ÎLE
DE
FRANCE
EMPIRE
NORMANDY
CHAMPAGNE
Paris
BRITTANY
MAINE
BLOIS
ANJOU
TOURAINE
POITOU
FRANCE
FRENCH
ROYAL
DOMAIN
987
AQUITAINE
AUVERGNE
GASCONY
TOULOUSE
NAVARRE
CORDOVA
100 MILES
BARCELONA
1

Paris
FRENCH
ROYAL
DOMAIN
1180
2

GROWTH OF FRANCE, 987 AND 1180

which Hugh Capet ruled had grown into a great and powerful state, stretching from the Rhine to the Channel, from the North Sea to the Mediterranean. The feudal suzerainty which Hugh had held had become the strongest and most centralized monarchy among the secular states of Europe.

The Growth of English Royal Government

While France had been moving towards royal absolutism, England had been slowly developing the institutions and procedures which would in time produce the most significant constitutional monarchy—a monarchy limited by parliamentary power—in the modern world. This development, however, was slower and more haphazard than the development of French absolutism. Of importance at the beginning of the English development was the preoccupation of the Norman and Angevin kings with their continental lands. Continental crises repeatedly forced these kings to make concessions to their people, especially since the kings were prepared to exchange rights and grant privileges in return for money to prosecute their French wars.

Even so, what we see in the England of the High Middle Ages is little more than the dimmest anticipation of limited monarchy. What is

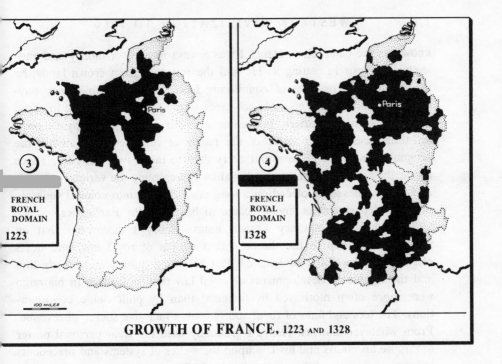

GROWTH OF FRANCE, 1223 AND 1328

obvious in this period is the strength of the English monarchy rather than limitations on it. Indeed, much that was in time to be associated with English popular government actually began at the behest of the crown.

We have already seen how solidly William the Conqueror established himself in England. He was probably able to function more nearly as a monarch than any of his royal contemporaries in western Europe. He passed on this tradition to his sons, especially to Henry I (*1100–1135*). Out of that tradition Henry built the first true English government. Henry inherited not only his father's evil temper but his Norman sense of order and efficiency. He inherited, too, the germinal institution of royal government, the *curia regis,* the council of vassals gathered with their overlord, the same institution we have seen operating everywhere in feudal Europe. To this body Henry appended a smaller group of royal officials, as the housekeeping tasks of his government grew more pressing and complex. This was—in contrast to the feudal curia which met intermittently—a continuous body of officials, and from the gradual differentiation of its tasks came the various departments of government which were to play such an important role in the domestic history of England.

The proliferation of royal business and royal records necessitated a chancery, the "secretarial staff" of the king under the powerful official known as the Chancellor. Henry I was always in need of money and end-lessly ingenious in getting it. He had the revenues from crown lands; he made a regular practice of commuting feudal services into money pay-ments; he had the revenues of such taxes as the Danegeld; he also imposed fines and granted charters. It became necessary to employ officials on a full-time basis to keep track of the tangle of revenues, to maintain the accounts, and to make sure that every debt to the crown was paid. Twice a year the accounts were received. Tallies representing the various accounts and their values were placed on a long table divided into colored squares: thus the department of finance came to be called the Exchequer.

Like his contemporary French kings, Henry I discovered that an indispensable prop to the throne was a system of royal law, and he is often called the "Lion of Justice." But he was a hungry and greedy lion and the significant developments of royal law that took place in his reign were more often motivated by financial than by philosophic considera-tions. The fees and fines of royal courts were a lucrative source of revenue. From whatever motives, Henry I gradually used his great personal power to impose his courts and his law upon the welter of systems and precedents in operation in twelfth-century England. The result was the first form of the Common Law, law which applied in every instance and in every part of the realm.

By the end of his reign Henry I had created the basic machinery of a royal administration, a royal financial system, and a royal law.

The chaotic reign of Stephen (1135–1154) was disastrous enough to prove the virtue of strong royal government—and not long enough to destroy completely the beginnings that Henry I had made. The Angevin Henry II (1154–1189) established order again and the development of English government resumed. The greatest achievements of Henry II's reign came in the realm of law and its extension. Through his laws, writs, and legal enforcement Henry extended the king's justice as never before. The old sworn inquest of Anglo-Saxon times was transformed into the jury trial. The machinery was set up by which, in response to a complaint, the sheriff of a shire was to bring both parties in the complaint before the king's justice, along with twelve men who had reason to know the facts in the case. The twelve were placed under oath and asked which party spoke truly. On this basis the justice decided the case. The ease and equity of such a system commended it to the people and it was an im-portant factor in making the king's law nearly universal. Closely related to the trial jury was the grand jury, which also took form in this time.

The sheriff was directed to bring before the king's justice a group of responsible men who would report any serious crimes in the shire and name the offenders, whereupon writs could be drawn, prosecution begun, and fines collected. As Henry's legal procedures brought more cases under his hand, he increased the number of courts. Itinerant justices went out on regular rounds carrying the justice of the king's court into the countryside. The decisions of these justices and others gave further form and larger scope to the Common Law.

To Henry II, as to his Norman predecessors, royal justice was an important source of cash. Money was as crucial to the crown as it had ever been. Henry's vast and turbulent continental holdings had to be policed, and the cost was great. He extended and developed the Norman financial system as he did the legal system. Much of the business of the royal courts was the collection of crown revenue and the fixing of assessments. For the first time regular property taxes were collected. One was called the "Saladin Tithe," ostensibly to be used for a crusade.

Henry II's governmental reforms, to which history attaches such archsignificance, were made in the midst of the furious action that typified his reign and his nature. His most pressing concern was the preservation of his French lands. Related to this concern was Henry's trouble with the church. Since the time of William the Conqueror, the English kings had carried on an intermittent struggle with the church over the same issues that we have seen fought out in Germany. As the reforming papacy pressed its claims to universal sovereignty the conflict between the church and state—whether the Empire, France, or England—intensified. William the Conqueror categorically denied the claim of papal suzerainty over England. He refused to allow any papal order to be obeyed in England without his express permission. He appointed high churchmen and demanded feudal service of them. He was willing to reform the English church after the Cluniac model, but he did it as the master of his state church, not as the servant of the papacy. William Rufus and Henry I handled the church as roughly as their father. But Henry II shared his age with that line of able, powerful, reforming popes that ended with Innocent III. When Henry tried to recover the many areas of royal jurisdiction that Stephen's reign had allowed to lapse to the church he came into head-on conflict with the papacy.

The contest with Becket capped that conflict. Thomas à Becket (c. 1118–1170) had been one of the small circle of the king's cronies, trusted men who were invaluable to his service. Becket had risen to the office of chancellor. In 1161 the see of Canterbury fell vacant and Henry triumphantly installed Becket as archbishop and primate of England. At last the king had a powerful ally in his struggle against the church! But he was mistaken; the spiritual office transformed Becket and Henry found instead an implacable enemy and champion of the church in his old friend. His short temper flared. For six years they fought bitterly, and Becket was in and out of exile. His cause was a rallying point for every enemy of the king. Henry uttered a threat in anger against his difficult archbishop, and four of his knights taking him at his word, to "rid" him of "this upstart priest," murdered Becket at the altar of his cathedral of Canterbury. Henry was engulfed by remorse and by a wave of popular indignation both in England and on the continent. He was forced to accept the jurisdiction of church courts, allow appeals to Rome, and reverse his policy of clerical control. Thomas à Becket almost overnight became a saint and the scene of his martyrdom the most holy shrine in England.

Henry's troubles with Becket and his humiliation by the church played into the hands of his rebellious sons. To the end of his reign he was never free of their disturbances.

Richard I (*1189–1199*) reaped the benefits of his father's reforms and careful administration. He spent only six months of his reign in England, but in person, in absentia, and in prison he mulcted it of every cent of revenue it would yield. He increased taxes, sold rights, granted charters, and pitilessly persecuted the industrious Jews of England for their wealth. His father's financial system rewarded his ungrateful son more handsomely than he deserved.

Richard's long absences and his outrageous exactions prepared the general ill-will which fell to his brother and successor, John (*1199–1216*). And John's arbitrary and tyrannical rule richly justified it. His enemies were legion. Pope Innocent III, taking advantage of John's unpopularity and misfortunes, forced him to acknowledge that he held his lands as a fief of the pope. Two generations of strong kings had made serious inroads on the privileges of the nobility. John's weakness invited their retaliation. His troubles with Philip Augustus and Innocent III provided the opportunity. Returning from the fiasco of Bouvines, he faced a nation united in hostility toward him. John's restive barons took the initiative. A murmur of rebellion had forced John to dismiss a feudal levy in 1212. His vassals, almost to a man, had refused to support his French campaign. In the face of certain civil war, John met the demands presented by his barons in the Magna Carta (1215), the most famous of all medieval constitutional documents. While it was principally a feudal document, it carried as well the protests of the clergy and the towns. Its intention was to correct the abuses which John had practiced, largely in his capacity as feudal overlord. It was only by extension that it came to be regarded as the charter of personal liberty for all Englishmen. But one great principle was clearly contained in it—the principle that the king is subject to law, not superior to it. Beyond that, Magna Carta is a complex of specific feudal rights and claims which have long since lost their meaning. The charter worked no miracle either upon John or his baronial opponents. Civil war broke out almost immediately and the rebels called upon the son of Philip Augustus to take the throne. When John died, a year after Magna Carta, his capital was in the hands of a hostile prince, the great continental empire of his family was gone, and his son was a nine-year-old child.

The Emergence of English Popular Government

The century that followed the death of John was the most significant in the constitutional history of medieval England. It was divided between

THE NATIONAL MONARCHIES

ENGLAND	FRANCE	GERMANY
STEPHEN (*1135-1154*)	LOUIS VII (*1137-1180*)	*Hohenstaufen Dynasty*
Angevin-Plantagenet Dynasty		CONRAD III (*1137-1152*)
HENRY II (*1154-1189*)		FREDERICK I (*1152-1190*)
RICHARD I (*1189-1199*)		HENRY VI (*1190-1197*)
		FREDERICK II (*1197-1250*)
JOHN (*1199-1216*)	PHILIP II (*1180-1223*)	
HENRY III (*1216-1272*)	LOUIS VIII (*1223-1226*)	
	LOUIS IX (*1226-1270*)	
		CONRAD IV (*1250-1254*)
		(Great Interregnum)
	PHILIP III (*1270-1285*)	RUDOLPH OF HAPSBURG (*1273-1291*)
EDWARD I (*1272-1307*)	PHILIP IV (*1285-1314*)	

the long, weak reign of Henry III (*1216–1272*) and the long, vigorous reign of Edward I (*1272–1307*): both the weakness of the one and the strength of the other were important to the progress of constitutionalism. Henry III, the son of John, began and ended his reign under regencies. The intervening period of his personal rule was divided among a series of personalities who dominated the king and dictated his policies. Henry III was one of the most attractive, learned, and pleasant of English medieval kings. But his lack of decisiveness destroyed the chance for a strong monarchy and the barons kept the ascendancy they had gained under John. The regency was strong enough to keep the peace. The foreign invasion with which John's reign had ended dwindled away to nothing and restive order replaced civil war. The king was torn first one way, then another by noble factions, foreign favorites, and papal legates. Civil war was never far below the surface. The limitations on the crown which had been won from John by the threat of arms were confirmed, and the spirit of Magna Carta became part of the English constitution. Henry's policies, or lack of policies, succeeded in alienating virtually every source of support he might have had. In 1258 the barons actually seized power from their inept king and established a series of councils to make policy for him and keep him under surveillance. It is a measure of Henry's inability that the barons were strongly supported in their coup by both the clergy and the townsmen, the traditional supporters of the crown.

The barons could not hope to rule well or securely, for as long as there was a king there would be a royal faction. Again civil war loomed and, in its course, appeared one of the most fascinating figures of English medieval history, Simon de Montfort. He was a French baron who had come to England, like so many others, to press some vague claim to property and seek his fortune. He had begun as a favorite of the fickle Henry III, but had come to support the cause of the barons. He led their forces, defeated and captured the king, and in 1264 was the effective head of the government. Simon de Montfort proved to be more than the leader of a rebellious faction; he became the first champion of the people. In 1265 he called a meeting of the great council and to that session he added two knights from every shire to represent the country people and two representatives from every town and "borough" (from *burg,* a fortified town). This meeting, called the Simon de Montfort Parliament, marked the first formal representation of the people in the government of England. But Simon's liberality had already begun to alienate a large number of the barons. When Henry III's able and vigorous son Edward escaped captivity and raised his banner, a great host flocked to him and in the same year that Simon de Montfort had called his epochal parliament, he was killed in battle and the monarchy returned to the throne. But the precedent of national participation in the making of policy had been established.

Prince Edward continued to rule for his weary and inept father. In 1272, at Henry's death, Edward I became king. Ironically, his policies were to embody the same vision of English nationality that had distinguished Simon de Montfort's brief rule. The difference between them was a crown. Edward followed the example of his strong predecessors in seizing the administrative machinery of government and making it serve him. It was finally in his reign that men of humble birth, well-trained and loyal to the crown, came to dominate the day-to-day business of government. (We have seen the same thing happening in the court of Edward's contemporary, Philip IV of France.)

But it was in the realm of law that Edward I made his greatest impact. He has been aptly called "the English Justinian." It was in his reign, and largely as a result of his legislation and codification, that the medieval form of the English Common Law was finally achieved—the law of property, the law of contract, criminal and procedural law. Not only the law but the organs of government which administered it were affected by Edward's reforms. He resolutely attacked the judicial immunities of the baronage and extended royal authority, largely through the courts. He widened the scope of the traveling justices and improved the organization of the central courts. He gave definite form to the three basic courts of Common Law, which had slowly been emerging out of the differentiation of the great council's work. The Court of Exchequer dealt with cases involving royal revenue, then, in time, any issue of finance, and finally any individual grievance of a financial nature. The Court of Common Pleas had been developing since before the reign of John—it was specified in Magna Carta—as a central court for civil cases on any subject. Its separate and definite form was achieved under Edward I and the roll of its precedents dates from that time. Finally, a parallel court was separated out to deal mainly with criminal cases, the Court of King's Bench. Despite this specialization of judicial functions, the great council, the *curia regis,* still remained the parent institution of the special courts and the ultimate court of the realm—what has been called the "High Court of Parliament." Many legal matters still remained within the generalized jurisdiction of the great council.

A more important function of the great council, however, began to become clear under Edward I—its function as parliament. When the council met to deal with largely judicial business under the authority of the king it came to be called parliament. To this extent it differed little from the French *parlement* that appeared in the same period. But Edward I put its meeting on a regular basis and made its great powers usable as never before. Parliament became the place where the people could present petitions, request redress, and denounce wrongs. It became the body to which the king increasingly turned for support in the making of policy and consent to taxation. It was largely this last function that turned the great council of feudal tenants-in-chief into the national representative body which is the ancestor of the modern parliament. Kings before Edward I had appealed to the commons and requested their representatives to sanction levies upon them, and there was the precedent of Simon de Montfort's parliament. Edward I, at various times through the earlier part of his reign, called upon representatives of various segments of his growing middle class. In 1295 Edward, involved in wars in France, Scotland, and Wales, and desperately in need of money, summoned what has come to be called the Model Parliament. It represented the great barons (the permanent members of the royal council), the counties, towns, and clergy. It was the most widely representative assembly ever called until that time. A similar meeting was held in every successive year of Edward's reign and, by the end of it, the participation of the people in the deliberations of government had been inalienably established. The king still ruled —parliament did not even have the power to initiate legislation—and it was clearly dominated by the privileged and the powerful: but an important beginning had been made.

Edward's judicial, administrative and deliberative reforms won him broad popular support, and played a large role in giving his people a positive sense of nationality. He was a national king as none of his predecessors had been, and quite knowingly so. The value of popular support soon became apparent. First it enabled him to oppose the "foreign" exactions of the church. Edward was as hostile as Philip IV of France to the claims of Pope Boniface VIII.[4] He outlawed the clergy who obeyed the papal bull, *Clericos Laicos*,[5] prohibiting clerical payment of secular

4. See p. 373.
5. Papal bulls were so called because of the seal (in Latin, *bulla*) affixed to them. They are usually designated by the first word or two of the text. Bulls were one form of official decree of the pope as head of the church. Originally domestic and largely spiritual in nature, they had long since come to be employed as political instruments

taxes, and confiscated their temporal goods. This proved a popular measure in the growing climate of anticlericalism.

Popular support also enabled Edward to conduct a series of campaigns to enlarge the realm. The rugged, stubborn Welsh were finally subdued after more than a century of nominal English rule. Edward involved himself, as well, in the tangled affairs of Scotland. A disputed succession to the Scottish throne gave him the chance to arbitrate among the contenders. The price of his service was Scottish recognition of his overlordship. His insistence upon this drove the Scots to an alliance with France; this was to be one of the constant problems of English foreign relations for the next three centuries. Edward invaded Scotland, defeated the king he had previously selected, and declared the crown his in 1295. Within two years Scotland was in flames again. The rebel chieftain, William Wallace, was defeated and a second English invasion followed, only to be upset by Robert Bruce, another champion of Scottish nationalism. The hostility that grew from Edward's Scottish campaigns was to be a troublesome problem for England until the seventeenth century. While Edward fought to "round out" his kingdom to its natural frontiers, he carried on an intermittent and desultory war with France over the remaining English holdings on the continent. Edward was unable to see that this was a lost cause.

In the century and a half that separated the accession of the Angevin Henry II from the death of Edward I in 1307, England had been created. The successive loss of French lands had transformed Norman-French dukes and counts into English kings. Henry of Anjou knew no English and "Good King Richard" probably knew none, but by the time of Henry III royal proclamations had begun to be issued in that language. Edward I may be called the first truly English king and much of the success of his reign may be attributed to his recognition of a sense of nationality. In the country at large the earlier distinction between Norman and Saxon had practically disappeared, to be replaced by a spirit of national unity. At the end of Edward's reign England was a strong and prosperous realm, beginning to form a national culture. It had an effective national militia and a national government which combined a responsible kingship with the still inchoate instruments of popular will.

—and with considerable effect—by the great papal politicians of the High Middle Ages. Their effectiveness derived from the threat of spiritual sanctions which they carried, excommunication, or interdict, and in an "Age of Faith" such punishments were not taken lightly.

THE ECONOMIC REVOLUTION

We have seen that in the course of the eleventh and twelfth centuries several of the feudal monarchs of western Europe expanded their authority and paved the way for the establishment of the modern state system. Contributing to these political changes, and in turn, stimulated by them, were revolutionary social and economic changes. These were to be found in the revival of town life, the increase of trade and manufacture, the expansion of money economy, and the creation of a new and significant set of urban classes in European society.

The Rise of Towns and Townsmen

The medieval towns grew from varied origins. In Italy and the south of France the old Roman cities provided the nuclei around which urban life began to develop once more. In the earlier Middle Ages most of them had been reduced to villages by economic decay. Some few had retained their connection with the Byzantine Empire and the eastern trade; many had become centers of church administration, the seats of bishops, and had been kept alive by the economic demands of the episcopal community. Agricultural laborers were needed to work the estates of a bishop: artisans and craftsmen, weavers, candlemakers, stonecutters, metalworkers, and many others were necessary to the life of the diocese. They were attracted to these centers by the opportunity for work and by the protection that the wealth and power of the bishop gave them. The bishop maintained a market for the petty exchange of local goods; he had barns and storage houses for the produce of his estates; and there were courts and officials to keep the peace and arbitrate disputes. Not only in Italy and the south of France, but throughout western Europe episcopal towns grew up. As the monastic movement spread, towns also tended to develop around the rich monasteries, which had many of the same needs as the bishoprics. They too were centers of extensive agricultural holdings that attracted artisans and craftsmen. Settlements grew under the protection of their walls and their privileges. Many places, particularly wealthy manors that had a unique commodity such as salt or iron ore, took on the look of towns. Other settlements grew at strategic locations—at a river crossing, a ford or bridge (Oxford, Frankfort, and Cambridge, for example); at the foot of a mountain pass; or on an island, like Paris. As feudal lords built castles for military defense, communities sought the protection of their castle walls and existed by serving the needs of the noble household. Many of these incipient towns never became more than villages. But many did, and the predominantly rural aspect of feudal Europe began to change.

The towns attracted people, and the company of people was stimulating. The burgeoning needs and wants of the town stretched their ingenuity. The crafts and skills of urban life, so long neglected, began to spring to life once more. The men of the towns had things to sell, first to each other, then to traveling merchants, who bought the produce of one town to sell to the people of another. At first these merchants were pack-carrying peddlers. But as their profits grew so did the scope of their business, and in turn this took them to more distant places. Eventually they settled down, in some convenient town, built warehouses, opened offices, and hired workmen. Where the increasing populace came from remains a matter for speculation. Both the merchants and the workers of the towns were generally of humble birth, which usually meant servile birth. How did they free themselves from their manors and the service of their lords? Were they runaway serfs? Some probably were. Were they in some way able to purchase their freedom? This was probably possible for some. But from the beginning freedom was a necessity for the townsman. It became as increasingly necessary for the town as for its individual citizens.

As the towns took shape under the walls of castles and churches and monasteries, they requested permission of their lords to build walls for their own protection. These walled settlements were called *faubourgs* (from Latin, "outside the burg" or fortress) and *suburbs* (from Latin, literally "under" the fortress or fortress walls). The sections of these early "towns" grew in tumbling, haphazard fashion, one pushing another, until the area surrounding the original fortress was crowded with dwellings and shops and stores of "burghers," as the townsmen came to be called. As early as the end of the eleventh century towns were beginning to secure the liberties necessary to their continued existence. Sometimes they gained them by outright rebellion, forcing their lord to grant them charters; sometimes they bought their privileges; sometimes their charters were freely granted by lords intelligent enough to see the enormous advantage in encouraging such prosperous communities. Some lords even created new towns and advertised special privileges to attract citizens. The Capetian and Angevin kings were quick to see the advantage of the towns and were generous in granting privileges and charters. But whether by force, purchase, or grant, the towns moved toward freedom. Some achieved it in greater degree than others. We have already noted the role of the Lombard communes in the political history of Germany and Italy in the twelfth century. Town liberties were essential and inevitable. The townsmen could not be bound by the static laws of serfdom, by the personal code of chivalry, or the services of the feudality. They demanded and received not only their personal freedom but the right to marry and inherit without interference, the right to travel and trade, the right to govern themselves, and legal status for their communities. From an early time the town governments moved toward the form of the republic, a form of government virtually unkown for more than a thousand years in western Europe. The towns beckoned to the serfs of the countryside and one of the common clauses of a town charter provided that if a serf remained in the town for a year and a day without being caught by his lord, he was a free man. The men of the towns were a new element in medieval society. They were not nobles and yet they were not serfs. They came directly between the older divisions of the privileged and the nonprivileged orders, partaking of elements of both, and thus they were often called the "middle class."

The Guild Organization

The townsmen were artisans and merchants. It was this economic identification that made them most clearly distinct in medieval society. Nothing, therefore, was more natural than that they should organize themselves into economic associations. These *guilds* were the most characteristic of medieval urban institutions.

The earliest guilds were the merchant guilds, made up of all the merchants and sometimes also the artisans of a town. Little is known about their origins. In some cases they grew out of the political action groups that secured the town charter. They were almost always religious confraternities and mutual protective societies as well. The same men who were the guild masters tended to be the officeholders, *aldermen,* the ruling group of the town. The purpose of the merchant guild was to protect the market of the town and its products from outside competition. They supervised trade, set prices, and even taxes, and saw to it that all members had an equal opportunity to buy and sell. Monopoly was the aim of the guild but it must be stressed that modern capitalism was not. This was a phenomenon of the later Middle Ages, when medieval ideas and institutions were already yielding to new ones. The medieval guild did not countenance the practices that modern society dignifies with such terms as private enterprise, rugged individualism, and initiative. For this reason many of the guild practices and prohibitions seem strange and unrealistic to us. They were concerned with keeping profits at the level of a "just price," that is, materials, labor, and a profit sufficient to enable the producer to live decently. They were concerned with giving each guild member equal opportunity to exploit a market. The same sort of practices carried over to the later craft guilds. Many labor-saving devices were prohibited when they appeared simply because they were not available to all guild members and their use would be "unfair." Much of this attitude was simply institutional conservatism; but much of it was also a matter of moral principle.

In time, as products became diversified, as prosperity and techniques advanced, and social levels began to be clearly defined, associations of craftsmen split off from the merchant guilds. Men who made the same product banded together on the model of the older associations and often to protect themselves against the economic power of the merchant guilds. This was the origin of the craft guilds. Within each craft guild—unlike the merchant guilds—there were three divisions: masters, journeymen, and apprentices.

The masters were producing shop owners, butchers, bakers, candle-stick-makers, and dozens, even hundreds of others. The masters were also the men who controlled the guild, inspected and passed on the quality of the guild product, hours and conditions of work, prices, discipline and punishment for infractions or sharp practices.

Their shops were the training schools for their trades. Young boys were apprenticed to established masters to learn their skills. This relationship was governed by a strict and regular contract. The boy worked and learned in his master's shop. His period of apprenticeship in most crafts was seven years. During that time he lived under hard and demanding discipline; but he learned the craft from its most gross and general aspects to the refinement and finish of its final product, whether good miller's flour or a fine gold salt-dish. The master usually had the obligation to feed, clothe, house, and instruct his apprentice. The latter he sometimes did by sending him to a guild school—the first secular schools since antiquity— more often by naive and pious exhortations to commonplace virtues; and sometimes by regular beatings. Still the town records of every generation preserve the complaints against tumultuous bands of apprentices making the streets unsafe and a general nuisance of themselves. In the small shop of the typical master the apprentice was treated like a member of the family. The master shared his home and his skill with the boy and, more often than not, patiently instilled in him the respect for materials and workmanship so patent in the medieval guild products which have come down to us.

When the boy finished his apprenticeship he progressed to the status of journeyman—that is, a free laborer to be employed at a daily wage (from French *journée,* "day"). The skilled journeyman was employable wherever the work of his guild was done. Frequently he went on a year's journey, working his way from one town to another, seeing the world and learning its ways. Sometimes he simply stayed on in the house of his master as an employee. But, in any case, he looked forward to the time when he could open his own shop and become a master. This necessitated his saving, or borrowing, the capital to finance his enterprise. Sometimes it took him many years. Sometimes it was as simple as marrying the boss's daughter. He also had to satisfy the standards of the guild. This required an examination, sometimes the creation of a "masterpiece"—the proof of his proficiency at his craft—and always the payment of a master's fee. In the later Middle Ages it became increasingly difficult for the journeyman to break into the master's circle. The masters tended to become capitalistic manufacturers: they raised the entrance fee beyond the hopes of any ordinary craftsman; they controlled the flow of raw materials and credit and manipulated markets, sometimes on a world basis. The journeymen became simply workers and their numbers swelled the proletariat of the medieval towns. But this is part of another story.

All aspects of town life in the High Middle Ages were dominated by the guilds. They participated in town government; in many instances their representatives *were* the town government. They played a prominent role in the social life of the town and they contributed to the celebrations of the local churches. Often the stained glass windows and decorative statuary of churches would be the gifts of guilds. As the lay-Christian "mystery plays" developed as popular entertainment, the guilds came to present plays on appropriate Biblical themes: the wine-maker's guild presented the Marriage at Cana; the carpenters' guild, Noah and the Ark. The guilds also provided a form of social security, caring for the widows and orphans of deceased members. They established chantries for perpetual prayers for their dead, endowed chapels, and hospitals.

The Life and Look of the Medieval Town

The medieval town was crowded, dirty, dangerous, busy, and a place of infinite excitement. It was surrounded by a wall, more or less elaborately fortified with towers and bastions and drawbridges. The space within the town, limited by the circuit of wall, was at a premium. Every inch of room was used with little or no civic planning. As the towns grew in population they often had to tear down the old defensive walls and build new ones incorporating new *suburbs* and *faubourgs* that constantly mushroomed at the foot of the walls. Even bridges, like London Bridge or the Ponte Vecchio in Florence, were crowded with shops and dwellings. They even cluttered the tops of the defensive walls of many cities. Houses crowded together and shot up many stories to a wilderness of spires, gables, and chimney pots. Their upper stories overhung the narrow twisting streets that threaded their way through the town. Occasionally the streets broadened into the courtyard of a church or guildhall or town square; and the streets giving access to the defensive wall were usually straight and direct.

In the course of the twelfth century the prospering towns began to pave their main streets. In the reign of Philip Augustus some of the streets of Paris were paved (but one of the common Latin names of that city continued to be Lutetia, from *lutum,* "mud"). The streets of a town also served as sewers: people simply dumped their trash, garbage, and offal out into the streets where dogs and pigs disposed of it. The statutes that nearly every town had against such practice were cheerfully ignored. Occasional rains cleaned the streets and swept their refuse into the streams or wells from which the people drew their drinking water. Pestilence and fire were frequent and were taken for granted.

The members of the various guilds settled in separate quarters of the city. Their shops occupied the street level of their houses. Board shutters let down to form the counter over which the master sold his goods and haggled with his customers. At night the shutters were folded up and locked. The upper stories of the buiding were the living quarters of the family—the garret rooms usually reserved for the junior apprentices. There might be a guildhall nearby. Some of the guildhalls of the later Middle Ages were splendid and ornate structures. But usually the chief buildings of the towns were the churches, which were numerous and lavish. In the later twelfth century London, with a population of close to 40,000 had 126 parish churches and 13 great conventual churches. An episcopal town would have its massive cathedral.

The towns teemed with life. Every trade, profession, and rank had its colorful costume. People of every sort jostled and crowded each other in the narrow streets. Thieves and pickpockets busily plied their trade. Pitiable, maimed, and disfigured beggars added their insistent whine to the cries of vendors. Priests, friars, merchants, students, town officials, rich and poor mingled together. There was scarcely a day unmarked by some religious procession winding through the streets with pomp and color. The prosperity of the towns attracted people in ever-increasing numbers. By the thirteenth century Paris had some 80,000 people; London had perhaps 40,000; the cloth towns of Flanders such as Ypres and Lille had between 20,000 and 40,000; and some of the Lombard and Tuscan towns, such as Florence and Milan, had as many as 100,000. As towns grew in size and prosperity, rivalries developed among them, sometimes to the point of war. Some of them formed leagues. Their animosities provided a cross current to the larger flow of national rivalries among the great emerging states of western Europe.

The Revival of Trade

The rise of towns in medieval society was closely related to the general revival of trade. Neither could flourish without the other. In their origin, as in their development, towns and trade were related. Both began their revival along the Mediterranean coast, especially in Italy. We have already noted that in Italy and the south of France the urban tradition of Rome was never entirely destroyed. A handful of cities there continued to enjoy the trade and industry that has always distinguished the city from the village. The most important of these was Venice.

The city of Venice fell heir to the ancient connection between Italy and Byzantium, and to the thin trickle of trade that continued to flow from Constantinople to the west. In spite of the incredible hardships and uncertainties of the Mediterranean trade, the profits were enormous, and Venice flourished. Her trade was almost entirely in expensive luxury goods —spices, fine metalwares, exotic and colorful textiles, jewels, perfumes, glass, gold, and silver. The church and the feudal nobility were the consumers, and Venice was practically the only purveyor. By the late eleventh century Venice was a formidable power in the Adriatic and the eastern Mediterranean. She allied herself with the Byzantine Empire against the ambitious Normans of Sicily, and was instrumental in thwarting the Norman scheme to conquer the whole eastern trade complex of Byzantium. In grateful return for what was really economic self-interest, the eastern empire rewarded Venice with a monopoly of her western trade.

Across the Italian peninsula, Genoa and Pisa matched the ambition of Venice. When the Norman invasion of Sicily and southern Italy upset the Mediterranean balance of power, these two cities seized their oppor-

View of Old Shetland croft with roof light (Gleggr) above the modern windows. The straw thatch covering turf shingles is secured by simmonds or ropes (old Norse sima-rope). Jarlshof, Shetland Islands.

Hunting Scene from *Manessischen Handschrift*. 1260.

Above: *Death of King Harold,*
from the *Bayeux Tapestry.* c. 1073—83.
Below: The Mainhold at Assisi.

St. Martin and the Beggar. St. Martin Cathedral.

tunities. As circumstances dictated, they allied or fought with the Normans and the various scattered Saracen powers. By the end of the eleventh century they shared valuable trading rights and strategic economic bases all around the western basin of the Mediterranean, and their "Christian" merchant companies traded indiscriminately with Christian and Saracen alike.

The enormous economic profits of the Crusades fell almost entirely to the Italian cities. We have already noted their role in the great adventure of militant Christendom. As the crusaders secured the Levantine coasts and the Byzantine Empire tottered, Italian merchant companies dug in. They fought each other bitterly for trading rights and advantages. The eastern trade beckoned them on; they established themselves around the Black Sea, in Armenia, in Egypt, Cyprus, and a dozen other places. The famous Polo family of Venice tracked the eastern trade all the way to China in the hope of profits, monopolies, or concessions for their family and city. The son, Marco Polo, left a fascinating record of this incredible journey. As the profits of the eastern trade enriched the cities of Italy, their markets across the Alps in Europe expanded in equal measure.

But the north of Europe was also developing a complex of exchange second only in volume and profit to that of Italy. It was centered in the towns of Flanders, the region that is now roughly Holland and Belgium. The Flemish towns were as admirably located for the northern trade as Venice, Genoa, and Pisa were for the trade of the Mediterranean. Flanders commanded the mouth of the Rhine River, with its tributary system that drained central and western Europe. Across the narrow sea lay the British Isles, both a market and source of raw material. To the north and east lay the Baltic, and Flanders was in a position to tap its trade and resources. In the eleventh and twelfth centuries, economic life began to quicken in all these areas. No small factor was the far-ranging activities of the Vikings. The goods of Byzantium and the east traveled the Varangian route up the Russian rivers to the Baltic, then to the North Sea and the far outposts of the Viking world. The heavy wares and raw materials of northern Europe found their way to the Flemish market towns, where they were exchanged for products brought in by the eastern trade and, increasingly, for products of native European manufacture.

The staple of Flemish economy was the textile trade. Since Roman times Flanders had been known for its cloth. The Flemish textile trade had even survived to Carolingian times. With the economic revival of the eleventh and twelfth centuries, the manufacture of Flemish cloth began to flourish once more, its products to pass out along the routes of northern trade as an important item of exchange. By the fourteenth century, nearly half the people of Flanders worked in the cloth industry. As the textile trade expanded, Flemish weavers and merchants needed new sources of raw material. English wool became so important that a significant political-economic bond was forged between England and Flanders which lasted well into modern times. England became the chief wool-producing area in northern Europe, and the wool trade became the most important single source of English prosperity. Second only to the textile trade was Flanders' trade in wines. With the Norman conquest, the continental taste for wine was transported to England, where the demands were increased by the Angevin succession. The trade in salt fish was almost equally profitable. Indeed, every conceivable commodity was to be seen on the docks and in the warehouses of the Flemish towns—everything from a shipload of lumber and bales of cloth to a coop of hunting falcons. Every product introduced into a virgin area created a new demand and an expanding market. Expansion was the prime characteristic of the reviving economy of Europe —expansion of towns, expansion of trade, expansion of manufacture.

Inevitably connections were made between the two great centers of reviving economic activity. Merchants from Italy took their wares overland across the Alpine passes, then along the river routes north; they shipped them to Marseilles, then by river boat up the Rhone to the Loire, the Seine and the Moselle. Flemish goods moved inland along the Rhine, the Meuse, the Moselle, and overland across northern France to the Seine and the Loire. Overland travel was extremely primitive and dangerous; most roads were little more than trails, choked with dust or clogged with mud. Travelers were at the mercy of bandits, both humble and noble, so the merchants banded together in caravans for mutual protection. In some areas transport companies were formed to assume the risks of travel for a percentage of the cargo. Not only was travel hazardous, it was also expensive. The merchants paid fees to cross bridges, to use fords, to cross feudal boundaries. In spite of these obstacles the long caravans of merchants' pack horses became a common sight on medieval roads, and gradually the roads were improved by toll-conscious lords, by the merchants themselves, their cities, and even by the church. Political authorities from kings to local counts began to supress banditry in the interest of general order and profitable trade. By the later Middle Ages travel had become much easier and safer, but where possible the merchant still found it preferable to transport his goods by river boat.

The routes from the north and south met in the lands of the counts of

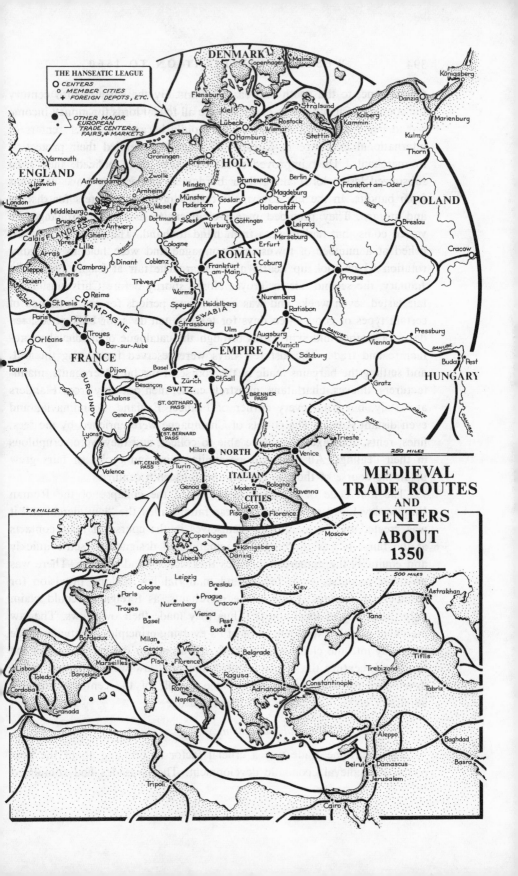

MEDIEVAL
TRADE
ROUTES
AND
CENTERS
ABOUT
1350

THE HANSEATIC LEAGUE
○ CENTERS
◎ MEMBER CITIES
+ FOREIGN DEPOTS, ETC.

● OTHER MAJOR
EUROPEAN
TRADE CENTERS,
FAIRS, & MARKETS

DENMARK
Copenhagen
Malmö
Königsberg
Flensburg
Kiel
Stralsund
Danzig
Lübeck
Rostock
Kolberg
Kammin
Marienburg
Hamburg
Wismar
Stettin
Kulm
HOLY
Thorn
Yarmouth
Groningen
Bremen
Ipswich
ENGLAND
Amsterdam
Zwolle
Minden
Brunswick
Berlin
Frankfort am-Oder
London
Arnheim
Münster
Magdeburg
POLAND
Middleburg
Dordrecht
Wesel
Paderborn
Goslar
Halberstadt
Breslau
Bruges
Dortmund
Soest
Göttingen
Leipzig
Calais
FLANDERS
Ghent
Antwerp
Cologne
Warburg
Merseburg
Cracow
Ypres
Lille
ROMAN
Erfurt
Arras
Dinant
Coblenz
Frankfurt
am-Main
Coburg
Dieppe
Amiens
Cambray
Trèves
Mainz
Nuremberg
Prague
Rouen
Reims
Worms
Ratisbon
Paris
St.Denis
CHAMPAGNE
Speyer
Heidelberg
SWABIA
Provins
Strassburg
Ulm
Augsburg
Pressburg
Orléans
Troyes
Bar-sur-Aube
EMPIRE
Munich
Vienna
Tours
FRANCE
Dijon
Basel
Salzburg
HUNGARY
Besançon
Zürich
St.Gall
Gratz
Chalons
SWITZ.
ST.GOTHARD
PASS
BRENNER
PASS
Geneva
GREAT ST. BERNARD
PASS
Lyons
Milan
NORTH
Verona
Trieste
Venice
Valence
MT.CENIS
PASS
Turin
ITALIAN
Modena
Bologna
Genoa
CITIES
Ravenna
T.R MILLER
Pisa
Lucca
Florence

250 MILES

Copenhagen
Moscow
London
Königsberg
Hamburg
Lübeck
Danzig
Leipzig
Cologne
Breslau
Kiev
Paris
Nuremberg
Prague
Cracow
Astrakhan
Troyes
Basel
Vienna
Buda
Pest
Tana
Milan
Genoa
Venice
Belgrade
Tiflis
Bordeaux
Pisa
Florence
Trebizond
Lisbon
Marseilles
Ragusa
Toledo
Barcelona
Rome
Adrianople
Constantinople
Tabriz
Cordoba
Naples
Granada
Aleppo
Baghdad
Beirut
Damascus
Basra
Tripoli
Jerusalem
Cairo

500 MILES

Champagne, to the south and east of Paris. By the early twelfth century the counts of Champagne—eager as were all feudal lords for money income —had begun to establish fairs which rapidly became the chief centers of international exchange in Europe. The counts extended their protection to merchants. They improved roads and kept them policed; they even subsidized lesser lords along their borders to protect the trade caravans from bandits. In the fair towns, the counts provided quarters for display and storage. They provided money-changers to assay and exchange the varied coins that had to pass from hand to hand. The fairs were established at a number of towns in Champagne and were held in a regular rotation which took up nearly a full year. The fair at Lagny opened in January, the second fair in Troyes closed shortly before Christmas. Each fair lasted seven weeks and was broken into periods for the exchange of certain types of goods—ten days for textiles, ten days for bulk goods, ten days for leather and skins, thus through the catalogue of medieval manufacture and trade. The last few days were reserved for paying the bills and settling the bargains made in the course of the fair. Merchants, manufacturers, thieves, charlatans, minstrels came; men not only from Flanders and Italy, but from every corner of France, England, Scandinavia, and even distant Russia. The counts of Champagne were enriched by the fees, fines, rents, and taxes they were able to collect; and they were scrupulous in their dealings. All over Europe similar fairs and cycles of fairs grew up in the course of the late twelfth and thirteenth centuries.

The first code of commercial law since the collapse of the Roman Empire developed as a result of these fairs. Called the "law merchant," it was created by the merchants themselves in the course of their contacts at the fairs. It was thoroughly pragmatic and designed to settle quickly and equitably the numerous disputes that were bound to arise. There was no other recourse, since feudal and manorial law had no provision for commercial disputes. Besides, the merchants, as foreigners, could claim only the mercy of local courts. Thus they made their own laws. The law merchant rapidly expanded; most of its evolving principles eventually made their way into the civil codes of modern Europe. In the early years of the fourteenth century the principles of commercial law were extended to the developing maritime trade and by the middle of the century extensive admiralty codes had come into general usage.

The Rise of Medieval Capitalism

This maritime trade was a crucial factor in bringing about the next phase of medieval economic development. The Crusades had stimulated sea travel; ships were growing in size, and navigators in skill and knowledge. Some Italian cargo ships could load five hundred tons of goods. The Genoese had a fleet of two hundred vessels. As the Atlantic trade opened, new types of ships were built to replace the Mediterranean *galley,* which had changed little in design since Minoan times. The high-prowed, short, box-like *carracks*—the ships of Columbus and the early explorers were of this type—carried the ocean trade from the Canary Islands to the Baltic. The greater carrying capacity of ships, the absence of tolls, and its relative speed commended sea travel to merchants and merchant cities. In the early fourteenth century, the Venetians opened a direct sea route to Flanders and after 1317 great armed fleets made regular annual voyages to the north of Europe. Shortly afterwards, a group of German Baltic cities banded together to form a commercial union known as the Hanseatic League. The Spanish kingdoms were also becoming maritime powers: in 1282 Aragon seized Sicily and established important Mediterranean trade connections; the city of Barcelona competed with the older Italian centers of trade; Castile, in the late thirteenth century, pushed her conquest to the sea. The Christianization of coastal Spain mitigated the dangers of Saracen pirates that had long closed the Atlantic to Mediterranean shipping. Within a relatively short period, by the mid-fourteenth century, the growth of the maritime trade strangled the inland fairs and short-circuited the older land routes of commerce.

The increase in speed and volume of exchange reflected in maritime trade was closely related to other basic changes taking place in the European economy. The commercial revolution, which had stimulated the economic resurgence of Europe, inevitably became an industrial revolution. The surplus capital that commerce produced began to be invested in manufacturing. We have already seen that the operations of the merchant and the producer were closely related in the cloth industry of Flanders. But it was in Italy that the most significant steps were taken toward the development of medieval capitalism.

The Italian cities began to produce the exotic goods they had for so long carried from the east. Often they simply stole the secrets of manufacturing processes. The enormous profits of their trade enabled them to finance their manufacturing ventures for which they already had a world market. By the middle of the thirteenth century Venetian glass, Milanese metalwares, Luccese silk, Florentine textiles, and other products of Italy were competing in the markets of western Europe. The control of goods, machinery, processes, and markets passed into the hands of a small group of merchant princes in the various Italian cities. These were the old guild masters slowly transforming themselves into industrialists. In 1297 the great council of Venice was closed and no more masters of the merchant guild of that city were to be elected. Before the middle of the fourteenth century 30,000 people worked for the Florentine cloth industry, which was controlled by some 200 magnates. The free workers and small shop owners who had once been protected by the guild system were destroyed by budding industrial capitalism and reduced to a laboring class.

Italian capitalism spread out along the trade routes of Europe. Italian companies opened branch offices and entered into complex negotiations for market control and raw materials. An inevitable corollary of such industrial and commercial expansion was the development of banking. In the mid-thirteenth century a beautiful and stable gold coinage reappeared in Europe, the Florentine *florin* and the Venetian *ducat*. No such coins had been minted in Europe since the seventh century. The needs of expanding business were outgrowing the silver penny of local mint and varying value all through Europe. Furthermore, trade could no longer depend upon the capricious fluctuations of local monetary values. The national monarchs and some great territorial lords quickly followed Venice and Florence in minting good, stable coins. The money-changer was transformed into the banker. His practice of keeping money for others and loaning it out at interest grew into the complex practices of large-scale credit, notes, discounts, and financial paper so familiar in modern banking. At the opening of the thirteenth century the city of Florence had a money-changers' guild and the rudiments of a banking system. Great family banks operated through the thirteenth and early fourteenth centuries. Two Florentine family banks, for example, the Bardi and the Peruzzi, practically controlled the national finances of England through loans to Edward I. They were equally busy all over Europe. Genoa's "national" bank, the Bank of St. George, operating both as a private corporation and a state treasury, lent and invested on such a scale that it was called the greatest single financial institution of the Middle Ages. The Jews, who had so long monopolized the trade of money-changing, were all but replaced by the Italian banking firms. The church modified the hard position it had previously taken on usury to accommodate itself to the new economic situation. Indeed, the management and manipulation of the enormous church revenues was a rich source of profit for bankers. Even some clerical groups carried on banking services. The semireligious, crusading order of Knights Templars used its great wealth and international connections to loan money, receive deposits, and to create credit on a large scale. As we have seen, it was chiefly this activity that aroused the avarice of Philip IV of France and led to the destruction of the order.

The revival of towns and the rebirth of trade, industry, and large-scale money economy were fixed in medieval society by the middle of the thirteenth century, and in their train came social changes of great significance. The townsmen had shouldered their way into society to become a middle class. Whether such townsmen were modest local guild masters, pack-carrying peddlers, or merchant princes, they had more in common with each other than with any other class in society. They stood for peace and order, without which they could not carry on their business; and they were willing to pay for it. In France and England they allied with strong kings against their common enemy, the feudality. In less united lands—Germany, Flanders, Italy—they formed themselves into strong city leagues. From their ranks, kings and lords, even the church, had begun to draw officials who were loyal and intelligent. As a class they were beginning to gain a voice in political council. The greatest and the richest among them were able to vie with the most powerful princes in display and influence. Many bought land and titles and married their sons and daughters into noble families. Notably in the Italian cities the old, vested nobility was absorbed into the merchant class to form a new kind of aristocracy. The enterprise of merchants, industrialists, and bankers had split the growing cities between the "haves" and the "have nots," creating a depressed and resentful working class whose riots and wars were to scar the following centuries.

Even the peasantry could not escape the implications of change. The towns and cities demanded greater supplies of food. For the first time, large groups of peasants had an incentive to produce a surplus for sale. And with the money earned by these sales they were able to buy freedom from oppressive manorial service. Increased incentive brought improved techniques of agriculture, improved equipment and stock. Most landed lords, caught in the spiral of increasing prices, were glad to commute services for rents in cash. Some even encouraged free peasants to colonize marginal lands and bring them under cultivation. The great forests of Europe began to be cleared, marshes drained, river valleys opened, and village colonies planted to grow into towns and cities. Early in the twelfth century the Flemish and Dutch began to win lands from the sea by building dikes and dams.

Medieval Europe was in the process of transformation.

SUGGESTIONS FOR FURTHER READING

≥⊱⊰≤

The National Monarchies

G. G. Coulton, *Life in the Middle Ages,* cited for Chap. 8.

P. Henderson, *Richard Coeur de Lion* (New York: Norton, 1959), a popular biography.

J. E. A. Jolliffe, *Angevin Kingship* (New York: Barnes and Noble, 1955).

E. Kantorowicz, *Frederick II, 1194–1250* (New York: Ungar, 1957), a massive and demanding biography of a fascinating figure skillfully set in his age.

*A. R. Kelley, *Eleanor of Aquitaine and the Four Kings* (New York: Vintage, 1958).

A. Luchaire, *Social France in the Time of Philip Augustus* (New York: Ungar, 1957).

C. H. McIlwain, *The High Court of Parliament* (New Haven: Yale University Press, 1910), one of the basic medieval institutional studies.

S. Painter, *The Reign of King John* (Baltimore: Johns Hopkins Press, 1949), a standard work.

————, *The Scourge of God: Peter of Dreux, Duke of Brittany* (Baltimore: Johns Hopkins Press, 1937), a fascinating portrait of a typical feudal magnate.

————, *William Marshal, Knight Errant, Baron, and Regent of England* (Baltimore: Johns Hopkins Press, 1933), comprehensive and authoritative account preserved in contemporary records.

F. M. Powicke, *The Thirteenth Century, 1216–1307* (Oxford: Clarendon Press, 1953), largely political history.

G. O. Sayles, *The Medieval Foundations of England* (London: Methuen, 1948).

C. H. Walker, *Eleanor of Aquitaine* (Chapel Hill: University of North Carolina Press, 1950).

The Medieval Economic Revolution

*S. Baldwin, *Business in the Middle Ages* (New York: Holt, 1937).

P. Boissonade, *Life and Work in Medieval Europe,* cited for Chap. 8.

*R. S. Lopez and I. W. Raymond, eds., *Medieval Trade in the Mediterranean World* (New York: Columbia University Press, 1955), a valuable collection of documents.

*J. H. Mundy and P. Riesenberg, eds., *The Medieval Town* (New York: Anvil, 1958), a collection of documents with an excellent introduction.

*H. Pirenne, *Medieval Cities* (Garden City, N. Y.: Anchor, 1956), a famous book on the revival of town life.

E. Power, *The Wool Trade in Medieval History* (Oxford: Oxford University Press, 1941).

F. Schevill, *Siena: The Story of a Medieval Commune* (New York: Scribners, 1909), an attractive study of a typical medieval town.

C. Stephenson, *Borough and Town* (Cambridge: Medieval Academy of America, 1933).

*Sylvia Thrupp, *The Merchant Class of Medieval London* (Ann Arbor: University of Michigan Press, 1962).

The Travels of Marco Polo, tr. by R. E. Latham (Baltimore: Penguin, 1961), an inexpensive edition of this much-published classic.

*Paperbound edition. In the case of reprint editions, publisher and date of publication given will be that of reprint rather than the original.

⇗10⇖

The High Middle Ages:
The Triumphant Synthesis

THE ZENITH OF MEDIEVAL CHRISTIANITY

As men began to give their loyalties to towns and to nation states; as they began to feel that they were Englishmen, Frenchmen, or Italians, Londoners, Parisians, or Florentines, there remained one call upon their loyalties that transcended the walls of towns and the frontiers of nations —the universal church, greatest of medieval institutions.

Reform and Recovery

By the twelfth century the Cluniac reform movement had lost its momentum. Its very success had brought corrupting power and wealth, and from the grass roots of the church came a wave of protest and reform. Leading the reform movement was a new order, the Cistercian, named after its place of origin, Citeaux in Burgundy. Directing the order was St. Bernard (1091–1153), the most commanding religious figure of the twelfth century.

Bernard joined the order in 1112, shortly after it was founded. Within a short time he had become the abbot of one of its houses at Clairvaux and the living example of its ideals. He kept every monastic vigil and fast, and in his fervor ruined his health and almost destroyed his body. A mystic, he sought with all his strength of spirit to cross the gulf that divides man from God. His very sense of the holy made him bitterly conscious of the imperfections of the world. If he failed to cure any imperfection of his own, it was the sin of spiritual pride; yet this was the driving force that made him the vocal critic of prince, monk, and peasant, church and state alike. He involved himself in the internal affairs of nations and the dynastic and territorial rivalries of kings and lords; he intimidated even the papacy. The Second Crusade was almost entirely his doing. He cajoled, bullied, and threatened Louis VII and the emperor, Conrad III, into taking the cross. Then he flayed them for their failure. But Bernard reserved both his greatest devotion and his choicest venom for the church. Its most effective champion against political and intellectual criticism, he was himself the most bitter critic of clerical abuse.

The Cistercian reform was not the only protest against monastic corruption. Prominent among the host of parallel movements in the twelfth century were a number of ascetic "hermit orders." Settling in inaccessible places and practicing the most extreme severities, they attracted thousands of followers. The most influential of these foundations was the Carthusian order, formed in the closing years of the eleventh century in a remote corner of the Alps. It was an order of silence and loneliness: each monk had his own cell, observed his hours and prayers alone, and ate his coarse and meager fare in solitude. Only once a week did he speak with his fellow monks.

From the monasteries the reform movement spread to the busy, secular cathedral chapters. Using the model that St. Augustine was alleged to have devised for the monks of Hippo in the fourth century, these chapters called themselves Augustinian Canons Regular. They lived by a "rule" like monks and practiced many of the same austerities.

Eventually the zeal for reform once again reached the papacy itself. The century between the death of Urban II (1099) and the accession of Innocent III (1198) had been a troubled one for the papacy. The popes had had to contend with the ambitions of the German emperors, the arrogance of their own Italian subjects, the election of antipopes, and the activities of demagogic heretics. The continuing state of crisis offered plenty of opportunity for the abuse of power and the corruption of ideals, bitterly catalogued by reformers like St. Bernard. The popes of the twelfth century had to be diplomats, politicians, even warriors. Though saints were scarce among them, they were sufficiently astute to preserve the papacy from its many enemies. With the accession of Innocent III, a new and brilliant era opened for the medieval papacy.

Innocent III, the Church, and the Papal Monarchy

A vigorous and intelligent Italian nobleman, Innocent had become a cardinal before he was thirty. He was a trained canon lawyer, a learned theologian, and an experienced diplomat and administrator. In 1198, at the death of his predecessor, he was only thirty-seven, yet already so eminent that he was elected pope almost without question. Having served four popes, Innocent, like Gregory VII, had had an important voice in papal decisions long before his elevation to the papacy. He was familiar with the intricate workings of church machinery and thus able to use it effectively in fulfilling his aims. These were the same as Gregory VII had cherished: the achievement of church supremacy among men and the establishment of papal supremacy within the church. More than any other medieval pope, Innocent was able to approach this ideal.

Innocent III gathered into his capable hands all the vast powers of the church to form the papal monarchy. Its center was the *curia*, the monarchical court of the church. The ranking members of the curia were the cardinals, who had been designated as the papal electoral college in the eleventh century. The College of Cardinals had inevitably grown in power and prestige; it constituted the high court of church law. Its members held important administrative posts. Moreover, it had become an international body: cardinals were chosen from among the most able and distinguished churchmen in Europe, each representing papal authority in his own country. Cardinals were often sent out by the pope as his special diplomatic or spiritual agents, called "legates."

The work of the papal curia was done in three administrative departments: the chancery, the penitentiary, and the camera ("chamber"). The chancery prepared all papal documents, including papal bulls. The penitentiary was responsible for punishments or penance; through this agency the pope wielded his enormous spiritual powers, the excommunication and the interdict. The penitentiary was also responsible for dispensations from papal power and exceptions to canon law. The third department, the camera, was the papal treasury, responsible for the collection and administration of the revenues that poured into Rome from every corner of Europe. In and around the papal curia swarmed a host of lesser officials— lawyers, notaries, secretaries—the dedicated, the ambitious, the hopeful, and the corrupt.

Below the level of the pope and the curia in the hierarchy of the church stood the archbishops, the governors of the spiritual "provinces" of Europe.

They maintained their own courts, in function—if not in size and magnificence—like the papal curia. They heard cases and appeals from those below them and enforced the decrees of the papacy. The archbishops were powerful and important personages; often their provinces were vast in extent and they themselves ranked with the greatest of secular princes.

Below the archbishops were the bishops, the key figures in the organization of the church. We have already noted their significance, as the champions of civilization and order in a barbaric society, as feudal lords, and as royal counsellors. Most of the material resources of the church were held by the bishops and the network of episcopal dioceses spread over the map of Europe; the great bulk of the church's legal work was done in the bishops' courts; a large portion of its revenue came from diocesan taxes, payments, and fines—passing through the hands of the bishops; the ordination, discipline, and control of the local clergy were also in their hands. Every church in his diocese was the bishop's responsibility, and often he was responsible for local monasteries. The center of the diocese was the cathedral, the bishop's church. He shared the responsibilities of his office and its endless day-to-day details with his cathedral chapter, the clergy of his church who made up the bishop's curia.

Finally, at the base of the great pyramid of the church were the thousands of parish priests. Each episcopal diocese was subdivided into parishes, often coterminous with manorial holdings, so that the church reached down into the basic patchwork of medieval society with its services, its taxes, its jurisdiction, and its consolation. Ultimately the burden of the church rested upon the shoulders of the parish priest: it was from his hands that the great majority of Christians received the sacraments; it was from the pulpit of his modest church that the common lessons of morality were preached. The village church was the hub of the community and the focus of community celebrations, which were almost always religious in character—the feasts of the church, the celebration of relics, and the tribute to patron saints. In most instances the secular intruded frankly upon the religious, for the medieval Christian saw no harm in enjoying his religion and making it part of his ordinary life. The courtyard of the church was often the local market, the local theater, and the local forum. The priest, limited though his learning might be, was nevertheless the most learned man of the village and acted as the notary, secretary, confidant, and sometimes even the banker for his flock. He bore both the responsibility and the odium of the church's taxes, for he stood at the source of its wealth. The church, like the state, exacted fees and fines for every conceivable service. There were baptismal fees, confirmation fees, marriage fees, and even a burial tax which took the form of the second-best piece of clothing, furniture, or livestock in the bereaved household. The most burdensome exaction was the tithe, not a voluntary contribution, but a full-fledged and often oppressive tax. It was the obligation of the parish priest to assess the tithe and see that it was paid in full by each member of his congregation—one-tenth of one's profits, whether from land, in products, or money.

It was upon this structure that Innocent III resolved to impose his monarchical powers. He used his spiritual authority as the secular monarchs used their legal authority. He claimed for the see of St. Peter a vast array of financial rights. He claimed from archbishops and bishops an oath of allegiance, binding them to the papacy.

Perhaps the strongest centralizing force at his disposal was the canon law, the law of the church. This had grown with the increasing institutionalization of the church. Much of it was an adaptation of Roman law. Most of it grew up as the church took over many of the functions of civil authority following the collapse of the Roman Empire. Church courts had jurisdiction over everything pertaining to church property or members of the clergy. They encroached upon secular society when the church became the recorder of births, wills, and deeds of property; all sworn contracts were sealed in church courts. They claimed jurisdiction over all wrongs, civil and criminal, which involved morality; they virtually held a universal jurisdiction. A hierarchy of courts grew up to correspond with the administrative hierarchy of the church, and with it the concept of appellate jurisdiction. With the growth of a monarchical papacy, the pope could claim final justice at canon law. The structure of the ecclesiastical courts was nearly complete by the time of Innocent III, and he was the most significant in a long line of popes trained specifically in the canon law. The law of the church, as well as its courts, was becoming regularized at the same time. At various points in the earlier Middle Ages, partial codifications had been made. Its sources in Scripture, tradition, and the official acts of the church had been defined and the categories of its jurisdiction set down. In the eleventh century the revival of interest in Roman law and the recovery of the Code of Justinian provided an example soon followed in the law of the church. In the mid-twelfth century the canon law was reduced to a code which was soon generally accepted. It quickly received the blessing of the papacy for, in its reflection of Roman imperial influence, it stressed the monarchical character of the pope within the legal framework of the church. Canon law, rather than theology, was to be the chief prop of the papal throne in the time of Innocent III and beyond.

Innocent exercised his power through the complex papal bureaucracy for which he was in part responsible. The agents of papal law, papal finance, and papal administration were to be found everywhere. Innocent had a powerful ally in the monks. Monasteries sought the protection of the pope and put themselves under his authority at the expense of local bishops. Further, the vigorous spirit of monastic reform fell in perfectly with Innocent's own ideas of reform. He succeeded in tying reform to papal authority. Up and down the hierarchy of the church he interfered, directed, and commanded reform and obedience—and the church as a whole responded.

In 1215 Innocent III summoned the Fourth Lateran Council to put the stamp of the church upon his achievements. There were four hundred bishops, eight hundred abbots and priors, seventy-two archbishops, and the patriarchs of Jerusalem and Constantinople; envoys from practically every Christian court, royal and noble, and representatives of towns and cities —convened to honor the supremacy of Innocent III within the church. The work of the Fourth Lateran Council clearly reflected the wishes of the pope. As a reforming council, there were decrees against every kind of abuse and directives to tie the church more tightly together. Bishops were ordered to take personal charge of the instruction and discipline of their clergy. Plurality—the holding of several church offices by a single person —was specifically condemned. Clerical elections, whether of cathedral deans, bishops, archbishops, or popes, were to be held with scrupulous regard for the regularities of canon law. The alienation of church property and lay interference in the affairs of the church were condemned. Clergy were not even to pay taxes outside the church. Measures were passed to restrict such doubtful practices as the sale of holy relics. Opinions at variance with those of the "one and universal Church" were solemnly condemned.

The Sacramental System

Perhaps the most significant measures of the council were those touching worship and theology, measures that gave to the spiritual purpose of the church the same sort of regularity that canon law and papal headship gave to its administration. The essence of that regularity was the sacramental system, officially approved by the Fourth Lateran Council and by it made the machinery of salvation. The council pronounced the doctrine of transubstantiation, officially declaring that, in the ceremony of the Mass, the emblems of the bread and wine were changed into the actual body and blood of Christ. Further, the council decreed that every Christian must confess his sins to an ordained priest at least once a year, and receive the Eucharist (the Holy Supper of the Mass) at least once a year. The effect of these decrees was to emphasize that through the sacraments, and only through them, could man attain salvation—and the sacraments could be administered only by the church. Thus every Christian was bound to the church in the very hope of his salvation.

The sacramental system had a long and tangled history stretching back into the early church and involving nearly all the complexities of medieval theology. Most simply, sacraments were sacred acts; more properly, they were sacred ceremonies or rituals intended to convey the grace of God to man. Originally numerous, such ceremonies had, by the opening of the thirteenth century, been reduced in general usage to seven, one of the favorite symbolic numbers of medieval theology. These were: baptism, confirmation, marriage, extreme unction, holy orders, penance, and the Eucharist. Five of the sacraments were to be taken only once in a lifetime. Of these baptism, confirmation, and extreme unction were universal, while marriage pertained to the laity and holy orders to the clergy.

The sacrament of baptism was based upon the assumption of universal human guilt, the doctrine of original sin. Through baptism an infant, already stained by his inheritance of sin, was able to share in the grace of God. It was the rite signifying his membership in the Christian community. Confirmation was the parallel rite, usually administered when the communicant was about twelve, by which the grace of baptism was literally "confirmed." An important and solemn ceremony, it could be administered only by a bishop. Its significance lay in the full acceptance of Christian responsibility. As the church attended man's birth with baptism and his coming of age with confirmation, so it attended his last hours with the ceremony of extreme unction. Consisting of the anointment of a dying person with consecrated oil, this "last rite" removed all the vestiges of sin and prepared him for the eternity he faced so imminently.

In earlier times marriage had been an essentially civil matter to which the church simply gave its blessing. But the blessing of the church came more and more to define the ceremony itself and marriage was sanctified. The bond between man and wife came to symbolize the bond between Christ and his church and to be regarded, therefore, as indissoluble. From the tenth century on, the control of marriage by the church became normal; thus the church brought within its scope the whole area of domestic relations.

The sacrament of holy orders set the priest apart from ordinary men and the hierarchy of the church apart from the order of secular society. Again, holy orders could be conferred only by a bishop, thus attesting the extreme seriousness of the sacrament. There were several degrees of holy orders and a man or woman might be a member of the clergy without having priestly orders. (This was generally true of the monastic clergy.) But the essence of holy orders was the power of the priest, whether that of the pope or that of the village parson. By virtue of his office, the priest could forgive sins and dispense God's grace. In this sense the priest was the church, armed with its immense powers. Its sacraments were administered by its priests, and in the ordinary life of the medieval Christian the office of the priest was most securely attached to the sacraments of penance and the Eucharist.

The sacrament of penance was fundamentally a bridge between the grace of God and the basic human condition of sinfulness. Christianity, from its beginnings, was laden with a sense of guilt, rising from its belief in human imperfection. In the early church it was a regular practice to confess one's sins publicly and do public penance. This continued to be the practice until, in the sixth, seventh, and eighth centuries, the missionary activity of the Irish monks introduced the idea of private confession, i.e., auricular confession, literally "into the ear" of a priest. While most of the practices of Celtic Christianity were abandoned, this confessional concept was retained. For most people the practice of private confession was infinitely superior to a public proclamation of guilt. Even the confessional priest was bound to honor the sinful confidences revealed to him.

As private confession became general practice in the church, the whole concept of penance grew. The power of the priestly office was sufficient to remove the guilt of the confessed sinner. But even after the damning guilt was removed, God still exacted punishment—the temporal consequence of sin. This gave rise to the doctrine of purgatory, the belief that there exists after death a place of punishment, intermediate between hell and heaven, in which the souls of the dead are literally "purged" of the stains of sin still attaching to them. The idea of purgatory had long existed in the church. It had frequently been part of the doctrine of the extremist sects, but by the thirteenth century it was generally accepted by theologians as part of the mystic geography of the afterlife. More immediately, the repentent sinner could suffer his punishment, in part at least, in this life. Indeed, it was normal practice for the confessional priest to assign a penance after absolution. This might consist of prayer, fasting, or almsgiving. A common penance was to say a designated number of prayers over a certain period of time. Another was pilgrimage. The concept of alms was extended to include very material fines, to be paid in money or property, for serious spiritual transgressions.

A related concept, that of indulgence, attached itself to the sacrament of penance. The indulgence was simply a substitute penalty for assigned penance. The full doctrine as well as the wholesale abuse of indulgences came later. During the Crusades, an indulgence might be granted to a crusader as a blanket removal of the punishment for sin. As the crusading spirit waned, the idea of indulgences remained. The concept was supported by the "treasury of merit," the belief that the excess grace of Christ, the apostles, the saints, and of pious people of every age was at the disposal of the church and that the church could tap this reserve of holiness for the benefit of the penitent sinner. Indulgences, drawn like a bank draft against the treasury of merit, came to be sold by the church as a substitute for penance to those who could afford to buy them. Such a doctrine was easily misunderstood and even more easily abused. Many honest churchmen were doubtful about it from the beginning. But greedy indulgence sellers, promising wonders for their wares, a gullible public eager to buy "tickets to heaven," and a papacy chronically in need of money were sufficient to maintain the popularity of indulgences.

The remaining sacrament, the Eucharist, was the most important of all, for it was the central rite of the Mass that formed the basic medieval Catholic church service. To celebrate the Mass was the most common duty of the priest, and it was the sacrament which most clearly defined the priestly office. The sacrament, strictly speaking, was that part of the Mass in which the emblems of the Last Supper were taken by the priest and worshipers. This was the most solemn moment in which a stupendous miracle took place. Whether in the impressive pontifical High Mass, performed by the pope himself, or in the humble service of the village church, the miracle was the same: the repetition of Christ's sacrifice upon the cross. When the officiating priest spoke the words of Christ, ". . . this is my body . . . ," the consecrated wine and bread of the service were transformed into His blood and body. Through the ritual partaking of these elements the worshiper could actually take within himself the divinity of Christ. The form of the Mass changed in details over the medieval centuries. By the High Middle Ages the communicant normally received only the bread or consecrated wafer while the officiating priest received the cup. On no doctrine did the church lavish so much symbolism, nor was any doctrine so encased in theology as this.

The sacramental monopoly was the core of the great spiritual authority of the church: excommunication was the withdrawal of the sacraments from an individual; interdict was the suspension of some or all the sacraments in a district, even a kingdom. No secular punishment was so generally dreaded, neither death nor imprisonment. Since the sacraments were essential to salvation, they constituted the most important consideration in the life of the medieval Christian.

Innocent III and the Secular Monarchs

The Fourth Lateran Council was an impressive demonstration of the power of the pope within the church. It was equally demonstrative of the political power that Innocent III and the papacy wielded in European affairs. Among its several acts were the deposition of Otto IV, the emperor of Germany, and the condemnation of Magna Carta on behalf of Innocent's vassal, King John of England.

For more than twenty years Innocent III had worked to elevate the papal above the royal powers of Europe. He claimed feudal suzerainty over Poland, Norway, Sweden, Denmark, Bohemia, Bulgaria, Serbia, Armenia, the Spanish Kingdom of Aragon, the Kingdom of Jerusalem, and the Byzantine Empire. Even the great states at the "core" of Western Europe did not escape the political influence of this vigorous pope. He inherited what had become a traditional enmity toward the German empire. In the year before Innocent became pope, Emperor Henry VI died. His scheme to unite the Norman south of Italy (his wife's inheritance) with the German empire came to nothing, and Innocent III did everything to perpetuate this division of the empire by supporting the various enemies of German unity. Moreover, Innocent claimed the right to decide between the claimants to the imperial throne in the civil war that followed Henry's death.

After delaying as long as possible he chose the Welf, Otto of Brunswick. But when Otto revived the traditional imperial policy in Italy, Innocent excommunicated him and commended the young Hohenstaufen heir, Frederick II. In return for papal support, Frederick made sweeping concessions of power to Innocent. As we have seen, however, this victory was also short-lived, since Frederick II in turn revived the traditional imperial policy with its opposition to papal claims of supremacy. It was left to Innocent's successors of the mid-thirteenth century to see the hated empire laid in ruins.

The Angevin-Capetian rivalry gave Innocent the chance to intervene in France and England. Realizing that Philip Augustus' ambition and ability were more dangerous to the papacy than John's weakness, he tended to favor the English king. As we saw in the preceding chapter, Innocent failed to impose his authority on Philip Augustus; he was more successful with John. His opportunity came when John capped his tyranny by interfering in a disputed election of the Archbishop of Canterbury. Innocent rejected all the claims in this complex case, including John's, and imposed his own choice of archbishop upon the cathedral chapter, the English bishops, and the king. John refused to accept the papal appointment, attacked the English church, and was promptly excommunicated. Innocent declared John's subjects freed of their obedience to him and offered the English throne to Philip Augustus. John found himself friendless and his kingdom about to be invaded. He capitulated by restoring the church property he had taken, accepting all Innocent's conditions, and rendering homage to the pope for his kingdom and acknowledging himself a papal vassal. It was the medieval papacy's greatest political victory and raised Innocent to the pinnacle of his power.

Medieval Popular Religion

At the same time that the church under Innocent III was winning its temporal victories, it was losing an even more significant spiritual battle against the ingrained paganism of popular religion. At best, the official theology of the church had never penetrated much below the surface of society; and the church had always had to fight for the enforcement of even the forms of religion. More often than not this fight was lost at the parish level, and the ceremonies, the theology, and the traditions of the church were grotesquely blended with the older, local pagan traditions of the people.

The source of this critical problem was the weakness of the parish priesthood. Priests were often immoral and even "criminous." The records of parish visitations are filled with charges of clerical drunkenness, lechery, theft, and brawling. Marriage and concubinage were prevalent among village priests. Even when the parish clergy were honest, moral, and well-intentioned—as the great majority probably were—they were still almost universally ignorant and untrained. The church had never been able to win the battle of investiture at the local level and the appointment of parish priests remained in the hands of secular lords. It is true that one of the primary duties of the bishop was to examine, confirm, instruct, and discipline local priests. But this task, difficult enough under the best of circumstances, was virtually impossible when the bishop was a busy nobleman, concerned for his lands and feudal obligations and himself often as unlettered as his parish clergy. Even more significantly, the medieval church, like medieval society generally, was split by the decisive line that divided the noble from the non-noble. It is true that the church always held out the hope of preferment to men of ability, regardless of their origin, and that many men of humble birth became important ecclesiastical lords. But more generally the parish priest was of humble birth and the bishop almost invariably a nobleman. The priest thus was separated from his immediate superior by a difference of kind rather than of degree.

In the hands of the parish clergy the ceremonies of the church, even its essential sacraments, slipped easily from religion into magic. The often subtle distinctions between orthodoxy and heresy were blurred by the simplicity of the clergy.

One of the most important aspects of popular religion was the veneration of sacred relics. From an early time in the history of the church the belongings, clothes, even the bones of holy men, had been cherished, and had brought fame to the churches that housed them. The belief in relics was by no means confined to the peasant. Knights bound sacred relics into the handles of their swords and great lords made presents of them to favored churches. With the Crusades, the holy places of the east were opened and the traffic in relics flourished. Hundreds of churches boasted such mementos as finger bones of the apostles, skulls of martyrs, splinters from the true cross, even the milk of the Virgin Mary! Enlightened clergy preached and reasoned in vain against the excess of zeal for relics.

Related to the veneration of relics was the cult of the saints. Many of these were simply faded local gods, transmuted and Christianized; others were historical personages whose virtuous lives or spectacular martyrdoms fixed them in popular imagination; still others were the personages of Scripture who became easily confused with pseudo-history, tradition, and romance. What commended the saints was their power of intercession. God was always a remote and dangerous force; even the appealing personality of the historical Jesus was obscured by medieval theology, popular superstition, and ignorance. Men were so preoccupied with their own sins that they tended rather to see Jesus as a righteous judge than a compassionate Saviour. The saints came to represent intermediate powers who could be approached, reasoned with, even bribed and threatened, to speak on one's behalf before the eternal tribunal. There were specifically local saints, saints of trades and professions, saints for every activity of life from travel and a good-night's sleep to the begetting of children. The thousands of saints' lives and stories that abound in the literature of the Middle Ages attest to their popularity. Of all the saints, none was more popular, more universal, more varied in function than the Virgin Mary. Popular imagination made her Queen of Heaven, the universal mother who could soften the heart of her Son for the sake of sinful humanity. St. Bernard wrote in a sermon, "Dost thou fear the divine majesty in the Son? Wilt thou find an advocate before Him? Flee to Mary: in her humanity is pure. The Son will listen to the mother, and the Father to the Son."[1] In a society that still honored the monastic life, she appeared as the very embodiment of the virtue of holy virginity. She was the giver of life as Eve had been the giver of death. She was enshrined in songs, stories, and art.

Heresy and Heresy Hunters

While Innocent III had struggled to assert his control over the church and the secular powers, various heretical groups became increasingly numerous and popular. There were striking similarities both in their doctrines and in the dangers they presented to the church. These heresies flowed, curiously enough, from many of the same sources as the orthodox reform movements of the twelfth century. The failure of monasticism, the unworthiness of many clergy, the preoccupation of the church with political goals and material administration, led many men into the various reforming orders; others were led beyond the legitimate avenues of protest and reform into heresy.

The profound economic and social changes which were beginning to affect medieval society contributed to the creation and spread of heresy. The church had failed to meet the challenge of the town. The great increase in the number of the poor and the ruthless concentration of wealth and power in the hands of guild masters produced tensions that the church did not, or could not, resolve. For one thing, the church was itself too deeply involved in medieval economy: it was the greatest landholder in western Europe, and in the rising towns its enormous financial resources fostered an alliance with the moneyed and propertied classes. Who was to champion the cause of social-urban reform? The concentration of people in towns quickened the intellectual currents of medieval society. Men

1. New Schaff-Herzog *Encyclopedia of Religious Knowledge*. VII, 221.

talked and questioned more freely; exchange and diversity stimulated questions, and the church provided no adequate answers. From the growing schools that flourished in the towns came intellectuals with their doubts and questions. Medieval heresy was, in short, an urban phenomenon.

As the routes of trade were once more established, heretical ideas spread along them from town to town. The germs of the old heresies of the third and fourth centuries had stayed alive in the east. They began to travel the trade routes to the west—up the Danube valley to Hungary, from Syria and Greece to northern Italy, along the Alpine and river routes to southern France, to the Rhine valley and ultimately to Flanders and England. In no area was the conjunction of ancient heretical ideas and local conditions more productive of heresy than in the south of France. There, in the town of Albi, originated the most important heretical sect of the twelfth and thirteenth centuries, the Albigensians.

The Albigensians revived the old Manichaean dualism that had come into early Christianity from Persian philosophy and theology, and so mightily tempted St. Augustine. They conceived of a constant struggle between a god of light, goodness, and spirit and a god of darkness, evil, and matter. Man was caught in this struggle: his spirit pertained to light; his flesh, to darkness. Out of this extreme dualism the Albigensians preached a doctrine of purification: they advocated celibacy; refused to eat meat; and would not take oaths or tell lies. They rejected the existing forms of society—the administration of justice, capital punishment, even war! In conventional religion they saw the servant of evil: the church, with its wealth and power, its material concerns and organization, they rejected completely. Since it was the aim of every believer to gain perfection and since this could be attained only by extreme purification, the group was frequently called the Cathari, the "pure." It was darkly rumored that those who gained perfection sometimes took their own lives lest they fall back into the toils of the flesh. The logic and simplicity of their doctrine, the purity and virtue of their lives, and their zeal in converting others, spread the Albigensian heresy like a brush fire. The Albigensians performed the services of charity that the church would not perform. They even set up their own schools. In some towns and cities the orthodox clergy were driven out completely. The Albigensian heresy spread in every direction, even across the Alps to Italy, in the very shadow of the papacy.

As this contagious heresy spread, it became confused with other similar movements and groups. The most important of these was the

Poor Men of Lyons, founded in the late twelfth century by Peter Waldo, a wealthy merchant. Peter gave all his money to the poor and was joined by others who followed his example. They traveled about barefoot, dressed in coarse and simple garments. When they could they helped the poor, but primarily they preached from Scripture in the language of the people, and with a fervor that won them audiences everywhere. The Waldensians, as they were called after their founder, gained the status of a lay order and official recognition by the church. But they remained suspect, the clergy being almost universally hostile to them because of their preaching and the damaging example of their poverty and zeal. Gradually the Waldensians drifted over the line into heresy.

For almost half a century before Innocent III, the church had fought a losing battle against the heresies; and Innocent inherited its failure. Thousands of people, whole districts and towns in southern France and northern Italy, were under the control of heretical groups. In many areas they were joined by secular lords, some of whom were probably stirred by lofty motives. Their other motives were the desire to confiscate rich church properties and overturn established order. The spiritual threats and weapons of the church were of no avail. In 1208 Innocent III took the ultimate step of proclaiming the Albigensian Crusade against these heretics. The call to holy war was answered by the hungry baronage of northern Europe and whatever high, spiritual purpose the Crusade might have had was lost in the bloody scramble for lands. Heretics and non-heretics alike were murdered and their estates taken. The feudal lords of the south made common cause with the heretic communities for their very survival. But the force of the Crusade was too great. Towns fell and districts were overrun; order disintegrated. The flourishing agriculture and trade of this whole prosperous region were destroyed along with its rich secular culture. As the control of the church failed and the momentum of the Crusade slackened, the shrewd and watchful Philip Augustus of France began to move. What was left of the Crusade was taken over by the French crown and within half a century the Capetian monarchy was solidly established in the south of France. The Albigensian Crusade had destroyed almost everything but heresy; the violence of the Crusade scattered the heretics all over Europe, where their doctrines blended with a hundred local causes to generate new heresies with which the Christian community was beset for centuries. Even in the blasted land of the south of France heresy continued, for neither the church nor the state had removed the causes from which it sprang.

Many of the causes responsible for the heretical crisis of the High Middle Ages were also responsible for the founding of the mendicant or "begging" orders, chiefly those of St. Francis (1182–1226) and St. Dominic (1170–1221).

St. Francis was the son of a rich merchant in the Italian town of Assisi. Quite suddenly he experienced a deep personal conversion, turned his back on the worldly life he had known, and resolved to follow the example of Christ. Like Christ, he dedicated himself to poverty and service: "He suffered to see any poorer than himself." He regarded having possessions as no better than theft from the needy. To those needy he dedicated his life—to the helpless, the hopeless, the diseased. He provided for them what he could. He begged, worked, and prayed for them; and he preached to them the purest, simplest, and most naive gospel that Christianity had known in a thousand years. Francis was himself as magnificently simple as his gospel. He gloried in God. He saw himself as "God's troubador." We are told that though often hungry, he was never sad. He sang and preached to the birds and beasts, and indeed, all things in nature drew his love, "our brother the sun," "our sister the moon," "brother wind," "brother fire," "our mother the earth," and even "our sister, the death of the body, from which no man escapeth."

The power of his example brought him disciples; but he was bewildered by them. He had nothing but his example and the charge of Jesus to give his disciples:

". . . and [He] gave them power and authority over all devils, and to cure diseases. And he sent them to preach the kingdom of God, and to heal the sick. And he said unto them, Take nothing for your journey, neither staves, nor script, neither bread, neither money; neither have two coats apiece (Luke IX:1-3).

. . .

If any man will come after me, let him deny himself, and take up his cross, and follow me. For whosoever will save his life shall lose it: and whosoever will lose his life for my sake shall find it. For what is a man profited, if he shall gain the whole world, and lose his own soul (Matthew 16:24-26).

Innocent III, troubled with heretics, many of whom were suspiciously like Francis in beliefs and behavior, gave his sanction reluctantly to the order that was already forming around Francis. The Franciscan Order was, to a remarkable degree, the extension of its founder. He insisted that it be a minor order and he called his followers the *Fratres Minores,* "Little Brothers," hence the term "friar." They were to be neither monks nor priests, yet they were like both. They lived under the same kind of vows as monks, but not in monasteries. They preached like priests and lived in the world, yet they had no parishes and could not, at least originally, administer the sacraments.

The Franciscans were essentially an order of service; they avoided the spiritual exercises of the ascetic and the isolation of the hermit. They avoided learning and wealth; Francis was so ardent in his pursuit of "Our Lady Poverty" that he forbade his order even to own corporate property. The brown-robed, bare-footed Franciscans became a part of European society. Where they could they earned their living and gave from it to the poor. Where they could not work they humbly begged. While Francis himself loved nature and the countryside, his order was essentially an urban one, for it was in the crowded, squalid towns that the work of Christ most needed to be done. The slums of the growing cities bred not only poverty and disease, but heresy, and here the church found the Francisans a more effective weapon against heretics than fire or arms. Heretics inveighed against the wealth, luxury, and power of the church: they condemned its ceremonials and lack of social service. The Franciscans were a living refutation of these charges.

Yet the very success of the Franciscans was to lead them away from the ideals of their founder. The Franciscans were too valuable to the church to be allowed to go without rules and order, and eventually the papacy insisted that they adopt a formal rule of discipline. From then on the order ceased to be really "Franciscan." The evangelical example of St. Francis became increasingly suspect. Property and wealth flowed into the order and before the end of the thirteenth century there were more than a thousand Franciscan houses. The mendicant order dedicated to poverty and service had become an order of wealth and learning. Bitter factions grew up and, ironically, the faction which adhered most faithfully to the precepts of St. Francis—the Spiritual Franciscans—was declared heretical and hounded out of existence.

The Franciscans had become heresy fighters by fortunate coincidence. The other great mendicant order, the Order of St. Dominic, was designed from the beginning to do this work. (The Latin form of the order's name, *Dominicanes,* was popularly split into the sinister pun *Domini canes,* "the hounds of God.")

St. Dominic was an aristocratic and learned Spanish cleric. For many years he worked in the heresy-ridden towns of the south of France, and witnessed the horror and the failure of the Albigensian Crusade. In the year following the death of Innocent III Dominic proposed a new order, which was confirmed by Innocent's successor, Honorius III. It was called officially the Friars Preachers, and its special task was the conversion of heretics. Dominic was convinced that heresy flowed primarily from ignorance and that it had to be combated with persuasion and reconversion. St. Dominic lacked the personal magnetism of St. Francis, but he made up for this by his keen intellect and genius for organization. The Dominicans were from the outset preachers and theologians; they traveled widely preaching in the language of the locality. Combined with their dedication, their intellectual accomplishments made them the foremost learned order of the later Middle Ages.

Well-organized, zealous, and learned, the Order of St. Dominic, dedicated to the missionary conversion of heretics, put itself at the disposal of the papacy and so became identified with the most infamous institution of the medieval church, the papal Inquisition. The Inquisition was the end product of a series of failures and limited success in dealing with heresy. In spite of every effort, including the pious example of the Franciscans and the preaching of the Dominicans, heresy not only remained, it grew. The Inquisition was instituted in 1233 by Pope Gregory IX and rapidly became international in scope. Wherever heresy, or witchcraft, or evangelical piety appeared—even the vaguest charge or suspicion from the most irresponsible source—the Inquisition reached.

The word "inquisition" has an innocent enough meaning, simply "inquiry." In practice, however, the Inquisition became a most fearful instrument of tyranny: when it moved into an area, all heretics were called to confess and repent. Those who did so within the thirty days of "grace" were absolved, given light penances, and released; those who did not were then hunted down. All faithful believers were adjured to denounce them; all charges were accepted (the denunciation of two witnesses was enough, including the testimony of children, criminals, heretics themselves, and the jackal pack of professional informers that inevitably followed in its wake). Trials, held in complete disregard for the normal rules of equity that held even in the crudest village courts, were set up so that the accused person was never confronted with his accusers. He was not even told who they were; he was permitted only to submit a list of his personal enemies, and if any accuser appeared among them his testimony was thrown out. The accused was charged with his crimes and persuaded to confess. If he persisted in his putative heresy, he was taken to prison where he was kept in filth, hunger, and isolation until he was ready to confess. As the Inquisition took hold, the use of torture became routine. The pain of fire or rack or lash would frequently bring confession—only to have it repudiated. Sometimes torture was applied again and again until a prisoner would have to be carried or dragged before the Tribunal (high court), every joint of his body pulled apart by the pressure of the rack, or his feet burned into shapeless lumps of charred flesh. The heretic who persisted, or survived, was turned over to the secular powers for execution, normally burning at the stake.

THE CHURCH AND THE WORLD OF LEARNING

The Renaissance of the Twelfth Century

The renaissance of the twelfth century stemmed largely from the combination of circumstances that made possible the recovery of much of the learning of the classical world. The Crusades, the Christian reconquest of the Mediterranean, and the general revival of trade brought western Europeans once more in contact with the sources of classical learning. To the minimal remnants of classical learning preserved by the church in the west were added the riches of the Byzantine-Greek tradition of the eastern empire, the Saracen-Hellenic tradition of the Mediterranean, and the Saracen-Hellenic-Judaic tradition of Spain.

From the age of the church fathers to the sixteenth century, medieval literacy was chiefly Latin, since this was the only language available to the west in a stable, written form. In this long period a number of individual writers had used the language with style and polish—Augustine, Boethius, Bede—and there had been brief interludes of its more general literary use at the courts of Charlemagne, Alfred, and Otto the Great. But over the centuries it had lost most of the elegancies of its golden age; it was simplified, perhaps vulgarized, but it retained the vitality of a language in use.

The chief use of Latin was religious, since the church was the only major medieval institution that found continuous literacy necessary. The schools of the Middle Ages were almost exclusively church schools. At first they were largely monastery schools, but from an early period the bishops began to establish cathedral schools. As the role of the bishops in the church became more significant, their schools became the chief centers of learning. And as secular society developed an increasing need for educated men, these schools began to serve its needs as well as those of the church. It was a handful of cathedral schools—notably those at Paris, Chartres, Orléans and Canterbury—that led the classical revival of the twelfth century. In these schools teacher-scholars like the famous Englishman, John of Salisbury at Chartres—taught a vigorous Latin style. But beyond their interest in the forms of Latin, these scholars revived the study of an expanded canon of classical Roman authors.

The earlier Middle Ages had carried over from ancient classicism a pitifully small handful of actual works. The early Christian frame of reference had no place for the great bulk of ancient writing. Much that was retained was distorted; many works were lost or scattered, preserved by the incidental interest of individual scholars. As the localism of the early Middle Ages began to disappear under the impact of the Crusades and revived trade, many of these works came to light again.

During the long period of relative quiescence of learning in the west, the Greek heritage had been kept alive in Constantinople. Byzantine libraries contained thousands of manuscripts by classic and Hellenistic writers in every field of ancient knowledge. Byzantine scholars had studied and commented on these works for centuries, building up a huge body of critical literature. In the course of the twelfth century, crusaders, pilgrims, and merchants began to visit Constantinople and the east in numbers. The treasure house of Byzantine-Greek learning was now open to the west.

The Mohammedans, in their conquest of the east, had swept up large portions of the classical intellectual heritage along with lands and booty. In the vast empire of Islam this tradition blended with the currents of Persian astronomy and metaphysics and Hindu science and mathematics to produce the impressive works of Arabic science, mathematics, medicine, and philosophy. In Spain, at the antipode of the Saracen world, the medieval Arabic intellectual culture found one of its most significant focal points.

In the rich and tolerant Saracen courts and flourishing cities of Spain, Arabic learning met and blended with the vigorous tradition of medieval Judaism. Through a checkered political history, through dispersion and persecution, Judaism had preserved its spiritual-intellectual inheritance. The synagogue was a fixture of every Jewish community, as much a school as a center of worship. Within these schools Jewish scholars had labored over the centuries to understand and explain their holy law and Scripture. The result of these labors was an elaborate tapestry of commentary known as the Talmud. Inevitably, Talmudic scholars were led from religion and sacred legalism to commentary upon the bits and pieces of a hundred other disciplines, and ultimately to philosophy. In the permissive atmosphere of Moslem Spain, Jewish learning and philosophy flourished. It enriched and

was enriched by the diverse currents of Islamic thought. Jews became famous physicians, teachers, and scholars. Their wit and learning were
matched by the salons of wealthy and learned patrons, both Jewish and
Moslem.

Moslem Spain produced the greatest of Hebrew scholars, Moses ben
Maimun (1135-1204), known to the Christian world as Maimonides, possibly the most learned man of the twelfth century. He traveled widely,
finally settling in Egypt as the court physician of Saladin. But his ideas
traveled more widely still. He was not only a physician, but a scientist, a
Talmudic scholar, and philosopher. Before he reached middle age he had
already written the most renowned religious work of medieval Judaism, a
massive, multivolume commentary on the entire law and tradition of his
people. But the work that was to bring his opinions to bear most heavily
upon both Islam and Christianity was a later one, the *Guide to the Per-
plexed*. It was a curious book, at the same time a tract against Jewish
heresy, a commentary upon Scripture, and a keenly reasoned work of
philosophy. Its influence can be traced in many of the crucial arguments of
Christian scholasticism. Maimonides maintained that reason and revealed
religion are not enemies. He saw God as the supreme intelligence and
Aristotelian first cause. He rejected the cruelty of original sin and
insisted that each man carried a sufficient burden in his own sin without adding to it the onus of the sin of his ancestors. He moved a step
beyond the perplexity of St. Augustine to hold that the human will must
be free in its choice of either good or evil. The omniscience of God must
foresee man's choice, but must not be thought to determine it. He saw no
particular reason to hope for personal immortality; the soul of man comes
from God to man and returns to God, but there is no continuity of that
momentary human personality into eternity.

At the very time that western Christendom was approaching the intellectual maturity of the High Middle Ages, these vigorous traditions of
nonwestern thought challenged and stimulated the intellect of the west. In
Constantinople and the Near East, in Sicily and Naples, in the zone of
contact between Christian and Saracen in southern France and northern
Spain, Christian-Catholic scholars came under the spell of the "new learning." As they learned they began to translate the works of Arab and Jewish
scientists, commentators, and philosophers; but most of all of the long-lost
writings of the Greeks, and none more eagerly than the works of Aristotle.
These clumsy, early translations were seized upon and eagerly copied. They
quickly made their way across Europe. The translations increased in accu-

racy and number and the west was inundated with an alien flood of learning, along with considerable nonsense and superstition to add to its own.

For almost a thousand years the core of western learning had been theology. It was not only the "queen of the sciences," it was virtually the only "science." Thus, the impact of this intellectual revolution was most profoundly felt in theo-philosophy. The effects of Arab science and Hebrew learning were disturbing, but at the center of the revolution was Aristotle. In the course of the twelfth century practically the whole corpus of Aristotelian philosophy—his scientific, logical, ethical, and metaphysical works—became available to western scholars, along with the learned Arab and Jewish commentaries and adaptations of the Aristotelian system. It is almost impossible to overemphasize their effect. The recovery of Aristotle gave the west a countersystem to its own rather limited and static theo-philosophy—a system created and established before Christianity and completely outside the Judao-Christian tradition. In many serious respects it was at variance with Christianity as, for example, on personal immortality, on the eternity of the natural order, and, of course, on the whole question of Christology. Yet, Aristotle's impressive knowledge was coupled with a rigorously logical methodology that seemed to bring order to the phenomenal world and within which all experience could find a place. Aristotelian knowledge, and the categories which he had devised for it, became an authoritative canon. Aristotelian logic became an intellectual tool of almost universal use. It was the "modern" method and the scholarly men of the twelfth century mastered in it detail. Inevitably they applied it to Christian doctrine.

The preoccupation with Aristotelian logic led to one of the most basic controversies of medieval intellectualism, the nominalist-realist controversy. It was an echo of the ancient divergence of Aristotle and Plato on the question of the nature of reality, an echo mounting to a reverberating din as the implications of Aristotle's system began once more to be examined. Aristotle had opposed Plato's famous "Doctrine of Ideas," holding that such ideas had no separate, governing existence, but were simply categories of logical classification, mere names. The medieval arch-Aristotelians followed their master to this conclusion and were thus called "nominalists" (from Latin *nomina,* "names"). The more traditional view of reality had come into Christianity from Plato through Christianized Neoplatonism and, since it comported so well with the transcendentalism of Christian thought, it became blended with it. As the Aristotelian nominalists sharpened their new definitions, they were opposed by the Platonic "realists"—those who held that the only realities were abstract generalities or "ideas." Throughout subsequent medieval history this argument raged. It involved every discipline and every field. But, as we shall see, its most important implications were for theology.

No figure is more representative of this turbulent age of intellectual excitement and philosophic revolution than Peter Abélard (1079–1142). Abélard was the eldest son of a Breton noble family, but turned his back upon his feudal inheritance to become a scholar. He studied and traveled, seeking out logicians and philosophers, and inevitably he drifted to Paris, already the rising intellectual center of France and northern Europe. He became a teacher of logic at the Cathedral School of Notre Dame and then, with equal aplomb, of theology. He was brilliant, attractive, and egotistical. His students loved him, flocked to his courses, and paid him handsomely in fees; his colleagues hated him. At the height of his fame, Abélard became involved with a young woman named Héloïse, a private pupil. Her family had Abélard attacked, beaten, and emasculated. He fled from Paris to become a monk, and continued to teach, dispute, and write. His brilliance led him to the verge of heresy.

Of his several books, one especially was condemned, his *Sic et Non,* "Yes and No." The book was an exercise manual in logic in which more than 150 propositions were listed with statements pro and con, taken from authorities. Innocent enough! However, the propositions were all theological and religious and the authorities were the church fathers, the decrees of the church, and Scripture itself. Its author twisted evidence, loaded propositions, and—while he drew no specific conclusions—encouraged his reader to question religious authority. On the basis of this and other works, and because of his attitudes generally, Abélard was censured by the church in an attack led by the formidable St. Bernard of Clairvaux. Before the censure could take punitive form Abélard died. He had articulated one of the most serious problems of his time: the conflict of faith and knowledge.

The church already faced the criticism of mystics and social-revolutionary heretics. Was it to face once more, as in the fourth century, the threat of intellectual schism? Recognizing the strength of these new currents of thought, the church decided to turn them to its own advantage. Instead of courting the dangerous enmity of intellectualism by rejecting it, the church would seek to control it. This compromise provoked considerable criticism from within the church—St. Bernard, among others, was strongly opposed to it. But while the police powers of the church remained alert for the logician who encroached too boldly on cardinal doctrines, the church by and large accepted the challenge of the new thought; and so made possible the brilliant accomplishments of the medieval scholastics.

In the century following the death of Abélard the dialectic methodology that he loved so well was perfected. The study of Aristotle quickened interest in other areas of classical knowledge. An expanding society called insistently for greater and more varied intellectual skills.

Thus the revival of ancient authorities and the stimulus of Saracen and Judaic works led to the systematic study of medicine in the Mediterranean lands. The first important European center of these studies was Salerno, largely due to the patronage of Emperor Frederick II. Branching out from Salerno, other centers were soon established.

About the same time, the Italian city of Bologna became the center for the systematic study of Roman law. This had continued to be applied, though in a very fragmentary and simplified fashion, in the Mediterranean lands where Roman influence was most tenacious; but by the mid-twelfth century several scholars had revived the Code of Justinian and were studying the Roman legal system as a whole. These scholars developed a method and approach to their study that rivaled the popularity of the Aristotelian method and that attracted students from all over Europe. The impetus to the study of Roman law came not only from the intellectual attractions of the system, but also from the possibility of its practical application. The revival of trade and communications, the development of national states, and the revived sense of broad territorial sovereignty called for a "new" law. Neither the personal code of feudalism nor the varying bodies of local custom could satisfy these new needs. The Roman law, however, offered a logical, legal system created for the very kind of socio-political order toward which Europe was moving once more. Men trained in the Roman law found positions in national courts and city councils. We have seen the part they played in the growth of royal absolutism.

Paralleling the interest in Roman law was the attempt to rationalize the law of the church. About the middle of the twelfth century, Gratian, a learned monk at Bologna, compiled a work entitled *Concordantia discordantium canonum*. "The Harmonizing of Conflicting Canons," usually referred to simply as the *Decretum*. This succeeded in reducing the mass of canon law to a logical system which bears comparison with the *Corpus Juris Civilis*. Its study became extremely popular. Education in canon law was as sure a means to church preferment as education in the Roman law was to a career at court in the secular states.

In spite of the appeal of law and medicine, theology remained the most popular and revered study. The church was still the most commanding institution of Europe, and the cure of the soul the most abiding concern of men.

On the eve of the thirteenth century the framework of medieval scholasticism was complete. A logical methodology based upon Aristotle was generally accepted. The standard texts and authorities were established. The three great learned professions of medicine, law, and theology were already solidly based. It remained only to supply for medieval learning an appropriate institutional setting. This was the institution of the university, one of the truly unique contributions of the Middle Ages to the history of western man.

The Rise of the Universities and Medieval University Life

The universities began as private concerns. They were a practical answer to the problem of managing the instruction of large groups of people in some systematic way. The earliest universities were at Bologna and Paris, and the subsequent form of university organization, in southern and northern Europe, respectively, grew from these two early centers. In both instances the university was modeled closely upon the organization of the guild.

Thousands of students were attracted to Bologna to study civil and canon law. In order to protect themselves from exploitation—high rents, bad food, and even local police powers—they formed a student organization. This was called *universitas,* a Latin word often used as a general term for either guild or commune. This student corporation was highly successful as a bargaining instrument, so much so that it began to control not only the environment of student life, but the curriculum and the faculty as well. This body set the fees for courses; it ruled on how courses were to be taught, the length of lecture time, and frequency of examinations; a professor could be fined if he were absent from class, if he held class too long, if he digressed from the subject. For protection against their students the professors formed their own guild of masters and between these two bodies they established the government which was the ultimate form of the University of Bologna. It was given legal status by a grant of Frederick Barbarossa in 1158; the University of Padua was formed in 1222 by the secession of a group of students and faculty from Bologna. Other Italian universities founded in the thirteenth century, as well as schools at Salamanca in Spain and Montpellier in the south of France, took the Bolognese form.

The organization of the University of Paris grew out of the cathedral school of Notre Dame. This school, staffed by cathedral canons, was already organized as a "faculty." In the course of the twelfth century the number of teachers and courses expanded beyond the limits of the cathedral school. Masters and students congregated across the Seine from the little island on which the cathedral stands, on the "left bank," which came to be known as the "Latin quarter"; for Latin was the language of instruction. The overflow group of students and masters across the Seine maintained their close connection with the cathedral school. A guild of masters—including those at the cathedral school—was eventually formed and headed by a rector, and the association formally chartered as a university by Philip Augustus in 1200.

As the University of Bologna was noted for its courses in law, Paris became famous for theology. It attracted the finest scholastic minds in Europe and, like the faculty of a great university today, these men were not only teachers, but scholars. Their writings, disputations, and speculations made Paris the theological, and thus the intellectual, capital of Europe in the High Middle Ages. But Paris was also widely famed for its college and faculty of arts (what we might consider the undergraduate college). The prestige of Paris spread its influence broadly. Other French universities copied its organization and courses; a disaffected group of English students withdrew from Paris and formed the first English university of Oxford before the middle of the thirteenth century. Practically all the German universities were modeled on Paris.

The basic arts course of the medieval university, leading to the baccalaureate, or bachelor's degree, was the equivalent of the guild apprenticeship, the first prerequisite for entrance into the teachers' guild. It provided for instruction in the *trivium,* the three cardinal subjects of grammar, rhetoric and logic. All discourse was in Latin. The old, late Latin texts of Donatus and Priscian were the basic books of grammar, and the student was drilled in their contents as well as their application to general study. Rhetoric was learned in lectures and debate. Logic was based upon Aristotle and, to a lesser degree, upon other classical writers, and was employed as a method in all the subjects studied. The baccalaureate course in the medieval university was intensely practical—for in effect, the trivium consisted of important tool subjects: how to write, how to speak, and how to think.

Practically all university instruction was oral. Books were scarce and expensive. Parchment and even wax tablets were beyond the means of many students. Memory was exercised much more arduously than in modern university training. Often courses were taken two or three times so that nothing would be missed. The courses were organized in series of "lectures" (meaning "readings"). The professor "read" the basic text of the course—a practice unfortunately still not completely abandoned—and the students copied or memorized it as the professor read. He incorporated in his lecture the standard "glosses," or commentaries, on the work as well as his own interpretations. When the course was over the student had his own copy of the text either in his memory or in his notes. The normal arts curriculum took four or five years; the student took a number of courses, absorbed a body of learning, and learned to put it to use. He might travel about to several universities to get all the courses he wanted. The completion of the baccalaureate was a comprehensive examination on the material of the trivium. It was usually a grueling oral examination and might include disputation on set topics. For the successful candidate the apprenticeship was over and he was prepared to "commence" professional training (a concept we retain as part of the ritual of university graduation or "commencement").

The curriculum of the master's degree was the university equivalent of journeyman's training in a craft guild. Having "mastered" the basic skills and knowledge of his trade, the student was ready for more extensive learning. The master's program was organized around the *quadrivium,* consisting of the four disciplines of arithmetic, geometry, astronomy, and music. Together with the trivium, these formed the Seven Liberal Arts. Even with the expansion of learning in the twelfth century, much of the quadrivium still depended upon the old standard works of Boethius on arithmetic, astronomy, and music. But to these were added Moslem works in mathematics, the text of Euclid's geometry, and the *Almagest* of Ptolemy.[2]

Music was practiced in the church services where students, as clergy, were expected to chant and sing the many services of the religious calendar. It was also a theoretical discipline more akin to philosophy and mathe-

2. This book was the Arabic version of the astronomical theories of the second-century Alexandrian scientist, Claudius Ptolemy. It was of great importance to medieval science and learning, almost equally because of its great authority and its basic errors. Ptolemy rejected the earlier, correct Greek theory (heliocentric) that the sun is the center of the universe. His works argued for a geocentric or earth-centered universe, and he argued so persuasively that first Arabic and then Christian scholars accepted him with little question. His theories were not only the core of medieval astronomy, but were accepted by the theologians as the official Christian cosmology.

matics than to music in the modern sense. Here the theories of Aristotle were largely followed. Indeed, the study of Aristotle touched every subject in the master's course, and he was the ultimate authority of the medieval school. The master's course usually took four of five years and again might take the scholar to several universities. The end of the course was an examination, usually the defense of a thesis—some logical, metaphysical, or theological proposition which the candidate undertook to debate with a board of examiners. The thesis is still a fixture in university graduate study, even though its form has been completely changed. For the medieval master's candidate, the defense of the thesis was literally the proof of his proficiency in knowledge and method. If he satisfied the examiners he received the coveted degree, which was his license to teach the arts course, and represented his cooptation into the masters' circle of the teachers' guild.

Some scholars, in addition to the master's degree, or instead of it, took the course leading to one of the three professional degrees; the doctorates of law, medicine, or theology. These were, like the master's program, demanding disciplines, difficult, expensive, and time-consuming. The theological course took no less than eight years and frequently as long as twenty.

That the pinnacle of medieval education should have been theology is entirely appropriate. The church was more intimately connected with medieval learning than any other institution. The church, in its monastic and cathedral schools, had laid the foundations of the medieval university. Virtually every literate person in western Europe was a cleric. Moreover, the church had more need both to promote and to control literacy than any other institution. The vast and complex administrative, financial, and legal machinery of the church demanded men of learning. The far-ranging battle against the heresies of the twelfth and thirteenth centuries was most effectively waged with learning and argument. Further, the church had more cause to be wary of the untrammeled exercise of reason than any other institution, for its existence rested, in the final analysis, upon a theory and a body of conviction, a base more easily overturned by the logic of a scholar than the sword of a conqueror. Thus, as the universities came into existence, the church moved to control them.

Since the university faculties were made up chiefly of men in various religious orders the church, through the orders, maintained an important hold upon them. Not only the faculty but, by long tradition, the students of the typical university were members of the clergy. They received the tonsure; they were sworn, in theory, to clerical celibacy. They wore the clerical garb that is the remote ancestor of the academic dress still aired occasionally on modern university campuses. The clerical status of the university personnel gave the church an important means of control over them; it also gave to university faculty and students certain solid advantages. They were sometimes freed of local ecclesiastical control and given self-governing status by the church. Noted scholars were sometimes handsomely rewarded in church preferments. Both students and faculty could claim "benefit of clergy," which meant that they could be tried at law only in church courts.

The medieval student worked hard, lived meagerly, and took his pleasures when he could. His courses were formidable, demanding the highest intellectual discipline. The lecture halls were cold and drafty; there were seldom desks or chairs, and the students often sat on the straw-covered floor while they followed the spidery evolution of logical arguments through a classroom day of some eight hours. Some of the early colleges were founded to provide student living quarters, but there were always more students than places, and students were almost universally hard-pressed for funds. The rigor of their studies and their clerical status made it almost impossible for them to "work their way through college"; some few were able to secure "livings," usually nominal positions in local churches; some could depend upon their families; many were desperately poor.

Yet the very rigors of their life gave medieval university students a fierce sense of community. Their tattered robes and Latin speech became the proud marks of their profession. They were a truly cosmopolitan brotherhood, wandering about from one university to another, searching out famous masters or courses: Oxford, Paris, Bologna, Salamanca, Montpellier, Leipzig—the world of learning was undivided. The "wandering scholars" were very much a part of the wayfaring life of the Middle Ages. They traveled in small groups for protection. They worked and begged and—so we are told—they stole. They frequented inns and taverns when they could; monasteries, churches, barns, and haystacks when they could not. They lived by their sharp wits and sharp tongues and, if only for their footloose life, were universally suspect. Medieval society had not yet lost its parochial prejudices. A self-respecting cleric stayed put—away from the temptations of the strange and the unfamiliar. Yet, those very temptations were attractive to the wandering scholars.

There developed among this cheerful company a mock order. It had no formal membership, few rules, and great vitality. It was called the *Ordo Vagorum,* "the vagabond order," and was, by its very existence, a jibe at the traditional orders of the church. Like all good orders, it had its patron saint, the mythical St. Golias, a disreputable, shabby, drunken, gambling, irrepressible composite of all the virtues of the open road. His followers called themselves *Goliardi.*

Nearly all that survives of them is a body of their Latin verse, known as Goliardic poetry. Some of it is doggerel composed on the spot for a flagon of wine; some of it is among the finest of all Latin poetry; most of it is outrageous. Nothing was sacred to these versifiers—neither saints, nor sacraments, nor doctrines, nor the church itself. One famous Goliardic poem parodied the Apostles' Creed, placed in the mouth of a dying poet. Instead of believing "in God, the Father almighty, creator of heaven and earth; in Jesus Christ His only son," the poet, punster and cynic to the end, believes in dice

> That got me often bite and sup,
> And many a time hath had me drunk,
> And many a time delivered me
> From every stitch and every penny.

His thoughts turn not to his sins nor the hope of heaven but to

> Watch the roast turn on the spit,
> And the wine that's clear and green.
> Orléans, Rochelle, Auxerre . . .

and

> Paris, by my soul
> There was a girl there, she was fair. . . .

The thought of Resurrection does not intrigue him,

> Sir Priest, I chafe
> At thinking of that other life.
> I tell you, 'tis not worth a straw.
> And I would pray to the Lord God
> That he will in no kind of way
> *Resurrectionem* make of me. . . .[3]

Almost all the verse of the wandering scholars had this same bitter quality. Much of it turned to satire, especially satire of the church. Immoral and

3. Helen Waddell, *The Wandering Scholars,* by permission of Constable Publishers, London.

indecent the poets might be, but they had at least the virtue of honesty and the strength of their carnal convictions. They were merciless toward the hypocrisy of the well-fed monk, the well-horsed priest, and the venal bishop. In this sense the wandering scholars made common cause with the popular heretics to harass the church. Councils and synods and anathemas finally condemned the *Ordo Vagorum*. But medieval students continued to go from university to university; they sang their ribaldries; and their spirit was, in part, always the spirit of Golias—from John of Salisbury in the twelfth century to Erasmus in the sixteenth.

The Profession of Learning: Medieval Scholasticism

While the universities produced the disreputable votaries of Golias, they also produced the scholars who created, in the twelfth and thirteenth centuries, the impressive system of theology and philosophy known as Scholasticism.

In the generation after Abélard one of his students, Peter Lombard (*c.* 1100–1160), used his teacher's logical method—though not his irreverent attitudes—in preparing the most famous of all medieval textbooks, *The Four Books of Sentences*. Lombard was a careful, moderate, and well-trained scholar, and his work provided a framework within which the problems of theology could be considered. The *Sentences* present the substance of Christian theology in a systematic way: the concepts of the Trinity, God, Providence; Christian cosmology, grace, and free will; the work and promise of Christ and Christian virtue; the sacraments and salvation. Each principal point is subdivided and, for every question the authorities are cited as in Abélard's *Sic et Non*. But, unlike his teacher, Lombard did not leave the student confused by the inconsistencies and contradictions of these authorities; he provided explanations and resolutions in orthodox terms. The *Sentences* were to theology what Gratian's *Decretum* was to the study of canon law.

But distinguished as Lombard's work was, it did not come to grips with the crucial theological problem of the time: the nominalist-realist controversy. The problem of reconciling the rationalist non-Christian Aristotelian system with the basic tenets of Christianity remained, and with it the danger that the Aristotelians might sweep the field. The extreme nominalists were constantly led to deny the fundamental generalities of Christianity, and despite the vigil of the church, heresy was beginning to bud from the searching theological speculations at the universities. Early in the thirteenth century a group of scholars at the University of Paris subscribed to the views of the Moslem philosopher Averroës. Known as Averroists, they blatantly challenged the church on philosophical grounds. The hard-pressed church might well have repressed the heresy of the learned as harshly as it quashed that of the humble. But in this crisis of Christian learning two men came forward to resolve the apparently irreconcilable differences between faith and reason and virtually to create the formal theology of the High Middle Ages—two Dominican scholars, Albertus Magnus (Albert the Great), and his pupil, St. Thomas Aquinas.

Albertus (1193–1280) was a German nobleman who became a Dominican friar and devoted his long life to the church, and especially to scholarship. The task he undertook and completed, in a massive set of more than twenty weighty volumes, was a commentary upon the whole works of Aristotle, a commentary which would place these dangerous writings in a Christian setting and remove from them all non-Christian elements. Albertus realized that it was not possible to deal with only this or that point of Aristotle. He had to explain the entire system. And since that system embraced all the categories of the world's knowledge, the explanation had to describe an equally universal system. His learning was prodigious and he was known as the "universal Doctor." His work influenced the course of much medieval thought. But by far his greatest influence was on his friend, pupil, and fellow-Dominican, Thomas Aquinas.

Thomas (1225–1274), like his master, was a nobleman, but born in the Kingdom of Naples of German-Norman ancestry. As a young man he joined the Dominican Order over the protest of his family and went to Cologne to study with Albertus Magnus. He followed Albertus to the University of Paris, continued his studies there, and took the next step beyond the work of his teacher. It was Thomas Aquinas who devised a comprehensive theological system that reconciled reason (Aristotle and the rational tradition of Hellenism) with revelation (Scripture and the Christian tradition).

Thomas founded his system on the assumption that there is no possible contradiction between the truth of reason and the truth of faith. The natural world is properly known through the senses and understood by reason; but beyond the natural world such truths as the last judgment, redemption, the incarnation, or the Trinity can be known only by revelation. The one does not contradict the other, but rather completes it, and all truth is actually one. This assumption enabled him to go to the heart of the nominalist-realist controversy, for these distinctions were ultimately based upon the opposition of faith and reason. Thomas argued, like Plato, for a hierarchy of realities, reaching from the lowest-created being to the perfection of God; and, like Aristotle, that all things are composed of "being" and "becoming," actual and potential. God alone is pure actuality, i.e., reality with no potential. (To argue otherwise is to limit that which must be defined as without limit.) Below God all reality is ranked in the order of its capacity for being realized, and all reality is animated by the dynamic process of "becoming," i.e., becoming as much like God (complete being) as its nature allows. "Wherefore, if all things tend to God as their last end, so as to acquire His goodness, it follows that the last end of things is to become like unto God."[4] Thus, in very literal terms, "the earth is the Lord's and the fulness thereof," and the order of the universe is an ethical order.

This concept of the dynamic of the universe accorded perfectly with the "scientific" picture of the medieval universe derived from the mistaken notions of Ptolemy. The limit of the universe, in both a spatial and a metaphysical sense, was God. Below Him ranked the complex order of angels and supernatural, heavenly powers. At the farthest point from Him —at the center of the earth—was Satan, also God's creature. In the midst of creation stood man.

In his conception of man Thomas rejected the ancient and troublesome dualism which separated the body and the soul, demeaning the one and ex-alting the other. He saw no way that man could be complete without body as well as soul. In this he clearly followed Aristotle, as in the companion idea that the soul is the "form," the dynamic, "becoming" quality of man while his body is his "being" or "matter." But on the point of the soul's immortality, Thomas had to abandon Aristotle and the classical "end" of man in the good life. Even the best of lives must be imperfect in the context of Christianity; perfection may be gained for man only in God. Thus, the "end" of man lies outside this life, and this life must perforce be a preparation for a supernatural end. The rational soul must prepare man to know God. But there is an impediment between man and the rational search for perfection, the peculiarly Christian doctrine of original sin, which disposes man to seek ends other than God. This doctrine led Thomas to deal with the classical religious question of free will and predestination. And his whole system dictates that he make man a creature of free choice; not only for the sake of human dignity, but to preserve the concept of God

4. "Summa contra Gentiles" in *Selected Writings of St. Thomas Aquinas,* ed. d'Arcy (New York: E. P. Dutton, 1950), p. 88.

from the taint of authoring evil. To be truly free, man must be able to choose evil as well as good and, while God knows the choice man will make, he does not dictate the choice. Human sin is the result of human action. Thus, man, the favored creature of God, struggles to attain the knowledge of God through a world which was of God's making. God is the first cause, pure essence, immovable, immutable, eternal, one—and the very heart and center of the Thomist system. Thomas proves His existence both by logical argument and by the truth of sacred revelation: the truth of God is one.

Thomism is a system in the truest sense, for it is complete. The sketch outlined above suggests only a handful of the most important ideas of a vast, orderly, closely reasoned structure, touching such things as the attributes of God; the persons of the Trinity; the structure of the church; the sacraments; divine astronomy; the numbers, properties, and ranks of angels; the hierarchy of sins and virtues; natural, human, and divine law; and warnings against magicians and false miracles. The works of Thomas fill seventeen large volumes and include Aristotelian commentaries, hymns, sermons, and even a treatise on mechanical engineering. The most important of his works are the *Summa contra Gentiles,* a polemical work, and the great, systematic *Summa Theologiae* (Summation of Theology), of which no book ever more deserved the title.

The Thomist system was by no means unopposed. Countersystems, bitterly argued and learnedly compiled, continued to appear throughout the later Middle Ages. The universal implications of scholasticism were never really exhausted. Universalism itself led to a series of developments of special interest and significance to the modern world, what we would call "general science." There were no science courses as such in medieval formal education. But many scholars, including Albert and Thomas, had dealt with the body of knowledge that we know as the sciences. Further, scholasticism did not separate nature and the supernatural. Every jot and tittle of creation had to be explained and systematized. This led to the writing of the great medieval encyclopedias, such as that by the thirteenth-century scholar, Vincent of Beauvais. His work was a systematic treatise ranging from the natural and supernatural to the factual and nonsensical.

Even the best of the medieval writers on the sciences were nevertheless children of wonder, and what appear to us as penetrating insights into the "nature of things" were lodged side by side with the most childish absurdities. Medieval physicians, investigating the pulse, came close to discovering the secret of the circulatory system. Yet those same physicians retained the theory of "humors" or body fluids by which the various tempers and dispositions were explained. The champions of "natural studies" were, somewhat incongruously, Franciscan scholars, especially those at Oxford. The two most outstanding of these were Robert Grosseteste (c. 1175–1253) and Roger Bacon (c. 1214–1292). Both were interested in mathematics, astronomy, optics, and physics; and both wrote books and constructed experiments in the best tradition of empirical science. Their belief in the method of experimentation was probably more important than their actual discoveries.

Astronomy and astrology were hopelessly mixed, as were chemistry and alchemy. But many positive advances and practical discoveries were made: in mathematics, early in the thirteenth century, a form of Arabic numerals came into use, including the zero. Not much later mathematicians began to handle the concepts of the analytical geometry, although its "system" was not stated until the seventeenth century. Also in the thirteenth century, work in metallurgy led to the invention of the magnetic marine compass, work in alchemy to gunpowder, work in optics to eyeglasses. The same century produced paper of European manufacture, the mechanical clock, and the ship's rudder. But medieval scientists were unable to take the final step necessary to a true age of science—the isolation of data and the study of natural phenomena in context. They remained theologians even when they were scientists. Yet Grosseteste, and especially Bacon, insisted that authority, the authority of Galen, Avicenna, or even of Aristotle, should not be accepted without question. They pleaded that tradition must be constantly reexamined and advocated experimentation and criticism. They held the end of a thread that was not to be picked up again for almost four centuries.

THE SECULAR LEARNING OF THE HIGH MIDDLE AGES

The intellectual renaissance of the High Middle Ages was by no means exclusively the creation of Latin-speaking churchmen and scholars. Side by side with the philosophic speculations and learning of the universities there developed a rich and varied secular literature. It was not closed off from, nor antagonistic to, the influences of the church and the learned world. But its primary emphasis was secular and its language, the vernaculars—the earliest written forms of French, German, Spanish, Italian, English, the parent forms of the languages of modern western civilization.

These languages had been long in formation. Over the centuries the spoken Latin of the western provinces was gradually transformed into the Romance languages and dialects. The great migrations carried Germanic languages across much of northern Europe. There were cross influences, contact, and amalgamation. By the ninth century Anglo-Saxon had crystallized as a written language. In the tenth century French was beginning to take form along with Spanish and Italian. In the following century the formative impact of Norman-French began to be felt upon Anglo-Saxon in England.

The vernaculars took shape out of an oral literary tradition as old and as varied as the languages themselves. Bits and pieces of classicism survived the general ruin of classical secular learning and filtered down to the people. The hopes and fears of magic, superstition, witchcraft, and fairy lore became fixed in popular literature. The wild, beautiful, and somber mythology of the Germanic peoples became a part of this tradition; the genealogical records of barbaric kings were fixed in metrical form and their deeds and those of their ancestors were turned into lyric ballads that constituted an epic history. Charlemagne loved to hear the "old deeds" sung, and encouraged their collection. The Vikings carried their hero tales, their mythology, and their epic history to Iceland where, in the High Middle Ages, they were written down in probably the most undiluted versions of Germanic traditional literature.

The Medieval Epic: The Literature of Feudalism

The earliest major literary form to be written in the vernaculars was the epic. This grew naturally out of the raw materials of the heroic oral tradition stemming from the Germanic migrations. The Icelandic sagas and eddas assumed their permanent forms in the isolation of the Viking "westland." But on the continent fragmentary works like the *Hildebrandeslied,* and in England the Anglo-Saxon *Beowulf,* were gradually refined and expanded. By 1200 some unknown German "Homer" had put into writing the greatest of the Germanic epics, the *Niebelungenlied,* relating the adventures of Siegfried.

The *Niebelungenlied* was probably part of an ancient epic cycle retold and expanded by generations of bards. It was almost certainly part of the protohistory of one of the Germanic peoples—probably the Burgundians. But it had been appropriated by other peoples and attached to other traditions, absorbing other heroes in the process, until Siegfried came to represent a generalized ethnic hero of the Germans, and his story their preeminent epic. It spread as far as Norway and Iceland, where it became part of Norse literature.

Even more than the *Iliad* or the *Odyssey*, the *Niebelungenlied* is a true folk epic. Though the shaping hand of a master poet is evident, the lapses and incongruities, and the fact that the incidents are poorly joined, suggests that tradition outweighed conscious art. The heroes are grim and bloody —even more so than Achilles—and none of them attains the full dimensional complexity of Odysseus. They have few conflicting traits, and never transcend the limitations of allegorical figures. The most ancient folklore appears practically undigested in this epic. Siegfried is rendered invulnerable by the blood of a dragon, *except* for one spot where a linden leaf falls on his back. It is here that his assassin strikes. In one version he is handily equipped with a magic cloak of darkness. The maiden Brunhild has supernatural strength that resides in her virginity. Many of these concepts recall Greek mythology.

Superimposed on these primitive elements are values of a much later time, reflecting the taming of Germanic barbarism. Thus, the story of a Siegfried is transposed from its original pagan to a Christian setting. Moreover, in many ways the *Niebelungenlied* mirrors feudal society and the values of chivalry, rather than the primitive society that gave birth to the heroic oral tradition. But it must be remembered that this epic was committed to writing at the feudal courts of central Germany in the generation of Frederick Barbarossa, when feudalism was at its strongest. And in medieval Germany, as in archaic Greece, the epic tradition was the special tradition of the nobility, and so reflected their aspirations.

At about the same time, a parallel literary form, the *Chanson de Geste* (Song of Deeds) came to maturity in France. Its most famous example is the *Song of Roland*. Like the German court epics, this grew from a kernel of historic fact, the death of Hruodlandus in a rear-guard skirmish at the Pass of Roncesvalles during Charlemagne's withdrawal from Spain in 778. But as in the German epics, sober history was soon overwhelmed by romantic and heroic fantasy. In the dark days following the fall of the Carolingian Empire, many legends had grown up around the figure of Charlemagne. One of these took him on a fantastic pilgrimage to Jerusalem; another endowed him with a troop of knights, the Paladins, who fought for right and justice like King Arthur's Knights of the Round Table—on whom they were probably modeled. This is the legendary setting of the *Song of Roland*.

The *Chansons de Geste,* including the *Song of Roland,* were clearly

related to feudalism, the Crusades, and the first stirring of French nationalism. Even the motivation that moves the plot is feudal. The pride of Roland,
which will not let him call for help, is the stubborn and foolish self-esteem
of the typical feudal knight. His friend Oliver says,

"Great is the host of the heathen, . . . and few is our fellowship. Roland, fair
comrade, I pray thee sound thy horn of ivory that Charles may hear it and return
again with all his host."

"That were but folly," quoth Roland, "and thereby would I lose all fame
in sweet France. Rather will I strike good blows and great with Durendal, that
the blade thereof shall be blooded even unto the hilt. . . ."

[Says his friend] "I see no shame herein. I have seen the Saracens of Spain,
they cover the hills and the valleys, the heaths and the plains. Great are the
hosts of this hostile folk, and ours is but a little fellowship."

And Roland makes answer: "My desire is the greater thereby. May God and
His most holy angels forfend that France should lose aught of worship through
me. Liefer had I die than bring dishonour upon me. The Emperor loves us for
dealing stout blows."[5]

At last, overwhelmed by his wounds and surrounded by the havoc his
sword has wrought, Roland dies. Even his final gesture is a feudal act; he
offers his glove to God, a traditional sign of vassalage.

The *Chansons* were not only the epics of feudalism, they were, more
specifically, the epics of the Crusades. At the very time that the *Song of
Roland* was taking its final form, the fever of the First Crusade was sweeping across Europe. The edge of its religious zeal had not yet been blunted
by reality. Men sought an analogue to the great contest of Christian and
Saracen in the Holy Land. They found it in the shreds of Carolingian
history and heroic tradition preserved in the *Chansons*. Thus, a principal
motivation in the *Song of Roland* is the fanatic spirit of religious war.

Finally, the *Song of Roland* is the great national epic of France. As
Charlemagne was transformed from a Germanic tribal king into a chivalrous, crusading champion, he was also transformed into a national monarch
of "sweet France." At the moment of its greatest triumph, French feudalism
was already beginning to submit to the ideal that was ultimately to destroy
it, the ideal of national unity. The *Song of Roland* is a document of that
beginning.

In Christian Spain much the same spirit produced a counterpart to
Roland in "el Cid." Like Roland, and possibly Siegfried, the Cid was a

5. Quoted in *Masterworks of World Literature*. ed. Everett, Brown, and Wade,
I, p. 476.

historical figure, Ruy Díaz de Bivar. A minor Spanish noble living in the latter half of the eleventh century, he was a professional soldier and military commander of great ability and took a leading part in the expansion of Christian Spain. The name Cid is derived from a Moslem term meaning lord and was sometimes coupled with the Spanish *Campeador,* "Champion." Ruy Díaz was a dashing feudal figure, strong, ruthless, and almost completely amoral. Though a Christian champion, he also fought for the Saracens, plundering Christians and Saracens with equal zeal. He was the hero of the *Poema del Cid,* which appeared in the twelfth century, and a host of ballads, songs and chronicles that developed in the thirteenth and subsequent centuries. He became the national hero of Spain and his literary character was molded into an archetype of the noble Spaniard. His exploits symbolized the most crucial historical experience of Spain, the great domestic crusade to expel the Saracens that formed not only Spain but the Spanish national image.

The Troubadors and the Songs of Love

Western feudalism produced another form of literature strangely unrelated to the epic temper, the poetry of the troubadors. It originated in the highly Romanized area of northern Italy, northern-Christian Spain, and especially the south of France. Despite successive waves of barbarism, civil war, "foreign" rule, and the passage of centuries, some important vestiges of cultural unity had survived in this wide area. The influence of Moslem Spain and of reviving trade may have helped to set this region apart from the rest of western Europe. In any case, Provence—as the central region of the south of France came to be called—became the home of the most elegant and sophisticated secular culture of the High Middle Ages.

Concentrated in the feudal courts of the south, its most typical expression was the lyric poetry of the troubador. Like the epics, chansons, and battle ballads, it was a feudal literature; but its theme was not war and feats of arms, it was love. Almost all the intricate, conventionalized forms of troubador poetry were concerned with this theme, but in a very special context: it has been called the glorification of adultery. The typical troubador lyric was addressed to a married woman, usually a noble matron, and it expressed the troubador's desire for her. (It must be added, however, that this was a literature primarily of unrequited love.) It was an elaborate game in which ardent pursuit never—or seldom—attained its object. Yet, this literary pretension affected profoundly the entire feudal society of

Provence. There are almost five hundred Provençal troubadors known by name. Some of them were professional poets, but an impressive number were noblemen, some among the greatest of European feudatories. How, or why, such delicate sentiments came to be part of the normally brutal and insensitive life of feudalism remains a mystery. Troubador poetry created the "cult of the lady." Grandames held courts of love in which delicate questions were debated in an amatory parallel to the courts which debated the grim issues of military-political feudalism. Almost the entire "chivalrous" content of chivalry stemmed from the influence of the troubadors.

From the south of France, the troubador tradition, its manners and its poetry, spread. It took root in the court of Frederick II in Sicily, where the noble brother of St. Thomas Aquinas was an accomplished troubador. It was deeply influential in the minuscule courts of north-central Italy, where it survived to contribute to the literature of the Renaissance. Eleanor of Aquitaine brought to her marriage not only her southern lands but their society and culture. In her train the ways of the troubador, and a good many troubadors themselves, were introduced into northern France and later to England. Her son, Richard the Lion-Hearted, was an accomplished poet. In Germany the troubador tradition produced a parallel in the *minnesingers,* "love-singers." Some of the most important medieval secular poetry was composed by this group. Wherever the troubador songs went their influence blended with other currents of secular, vernacular literature. But in the spiritual homeland of every troubador, the south of France, the society that had produced this exotic culture was brutally destroyed. The carnal tastes and "gay wisdom" of the Provençal nobility had long been a scandal to the church, especially since this was often coupled with widespread contempt for the clergy, and even for the mysteries of religion. The culture of Provence blended with the dangerous heresy of the Albigensians to provoke the Albigensian Crusade, which was an attack not only on heresy but on every aspect of Provençal culture; the south of France never recovered from its blasting effect.

Middle-Class Literature: Entertainment and Social Commentary

In the twelfth and thirteenth centuries the rising middle class of the towns and cities began to challenge the place of the nobility. Trained lawyers became a powerful support to royal absolutism and stood with the high nobility beside the thrones of Europe. Wealthy merchants bought land and titles and married their well-dowered children into great feudal families. Wealth created leisure and leisure created taste. A middle-class culture began to form. Its literature, like its pretensions, was modeled on that of the old nobility. The battle songs and epics, even the chivalrous songs of noble love, were taken over by the non-noble. But the first true middle-class literature was the Romance.

This form had begun as another variety of the aristocratic *chanson,* and its earliest subject had been the story of King Arthur and his knights. Arthur was the half-legendary, half-historical hero of Celtic tradition, dating from the sixth-century resistance to the Anglo-Saxon invasions. He had lived on in the Celtic fringes of the British world and his exploits had grown with the embroidery of fancy. In the middle of the twelfth century, the Anglo-Norman-Welsh Geoffrey of Monmouth included the basic tale of Arthur in his *History of the Kings of Britain.* It was taken to the continent and, for some inexplicable reason, caught the literary fancy as almost no other medieval theme had.

To the popularity of the Arthurian legend attached other cycles and stories, such as the famous love story of Tristan and Iseult. Even the distorted historical tradition of antiquity was romanticized. Alexander the Great and the heroes of the Trojan War became knights and champions of chivalry. These were mixed with Byzantine and Saracen tales. There was no medieval literary form so universal as the Romance. The blood and honor of the feudal epic became part of the Romance, along with the value-system of the knight. The love lyrics of Provence were an important influence. Popular superstition, witchcraft, magic, and Celtic fairy lore were woven into the Romances, which abound in love potions, curses, spells, dragons, and magic swords.

At the same time, the reforming temper of the age played an important role in the shaping of the Romance. Thus, the ideal of the loyal vassal was transformed into that of the perfect knight, represented by Sir Galahad, half-knight, half-monk, seeking religious perfection in the quest for the Holy Grail. The crusading ideal of the soldier for Christ gained its triumph in Romantic fiction, even as it failed in the hard reality of the Crusades. And even the worldly love of woman, which had come to the Romance from the lyrics of the troubadors, was transformed under the influence of the cult of the Virgin Mary.

Almost from the beginning the Romance belonged as much to the middle class as to the nobility. Much of the shrewd and realistic spirit of the townsman and merchant was absorbed by it, as was the earthy humor and homely wisdom of the peasant that still clung to the townsman. One of the most durable characters was Renard the Fox, who was taken from the popular stories of the High Middle Ages to become the center of a Romance which enshrined the middle-class businessman's ideals of self-reliance and shrewd resourcefulness.

The final form of the popular Romance was achieved in the famous *Roman de la Rose.* This was the work of two thirteenth-century French poets, Guillaume de Lorris and Jean de Meun, but it was, at the same time, an animated reflection of all the varied forms of popular literature. The basic story is a dream of love. A lover, smitten by Cupid's arrow, strives to pluck a beautiful rose, the symbol of his love and of his lady. After overcoming a succession of obstacles, he at last possesses the rose. Upon this simple thread are strung almost twenty-thousand lines of allegorical poetry. Allegory is heaped upon allegory until the poem becomes a Pilgrim's Progress of the flesh. The lover is aided by Fair-Welcome and opposed by False-Seeming and Jealousy. The poem swells out in digressions upon every imaginable subject—history, philosophy, natural science, social commentary—to become a veritable *Speculum Naturale,* a mirror of the world into which nearly every subsequent medieval popular writer would look for inspiration.

It was in the lively atmosphere of the medieval town that the most lively of popular arts, the drama, was revived. The medieval drama was profoundly and often incongruously affected by the currents of secular life, but its basic sources were popular religion and the liturgy of the church. The medieval, like the classical drama, was the child of worship. The very central act of the Christian faith, the Mass, was a symbolic re-enactment of the sacrifice of Christ. Other services of the church were also enactments or representations. From an early time the seed of drama was present in the forms of religious liturgy.

It was in the towns of the twelfth and thirteenth centuries that the sacred-secular drama became the most broadly based of medieval literary forms. Like the symbolic sculpture of the cathedral or the romanticized figures of hero tales, the medieval drama was clothed in the garments and the meaning not of Biblical times but of "modern." In this way the "mystery plays" were born, representing the Story of Adam, of Daniel, of Noah and the Ark, and the Miracles and Parables of Christ. They were crowded with the high-piled symbolism that medieval men loved. They innocently mixed sacred texts with their own misconceptions of their meaning and even with their gamy humor. Eventually the plays were moved outside the church to the porch and then to the market place; from the Bible to the vast treasury of saints' lives and miracles; and from the clergy to the laity. The miracle plays became a fixture of medieval public entertainment. Troups of players were formed. As has been said, the guilds often performed particular plays whose themes were appropriate to their crafts—for example, the carpenters' gild might present the story of Noah and the Ark. As the plays moved out of the church they moved out of religious favor (the church had learned how easily anything connected with religion that was not under its control could lead to blasphemy or even heresy). But despite the suspicion with which the church continued to regard the nascent drama, it flourished to become the lineal ancestor of the modern European theater.

Dante and the Eternal Vision

The greatest philosophic poem of the Middle Ages, perhaps of all time, is the work of the Florentine-Italian poet Dante Alighieri (1265–1321). But even more, this man and his work represent a profound synthesis of medieval thought and art. Like Aristotle, Dante stood at a dividing line between two culture worlds and looked back to summarize that which was about to pass.

Dante was born into the plutocracy of the bustling Italian city of Florence, one of the key centers of the revival of trade and money economy. We know very little about his early life, and much of that is contradictory. His family had lost its wealth and Dante was orphaned at about fifteen. Yet he seems to have been an accepted member of the young élite of the city and to have enjoyed the education typical of his class. No small part of that education was the intricate courtly poetry which had been vigorously transplanted from Provence. Like every good troubador, the young Dante found his lady, the maiden Beatrice; and, again in this tradition, his passion for her was impossible to realize. He loved her from afar; saw her apparently only twice; and mourned her death at the age of twenty-four. The love of Beatrice was a constant influence in Dante's life, an influence that moved from flesh to symbol until, in his mind, she was transformed into the perfect love of God. Dante early gained some fame as a poet, largely through his poems to Beatrice, most of which he collected into a work he called the *Vita Nuova,* the "New Life."

Secular learning was probably stronger in the Italian cities of this period than anywhere else in Europe. Universities, schools, and academies flourished, as well as individual scholars who accepted pupils for instruction. We know that Dante studied with at least one such scholar, Brunetto

Latini, and that he was admitted to the Florentine guild of Apothecaries and Physicians, a guild of professional scholars. An accomplished Latinist, he knew the ancient poets as thoroughly as any university classicist, and his love for Vergil was almost as consuming as his love for Beatrice. He had mastered the whole field of medieval formal knowledge. His works bristle with allusions to the great works and figures of medieval intellectualism, and he made contributions not only to philosophy and theology, but to such diverse fields as political theory and linguistics.

Active political participation was traditional to his class, and Dante entered the maelstrom of Florentine politics. For a time he had a successful political career, even rising by 1300 to be one of the priors or municipal counsellors of Florence. Then in 1301 his life was overturned by one of those unpredictable party revolutions that unsettled the history of every Italian city; a rival faction suddenly seized power and Dante found himself an exile. This acutely patriotic man no longer had a "country" in which to exercise his patriotism. For the next nineteen years he wandered about Italy from one city or court to another. In his exile he turned his mind to the great theme of the *Divine Comedy*.

The *Divine Comedy* is, in many ways, the secular-poetic counter-part of the *Summa* of St. Thomas.[6] Their core and purpose are the same. As Dante expressed it in a prefatory letter, the subject of his work is "the state of souls after death"; its intention, "to remove those living in this life from a state of misery, and to guide them to a state of happiness"; its theme, salvation. The poem is constructed, like the *Roman de la Rose,* in the framework of a complex allegory: there is scarcely a line that does not carry more than its superficial meaning. It is permeated throughout by the mystery of number symbolism—three, seven, nine, ten, one hundred, all of them heavy with meaning for the medieval Christian. The poem is divided into three major sections, each containing thirty-three cantos or verses which, with the introductory canto, total one hundred. The

6. The *Divine Comedy* is obviously not secular in theme or purpose: it is moral, religious, and profoundly theological. It represents the fusion of religion with the secular life that was so much a part of the Middle Ages. The poem may be called secular, however, because the poet was not a member of the clergy and because it was written for the laity. For this reason Dante, after some hesitation, decided to write it in the vernacular dialect of his native Florence. The subsequent popularity of the *Divine Comedy* and its high literary quality tended to stabilize its language as the "official" form of Italian. In this sense, perhaps more than in any other, the *Divine Comedy* must be regarded as a secular poem for, by its use of the vernacular, it stands with the other great literary monuments, previously discussed, which mark the emergence of Europe's modern languages.

geography of Dante's afterworld is also formed by numbers—the seven mortal sins, the seven virtues, and the varied states of blessedness. Even the rhyme scheme is based upon the sacred number of the Trinity. The opening lines of the poem set the allegorical scene:

> In the midway of this our mortal life,
> I found me in a gloomy wood, astray,
> Gone from the path direct. . . .

Dante is speaking not only of the years of his life, but of the turning point of every man's life. The gloomy wood is not only an actual forest; it is equally the tangled wood of sin and human error in which all men are lost. Shortly, Dante is frightened and his way blocked by a leopard, a lion, and a she-wolf, the conventional symbols of lust, pride, and avarice that again block the path of man to virtue and salvation. Help comes when he meets the ghost of Vergil, who symbolized for him the perfection to which reason alone could lead man. With his phantom guide Dante turns to the only path left him, that which leads through Hell to Purgatory and eventually to the sight of God.

Hell is a great descending cone in the conception of which medieval theology and cosmology were equally mixed. Hell is separation from God: if God is the limit of the finite universe, then the pit of Hell must be the point farthest from Him, the center of the earth. And, since sin and Hell are inseparable Satan, the most terrible of sinners, is at the very bottom of the pit, lodged fast in a lake of blood-streaked ice. It is toward that terrible apparition that Dante and his guide make their way. The murky cone of Hell is divided into gulfs in which sinners are eternally punished. Each region is symbolic of one of the mortal sins, arranged in a descending order of severity.[7]

The punishments themselves are graphic in their detail and hideous in their appropriateness. But all who suffer in Hell suffer alike the greatest of all punishments, the absence of hope; for their sins have cheated them of the opportunity to know God. Each character of history or of legend, each punishment, and each level carries its part of the infernal allegory.

---

7. The mortal sins of medieval theology were pride, anger, envy, sloth, avarice, gluttony, and lust. Opposed to the mortal sins were the seven cardinal virtues: wisdom, justice, temperance, courage (the so-called moral virtues); and faith, hope, and love (the theological or distinctly Christian virtues). Dante uses the virtues in the structure of Heaven as he uses the vices in the structure of Hell and Purgatory.

At last, fainting with horror, Dante is led past the towering, loathsome figure of Satan and, by a "hidden way," mounts to the surface of the earth once more and to the foot of the mount of Purgatory—the second division of the poem. Purgatory continues the allegorical cosmology of Dante. It is a high hill reaching up toward the lowest ranks of Heaven and topped by an earthly paradise. The hill is mounted by seven climbing levels, again, as in Hell, symbolic of the seven mortal sins. The punishments of Purgatory do not differ materially from those of Hell—but what a difference in atmosphere! Instead of moans and wails, Purgatory is filled with joyous singing. It is divided from Hell by hope. The souls in Purgatory have been saved from Hell by the sacrament of penance. The torment that they undergo is the "debt" of temporal punishment that remains after guilt is removed. As Vergil explains,

. . . God wills that the debt be paid. Heed not the form of the pain; think what followeth, think that at worst beyond the great judgment it cannot go.[8]

Purgatory is a progressive state. The souls gradually make their way from one level to the next, leaving the burden of their sins and the weight of their carnal bodies behind them until at last, purified and ethereal, they mount to heaven. At last Dante is brought to the top of the hill of Purgatory where Vergil must leave him to another guide, for earthly wisdom can only go so far. His new guide is none other than the maiden Beatrice, who again appears as love's symbol and who, along with St. Bernard, will take Dante into the realm of Heaven.

Heaven completes the scheme of the *Divine Comedy.* The poet is drawn upward through the glowing spheres of blessedness until he sees God, "the goal of all my longings."

O grace abounding, wherein I presumed to fix my look on the eternal light so long that I consumed my sight thereon! Within its depths I saw ingathered, bound by love in one volume, the scattered leaves of all the universe; substance and accidents and their relations, as though together fused, after such fashion that what I tell of is one simple flame. . . . Thus all suspended did my mind gaze fixed, immovable, intent, ever enkindled by its gazing . . . [and] my desire and will were rolled—even as a wheel that moveth equally—by the Love that moves the sun and the other stars.[9]

8. *Purgatory,* Canto X.
9. *Paradise,* Canto XXXIII.

THE ART OF THE HIGH MIDDLE AGES

The revival of learning in the twelfth and thirteenth centuries was accompanied by an equally impressive revival of art—particularly in architecture. As throughout much of the history of art, religion provided the chief inspiration and impetus. Men built houses, manors, and castles in every period of the Middle Ages. They painted, carved, whittled, and created many useful and beautiful things. But the principal forms of painting, calligraphy, sculpture, and architecture were ecclesiastical.

We have seen that, as Christianity became institutionalized in the late days of the Roman Empire, the place of worship became the focus of religion and architecture the chief of the Christian arts, with every other art attached and subordinate to it. When in the course of the eleventh century some degree of order returned to western Europe, it was soon followed by a general and vigorous revival of church architecture. This reached magnificent maturity in the synthesis of two basic styles, the Romanesque and the Gothic.

The Development of Romanesque

It is somewhat misleading to speak of a single Romanesque style. During the eleventh and twelfth centuries, feudal regionalism still tended to be strong. Thus architecture developed regionally in accordance with local needs and in reflection of surviving local traditions. In southern Italy, for example, Romanesque building retained many basilican features. But in northern Italy, where the German-imperial forces were entrenched, there were modifications. Conversely, the southern German Romanesque style was profoundly influenced by the close connection with Italy. Farther to the north in the Rhine valley, the "typical" Romanesque church was a much heavier, more fortress-like structure. In the south of France Romanesque tended to a plain rectangular plan with a shallow porch and deeply recessed doorway arches. The Norman and Anglo-Norman styles developed some of the skeletal angularity and loftiness of the later Gothic, and clearly resembled none of the other continental styles.

In spite of this diversity we can distinguish certain characteristics as typically "Romanesque." The term itself suggests the basic common element, the use of the round, or "Roman" arch. As men once more began to build massive stone structures, they turned to the only clear model before them, the architectural tradition of Rome. Along with the Roman arch, the Romanesque builders adopted the Roman barrel- and cross-vault. Like the arch, these forms were dictated by structural necessity which, coupled with technical inexperience, produced the massiveness and structural simplicity of Romanesque. The Romanesque builder made his side walls heavy and thick to bear the crushing weight of the stone roof vault. As he pushed the side walls to any height, stresses multiplied disastrously. He was careful not to weaken the supporting walls with large or numerous window openings; the same well-grounded fear forced him to support interior openings—the passages between the nave and the arcade, for example—with heavy, stone piers. For these reasons, Romanesque buildings, of whatever regional style, tended to be low and horizontally organized rather than lofty and vertical; and they tended to be poorly lighted and to have vast expanses of structural wall space.

Romanesque churches also developed a somewhat characteristic ground plan in response to the growth of church liturgy. Some of the earliest Romanesque buildings were the work of the reformed monastic orders and the form of early Romanesque reflected monastic influence. Monastic buildings were made specifically to serve the purposes of the monastic clergy; these called for an apse to house the alter and a choir to accommodate the singers of the monastic offices. As these monastery churches became centers of general worship, of pilgrimage, or miracle cults, they had to expand. They added a nave for the laity—often completely separated from the choir, which was for officiating clergy. Then, as more space was needed, they added the transept wings to give the typical cross-form to the church plan. They were forced to add chapels to house the relics and celebrate the saints then beginning to dominate popular religion. Secular churches imitated, modified, and extended monastic forms, preparing the way for the great cathedrals of the late twelfth and thirteenth centuries.

Finally, Romanesque church architecture may be characterized by its surface decorativeness. The forms of decoration were as diverse as the buildings themselves and as responsive to local stimuli. In Italy, the mural decoration of the older basilican-style churches was probably influential. Though there, as in other areas, the challenge of empty wall space may well have been sufficient stimulus to the art of decoration. In some cases this challenge was met by the use of various kinds and colors of stone; in others the walls were painted; in many, relief carving was used. In the earlier churches this took the form of little more than surface piercing, but in time sculptural decoration became one of the most characteristic features of the Romanesque style. The austere St. Bernard protested it vigorously:

> To what purpose are those unclean apes, those fierce lions, those monstrous centaurs, those half-men, those striped tigers, those fighting knights, those hunters winding their horns? Many bodies are there seen under one head, or again, many heads to a single body. Here is a four-footed beast with a serpent's tail; there, a fish with a beast's head. Here again the forepart of a horse trails a goat behind it, or a horned beast bears the hinder quarters of a horse. In short, so many and so marvelous are the varieties of divers shapes on every hand, that we are more tempted to read in the marble than in our books, and to spend the whole day in wondering at these things rather than in meditating the law of God.

And on church splendor generally,

> Hence the church is adorned with gemmed crowns of light—nay, with lustres like cartwheels, girt all round with lamps, but no less brilliant with the precious stones that stud them. Moreover we see candalabra standing like trees of massive bronze, fashioned with marvelous subtlety of art, and glistening no less brightly with gems than with the lights they carry.[10]

In general, if not in detail, the very decorations which St. Bernard deplored flowed from the same source as his own religious zeal, the spirit of the reformed monasteries. The place of worship was a place appropriate for moral-intellectual instruction. Thus the decorations of the monastic church had a didactic purpose; to set before the eyes of the monks "sermons in stone." These took the forms of Biblical stories, incidents from saints' lives, moral tales, and symbolic themes. One of the favorite subjects was the enthroned Christ, sometimes blessing man, more often judging him, and often surrounded by the animals which had come to symbolize the four evangelists. Probably the most frequent theme was the Last Judgment, graphically depicting the separation of the damned and the saved. The vigor and freshness of Romanesque sculpture could not, however, be bounded entirely by the sacred and the canonical. The challenge of wall or capital or doorway was always before the Romanesque sculptor, as was the temptation to make use of his own growing skill. Thus he was led to carve the beasts and fantastic creatures he had never seen but knew so confidently from the pages of his bestiaries and encyclopedias. Serpents and monsters, lions, griffins, and eagles—and even "un-

10. St. Bernard's "Apologia" to William, Abbot of St. Thierry, in *A Documentary History of Art,* ed. E. G. Holt, Princeton: Princeton University Press.

clean apes"—glowered and chittered in the foliage of his columns surrounding the figures of Moses or St. Paul or St. Anthony.

The irrepressible spirit of its sculpture was part of the general vigor of Romanesque art, reflecting a restless and energetic age. Romanesque often went to excess and often failed in its designs, both of sculpture and of structure; it was often clumsy, blunt, ugly, or grotesque—but it was never dull and seldom static.

The Emergence of Gothic Structure

The legacy of Romanesque art was the basis of the Gothic style, which began to appear in the latter half of the twelfth century. In a structural sense, Gothic architecture is traditionally separated from Romanesque by the introduction of three elements: the ribbed vault, the pointed arch, and the flying buttress. Yet even here Romanesque had set the problems and already suggested the solutions.

Most later Romanesque churches had been built in sections called bays, one at a time until the structure was completed. Bay construction saved the cost and labor of scaffolding, since the same supporting timbers could be moved along with the construction, and it had a definite structural advantage because it divided thrusts and pressures. Instead of one continuous roof vault, the bays were a series of self-contained vault systems. Each bay was defined and stabilized by a heavy masonry framework of ribs. In the early barrel vaults these were simply transverse ribs, but as cross vaults were used, diagonal ribs were added for strength and stability. These defining ribs carried the thrust of the roof arches to the sides of the building and down into the heavy supporting piers and side walls. But problems remained in this Romanesque vaulting system: as we have already noted, the interiors tended to be low and poorly lighted, and the round arch form created a series of ceiling domes that interfered with the spatial unity of the whole roof vault.

Gothic architects found a way to reduce the crushing weight that had always limited the height of the vault. By reducing the structural elements of the vault to the ribs themselves, and allowing the ribs to cluster together like the trunk of a great tree, they could produce a stable framework of ribs and piers that would stand by itself. The intervals in the ceiling vault and the side wall spaces could be filled with a light, nonstructural membrane of stone. By thus reducing the weight of the roof vault, its height could be increased. At the same time, the heavy clustered piers of interior support did the work that thick walls had had to do for the Romanesque building. The Gothic architect found that the walls, like the solid vaults, could be reduced to a skeletal outline, almost eliminated. In place of structural walls the Gothic builder could fill the wall space with a hanging curtain of delicately pierced stone to hold the colored glass windows that are the decorative glory of the Gothic style.

With the problems of weight and height resolved, the necessity for the round arch also disappeared. The Gothic architect was able to flatten and point the structural arches, so that the arches of both a wide and a narrow opening could rise to the same height, giving a continuous roof vault. These narrow, delicately pointed arches could carry windows to unprecedented heights. With the skeletal ribbed vault and the pointed arch, true Gothic needed only to develop a system of exterior counterbalance in the flying buttresses.

Like much else in Gothic, the flying buttress was actually implicit in the Romanesque structure. In earlier and smaller Romanesque buildings, the heavy walls had absorbed the thrust of the roof arches. But as buildings grew in size, a limit was reached. Massive piers were added to the walls at the points of severe thrust. In some of the Lombard churches, but especially in the daring style of the Normans, these piers were placed outside the church walls at the necessary intervals and engaged to the walls as extra weight to absorb the thrust. In such a Norman church as the Abbé aux Hommes of William the Conqueror in Caen, the loftiness of Gothic was already anticipated. It remained to Gothic builders to cut the engaged piers away from the side walls, let them rise from the ground outside the shell of the structure, then reach across to support the bay vaults precisely at the points of thrust. With the flying buttress, structural support was removed entirely from the interior of the building and the Gothic style had its final basic characteristic.

The Gothic Flowering

The clear transition from Romanesque to Gothic is best seen in the Abbey Church of St. Denis, rebuilt about the middle of the twelfth century. It was conceived and begun by the Abbot Suger, brilliant and energetic minister of the French kings Louis VI and Louis VII. His church was the religious focus of the emerging nationalism of France. The abbot's wealth and position attracted the finest craftsmen and materials to his building project. His own taste and intelligence enabled him to pick out of the varied experiments of late Romanesque precisely those elements that we have seen as the defining characteristics of the Gothic style; Suger brought them together in a single structure. From its beginning at St. Denis, the Gothic styles moved to the cathedrals of Sens and Chartres, which were built in the latter half of the twelfth century, then to Notre Dame of Paris, then to Amiens in the mid-thirteenth century—becoming more complete and more confident at every step.

While Gothic was, in a structural sense, a continuation and completion of Romanesque, in many ways it was not so much a continuation as an antagonistic countermovement. Romanesque had been molded by the spirit of the reformed monasteries and, in a large degree, reflected the needs and tastes of the monastic community; Gothic was the style of the secular church and its most characteristic structures were the cathedrals. Finally, the symbolic forms of Romanesque tended to reflect the narrow fervor and limited theology of the monk; Gothic reflected the more varied and universal forms of secular religion.

When we think of Gothic we think appropriately of the church architecture of north central France—of the cathedrals of Chartres, Rheims, Amiens, Rouen, and Paris. Virtually all other Gothic forms emigrated from this area. In the course of the High Middle Ages the French Gothic style reached the fringes of Germany along the Rhine, as is evident in the cathedrals of Strassburg and Cologne. Across the Channel and the North Sea it is found in the cathedrals of Salisbury and Gloucester in England. Later it crossed the Pyrenees, to be used in the cathedrals of Burgos and Seville in Spain. There was much less diversity in the Gothic than in the Romanesque styles; nonetheless, as Gothic influences migrated from north central France they were inevitably modified by different regional tastes and artistic and liturgical traditions. Yet, beautiful and impressive as English, German, or Spanish Gothic architecture is, the most perfect expression of the Gothic style is to be found in the region of its birth, in the churches of the Île-de-France, the realm of the Capetian kings.

It is no coincidence that the fury of Gothic building took place in this area, and principally in the reigns of Philip Augustus and Louis IX. These great Capetian monarchs ruled the most dynamic state of western Europe. Paris was the center of a growing national spirit; Capetian France was the focus of the civilization of the High Middle Ages and the Gothic cathedral was the most solid evidence of its primacy. Between the accession of Philip Augustus and the death of Louis IX, a span of ninety years, no less than eighty cathedrals and almost five hundred abbey churches of cathedral size were built in north central France.

Façade, Chartres Cathedral.

Right: *The Taking of Jerusalem by the Crusaders,* from *Grandes Chroniques de France-Festin.* 14th century. Below: *The Virgin and the Liberal Arts,* Tympanum over the Royal Door. Chartres.

34

Amiens Cathedral.

Edward III of England.

Nave, Amiens Cathedral.

Façade, Cathedral at Bourges.

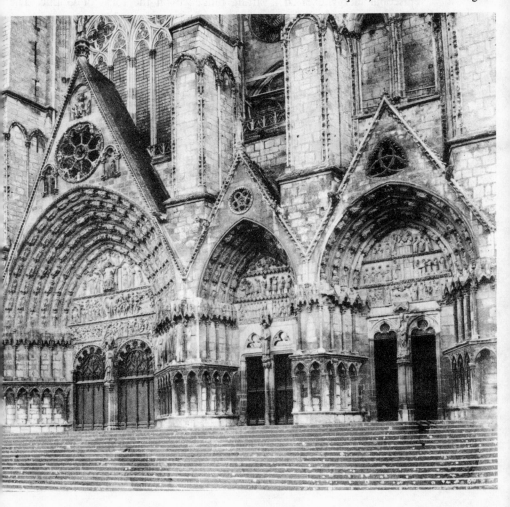

The cathedral is peculiarly the church of a bishop, and the bishops of the Île-de-France played a determining role in the development of Gothic art. The Capetian kings had found their strongest support in the high clergy, who had helped significantly in the building of France; they were rewarded accordingly in wealth and prestige. At the same time the religious initiative of the High Middle Ages was passing from the reformed monastic orders to the secular clergy under the direction of a monarchical papacy; and here too the bishops were the key figures. Thus the cathedral was a clear expression of the position, pride, and wealth of the bishop, its grandeur and size a measure of his significance. It was the administrative, and often the intellectual, center of his diocese. But its prime function was as a center of worship, and so the needs of the secular, episcopal clergy exerted a strong influence on the form of Gothic. The Romanesque cruciform ground plan was expanded, and the transepts were broadened and the nave lengthened to give more space. The cathedral was no longer primarily the church of a monastic chapter; it was the church of a congregation.

The increasingly popular cults of relics and saints tended to center in the cathedrals. Bishops vied with each other for them. Cathedrals which had especially efficacious relics were centers for lucrative pilgrimages. Chartres was a miracle shrine of great curative power. After the Christian sack of Constantinople in the Fourth Crusade the thousands of sacred relics from that city were "auctioned" to the churches of the west, among them the famous skull of St. Anne, which was acquired by Chartres. But its most prized relic was the tunic that the Virgin was supposed to have worn at the time of Christ's birth. It had been given to the church by Charles the Bald and had acquired a long record of miracles, making it one of the most famous relics in the world, and Chartres one of the leading centers of the Cult of Mary. In the later thirteenth century Louis IX paid a fortune for the Crown of Thorns and built a beautiful chapel, Sainte Chapelle, to house it. In every major cathedral chapels were built to house their prized relics and the mementos of their special saints. These chapels clustered around the altars of the apse and transepts, while the side aisles were doubled to provide a separate "ambulatory" or passage through and around the church leading to the relic chapels.

While the Gothic cathedrals belonged indisputably to their bishops, they also belonged to the townspeople, reflecting their pride and prosperity. Physically the cathedral dominated the town, rising above the jumble of dwellings and twisting narrow streets that converged on its broad courtyard apron. More than the guild hall, more even than the city hall or palace, the cathedral was the center of town life, the scene for the celebration of holidays and festivals. It is no wonder that the medieval townsmen were willing to contribute their wealth and labor to these buildings—from generation to generation, from century to century. The Cathedral of Chartres, for example, was begun in 1134 when fire destroyed an older structure. Half a century later, the partially completed cathedral burned once more. Again it was rebuilt and substantially completed by the end of the thirteenth century; but the north spire was not added until the early sixteenth century—almost four hundred years after the building was begun.

The towns provided the wealth and labor for the cathedrals. The broadening urban culture of the High Middle Ages provided the artistic, architectural, and engineering skills for their construction. The actual builders of the cathedrals were master craftsmen and architects who were experts in Gothic construction. They were respected and educated men, often university trained, with a knowledge of mathematics, engineering, materials. Most of the labor was done by bands of skilled artisans—stonecutters and masons, sculptors, glaziers, carpenters—who migrated from one job to another. We can follow certain groups by the traces of their styles. These artisans were townsmen also, and their skills the result of the division and specialization of labor that had become possible only with the rise of towns.

As the cathedral belonged to both the episcopal clergy and the townsmen, so its elaborate symbolism flowed both from the clerical world of liturgy and learning and from the vital sources of popular religion. The widespread number symbolism that we have noted in the poetry of Dante became part also of the building and decorative scheme of the cathedral: for example, the employment of the number three, for the Trinity, in the three-aisle division of the ground plan and the three levels of interior elevation. The adoration of saints and relics was one of the most conspicuous features of popular religion and the Cult of Mary was the most popular of all. In one sense the cathedrals may be viewed as the products of this popular adoration. Virtually every major cathedral church bears the name Notre Dame, "Our Lady." They were the palaces of the Queen of Heaven. The "Lady Chapel" normally occupied the place of honor in the center of the cluster of chapels behind the cathedral apse. The rose windows that glorify the entrance façades and transept faces of so many cathedrals are symbolic of Mary's flower, the rose. Often the controlling theme of the decorative exterior sculpture of the cathedral was the life of the Virgin and of Christ, her son.

Gothic Sculpture

Many of the circumstances that influenced the development of Gothic architecture were also reflected in the decorative and symbolic sculpture of the cathedral. We may take Chartres as an example. More than two thousand pieces of statuary are in its scheme of decoration, almost all of them outside the building, clustered around the chief entrance on the west and the two transept entrance porches. The north porch is dedicated to the Virgin. Its sculptural program deals with her life, that of her parents, especially St. Anne, and foreshadows the life of Christ. The south porch is devoted to Christ and his work. The west façade sculpture—earlier than either of the transept porches—participates in both these themes and is one of the most renowned groups of Gothic sculpture.

The west façade sculpture is set around the triple doorway opening into the nave and two aisles of the cathedral. The larger central doorway is dominated by the tympanum[11] figure of Christ, surrounded by the evangelistic figures. In this setting Christ is shown enthroned as the King of Heaven and the portal is thus called the royal portal. Around this group of figures the deep recesses of the doorway dissolve into three bands of sculpture, which contain the figures of Biblical elders. Below the tympanum and immediately above the door is a heavy slab deeply carved with the figures of the Apostles, seated in a narrow Gothic space, each figure under an arched opening.

The smaller doorway to the south, the Virgin portal, depicts Mary as the Queen of Heaven, enthroned with her infant son and attended by two angels. Two bands of sculpture below depict the nativity scene and the presentation in the temple. The figures are drawn from the daily life of the medieval town and countryside. The shepherds adoring the Christ child are the shepherds who herded their flocks in the meadows near Chartres; the elders and doctors of the temple wear the robes of the canons and teachers in the cathedral school. In the recesses of the Virgin portal appear the Seven Liberal Arts, composing a series of delightful vignettes of the scholarly life: Grammar holds an open book and a bundle of switches (which she is about to apply to two curly-headed children

11. This term refers to the stone "filler" in the arched space above the door lintel and under the arch of the larger door opening. From an early time this was one of the favored spots for sculptural decoration.

who are scuffling rather than studying), Music, represented by Pythagoras, is depicted as a robed and bearded medieval scholar writing on a lapboard desk. At the symbolical level these figures assert the claim of the Scholastics that Mary was perfect in her learning as well as in her divinity. And more generally, the very presence of this group emphasizes the eminence of the cathedral school of Chartres on the eve of the thirteenth century, and the significant role of learning in medieval Christianity.

The north portal depicts the ascension of Christ—the end of his earthly life—corresponding to its beginning in the Virgin portal. Here the signs of the zodiac and a portrayal of the labors of the agricultural year balance the depiction of the Seven Liberal Arts in the Virgin portal. Below all three of these tympanum scenes, flanking the doorways, are a series of figures which represent the kings and queens of Judah, the ancestors of Mary and Christ.

There are some seven hundred figures in the west façade sculpture, but so perfectly are they integrated with the architecture that they do not intrude upon the viewer—rather they allow themselves to be discovered by him. The kings and queens are rendered in columnar form and serve as columns as well as decorations and representations of Biblical personages. The scenes and figures of the recessed doorway serve to define its structural arches. Even the tympanum scenes serve the architectural function of closing the space at the tops of the doors. Seldom have architecture and sculpture been in more perfect accord than in the Gothic style.

The ultimate symbolism lies in the upward thrust of every part of the great structure itself; in the spires of the flying buttresses, in the sharply pointed, narrow windows, and even in the steep pitch of the shed roof. The west façade towers complete the vertical thrust—the major effect of the Gothic style. The vertical stress of the exterior skeleton is repeated inside the cathedral in the great clustered piers and, most of all, the towering roof vault with its supporting ribs lost in the shadows more than a hundred feet above the floor.

The interior of the Gothic cathedral was designed for illumination. All interior decoration except that inherent in the structure itself was removed. There was little or no sculpture, no mosaic, no mural painting. Their place was taken by the light of the sun filtering through the transparent tapestry of stained glass windows. The constantly changing light clothes the interior of the cathedral with glowing patterns as carefully contrived as the symbolism of the exterior sculpture. Again we may choose Chartres as an example because its glass has no equal. Behind the altar, in the apse, a series of narrow lancet windows almost fifty feet tall are glazed in a deep blue to catch the brilliant morning sun. Along the sides of the cathedral in the tall clerestory windows and transept roses the spectrum unfolds until we reach the three lancet windows of the west façade and the great rose window above it in tones of predominant reds to emphasize the last dying rays of the western sun. The symbolic scheme of the windows was fully as complex and as encyclopedic as that of the sculpture, and as closely integrated with the structure. And, like the sculpture, the windows were the work of some of the most skillful masters in an age of master craftsmen.

Each of the great cathedrals has its own perfection. No two of them are alike and none of them was ever completely finished. Most of them have the typical, massive twin towers flanking the west façade. Some have spires atop the towers; some have a lofty "lantern tower" over the nave-transept crossing; some have porches. The cathedrals vary greatly in size and proportion, each having wide variations of style and form even within itself. In almost none of them do the towers and spires match each other perfectly. Differences in pier and rib styles often appear side by side in the same nave or choir. Each architect who inherited the supervision of a cathedral building expressed himself and the building and decorative vogue of his own generation. But the massiveness and grandeur of the structure itself absorbed the diversity of its parts to create an overpowering sense of unity.

SUGGESTIONS FOR FURTHER READING

≈✦

The Church and the World of Learning

W. Allman, *The Growth of Papal Government* (New York: Barnes and Noble, 1955).

F. Artz, *The Mind of the Middle Ages* (New York: Knopf, 1953).

*M. W. Baldwin, *The Medieval Church* (Ithaca: Cornell University Press, 1933).

*S. Baldwin, *The Organization of Medieval Christianity* (New York: Holt, 1929).

Basic Writings of St. Thomas Aquinas, ed., intro., and notes by A. C. Pegis (New York: Random House, 1945).

M. H. Carré, *Realists and Nominalists* (Oxford; Oxford University Press, 1946).

G. G. Coulton, *St. Bernard, His Predecessors and Successors,* Vol. I of *Five Centuries of Religion,* 3 vols. (Cambridge: Cambridge University Press, 1923).

E. Gilson, *The Philosophy of St. Thomas Aquinas* (Cambridge: Heffer, 1924).

C. H. Haskins, *The Renaissance of the Twelfth Century* (Cambridge: Harvard University Press, 1927), an important "thesis" book in medieval intellectual history.

————, *The Rise of the Universities* (New York: Holt, 1923), delightful series of essays.

Introduction to Saint Thomas Aquinas, ed. and intro. by A. C. Pegis (New York: Random House, 1948).

H. C. Lea, *The History of the Inquisition,* (New York: Harper, 1888), 3 vols., a classic liberal-Protestant work, tending to polemic.

Little Flowers of St. Francis and St. Bonaventura's *Life of St. Francis,* both in many editions.

A. C. McGiffert, *History of Christian Thought,* Vol. II. Fine treatment of the major figures and schools of medieval thought.

R. C. Mortimer, *Western Canon Law* (Berkeley: University of California Press, 1953).

*S. R. Packhard, *Europe and the Church under Innocent III* (New York: Holt, 1928).

S. Runciman, *The Medieval Manichee* (Cambridge: Cambridge University Press, 1947).

P. Sabatier, *The Life of St. Francis of Assisi* (New York: Scribners, 1894), the standard, modern biography.

Selected Writings of St. Thomas Aquinas, ed. by M. C. D'Arcy (New York: Dutton, 1950).

A. C. Shannon, *The Popes and Heresy in the Thirteenth Century* (Villanova: Augustinian Press, 1949).

Singer, Holmyard, and Hall, *A History of Technology,* cited for Chap. 1; refer to chapters on alchemy, chemistry, etc.

J. A. Symonds, *Wine, Women, and Song* . . . (London: Chatto and Windus, 1884), a collection of medieval student songs.

H. O. Taylor, *The Medieval Mind* (London: Macmillan, 1911), 2 vols., a classic work of medieval intellectual history.

L. Thorndike, *A History of Magic and Experimental Science,* Vol. II., cited for Chap. 6.

A. S. Turberville, *Medieval Heresy and the Inquisition* (London: Lockwood, 1920), a good popular treatment.

E. Vacandard, *The Inquisition* (New York: Longmans, 1908).

H. Waddell, *Peter Abélard* (London: Constable, 1933), a novelized biography of one of the most colorful of medieval schoolmen.

*————, *The Wandering Scholars* (Garden City, N. Y.: Anchor, 1955), a fascinating book of medieval student life.

Medieval Secular Literature

The Arthurian Cycle, Tristan and Iseult, and *Aucassin and Nicolette,* the most popular romances, are available in many editions.

Beowulf, ed. by C. W. Kennedy (New York: Oxford University Press, 1940).

E. K. Chambers, *The Medieval Stage* (Oxford: Oxford University Press, 1903), 2 vols.

*Dante, *Divine Comedy,* many editions; see especially the translation of Dorothy Sayers (Baltimore: Penguin, 1955).

The Epic of the Cid, tr. and ed. by J. G. Markley (Indianapolis: Bobbs-Merrill, 1961).

E. Gilson, *Dante the Philosopher* (New York: Sheed and Ward, 1948).

*W. P. Ker, *The Dark Ages* (New York: Mentor, 1958).

*———, *Epic and Romance* (New York: Dover, 1960).

Roger S. Loomis, *Arthurian Tradition and Chrétien de Troyes* (New York: Columbia University Press, 1949), basic critical work.

R. Menendez Pidal, *The Cid and His Spain,* tr. by H. Sunderland (London: Murray, 1934).

The Romance of the Rose, tr. and ed. Ellis, 3 vols. (London: Dent, 1926-28).

Song of Roland, tr. and ed. by C. K. Scott Moncrieff (Ann Arbor: University of Michigan Press, 1959).

K. Vossler, *Medieval Culture: An Introduction to Dante and His Times* (New York: Harcourt, 1929), 2 vols., a basic cultural history of the High Middle Ages.

Medieval Art

*Henry Adams, *Mont-Saint-Michel and Chartres* (Garden City, N. Y.: Anchor 1959), one of the most famous of medieval studies, not only of architecture but of medieval life and society.

*Emile Mâle, *The Gothic Image* (New York: Harper, 1958).

*C. R. Morey, *Christian Art* (New York: Norton, 1958).

———, *Medieval Art* (New York: Norton, 1942).

Otto von Simson, *The Gothic Cathedral* (New York: Pantheon, 1956).

*A. Temko, *Notre-Dame of Paris* (New York: Viking, 1955).

*Paperbound edition. In the case of reprint editions, publisher and date of publication given will be that of reprint rather than the original.

❧ 11 ❧

The Waning of the Middle Ages

THE DECLINE AND FALL OF THE PAPAL MONARCHY

The century and a half before the year 1300 had been a time of accelerating growth and accomplishment in the history of medieval Europe. Towns had sprung up and prospered; a flourishing network of trade had knit them together and quickened material life; the chaos of feudalism seemed to be giving way before the wealth and power of the national monarchies. In every field of activity there had been a reaching out and a sense of optimism. The forms of Gothic art had evolved and been perfected. The genres of vernacular literature had multiplied as never before. And the scholastic philosophy had met and absorbed the challenge of the Aristotelian revival.

The century and a half after the year 1300 presents almost exactly the opposite picture. It was a time of general war and devastation, of revolution and upheaval, of social instability and violent religious protest, of famine, pestilence, and a general attitude of despair and resignation. This pattern of the "waning" of the Middle Ages was common to Europe although, as we shall see in the next chapter, Italy must be regarded as an exception. The pattern took its most characteristic form in precisely that area of northwestern Europe where the highest development of the culture of the High Middle Ages had taken place.

Insofar as such complex patterns of events may be said to have a common cause, that cause seems to have been a prolonged and serious economic depression. The precise cause-and-effect relationship between economic and social or political or intellectual phenomena cannot yet be clearly seen through the complexity of events. But what we can see is a profound conditioning effect produced by economic crisis virtually throughout northern Europe. The curve of prosperity plunged sharply downward from its height of the late thirteenth century and did not recover until well after the mid-fifteenth century. In this period there was a general decline of agricultural productivity. Much of the land which had been reclaimed and settled in the thirteenth century reverted to forest and waste. Even land which had been in cultivation for centuries was abandoned. Manorial villages withered and disappeared. This was in part caused by a steady decline in population, massively accelerated by the Black Death that struck Europe in the mid-fourteenth century and continued to recur for another century. Labor shortage, of course, aggravated the problems of agricultural production as many laborers either demanded better conditions of tenure or fled their plots to seek work in the cities.

But towns and cities, even more than the countryside, were declining in population. They were hardest hit by epidemics, but of almost equal importance the trade and exchange that was the lifeblood of the city had declined also, to such an extent that the volume of trade in northern Europe in 1400 may actually have been less than it was a century before. Such conditions as these spread alarm in every direction and triggered savage social revolts and equally savage reprisals. At the same time as economic conditions had their effects in other spheres, military, political, and social events contributed heavily to the pattern of economic troubles. The chronic military anarchy of Germany and the intermittent progress of the Hundred Years War certainly had their effect upon every aspect of north European economy through much of this period and contributed to such things as the decline of trade and the depopulation of vast stretches of the countryside. The chronic insolvency of rulers, owing largely to the cost of war, contributed to the disastrous cycles of "boom and bust" which characterized large-scale, international finance in this period. Even the pressure for centralization of the national monarchies had its unsettling effect upon the general European economy. The French crown, for example, virtually ruined the Champagne fairs by taxation, and English merchants successfully demanded of their kings an end to the trading privileges of foreign companies in England and the extension of English trade privileges in Flanders. Each of these moves had profound effects upon the economic patterns of the age, and in each case the people whose material lives were based upon that economy found themselves less well off than their fathers had been. We can, of course, see these events somewhat more clearly than the men of the fourteenth and fifteenth centuries. They, in contrast, saw no rhyme nor reason to their problems. The very senselessness of things led men to anger, frustration, and despair. On the one hand they violently rejected many of the most substantial portions of their value system; on the other, they embraced the most extreme and neurotic expressions of religious fervor. Had the church been able to seize and mold this blind and desperate religious fervor the history of this period might have been very different indeed. But the church as an institution was too deeply involved with the very forces we have been discussing. It was too much of the world to seize the leadership of an otherworldly reaction.

In the course of the thirteenth century the church, directed by the monarchical papacy, became the greatest "state" of Europe. Yet its very success as a temporal power proved its greatest danger. To begin with, it undermined the church's spiritual purpose and leadership. Moreover, it inevitably aroused the hostility of the strong secular rulers of Europe. By the close of the thirteenth century the church found its authority challenged on all sides, and throughout the later Middle Ages the popes fought desperately to retain even the shadow of their power. We turn now to the story of that struggle.

Boniface VIII and the Kings

Boniface VIII (*1294–1303*) came to the papal throne in the last decade of the thirteenth century. He was a vain, ill-tempered, and imperious old man whose long life had been spent chiefly as a canon lawyer and papal diplomat. His interest in spiritual matters was slight; instead, he used the powers of the office to crush his personal enemies and its wealth to advance his own family. So strong was his love of power that he often discarded his priestly robes for the traditional garb of the emperor. His desire to play the autocrat led him to make extravagant claims for papal supremacy, surpassing even those made by Innocent III. His fatal error was to confuse the well-reasoned arguments of canon law and the pompous phrases of the papal chancery with the tough realities of politics.

Shortly after his accession, Boniface seized an opportunity to press his claims to supremacy. Both Edward I of England and Philip IV of France were involved in expensive and protracted wars—Edward against the Welsh and Scots, Philip against the Count of Flanders and the remaining English holdings in southwestern France. Both Philip and Edward demanded taxes of their national clergy; Boniface intervened with the bull, *Clericos Laicos,* in which he denied the right of any power but the pope to levy taxes upon the clergy.[1] Both kings struck back: Edward virtually outlawed any clergy who refused his demands; Philip prohibited the export of bullion from France and thus cut off the flow of papal revenue from the French church. Both kings were solidly supported by public opinion, and even the majority of the clergy could not stomach the pretensions of the pope. Boniface gradually allowed his prohibitions to lapse, but not his claims.

On the heels of the taxation crisis came another. Philip IV arrested a treasonable bishop in the south of France and held him for trial in the royal courts. The French clergy, fearful of the consequences of such a precedent, appealed to Rome and Boniface. The battle over the issue of jurisdiction was thus joined. Boniface revived the arguments of the former bull, issued another claiming the right to intervene in the temporal affairs of an "impious and wicked" ruler, and threatened Philip with a synod of the French clergy to undertake "the reformation of the kingdom and the amendment of the king." It was this crisis that led Philip to summon the first assembly of the Estates-General.[2] He had shrewdly judged the popular temper and with equal shrewdness he played upon it. The Estates backed the royal claims and protested the interference of the papacy; Boniface responded with the bull, *Unam Sanctam,* in 1302, the climactic statement of papal supremacy over the secular state. Of the "two swords" of medieval political theory, Boniface claimed "it is necessary for one sword to be under the other; and the temporal authority to be subjected to the spiritual." The papacy had made such assertions before, but Boniface pressed on: "Therefore if the temporal power errs, it will be judged by the spiritual power, and if the lower spiritual power errs, it will be judged by its superior"—an argument for supreme papal authority, subject to no man nor human agency—"it cannot be judged by men, but by God alone." The bull ends with the resounding conclusion, "We therefore declare, say, and affirm that submission on the part of every man to the bishop of Rome is altogether necessary for his salvation." The claim to supreme papal authority was thus elevated to the dignity of an article of faith.

The extravagant posture of the pope and the claims of *Unam Sanctam*

1. See p. 373.
2. See pp. 372-73.

drew a swift reaction from France. Against the pope and his arguments Philip IV raised a storm of propaganda in which he concealed an audacious scheme. Philip's chief adviser in this crisis was Guillaume de Nogaret, a clever, unscrupulous lawyer, one of the group of "new men" who had begun to replace the feudal lords and bishops in the royal councils of Europe. Philip and Nogaret drew up a list of charges against the pope, attacking his character, his personal life, his election, and the legitimacy of his claims. Nogaret then hastened to Italy, raised an armed band from among the pope's bitter personal enemies, and broke into the papal summer palace at Anagni to take Boniface captive. Nogaret was hardpressed to keep his "allies" from killing the aged pope; indeed, one of them struck him across the face with his mailed glove. The plan was to capture the pope and bring him back to France, where he could be tried before a general council that Philip IV would summon under his own presidency. The scheme might have succeeded had not the local villagers gathered and driven off the attackers. Boniface returned to Rome, where he died within a few weeks, never recovering from the shock and humiliation of "the terrible day at Anagni." That day belonged to Philip IV and with it the initiative in his long struggle against the pope.

Boniface's death was followed by a period of confusion. A successor died almost immediately under circumstances that strongly suggested he had been poisoned. Then almost a year of wrangling passed before the cardinals could agree on a successor. In 1305 they finally elected a French archbishop as Clement V.

"The Babylonian Captivity"

Instead of going to Italy to assume the papal office, Clement decided to take up residence at Avignon, the southern frontier of the French realm on the east bank of the Rhone. Now a French pope reigned in a city well within the long reach of the French king. Clement filled the College of Cardinals with his relatives, his personal friends, and "friends" of Philip IV. Thus began the period of French domination of the papacy that was to last for three-quarters of a century, through seven pontificates, and to be known, in the phrase of the Italian poet Petrarch, as "the Babylonian captivity" of the church. With each passing year Italy, torn with the factional strife in which Boniface had so vigorously competed, became less attractive to Clement. Moreover, the timid pope came increasingly under the power of the aggressive French king. He backed Philip in his systematic destruction of the Knights Templars. He not only revoked the

Pope Boniface VIII.

BONIFTIVS
PP·VIII

Carcassone.

offensive bulls that had been the undoing of Boniface, but even declared that the secular state was a divine foundation. Finally, Philip was found innocent of any part in the Anagni affair!

The interests of the French king as well as his own led Clement V to open once more the ancient contest with the German Empire. Emperor Henry VII, on the precedent of Philip IV, declared his superiority to papal authority and marched into Italy. For dynastic reasons and with sublime inconsistency, Philip supported the traditional anti-imperial position of his captive pope. The ensuing contest between empire and papacy was a ghostly echo of the twelfth century—a shadow struggle between an empire that could not hold Italy and a papacy that had abandoned it—but the hostilities were no less real. Indeed, through the reigns of four popes and into the middle of the fourteenth century, the Italian-imperial question remained a more or less constant papal preoccupation and a focal issue in the complex affairs of Germany and central Europe.

Henry VII died in 1313 in Italy, still trying to revive the moribund claims of the empire. His death brought the curse of another disputed election. The imperial title was seized by Louis, the Duke of Bavaria, who was opposed by the Hapsburg Duke Frederick. Since Louis of Bavaria took the traditionally strong secular position of the empire, he was the object of special attack by Pope John XXII, Clement's successor and one of the most vigorous and venomous of medieval popes. In response, Louis extended the protection of his court to any enemy of the papacy or the church. The papal-imperial quarrel provoked widespread criticism of the church, not only for its political activities, but for its numerous other shortcomings, many of which stemmed from its wealth and temporal ambitions.

One of the most important of the critics of the church was the English Franciscan scholar, William of Occam (c. 1300–1349), a leading spokesman for the extreme purist wing of the Franciscan Order, the Spirituals. The group had already been condemned by John XXII for its insistence on clerical poverty. Indeed, John had actually gone to the length of declaring it heresy to claim that Christ and the Apostles lived in poverty! William of Occam, in opposing the wealth of the church, also opposed its political power and thus, rather obliquely, became the advocate of the political supremacy of the state over the church as the only way in which the church could be returned to the true concerns of religion.

A more direct and vigorous champion of secularism was the Italian scholar, Marsilio of Padua (c. 1290–1343), author of *Defensor Pacis*

("The Defender of Peace"), one of the most significant works of medieval political theory. The "defender," maintained Marsilio, should be the emperor, the secular power ruling for the people, in their interest, and under their law. The church, he argued, should be under the state, concerned only with man's spiritual governance and having neither political power, independent wealth, nor legal jurisdiction. He rejected the narrow clerical definition of the church altogether, and with it the special status of clergy, and even the Petrine theory, the basis of the pope's status. (The theory of the dynastic succession of the popes from Peter, pp. 190–91.) To Marsilio the church was the community of the faithful, the whole body of Christian believers; its spiritual authority was Scripture; and its coercive authority was a general council, a body representative of and responsible to the community of the faithful. These remarkable theories were to play a significant role in the reform schemes of individuals and councils through the fifteenth century, and to be taken up by the Protestant revolutionaries of the sixteenth.

The papacy at Avignon found itself opposed not only by the German emperor and his secular theorists, but by other kings. The powerful monarchs of France and their royal kin on half a dozen minor thrones throughout Europe generally challenged the temporal power that the papacy had once claimed. In distant Bohemia and much of eastern Europe kings championed rising national sentiment in opposition to the western-Latin-Catholic tradition which had been so long identified with tyranny over them. In England the vigorous Edward III took advantage of popular resentment against the church and the papacy. In the mid-fourteenth century the king and Parliament passed the antipapal statutes of *Provisors* and of *Praemunire*. The *Statute of Provisors* prohibited papal appointment to vacancies in the English church, i.e., the papal claim to "provision." The *Statute of Praemunire* similarly prohibited judicial appeal from English church courts to the pope. Both these important statutes reflected the popular hostility to the papacy as a "foreign power" in league with France, the national enemy of England in the Hundred Years' War.

Despite such attacks upon the papacy by kings, parliaments, scholars, theorists, reformers, and plain people, the popes at Avignon continued the same practices and condoned the same abuses that had been criticized with increasing temper for two centuries. Some of them were sincerely interested in clerical reform and some were men of deep personal piety. But they were all committed to a direction the papacy had charted long before them and were trapped in the crisis of their time. The papacy had become, for better or worse, a monarchical state. It had to behave like a state and it had to compete with the growing strength of the secular monarchies as they assumed more aggressive form in the fourteenth century. The papal monarchy was committed to political, diplomatic, and administrative responsibilities that constantly became heavier. The essentially secular tasks of papal government were increasingly the primary concern of the popes and their spiritual responsibilities were necessarily either neglected or subverted. This secularization of the papacy was radically accelerated in the fourteenth century, and an increasing din of criticism accompanied the process.

The most strident criticism was leveled at papal finance. With the abandonment of Rome and the papal states a large portion of the regular papal revenue was lost and the popes of Avignon had to find new sources of income. The result was a financial administration at once the most advanced, the most efficient, the most lucrative, and the most ruthless in Europe. Its guiding genius was John XXII (*1316–1334*), who had succeeded Clement V in 1316. He was a French cardinal, almost seventy years old when he became pope. But neither his years nor his extreme personal mysticism lessened his vitality. He was an unflagging advocate of papal supremacy and the champion of the "French party." He fought with Louis of Bavaria, with the Italian barons who threatened the remaining papal interests in Italy, and with the Spiritual Franciscans.

In order to maintain his position of supremacy John needed money, and he forced the administrative machinery of the church to yield it. The way had been prepared for his reforms. The theory of papal supremacy within the church had long been stated and was generally accepted. The administrative and financial structure was already established. He had only to extend its province and improve its efficiency. John vastly extended the right of papal "reservation" or "provision," that is, the right of direct appointment by the pope to local church positions. By the end of the Avignonese period there was almost no church benefice above the parish level left unclaimed by the pope. These offices were, of course, for sale. In anticipation of vacancies the papacy would receive generous gifts from hopeful applicants. Many church offices were created for no better reason than to be sold. The most frequent charge of outraged reformers in the later Middle Ages was the charge of *simony*—the sale of spiritual offices. The principle of papal reservation was applied not only to church offices, but to the vast number of taxes, rents, fees, and other money payments up and down the hierarchy of the church. More and more cases at canon law—

and consequently their judicial fees—were brought under direct papal jurisdiction. Through his "plenitude of power" the pope claimed the right of supervision and "visitation" formerly exercised by bishops and regional church officials. Local churches and foundations were seldom visited, but they were regularly taxed for visits. The pope, as interim administrator, collected the revenues for church offices that were vacant, and there were many vacancies left unfilled for years to the profit of the papacy. Closely related to "vacancies" was the new papal tax, called *annates,* "first fruits," a portion of the first year's revenue from a papal benefice. In all, the treasury of John XXII collected more than four hundred specific fees and the annual papal income far exceeded that of any secular monarch.

The financial and administrative abuses of the papacy spread downward through the church: unscrupulous and profiteering papal collectors were legion; hard-pressed church officials passed their financial burdens along to the resentful public; absenteeism was prevalent among the high clergy (we have already noted the hostile action taken in England against papal provision); dispensations from canon law were as easy to buy as offices; thus, no corner of Christendom was free of complaints against clerical immorality and abuses.

There had been persistent and well-founded pressure on the popes to return to Italy. But central Italy was a jungle into which the French popes of Avignon had no great desire to venture. The towers of bandit lords dominated every hamlet in the papal states, and Rome itself was divided into petty sectors, each the province of some warlike noble family. During the pontificates of Clement VI (*1342–1352*) and especially Innocent VI (*1352–1362*) some headway was made against this disorder, the warlike and efficient Cardinal Albornoz successfully clearing many of the war lords from papal lands. Moreover, the ravages of the Hundred Years' War were beginning to reach toward Avignon. Urban V (*1362–1370*) actually returned the papacy to Rome, but the city was still a ruin and life there still compared unfavorably with the luxury and security of Avignon, especially for the predominantly French cardinals. After three years Urban was constrained to move his court back to Avignon. His successor, Gregory XI (*1370–1378*), once more returned to Rome and died there. Thus the electoral conclave was held in Rome for the first time in more than seventy-five years. While the cardinals deliberated on their choice of a pope an unruly mob of Romans milled outside and demonstrated for an Italian pope and, for the first time in more than seventy-five years, the cardinals elected one, the Archbishop of Bari, who became Urban VI (*1378–1389*).

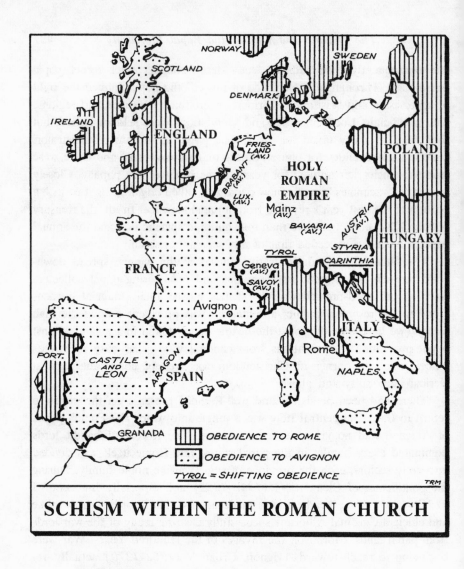

OBEDIENCE TO ROME

OBEDIENCE TO AVIGNON

TYROL = SHIFTING OBEDIENCE

SCHISM WITHIN THE ROMAN CHURCH

The Great Schism

Urban VI, to the chagrin of his cardinals, immediately announced a severe reform program. Furthermore, he ruled with tyrannical force and, as a native Italian of humble birth, he savagely attacked the pleasure-loving and aristocratic French cardinals. Their every interest threatened, they withdrew from Rome, declared the election of Urban VI invalid because of coercion, elected one of their own number as Clement VII (*1378–1394*), and returned to Avignon. Urban refused to accept either his deposition or the election of his rival. He proceeded to fill the College of Cardinals with

Italian clerics. Clement VII in Avignon maintained the French majority in *his* College of Cardinals. Thus Christendom was confronted with two popes, two sacred colleges, and two papal courts, at Rome and Avignon. Each pope excommunicated the other. Curses were hurled back and forth as each claimed supremacy over the other. The Great Schism had begun.

The nations of Europe were now faced with a choice. Divided by the Hundred Years' War and a number of lesser conflicts, their decisions tended to follow the dictates of political expediency. England supported the Roman papacy; France, the Avignonese. The minor states moving in the orbit of either of these major powers followed suit. Political motivation similarly influenced the decisions of the German and Italian principalities and the states of eastern Europe. The papacy had fought to establish itself as a state, it was now reduced to nothing more than one. The abuses financial, moral, and otherwise, which had been the scandal of the "Babylonian" papacy continued. Indeed, they became more flagrant as two popes contended for wealth and power and neither was able to enforce general clerical discipline.

The Great Schism provoked an unprecedented wave of criticism and popular hostility to the church. The arguments of Occam and Marsilio were revived and augmented. One of the most important critics of the church and papacy was the English scholar John Wyclif (*c.* 1320–1384). Although his principal interests were theological, he resolutely followed their implications into socio-political doctrines. As Luther, Calvin, and Zwingli would do in the sixteenth century, Wyclif rejected the traditional Thomist Scholasticism. Going beyond William of Occam, he denied the sacraments, the priestly power, and the special nature of the church. He based his concepts of religion upon the authority of Scripture, literally interpreted, rejecting the canonists, the glossators, the interpreters, the allegorists, and the Aristotelians. He maintained that the simple word of God revealed in the Bible and available to any who heard or read was a sufficient guide for the Christian. Such an argument denied to the church that monopoly of grace which it claimed as the special agent of God. To Wyclif, as to Occam and Marsilio, the church was the community of believers. But again Wyclif went further and anticipated the Reformation by including in his definition of the church the Calvinist notion that it was also the community of the elect, those souls predestined by God for salvation.

Having attacked the theological foundation and, indeed, the theoretical necessity of the church, he attacked its temporalities. He advocated a return to the simplicity of the early church, again anticipating the "primitivism" of the Reformation. He hated the wealth and power of the church and saw them as the source of its corruption. Consequently he championed the supremacy of the state over the church in such temporal concerns. It was this advocacy that enabled Wyclif to survive. The English state was most tolerant toward any theory that justified its seizure of church property and ecclesiastical powers. But it was his simple, uncomplicated, and persuasive religious doctrines that won Wyclif his popular following. He translated the Bible into English for the first time, and much of his writing was in English. His followers, the Poor Priests, were better known as the Lollards. They continued to preach Wyclif's doctrines but, like many such groups, they tended to become associated with social revolution and be discredited. Nevertheless, some traces of Lollardry survived in England into the sixteenth century.

Wyclif's most telling influence was not in England, but in Bohemia. A dynastic marriage had brought a Bohemian princess to England as the queen of Richard II, and with her came many Bohemian scholars, among them Jerome of Prague. Jerome was deeply affected by Wyclif's teachings and carried them back to the University of Prague, where they became associated with the ardent nationalism of Czech students and masters. One of the latter was a fiery young reformer named John Hus (c. 1369–1415). The arguments of Wyclif supported the attacks that Hus had already begun to make upon the temporalities of the church and clerical immorality. Hus became rector of the University of Prague, largely on the basis of his leadership in the anti-German, nationalist cause. But he slipped easily from criticism into heresy and attacked not only the corruption of the clergy and the pope but the whole theory of the clerical state, as well as the theory of the sacraments, indulgences, and the sacrifice of the Mass. In spite of his heretical opinions—perhaps because of them—Hus grew in popularity and behind him grew an extreme nationalist, ascetic, reforming party known as the Hussites. In 1414 he was summoned to the church council in Constance to present his views. He had been given a safe-conduct by the Bohemian emperor, Sigismund, but once in Constance the emperor deserted him. Seized by the orthodox party, he was tried and burned at the stake in 1415. He was shortly followed by Jerome of Prague. Their martyrdom only succeeded in transforming the Hussites into a revolutionary party. Hus became the symbol of Czech nationalism and in his name the sturdy Hussites maintained their independence in central Europe until they joined forces with the Protestant Reformation a century later.

Trenchant criticism of the church by men like Wyclif and Hus not only encouraged the spread of new heresies, but revived older ones. The teachings of the Albigensians, the Waldensians and the Spiritual Franciscans began to enjoy renewed popularity throughout Europe. Groups preaching apostolic poverty and evangelical purity sprang up in Bavaria, the Rhine valley, and eastern Europe. Groups resembling the English Lollards appeared in the Low Countries under a dozen names. Every peasant revolt or proletarian uprising of the later Middle Ages had its companion heresy and fanatic religious leaders. There were quietist groups who harbored suspicious views and service groups who practiced organized charity and practical mysticism as semireligious lay orders. The most significant of these were the Brethren of the Common Life.

The Brethren were founded by Gerard Groote (1340–1384) in the Low Countries. By the end of the fourteenth century there were Brethren Houses in many Dutch towns and the movement was spreading to Germany. The members lived in common, sharing what goods they had. They organized charity and, especially, schools. Their schools, founded to spread a renewed spirit of religious devotion, were probably the best of their time in northern Europe. They were responsible for the education of many of the great religious figures of the late fifteenth and sixteenth centuries, including Erasmus and Luther. However, the very purity of their lives and teaching rendered the Brethren a reproach to the clergy and consequently made them suspect in the eyes of the official church. Moreover, their teachings shared with a number of mystic movements an emphasis on personal religion and union with God, which again scarcely endeared them to the orthodox.

The Conciliar Movement

Much of the religious criticism and anticlerical sentiment of the late fourteenth and fifteenth centuries stemmed from the Great Schism. The Roman Urban VI was succeeded by Innocent VII and Gregory XII; the French Clement VII, by Benedict XIII. The general opinion of Europe swelled in protest against the continued division of the church and many voices joined the shouts of heretics and reformers. Neither papacy would admit the competence of the other and neither would submit. Gradually a movement developed advocating the convocation of a council to resolve the great controversy and heal the schism. Marsilio and others had already denied the absolutist claims of the papacy and argued that the will of the church as a whole must bind even the pope. That will was best expressed through a representative council, as in the early centuries of Christian history. Councils were proposed and threatened several times in the closing years of the fourteenth century. Finally a party within each of the sacred colleges joined to call the Council of Pisa in 1409, ushering in the "age of the councils."

The Council of Pisa was a splendid and hopeful assembly, attended by delegates from every important secular court, from both Rome and Avignon, from the universities—especially Paris and Bologna—and by thousands of ecclesiastical dignitaries. The council sessions heard the cases against both ruling popes, the Roman Gregory XII and the Avignonese Benedict XIII, and declared them both deposed as schismatics, heretics, and consorters with heretics. The council then chose a unitary successor as Alexander V and the delegates departed, their work well done, leaving the task of reform in the hands of the new pope. But the problems of the conciliar age had only begun. Almost immediately Alexander V died and the unitary cardinals chose the most forceful of their number to replace him, Cardinal Baldassare Cossa, as John XXIII.[3] They could not have chosen more badly. The new pope was a man of notorious reputation for violence and wickedness and had not the slightest vestige of spirituality. He was a highly successful general and diplomat, akin to the tyrants of many north Italian states. In the meantime, both the deposed popes had denied the jurisdiction of the council and refused to abdicate. Thus the Council of Pisa had succeeded only in creating three popes where two had been before; and the new pope who carried the conciliar banner was even more disgraceful and intractable than the other two.

The scandal of John's election, the obvious subversion of reform, the prospect of new abuses, and the aggravated schism raised a clamor of nearly universal complaint. In this crisis the newly elected Emperor Sigismund stepped forward to call another council. It pleased his imperial ambition to invoke the precedent of Constantine and Nicaea. Furthermore, he was sincerely interested in healing the troubles of the church and the European community of nations held him in respect. John XXIII, seriously threatened by his enemies in Italy, was forced to publish the bulls sanctioning the council which was to convene at Constance in 1414.

It was an even more splendid assembly than the Council of Pisa, more broadly representative, and with a more definite program not only to end the schism but to reform the church "in head and members," and

---

3. Since the "official" list of the Roman Catholic Church rejects such conciliar popes, the recent pope (1958-1963) was free to assume the name and number of John XXIII.

to stamp out the heresy which, as we have seen, had flamed up once more, particularly in Bohemia. The condemnation of Hus was an auspicious symbol of the serious intention of the council as a whole. It turned with equally stern purpose to the problem of the schism. Pope John had lent his dignity to the council in the hope of manipulating it into confirming him in his office. But when it became apparent that not only Gregory and Benedict, but he too was to be deposed, he fled Constance, hoping to paralyze decision by his absence. But the council proclaimed its superiority to papal power and had John arrested and brought back to Constance to answer a long list of charges. He was tried, convicted, deposed, and imprisoned. Close on the heels of this radical action, Gregory XII resigned. Appeals were made to Benedict XIII to follow suit. Emperor Sigismund met with him and the council argued for two years on the question. Benedict remained adamant and finally in 1417 he was simply declared deposed. (Until his death six years later Benedict continued to style himself pope, but he had lost all support and all prestige and was largely ignored.)

Thus, in 1417 the council and the cardinals finally proceeded to the election of a new unitary pope, this time an adroit politician and cardinal of the Roman family of Colonna who took the name of Martin V *(1417-1431)*. A list of reform articles had been drawn up by the council and accepted by Martin before his election. But the hope for reform was completely frustrated in the months that followed. The parties to the council had already begun to leave. Those who remained could not agree on the implementation of reform and Martin V skillfully divided their opinions. In the spring of 1418, after more than three and one-half years, Martin V dissolved the Council of Constance with the promise of convening another at Pavia in five years.

In the years that followed Martin V sought every means to evade another council and to repair the arguments as well as the substance of papal supremacy. The promises of reform were completely ignored. A truly effective council was stalled off until after Martin's death. His successor, Eugenius IV, another ambitious Italian politician, was equally opposed to the conciliary theory. But he was unable to avoid sanctioning another council, which met at Basel in 1431. The princes of Europe had already threatened Martin V with the fate of John XXIII.

The most pressing business before the council, and one of the principal reasons it was called, was the Hussite problem. The militant followers of Hus, under able leadership, had consistently defeated the armies sent against them. Their successes spread their heresies and all of eastern

Europe was threatened with contamination. But before much could be done either against heresy or for reform the old issue of jurisdiction was raised once more, with delays, maneuvering, and charges of bad faith. Some headway was made against the Hussites, more because of their own dissension than because of any positive action by the council. But the council claimed the victory and its prestige was enhanced. Eugenius IV, still refusing to deal with heretics on equal terms and hoping to steal the initiative from the council, declared it dissolved and called another at Ferrara. The Council of Basel, seeing its advantage slipping, damaged its cause further by electing a rival pope, the widowed layman Amadeus, Duke of Savoy, in 1439. It could now be charged with reopening the schism that a former council had healed with such pains. The conciliators at Basel dwindled in number as more and more members defected to Eugenius and his council at Ferrara (it was later moved to Florence). Furthermore, the pope had found an important propaganda issue, the reunion of the Greek and Latin churches, a papal dream for more than three centuries. The representatives of the Greek Church were induced to come to the council and to hold out the possibility of reunion because of the increased pressure of the Turks and the forlorn hope that compliance on religious questions might bring military and financial help from the west. But the hope of such help—never very strong—faded, and the theological issues dividing east and west were hopelessly muddled. After months of argument and fragile agreement the pope declared that Christendom was once more united under his hand; and the Greek clerics agreed. It was a triumph for Eugenius in spite of the fact that the act of reunion was never accepted by the Greek church as a whole, and little done to implement it in the west.

The great hope of conciliar reform faded and the papacy reasserted its supremacy over the church. At the same time it lost the last vestige of its claim to supremacy over the national states. As the Council of Basel wrangled, the French king Charles VII convened a synod of his clergy at Bourges. This group, dominated by the French conciliar party, took the initiative that the delegates at Basel had lost and proclaimed that the decrees of a council are superior to the pope. The proclamation was called the Pragmatic Sanction of Bourges (1438) and was, in effect, a declaration of independence for the French national church. This document accepted the principal reform items which the councils had debated for thirty years—denial of papal "provisions" in France, the prohibition of "annates," and the restriction of papal legal jurisdiction. Almost point for point, Philip IV's arguments against the claims of Boniface VIII more than a century earlier now triumphed. In the following year, the German Imperial diet adopted a similar arrangement, the Pragmatic Sanction of Mainz. Less than half a century later, by the Concordat of 1482, the Spanish church was largely freed of papal control and became a national church. The English church won virtually the same status by default.

In 1449 the rump sessions of the Council of Basel were terminated by its own members after almost twenty years of fruitless deliberation. The conciliar movement had failed. It had produced no significant body of reform and the same abuses in religion scandalized the general opinion of Europe in 1450 as in 1400. It had failed in its design to change the fundamental constitution of the church and make of it a limited monarchy. The popes, even those created by the councils, consistently opposed every item of conciliar theory and relentlessly maintained the position of papal supremacy. The failure of the conciliar movement to effect a general reform of religion left open only the avenue to revolution, and that revolution came with Luther and the Protestant Reformation.

FRANCE, ENGLAND, AND THE HUNDRED YEARS' WAR

The Causes of the War

The roots of this conflict reached back to the link forged between France and England by the Norman conquest. Although the great Capetian kings of the thirteenth century had taken from their Angevin cousins most of the French lands held by Henry II, the English still retained a foothold in southwestern France—principally Guienne and Gascony. However, they held these lands as vassals of the French crown, and the performance of vassal duties constituted a continual source of friction. The situation was aggravated by the economic importance of the region for England. One of the chief wine-growing areas of Europe, it produced most of the wine consumed in England and at the same time provided a lucrative source of taxes for the English crown.

An economic tie also bound England to another French fief, that held by the counts of Flanders. The Flemish cloth towns were the principal buyers of raw wool, England's chief export. By the opening years of the fourteenth century these towns were in constant political turmoil caused by the conflict between the merchant oligarchies and the commons of the towns. The merchants, fighting to preserve their position, appealed to the

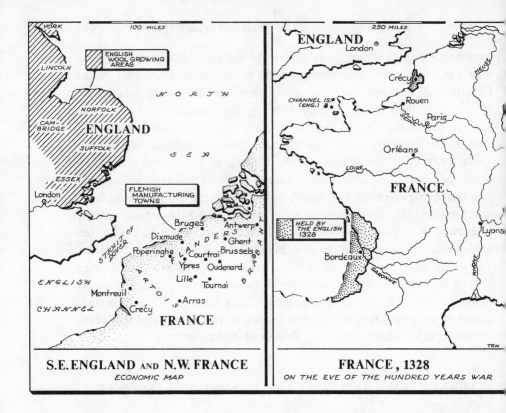

Count of Flanders to keep order; he, in turn, appealed to his overlord, the French king. The commons of the town, fighting for political rights and economic equality, appealed to the English (who could ill afford open French intervention in this region so vital to their economic well-being).

Other circumstances also contributed to fan the antagonism between the French and the English. Scotland encouraged the French to war on its aggressive southern neighbor, while exiled French barons encouraged the English kings to war against those who had driven them out of their lands. French, English, and Flemish sailors constantly clashed in piratical encounters in the Channel and the North Sea. Only a pretext was needed to precipitate open war, and that presented itself in 1328.

In that year the third son of Philip the Fair of France died. He was the last member of the direct Capetian line and was succeeded by his cousin, Philip VI of the House of Valois. In this French dynastic crisis the young, vigorous, and ambitious Edward III of England saw an opportunity for the Angevins. His mother had been the daughter of Philip IV, and

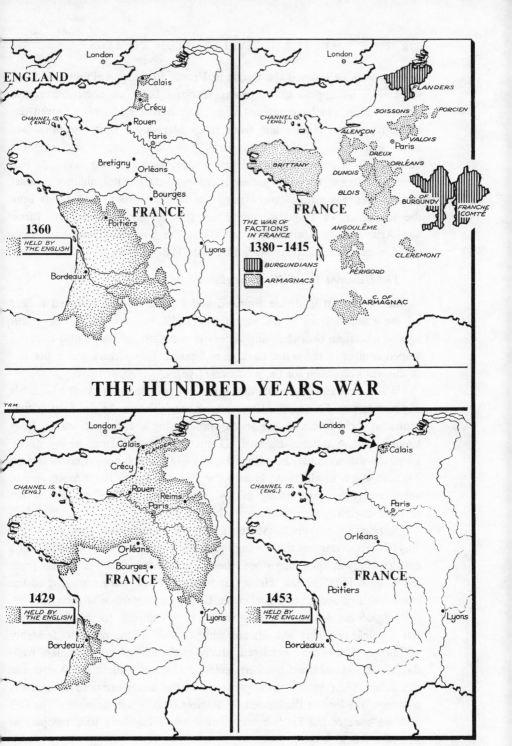

THE HUNDRED YEARS WAR

on that basis he claimed the throne of France for himself. Philip VI countered with an appeal to the so-called Salic Law, an ancient Frankish statute which had been revived some time before and which barred descendants in the female line from royal succession. Both positions had some legal basis. Philip VI answered Edward's claim by declaring the latter's fiefs forfeited and marching an army into Guienne in 1338. Edward had begun to put together a complex continental alliance against France that was already threatening the Rhine frontier. About this time the townsmen of Flanders, under an able revolutionary leader, Jacob van Artevelde, recognized Edward III as the king of France and negotiated a commercial treaty with England. The war was on.

The Hundred Years' War: English Phase

In an attempt to divide England and Flanders the French put a fleet off the Flemish coast in the summer of 1340. But the English fleet sent against it won an overwhelming victory in the Battle of Sluys, and England gained control of the water passage to France. This victory was a presage of the war's direction for the next twenty years.

With command of the sea and a base of operations in the feudal lands of southwestern France, the English took the initiative. As the French concentrated their forces in the south, anticipating a concerted attack from English-held Aquitaine, Edward III opened a second front in the north. Landing in Normandy, he planned a ravaging march across northwestern France, which would bring him to the Flemish coast. The French forces, some twenty thousand strong, hastily moved north and the two armies met in 1346 at Crécy, near the Flemish border.

Although the French had the advantage of numbers, they found the English in a strong position on high ground. As the heavily armored French cavalry charged up a long slope, they were met by a rain of arrows from the English longbowmen. Horses and men fell and were trampled as the cavalry charge broke up in confusion. Under the protection of their archers, the English cavalry and pikemen moved in to complete the rout. At nightfall the field of Crécy was littered with the ruin of the proudest feudality of Europe. The victory belonged largely to the English longbowmen, well-diciplined and seasoned by their recent campaigns against the Welsh and the Scots. Their effectiveness proved that the heavy-armored knight was no longer the lord of the battlefield. Almost equally significant was the fact that the core of the English army consisted of regularly paid troops and not of a feudal levy.

At Crécy, the English gained a military reputation that was to last for centuries. Of more immediate consequence, however, was the winning of Calais. After Crécy, Edward moved directly west and besieged this important coastal city. The fall of Calais in the following spring may well have been the most important victory of the war. Through the later changes of fortune, Calais remained in English hands—a secure entry port into France, an economic center for the continental wool trade, and a symbol of the formidable power of English arms.

The campaigns of 1346–47 were followed by a truce which lasted for nearly ten years. But, for the French, the period was scarcely distinguishable from open war and in many ways worse in its effects on the populace. Marauding bands of unemployed soldiers ravaged the countryside, living off the helpless peasantry. This kind of devastation became the most characteristic feature of the Hundred Years' War, more telling in every way than the few pitched battles and formal treaties that mark its course.

In 1356 the French again gathered their forces, this time under the command of John II (*1350–1364*), Philip's successor. A small English raiding force under Edward the Black Prince, the eldest son of Edward III,

---

THE POWERS OF THE HUNDRED YEARS' WAR

ENGLAND	*FRANCE*	*BURGUNDY*
EDWARD III (*1327-1377*)	PHILIP VI (Valois) (*1328-1350*)	
	JOHN THE GOOD (*1350-1364*)	PHILIP THE BOLD (*1363-1404*)
RICHARD II (*1377-1399*)	CHARLES V (the Wise) (*1364-1380*)	
HENRY IV (*1399-1413*)	CHARLES VI (*1380-1422*)	JOHN THE FEARLESS (*1404-1419*)
HENRY V (*1413-1422*)		
HENRY VI (*1422-1461*)	CHARLES VII (*1422-1461*)	PHILIP THE GOOD (*1419-1467*)
		CHARLES THE BOLD (*1467-1477*)

---

was caught by the French at Poitiers. It was the story of Crécy once more: the French feudal cavalry charged the English defensive position; the English archers broke the attack as before and the battle became a slaughter. King John, his son, and a great number of other high nobles were captured; thousands of others were killed; and the survivors fled in wild confusion. The Black Prince returned in triumph to England with his prisoners. After three years of desultory campaigning and false truces, a general peace was arranged in 1360 by the Treaty of Bretigny-Calais. By its terms Edward III received substantial concessions in French lands, an expanded area in the southwest, and the lands around the port of Calais, roughly what the English actually held after Poitiers. Further, the vexing problem of feudal obligations was resolved: Edward was to hold his French lands in sovereign right. The ransom for King John was set at the equivalent of thirty million dollars. In return, Edward was to renounce his claim to the French throne. This treaty ultimately proved to be as meaningless as the several truces already made and violated in the course of the war.

The Recovery and Relapse of France

The acceptance by France of the humiliating terms of Bretigny-Calais reflected the chaotic state of her affairs. King John II had been captured at Poitiers, leaving government in the hands of the Dauphin[4] Charles, his eldest son, a weak and sickly boy of eighteen. Moreover, the coterie of nobles that, in effect, had constituted the government of France, had been either killed, exiled, or disgraced as a result of the encounter at Poitiers. The remnant of the government bureaucracy was dispersed, its operation paralyzed by the absence of the king; the court had no head, no army, and almost no financial resources.

In this crisis the French Estates-General made its long-delayed bid for a voice in the management of the realm. The renewal of the English advance in 1355–56 had forced John II to call the Estates to ask for taxes. Seizing this opportunity, the Estates demanded a measure of control over the expenditure of the tax money they voted. A wealthy merchant and popular spokesman for the Parisian middle class, Étienne Marcel, led the Estates in this radical demand. After the disaster of Poitiers the demands

---

4. This title had come to designate the heir apparent to the French throne; the Prince of Wales is the English equivalent. It was the result of a succession arrangement made by Philip VI with the last ruler of the Dauphine, a territory in the south of France.

of the Estates were stated even more emphatically, and the hard-pressed Dauphin was forced to the concession known as the Great Ordinance. By its provisions, a permanent committee of the Estates-General was to supervise the expenditure of all tax funds; the Estates were to meet regularly and frequently, and some general social reforms were to be undertaken.

The Estates-General seemed about to follow the English Parliament in gaining a voice for the people in the affairs of government. But Marcel pushed on too fast and too far; he crossed the line into revolt against the crown. Marcel planned to replace the weak Dauphin with Charles of Navarre, one of several royal cousins of the Dauphin. He had already begun these negotiations and, to bring additional pressure upon the court, had raised the people of Paris in a revolutionary commune. Marcel's leadership faltered and the captive Dauphin escaped from the barricades of Paris to the comparative safety of the provinces. He summoned an ad hoc assembly that voted him the funds necessary to recapture Paris and, on the eve of the Treaty of Bretigny-Calais, Charles returned in triumph to his capital. Marcel was murdered and royal government was reestablished. The Dauphin had grown into King Charles V (*1364–1380*) whose bitterness and suspicion passed for wisdom (he was called Charles the Wise) in a time when the French realm could boast little better. Marcel's intrigues and his identification with the cause of the Estates-General had produced a reaction against popular government. In the decade following 1359 the liberty and initiative of the Estates were further compromised. In 1369 the king extracted from them a virtually perpetual right of taxation, and the control of the national finance passed to the royal treasury. The Estates-General had lost its moment; not for another four hundred years and a bloody revolution would France have a representative assembly and popular liberty.

Significant in the discrediting of popular government was its association with a massive peasant revolt that broke out in 1358—a revolt that had been brewing for generations. Earlier in the century, immediately following the opening campaigns of the war, a virulent plague, the Black Death, had spread to France from Italy. Perhaps as much as a third of the population of western Europe had perished from it and the periodic outbreaks that recurred into the next century. On the heels of the disease came the ravages of war, and it was the helpless peasantry that was hardest hit not only by the raids but also by the plundering of the marauding bands of French soldiers. Unprotected, the peasants were kidnaped and impressed for military service, tortured and killed. Their villages and crops went up in flames. To these miseries, including famine, the government added the burden of war taxes.

With no leadership, no strategy or arms, the peasantry rose in ferocious rebellion in the summer of 1358. In blind fury they turned on the nobility, their traditional masters and oppressors. The indifference of the nobility to the widespread suffering of the peasants no doubt helped fan the flames. And perhaps the defeat of the nobles at Poitiers encouraged the peasants to attack those who had for so long seemed invincible. The uprising spread throughout western France. Étienne Marcel, already engaged in intriguing with Charles of Navarre, now sided with the peasant revolt, no doubt hoping to use it in his attempt to unseat the Dauphin. Although the Estates-General neither tried nor claimed to represent the peasants, Marcel's activities linked that body with the brutal revolt. When it was finally put down—with great cruelty and severity—there was an almost universal reaction against the peasantry in favor of stable royal government. In spite of the fact that its connection with the revolt had been slight, the Estates-General was included in the popular reaction against it.

The widespread support that Charles attracted throughout France in those troubled years became the basis of a slow and steady recovery. There was a reassertion of royal absolutism, but there was also a return of confidence in the crown and in the state. This was further bolstered by a slow but favorable turn in the fortunes of war. The French were finally profiting from the lessons taught them by English arms during the previous thirty years: the French army was reorganized; Charles retained a semi-permanent force of regular troops and began to turn to disciplined infantry in preference to the gallant and ineffective feudal cavalry; further, for the first time in the war, the French had an able general in Bertrand du Guesclin, who was made marshal of the French armies by Charles V. Under his command the French began to regain both their captured lands and the initiative in the war. Meanwhile, the English lost their boldest general, the dreaded Black Prince, in 1376. The following year Edward III, his father, died, leaving the throne to the ten-year-old son of the Black Prince, Richard II, and to the several ambitious lords who vied for control over the young king. The English were virtually out of the war and by 1380 their continental holdings had once more been reduced to a coastal foothold in the south and Calais in the north.

At this crucial point the French advantage was lost again. In 1380

Charles V was succeeded by his young son, Charles VI. In his minority the powers of the crown fell into the hands of his three unscrupulous uncles, the dukes of Berry, Anjou, and Burgundy. These men, already powerful magnates, virtually divided France among them and among their selfish private interests. The three centuries of Capetian struggle against feudalism seemed lost with the emergence of the new feudalism of royal factions. For a moment the dukes were threatened when the king reached his majority. Then in 1392 Charles VI became violently insane. Factionalism reasserted itself and civil war rapidly approached.

As the factions struggled for power, two parties formed: one around Philip, the Duke of Burgundy, and the other around Louis d'Orléans, Charles VI's handsome, wastrel brother who had become the closest adviser of the mad king. Louis d'Orléans drew his support largely from his family lands in the south and the east of France. The opposing power of the Duchy of Burgundy had been ominously growing since mid-century. The same King John who was defeated and captured at Poitiers had given the nucleus of the duchy to one of his sons, on the thirteenth-century Capetian precedent of endowing royal sons with *appanages,* feudal holdings of some consequence. This was a precedent dangerous enough for a strong king; with a weak, absent, or insane king it was disastrous. The Duke of Burgundy, with a fine eye to his own advantage, had secured the succession to the County of Flanders and added to his already considerable state the richest economic concentration in northern Europe. By the opening of the fifteenth century Philip of Burgundy had, in fact if not in name, revived the ancient "middle kingdom" of Lothair, and had made it one of the richest and most powerful states in the European community.

In 1404 Philip of Burgundy was succeeded by his son, John the Fearless. John was not only fearless, he was as ambitious as his father and even more unscrupulous. In the fall of 1407, the leader of the opposing faction, Louis d'Orléans, was murdered in a Paris street. Duke John of Burgundy freely confessed that he had hired the assassins. A coterie of sympathetic barons joined together to lead the party of the murdered Louis against the Burgundian faction. The leader of this group was the fiery Count of Armagnac, from whom the party took its name. Burgundians and Armagnacs thus divided France, with the mad king caught between them and his unhappy land their prize. Civil administration was crippled and order practically disappeared in large sections of France. The nobility throughout the land chose sides as their interests dictated and raised bands of soldiery to add their terror to that of the "Free Companies." The peasants and commons not only bore the brunt of military devastation, they were forced to remit ever-increasing taxes to support their oppressors.

The War Resumed

The civil war in France offered a tempting opportunity for the English to reopen the war, especially since the domestic troubles that had crippled England in the late fourteenth century were now resolved. The incompetent Richard II had been deposed in a palace revolution that brought Henry IV and the new Lancastrian dynasty to the throne in 1399.[5] In 1413 the second Lancastrian king, Henry V, saw in the prostration of France the chance to submerge the problems of his own nation and dynasty in the glory of a successful foreign war.

On the continent the Burgundian faction was already seeking an alliance with England, largely because of the important Anglo-Flemish economic connection. With Burgundian support, Henry V revived the English claim to the French throne and opened the war once more in 1415, with an invasion through the Norman port of Harfleur. Henry V's invasion was a repetition of those of 1346 and 1356, a plundering march across western France to Calais. The Armagnac faction had gathered a large and impressive army, which forced a battle at Agincourt. It was a repeat of the slaughter of Crécy and Poitiers. The English archers and men-at-arms were again the victors. The foolish Armagnac nobles had thrown away the military reforms of Charles V and once more relied on traditional feudal cavalry tactics. In the carnage at Agincourt more French nobles were killed than the number of the entire English army, over ten thousand, while the English lost no more than a few hundred men.

After Agincourt the civil and the foreign wars merged. The Burgundians gained the upper hand following the English victory; they seized Paris and the king while the Armagnac party entrenched itself in the south. With the Armagnacs stood the Dauphin, the future Charles VII. The Burgundians and English entrenched themselves in Paris and northwestern France and in 1420 arranged the Treaty of Troyes. By its terms Henry V was to be the regent for the insane Charles VI while he lived, and then to succeed him as king of France and sovereign of all territory then in his hands. The captive Dauphin was repudiated; the treaty was sealed by the marriage of Henry V to the French princess, Catherine. Be-

5. See pp. 490-91.

fore the Treaty of Troyes could effect the dynastic revolution it had an-
nounced, both the old Charles VI and the young Henry V died in 1422
The English king left an infant heir, Henry VI, for whom the Duke of
Bedford, his uncle, ruled as regent.

At this juncture, the most striking personality of the Hundred Years'
War, Joan of Arc, made her appearance. Joan was a simple young peasant girl, naive and superstitiously religious, from the province of Lorraine
on the border between the two pieces of divided France. She came to
believe that the patron saints of her village were speaking to her, telling
her to go to the Dauphin to secure his coronation. Armed only with the
faith in her voices, Joan traveled to Bourges in 1429 and presented herself
and her plan to the Dauphin Charles. She found him living like a servant
in his own court, robbed and bullied by the nobles who surrounded him.
Joan's very simplicity gave her a peculiar strength: her conviction gave
conviction to others; perhaps innocence and faith could still work miracles!
She was given a horse, a banner, and a suit of white armor. Supported by
a small band of soldiers, she joined the forces raggedly attacking the
stronghold of Orléans, a key city besieged by the English and Burgundians.
Her presence infused new spirit into the discouraged French armies. Orléans was relieved; other successes followed; and the course of the war
began to turn. Joan secured the coronation of the Dauphin as Charles VII
in the liberated city of Rheims, the traditional site of royal investiture. Less
than a year later Joan was captured by the Burgundians and sold to the
English. For a year she was held in prisons and subjected to repeated and
persistent questioning. Even her faith and her simplicity could not save
her; she was found guilty of witchcraft and executed. An English soldier
standing near the stake said in awe, "My God, we have burned a saint!"

The career of "the maid" may not have been the turning point in the
last phase of the Hundred Years' War, but the temper of the war did
change. The first to take advantage of it was the shrewd Duke of Burgundy, now Philip the Good, his father, the "fearless" John having been
murdered in 1419. Philip was in an enviable position; indeed, he held the
balance of power in the war. He could thus threaten the English that he
would break his alliance with them and be bribed by the French for his
threats. The result of Philip's manipulations was the Treaty of Arras
(1435). By its terms Philip of Burgundy broke his English alliance and
received concessions in valuable lands bordering his duchy. The English
were offered reasonable terms but refused anything short of absolute sovereignty in northern France, which they were already in the process of

losing. The empty demands of the English were accompanied by more losses as France continued to recover her strength: Charles VII regained Paris in 1439; in 1442 much of southwestern France was taken; by 1445 he had been able to effect some military and financial reforms and was gathering up the strands of royal authority once more; and in 1449 and 1450 the English were driven from Normandy and by 1453 they held only Calais, the last remnant of those French lands which had been the pride of William the Conqueror and the "empire" of the Angevin Henry II.

The year 1453 may be taken as the end of the war. There was no formal treaty of peace. The English persisted in their claims and intermittent fighting continued. But the outbreak of the domestic Wars of the Roses prevented the English from pursuing any effective continental campaigns.

The Hundred Years' War had been a costly, and useless, conflict marked by barbaric cruelty and senseless destruction. In every campaign there had been mass executions, retaliation against the innocent, betrayal of allies, and slaughter of prisoners. The Black Prince ordered the complete destruction of a French city that had resisted him, including the burning of the cathedral, and watched the slaughter of the townspeople while he lay sick in a litter. After Poitiers there were so many prisoners that he ordered the common soldiers murdered for fear of their very numbers. At Agincourt, a belated and ineffectual counterattack alarmed the English, burdened as they were with their prisoners, and Henry V ordered the massacre of all but the highest-ranking captives whose ransoms would be most lucrative; thousands of men were put to the sword. These atrocities were committed by men who gave lip service to the ideals of chivalry.

Nothing else speaks so clearly of the real passing of feudal knighthood as this disparity between ideal and behavior. The normal tactic of the English in their periodic invasions was devastation. It was regular practice to give over conquered towns to rape and pillage by the soldiery in lieu of their pay. In the intervals of peace the French countryside was never free of marauding bands of soldiers. In the latter years of the war these were often organized as professional soldier companies under ruthless mercenary commanders called by the people the écorcheurs, "flayers." In the wake of military devastation and in the collapse of general order, whole districts throughout western France were taken over by outlaw bands sometimes numbering in the thousands. The cost of the Hundred Years' War in human life can never be counted. Villages were wiped out and towns reduced to villages. At the war's end only five people survived among the ruins of the once populous city of Limoges. Even Paris was so depopulated that wolves prowled the suburbs and attacked women and children.

Yet with all its misery and cost the Hundred Years' War was instrumental in achieving the unity of the French nation. This war that began as a dynastic conflict over the obligations of feudal magnates gradually took on the aspect of a struggle for national self-determination. It was ultimately the French people as a whole who united against the English devastation and the greedy separatist ambitions of their own nobility. The support they gave their king made possible the recovery of France, and at the same time brought about the restoration of strong royal government. Within a generation after the end of the war France was again the most prosperous and powerful state in western Europe under a king, Louis XI (*1461–1483*), who was more of a popular sovereign than any king before him.

Finally, the Hundred Years' War produced a new state, the Duchy of Burgundy, to take its place in the political economy of Europe and to be a significant factor in European history at the beginning of modern times.[6]

England: The War and the Peace

While in France the Hundred Years' War ultimately confirmed royal absolutism, its effect in England was to help bring about a decline of royal authority.

The reign of Edward I had been a high point in the history of medieval England. In 1307 he was succeeded by his weak and incompetent son, Edward II, and for the twenty years of his reign the initiative passed once more to the selfish baronage. Many of the internal political advances that England had made under Edward I were lost, along with much of the territory that he had won. But the most significant advance remained; Parliament continued to meet and to have an important part in the government of England. In 1327 Edward II was deposed and murdered by a clique of nobles and the throne passed to his young son, Edward III (*1327–1377*).

The third Edward almost immediately established a reputation as a swashbuckling, chivalrous warrior-king, and this remained the popular image of him throughout his long reign. The French war which he began was not unpopular. On the whole it was not considered only as "the king's

6. See pp. 581-83.

war," but accepted by the English as a national war also. What is perhaps of greater long-range importance, it was an expensive war. Furthermore, the economic changes—the growth of trade and manufacture and the decline of manorialism—that were taking place at an accelerated pace during these years, tended to place the control of finance increasingly in the hands of the middle class, the class whose representatives now sat regularly in Parliament.

In the half-century reign of Edward III from 1327 to 1377 Parliament was called forty-eight times. The war made it impossible for the king to live "of his own" or from his rapidly dwindling feudal revenues. He had to have money voted by Parliament. Edward bought this financial support with concessions made to parliamentary petitions. Royal concessions gradually gave way to parliamentary privileges, which were then turned into parliamentary rights. For temporary financial relief the crown was relinquishing permanent rights. By the last years of the fourteenth century the Parliament was in fact the principal source of law and its controls had been extended to embrace a broad spectrum of policy; economic regulation and social legislation, the relations of church and state, and even the royal household, from which Parliament could demand the removal of incompetent or unworthy advisers. However, the king could and did still legislate by royal ordinance and the growing machinery of justice and administration remained under his control.

Edward III died in 1377. The Black Prince having died the year before, the hope of a strong succession was lost. During Edward's last years he had been dominated by his unscrupulous brother, John of Gaunt, who continued to dominate the boy-king, Richard II, the son of the Black Prince. The self-seeking policies of Gaunt, his military failures, the increased cost of the war, and the reckless imposition of taxes triggered the forces of social violence.

England was still suffering from the effects of the Black Death (which had struck there as on the continent at mid-century a generation before). The pestilence had taken a fearful toll in lives, certainly a quarter of the English people, perhaps more. With labor in short supply, an economic revolution began. The nationwide demand for labor broke through the remaining barriers of traditional manorialism. The gradual process of commutation had been going on for two centuries, making large numbers of peasants renters instead of serfs. In the years following the Black Death peasants were in a position to bargain with their lords for freedom, for wages, and for rents. When bargaining failed they took to the roads in great numbers, offering themselves to any employer. The same was true of the laborers in the towns where skilled workers, for example in the budding cloth industry, were at a premium.

The king and Parliament, alarmed at the revolutionary direction of these changes, attempted to fix wages and prices. In 1351 the Statute of Laborers was passed, obliging every free worker to take work when it was offered him and at a wage customary before the Black Death. Despite the heavy penalties attached to violation of the statute, it was never regularly enforced. The tide of economic change was too strong. The labor crisis was effectively met not by government action but by a shift in the socio-economic structure of the nation. The war had produced an artificial prosperity that had benefited the commercial and industrial middle class at the expense of the landed nobility. Faced with ruin, many of the large landowners took advantage of urban demands and the labor shortage to enclose their manor lands and turn farms into sheep runs. Wool was still the staple of English prosperity, and as the "enclosure" movement spread, the increased supply of wool stimulated further production. Great fortunes were made; many wealthy city dwellers and enterprising yeomen invested in rural lands for sheep-raising. The result was an increase of the aristocracy of wealth that had been growing in importance for several centuries.

Such economic changes had their inevitable social consequences. As men of substance prospered they closed ranks. The peasantry of the countryside and the laborers of the towns found themselves the victims of the economic revolution for which they had been partially responsible. In many areas the old, predictable pattern of agricultural village life was shattered forever. Everywhere the lowly were at the mercy of the rich and powerful who had, at the same time, the support of government. The rumblings of social and economic discontent inevitably took on a heretical and anticlerical tone. The disgrace of the papacy, the schism of the church, and the general collapse of clerical life seemed in some way related to the changes that threatened the social order. Voices were raised in angry protest.

One such protest was the *Vision of Piers the Plowman,* a long allegorical poem depicting the plight of the peasant (he was commonly called Piers in England, as he was called Jacques in France). It was probably originally written by William Langland, a poor country parson close to the miseries of the peasants. It was, however, so popular and so often revised, rewritten, copied, and spread that it became less the work of a single author than a nearly universal plaint. Other voices belonged to the radical Franciscans of the Spiritual branch of the order, preaching the imitation of Christ and the equality of poverty. Radical preachers of every type joined them and people listened and agreed. The teachings of John Wyclif were taken out of their religious context and converted into a socio-economic doctrine, his ideas on religious equality and the community of believers becoming the basis for a primitive form of communism.

In this critical climate the government of the regent, John of Gaunt, demanded a series of poll taxes which fell hardest upon the lower classes, already oppressed and already resentful. The attempt to enforce these tax levies resulted in widespread uprisings. The news spread rapidly and in 1381 perhaps as many as one hundred thousand peasant rebels descended upon London. They burned and looted as they came; there were demonstrations, threats, and even the murder of high officials in London itself. The fifteen-year-old king went out to the rioters and, with more courage than his elders, put himself at their head until he succeeded in dispersing them. Once the peasant revolt was over, reprisals began. None of the temporary concessions that had been made was left in force. The revolt itself failed to gain its end.

The violence of the peasant revolt was matched by the arrogant lawlessness of the nobility. Partly as a result of intermittent war, partly from the failure of effective domestic government, the nobility everywhere maintained corps of troops and retainers, which threatened the order and safety of large sections of the realm.

In their ruthless economic individualism the rising class of English capitalists, merchants, and industrialists were as selfish and irresponsible as the nobles. The Statute of Laborers and the repressive measures against both peasantry and urban workers were reflections of their influence. But at the same time they were behind legislation to exclude foreign merchants from English internal trade, to restrict English trade to English ships, and to curtail the exportation of bullion.

Much of the trouble that bloomed in the minority of Richard II grew from the weakness of the crown and the many failures of the regency. In 1389 Richard II declared himself of age, but there was no conspicuous increase in the effectiveness of government. Richard had trouble with a series of parliaments until, in 1397, he moved to break the powers of Parliament altogether and turn back the clock. He attacked the freedom of petition, packed the Parliament with his own favorites, and revoked the basic rights of popular government. Within a year Richard found himself without a country, and his people, under parliamentary leadership, solidly rallied behind a rival, Henry of Lancaster, the son of Gaunt, whom Richard had previously exiled. Richard's experiment in absolutism had failed. Parliament convened once more; Richard was forced to abdicate; and Lancaster became Henry IV (*1399–1413*), the first of his dynasty.

The year 1399 marks a high point in the history of Parliament. It had vindicated the principle that Parliament was a real partner in the government of England. It had unmade one king and made another. Through the first half of the fifteenth century Parliament consolidated the gains it had made. Regular sessions continued and each Parliament extended its rights and jurisdiction. At the same time, and in conjunction with Parliament, the whole system of English government was extended and rationalized. The judicial structure was largely completed; the functions of the royal council were redefined and its power limited.

In the course of the fourteenth century a new royal official had appeared at the local level of government, the Justice of the Peace. By the fifteenth century there were justices in every county and they had nearly superceded the older office of sheriff. They were chosen from local gentry, who accepted the position both as an honor and as an obligation. The justice was both the head of the local police force responsible for investigating crimes and a police judge with regular quarterly sessions of court. The administration of local government was almost completely in his hands.

The victory of Parliament was not an unmixed blessing for, hampered by Parliamentary restrictions, especially in money matters, Henry IV was faced with a number of serious crises: a rebellion in Wales; Scottish raids across the northern border; and dangerous insurrections among the nobility. Only gradually, and with great difficulty, was Henry IV able to bring order to his realm and to establish his new dynasty. By the time his son, Henry V (*1413–1422*), succeeded to the throne, he was able to assume the role of a national monarch and, as we have seen, to engage once more in the great national contest with France. English prestige was never higher than in the reign of Henry V, but his early death plunged both his nation and his dynasty into the factional conflict that marked the passing of medieval England.

The Hundred Years' War dragged to a close in the inglorious reign of Henry VI. Since he was an infant at the death of his father, the first fifteen years of his reign were again in the care of a regency. Within the council of regency the ambitious lords, most of them relatives of the king, struggled for power over him. The situation, which might have been improved by a strong king, was only worsened by the weakness of Henry VI when he did reach maturity. As the king's weakness degenerated into intermittent insanity, the struggle for power spread from the council down into the entire realm. By 1450 England was on the brink of the civil conflict known as the Wars of the Roses.

Attempts to control the king gave way to attempts to seize the crown. The parties that quickly formed found their leaders in the houses of Lancaster and York, with their romantic symbols the red and white rose. The royal contenders of the next thirty-five years were all descendants of the several sons of Edward III, and they were able to dispute for the crown because they had been provided with great wealth and position. Edward III had made his younger sons the most powerful barons of the land. In England, as in France, the royal appanages became a source of civil war as royal relatives fought for the powers of a mad and feeble king. As the parties formed, almost the entire English nobility was drawn into the conflict in one way or another, for one cause or another.

The fortunes of war brought the Yorkist Edward IV (*1461–1483*) to the throne and the Lancastrian Henry VI died in captivity, probably by murder. The death of Edward IV again left a boy-king, Edward V, who never really reigned and who was immediately imprisoned and succeeded by his cruel and able uncle, Richard III. Edward was later murdered along with his younger brother (they were the "little princes" in the Tower). Within two years great numbers of the nobility were alienated by Richard and flocked to the banner of a new contestant for the throne, Henry Tudor, Earl of Richmond. In the summer of 1485 Richard met the invading army of Henry Tudor on the field of Bosworth and was killed. According to a hardy tradition, the new king picked up the crown from a bramble bush where it had fallen from Richard's head.

For a generation England had been torn by dynastic civil war and while the population as a whole had not participated in this prolonged passage at arms, the entire nation had suffered from it. The gains that Parliament had made under the Lancastrians in the early part of the century seemed lost. The thriving economic life of England was paralyzed by the uncertainties and confiscations of war. General peace and order had disappeared. The turbulent old nobility had all but destroyed itself in the course of the Wars of the Roses—the last feudal conflict in English history. With the new dynasty of Henry Tudor, England gradually became a nation of shops and shopkeepers, of bankers, industrialists, and gentlemen, one of the most powerful and prosperous nations of modern Europe.

THE RISE AND FALL OF EMPIRES:
GERMANY AND THE EASTERN FRONTIER

The Triumph of Constitutional Disorder

Within a generation after the death of Frederick II in 1250, the German Empire lay in ruins and the papacy could look with grim satisfaction on the destruction of that "nest of vipers," the Hohenstaufen dynasty. The papacy had been supported in its struggle against the empire by the German princes. In the "interregnum" that followed Frederick's death these princes seized the political initiative and gained the territorial sovereignty that was to reduce Germany to a geographic expression for more than six hundred years.

In 1273, confronted by the threat of the French, the papacy took the lead in bringing the interregnum in Germany to an end formally. The aggressive Capetian monarchy was expanding toward the Rhine at the expense of Germany, and to the south of France toward Italy. A junior branch of the Capetians held the old Hohenstaufen Kingdom of Naples and had begun to revive the expansionist designs of Henry VI and Frederick II; the papacy needed the weight of Germany to balance the rising power of France. Under the threat of papal intervention, the German princes elected Rudolph I of Hapsburg (*1273–1291*) to the kingship, which they had reduced to a virtually meaningless dignity. Rudolph seemed an ideal choice for the princes. He was not from one of the traditional "imperial" families, nor was he a great territorial lord. He was a south German count holding lands in Swabia and Switzerland. Personable, and a man of presence, he seemed, above all, a "safe" candidate.

Rudolph of Hapsburg was also a shrewd and realistic politician. He realized as fully as any electoral prince that the empire was only a venerable fiction and that any serious attempt to revive its power was quixotic folly. He turned instead to the creation of a strong dynastic state within the framework of the German state system; and he used the royal-imperial dignity as a means to this end. The princes had helped themselves to imperial lands and violated feudal rights. Among others, Ottokar of Bohemia had seized a large wedge of imperial fiefs from the middle

Danube to the Balkans and the Adriatic. He refused to recognize the election of Rudolph, thus providing a pretext for his condemnation at feudal law and for the confiscation of his fiefs. With papal support and money, Rudolph was able to enforce this confiscation, and Ottokar was killed in battle in 1278. At one stroke the modest lands of the Hapsburgs had been multiplied many times, establishing them as one of the most powerful princely families in southeastern Germany.

Rudolph had every intention of keeping the imperial title in his family by setting the dynastic principle once more above election. But the German princes were already alarmed at the growth of Hapsburg power, and fearful of losing the electoral privilege on which their chaotic independence rested. Thus, at the death of Rudolph in 1291 the princes turned not to his son, Albert, but to another powerless princeling, Adolph of Nassau (*1292–1298*).

Adolph was able and ambitious. He adopted a vigorous anti-French imperial policy, but the diplomatic arrangements on which its success depended were too complex. Philip the Fair of France was too powerful, the papacy too preoccupied, the small princes of Germany too jealous and too impoverished, and the House of Hapsburg too strong. Adolph's designs crumbled and, faced by the prospect of a civil war, the electors deposed him in favor of his Hapsburg rival, Albert I (*1298–1308*).

The direction of European affairs favored the dynastic policies of Albert as it had frustrated the imperial policies of Adolph. Philip the Fair of France wanted a free hand along the Rhine frontier. Albert of Hapsburg was happy to cooperate with Philip against the Rhenish archbishops, who led the party opposing Hapsburg dynastic plans. Any opposition from the papacy was soon neutralized by Philip's coup against Boniface VIII and his subsequent "capture" of the Avignonese popes. With the tacit support of the French king and the French pope, Albert was able to strike vigorously against the electoral princes of the Rhine in the west, and to continue the aggrandizement of his house in the east. In 1306 he claimed the inheritance of Bohemia and Moravia following the failure of the previous ruling line. Suddenly, in 1308, Albert was murdered. The French policy he had been responsible for worked against his dynasty and his hopes; the Rhineland was filled with pro-French appointees of the French pope, and more German princes retained their traditional preference for a weak king. These circumstances combined to bring about the election, in 1308, of a minor Francophile noble, Henry Count of Luxemburg, as Henry VII (*1308–1313*).

Like the Hapsburgs, Henry VII made no real effort to revive the force of empire but turned instead to the east. There he managed to unseat the Hapsburg claim to Bohemia-Moravia and to establish his family on the Bohemian throne. Thus a new dynasty sank its roots on the eastern frontier and a new rivalry rose to torment Germany for the following century, the rivalry of Hapsburg and Luxemburg, not only in their claims to eastern lands but in their claims to both the royal and imperial crowns. Having successfully followed the dynastic policies of his Hapsburg rivals, Henry VII was next deluded by the hope of imperial revival in Italy. He was led to Italy by the half-promises of the popes at Avignon, but once

---

HAPSBURG AND LUXEMBURG

HAPSBURGS	*LUXEMBURGERS*
RUDOLPH OF HAPSBURG *(1273-1291)*	
ADOLPH OF NASSAU *(1292-1298)*	
ALBERT I *(1298-1308)*	
	HENRY VII (Luxemburg) *(1308-1313)*

C I V I L   W A R
FREDERICK THE HANDSOME (Hapsburg) and LOUIS OF BAVARIA

	CHARLES IV *(1347-1378)*
	WENCESLAS *(1378-1400)*

C I V I L   W A R

	SIGISMUND *(1410-1437)*
ALBERT II *(1438-1439)*	
FREDERICK III *(1440-1493)*	
MAXIMILIAN I *(1493-1519)*	

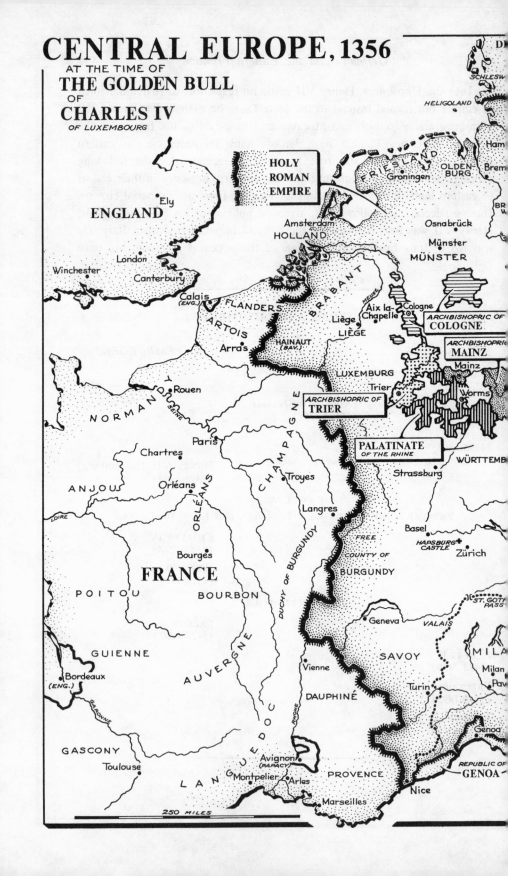

CENTRAL EUROPE, 1356

AT THE TIME OF
THE GOLDEN BULL
OF
CHARLES IV
OF LUXEMBOURG

HOLY ROMAN EMPIRE

ENGLAND

Ely

London
Winchester
Canterbury

Calais
(ENG.)

FLANDERS

ARTOIS

Arras

HAINAUT
(BAV.)

NORMANDY

DU SEINE

Rouen

Paris

Chartres

ANJOU

Orléans

ORLÉANS

LOIRE

Bourges

FRANCE

POITOU

BOURBON

GUIENNE

Bordeaux
(ENG.)

GARONNE

GASCONY

Toulouse

LANGUEDOC

AUVERGNE

RHONE

Avignon
(PAPACY)

Montpelier
Arles

Marseilles

250 MILES

SCHLESW

HELIGOLAND

FRIESLAND
Groningen

OLDEN-
BURG

Ham
Brem

BR

Amsterdam
HOLLAND

Osnabrück

Münster
MÜNSTER

BRABANT

RHINE

MEUSE

Aix la-
Chapelle

Liège
LIÈGE

Cologne

ARCHBISHOPRIC OF COLOGNE

ARCHBISHOPRIC MAINZ

LUXEMBURG

Trier

Mainz

Worms

ARCHBISHOPRIC OF TRIER

PALATINATE
OF THE RHINE

WÜRTTEMB

Troyes

CHAMPAGNE

Strassburg

Langres

Basel

FREE
COUNTY OF
BURGUNDY

HAPSBURG
CASTLE

Zürich

DUCHY OF BURGUNDY

ST. GOTT
PASS

Geneva

VALAIS

MILA

DAUPHINÉ

SAVOY

Vienne

Milan

Turin

Pav

Genoa

PROVENCE

Nice

REPUBLIC OF GENOA

DI

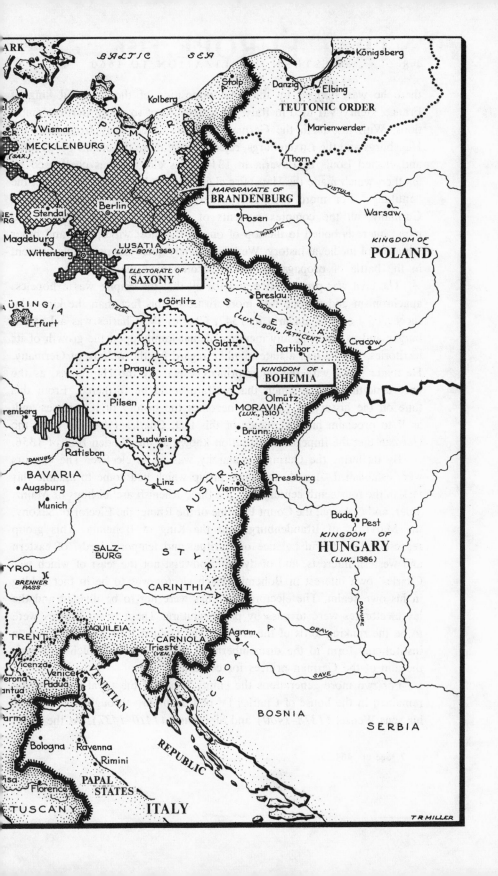

there he was stopped by the solid opposition of the powerful king of France. Henry VII died in Italy, the graveyard of so many German ambitions. With his death the German electors turned away from both the Hapsburgs and the Luxemburgs, rejected once more the claims of heredity, and elected Louis of Bavaria in 1314. This election was challenged by another, which made the Hapsburg claimant, Frederick the Handsome, the "antiking." For more than thirty years civil war raged once more in Germany; all the complex currents of imperial, German, French, and papal interests boiled to the top of one of the most widespread and bitter struggles of medieval history. We have already noted the papal involvement in the battle of propaganda which accompanied the dispute.[7]

The civil war proved once and for all that the empire was a hopeless anachronism and no one was more aware of this fact than the king who succeeded Louis of Bavaria in 1347, Charles IV. Charles was a Luxemburger and as intent as any member of that family upon the growth of its territories. Yet he had a statesmanlike regard for the welfare of Germany. He made peace with the other princes, especially the Hapsburgs, as the only condition under which that welfare could be furthered. From this time on the history of Germany becomes the history of its princes and, as if to proclaim his acceptance of this fact, Charles IV urged upon the German diet the imperial constitution known as the Golden Bull of 1356.

By its terms the German monarchy was to be elective. The electors were established—largely the same group which had come to assume this task in the fourteenth century—as the three Rhenish archbishops of Mainz, Trier, and Cologne; the Count Palatine of the Rhine; the Elector of Saxony; the Margrave of Brandenburg; and the King of Bohemia. This group represented a careful balance of spiritual and temporal lords, of eastern and western interests, and of dynastic powers, not the least of which was Charles' own interest in Bohemia. Each elector was to be in fact a king in his own realm. The electoral holdings were not to be divided and the lay electorates were to pass by primogeniture. These seven princes were to be the ranking lords of the empire. The Golden Bull gave the ultimate institutional form to the dismemberment of the empire, which had been the aim of the German princes for centuries.

For two more generations the empty honor of the royal-imperial title remained in the house of Charles IV of Luxemburg through the reigns of his sons Wenzel (*1378–1400*) and Sigismund (*1410–1437*). At the death

7. See pp. 464-65.

of Sigismund the imperial title passed once more to the House of Hapsburg, where it was to remain until the dissolution of the empire in the twentieth century. It had become a burden that only the greatest of territorial princes could bear, and a Hapsburg monopoly largely by default. Over the centuries it gained the force of a tradition.

Imperium in Imperio: The German State System and the Domestic History of Germany

The Golden Bull of Charles IV recognized the fact that there was no longer either an empire or a monarchy in Germany with effective coercive force. The role of the state was thus assumed not by a national unit—as in France and England—but by the many regional territorial units of Germany. Some of these, like Bohemia, Bavaria, and Austria, were powerful and expanding states in their own right. Others were minuscule postage-stamp principalities. The relations among these states were as chaotic and unprincipled as those which prevailed between France and England. The result was continual lawlessness and disorder; though the smaller states tended to band together into leagues for mutual protection, conflicting self-interest made even these relations unstable. One exception to this was the confederacy of the Swiss.

The several small districts or *cantons* (literally, "corners") of Switzerland were typical peasant communities, inhabited by sturdy mountaineers. With the revival of trade and the creation of a network of exchange between Italy and the north of Europe, the Swiss found themselves in a strategic position to dominate the flow of overland trade through the Alpine passes. By the thirteenth century several cantons had come within the feudal claims of the nearby Hapsburg lords and, as the Hapsburgs attempted to tighten their controls over them, the Swiss fought back. Throughout the latter part of the thirteenth century this struggle went on intermittently. While the Hapsburgs struggled on other frontiers to establish their monarchical-imperial position, the Swiss doggedly maintained their independence. The three "forest cantons" had gained a form of self-determination by 1291, and were legally subject only to the emperor. This meant, in effect, the absence of any external control.

These three cantons became the nucleus of further Swiss independence as other cantons, both urban and peasant, were drawn into the growing Swiss union. With nearly every accretion of territory the Swiss had to fight off their feudal lords and would-be masters. This they did in 1315 at Morgarten, in 1386 at Sempach, in 1388 at Näfels—armies of Swiss militiamen defeating feudal levies sent against them. By the last quarter of the fifteenth century the Hapsburgs had abandoned their futile efforts to conquer the Swiss and had granted them legal independence. By this time the Swiss had organized their conglomerate, tri-lingual territories into one of the most unique "states" in Europe. It was a confederacy in which each separate canton maintained the greatest possible independence and was in effect a tiny state; but in which, also, matters of common concern were decided in a federal diet. The Swiss have maintained both their independence and the substance of their system of government into modern times.

What the Swiss did out of the spirit of independence, the cities of Germany and central Europe were forced to do for bare survival. In the thirteenth and fourteenth centuries the natural alliance between the urban middle class and the central government against feudalism had been frustrated by the chronic weakness of central government in Germany.

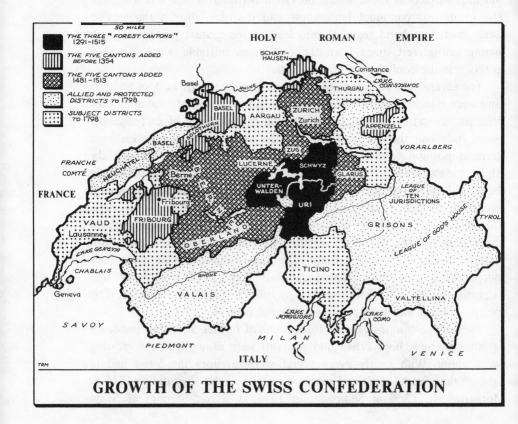

GROWTH OF THE SWISS CONFEDERATION

Thus the cities gathered into leagues to preserve themselves against territorial feudalism and to gain the order for which they looked elsewhere in vain. During the interregnum, what little remained of the organization of government was in the hands of a league of Rhineland cities. Other city leagues sprang up in various sections of Germany as the hope of national government failed. One of these was the Hanseatic League, probably the most famous of urban confederacies and, in the fourteenth century, the most significant economic force in northern Europe.

Like other such leagues, the Hansa was an unofficial, semivoluntary association with no fixed membership and no continuous executive authority. The league grew in piecemeal fashion. As early as the twelfth century merchants from the various German cities residing in London secured a corporate status. The same thing occurred in Bruges, then in Scandinavia, and at Novgorod in Russia. These merchant communities became the chief outlets for the carrying trade of the home cities and rich centers of economic life. As a network of exchange developed to tie together this growing empire of northern trade, the cities, settlements, and associations that formed its parts drew together. Two of the most important cities of northern Germany, Lübeck and Hamburg, assumed a leading role in this process. The cities that were becoming the Hanseatic League took common action against pirates and bandits to protect their routes of trade: they adopted a common currency and a common commercial law; they stood together on matters of collective bargaining, economic sanctions, and even boycotts. Their common interests grew as their trade grew. The merchants of the Hansa controlled a significant portion of the external trade of England and even of such a highly developed economic area as the Low Countries. In the more backward regions of Scandinavia and Russia the league operated with the self-determination of a nation-state, demanding and receiving from native princelings the privileges of virtual independence.

In the mid-fourteenth century the position of the Hansa in the Baltic was threatened by a resurgence of Denmark. In this emergency the league operated with all the dispatch and efficiency of a great state. It gained diplomatic alliances and played the game of political maneuvering. It marshaled the vast resources of its member cities and attacked, and defeated, Denmark. The Treaty of Stralsund in 1370 restored the Hanseatic monopoly in the Baltic and humbled Denmark. It also marked the high point in the history of the league, which now included some two hundred cities, towns, villages, factories, and settlements—from frontier fortress-cities like Novgorod and Bergen to the great "central cities" of Hamburg,

Rostock, and Lübeck, to Dutch, Flemish, and English Hansa "factories." It drained the goods of half the world. Its merchant princes loaned money and took interest on an international scale.

With the fifteenth century the decline of the Hanseatic League began. As in the case of nearly every large and complex institution, this decline was already under way at the time of its greatest success. A weakness of long standing was the league's lack of any effective central organization. Common enemies and common problems had led the member cities to cooperate at times of crisis, but the cities remained sovereign units. Bitter commercial rivalry on both the local and international level developed among these units. In the absence of a central league, the governments of some of the more powerful cities from time to time exercised a form of hegemony over neighboring towns, thus aggravating their differences with rival cities—such was the case with Lübeck, Cologne, and Danzig. This intercity rivalry sapped away at the vitality of the league. At the same time internal class conflict boiled to the surface in many of the Hansa towns as the lesser guilds and laborers challenged the dominant position of the merchant aristocracies. These outbursts, like the ones already noted in the Italian and Flemish towns, were marked by bloody turbulence.

Already weakened by these problems, the league found its activities further hampered by the growth of the centralized national economies. In England, for example, the fifteenth century saw the development of native commerce and the rise of the "new men" bent on chipping away at the Hansa privileges. The Scandinavian nations were also coming to resent the place of the Hansa in their material life. Many of the Hansa towns themselves came under the control of the growing territorial states in northern Germany. At the end of the fifteenth century the princes of Moscovy were able to break the Hanseatic control of trade at their end of the Baltic axis. The growth of Burgundy robbed the Hansa of its privileges in the Flemish ports. All across northern Europe the chronic war and devastation of the early fifteenth century diminished the trade that was the lifeblood of the Hansa, as did the Hundred Years' War in the west and the bitter conflict of Slav and German in the east. At the same time the principal routes of European trade began to shift away from the north and the Baltic, and the cities of southern Germany developed their trade from across the Alps, becoming commercial centers rivaling the wealth of the Hansa towns. The Venetians opened a water route to England and Flanders early in the fourteenth century. The vigorous international trade of Florence, Genoa, and Milan reoriented the trade connections between the north of Europe and the Mediterranean.

The expansion of German trade to the east in the great days of the Hanseatic League was part of a larger pattern of German eastward expansion—one of the great adventures of the medieval period. Since the time of Clovis the west German peoples had reversed the direction of the great migrations and had begun the *Drang nach Osten,* "The Drive toward the East." The result was a constant encroachment upon the eastern frontier and the gradual eastward shift of the center of Germany. The Saxon, the Bavarian, and the Avar wars of Charlemagne were part of this process. They were continued by the Saxon and Salian emperors. In the time of Barbarossa and the Hohenstaufens the eastern marks of the empire had been further extended by the feudal ambition of such great territorial lords as the Welf duke, Henry the Lion.

With the growth of a powerful French monarchy the Rhine frontier was established as the western limit of Germany. With the stabilization of the west German state system a sharp limit was set to the domestic expansion of the German states. Thus, in the later Middle Ages the broad, ill-defined eastern borderlands beckoned to German ambition as never before. We have seen how, with the failure of imperial power, the Hapsburg and Luxemburg dynasties founded their fortunes by seizing or dominating lands in the east—Austria, the Balkans, Bohemia-Moravia, Hungary. Farther to the north such territorial states as Brandenburg did the same thing, and in the Baltic the commercial-political expansion of the Hanseatic League was largely at the expense of non-German lands to the east. But the spearhead of the German eastward expansion in the later Middle Ages was the Teutonic Order.

This crusading order, like the Templars and the Hospitalers, had been forced out of the Holy Land by the progressive failure of the Crusades in the thirteenth century. There was no more logical place for their zeal and their activities than the German eastern frontier. With the nominal cooperation of Poland, the Teutonic knights began the systematic conquest of Prussia. Within half a century the order had conquered most of pagan Prussia, converted its people at sword's point, and expanded into the broad lands and ethnic patchwork of peoples at the eastern end of the Baltic— Balts, Slavs, Letts, Finns. This phenomenal expansion of the Teutonic Order attracted the cooperation of territorial states and kingdoms, of other semireligious orders, of the church, and of the commercial cities of north-

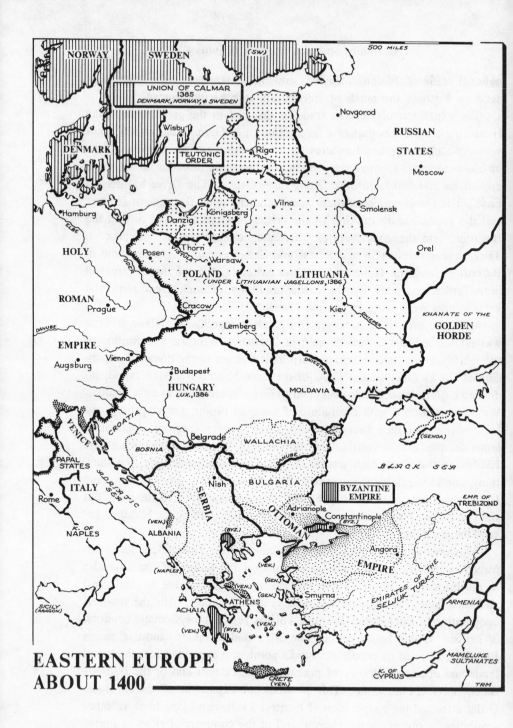

EASTERN EUROPE
ABOUT 1400

ern Germany. Behind the moving front of conquest came colonists to take up the devastated land, to found cities, and to exploit the wealth of this conquered area. German influences flooded into eastern Europe.

In the face of wholesale Germanization, native Slavic resistance began to form, centered in the kingdom of Poland. This resistance took a threatening form in 1385, when a simultaneous dynastic marriage and mass conversion united the kingdoms of Poland and Lithuania into a monster state almost as large as Germany and France put together. The conversion of the Lithuanians also put an end to the need for crusading, by which the Teutonic Order had justified its activities. In the opening years of the fifteenth century Slavic resurgence began to roll back the German advance. At Tannenberg, in Prussia, a huge pan-Slavic army recruited from the Baltic to the Black Sea disastrously defeated the Teutonic knights in 1410, in the name of Poland-Lithuania. On the heels of this defeat the order rapidly declined. Within a generation a native Prussian rebellion was the pretext for the resumption of the war. By 1460 the Slavs had completely broken the power of the knights. And by a peace treaty of that year, the Second Peace of Thorn, Prussia was divided, the western portion going to Poland, the eastern remaining in German hands, but under the feudal domination of the Polish crown.

Thus, on the eve of modern times, the *Drang nach Osten* had been stopped and the edge of its military penetration blunted. But German influences in eastern Europe remained. Indeed, civilization, however painful and costly the process, had come to eastern Europe in German form. Throughout the vast extent of Poland-Lithuania the nobles adopted German feudalism with its destructive notions of princely sovereignty, and reduced their peasantry to a German-type serfdom which was to persist for centuries. In the borderlands of Germany the savage conquest-conversion of the Teutonic Order had virtually depopulated huge tracts which were subsequently filled with German colonists who stayed on even when the lands were rewon by Slavic states. The cities—like Danzig, Marienburg, and Königsberg—which had grown up under the protection of Teutonic castles, remained German. The deep-seated conflict between Slav and Teuton was inherent not only at the ethnic and national levels in the complex politics of eastern Europe, but at every level of society and culture. It was a conflict that was to be perpetuated into modern times.

Tartars, Turks, and Boyars

While German eastward expansion was halted by the Slavs in the Baltic, the penetration of German-Hapsburg-Luxemburg influence down the Danube valley was halted and reversed by the Turkish-Moslem advance into Europe in the first half of the fifteenth century. The establishment of a Turkish hold in Europe was the ultimate result of disturbances far to the east, which had implications along the entire frontier between Europe and Asia.

In the opening years of the thirteenth century Genghis Khan (*1162–1227*), the greatest of all Asiatic nomad kings, had begun the conquest of the greatest of all Asiatic empires. Before his death he held most of farther Asia, and his armies had overrun Persia, the Caucasus, and the Russian plain north of the Black Sea. Genghis ruled millions of square miles of territory and millions of people. Yet he was not simply a lucky war lord; he was an able ruler. His empire did not fall to pieces at his death, but continued to grow under the leadership of his descendants. Of most immediate concern to Europe was the advance of the conqueror Batu Kahn into the Russian steppe and the highlands of western Asia. The terrible force of the Mongol-Tartar advance consumed whole nations and drove others before it.

One of the latter were a group of Turks later known as the Ottomans. These people, pressing against the Seljuk frontier in Asia Minor, were permitted to cross over and take up land within the Seljuk-Turkish empire. It was the story once more of the Huns, the Goths, and the Romans. The presence of the Ottomans upset the balance of affairs in the Near East. The Seljuk state was already in decline and the admission of the Ottomans proved the final blow. Within a generation of their settlement in the empire, the Ottomans had launched a series of attacks upon Asia Minor. The whole structure of Seljuk authority crumbled and the even weaker remnants of Byzantine power fell before the Ottoman advance. By the mid-thirteenth century the subcontinent of Asia Minor was in their hands and the expansion of Islam was under way once more under a new and vigorous set of masters.

Thus the tottering Byzantine Empire found itself threatened by the greatest menace in its history and at a moment when it was least able to defend itself. Constantinople had never recovered from the devastation of the Fourth Crusade. The loss of its essential Asiatic provinces had further weakened the empire's economic position. The commercial inroads of the Italian cities after the Crusades had been another blow to Byzantine prosperity. Under such pressures there had been, for three centuries, a steady deterioration of social and economic stability, a decline in production and consumption, and a weakening of the civil and military institutions upon which the health of Byzantium depended. Only the shell of an

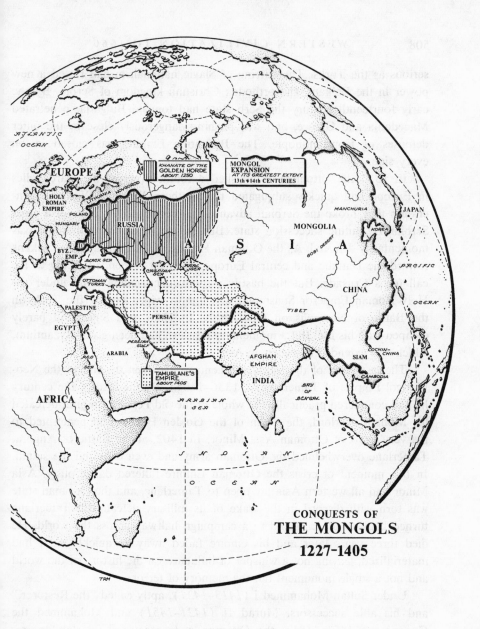

empire remained, and within that shell the dry corpse of the Hellenic-Byzantine tradition. The Byzantine state had entered the twilight of its long history. For more than a century it had been preserved rather by the weakness and inactivity of Islam than by its own efforts. With the fourteenth century Byzantium faced a reinvigorated Islam once more across the narrow straits and an aggressive Moslem-Ottoman military state.

Furthermore, on the European side the empire faced a menace as serious as the Turks. The stirring of Slavic nationalism had raised a new power in the Balkans, the orthodox Christian kingdom of Serbia. By the early fourteenth century the Serb state had toppled Bulgaria, penetrated Macedonia and Greece, and was pushing dangerously close to the outer defenses of Constantinople. The Byzantine Empire was closed in on every side.

In 1354 the Ottomans established a foothold across the Dardanelles in Europe and quickly subjugated the southern Balkans. Within a generation they broke the Serbian advance and destroyed the hope of a great Serbian-Byzantine succession state. But the doom of Constantinople was momentarily deferred. As the Ottoman Empire pushed through the Balkans toward the Danube and central Europe, the west responded feebly to the call for a Crusade. But the hastily assembled crusading army under the Holy Roman Emperor Sigismund was almost wiped out by the Turks in the Battle of Nicopolis on the Danube in 1396, and Sigismund barely escaped with his life. But a momentary reprieve had been given Byzantium, which was extended by events in Asia.

The last years of the fourteenth century had seen the rise of the Neo-Mongol Empire of Tamerlane(c. 1336-1405). By the turn of the century he had conquered practically the whole of the old Persian Empire; defeated his Mongol overlord, the Khan of the Golden Horde; and penetrated to the very heart of Ottoman Asia Minor. In 1402, at the Battle of Angora, Tamerlane overwhelmed the Ottoman army and even captured the sultan. In this moment of crisis the Ottoman Empire faltered dangerously. Asia Minor and all western Asia lay open to Tamerlane, and the Ottoman state was torn with discord in the wake of its military defeat. But Tamerlane turned back to the east and to a campaign halfway across the world. He died three years later and his empire faded away as quickly as it had materialized, leaving not a whisper of influence on the history of the world and not a single monument but the memory of terror.

Under Sultan Mohammed I (*1413-1421*), aptly called "the Restorer," and his able successors, Murad II (*1421-1451*) and Mohammed the Conqueror (*1451-1481*), the Ottoman state recovered its stability, reconquered Asia Minor, confirmed its position in the Balkans, and defeated another crusading army from the west. In 1453, almost a century after their first appearance on the continent of Europe, the Ottoman Turks closed in from every side on Constantinople. In May of 1453 the Golden City was taken. The citadel of the Christian east was at last in Moslem hands, and the Ottoman Empire firmly established on the eastern flank of Europe.

For at least two centuries after the fall of Constantinople the Ottoman Turks posed a threat to the west by their very existence in a viable form on the flank of Europe. Much of their success must be attributed to the stability, simplicity, and efficiency of the state they created. To an extent they adopted Arab and Byzantine devices and practices. But, essentially, the Ottoman state retained the primitive form of a nomad military monarchy. The sultan was the commander of the military and what civil powers he cared to exercise derived from this function. His council of state was made up of his *pashas,* subordinate military commanders. And the backbone of the state was the army.

The army was divided into three contingents or services. The most

GROWTH OF THE OTTOMAN EMPIRE

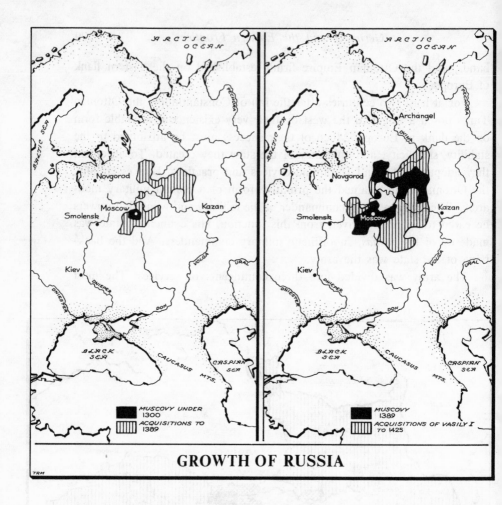

GROWTH OF RUSSIA

notable of these was the bizarre force known as the Janissaries. They were largely infantry troops made up of Christian boys taken from subject peoples in Asia Minor, the Near East, and the Balkans as tribute. They were trained in Moslem schools and barracks, and subjected to military discipline from an early age. Their lives and training were a combination of Spartan militarism and monastic asceticism. They were not permitted to marry, and they had no sentimental attachments or loyalties except to the state, which was their master. The Spahis were the major cavalry force, recruited mainly in the Asiatic portions of the empire and almost entirely from the Turks themselves, who owed this traditional mounted service to their sultan. Finally, the Timariots were a kind of militia service used almost entirely in the European parts of the empire. Their origins may go back to Persian-Arab roots or may represent a borrowing from Euro-

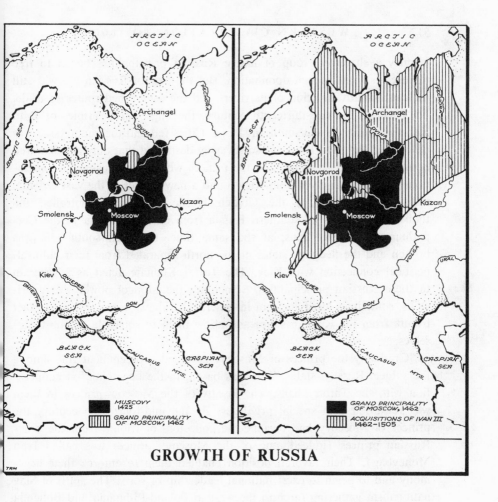

GROWTH OF RUSSIA

Map legend (left): MUSCOVY 1425; GRAND PRINCIPALITY OF MOSCOW, 1462

Map legend (right): GRAND PRINCIPALITY OF MOSCOW, 1462; ACQUISITIONS OF IVAN III 1462-1505

pean feudalism. They were nominally Turks—some were certainly renegade Christians—and they held lands from the sultan on condition of knights' service. Aside from the military forces thus constituted, there was virtually no Ottoman state, only an aggregation of subject peoples. Such a state lived literally "by the sword"—by conquest, expansion, and exploitation. And this was precisely the danger to Europe; for the European frontier remained the leading edge of Ottoman conquest, always in peril.

The Mongol expansion, which had been indirectly responsible for the creation of the Ottoman Empire, played a similar role in the creation of modern Russia. In the explosive age of the Vikings, as we have seen, Swedish merchant-adventurers had established a stronghold at Kiev and constructed an important trade route from Byzantium to Kiev, Novgorod, and the Baltic. Kiev was the first nucleus of medieval Russia. By the twelfth century a shadowy group of native Russian principalities began to free themselves from Kievan domination. But the axis of Russian life was still the north-south direction of its rivers and the established routes of trade.

Then, in the mid-thirteenth century, the huge Tartar armies of Batu Kahn swept across the southern steppe. Cities fell and the countryside was devastated. In 1240 Kiev was so savagely destroyed that only two hundred houses remained standing, and the princes who had struggled for generations to free themselves from Kiev found a new master in the vast Oriental state—the Khanate of the Golden Horde—that now controlled the thousands of miles of southern Russia from outer Mongolia to the Carpathian mountains. Thus, at the same time, the north-south axis was broken and the fledgling states of the north separated from their cultural-political connection with Kiev. The Tartar Khanate acted as a suzerain to these Russian principalities. Sometimes the Mongol power was capricious, sometimes terrifying, but in general the khans were content to exact tribute from the Russian states and allow them to squabble among themselves.

Gradually the princes of Moscovy assumed a preeminent role among the subject Russian states. This was based, in the beginning, on cooperation with the Tartar khans. The loyalty of the Moscow princes to them was rewarded with special privileges. By the mid-fourteenth century the princes of Moscovy had become the collectors of tribute from the other Russian princes (indeed, one of the Moscovy princes was called Ivan Moneybag). Their favored position enabled them to enforce their hegemony and to begin to exert national leadership of sorts. The spirit of Slav nationalism gathering force to the west in Poland-Lithuania and Bohemia also began to stir in Russia. With the growing strength of Moscow, subservience to Tartar domination gave way to hostility. As the Tartar power began to fade in the last decades of the fourteenth century and Tartar lands were battered by Tamerlane, the princes of Moscovy seized the leadership in what was becoming a national-ethnic reaction.

In 1380 Prince Dmitri Donskoi (*1359–1389*), at the head of a Russian army of perhaps a quarter of a million men, defeated a Tartar force at Kulikovo and shattered the myth of invincibility which had been an important part of the Mongol terror. The military prestige of Moscow and its growing power over its neighboring states rapidly turned it into the expansive center of a new Russian nation. With the second half of the fifteenth century we may accurately speak of a Russian state and of Ivan III (*1462–1505*) as a national monarch. His long reign saw the completion of a solid Russian territorial state. His armies took the independent fortress of Novgorod and thus reduced the most troublesome center of opposition to the rising national power in the north. In the last decade of the fifteenth century Ivan closed the Hanseatic factory at Novgorod and declared his state's independence of foreign economic domination.

Even before the fall of Constantinople, in the long senility of the eastern empire the princes of Moscow had begun to claim the religious and cultural leadership which Byzantium was losing. As early as 1440 these princes succeeded in posing as the champions of eastern orthodoxy and in making their state the center of a new and vigorous orthodox church. With the fall of Constantinople Moscow was left as the only significant cultural descendant of Byzantium and was more than ready to make the most of this role. The dynastic marriage of Ivan III to Princess Zoë, the last descendant of the imperial house of Byzantium, gave grounds for claiming direct connection with the Byzantine Empire. Indeed, it enabled Ivan to devise a theory of succession—upheld by his successors—to legitimize the claim that his state was heir to the Byzantine Empire. Prince Ivan transformed himself into Tsar Ivan (from Caesar), and hailed his city of Moscow as the "third Rome." On the eve of the sixteenth century Russia was ready to take its place as a European power.

SUGGESTIONS FOR FURTHER READING

General and Political History

E. P. Cheney, *The Dawn of a New Era, 1250–1453* (New York: Harper, 1936), more a series of reflective, interpretative essays than a narrative history; excellent.

E. Emerton, *The Beginnings of Modern Europe (1250–1450)* (Boston: Ginn, 1917), narrative of the complex political history.

R. Lodge, *The Close of the Middle Ages* (London and New York: Macmillan, 1901).

W. T. Waugh, *A History of Europe from 1378 to 1494* (New York: Putnam, 1932), detailed narrative history of the period but very readable.

The Decline of the Medieval Church

T. S. R. Boase, *Boniface VIII* (London: Constable, 1933).

G. G. Coulton, *Five Centuries of Religion* (New York: Cambridge University Press, 1950).

L. E. Elliott-Binns, *History of the Decline and Fall of the Medieval Papacy* (London: Methuen, 1934).

A. C. Flick, *The Decline of the Medieval Church* (New York: Knopf, 1930), 2 vols.

P. Hughes, *A History of the Church*, Vol. III (New York: Sheed and Ward, 1947).

W. E. Lunt, *Papal Revenues in the Middle Ages* (New York: Columbia University Press, 1934), 2 vols., a distinguished special study.

M. Spinka, ed., *Advocates of Reform, From Wycliff to Erasmus* (Philadelphia: Westminster, 1953), a series of substantial and well-selected readings from Wycliff, Hus, and the Conciliasts.

———, *John Hus and the Czech Reform* (Chicago: University of Chicago Press, 1941).

W. Ullman, *The Origin of the Great Schism* (London: Burns and Oates, 1948).

England, France, and the Hundred Years' War

A. H. Burne, *The Agincourt War* (London: Eyre and Spottiswoode, 1956).

———, *The Crecy War* (London: Eyre and Spottiswoode, 1955).

O. Cartellieri, *The Court of Burgundy: Studies in the History of Civilization* (New York: Knopf, 1929).

*John Froissart, *Chronicles of England, France, and Spain*, intro. by C. W. Dunn (New York: Everyman, 1961), a handy edition of a standard source for the Hundred Years' War as well as a classic of chivalry.

F. A. Gasquet, *The Black Death of 1348 and 1349* (London: Bell, 1908), a special study that is pertinent to the whole topic of this chapter.

V. H. H. Green, *The Later Plantagenets: A Survey of English History Between 1307 and 1485* (London: St. Martin's, 1955).

*J. Huizinga, *The Waning of the Middle Ages* (Garden City, N. Y.: Anchor: 1954), a brilliant analytic study of the late medieval civilization of France and Burgundy.

E. F. Jacob, *Henry V and the Invasion of France* (New York: Macmillan, 1950).

*D. B. Wyndham Lewis, *François Villon* (Garden City, N. Y.: Anchor, 1958), a famous biography.

*A. R. Myers, *England in the Late Middle Ages* (Baltimore: Penguin, 1952), well-paced, mature, interpretive.

E. Perroy, *The Hundred Years' War* (London: Eyre and Spottiswoode, 1951), the best brief, general account of the war.

V. Sackville-West, *Saint Joan of Arc* (Garden City, N. Y.: Doubleday, 1936), an unusually sensitive and perceptive study.

H. D. Sedgwick, *The Life of Edward the Black Prince* (Indianapolis: Bobbs-Merrill, 1931).

G. M. Trevelyn, *England in the Age of Wycliff* (New York: Longman's, 1899), a pioneering and still-classic work of social history.

Germany and Eastern Europe

G. Barraclough, *Origins of Modern Germany,* cited for Chap. 8.

Charles Diehl, *Byzantium: Greatness and Decline,* cited for Chap. 6.

*F. Nowak, *Medieval Slavdom and the Rise of Russia* (New York: Holt, 1930).

A. A. Vasiliev, *History of the Byzantine Empire,* cited for Chap. 6.

G. Vernadsky, *Ancient Russia* (New Haven: Yale University Press, 1943); *Kievan Russia* (New Haven: Yale University Press, 1948); and *The Mongols and Russia* (New Haven: Yale University Press, 1953), the best general account of medieval Russia.

P. Wettek, *Rise of the Ottoman Empire* (London: Royal Asiatic Society, 1938).

H. Zimmer, *Hanse Towns* (New York: Putnam, 1899) almost the only substantial work in English on the subject.

*Paperbound edition. In the case of reprint editions, publisher and date of publication given will be that of reprint rather than the original.

❧ 12 ❧

The Renaissance

THE GENIUS OF FLORENCE

In the two centuries between 1300 and 1500, during which northern Europe was gradually being transformed by political, economic, and cultural changes, a new era was already well under way in Italy. The Renaissance (literally, "rebirth") stemmed from a renewed interest in antiquity, in classical literature and art. But unlike the rediscovery of the classical world by the church scholars of the Middle Ages, the Renaissance revival of classicism was secular and humanistic in spirit. It represented a new way of life, a new mode of viewing both this world and the next. Beginning in the minuscule courts and rich bustling cities of Lombardy and Tuscany, it set Italy apart from the rest of contemporary Europe. By the time the Hundred Years' War had come to a close and the Wars of the Roses had placed the Tudor dynasty on the English throne, by the time the princes of Moscovy had turned themselves into Russian kings and Constantinople had fallen to the Turks—the Italian Renaissance was already on the threshold of its golden age.

The Material Basis of the Renaissance

The economic revolution that had brought towns and trade once more to Europe had begun in Italy, where conditions had been especially favorable to it. Though Italy had had more than its share of local wars and rapacious minor barons, it had never been extensively feudalized. Nor was it caught up in the movement toward the establishment of a strong centralized national monarchy—as was France. The papacy, which would have been the logical focus for Italian nationalism, was not strong enough to unite Italy into a single papal-Italian state. Moreover, any secular power that might have attempted such a move would have had to contend with the opposition not only of the papacy but with that of the German Empire, with its hold on Lombardy in the north and that of the Norman-German kingdom of Sicily in the south.

Throughout the Middle Ages, Italian intellectuals had mourned the lack of an Italian state; but in the absence of such a state both they and the populace at large had given their loyalty to the only strong political units that did exist—their towns and cities. In a way this went back to the classical tradition which had never been completely destroyed in Italy, the classical city retaining its vitality longer there than anywhere else in the western world.

Also, unlike the rest of Europe, Italy had retained a connection with the Byzantine Empire. Justinian's ephemeral western reconquests had slipped away everywhere else except in Italy, where the exarchate of Ravenna had remained a Byzantine foothold until the eighth century and where parts of Sicily had remained Byzantine until the Norman conquest of the eleventh century. Thus, while most of Europe was frozen into immobility and isolation by the feudal system and Saracen control of the western Mediterranean, Italy held open a thin trickle of trade with the east. This commerce nourished the cities of Italy—the trade in spices, jewels, fine metalwares, exotic fabrics, rare woods, and perfumes. The Crusades turned this trickle into a flood of products and wealth.

The Italian commercial cities commanded the sea routes to the Holy Land. In exchange for transporting and supplying the crusading armies, they received extensive economic privileges in the Latin states of the Near East—at the expense of Byzantium. In the opening years of the thirteenth century the city of Venice, as we have seen, manipulated the scandalous Fourth Crusade to its own advantage. Its intrigues resulted in the sack of Constantinople, and in the Venetian seizure of key holdings in the eastern Mediterranean. Genoa fought viciously with Venice for trading rights and monopolies all through the thirteenth century. In the previous century the Lombard towns had doggedly opposed the Italian schemes of the emperor Frederick Barbarossa and had succeeded by their wealth and courage in winning virtual independence under imperial charters. The

Saracen sea power, which had denied the western Mediterranean to European commerce for so long, was unable to stand against the vigor of the Italian maritime cities. By 1300 Italy was the center of a flourishing new economy in western Europe.

The very nature of this economy was revolutionary. From the outset Italian trade was international in scope, with the whole of western Europe as its market. The cost and risk of this trade were enormous—but so were its profits. Before long every aspect of economic, social, and political life in the Italian cities was affected by this development. The traditional guild system—with its emphasis on corporate protection, its guarantees of equal opportunity, equal profits, and just prices—soon proved inadequate to the needs of the new economy and began to transform itself under the pressure of the most powerful and enterprising merchants. In 1297, for instance, the masters of the merchant guild of Venice, who constituted the Grand Council of Venice, abolished that institution and, as a closed oligarchic group of merchant princes, assumed the government of the Venetian Republic.

As the commercial revolution became an industrial revolution as well, and the cities of Italy began to produce their own luxury goods for the markets of Europe, the transformation of the guild system continued. The masters of the "great guilds" in Florence became a patriciate, and moved to limit access to their rank. The rank of guild master became a privilege for a handful of families and individuals. It had little of the traditional connection with skill or craftsmanship; rather, it represented the ability to finance capital investment, to acquire industrial processes and machinery, and to establish international business connections. The Florentine cloth guilds were dominated by two hundred masters who, in turn, controlled about twenty-five lesser guilds and some thirty thousand people. The many men who had once been free workmen and small shop owners became, in effect, factory laborers.

The growth of great financial institutions paralleled that of industry, and the masters of the moneychangers' guild became the powerful bankers and banking families of Renaissance Italy. The Florentine family banks of the Bardi and Peruzzi manipulated an international network of credit. They loaned vast sums to Edward III of England and in return controlled a significant part of English economic life. Philip IV of France was almost equally in the debt of the Florentine bankers. The gold florins of Florence and ducats of Venice—first minted in the thirteenth century—became the common currency of large-scale business throughout Europe. The extent and complexity of Italian business operations called into existence new methods of bookkeeping and accounting, new concepts of credit and exchange: all of which added to the revolutionary aspects of these economic changes.

The agents of Italian business and finance were to be found throughout Europe. One might see at the fairs of Champagne wool-buyers from Florence, silk merchants from Lucca, and the representatives of Genoese and Florentine banking houses. In 1317 the Venetians opened a direct sea route to the north and each year the "Flanders Galleys" carried the goods of the Mediterranean to the markets of the Flemish towns and returned with the products of northern Europe: the rough cloth of Flanders, English wool, and the goods of the Baltic bought from the merchants of the German Hansa.

The Social Consequences of Economic Revolution

The merchant-princes whose ruthless vitality had changed the economic face of Italy were also the ruling class of its cities (indeed, as often as not, they had "made" their cities). Through the thirteenth and fourteenth centuries, when anarchy reigned in the disputed Kingdom of Naples and in the lands of an absent papacy, and bandit lairs crowned nearly every hill in central Italy, the only responsible government that was to be found was the government that these merchant-aristocrats created for themselves and their communities. To the new aristocracy were joined the remnants of the old. The Italian nobles had never entirely abandoned the towns. Some of them had become wealthy as the landlords of burgher tenants; some, throwing away the prejudices of their northern cousins, had actively joined in the commercial adventuring of the merchant companies; many had married their sons and daughters into the families of the rising middle class. The result was a fairly homogeneous plutocracy, dedicated to the exploitation of the new economic world that was opening before them.

The ruthless profiteering of the great and wealthy and the revolutionary changes in the social structure produced almost constant warfare within the walls of the Italian cities. The parties in this conflict took the names of worn-out causes and half-forgotten political factions, and the towns rang with the cries of Guelf and Ghibelline, White and Black, Gaetani and Colonese, Grandi and Popolo! But under whatever names, the parties were always the same—the "haves" and the "have nots." The fourteenth century was one of social violence everywhere in Europe, in Wat Tyler's England and the Flemish towns of Jacob van Artevelde; but in Italy it was especially savage. A greater gulf separated the rich from the poor and the narrow arena of the city set them at each other's throats more readily. In Florence the Ciompi, the day laborers of the cloth trade, rose in bloody rebellion in 1378 and succeeded in imposing their will upon that city for almost four years. Elsewhere, in greater or lesser degree, there were similar uprisings.

Incessant warfare within the cities was coupled with hostility among the cities and states. Each tiny state was a sovereign unit, each was jealous of its rights, and each demanded expansion at the expense of its neighbors. The political pattern of Italy was thus a microcosm of the hostilities and alliances involving the larger states of Europe.

The wars of Venice and Genoa that we have already mentioned continued through most of the fourteenth century. Florence and Milan were at war during most of the same period, and Venice joined this conflict as well; Florence fought against Lucca and Pisa as well as Milan, and at the end of the century Florence and the Kingdom of Naples were at war. This constant turmoil attracted the growth of tyrants and despots. There were always opportunities for ambitious men of skill and nerve. In some states, like Milan, local noble houses seized power. Other states turned to outside rulers, *podeste,* to seal the rifts between their factions, only to find that in many cases they had simply hired a master. Increasingly, the Italian states called into their service professional soldiers, *condottieri,* captains of mercenary companies who fought their battles for pay. The Hundred Years' War produced such men in abundance, and they drifted down into Italy to offer their questionable services to the warring city-states. The more successful mercenary captains were able to seize states of their own and rule by conquest, and not always badly. The result of the bewildering political flux of Italy was that the Renaissance state, whatever its particular form, was ruled by the powerful, the ambitious, and the ruthless few—the closed circle of a merchant oligarchy or a motley aggregation of local despotic princes. These men were the makers of the Renaissance. Their wealth paid for its works of art and supported its men of letters. But equally important, these new patrons of Italy were instrumental in creating the climate that was essential to the Renaissance. They were responsible for its secularism, its vitality and, to some degree, its greatness.

The Awakening

The Italian Renaissance began with the work of four men—the writers Dante, Petrarch, and Boccaccio; and the artist Giotto. Their lives spanned most of the fourteenth century: Dante was an established poet and respected political functionary of Florence in 1300; Petrarch and Boccaccio died within a year of each other in 1374 and 1375.

In most respects, as we have seen, Dante was a thoroughly medieval figure. But he was also the first significant figure of the Renaissance. His passionate love of Vergil and the classics anticipated the Renaissance cult of ancient letters. The awe-inspiring breadth of his knowledge and interests anticipated the Renaissance ideal of the universal man. Both his life and work were touched by the forces that helped shape the Renaissance. His life was scarred by the violence of Florentine city politics that condemned him to bitter exile in first one and then another of the jewel-like cities which were to be the scene of the Renaissance. He knew their dukes and despots and was honored by them. Yet Dante turned his back on the new world, for the spirit of his work embodies the theological values of the Middle Ages rather than the secular humanism of the Renaissance.

Petrarch and Boccaccio, however, were very much the products of this new world. Their lives and works epitomized what was merely suggested in Dante. Their tastes and attitudes and their expression of them created the Renaissance as a literary age. Like Dante they were Florentines, and like him they spent much of their lives in exile.

Francesco Petrarca (1304–1374) was born in Arezzo, the son of a Florentine notary and friend of Dante who had fled from Florence in the same political crisis. Ser Petracco (the son later euphemized the original name) finally settled in Avignon, where he found work in the endless legal business of the French popes. The precocious genius of the young Petrarch soon bloomed and by his middle years he was the most famous literary man of his generation, a virtual dictator of letters and art. He knew every important personage of Italy; he was courted by cities, dukes, kings, and popes. His fame helped to establish some of the most prominent features of the Renaissance, none more significant than the twin cults of personality and classicism.

Convinced that he was a most remarkable man living in a most remarkable age, Petrarch gloried in self-knowledge. Indeed, his introspection provided the subject for much of his writing—essays, verses, and especially letters which number in the thousands. With great diligence he collected copies of these and lovingly compiled them during the last years of his life. By then many of them had become, as it were, sacred relics of the cult of personality for which Petrarch was largely responsible and of which he was the hero. It is not surprising that he should have written the first autobiography of modern times, nor that he should have begun thus:

Greeting.—It is possible that some word of me may have come to you, though even this is doubtful, since an insignificant and obscure name will scarcely penetrate far in either time or space. If, however, you should have heard of me, you may desire to know what manner of man I was, or what was the outcome of my labours, especially those of which some description or, at any rate, the bare titles may have reached you.

To begin with myself, then, the utterances of men concerning me will differ widely, since in passing judgment almost everyone is influenced not so much by truth as by preference, and good and evil report alike know no bounds. I was, in truth, a poor mortal like yourself. . . .[1]

That he did not really consider himself a "poor mortal like yourself" is quite apparent. He thought, rather, that he was the first man since antiquity really to perceive and understand the magnificence of nature. To Laura—who was to Petrarch what Beatrice had been to Dante—he addressed a series of sonnets in which he displayed this perception. Of her death he wrote:

> Alas! that liquid look, that lovely face!
> Alas! the poised grace of that golden head!
> Alas! the sweetness of the words she said
> That soothed the savage breast, raised up the base!
> Alas! the smile—that dart which I embrace,
> Whose hope is death now that all hope is dead;
> O hadst thou not so late inhabited
> This earth, how queenly would have been thy place!
> In thee I burn, in thee still draw my breath,
> Being all thine. Death now has disciplined
> All lesser pain to nothing; no sharp teeth
> Can gnaw the constant grief-bright music dinned
> By thy last words, snatched up by jealous Death
> To vanish with their hope upon the wind.[2]

Petrarch sees his love as a flesh-and-blood creature of earth, "that lovely face" and "golden head" not as a wraith or a philosophical symbol as the medieval poets might have done.

More than anyone else Petrarch must be credited with the revival of classical learning that was the mainspring of the Renaissance. Though his actual knowledge and judgment of classical authors were often faulty,

1. In J. H. Robinson and R. W. Rolfe, *Petrarch, the First Modern Scholar and Man of Letters* (New York: Putnam, 1898), p. 59.
2. Joseph Auslander (trans.), *The Sonnets of Petrarch,* p. 229. Used by permission of David McKay Company, Inc.

his enthusiasm and devotion to classicism were unmatched. His Latin prose, while vigorous and effective, was certainly more medieval than classical, and though extravagantly honored in his own time, his Latin writings have little enduring value. Even his most ambitious work, a lofty epic based on the career of Scipio Africanus, is a tiresome, artificial, and pedantic piece. What was significant about Petrarch's classicism was its zeal. Tradition records that he wept over the pages of a Greek Homer that he could not read. The story is probably false but the gesture rings true. Learning was an affair of the heart to Petrarch; antiquity was immediate and alive to him, and the writings of the ancients represented the very quintessence of wisdom and moral goodness. He looked forward to a time when the classics would reign again and replace the babble of vulgar tongues that his time knew. To this end he dedicated his life. The exalted value that Petrarch placed upon the classics became part of the classical cult of the following centuries. With Petrarch began the enthusiastic search for classical manuscripts that would become a fever in the following generations. He himself discovered a manuscript copy of some of Cicero's correspondence.

Petrarch set the pattern for his age and established the archetype of the Renaissance humanist. Yet there were forces at work in the formation of Humanism of which neither Petrarch nor his enthusiastic supporters were fully aware. In a large sense Humanism, which he can justly claim to have fathered, was the reaction of the emerging secular-oriented society of Italy against the ascetic ideal of the Middle Ages. This was by no means a simple, clear, causal pattern. For generations the economic materialism which had come with the growth of towns, trade, and a money economy had created values incompatible with the church-dominated value system of an earlier age. Petrarch and the humanists who followed him provided their society with a "new" set of values derived from antiquity. Humanism-classicism offered ready-made arguments and standards for such a society. The classical ideal of citizen-man was thoroughly acceptable to the new urban society; and to this was joined a whole list of classical ideals and values. Furthermore, the tradition of classicism was more readily at hand in Italy than elsewhere to suggest itself as a frame of reference for the new ideals of Humanism. The homeland of the classical Roman Empire became the homeland of the new urban civilization of the thirteenth and fourteenth centuries.[3]

3. Although one of the most important and pervasive of intellectual movements, Humanism is difficult to define. The term itself is Petrarchian, based on Cicero's

Petrarch's love for and identification with classical antiquity made him impatient with the barbarism of his own time and of his immediate, medieval past. He led the rejection of the medieval which the whole Renaissance would soon express. Even such terms as "medieval," "Gothic," and "Scholastic" were terms of contempt coined by the humanists. Yet neither Petrarch nor Renaissance Humanism could cut the string of time that held them to their medieval past. Between the Renaissance and the classical world lay the thousand years of Christianity which had become a part of the heritage into which the humanists were born. It was impossible for them to reject the experience of their religion. From Petrarch to Milton, Renaissance Humanism was involved in this great classical-Christian contradiction—the emphasis on man and this world in the classical tradition and the emphasis on God and the next world in the Christian tradition.

At the height of his power and fame, about 1350, Petrarch met and befriended a younger contemporary and fellow Florentine, Giovanni Boccaccio (1313-1375). This illegitimate son of a Florentine merchant-banker had already made a name for himself as the author of the *Decameron,* the work for which he was to become notorious. It was by no means a work his elegant and fastidious friend could approve. By Petrarch's austere standard the *Decameron* was not a work of Humanism. But in a larger sense, and perhaps a better one, it is. It was written in Italian, not Latin. Its style was simple, direct, and uncomplicated by the typical humanist literary devices. Its many subjects were chosen from the world in which men lived, not the fancifully reconstructed world of classical antiquity. In a purely literary sense it is alien to the dominant humanistic literary trend. Instead, it is part of a strand of harsh, earthy, cynical realism which, while sometimes recessive, is never quite absent from Renaissance life and letters; in all, it is a superb mirror of the human spirit.

The *Decameron* is a collection of tales held together by an external

concept of *humanitas*—the sum total of man's strictly human capabilities and talents as opposed to any kind of mystic supernaturalism. Deriving from the revived interest in antiquity led by Petrarch, Humanism tended to retain its connection with classicism in the sense that the identifying mark of the humanists was their cultivation of Latin and Greek and their preoccupation with classical "correctness" in speech and writing. But even from the beginning there was much more to Humanism than a petty concern for the niceties of grammar. The substance of classical thought also impressed the humanists, who tended to translate classical values into the terms of their own age. Thus, Humanism became the chief philosophical framework of the Renaissance and had much to do with creating (or at least justifying) the leading values of the age—secularism, concern for individual worth, love of fame, and demonic productivity.

device. The Black Death had come to Florence—the introduction to the *Decameron* contains a classic description of its ravages—and to escape it ten fashionable young people, seven girls and three boys, leave the city for their country estates. They resolve to pass the time in telling stories and each of the ten must tell one story each day for "ten days" (from Greek *deka* + *hemera*) to make up the hundred tales of the *Decameron*. The stories came from many sources: some were ancient Oriental tales that had been brought to Italy in the ships of Italian merchants; others were popular medieval tales; some were folktales with parallels the world over. But from whatever source, Boccaccio made them part of himself and made them reflect the image of the "Renaissance society" that we see fully for the first time.

He describes a society of cities: we see the luxury of a leisure class made possible by the labor, trade, and money of urban enterprise; we see the squalor and misery of the urban laborers; we see a society filled with gaiety and artificiality; and, in the recurring themes of the *Decameron,* we see a parade of the values, prejudices, and attitudes of Renaissance man. Many of the stories turn upon the immorality of the clergy. This was certainly no new theme to the generation of Boccaccio, but his handling of it was in a new spirit. It was not his intention to relate the unworthiness of some clergy in order to reform others. The unworthy priest, the lecherous friar, the monk out of cloister were part of life as he saw it. He accepted them and ridiculed them for their essential absurdity. Another theme frequently intertwined with Boccaccio's "anti-clericalism" is the admiration of wit and ingenuity. This too was part of the emerging value system of Boccaccio's Italy. The sly merchants who trick and cheat each other with outrageous cynicism in tale after tale have the flavor of reality. We see the shrewd and lively intelligence of Renaissance man as well as his casual cruelty and astringent humor. The great majority of the Decameron's stories deal with love, and in their treatment we discover the zest, verve, bawdiness, and heat of Renaissance man's love of life. It is as if Boccaccio had taken the courtly code of troubador love and turned it inside out! His goddess is the golden Aphrodite, not the ivoried Madonna.

While the *Decameron* bound Boccaccio to one aspect of the Renaissance, his friendship with Petrarch bound him to another, that of humanistic classicism. Boccaccio also turned to the classics and, in his last years, produced a veritable humanistic library. He wrote two long and discursive encyclopedias comprising the biographies of famous men and women of the classical period. In another work he catalogued the geographical references in Greek and Latin literature. In still another he made a compendium of classical mythology. These works, for all their faults, were welcomed and honored in their time as among the first "research tools" of classicism. Petrarch had wept for Greek; Boccaccio became its first serious Renaissance student. He became proficient enough to puzzle out some passages of the standard authors and was enrapt by the beauty his halting efforts revealed. Like his master he became an ardent searcher for classical manuscripts. In a famous passage he described how he found the priceless works of the ancients tumbled in confusion in the library of Monte Cassino, how the grass grew in the dust and debris piled upon the shelves, and how the ignorant monks had mutilated the vellum texts to make charms.

The other significant figure of the dawning Renaissance was Giotto di Bondone (c. 1276–1337), the peasant boy who became the first famous artist of the Renaissance. A friend of Dante, he stood in the same relation to Renaissance art as Dante and Patrarch stood to Renaissance letters. Closer to Dante than to Petrarch, Giotto represented both the old and the new. He was not a conscious innovator but, as he developed the canons of his art and his craft, he slowly opened the way to the most significant direction of Renaissance art, that of naturalism. In this sense we must think of Giotto as the founder of the great tradition of art which was to be fulfilled in Leonardo, Titian, Michelangelo, and Raphael.

Giotto was not an intellectual (few artists of his age were). We do not find in him the painful self-awareness which was so marked in Petrarch or in the artist-intellectual typified by Botticelli in a later age. Giotto was an honest and simple craftsman, but one of enormous ability. His themes were not much different from those of his more "medieval" predecessors —the life of Christ and the Virgin, the lives and deeds of the saints. But he painted them with such reality that, as Boccaccio said, ". . . they seemed not so much likenesses as the things themselves; whereby it often happened that men's visual sense was deceived, and they thought that to be real which was only painted."

The artistic effects which made Giotto the wonder of his age were achieved by the illusion of space, by simple modeling, by composition, and by perspective. In short, with Giotto, the devices of modern painting came into the history of art. But again in Giotto, as in Dante, we see more the anticipation than the realization. The realism which was so striking to his contemporaries seems naive and grotesque to us. His knowledge of anatomy was sketchy and his figures distorted and badly drawn; but he realized the three-dimensional mass of the figure and understood the play of light upon its bulk. He had no real understanding of the mathematical laws of perspective, his space is shallow and his proportions incorrect; but the figures of Giotto have mass and occupy tangible space. He must be regarded as the first great compositionalist of Renaissance art. His scenes have a powerful, self-contained unity. Unlike the medieval artists, Giotto painted real people doing real things rather than symbols or ideas. Every innovation in conception and technique that is attributed to him flows from this one simple notion. Yet this was the seminal idea of all Renaissance art, and it resulted in perhaps the greatest single period in the history of art. This simple, direct naturalism was the basis of what is often called the Humanism of Giotto, but its roots were not classical; they stemmed instead from the personal experience of the artist himself. In this sense the Humanism of Giotto is more closely related to the earthy realism of Boccaccio than to the scholarly classicism of Petrarch. It took generations after Giotto for the strand of conscious classicism to be joined to the naturalism which he fathered.

The Rise of Florence

It was by no mere coincidence that the four "founders of the Renaissance" were Florentine. The beginning of the Renaissance was centered in that city and responsive to the rise and fall of its fortunes.

Through the first half of the fourteenth century Florence managed to balance herself upon the narrow edge between freedom and chaos. Internally she was in constant turmoil from the class conflict that came with rapid economic growth. Externally her freedom was menaced by the rise of powerful tyrannies all around her. A series of disastrous military defeats undermined the leadership of the merchant-aristocracy. Two of the greatest Florentine family banks had loaned heavily to Edward III of England, draining the credit of the entire city. In 1339 Edward refused to pay the interest on these loans and four years later repudiated them entirely. The resulting financial panic not only broke the two banks, but shook the entire financial structure of the city. The bankers and merchants, facing social revolution, called in an outsider to assume the reins of government. This had been tried before without great success, and it failed again.

The new *signor* was a French military adventurer called the Duke of Athens. He shortly tried to establish a popular dictatorship on the basis of the widespread hostility to the merchant-aristocracy, but the merchants proved too strong and his coup failed. On the heels of this civil commotion came the horror of the Black Death, which struck Florence in 1347–48, almost paralyzing the life of the city. This disaster had much the same economic effect in Florence as elsewhere, creating a scarcity of labor. When the laborers tried to exploit this advantage they faced the solid hostility of the merchant-aristocracy. Troubles mounted through the middle years of the century until, in 1378, came the wholesale proletarian uprising, the Ciompi Revolt. It was a reaction doomed to eventual failure and within a few years the powerful and the wealthy had returned to power. But the cause of the people against their economic masters had been taken up by Salvestro de' Medici, and from this time on the Medici were identified with the "democratic" interests of Florence.

On this base the political fortunes of the great family rested. The Medici were bankers; their family fortune had grown out of the ruin of the greater family banks of the fourteenth century. From about 1410 to his death in 1429 Giovanni de' Medici was the head of the family. His shrewd financial practices made the family immensely wealthy and Giovanni used his wealth, position, and connections to become a power in the political life of his city, taking the leadership against the narrow oligarchy which continued to direct the city's affairs.

The costly and frustrating local wars that had plagued Florence for more than a century began to go even more badly than usual and Cosimo de' Medici, the son of Giovanni, made an open bid for power. He was supported by the people in their exasperation with the unsuccessful "war policies" of the old oligarchy. The city fell into his hands in 1434. The "rule" of Cosimo was that of a political boss. He carefully preserved the myth of popular government with which his family was traditionally associated. Superficially Florence was a fairy-tale democracy: Cosimo held no public office; he had no legal authority; he dressed in the somber black of the businessman and mingled freely with the people. His weapon was his wealth, which enabled him to put people in his debt and then to place them in strategic spots in the city administration. From behind the scenes he controlled the machinery of Florentine government, its apparently free elections, its apparently honest tax rolls. The Medici actually ruled the city and their enemies, both political and economic, found themselves taxed out of existence, banished from the city, and even harried in exile by Cosimo's long financial reach. In a narrow sense the Medici rule of Florence was as corrupt as that which it replaced. But in a broader sense, it was a benevolent and responsible paternalism, an economic variation on the familiar Italian theme of civic despotism.

The influence of Cosimo spread outside the walls of Florence to the affairs of the whole peninsula. In 1447 a political crisis occurred in Milan that gave Cosimo an ideal opportunity for intervention. The despotic line of the Visconti family, which had ruled Milan for more than a century and a half, came to an end. The Visconti had been both ruthless and able; they had created a powerful inland state in the Po valley that was a menace to the trade routes and political boundaries of both Florence and Venice. These two states had often been in alliance against Milan, but in the crisis of the Milanese succession Cosimo de' Medici abruptly changed sides. He supported the bid of a new Milanese tyrant, Francesco Sforza. Francesco was a condottiere, able and ruthless but with scant support either at home or abroad. The valuable patronage of the Medici became the chief prop of his upstart dynasty. Shortly thereafter Cosimo supported another disputed claim, this time to the crown of Naples, and bound the new and ambitious King Ferrante of Naples to Florence and Milan. Thus Cosimo created the triple alliance of Florence, Milan, and Naples which became the chief stabilizing influence in the Italian peninsula through the rest of the fifteenth century. This alliance isolated Venice, already in decline from losses to the Turks in the east; at the same time it neutralized French influence, which was a potential menace to Naples and an immediate threat to Florence; and finally it brought peace and order to Italy on a larger scale than that war-wracked land had known for generations. It is no wonder that the first great flowering of the Renaissance coincided with the age of the triple alliance nor that its collapse at the end of the century precipitated a basic change in the cultural leadership of the Renaissance.

On the eve of the golden age of the Medici, in 1469, the leadership of the house passed to Lorenzo, the grandson of Cosimo, justly called *Il Magnifico,* "the Magnificent," the most famous member of an illustrious dynasty. With each generation the Medici power had become more secure. Lorenzo continued the general policies of his grandfather but he abandoned Cosimo's bourgeois pose and frankly assumed the role of a prince. He kept a magnificent palace and married a titled wife. He was the most lavish and knowledgeable patron of Italy, constantly underwriting arts, letters, and scholarship, and making Florence the hub of Renaissance culture. With his family's international connections and enormous wealth and facilities, Lorenzo became the chief banker to the papacy—the choicest financial plum of the world.

In 1478 a rival family made a last desperate attempt to unseat the Medici in the conspiracy which is called, after them, the Pazzi Plot. It was a far-flung and tortuous intrigue culminating in an assassination attempt in the cathedral of Florence at the Easter service. Lorenzo was wounded and his brother killed, but the shabby attempt to gloss an oligarchic reaction as a popular uprising failed utterly. The people of Florence rallied to the Medici and the plot was crushed. The artist Botticelli celebrated its failure with a grizzly painting, since lost, of the broken bodies of the chief conspirators hanging from the tower of the city hall, one of them still in the episcopal robes of his high church office. In this domestic crisis the enemies of Florence struck—Venice, the new pope, Sixtus IV, who was probably involved in the Pazzi Plot, and even France. But Lorenzo's personal stature and courage, coupled with his brilliant diplomacy, enabled him to restore the triple alliance, to drive a wedge between Venice and Rome, and to forestall the intervention of France. Florence and Italy were in his debt, for he had maintained the conditions for order on which both the prosperity of Italy and the culture of the Renaissance depended. Lorenzo was the virtual dictator of Florence, unopposed, unthreatened, and immensely popular. The triumph of the Florentine Renaissance was in large part the triumph of Lorenzo de' Medici.

The Florentine Quattrocento: Midday of a Golden Age

The dominant formative influence in the making of the Renaissance was classical Humanism; every other cultural influence became secondary to this. Wealthy men were eager to fill their libraries with classical manuscripts and their households with retinues of scholars. This patronage was no casual thing; it assumed the proportions of a civic enterprise. The competition of the market place was transferred to the cultural sphere. Demand produced a supply of classical humanists trained in the "new scholarship." These humanists, as well as their patrons, ransacked monastery libraries and archives for the precious remnants of ancient writings. The celebrated Poggio Bracciolini, attached to the Council of Constance, spent much of his time searching for manuscripts in the nearby Swiss monasteries and copying those he could not take away with him. One Florentine magnate equipped an expedition to track down a single classical manuscript that had been reported to be in some north German town; another was so carried away by his collector's zeal that he consumed his fortune in the process. Although the latter had been a merciless competitor of Cosimo de' Medici, Cosimo so respected the value of his taste and literary judgment that he gave him unlimited credit at his own bank for the purchase and duplication of manuscripts. Thus began the great private book collections which would form the basis of modern classicism and literary study.

Books stimulated both ideas and style; wealthy patrons maintained salons in their homes; groups of humanists studied, talked, and taught together. A famous Florentine center of such talk and study was the monastery of San Spirito. But the spirit of Humanism was essentially foreign to the monastic spirit, and even in the quiet garden of San Spirito it was the genius of pagan antiquity that animated the men who gathered there. One of the most striking things about the humanistic movement was its secularism, often verging over into paganism. The "new learning" and the new secularism merged easily with many of the older strands of anticlericalism and, in Italy, as one of the most significant products of the Renaissance, there emerged the first secular-learned culture of modern Europe. The pattern of its instruction is probably the most enduring contribution of the humanistic movement, the revolutionary form and concepts of Italian humanistic education. By and large the universities were either unable or unwilling to accommodate the new humanistic studies. They were too deeply enmeshed in the long-established, traditional forms of medieval formal learning. In a way this worked to the advantage of the humanist educators, since they were forced to organize their schools completely outside the medieval university tradition. They turned instead to the congenial ideal of antiquity and to the practical aims of their own discipline. Consequently humanistic education took the form of the academy—ultimately reaching back to Athens and Plato—and the intimate tutorial pattern of the ancient, classical household. The humanist educator was typically a resident tutor to the sons, and often the daughters, of a wealthy, noble, or princely family. Thus Guarino da Verona (1370–1460) and Vittorino da Feltre (1378–1446) were the schoolmasters of the "palace schools" respectively at Ferrara and Mantua. Their subjects, like the forms of their instruction, were classical—the language, literature, and the values of antiquity. And here their aims became practical for they, like their fellow humanists everywhere, regarded antiquity as an ideal toward which they instructed their young charges in the confident hope that they would grow into the kind of demigods they knew from the pages of Livy, Cicero, or Quintillian. With surprising frequency they did. The humanist educators were responsible for introducing into the history of education such modern concepts as physical education, the systematic

Left: ANDREA DEL VERROCCHIO. *Lorenzo de' Medici.* Below: ANDREA MANTEGNA. *The Family of Marchese Ludovico II with attendants.*

41

Left: FRANCESCO BONSIGNORI. *Francesco Sforza.*
Below: RAPHAEL. *Pope Julius II.* 1511 – 12.

The inscription within the painting reads:

TEMPLA DOMVM EXPOSITIS; VICOS FORA MOENIA PONTES:
VIRGINEAM TRIVII QVOD REPARARIS AQVAM.
PRISCA LICET NAVTIS STATVAS DARE COMMODA PORTVS:
ET VATICANVM CINGERE SIXTE IVGVM:
PLVS TAMEN VRBS DEBET: NAM QVAE SQVALORE LATEBAT:
CERNITVR IN CELEBRI BIBLIOTHECA LOCO.

MELOZZO DA FORLI. *Sistus IV and His Familiars.* c. 1475—77.

Left: Pope Alessandro VI.
Below: RAPHAEL. *Leo X and
Two Cardinals.* 1517—19.

study of history, attention to individual differences of students, and above all the commitment of formal education to the classics of Graeco-Roman antiquity from which the modern academic disciplines were freed only yesterday. From Italy the ideas and books of the humanist educators spread with the spread of humanism to have a similar effect all through the north of Europe.

The roots of Humanism lay in the pre-Christian classics and the zeal to tap these roots led often to excess. It is difficult to recapture the spiritual-intellectual intoxication of the early cult of he classics. Men not only worshiped the ancient but those moderns, the professional humanists, who cultivated the "neoclassic" style—the Ciceronian or Vergilian elegance—in their own writings. More often than not these writings are of almost no consequence in themselves; but their stylistic purity made them treasures. The professional humanists were the pampered darlings of their society. They were often unprincipled opportunists who mulcted their patrons and brawled with one another. Often, however, the professional humanist merged with the man of affairs. At the opening of the fifteenth century Colluccio Salutati was the Latin secretary of the city of Florence, a public official as well as the leading spirit of its humanistic circle. In the next generation the secretary of state for the Florentine republic was the noted humanist Leonardo Bruni. Every state in Italy sought the services of humanists to ornament their chanceries and compose official correspondence in proper Latin style. Many sons of commercial princes, studying with the humanists, began to acquire the high polish of humanistic education so that Humanism thoroughly permeated the upper strata of society, not only in Florence but throughout Italy.

The Greek for which Petrarch had wept in vain and for which Boccaccio had labored so manfully began to become available in the generation following them. The beginning of the so-called Greek Renaissance was the work of Manuel Chrysoloras, a learned and charming Byzantine scholar who came to Italy in the last decade of the fourteenth century. In 1396 he arrived in Florence and was welcomed like a conquering hero. For four years he taught and lectured there to eager audiences of young and old, and his instruction prepared the first Italian generation of Greek scholars. In 1438–39 the Council of Ferrara-Florence brought a swarm of learned Byzantines to Florence to swell the tide of Greek enthusiasm. The eastern trade connections of the Italian commercial cities gave access to the great Greek collections of Constantinople, which fed the new enthusiasm of Italian Hellenism. Long before the fall of Constantinople most of the literary treasures of the Byzantine Greek tradition had already been recovered. Regular purchasing agents brought Greek manuscripts from the east by the shipload on commission for Italian merchant-princes, and Italian scholars translated and edited them for an eager audience.

In this general revival of Greek the open-handed patronage and discriminating enthusiasm of the Medici was again a prime factor in making Florence one of the centers of Greek study. As Aristotle had been the idol of the scholastics, Plato became the idol of the humanists, and the center of his cult was Florence. Cosimo de' Medici selected a young man from his household, Marsilio Ficino, who showed exceptional promise and was, like so many others, absorbed in the study of Greek. In exchange for his promise to spend his life in the study of Platonism, Cosimo settled upon the young Ficino a handsome income, a library, and a foundation. This was the beginning of the Platonic Academy, the most famous and productive of the Renaissance centers for Greek studies. Ficino brilliantly translated most of the writings of Plato, wrote commentaries and expositions, and developed the basic canons of Renaissance Neoplatonism. This became the fountainhead of Italian Renaissance philosophy, and with the generation of Ficino's pupils humanistic learning broadened its scope. Its emphasis shifted from what had been chiefly a concern with the forms, the styles of classicism, to a concern with classical values.

While a polished style, either Greek or Latin, remained probably the most characteristic mark of the humanist and while the worship of antiquity for its own sake continued, Humanism began to examine the values revealed in the study of antiquity, to become a philosophic frame of reference for the assessment of human life. One of the most remarkable associates of the Platonic Academy—a man who may be taken as the most exemplary type of the Italian humanist—was Giovanni Pico della Mirandola (1463–1494). He was wealthy and brilliant and, in the best humanistic tradition, "athirst for every new thing." He studied widely and informally, and his mind was bent by a dozen currents of inquiry including not only Neoplatonism, but Hebrew studies, of which he may be reckoned the first important Renaissance student. He was enormously productive and once offered to dispute in Rome no less than nine hundred theses that summed up for him the whole knowledge of the world. In such personal intellectual audacity was the very spirit of the humanistic movement.

Furthermore, none of his contemporaries expressed better than he the fundamental meaning of Humanism in its best sense when he wrote in his *Oration on the Dignity of Man:*

O supreme generosity of God the Father, O highest and most marvelous felicity of man! To him it is granted to have whatever he chooses, to be whatever he wills. Beasts as soon as they are born (so says Lucilius) bring with them from their mother's womb all they will ever possess. Spiritual beings, either from the beginning or soon thereafter, become what they are to be for ever and ever. On man when he came into life the Father conferred the seeds of all kinds and the germs of every way of life. Whatever seeds each man cultivates will grow to maturity and bear in him their own fruit. If they be vegetative, he will be like a plant. If sensitive, he will become brutish. If rational, he will grow into a heavenly being. If intellectual, he will be an angel and the son of God. And if, happy in the lot of no created thing, he withdraws into the center of his own unity, his spirit, made one with God, in the solitary darkness of God, who is set above all things, shall surpass them all. Who would not admire this our chameleon? Or who could more greatly admire aught else whatever.[4]

Lorenzo the Magnificent continued the learned patronage of the Medici. Unlike Cosimo who had never really ceased to be a merchant, Lorenzo was not only a true prince but a truly learned man. He was a discriminating critic, a writer of some reputation, and the intellectual companion of the many famous philosophers and men of letters who thronged his city palace.

Florence was the center not only of the literary-humanistic flowering of the early Italian Renaissance, but of perhaps even greater significance for the future, the center of its dominant school of art. The two were by no means unconnected, and the classical literary enthusiasm that we have seen was equally apparent in the visual arts. Underfoot and before their eyes the Italians had the ruins of Roman antiquity—its public buildings, its temples, its statuary—and as the humanists exalted the values of classicism, nothing was more natural than a classical revival of art. When the patrons of art and culture rebuilt their country villas and city palaces, they wanted them built in the style of antiquity. Architects and builders began to study both the actual remains of classical art and its literary-mathematical theories of proportion and construction. By the mid-fifteenth century humanistic scholarship was joined to art and architecture in the

4. In E. Cassirer, P. O. Kristeller, and J. N. Randall, Jr. (eds.), *The Renaissance Philosophy of Man* (Chicago: University of Chicago Press, 1948), p. 225.

learned theorist and practitioner Leon Battista Alberti (1404–1472), who was also a fine Latinist, a poet, mathematician, and sculptor.

With even greater consequences the same developments were taking place in sculpture and painting. The worship of antiquity underscored the value of classical forms—essentially realistic rather than symbolic representations of man and nature. The thread of naturalism that reached back to the work of Giotto was picked up once more by such a sculptor as Donatello (1386–1466) and such a painter as Masaccio (1401–1429) and joined with the intellectualism of the humanistic movement. These men epitomized the scholar-scientist-artist of the Renaissance. Where Giotto had simply attempted to render the general form of the human body, Donatello studied the body and its mechanics as carefully and enthusiastically as the humanists studied their precious manuscripts. At the same time he applied the poses, the drapery, and the proportions of antiquity to his figures. Donatello's young "David" was possibly the first free-standing major statue of its sort since antiquity, and his great equestrian statue of the condottiere, Gattamelata, at Padua, revived another classical type. The harsh, realistic, intellectual style of Donatello continued through the work of his younger contemporary, Andrea del Verrocchio (1435–1488), to culminate in the masterworks of Michelangelo, the greatest sculptor of the Renaissance.

Fully as important as the works of these Florentine artists was their constant experimentation with technique. This was of greatest significance for painting because of its inherent fundamental technical problem—to represent three-dimensional reality on a two-dimensional surface. The Renaissance painter had before him no clear precedents or patterns, either classical or medieval. For all practical purposes, the artists of the fifteenth century, largely Florentines, created the theoretical structure of all modern painting. At the opening of the century Masaccio carefully studied anatomy and experimented with the control of light and shadow. Piero della Francesca and Paolo Uccello were obsessed with the study of perspective and delved deeply into mathematics; Fra Lippo Lippi turned for models to reality itself—the people he could see and touch about him—to paint the traditional themes. Antonio Pollaiuolo was fascinated by the representation of the nude figure, once more considered the temple and not the prison of the human spirit. By mid-century, in spite of the lagging approval of the church, artists turned to the dissection of cadavers and the scientific study of the internal structure of the body. Other artists turned to the study of optics, many to the problems of spatial geometry and composition, and nearly all of them to the technical matters of pigments and surfaces.

Influences crowded together as the fifteenth century progressed. Out of the controlling interest in naturalism and classicism new themes came to the fore as painters turned to the representation of nature—flowers, trees, landscapes—incorporating these into the predominantly religious themes traditional in medieval art. A striking portrait art began to develop, one of the inevitable consequences both of artistic realism and the worship of personality. In art as in literature the lavish and understanding patronage of the great and wealthy was inseparable from the works that crowd the century. And again the Medici led all the rest. Cosimo assumed the expense of reconstructing the convent of San Marco and thus gave employment to the artist Fra Angelico and the architect Michelozzo. He commissioned Brunelleschi to rebuild the church of San Lorenzo, one of the first truly Renaissance buildings of Florence. Donatello was showered with commissions by Cosimo, as was the painter-mathematician Uccello, who painted his greatest panels for Cosimo. Under Lorenzo the Magnificent the Medici palace became a museum and studio and virtually every significant artist of the age came there to study, to talk, and to be rewarded.

The Eclipse of Florence

In 1492 Lorenzo the Magnificent died in Florence; his death triggered a series of events that changed the direction of European politics and exerted a profound effect upon the culture of the Renaissance. The triple alliance of Florence, Milan, and Naples had been maintained for nearly half a century, largely by the influence of Cosimo and then of Lorenzo de' Medici. At the death of Lorenzo the balance of Italian powers was already seriously threatened by a deepening rift between Naples and Milan. Ludovico Sforza (called *Il Moro,* "the Moor"), the Duke of Milan, was a usurper who had seized power at the expense of his nephew. He was also a classic example of the Renaissance despot—clever, talented, ruthless, amoral, and concerned with nothing so much as his own survival. The boy ruler whom Ludovico had replaced was related to the house of Naples; his mother was the sister of King Ferrante. With the death of Lorenzo de' Medici these personal and dynastic tensions broke into the open.

Ludovico, threatened with destruction, decided to exploit French in-

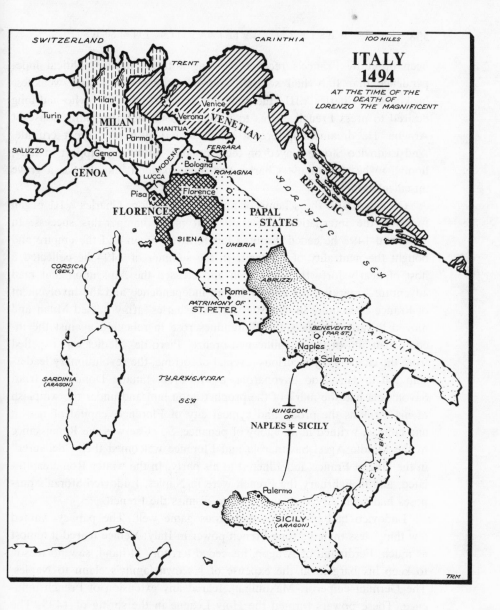

ITALY
1494

AT THE TIME OF THE
DEATH OF
LORENZO THE MAGNIFICENT

terests in Italy for his own purposes. France still retained a claim to Naples that went back more than two centuries to the breakup of the Hohenstaufen-Norman empire of Frederick II, further complicated by subsidiary claims. France had, furthermore, recovered from the ravages of the Hunded Years' War and, through the reign of the shrewd and economical Louis XI (*1461–1483*), had become once more the most formidable nation-state on the continent. The balance of power north of the Alps had been upset by France's recovery, posing a threat to the political independence that Italy had so long enjoyed. Italy's wealth and weakness beckoned to Charles VIII (the ambitious son of Louis XI), who had long desired to press French claims to Naples and replace the ruling house of Aragon. He dreamed of foreign conquest and even of a great crusade. And Ludovico Sforza played on these dreams, promising support in Italy, hoping to be able to use Charles and then abandon him. It was a grave miscalculation.

Obsessed with the scheme of an Italian invasion, Charles VIII began to settle the international accounts that might hamper his success. In 1492 and 1493 he ceded disputed territories to Spain and the empire and bought the neutrality of England. In the summer of 1494 he collected a host of nearly forty thousand men and crossed the Alps upon that mad adventure—marking the end of Italian independence and the involvement of France once more in dynastic war. As Charles' army passed Milan and moved toward Florence, the Florentines rose in rebellion against the incompetent son of the magnificent Lorenzo. Piero de' Medici was expelled from the city and, by a curious reversal of fortune, the revolutionary leadership fell to Girolamo Savonarola, a wild-eyed, fanatic Dominican friar. Savonarola had the mark of the prophet upon him and under the whiplash of his sermons the proud and cynical city of Florence, capital of reason and culture, writhed in an agony of penance. So close was the Renaissance to the Middle Ages! Savonarola and Florence welcomed their "deliverer" in the king of France and adhered to his party. In the winter Rome capitulated, and in February the French were in Naples. Ludovico Sforza's purposes had been served. It was time to dismiss the French.

Ludovico had played his dangerous game well. The papacy wanted few things less than a strong French power in Italy; Venice feared it almost as much. Ferdinand of Aragon, his ceded territory in hand, saw no reason to keep his bargain at the expense of his own family's claim to Naples. The German emperor, Maximilian, feared any extension of French influence. These powers formed the Holy League in the spring of 1495. The threat to Charles, while still somewhat veiled, was apparent. His long line of supply down the Italian peninsula could be easily cut by these potential enemies, and even France might be invaded. Charles began a hasty withdrawal; with each step northward his glorious conquests faded and his army melted away with disease. Only Savonarola's Florence remained faithful. Then, in 1498, the inevitable reaction set in even there. Savonarola fell from power, was tortured, hanged, and burned. The Medici returned to Florence and Ludovico Sforza seemed safe in Milan. But the French invasion, inconsequential as its results were at the moment, had broken the barrier between Italy and the north. Within two years Charles VIII of France died and was succeeded by his cousin Louis d'Orléans as Louis XII (*1498–1515*). Louis turned once more to Italy, this time, ironically, to press his family's claim to Ludovico's Milan, and Ludovico came to his end as a prisoner of the French. For more than half a century Italy became the battleground of European power-politics.

The struggle for power by self-serving politicians and the corrupt diplomacy of the period were brilliantly analyzed by Niccolò Machiavelli (1469–1527), the apostle of realistic, modern power-politics. The son of a Florentine lawyer, Machiavelli began his career in the upheaval attending Charles VIII's invasion of Italy and the collapse of Medici power in Florence. For more than fifteen years Machiavelli worked for the Florentine government as clerk, adviser, and diplomat, almost always behind the scenes and in a position to observe every sordid detail of the international politics of his time. In 1512 the republican regime in Florence ended with a Medici restoration, and Machiavelli was exiled along with the other functionaries of his party.

In exile he turned his hand to the political writings which, though they failed to restore him to position in Florence, have made for their author an almost unique place in the history of political theory. Machiavelli observed the world of politics around him. He did not censure it for its lack of morality; he did not even lament the lack of it. Instead, he took what he saw as the basis of a general principle: that this is the way politics must always be. He drew from his observations and, in the best humanistic tradition, from the examples of Roman history to create an empirical theory of politics. His whole system is based upon the assumption "that all men are bad and ever ready to display their vicious nature, whenever they may find occasion for it."[5] Within such a framework the only virtues that have meaning are greatness, power, and success. Machiavelli then turned to the types of states that might be acquired by force, fraud, or succession, and the problems of ruling them. He advocated for the successful ruler whatever is necessary for his success—the cynical use of religion as a tool of repression; reward and punishment and terrorism as instruments of policy—and documented his case from the successes and failures of history. His most famous work was the

5. In *The Prince and the Discourses* (New York: Modern Library, 1950), Discourses, III, p. 117.

little pamphlet called *The Prince,* a digest of his theories hopefully addressed to the restored Medici prince of Florence. It did not achieve its immediate purpose, but it introduced a new way of regarding politics—describing and analyzing political reality rather than dealing with abstract theories. Machiavelli did not teach his age: it taught him.

Ironically, though understandably, Machiavelli has always been associated with the means he advocated rather than with the end he hoped those means would ultimately serve: the achievement of Italian freedom. For Machiavelli was a passionate republican. But he contended that a strong, even ruthless, central government was necessary in order to gain and keep freedom. It is a tribute to Machiavelli's political acumen that almost four hundred years later this was to be the way in which Italian independence was finally gained. His republicanism appears quite clearly in the summary pages of *The Prince,* but is more fully developed in his larger work, *The Discourses on the First Ten Books of Livy.*

The same age that produced the sharpened political genius of Machiavelli produced also the universal genius of Leonardo da Vinci (1452–1519), the personification of the ideal Renaissance man. Leonardo was the illegitimate son of a Florentine notary and was apprenticed at an early age to the artist, scholar, and teacher Andrea del Verrocchio. He learned his artist's craft in the midst of that incredible burst of energy that characterized Medicean Florence—and he was a part of it. This was a time of exuberant, unbounded confidence and optimism. The world seemed on the verge of a golden age and all men knew it. Leonardo soaked up the energy and the multiple influences of his city to form his own universalism. He quickly became a young artist of note and caught the discerning eye of Lorenzo de' Medici.

In 1493 he applied for a position at the court of Ludovico Sforza in Milan and described his qualifications as a military architect, siege and hydraulic engineer, ordnance and demolition expert; as architect, sculptor, and painter, ending with the words, "And if any one of the above-named things seem to anyone to be impossible or not feasible, I am most ready to make the experiment in your park, or in whatever place may please your Excellency, to whom I commend myself with the utmost humility."[6] Humility indeed! Leonardo went to Milan and undertook not only such works as he had promised but many more. He was the Merlin of Il Moro's court.

6. Quoted in E. G. Holt (ed.), *A Documentary History of Art,* I, pp. 273-75.

The years in Milan were his most productive. Four of them he spent in painting the "Last Supper." It is typical of Leonardo that this masterpiece was not only a profound artistic expression but a great intellectual feat as well. His restless mind probed every corner of the dramatic meaning of his subject and his brush followed. He wanted to see the scene completely new, free of conventions. Few paintings have been more carefully planned.[7] In the midst of a dozen projects—major paintings, portrait commissions, architectural designs, monumental sculpture—Leonardo still had time to be interested in a universe of things. He studied the flight of birds and experimented with the possibility of human flight. He studied both plants and animals, and his notebooks are filled with careful nature drawings. He was fascinated with alchemy and mathematics. He studied anatomy and dissected cadavers. He wrote what was probably the most complete and scientific study of the technique of painting up to that time. The notebooks that he kept religiously reveal fragments of a hundred projects and a thousand interests. They contain drawings and notes which anticipate the airplane, the submarine, the military tank, explosive shells, the heliocentric theory of the universe, and the concept of gravitation.

When the French invasions destroyed the security of Ludovico's court, Leonardo left Milan and traveled widely through Italy. In these years he painted the "Mona Lisa," probably the world's best-known portrait. In Florence he worked on the preliminary studies for a great battle scene that he never finished. In Rome he was occupied for a time with the decoration of the Sistine Chapel. Finally he retired to spend his last years in France.

Time has not dealt kindly with the works of this most universal of Renaissance artists. His paintings and studies have been scattered. The plaster model of his great equestrian statue of Francesco Sforza was shot to pieces by the French troops when they occupied Milan. But Leonardo himself was too restless a genius. Many of his projects he simply abandoned when he had solved whatever special problem interested him. Life was too short and there was too much to be done and known. Leonardo wrote, "When an artist's aim goes beyond his work he will compose but

---

7. It is ironic that the very penchant for experimentation that made him a great artist has destroyed his greatest work. At the time he painted the "Last Supper" he was experimenting with a new painting technique, employed in the work. It was a failure and the painting had begun to deteriorate even in the artist's own lifetime. Today it is a hopeless ruin.

few works, but they will be such that men will gaze in wonder upon their perfection."

THE GOLDEN AGE

As the great age of Renaissance Florence came to a close in the last decade of the fifteenth century and all Italy was thrown into the confusion of war and invasion, the Renaissance achieved its final burst of creative energy. The setting was Rome; not the Rome of the austere, reforming popes of the High Middle Ages, but the secularized and opulent Rome of the Renaissance papacy.

The Renaissance Papacy

We have already traced the decline of the medieval church from the thirteenth century through the later Middle Ages. We have seen the effects upon clerical prestige of the Babylonian Captivity, the Great Schism, the conciliar movement, and the widespread protests and heresies. We have seen the papacy losing its stature as an international force to the advancing national states. On the eve of the sixteenth century the papacy still claimed its ancient rights and jurisdictions, but was actually operating as one of the community of Italian states. It was in this capacity that papal Rome became a force in the civilization of the Renaissance.

The popes faced a somewhat more difficult domestic problem than the rulers of other Italian states. During the fourteenth century the absence of the papacy from Italy had left the papal states at the mercy of a host of petty despots and bandits who seized virtually every town, village, or strong point. In Rome itself powerful noble families were a menace to papal government. In the early years of the fifteenth century papal energy was directed to fighting the claims of the conciliasts while rapacious neighbors in Italy made further inroads upon the states of the church. It was the middle of the century before the popes could turn seriously to the restoration of their authority in their own lands. The device they used most effectively was dynastic appointment. From the time of Calixtus III (*1455–1458*) the Renaissance popes regularly packed the temporal and spiritual offices of the papal states with their own relatives, often called "nephews," hence the term nepotism (from Latin *nepos,* nephew). Such dynastic politics created nearly as many problems as it solved, for each pontificate brought new appointments, displacements, and hostilities. By the beginning of the sixteenth century a dozen powerful and jealous families were involved in the in-fighting for the prize of the papal states. In the larger arena of Italian politics the popes preserved their traditional goal of a disunited Italy. They operated with the same ruthlessness and the same devices as the Italian secular princes, and consequently were classed with them by their contemporaries.

In 1492 Roderigo Borgia mounted the papal throne as Alexander VI. One of the favored nephews of Calixtus III, he had been a power in papal politics for more than twenty years. With his elevation the secularization of the papacy was complete. He lived like the political despot that he was and completely ignored the spiritual responsibilities of his office. Rich, able, and immoral, his chief purpose was to establish his family's rule in the states of the church and found a strong Borgia-papal dynasty. In his son Cesare Borgia, whom he publicly acknowledged and honored (along with his other children), he had a military commander second to none in Italy. But Alexander's plans were threatened by the blundering presence of the French. His enemies inside the papal circle wanted him deposed and their own parties elevated by the French king; and Charles VIII himself spoke ominously of a general council to reform the papacy. But time was on Alexander's side. Charles VIII passed on to Naples and Alexander could begin to intrigue with the host of other powers that now wanted to be rid of the French "barbarians."

When Louis XII mounted another French attack in 1499, Alexander welcomed him, for this French king sought Milan, not Naples. And Milan was precisely the state that stood in the way of Alexander's political ambitions on the northern border of the papal states. Once more the slippery diplomatic balance shifted as the papacy, Venice, and France combined against Milan. Within a year, in 1500, Ludovico was defeated and a prisoner of the French. Alexander profited handsomely: he got rid of an ambitious enemy in Milan; he supported a partition of his ancient southern enemy of Naples between France and Spain—neither of whom could afford to exploit it; and in the exchange he received the military and financial aid of the French in his own dynastic schemes for central Italy. Under the direction of Cesare Borgia, these schemes were rapidly moving toward success. Then the hope of a great Italian Borgia state failed. Alexander died in 1503 and, without the support of the papal office, Cesare was unable to complete his conquests. After the month-long interim reign of Pius III, Alexander VI was succeeded by his most implacable enemy among the papal intriguers, Giuliano della Rovere, who became Julius II.

Julius was fierce, energetic, and one of the greatest politician-diplomats of his generation. While he had hated and opposed the Borgias for most of a lifetime, his own program was little different from that of Alexander VI —the creation of a strong papal monarchy held by his own family. Nor were his methods and scruples different. The major powers of Europe, which were by now all deeply involved in the tangled affairs of Italy, united against Venice in the League of Cambrai (1508). Each member of the League had its own designs and selfish expectations. Julius wanted to reduce the power of Venice and seize certain key territories along the northern frontier of the papal states. While a French army defeated the Venetians, Julius struck quickly for the lands he wanted, taking the field in person at the head of his forces. Once the coalition had served his immediate purpose Julius abandoned it, turned against the French "barbarians," and "forgave" defeated Venice. By 1511 Julius had built such a formidable alliance system that the French were forced to abandon even Milan and, at Julius' death in 1513, the papacy stood stronger among the Italian states than ever before.

The new pope was the Medici Leo X, a son of Lorenzo the Magnificent; and with this succession Florence drew close to Rome. The Renaissance papacy seemed on the threshold of a glorious new age of political prestige. Italy was stabilized and a new balance of power was forming north of the Alps. Yet, within a generation the Medicean papacy was to be consumed in the conflagration of larger dynastic war involving the great powers of Europe.

Rome and the High Renaissance

In spite of the intrigues, broken treaties, murders, license, and immorality that marred their rule, the high Renaissance popes were, almost without exception, great patrons of arts and letters and deeply committed to the culture of the Renaissance. Nicholas V (*1447–1455*) was a highly trained professional scholar and humanist. his court attracted the leading humanistic figures of Italy and vied with that of Cosimo de' Medici in Florence. It was he who laid the foundations for the great Vatican library. Pius II (*1458–1464*) was the famous humanist Aeneas Sylvius, one of the greatest Latinists of his time and a pivotal figure of the world of learning. Paul II (*1464–1471*) was an eminent art collector. But the greatest gift of the papacy to the Renaissance was its patronage, and the greatest patrons were, paradoxically, precisely those popes who were the most scandalous in behavior and most secular in policy—Alexander VI,

Lorenzo Ghiberti. East Doors of the Baptistery, Florence. c. 1435.

Left: St. Peter's, Rome.
Below: MICHELANGELO. *The Slave*. c. 1516.

OPPOSITE
Left: GIOVANNI BELLINI
Portrait of Young Man.
c. 1500.
Right: GIORGIONE. *The
Cross Bearer.* c. 1505.

Right: LEONARDO DA VINCI. *The Last Supper.*
c. 1495—98.
Below: DONATELLO. *Equestrian Monument of
General Gattamelata.* 1445—50.
Opposite: ANTONIO DEL POLLAIUOLO. *Battle of
Ten Naked Men.* c. 1465—70.

Left: LEONARDO DA VINCI.
Self-Portrait.
Below: TITIAN. *Venus and Adonis.*
c. 1525.

Julius II, and Leo X. The very political and dynastic politics which demeaned the Holy Office made them the most rich and powerful among Italian princes. Operating as secular princes and retaining the ancient claims and forms of universal authority, there were no rulers of Italy more eager to glorify themselves in art and letters than these popes. Their wealth, generosity, and sophistication attracted talent from all over Italy.

Rome itself had so far produced no "school" of style either in art or letters. But the artists, sculptors, gem-cutters, musicians, humanists, lawyers, collectors, and agents who flocked to Rome in the last decades of the fifteenth century brought with them every regional form and variation that the Renaissance had already produced in Italy.

In the plastic arts these varied styles were synthesized to create a new species of ecclesiastical art, an art that reflected the majesty and might of the church rather than its spirit. The papal court was like an emperor's court, and the popes demanded an "imperial art." Thus the prevailing characteristic of the High Renaissance style was solemn grandeur. Nowhere else in the world were there such monumental projects to be undertaken and such successes to be won.

The artist whose work most clearly represents this culminating phase of the Renaissance was Michelangelo Buonarroti (1475–1564). This great and somber genius almost spanned the Renaissance with his long life. He was, like Leonardo, the product of Florence in its great age. He had worked in the studio of the brothers Ghirlandaio and was among the aspiring young artists who studied in the museum of the Medici gardens and was a special favorite of Lorenzo the Magnificent. He associated freely with the humanists and litterati of Lorenzo's circle and picked up many of their ideas, being especially impressed by the semireligious Neoplatonism of Ficino and Pico. During the years following the death of Lorenzo, Michelangelo traveled about Italy. He returned to Florence several times for a variety of commissions. By the age of thirty he had established himself as the leading sculpture of his time, and was sought out by the Pope Julius II to design and execute a monumental tomb for him.

Before this project was well under way the imperious pope demanded that his artist suspend plans for the tomb and undertake the decoration of the Sistine Chapel. Julius was especially interested in this work, for the chapel commemorated his relative and benefactor, the former pope Sixtus IV. Michelangelo refused. A terrible quarrel resulted and finally, after threats, scenes, and reconciliations, Michelangelo took up the project of the chapel, thus driven to do what became his greatest work. The chapel offered a unique challenge. A start had been made on a decorative scheme for it in the previous century, but the design lacked unity and was uneven in quality. The barrel-vaulted ceiling, ten thousand square feet of space, remained to be done. For months Michelangelo struggled with his drawings and schemes, searching for a principle of organization. He finally evolved a plan of painted architectural divisions to define and contain various levels of the work, and then began to fit into it the pieces of a gigantic allegory. He worked for almost four years under the most exhausting conditions—but the result was magnificent. In the top of the ceiling were nine panels of gigantic size, depicting the work of God in creating the universe and man. These appeared as though viewed through architectural skylights, opening into eternity. At the corners of these panels and lower down along the arched ceiling he placed twenty monumental nude male figures, painted with virtuoso skill and twisted into every imaginable posture of the human body. In the spaces between the high windows, on thrones painted into his architectural scheme, he placed massive figures representing Old Testament prophets and sibyls (prophetesses) of classical antiquity—those who foretold the coming of Christ. Closely related to these figures were a series of scenes from the Old Testament and the Apocrypha, symbolically foreshadowing incidents in Christ's life. In all, this great, crowded, contorted composition contained more than three hundred figures. Its meaning is a synthesis of the whole artistic and intellectual inheritance of the Renaissance. In the broadest sense it is traditionally Christian, dealing with the Creation, Fall, and Redemption of man. But these themes are presented in the anthropomorphic terms of classical Humanism and the Renaissance cult of man. And the whole is infused with a sense of dignity, power, and mystery owing in large part to the influence upon Michelangelo of Florentine Neoplatonism.

Michelangelo worked intermittently at projects for Leo X both in Rome and Florence, where he executed the massive figures for the Medici tombs. His later years were spent in Rome under the last of the Renaissance popes. He returned once more, twenty-five years later, to the Sistine Chapel to decorate the altar wall with an apocalyptic vision of the Last Judgment. By this time he was the most famous artist in the world.

With the astounding virtuosity which is the very mark of the Renaissance, Michelangelo turned from sculpture and painting to architecture. He built palaces, churches, and monuments; the "monumental style" and "grand scale" of High Renaissance architecture are largely his creation. Even the great Cathedral of St. Peter's, which had been under construction for almost half a century, owes much of its basic form to him. Thus the greatest artist of the Renaissance was instrumental in producing its greatest building.

The long lifetime of Michelangelo intersected the career of every significant artist of the High Renaissance. He knew the architect Bramante (1444–1514), who conceived the original plan for St. Peter's; he had a profound effect upon the short and brilliant career of the young Raphael (1483–1520).

The Glory of Venice

As the Italian Renaissance had its origins in Florence and reached its peak in Rome, it found its last great expression in Venice. In every way the glory of Venice in the late fifteenth and sixteenth centuries is a sunset glory. The Italy that had created the Renaissance was rapidly disappearing. In the early sixteenth century Europe was torn apart by the Franco-imperial wars of Charles V and Francis I, and dismembered Italy was both their prize and their battleground. The resurgence of Turkish power in the east began to limit the trade that had financed the culture of Renaissance Italy, and the center of European economic life shifted from Italy toward the coast of the north Atlantic.

The culture of the Venetian Renaissance reveals influences somewhat different from those that had shaped the Renaissance in the rest of Italy. Indeed, the Venetian Renaissance developed along almost independent lines. More than any other Italian state Venice was associated with the Byzantine-Moslem east, and nowhere is this more apparent than in the arts of the Venetian Renaissance. The monuments of Venice are more Byzantine than western—one has only to look at the Cathedral of San Marco. There is in nearly all Venetian art a love of color and display for its own sake, an emotionalism and flamboyance that contrast sharply with both the intellectualism of the major Florentine style and the sculpturesque monumentality of the Roman.

The main line of Venetian art began with the remarkable Bellini family. The father, Jacopo, was a contemporary and friend of the great Florentine innovators of the mid-fifteenth century; his youngest son, Giovanni, was the teacher of practically every important north Italian artist of the sixteenth century. It was Giovanni especially who laid the foundations in accurate, virtuoso drawing; dramatic, emotional composition; and richness of color on which Venetian art was to rest.

The two chief masters of the Venetian school were the products of the

Bellini shops, the painters Giorgione (1476–1510) and Titian (1477–1576). Their work must really be considered together. Giorgione was possibly the more talented of the two, but his early death left his influence to mature in the work of his friend, in whom all the influences of Venetian art were eventually to find expression. Titian did not have to fight for the acceptance of his art. Indeed, his paintings seemed to stand for the very qualities that people expected in great art. Furthermore, every stage in the development of his art flowed smoothly with the tides of taste and his fame and fortune grew steadily and easily.

Titian was neither an intellectual nor a scientific innovator; he was a painter, par excellence. He has no peer in this sense save Rembrandt, or perhaps Rubens or Velásquez. At every period his works are a delight to the eye, sumptuous and glowing. He moved easily from the most secular themes to traditional religious paintings. He was especially famous for his sensuous nudes; but his monumental, dramatic religious scenes are not essentially different in tone. He was much sought as a portrait painter; and his portraits rank among his finest works, his subjects a catalogue of the great men of the sixteenth century. He was the favorite artist of the emperor Charles V and painted him many times. Titian was carried off by the plague at the age of ninety-nine. His studio-factory had already supplied the roster of the next generation of European art, and his long life had already carried him well beyond the great days of Renaissance Italy. The cultural initiative had long since passed beyond the Alps and the Renaissance had become a general phenomenon of European culture.

THE EUROPEAN RENAISSANCE

The Migration of the Renaissance

Long before the French invasions of Italy at the end of the fifteenth century, the Renaissance had begun to filter across the Alps. For centuries the Alpine passes had carried the goods of Italy into southern Germany to the headwaters of the Rhine; and the great cities of southern Germany had grown with trade. From Genoa, Milan, and Florence the routes of commerce reached Marseilles and the Rhone. In every city of northern Europe there were Italian banks and merchant houses. For centuries Italian businessmen had brought their language, their ideas, and their tastes with them to the north, while thousands of people—soldiers, students,

scholars, churchmen, the sons of merchants and bankers from the north
—had gone to Italy and returned to report its marvels.

The same institutions of finance, business, and industry that had formed
the material basis of the Italian Renaissance were coming into existence in
the north in the centuries at the end of the Middle Ages, partly stimulated
by the trade and wealth of Italy, but growing also from native resources and
initiative. In the north, as in Italy, the new wealth produced a patronage
class, and their taste was deeply influenced by Italian models. This class
added its weight to the traditional patronage of nobility and royalty.

Well before the end of the fifteenth century Italian styles of architecture
and decoration had migrated as far as Poland and England. Italian artists
and architects were widely sought and richly rewarded. The domestic styles
of northern Europe began to be modified in emulation of the comfort and
luxury to be found in Italy. Rich men wanted their portraits painted by the
acknowledged Italian masters. A trip to Italy became a necessary part of
the "finishing" of every well-to-do young man and speaking Italian became
fashionable.

In the north, as in Italy itself, the classicism of the humanists led the
way to the Renaissance. The humanists claimed to be the purest exemplars
of the new Italianate way of life. And the educated as well as the half-
educated generally accepted their assertions. Thus Italian humanists filled
the courts and cities of northern Europe. They came as adventurers seeking
their fortunes. Some were attached to municipal or royal chanceries. Some
were in the trains of the Italian churchmen who received appointments to
German, French, or English benefices. Some came with Italian economic
missions. They were court poets, Latin secretaries, confidants, ambassadors
and spies, resident tutors, and sometimes even university professors. But
in whatever capacity, they spread their attitudes toward ancient literature,
their scholarship, and their criticism. They spread their books and ideas
and enthusiasm until Italian Humanism permeated the intellectual environment of Europe.

By the latter half of the fifteenth century the seeds of Italian classical
Humanism had begun to mature in the countries outside Italy. At the
German universities of Heidelberg and Leipzig Italian-trained German
scholars such as Rodolphus Agricola and Mutianus Rufus taught Greek
and "liberal studies." Lefevre d'Étaples brought the scholarly methods of
Ficino's academy to his philosophic lectures at the University of Paris. By
the turn of the century both Oxford and Cambridge were thoroughly im-

bued with Humanism and England had already produced a famous generation of its own learned men. In Spain the great Cardinal Ximenes founded
his reformed university at Alcala on generally humanistic principles. Native-
born humanists were beginning to establish themselves all over Europe.
There were poets like Ulrich von Hutten in Germany; scholars like Guillaume Budé in France and Thomas Linacre in England. Many of them
were considered eminent even by the snobbish humanists of Italy. By 1500
most of the cities of Europe had their circles of humanist writers and
enthusiasts. Sometimes they were affiliated with universities, often with
schools, sometimes with a noble or royal court. The humanist became
a truly international figure, at home wherever his clear, precise, and elegant
Latin speech was understood and wherever men discussed the classics,
the "new education," scholarship, and other scholars.

The ideas and works of the international humanists of the sixteenth
century traveled as freely as the humanists themselves, through the new
agency of the printing press. Indeed, one of the most significant factors
in the spread of humanism was the invention of printing. Actually, most
of the complex operations of printing had long been known in Europe.
Paper had been introduced from the east, ultimately from China, during
the Middle Ages. Along with paper came the idea of the block print; and
printed books, largely devotional pieces, had been printed from page blocks
for at least two centuries. The crucial step to modern printing was taken
some time around the middle of the fifteenth century, with the invention
of individual, movable, letter dies cast in metal.

Tradition attributes this final step to Johann Gutenberg of Mainz,
though on the basis of rather sparse and doubtful facts. A man named
Gutenberg was associated with the book trade and possessed some "secret"
process. His experiments with it were costly and he borrowed money.
When he could not pay his debts he lost both his business and his secret;
and he himself disappeared from the historical record. At some point in
this history of troubles either Gutenberg or his enterprising creditors produced the handful of the world's first printed books—a *World Judgment,*
several editions of the popular Latin grammar of Donatus, an *Astronomical Calendar,* and the crowning piece, the so-called forty-two line
"Gutenberg" *Bible,* probably printed in 1456.

Whether any of the shadowy figures who surround the Gutenberg
controversy deserve the specific credit for the invention of printing is
actually a rather pointless antiquarian question. The principal ingredients
of the invention were already there, and the first great age of modern

critical scholarship cried out for the precision and accuracy of the printed page. A rapidly broadening literate public clamored for books that could no longer be supplied in sufficient numbers by laborious hand-copying. Finally, the economic organization of western Europe made it possible for a man to operate a press as a business and for many to buy the books he produced.

The successors of Gutenberg printed well over a hundred books and trained a host of printers who carried their skills all over Europe. By 1500 there were fifty-one presses in Germany, seventy-three in Italy, thirty-nine in France, twenty-four in Spain, fifteen in the Low Countries, eight in Switzerland, and at least two in England. These early printing houses tended to become centers of scholarship. Often the printers themselves were respectable scholars and more often still their presses attracted other scholars. The reading public was imbued with the values and prejudices of Humanism and the first serious publications of early printing—save only the great volume of religious and devotional literature—were the works of humanistic scholarship. The most notable humanist-printer in Europe was Aldus Manutius of Venice. By 1490 his press was a flourishing business and he had embarked upon the great venture of his life, to prepare inexpensive, standard editions of the Greek classics. He gathered around him a corps of learned editors, artists, and technicians. His house became an academy of learning and wit. Nearly every important humanist of the age worked for the Aldine press at some time or other. The same thing was happening in printing houses all over Europe. A bond was forged between learning and printing. Indeed, much of the accomplishment of the international Humanism of the sixteenth century would have been impossible without the press.

Erasmus and the Rise of Christian Humanism

Both the printing press and the cosmopolitan brotherhood of Humanism played an important role in the life of the greatest figure in the history of Humanism, Desiderius Erasmus (*c.* 1466–1536). Erasmus was the illegitimate son of a Dutch cleric, born in Rotterdam. As a child he was placed under the care of the pious Brethren of the Common Life and had the advantage of study in their schools. The young Erasmus was orphaned at an early age; he had no money and was already showing the spark of a superior mind. There was no way open to such a boy but the church. His guardians placed him in an Augustinian monastery at Steyn, where he grew up. There is no indication that he ever had the slightest sympathy with either the disciplinary rigors or the spiritual exercises of his fellow monks. But the monastery had books and a certain tradition of learning, which did attract him. By this time the humanistic movement was spreading through northern Europe, and its values and attitudes penetrated even the walls of the monastery. Erasmus worked to cultivate a polished Latin style and devoured all the "new" books he could get his hands on. Although Erasmus was ordained a priest and committed himself irredeemably to the religious life, it became increasingly clear that he would never become either a conventional cleric or a contented monk.

He seized an opportunity to serve a neighboring bishop as Latin secretary, elated not only at the chance to leave the cloister but also at the prospect of accompanying the bishop on a journey to Italy, the very shrine of Humanism. The trip to Italy did not materialize but, under the sponsorship of the bishop, Erasmus did go to the University of Paris to study theology. At Paris he was enrolled in the rigorous reformed College de Montaigu and began the traditional program in theology. But he preferred the somewhat raffish society of the humanist circle of Paris. His writings, largely humanistic trivia at this point, began to attract some small attention, largely because of their style. Erasmus struggled after success. He fought against chronic ill health and the dismal prospect of returning to his monastery. He wrote, he studied, he taught—and he despaired.

Then in 1499, in the train of a wealthy young Englishman who had been one of his pupils, Erasmus traveled to England. This journey was in many ways the turning point in his life. He made friends among an eager and influential group of English humanists, including the young Thomas More. He made important contacts with a number of patrons; he was beginning to prosper and be known.

In 1500 a book appeared on which he had been working for some years, the *Adagia,* a collection of adages, maxims, epigrams, and quotable sayings culled from the classic authors. It was an immediate success and became a standard book of reference. It was regularly reprinted and expanded all through his life and became the foundation stone of his fame. Erasmus continued to write and study, producing a string of books: translations, humanistic commentaries and essays, and works of popular theology. In the meantime he diligently studied Greek and cultivated a wide circle of friends and patrons. In 1506 he finally made his pilgrimage to Italy as the tutor and companion of a number of children from the English court circle. He found that his growing fame had preceded him. The great Aldus of Venice welcomed him and published an expanded edition of his

Adagia; Florence opened its libraries and gave him the company of its learned men; Erasmus was honored in Rome and introduced to the rich and cultivated churchmen who stood close to the papal throne.

After some three years, word reached him of the accession of Henry VIII in England. Young Henry seemed the very exemplar of the humanist prince and Erasmus hastened once more toward England to enjoy the coming age of gold. He arrived sick and weary from the journey and was taken into the agreeable home and healing company of his friend Thomas More. There Erasmus wrote his most famous book, *The Praise of Folly.*

Its title and general form had been thought out through the tiresome journey from Italy. The book is a delightful satire, an address by the goddess Folly, who proves with impeccable logic and inexhaustible arguments that all men are her votaries. It is a gratuitous broadside of laughter at the human race. Folly claims wives, husbands, lovers; she claims the young and the old; the scholar, the tradesman, the peasant. This ingenious little book revealed the heart of Erasmus' talent, a genius for satire. He had the gift of penetrating to the very essence of things, the satirist's sensitivity to fraud, hypocrisy, pomposity, and vice. Men read his works and nodded and smiled in agreement. Not only in *The Praise of Folly,* but in a long list of popular books, he revealed the vicious and ignorant priest, the perpetual miracle hunter, the chaser after saints and relics, the pedantic Ciceronian humanist. There was not a single variety of meanness, ignorance, or depravity which he did not touch upon. His ability to say supremely well precisely what people were thinking made him the most widely read author of his century—and the most widely feared.

Yet the importance of Erasmus was not so much in his satire as in the purpose it served. The chief target of his criticism was the church; his chief purpose, the reform of the church and religion. Even *The Praise of Folly* was not free of this serious purpose. Indeed, the chief point of the book is contained in its argument for Christian behavior. Folly speaks:

. . . Christ himself, although he possessed the wisdom of the Father, became something like a fool in order to cure the folly of mankind, when he assumed the nature and being of a mortal. . . . He was made "to be sin" in order to redeem sinners. He did not wish to redeem them by any way except by the foolishness of the Cross, and by weak and simple apostles. . . .

. . .

The Christian religion on the whole seems to have some kinship with folly, while it has none at all with wisdom.

. . .

No people seem to act more foolishly than those who have been truly possessed with Christian piety. They give away whatever is theirs; they overlook injuries, allow themselves be be cheated, make no distinction between friends and enemies, shun pleasure, and feast on hunger, vigils, tears, labors, and scorn. They disdain life, and utterly prefer death; in short, they seem to have become altogether indifferent to ordinary interests, quite as if their souls lived elsewhere and not in their bodies. What is this, if not to be mad?[8]

Yet Erasmus was not such a reformer as St. Bernard or Savonarola. He had no vision of faith to bring to his fellow men. Erasmus never took the road to Damascus. Christianity represented to him the best mode of behavior that mankind had ever found and his approach to reform was essentially philosophic and moralistic. Religion was principally a "philosophy of Christ" and what he asked of man was that he behave in a manner acceptable to a humane and reasonable God. In this sense there was no separation between religion and learning. One could not reject the one for the sake of the other. This was the essence of Erasmian humanism.

Because of his concern for religious reform and because of his conviction that good religion and good learning go together, he bent his considerable ability to Christian and Biblical scholarship. In the course of a lifetime of learning he had equipped himself with the tools of humanistic criticism. Like the earlier Italian humanists he worked wth classical letters and edited volume after volume of the standard ancient authors. But his greatest works of scholarship were religious. He brought out critical editions of many of the church fathers. He labored for many years in preparing an edition of St. Jerome. But his most ambitious work was a critical text and Latin translation and commentary on the *Greek New Testament,* which appeared only a year before the outbreak of the Lutheran revolution in Germany.

The last years of his life were spent in Basel, Switzerland, where he was an editor for the press of John Froben. This was the sort of connection that Erasmus had sought for years. He did not have to teach or solicit patrons. In the printing press he had available the most powerful instrument of persuasion the world had ever known. He may be considered the first major figure in literary history to understand fully the implications of the press for scholarship and propaganda—and to use it. He was to his much wider world the same sort of literary dictator that Petrarch had been to his. His massive scholarship gave him almost unquestioned authority in the community of letters. His satiric works were read by prac-

8. Ed. and trans. by L. F. Dean (New York: Farrar, Straus, 1946), pp. 125-127.

tically every literate person in Europe. The textbooks that he wrote in considerable numbers were widely used in the new humanistic schools and academies everywhere, and they spread his ideas more effectively than anything else he wrote. He corresponded with every person of consequence in Europe—the pope, the emperor, and a half dozen kings and princes. His literary approval was sought by young writers and his company solicited by the great and famous everywhere. He richly deserved his title, Prince of Humanists.

The religious reforming purpose which was so close to the life of Erasmus was not simply an isolated, personal preference. On the contrary, the very eminence of Erasmus derived in large part from his being so thoroughly identified with the major intellectual currents of his time. The principal concern of northern scholarship and learning was precisely this kind of Christian Humanism: and it was this concern that most sharply distinguished northern from Italian Humanism. This is not to say that the Humanism of Italy was universally un-Christian. It is rather to say that, while the Italians had no specific quarrel with religion, they tended on the whole to take a rather realistic and secular view of the church, to accept Christianity as it actually was, and to be much more enthusiastic about classicism. Some beginnings of Biblical scholarship had been made, however, and Erasmus, for example, drew heavily upon the critical work of the fifteenth-century Italian humanist, Lorenzo Valla. But what had been at most a secondary and even casual concern of the Italians became a vital matter to the northern humanists. In the first place, the somewhat nationalistic, classical enthusiasm of the Italian had much less meaning for the northerner. The Italian could claim a descent, however removed in time, from classical Rome, which was absurd for the Dutch, German, or English humanist. Furthermore, the sophisticated and worldly view of the church that the learned Italian customarily took was not widely shared outside of Italy. The deep roots of Scholasticism were still fixed in northern learning and the memory of the conciliar movement was still strong. Many of the late medieval reforming movements and the remnants of several purist heresies lingered on in the north.

All this amounted to a countertradition which met and mingled with the current of Italian classical Humanism as it flowed northward. Thus, in England, the pious and learned John Colet, a friend of Erasmus, applied the principles of classical-historical scholarship to sacred Scripture in an epochal series of public sermons and spent his own fortune in establishing a school to educate young boys not only in the best of learning, but a distinctly Christian learning. In France the humanist Lefevre d'Étaples was also applying himself to Scriptural scholarship and beginning to ponder the same thoughts about justification by faith as his German contemporary, Martin Luther.[9] In Spain, under the patronage of Cardinal Ximenes, a group of scholars produced a great critical text of both the Old and New Testaments shortly after the publication of Erasmus' *Greek New Testament*. Everywhere learned men were fostering the study of Greek and Hebrew for the specific purpose of penetrating the secrets of the Bible.

In addition, and often in contrast to such positive scholarly reforms as these, there was trenchant criticism of the established church for its sins of secularism and its failure generally to promote either learning or piety. We have already seen the combination of scholar and satirist in Erasmus; and there were others like him. The famous *Utopia* of Thomas More was in part, a thinly disguised attack upon clerical abuse. The *Narrenschiff* ("The Ship of Fools"), by the German Sebastian Brandt was a much cruder and more direct attack. Under the whiplash of humanist criticism the old sentiments of anticlericalism grew once more, becoming more articulate than ever before. The secular preoccupation of the papacy had filtered down into the ranks of the clergy. The losing struggle of the church against the state had sapped its institutional energy. Everywhere forms and formalism tended to take the place of meaningful religious practice. The corruption that had festered in the church for centuries was breaking out on the surface of secular society. The humanist critics did not miss their opportunities. The church fought back against its critics; but the wit, the sarcasm, and the more than half-truth of the criticism made a difficult and elusive enemy. Often the clumsy tactics of the church were turned into new charges against it, as in the famous Reuchlin case.

Johann Reuchlin was one of Europe's most distinguished scholars of Hebrew. In 1506 a converted Jew wrote a zealous tract urging the condemnation of Hebrew studies as anti-Christian. Reuchlin answered this ridiculous book with a defense of the study of Hebrew and thereupon was summoned before the Inquisition in Cologne. Amid the prolonged hearings, charges, and countercharges of this sensational case, there appeared an anonymous book, equally sensational, entitled *Letters of Obscure Men*. Its authors were probably a group of German humanists led by Ulrich von Hutten, but the book purported to be made up of letters, largely from clergy, addressed to the members of the Cologne Inquisition, posing absurd

9. See p. 570.

Right: Hans Holbein the Younger.
Erasmus of Rotterdam. 1523.
Below: Albrecht Dürer. *Melancholia*.
1514.

Jan van Eyck. *Giovanni Arnolfini and His Bride*. 1434.

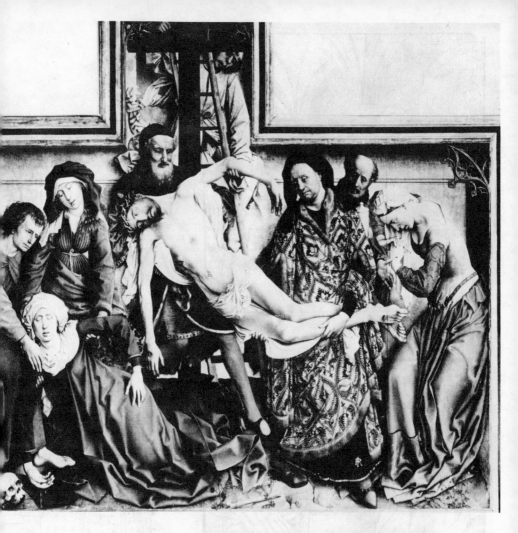

Above: ROGER VAN DER WEYDEN.
The Descent from the Cross.
c. 1435.
Right: ALBRECHT DÜRER.
Self-Portrait. 1498.

Top: HANS WEIDITZ. *Merchant*. c. 1519-20.
Above: *John Hus Being Burned at the Stake as
a Heretic*. 1415.

Venice in the 15th century.

Chambord, residence of King Francis I. 16th century.

and pettifogging questions of theology, commending the learning of the Inquisitors, and supporting them against Reuchlin—and all written in the most studiously bad Latin, with the worst possible logic, and bristling with ignorance. The book was a tremendous success. Reuchlin was eventually absolved but if the case against him had any point it was lost, and the authorities of the church further discredited.

The Renaissance of the Nations

While the religious countertradition of northern Europe profoundly modified the force and direction of Humanism, other native traditions modified still other expressions of the Renaissance outside of Italy. The forces which had created the civilization of the Italian Renaissance were, to a degree, closely related to the peculiar Italian environment in which they flourished. The northern European environment differed significantly from the Italian, and inevitably conditioned the expression of the Renaissance as it became a European rather than a strictly Italian phenomenon.

Of considerable importance in the northern environment, as distinct from the Italian context, were the lingering vestiges of feudalism and the growing sense of national identity. Like most important historical forces, neither of these can be discretely isolated. They often ran violently against each other; often they cooperated; more often still they functioned in relation to the many other forces of change operating in a vigorous and expansive society.

In Germany the centuries of the later Middle Ages had frustrated nationalism and seen the state surrendered to the princes. Social turmoil followed. Sometimes it was expressed in religious forms, heresies, and violent reform movements. Nearly all of these had nationalistic overtones.

In the neighboring Low Countries the house of Burgundy ruled a rich and powerful duchy, and at the court of Burgundy the decadent and meaningless forms of chivalry reached a level of refinement which may be legitimately called a Gothic Renaissance and which spread across the Rhine into Germany, across the Meuse into northern France, and even to England. It produced a magnificent flowering of the arts that included not only a vigorous late Gothic architecture and sculpture but a school of realistic, jewel-like painting, which reached its zenith in the work of the Van Eyck brothers in the first part of the fifteenth century. Thus, contemporary with the experiments of the Italian Renaissance, another countermovement was forming in the north.

Gothic realism was a world apart from the realism struggling into existence in Florence. The Gothic vision of reality was made up of a seemingly infinite number of perfect details painted with loving care. The whole was discovered in its parts—exactly the reverse of the visual conceptualism of Renaissance Italy. In the second half of the fifteenth century the influences stemming from Italy followed the bankers and merchants to the Flemish ports and began to blend with and influence the widespread Gothic style.

The same influences traveled over the Alps to meet that same Gothic style in southern Germany. They met in the life and work of the greatest of northern Renaissance artists, the German Albrecht Dürer (1471–1528). As a boy Dürer was apprenticed to an artist and learned the painstaking techniques of traditional German-Gothic realism. His first fame came as an engraver and wood-block cutter, which work further sharpened his vision and draftsmanship. Shortly after the turn of the century Dürer traveled to Italy and soaked up those intoxicating ideas and influences that had already begun to change the course of northern art. He fell in love with Humanism, with classicism, and with the Italianate ideal of the universal man. He became the Leonardo of German art. He experimented with and wrote about the same problems of proportion, perspective, measurement, and mathematics that had so intrigued the scholar-artists of Italy. The new influences did not destroy the native tradition of northern realism in Dürer, but were blended with it to produce his finest work. He was one of the most influential figures—not only in art—but in the intellectual world of his time.

Almost equal in fame was his younger contemporary and fellow German, Hans Holbein the Younger (1497–1543). Like Dürer, Holbein began his career in the flourishing book trade that the printing press had produced. He worked for the Froben press in Basel and executed the illustrations for the Froben edition of Erasmus' *Praise of Folly*. Holbein was attracted to Humanism and, again like Dürer, he was a respected member not only of his artist's trade but of the international community of the New Learning. He went to England, armed with letters from his friend Erasmus, and gained immediate fame as a portrait painter. In portraiture Holbein found a unique place in the history of art. His work combined the detail and finish of the best northern styles with the solidity and structural unity of the Italian. He was second only to the great Titian as a Renaissance portraitist.

As the cultural forms of late Gothic flourished in northern France they flowed together with the strong currents of religious reform and traditional Scholasticism. The University of Paris was still a force to be reckoned with, and theology had not yet been deposed as queen of the sciences. From the south came the currents of Italian Humanism, Italian artistic styles, and Italian manners; currents which increased in force with the end of the fifteenth century and the Italian invasions of Charles VIII and his successors. The memory of French cultural leadership in the High Middle Ages was still strong. The force of national consciousness was probably more pronounced in France than in any other state in Europe, though at the same time many of the vestiges of feudalism retained their tenacious hold. These crosscurrents produced intellectual ferment in the France of the Renaissance. It was an exciting, absorbing, and productive time; it produced artists, scholars, theologians, and poets. But the men who most exemplified both its diversity and its productivity were François Rabelais (1490–1553) and Michel Seur de Montaigne (1533–1592).

Their lives span the century of the Renaissance in France. When Rabelais was a child the French invasions of Italy began; at the death of Montaigne the disastrous wars of religion were nearly over and modern France was about to emerge under the leadership of Henry IV and the Bourbon dynasty. Yet while they shared their century, their lives represent two different aspects of the turbulent French Renaissance.

Rabelais reflected a confusing mixture of the tastes, prejudices, and values of both the Middle Ages and the Renaissance. He was a rebel, an arch-individualist, fascinated by his own remarkable many-sidedness: he had the insatiable curiosity of Leonardo; he was a learned man, a physician and scientist; he was a humanist, a monk and a priest; he was also a noisy skeptic, a dedicated reformer, and an incorrigible rake. The world to him was constantly new and exciting—no man has had a more voracious appetite for experience. He had a fantastic amount of knowledge tumbled together in the untidy, medieval encyclopedia of his mind. And this Rabelais expressed in his books, a series of volumes dealing with the lives and adventures of a family of frolicking giants, Gargantua and Pantagruel. The framework of his writing was the coarse, comic form of the medieval *fabliau*, but within that framework he used the incidents of his narrative to attack schools, universities, Scholasticism, and theology; to condemn the folly of war; and to ridicule the corruption of the clergy. Through the whole of his work runs the theme of freedom—freedom from traditional restrictions, freedom to do what one will, even if it is only to "drink deep!" and to destroy one's self. In the rich profusion of his writing Rabelais creates an admirable regimen of humanistic education. He relates the history of a war started when some shepherds of one king confiscate the cakes of some cake-bakers, subjects of another king. He implies that flesh-and-blood wars begin for no better and no more logical causes. He creates a mock monastery, a temple of the flesh, dedicated to man's self-respect as man and ruled not by asceticism but by decent moral principles distinctly Epicurean in tone. He takes his hero upon a great journey crowded with adventures and with allegory, a satire upon the notion of pilgrimage. He seeks the shrine of the Oracle of the Bottle. And not unexpectedly, when he finds it, the advice he receives is simply "Drink!"

Montaigne was outwardly the opposite of Rabelais. He was a gentle, sensitive, and courteous nobleman, condemned to fit an old way of life into the confusion of a rapidly changing time. At the age of thirty-eight he turned his back upon this impossible task and retired to his family estates. He devoted practically the rest of his life to writing and polishing the series of essays on which his fame rests. In his book-lined study and in the castle of his own mind he rejected the social activism of the Renaissance and turned his enormous curiosity inward upon himself. This study absorbed him, reflecting the fascination that Renaissance man had with man and Montaigne studied himself as an example, no better or worse than most men, but an example on which at least he was an expert. The essays superbly reveal a kind, compassionate, skeptical, and very wise man.

While both Rabelais and Montaigne were men of the Renaissance, they were peculiarly representatives of the Renaissance in France. They absorbed the substance of Humanism and rejected its artificial classicism. Both wrote in French, as did an increasing number of the intellectuals and poets of sixteenth-century France.

In Spain, as in Germany, the fury of religion overwhelmed the beginnings of the Renaissance. As Luther's Germany became the first citadel of Protestantism, the Spain of Charles V and Philip II became the center of the Catholic reaction. Everything and everyone in Spain was subordinated to the neo-orthodoxy of the Counter Reformation. The result was the blighting of Renaissance culture. The suspicion was widespread, not only in Spain but among the conservative and the orthodox everywhere, that there was some sinister connection between the skepticism and curiosity of the Renaissance spirit and the religious revolution that was breaking in Germany and threatening elsewhere. In Spain, however, the fanatical cooperation of a powerful monarchy and a strongly entrenched church made possible the wholesale repression of ideas. Spain had one holy mission, the defense of the church and the championing of orthodoxy. Any suspicion of humanistic or "Erasmian" leanings brought one before the Inquisition. Every intellectual and virtually every literate person in Spain was summoned before the Inquisition at one time or another. Almost the only significant work that may be claimed for the Renaissance in Spain is the *Don Quixote* of Cervantes (1547–1616), written at the end of the sixteenth century. Yet even this work must be regarded more as the product of peculiar forces of Spanish history than of the more familiar forces of the Renaissance. The mad Don was no more mad than the Spain of Philip II.

In distant England the Renaissance came with the Tudor dynasty and the triumph of Henry VII in 1485, part of the tremendous surge of energy which brought modern England into being. For a century before this time England had been in the "acquisitive" stage of Renaissance culture. Many Englishmen had gone to Italy and returned, like northerners elsewhere, impressed with the new culture of the Renaissance. Many influences continued to pour into late medieval England from Italy. Even as characteristically "English" a figure as Geoffrey Chaucer (c. 1340–1400) could not escape them. His *Canterbury Tales* has a cosmopolitan quality that derives in part from Chaucer's deep human sympathies and his contacts with the main currents of contemporary life. But this work also has an earthiness and zest which suggest the influence of Boccaccio— some of whose stories are actually part of Chaucer's collection. The range and spirit of his work, not only the *Canterbury Tales,* but such varied things as the translation of a scientific treatise on the Astrolabe, a book of "courtesie," and the romance of *Troilus and Criseyde,* all suggest some of the "lust for newness" and some of the confident versatility that were so much a part of the Renaissance spirit.

By 1500 Italian Humanism had been domesticated in England. It was established in the universities and could boast a circle of learned devotees in London. The English humanists, men like John Colet and Thomas More, were closely tied to the widespread pre-Reformation reforming movement. But the outbreak of the continental Reformation tended to discredit the idea of peaceful reform, even in England. In the religious conflict that was beginning there was no room for the middle ground held by the humanists. As the conflict heightened Henry VIII, who had once been the bright hope of the humanists, broke with the church over the question of a divorce and the dynastic necessity of a son to succeed him. While Henry wanted no doctrinal reform, his own action had opened the door to the very changes that he feared. In the two subsequent reigns of his Protestant son Edward VI (*1547–1553*) and his Catholic daughter Mary (*1553–1558*), the pendulum of religious change swung rapidly back and forth. Persecution, execution, and religious bitterness brought England to the brink of social and religious revolution.

In 1558 the third heir of Henry VIII, Elizabeth I (*1558–1603*), came to the throne. She was the daughter of Ann Boleyn, the woman for whom Henry had put aside his first wife and invited the Reformation to his realm. In the "age of Elizabeth" the Renaissance, which had been crushed and intimidated by a generation of religious violence, blossomed into the most magnificent and productive period in England's cultural history. In a reign of almost half a century Elizabeth identified herself with her age and its accomplishments to such an extent that her personality and her policies may be thought of as immediately responsible for the great period of the English Renaissance. Shakespeare cast his estimation of Elizabeth in the form of a prophecy in his play *Henry VIII:*

> . . . truth shall nurse her;
> Holy and heavenly thoughts still counsel her;
> She shall be lov'd and fear'd; her own shall bless her;
> Her foes shake like a field of beaten corn,
> And hang their heads with sorrow; good grows with her.
> In her days every man shall eat in safety
> Under his own vine what he plants, and sing
> The merry songs of peace to all his neighbours.
> God shall be truly known; and those about her
> From her shall read the perfect ways of honor
> And by those claim their greatness, not by blood.[10]

Elizabeth addressed herself to the deep-seated religious problem she had inherited with her throne.[11] Her settlement was not a theological but a politico-social resolution. She intended to unify her church as she would unify her state. The result was Elizabethan Anglicanism—doctrinally broad, theologically ambiguous, a faith that would not exclude any loyal Englishman save the most fanatic extremist, either Protestant or Catholic. Such an approach to religion had its immediate effects upon the cultural life of England. Scholars came out of intellectual hiding. A feeling of sureness came back to thought and expression. No longer did a man

10. *Henry VIII*, V, v, 18-39.
11. See pp. 646-47.

have to fear reprisal for what he wrote. A feeling of joy and freedom returned to life and letters.

To the intellectual security that Elizabeth gave her people she added economic and political security. Her shrewd diplomacy held at bay the threat of Spain and played off the continental powers against each other. Her consistent encouragement to commercial and financial enterprise gave to her people a great age of prosperity. In the summer of 1588 Philip II of Spain mounted his "Invincible Armada" for the conquest of England. He had exhausted his intrigues and come to the end of diplomatic patience. But Elizabeth had gained thirty years of precious time. The English could now summon the resources to counter the threat of Spain. The defeat of the Armada was a disaster for Spain. As the broken remnants of the great fleet limped back to Spain, England responded to her triumph with heroic emotion and soaring confidence. The great age of Elizabethan letters was at hand.

The preeminent form of the Elizabethan Renaissance was literature and, as on the continent, it was written in the vernacular. Englishmen had something to say about themselves and their world: and they had a language in which to say it, the rich, ornate, and expressive English of the sixteenth century, the product of the multiple influences that had been forming it for centuries. By the middle of Elizabeth's reign Edmund Spenser and John Lyly had fixed the forms of Elizabethan English and its greatest artist, William Shakespeare (*c.* 1564–1616), had been born.

The sketchy and controversial details of Shakespeare's life offer but a shadow of the man. He was probably of the provincial middle class, and most likely acquired little more than a common-school education. As a very young man he gravitated, like most Englishmen of talent and ambition, to London. There he found the stage: and this was to be the focus of his life. In London too he found the society of other poets, the excitement of a great capital, and the stimulation of a broad intellectual world. All these he consumed and made part of his own genius. In a comparatively short time Shakespeare was a busy and prosperous dramatist and the parade of his plays began to appear.

Shakespeare wrote live drama for live audiences and much of the shape of his poetry was determined by the limitations his medium set for him. The Elizabethan play was produced on a tiny, barren, apron stage, often with high-ranking patrons seated on it. The audience was filled with vendors and sometimes pickpockets and prostitutes, and was a

vocal and restless crowd. There was no realistic costuming and no stage
scenery. Young boys played the roles of women. In all, there had to be
the most willing suspension of disbelief. Shakespeare's plays are marked
by his necessary concessions to these limitations. Much of his extravagance of language and most of his outrageous puns may be considered
as bows to popular taste. His comedies and comic relief scenes are especially difficult because they lean so heavily upon current controversies
and personalities and ephemeral allusions.

Yet, within the framework of his demanding medium Shakespeare
managed to touch that quality of universality which marks all great
literature. His plots were seldom original; he took them from chronicles,
history, common stories and legends—and from other playwrights. But
in almost every instance Shakespeare made his plot, however hackneyed,
pose some problem of universal human concern. He took the plot of
Julius Caesar from Sir Thomas North's translation of Plutarch's *Lives,*
but he sharpened its meaning and made it deal with the questions of
tyranny, personal greatness, pettiness, and man's ingratitude. He took
Romeo and Juliet from an old Italian tale that was already a popular
play. But again he strengthened the plot and made it transcend its setting
to speak of the eternal conflict of age and youth, tradition and innovation.
Shakespeare saw deeply into human nature and, as a result, his characters
have a life of their own.

Shakespeare the man remained obscure to the end. His young contemporary, Ben Jonson, wrote of him:

> Soul of the age,
> The applause, delight, the wonder of our stage,
> My Shakespeare, rise! I will not lodge thee by
> Chaucer or Spenser, or bid Beaumont lie
> A little further to make thee a room:
> Thou art a monument without a tomb
> And art alive still while thy book doth live,
> And we have wits to read, and praise to give.

SUGGESTIONS FOR FURTHER READING

ᕮᏉᏓᕮ

General Works

*J. Burckhardt, *The Civilization of the Renaissance in Italy* (New York: Harper, 1958), the most famous single book on the Renaissance.

*G. DeSantillana, *The Age of Adventure* (New York: Mentor, 1956), readings from a series of Renaissance writers.

E. Emerton, *The Beginnings of Modern Europe,* cited for Chap 11.

*W. K. Ferguson, *The Renaissance* (New York: Holt, 1940).

H. S. Lucas, *The Renaissance and the Reformation* (New York: Harper, 1960).

New Cambridge Modern History, Vol. I, *The Renaissance,* ed. by G. R. Potter (Cambridge: Cambridge University Press, 1957), a much-improved volume in the new edition of this standard general work.

G. C. Sellery, *The Renaissance, Its Nature and Origins* (Madison: University of Wisconsin Press, 1950), a series of essays by a leading American medievalist stating a moderately "anti-Burckhardian" position.

The Renaissance in Italy

*C. M. Ady, *Lorenzo dei Medici and Renaissance Italy* (New York: Collier, 1962).

*Bernard Berenson, *Italian Painters of the Renaissance* (New York: Meridian, 1960), the basic work of this century's greatest critic and expert on Renaissance painting.

H. Baron, *The Crisis of the Early Italian Renaissance* (Princeton: Princeton University Press, 1955) 2 vols., brilliant restudy of the relationship between politics and intellectual-cultural history.

Boccaccio, *Decameron,* available in many editions.

*E. Cassirer, P. O. Kristeller, and J. H. Randall, eds., *The Renaissance Philosophy of Man* (Chicago: Phoenix, 1955), selections from some important Renaissance philosophers.

*B. Castiglione, *The Book of the Courtier* (Garden City, N. Y.: Anchor, 1954), a famous Renaissance book of "gentility."

*B. Cellini, *Autobiography* (Garden City, N. Y.; Anchor, 1960), a candid if somewhat scandalous and probably exaggerated contemporary work.

*K. Clark, *Leonardo da Vinci* (Baltimore: Penguin, 1959).

M. P. Gilmore, *The World of Humanism, 1453–1517* (New York: Harper, 1952).

*J. Lucas-Dubreton, *The Borgias* (New York: Dutton, 1954).

E. MacCurdy, ed., *The Notebooks of Leonardo da Vinci* (London: Reynal and Hitchcock, 1939), 2 vols., there is also an abridged version in paperback, ed. by P. Taylor (New York: Mentor, 1960).

Niccolo Machiavelli, *The Prince and the Discourses* (New York: Modern Library, 1950) a handy edition of a much-published work.

D. Merejkowski, *The Romance of Leonardo* (New York: Heritage, 1953), an exciting account of Leonardo da Vinci and his age.

P. Misciatelli, *Savonarola* (New York: Appleton-Century-Crofts, 1930).

J. H. Robinson and R. W. Rolfe, *Petrarch, the First Modern Scholar and Man of Letters* (New York: Putnam, 1898), a standard biography that also contains translations of much of his writings.

*R. Roeder, *The Man of the Renaissance* (New York: Meridian, 1957), a series of biographical sketches forming a composite portrait of Renaissance man.

F. Schevill, *The First Century of Italian Humanism* (New York: Crofts, 1928).

————, *History of Florence* (New York: Harcourt, 1936).

————, *The Medici* (New York: Harper, 1960).

*Geoffrey Scott, *The Architecture of Humanism* (Garden City, N. Y.: Anchor, 1954), art and the influence of Renaissance humanism.

Vasari's Lives of the Artists, B. Burroughs, ed. (New York: Simon and Schuster, 1959), the famous source of most of our contemporary information about Renaissance artists.

The Renaissance in the North

L. Batiffol, *The Century of the Renaissance in France* (New York: Putnam, 1935).

*Morris Bishop, *Ronsard: Prince of Poets* (Ann Arbor: University of Michigan Press, 1959).

D. Bush, *The Renaissance and English Humanism* (Toronto: University of Toronto Press, 1939).

M. de Cervantes, *Don Quixote,* available in hundreds of editions; see, for example, *The Portable Cervantes,* ed. by S. Putnam (New York: Viking, 1951).

*R. W. Chambers, *Thomas More* (Ann Arbor: University of Michigan Press, 1958).

Erasmus, *The Praise of Folly,* ed. by L. F. Dean (New York: Farrar, Straus, 1949), a handy and well-prepared edition of a standard classic.

E. H. Harbison, *The Christian Scholar in the Age of the Reformation* (New York: Scribner, 1956).

*J. Huizinga, *Erasmus and the Age of Reformation* (New York: Harper, 1957).

The Letters of Obscure Men, ed. by F. G. Stokes (London: Chatto and Windus, 1909), a definitive edition of this curious satiric work.

Michel de Montaigne, *Essays,* ed. by J. Zeitlin in 3 vols. (New York: Knopf, 1936), probably the best modern edition although, like most such classics, also available in paperbacks: *Michel de Montaigne, *Complete Essays,* tr. by D. M. Frame in 3 vols. (New York: Anchor, 1960).

Thomas More, *Utopia,* available in several editions, some of which contain other of his works as well.

E. Panofsky, *The Life and Art of Albrecht Dürer* (Princeton: Princeton University Press, 1955), the best work on Dürer.

M. M. Phillips, *Erasmus and the Northern Renaissance* (New York: Macmillan, 1950).

François Rabelais, *Complete Works* (New York: Tudor, 1955); there are many other editions including a *Viking Portable Rabelais,* ed. by S. Putnam (New York: Viking, 1946).

*P. Smith, *Erasmus* (New York: Dover, 1962).

E. M. W. Tillyard, *The Elizabethan World Picture* (New York: Modern Library, 1959).

*Paperbound edition. In the case of reprint editions, publisher and date of publication given will be that of reprint rather than the original.

❧ 13 ❧

The Reformation

LUTHER AND HIS GERMANY

The cultural revolution of the Renaissance was paralleled by the violent and tumultuous revolution in religion known as the Reformation. There are many things that tie the Renaissance and the Reformation together—the rapid economic changes taking place in Europe, the growing secularization of society, the climate of protest against the abuses of the medieval church. There is even some causal relationship between them. But in one sense it can be said that the Reformation stemmed from the fears and doubts and from the spirit of one man, an obscure German cleric and professor of theology named Martin Luther (1483–1546).

The Making of a Reformer

Luther's family roots reached back into the stolid, moral, orthodox, and superstitious tradition of the German peasantry. His father, however, had been resourceful enough to get into the flourishing mining industry of central Germany, and by the time Luther was born in Eisleben, his father had a comfortable fortune and all the attitudes and prejudices of the rising German middle class. Nevertheless, Luther retained a certain simplicity of thought and hard-headed judgment characteristic of his peasant forefathers.

The young Luther was raised in a stern home and sent to pious

568

and respectable schools, among them, the school of the Brethren of the Common Life in Magdeburg. At eighteen he went to the University of Erfurt. There, as at every university in western Europe, the ferment of humanistic studies and criticism was at work. Luther studied and loved the classics but, significantly, he was not swept away by the humanist enthusiasm and neither condemned nor abandoned traditional scholastic studies. Luther diligently worked through the master's degree (his father intended him to go on to study law, long established as a way of preferment for the sons of burghers).

Then suddenly, in July of 1505, as he was returning to Erfurt from a visit home, Luther was caught in a violent summer storm. A bolt of lightning struck near him, throwing him to the ground. He cried out in terror, "St. Anne help me! I will become a monk." Within two weeks he entered the rigorous Augustinian order at Erfurt. Within a year he took his vows and became a monk. Yet it would be wrong to suppose that his impulsive vow alone made him a monk. Rather it was his response to those deep-seated fears and doubts that have always beset the most ardent Christian believers. And his response was a traditional one. Even in the general decline of the church the true monastic vocation was still generally respected as the purest expression of the Christian life and the surest offering that man could make to God.

Once he had made his decision, a flood of penance nearly overwhelmed the young monk: he practiced every severity; he said every prayer and kept every vigil. Obsessed with a sense of his own sin and unworthiness, he almost destroyed himself in his desire to make himself acceptable to God. How could he, out of the depths of his own sin, approach the awesome perfection of God? How could he ever know when he had done enough, when God was satisfied with him? How long these fears had festered in his mind it is impossible to say, but once he had closed the door upon the world, they reached a new intensity. His kindly prior reasoned with him and tried to explain the God of love to the novice who could see only God's wrath and judgment.

Despite, or perhaps because of, Luther's fierce inner struggle, his superiors marked him out for success in his order, possibly seeing in his intensity the making of another St. Bernard. He took priestly orders and continued his studies, turning now to theology. He was sent on several official missions by his order, once even to Rome. Then, on the request of the Elector of Saxony, Frederick the Wise, the young scholar-monk was sent to teach in Frederick's newly founded university at Wittenberg.

By 1513 he had earned a doctorate in theology and held a key position at the university. As the world goes, Luther was a success. Any career he might choose lay open to him within his monastic order—teaching, administration, scholarship. But Luther still wrestled with his doubts. He was still caught in the "terror of the holy"; and he still could not feel that he was "justified" in the sight of God. The most fearful self-punishment had produced no inkling that God was satisfied with him. He found no more assurance in the sacraments. He confessed his sins, real and imagined, until the catalogue was exhausted—and still he could not know. "I was myself more than once driven to the very abyss of despair so that I wished I had never been created. Love God? I hated Him!"

Thus tormented, Luther turned to his teaching and his study. As he prepared a series of lectures on the Psalms he began to see a glimmer of hope. Then he turned to the New Testament and the letters of Paul; in the letter to the Romans he discovered, in a new sense, a passage he must have read hundreds of times before: "For therein is the righteousness of God revealed from faith to faith: as it is written, the just shall live by faith" (Romans 1:17). As Luther later said, "This passage of Paul became to me a gate to heaven." It became more: it became the basis of the Lutheran theology—the seed of the idea of justification by faith. Luther had found in his own bitter experience that he could not "earn" God's grace by his own works or merits. He had sincerely tried every traditional device—prayer, fasting, penance, alms—and he had no sense of salvation. Man was too wretched, too immersed in sin, too separated from the perfection of God to do any good thing acceptable to Him. But faith was something else. It was not a work of man; it was a free gift of God, given by the sacrifice of Christ. It was only through faith that the wrath and justice of God could be reconciled with His mercy. From this basic Pauline principle, Luther began slowly to work out a system of his own. Continuing to lecture and study, he was apparently not yet aware of the revolutionary implications of his speculations.

The Great Indulgence Scandal of 1517

Elsewhere in Germany, however, events were rapidly moving toward a crisis that would precipitate Luther into the role, not only of a reformer, but of a revolutionary. Albert of Hohenzollern was a rising young churchman who had collected an impressive number of bishoprics, including the electoral see of Mainz. This had been possible largely through the political influence of his brother, the Elector of Brandenburg, one of the key eletoral princes of Germany and a great and powerful lord, and through the cooperation of the Medici pope Leo X.

Leo was happy to have two of the German electors in his debt, for a new imperial election would be coming soon to replace the aging Emperor Maximilian I, and the papacy was always concerned over German politics. Nevertheless, it had been an expensive business to get all the dispensations necessary for the young Hohenzollern to hold his multiple offices, especially at his un-canonical age; and Leo X was not a man to let one penny slip by him. But this sort of political and financial maneuvering had long been accepted as a normal part of ecclesiastical life. Simony was not only accepted, it was a regular source of clerical revenue. The financial details were handled by the German banking house of Fugger, which was now challenging the Italians in the north of Europe. Albert of Hohenzollern got the money to pay for his offices; and to repay his bankers he received from Rome permission to extend into his new ecclesiastical lands a special sale of indulgences, one of the most lucrative sources of wealth for the church, and one of its most questionable practices.

The sale of indulgences was always popular and this one was carefully prepared. Everyone was to profit from it—the Fugger bankers, the archbishop Albert, the pope, and even the emperor. In the spring of 1515 the sale was solemnly proclaimed by a papal bull with Albert, as its chief commissary, offering most generous terms to the faithful. A famous indulgence preacher named Johann Tetzel was named subcommissary. The preaching and sale began; and by the early part of 1517 this efficient machine of salvation had moved into ducal Saxony. (Ironically, the sale had been prohibited in electoral Saxony, primarily because it might interfere with domestic sales of the same commodity.) Yet so popular and desirable were the indulgences that many people from Luther's part of Saxony traveled across the frontier to buy them.

At best the whole doctrine of indulgences was doubtful. It had been attacked by pious churchmen for centuries and was one of the favorite targets of church critics. It was a doctrine easily misunderstood and even more easily abused. Tetzel, in his zeal for a successful campaign, made extravagant claims and pushed the doctrine well beyond its limits, promising miracles and even preaching indulgences for the dead. As the campaign came closer to Wittenberg, Luther recoiled from it. He was groping toward a concept of faith out of his rejection of human works.

What more crass example of the folly of "works" could be found than this scandalous hawking of promises of salvation. Luther knew nothing of the careful and businesslike arrangements that had preceded the indulgence sale.

On October 31, 1517, Luther posted his famous "Ninety-Five Theses" on the door of the castle church in Wittenberg. They focused on the implications of the indulgence doctrine. Luther attacked the concept of the Treasury of Merit; he denied that the pope had any special power over purgatory or that he could remit the guilt of sin except as God remitted it; he defended the idea that every contrite Christian had full access to God's grace and thus had no need of indulgences. These theses were actually academic articles, items which Luther was willing to debate with other academicians. They were written in Latin and in stilted scholastic prose and were never intended to be either popular or inflammatory. But copies were made by friends; they were translated into German; they were printed and widely circulated.

Luther's attack upon indulgences hit a popular chord in Germany and a rumble of approval rose from the populace. Luther and his arguments were at once savagely attacked by Tetzel and his fellow Dominicans. Word reached Rome, but Leo X gravely misjudged the drift of affairs in Germany. It seemed no more to him than another of the interminable monkish quarrels over obscure points of theology. He ordered the general of the Augustinian order to reprimand and silence Luther. But Luther's growing commitment to a new theology would not let him keep silent. He was ordered to trial at Rome for his doctrines.

At this point his lord, Frederick the Wise, intervened on Luther's behalf to have the trial held in Germany at Augsburg, in conjunction with the meeting of the Reichstag in October of 1518. The church was placed in the uncomfortable position of arguing its case against a critic, very possibly a heretical one, before a secular assembly, all of which could be construed as an admission of the right of the Reichstag to judge the church in religious matters. The German princes were already hostile to the secular claims of the papacy and, as Luther argued the supremacy of Scripture and conscience, he found a sympathetic audience. Luther fled the session before any judgment could be rendered and fully expected to be followed by a papal condemnation. Yet he stubbornly held to his views and continued to examine their implications, even as those implications led him toward the brink of heresy.

The Break with Rome

Martin Luther might well have become another Hus, condemned and destroyed by the joint hostility of church and state—except for the complex political crisis that was developing in Germany. Luther, quite innocently, became an issue in that crisis. Neither the emperor nor the pope was willing to sacrifice a political advantage in order to silence Luther. The emperor Maximilian wanted nothing more than to secure the imperial succession for his grandson, the Hapsburg prince, Charles. But since Charles was also the heir of Spain, the pope wanted nothing so much as to prevent his election and thus curtail the growth of Spanish influence so dangerous to papal independence in Italy. To both these aims Frederick the Wise of Saxony was the key. He had enormous prestige among the other German princes; they might very well follow his lead in any electoral decision. Frederick had decided to protect Luther.

While the pope hesitated, the Dominican defenders of German orthodoxy pressed their attack. In the summer of 1519 Luther was forced into a debate at Leipzig. His opponent was the skillful and formidable dialectician, Johann Eck, who had long opposed Luther's views and now swore to expose him conclusively as a heretic. This is precisely what happened in the grueling debate that followed. Eck led Luther inexorably to the conclusion toward which his own thought had long been taking him; and Luther stubbornly accepted those conclusions. He was led to reject the authority of the pope or councils, indeed, any authority except Scripture. He was led to endorse many of the heretical teachings of Hus, in itself a sufficient heresy.

Even as the debates ended, the long-awaited imperial election had elevated Charles of Hapsburg to the Imperial throne as Charles V, the most powerful ruler of his age. The political impasse that had held the Lutheran question suspended was now resolved. Charles was dedicated to destroy this heretic—but the heretic was well on his way to becoming a national hero in Germany.

During the next two years Luther publicly proclaimed the cardinal tenets of a new religious sect. He held that man was saved by faith, not by works. In its fully developed form this was a blow at the most fundamental beliefs of traditional Catholicism, for it repudiated not only such fringe doctrines as indulgences and such obvious works as pilgrimages and the usual forms of penance, but the very nature of the sacramental system. In Luther's view, even the most faithful attendance upon the sacraments was inferior to faith and was again a matter of man's offering his works to God. Furthermore, with the exception of baptism and the Eucharist, Luther could find no satisfactory scriptural authority for the sacraments.

This line of argument had other serious implications. If the sacraments were not the means to salvation, then he had destroyed the special office of the priest, and with it the entire hierarchy of the church. If man is justified by faith, then the faith of one man is as acceptable as that of another, even of priest or pope. This became the Lutheran doctrine often called the "priesthood of all believers." Again Luther searched the Scriptures and the history of Christianity to support his arguments. He rejected the hierarchy of the church as the work of men rather than of God. He held that Christ is the head of his church and that the church itself is the community of believers. If the church is not the priestly hierarchy, then how can it justify its temporalities, its wealth, its property, and its preoccupation with the world? He called for a reforming council; he summoned the secular authorities to strip the church of its secular powers.

These ideas and many more were developed in Luther's writings between 1519 and 1521. They awakened echoes all over Germany. Heretics, mystics, and reformers had disputed the sacraments and attacked the secular activities of the church for centuries. The conciliasts had attacked papal supremacy and the power of the ecclesiastical institution. The humanists trumpeted the abuses of the church and advocated the purifying study of Scripture. Humanists and heretics had pointed back through the history of the church to the purity of primitive Christianity Luther's attack on Rome stirred German nationalism in the hearts of princes and peasants alike. Thus, while Luther's ideas represented little that was completely new, the synthesis of these various currents of thought had a broad and powerful appeal.

In the winter of 1520 the long-expected papal bull of warning, *Exsurge Domine,* arrived in Wittenberg, giving Luther sixty days to submit. He publicly burned the document. This rejection of the church's authority was followed by a solemn bull of condemnation. The church now depended upon the state to enforce its condemnation. A meeting of the German diet, under the presidency of the new emperor, Charles,[1] was

1. See p. 568.

scheduled for January 1521, and Luther was summoned to appear before it.

The rigidly orthodox young emperor had no love for the condemned heretic who had been summoned before him, but Charles was not entirely free to move as he wished. Public opinion was reaching a revolutionary pitch throughout Germany. In city after city where ecclesiastical authorities had tried to burn Luther's books there had been riots. There were ominous rumblings from the peasantry. The country was flooded with violent antipapal pamphlets and posted with Lutheran placards. Even in the city of Worms, where the Diet was sitting, there were attacks on the papal party and pro-Lutheran demonstrations. Of even greater importance was the attitude of the princes. Charles had been the reluctant choice of the electors. The lesser princes thoroughly distrusted him. He was bound by the severe restrictions of the imperial constitution, and the princes meant to invoke every one of those restrictions. Many of them saw in Luther a convenient weapon to use against imperial authority; many others saw at stake the principle of German freedom from the interference of both pope and emperor; others, like Frederick the Wise, were honestly swayed by Luther's arguments. There was, furthermore, the lingering hostility between the new emperor and the pope. Despite the paternal blandishments of Leo X, Charles knew that Leo had opposed his election. The pope was still his potential political enemy and he may well have considered how his own orthodoxy might serve papal political ends. In such an atmosphere Luther came to Worms, under imperial safe conduct.

In April of 1521 the simple, austere, emaciated reformer stood before the splendor of the emperor, his court, and the Diet. He was confronted with his own writings, which had already been examined, found full of heresies, and condemned. Did he intend to defend their contents? Once more Luther sought the protection of Scripture. Could his accusers prove that he had written anything contrary to Scripture? Thus did he reject the authority of the church to interpret the word of God and to control its own members. If he could not be refuted on his own ground he refused to budge from his position. Before this great and powerful assembly, which held his life in its hands, Martin Luther proclaimed, "Here I stand, for I can not do otherwise. God help me! Amen."

He was quickly bundled away toward the protection of Saxony. His defiant stand had shaken the whole Diet. With the goading of the papal legate and of his own Catholic conscience, the emperor drafted a strong condemnation of Luther to present to the princes. Many had no wish to declare themselves so unequivocally. The threat of popular violence was growing; the session began to break up. The emperor hastily revised his proclamation and the Edict of Worms was haltingly approved by the rump minority of the Diet that remained.

Revolution and Reaction

The emperor had been unable to seize Luther at Worms. In the months that followed the meeting of the Diet he was unable to pursue him. Even as Luther argued his case before the Diet the emperor's kingdom of Spain was in violent rebellion against him. The rebels there were broken by the time the Diet ended, but the revolt still smoldered; finances were in chaos and Charles was desperately needed in Spain. The German princes had made it clear that they would place at their emperor's disposal neither their unqualified loyalty nor their military-economic support. Charles was already at war with France in Italy and along the disputed border of the Low Countries; he had to look hastily to both his defenses and his alliances. Thus, "that devil in the habit of a monk" remained still unpunished.

Yet Luther was still in grave danger and no one knew how long the influence of the Elector Frederick could protect him, not even Frederick himself. On his way back to Saxony a band of armed men seized Luther and took him to a place of hiding, the Wartburg Castle in Thuringia. The elector had arranged this "friendly kidnaping," but even he did not wish to know where his captive was being held. For most of ten months Luther remained in hiding. It was a time both of serious inward doubts and great productivity. He continued to write, to attack the abuses of the church and its charges against him. He continued to develop his theology and began his epochal translation of the Bible into German. But while Luther was absent from Wittenberg the Reformation he had begun there threatened to become a revolution.

Luther had gathered disciples in Wittenberg. Some of them, like the delicate, scholarly, young Melanchthon, were moderates. Most, however, were zealots and with Luther gone, their zeal threatened to destroy the Reformation before it had well begun. There was agitation to throw over the Catholic Mass. Students and townspeople were incited to riot in the churches, to disrupt services, and intimidate priests. Carlstadt, one of the most radical of the Lutherans, celebrated the Christmas of 1521 in a thoroughly "Protestant" manner—without vestments, without recourse to confession, and with no more than a parody of the traditional Mass. His sermon stressed Luther's doctrine of faith and he distributed both bread and wine to the communicants. There were iconoclastic riots as mobs destroyed sacred images and smashed statues. Luther's congregation of Augustinians disbanded their house and abandoned their vows. From the ever-present lunatic fringe of religious radicalism reformers and "prophets" began to drift into Wittenberg to add their voices to the religious babble. The elector was alarmed and bewildered; he was genuinely concerned for the welfare of his soul and the souls of his people, and he believed in Luther. But how long could he tolerate the radicalism that might burst into social revolution at any moment? His orthodox neighbors had ample reason to invade Saxony.

At this point, early in the spring of 1522, Luther returned to Wittenberg. His tremendous personal authority made itself felt at once, as he began to guide his young Reformation away from violence and the certain discredit that would follow. He preached caution and understanding. He curbed the worst of the hotheads and order was restored.

In the meantime Luther's ideas had spread throughout the whole of Germany. To the peasantry the direction of the Lutheran movement had special significance: they were rapidly being pushed toward universal serfdom; their landlord-masters were encroaching upon their lands and rights while the new, inflated economy of the middle-class cities consumed their agricultural profits; they were the victims of every rapacious force in German society. There was no authority to which they could appeal. They saw in Luther a deliverer; his doctrines made them equal with their betters in the eyes of God. Why not in the eyes of men? If their faith was equal, why not their goods? Religion easily bridged the gap to revolution and in 1524 the storm broke in the benighted region of the Black Forest. It spread rapidly through southwestern Germany, involving not only the peasantry but the depressed proletariat of the cities. The demands of the peasants were, on the whole, surprisingly moderate. In substance they wanted no more than a return to the old, familiar patterns of their manorial tenure and guarantees against economic exploitation. All their demands were couched in religious terms and had a distinctly evangelical flavor. As their demands were refused by the feudality and as the revolt grew and spread, moderation was replaced by radicalism. Monasteries, castles, and country manor houses were invaded and looted. There were murders and atrocities as leaders arose to direct and exploit the Peasants'

Revolt. Some of them were natural leaders from the peasants themselves; other were penniless knights; many were religious fanatics of revolutionary temper. The peasant revolts assumed the burden of diverse programs and personal ambitions. Their violence threatened to destroy not only the economic order of German feudalism, but all order, both civil and religious.

Luther watched the chaotic progress of the movement with increasing alarm. He had been sympathetic with the peasants in the beginning. Then he despaired of them. Some of the radical peasant leaders turned bitterly against Luther and accused him of betraying their cause. As the wave of rebellion moved into Saxony and neared Wittenberg, Luther tried to moderate it. But when he saw the destruction of life and property and order he turned violently against the peasants and took his position by the side of established authority: ". . . let everyone who can, smite, slay, and stab, secretly or openly, remembering that nothing can be more poisonous, hurtful, or more devilish than a rebel. It is just as when one must kill a mad dog."[2] The authorities, however, needed no admonition from Luther. The initial fury of the peasant revolt subsided. It was not one revolt but many. There was no one program, no one leadership, and no communication among the various groups of peasant rebels. They not only lacked arms but a tradition of arms; their only weapons were their numbers and their frenzy. Order began to be restored. Then, in the spring of 1525, a large body of imperial troops, freed by the end of the war in Italy, ended the Peasants' Revolt. There were savage reprisals and artocities more terrible than any the peasants had committed. In the collapse of the revolts the traditional forms of religion reclaimed the peasantry. Luther had taken his stand against the peasants, declaring for order and authority, rejecting radicalism and social revolution.

As Luther lost the support of the peasantry he was losing the support of another group, the moderate humanists. He was too moderate for the peasants; too radical for the humanists. The humanists were, as we have seen, the most influential segment of the European intelligentsia. Most of them had long been the vocal advocates of church reform. In the early years of the Lutheran movement they had given Luther their support. His attacks upon the long-standing abuses of the church echoed their own criticisms. His appeal to history and Scripture followed the general lines of Biblical Humanism.

2. Quoted in Roland H. Bainton, *Here I Stand: A Biography of Martin Luther* (New York: Mentor Books, 1955), pp. 216-17.

Some were vaguely disturbed by the tinge of anti-intellectualism that clung to Luther's passionate doctrine of faith. In the years following the Leipzig debates, as Luther moved toward a definite break with the church, the great majority of the humanists took their stand against him in support of traditional religion. It was the abuses of the church that they had attacked, not its substance; and when they were forced to choose, they really had no choice. A few remained in the Lutheran camp—Biblical scholars like Melanchthon, the artist Dürer, and the radical nationalist Ulrich von Hutten. Most of the humanists, however, followed the lead of Erasmus, the most influential man of letters in Europe.

Erasmus had been offended as much by Luther's tactics as by his doctrines. He was at a loss to understand the stubborn, prophetic conviction that made Luther so uncompromising. Yet he insisted that Luther must be heard. He opposed the processes that the church used against him and refused a lucrative church office rather than declare against Luther. The moderate position of Erasmus was, in turn, condemned by both Lutherans and Catholics. In orthodox Louvain in 1519, Erasmus was attacked for having encouraged Luther in the past and for not condemning him now. From the Lutherans, led by Hutten, came the bitter charge that he had deserted the man who was putting into effect the program of reform he had himself advocated. He was, in his own words, "a heretic to both parties"; and it was becoming clear that his mederation was unacceptable to either.

That Erasmus would ultimately reject Luther's position might have been predicted from the first. Not only in the superficialities of taste, personality, and training, but in the most basic areas of belief they were diametrically opposed. In 1524 Erasmus directed at Luther his carefully reasoned *Essay on Free Will,* for it was on this issue that the difference between Erasmus and Luther turned. Erasmus argued for the freedom of the will, refusing to accept the notion of a God so cruel as to demand obedience and devotion of a creature deprived of the power to render them. Any other view seemed to him to make man not a thinking being, the very image of God, but a helpless and servile automaton. The reply came from Luther in a large and heavy volume, *On the Bondage of the Will.* Erasmus is a "babbler, a skeptic, an Epicurean hog, ignorant, stupid, and hypocritical." By holding to reason, argued Luther, Erasmus had missed the great idea of faith. Man's will is as depraved as the rest of him. He lacks the power to will his own good, as he lacks the power to save himself. With this exchange there was no longer a common ground between Luther and Erasmus. The Renaissance and the Reformation went their separate ways.

By 1525 the fundamental form of Lutheranism had been determined. It was established as a new religious sect, widely accepted and steadily growing in northern Germany. Luther, by his stand on the Peasants' Revolt, had rejected radicalism and social revolution. At the same time, by his break with Erasmus and the humanists, he had rejected intellectualism. Lutheranism was solidly planted in the middle ground of social and doctrinal conservatism. Its strength came from the prosperous, sober middle class. Gradually it acquired a structure of authority with its own clergy, but it remained fundamentally a layman's religion. Luther had broken once and for all with the Catholic concept of hierarchy, for the most fundamental articles of his belief denied the special function of a priesthood. The center of worship was moved from the altar to the congregation. The Lutheran concept of clergy moved also in a lay direction. The clergyman was a pastor, a congregational leader, and not a priest. As early as 1521 Luther had argued against clerical celibacy and shortly thereafter the more radical of his followers had begun to marry. Luther himself was married in 1525 to a former nun, Katherina von Bora, and their life created the pattern of the Protestant parsonage as the exemplary Christian home. Since Luther rejected the institutional form of the old church, he placed his new church under the institutional care of the secular state. He argued that the state was derived from God as clearly as the church, and he welcomed for his church the protection of the state that he had personally enjoyed for so long at the hands of the Saxon elector. Lutheranism became a state religion.

Luther continued to live in Wittenberg. His old Augustinian cloister was made over into a home for himself, his "Katie," and a growing brood of children. His door was always open to the poor, the sick, and to orphaned children, four of whom he raised with his own large family. His kitchen table was the center of the Protestant universe. Hardly a meal passed without company. Luther's fame attracted the great, the learned, and the curious; and after dinner he would talk on anything and everything. One of his sons made notes on these *Tabletalks,* and his many students and visitors contributed their memories of Luther to make one of the most valuable and lively documents of the Reformation.

The Reformation remained under Luther's personal direction until his death in 1546. From his hand poured out a torrent of pamphlets, letters, sermons, and tracts which guided his followers and shaped his sect. These works also had another importance, for together with Luther's translation of the Bible they represented the first significant use of the German vernacular in writing. In addition to his religious influence, Luther must be credited with virtually creating the modern German language.

In German, in Latin, and in translation, Luther's ideas spread far beyond Germany; the Reformation had become a European phenomenon.

RELIGION AND POLITICS

Luther's Reformation developed within the context of a complex balance of political forces that involved most of the European continent. The key figure in that balance was Emperor Charles V (*1519–1556*), the young Hapsburg who had faced Luther at the Diet of Worms.

Charles V and the Hapsburg Inheritance

When Charles of Hapsburg was elected emperor on June 28, 1519, he was the richest and most powerful monarch in Christendom, the heir to lands that made him an emperor in fact as well as in name. The tangled history of this vast inheritance does much to explain both the successes and the failures of Charles V.

The roots of the Hapsburg Empire reach back to Germany and Austria, to Burgundy, and to Spain. By the middle of the fifteenth century the Hapsburgs had once more gained the imperial title they were to hold in one form or another into the present century. The entrenched and recognized power of the princes, however, made it an empty if not ridiculous honor. Frederick III (*1440–1493*) saw even his own family lands seized by other powers in Hungary and Austria, and he himself lived a precarious, hand-to-mouth existence. But Frederick blithely ignored the hard realities of his state and clung stubbornly to the exalted theories of imperial supremacy.

In 1477 the Hapsburg fortunes suddenly took a happy turn. The reasons for this lay in the affairs of the Duchy of Burgundy. Throughout the earlier fifteenth century the dukes of Burgundy had been able to take advantage of the weaknesses of the empire and the involvement of France in the Hundred Years' War to create a powerful state between France and the empire along the lower Rhine. The shrewd policies of its dukes, its immense political importance, and the wealth of the Low Countries had made the Duchy of Burgundy one of the most important states in Europe. In 1467 the cautious and politic Duke Philip the Good was succeeded by his son Charles, called the Bold. He was not only bold, but rash and foolish. The court of Burgundy was the center of a late-blooming, artificial, and highly developed cult of chivalry; and Duke Charles, raised amid its forms and pretensions, easily confused appearance with reality. He cherished a grandiose scheme of re-creating the old Carolingian middle kingdom of Lothair, and to rule as its king, if not emperor.

The crux of Charles' scheme was the conquest of a belt of land along the middle Rhine. This led him into headlong conflict with the traditional French design to make the Rhine France's "natural frontier" on the east. And it led the quixotic Charles into contest with the wily, ruthless, and determined Louis XI of France, the "spider king." Louis had engineered the recovery of France after the Hundred Years' War. He had reconstructed French absolutism so skillfully and completely that he held in his hands practically the total resources of his nation. He was as dedicated to French security abroad as to royal absolutism at home. And the chief menace to that security was Burgundy; as Charles the Bold prepared to win his empire Louis began to intrigue. He encouraged the rebellion of Charles' Flemish towns; he neutralized a feeble Anglo-Burgundian alliance; he allied himself with the Swiss and the south German princes who were equally menaced by Charles' ambition in the Rhine valley. But Charles pursued his ambition to his death. He was killed in battle with the Swiss at Nancy in the winter of 1477. His body stripped and mutilated, and his face gnawed away by the wolves that ranged the battlefield, he was never even conclusively identified among the dead. He had wasted the substance of his state, impoverished his own people by his military folly, and aroused half of Europe against him. He left as his successor a defenseless young daughter, Mary of Burgundy.

Louis XI immediately pounced upon the complex of holdings that made up the Duchy of Burgundy. Some he invaded; some he claimed by feudal right; some he bought. The young duchess was virtually a captive, and Louis made plans for her marriage to his son, the future Charles VIII. Then suddenly his schemes fell apart. Mary had been betrothed to the Hapsburg prince and imperial heir, Maximilian, as part of an earlier, futile negotiation between her father, Charles the Bold, and Emperor Frederick III. In August of 1477 Maximilian appeared in the Low Countries and was immediately married to Mary of Burgundy. About the same time several of the Burgundian states, notably Flanders and Hainault, rose against French encroachment and cast their lot with Mary and her new Hapsburg husband. Louis XI had managed to seize some territory but his primary objective, the destruction of Burgundy, had been blocked. The Duchy of Burgundy was now attached, however tenuously, to the German imperial family.

This attachment was raised to another plane of importance in 1486 when Maximilian succeeded to the powers of his feeble father and in 1493 when he became emperor on the death of Frederick III. As far as the Burgundian Lowlands were concerned, however, Maximilian was never able to exercise full sovereignty. Most of the states had sided with him against Louis XI, but only because they saw in Maximilian a lesser evil. What they really wanted was freedom from any royal or ducal restraint. The seeds of the Dutch Republic were already planted. Before her early death Mary of Burgundy produced a son for Maximilian, the boy soon to be called Philip the Handsome.

While the Lowlanders could claim their freedom from the German Maximilian as regent, they had no such claim against Philip, their natural and legal prince. At the same time this prince was the clear heir to the vast, if disputed and rebellious, German holdings of the Hapsburg family. Through this Hapsburg-Burgundian Prince Philip another significant dynastic connection was established, with Spain. Modern Spain was itself only a recent creation among the family of European nations. Through the first half of the fifteenth century Spain was still a congeries of wrangling, independent states, involved in piecemeal wars with the rapidly declining Moslem power in the peninsula and in North Africa. Among the Spanish states the largest and most powerful was Castile. In 1469 this kingdom was joined with the Kingdom of Aragon by the marriage of its heiress Isabella to the Aragonese Prince Ferdinand. Shortly thereafter they succeeded to the rule of their respective states. While neither was sovereign in the lands of the other, their joint rule in effect created a single kingdom of Spain. Ferdinand inherited the foreign interests of his house, especially the claim to the Kingdom of Naples. To press that claim and to protect Aragonese foreign interests elsewhere, he was involved in constant diplomatic intrigue. A part of this tortuous diplomacy was the marriage alliance between the eldest daughter of Ferdinand and Isabella, Juana, and the Hapsburg Duke Philip the Handsome. In 1500 this marriage gave birth to the future Charles V, the heir to all the lands that attached to his diverse blood lines.

In 1516 the pieces of the great international Hapsburg Empire began

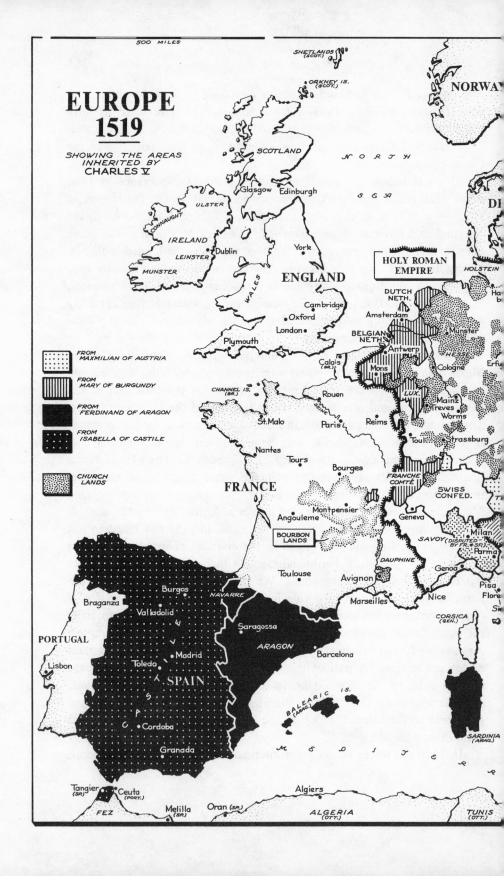

SWEDEN

Upsala

Wisby

Calmar

RK

Copenhagen

FINLAND
(S.W.)

ESTONIA

LIVONIA

Riga

Novgorod

Moscow

MUSCOVY
(RUSSIA)

KURLAND

Libau

BALTIC SEA

Smolensk

TEUTONIC
ORDER

Vilna

Danzig

PRUSSIA

BRANDEN-
BURG

Thorn

VISTULA

Posen

Warsaw

LITHUANIA

LUSATIA

Dresden

SILESIA

Hen-
?

ON

BOHEMIA

MORAVIA

P O L A N D

Lublin

VOLHYNIA

Kiev

ACQUISITIONS OF
CHARLES V'S BROTHER,
FERDINAND, TO 1526

Lemberg

PODOLIA

tisbon

ARIA

AUSTRIA

Vienna

STYRIA

Pressburg

GALICIA

Budapest

Tokay

MOLDAVIA

Jassy

CRIMEA

HUNGARY

TRAN-
SYLVANIA

NETIAN

Ravenna

DALMATIA

Belgrade

WALLACHIA

Bucharest

BLACK

SEA

REPUBLIC

BOSNIA

SERBIA

DANUBE

PAPAL
STATES

Assisi

ITALY

MONTE-
NEGRO

Nish

Sofia

BULGARIA

OTTOMAN

Adrianople

Constantinople

Rom?

NAPLES

AL-
BANIA

Salonica

EMPIRE

Naples

Janina

(VEN.)

Smyrna

(GEN.)

SICILY
(ARAG.)

(VEN.)

MOREA

DUCHY OF
NAXOS

CRETE
(VEN.)

TRM

to come into the hands of the young Charles. With the death of Ferdinand in that year and with the hopeless insanity of his mother, Charles became Charles I of Spain, uniting the claims to both Castile and Aragon. The opening years of his reign were filled with troubles. The Spanish were suspicious of Charles' foreign ways and his Flemish court. There was much local resistance to the effective union of Castile and Aragon. In the midst of this unsettled situation in Spain, the Emperor Maximilian died (1519), leaving to Charles the scattered Hapsburg lands of Germany and eastern Europe. In his later years Maximilian had tried to assure his grandson's succession not only to the family lands but to the title of emperor. With his death that title was open and Charles was the logical candidate. But there were others, the strongest being the young king of France, Francis I. The imperial election of 1519 was impossibly corrupt. The electoral princes took bribes from both Charles and Francis and at one time or another in the negotiations each had the promise of a majority of electoral votes. The pope was, of course, also concerned with the out-come of the election, and added his bribes to assure that neither Charles nor Francis would succeed. After months of profitable deadlock the princes unanimously voted for the Hapsburg Charles, who at long last became Charles V, Holy Roman Emperor.

In 1520 Charles came to Germany for his coronation and a few months later opened his first imperial Diet at Worms, in January 1521. It was here that Martin Luther stood in defiance before him. Yet Luther was only one of Charles V's many problems. Even as the Diet of Worms met, the Ottoman Turks had taken Belgrade and eastern Europe was open before them. Everywhere in the Near East Turkish strength was on the upswing. Turkish naval power made ominous headway against the Vene-tians. In 1520 Suleiman I, the Magnificent, became the Ottoman sultan, the effective head of a revitalized and aggressive Islam. Charles V and his fellow western princes faced another crusading age, this time to be fought not in the distant Holy Land, but in the very backyard of Europe.

Yet even in the face of the common menace of the Turks, Charles V could not expect more than passive hostility from the German princes. He was a powerful monarch and his non-German holdings could well provide him with the resources to break their long-standing independence and reverse the direction of centuries of German history.

To the Turkish and the German problems of Charles was added a serious rebellion in Spain. The moment Charles had left for Germany to accept the imperial title the so-called *Communeros* revolt broke out in Spain. It was in part directed against the Flemish foreign influences Charles had introduced into Spain. But more than that, it was a complicated protest of both the Spanish aristocracy and the Spanish cities against the centralization of which Charles was the symbol, and which threatened their traditional rights. Ferdinand and Isabella had moved fast and far toward a unified national monarchy. The dangerous feudal military "brotherhoods" that held over from the centuries of Spain's domestic crusade were suppressed and reorganized. In this work, as elsewhere in Europe, the Spanish monarchs had the support of the towns; but they bought that support by liberal grants of self-government. The probability that their status would be changed was the principal reason for their revolt against Charles.

Again, as in the rest of Europe, Ferdinand and Isabella had gained virtual control of the Spanish church. They exacted from the papacy extensive rights over the Spanish church and moved to make religion an instrument of national unification. Indeed, the church in Spain tended to be a department of state and the shrewd monarchs turned the inherent, fanatical orthodoxy of their people into a national channel. In 1478 the Spanish Inquisition was established to promote the orthodoxy that needed little promotion, and to stamp out divergencies of religious belief that might be politically dangerous. In 1492, as an offering both to nationalism and religion, the last feeble stronghold of Islam in Spain, Granada, was forced to surrender. The great crusade was over. In the same year the discoveries of Columbus opened the door to a vast new world for Spanish faith and Spanish arms. In the new climate of nationalism and nationalistic bigotry, the church and state moved not only against the Spanish Moslems but against the numerous Spanish Jews. More than two hundred thousand Jews were expelled from Spain and their property confiscated. The many Jews and Moslems who remained were forcibly converted and then constantly harried by the state, suspicious of their sincerity. In the interest of religious purity Spain had sacrificed, in her Jews and Moslems, the most industrious and productive elements of her people. Nearly all these rapid and radical changes that the past half century had brought played some role in the *Communeros* uprising against Charles V.

By the time Charles arrived back in Spain the revolt had split and his royal agents had managed to restore order. Partly as a result of these uprisings, partly from his own inclinations, Charles from this time made Spain his central concern. This is not to say that he ceased to be emperor on the continent. Indeed, the wars that filled the next forty years arose largely from imperial and not Spanish causes. But for all his concern with Turks and Lutherans, with French arms and papal treachery, Charles became increasingly in temperament and policy the successor to Ferdinand of Aragon. The courses of both the Reformation and the Counter Reformation were profoundly affected by the "Hispanicising" of the Emperor Charles.

Hapsburg and Valois

The concentration of lands, titles, and wealth in the hands of Charles V caused a basic and inevitable shift in the power structure of western Europe. The state most clearly endangered by the Hapsburg threat was France. In 1515 the aged Louis XII had been succeeded by the vigorous young Francis I (*1515–1547*) of another branch of the French Valois family. Francis was vain, ambitious, and a thorough Machiavellian. He ruled a compact and wealthy state, probably the most clearly differentiated national unit on the continent; and in his nation Francis probably came closer to realizing the ideal of royal absolutism than any other monarch of his age.

In the mere coexistence of Francis I and Charles V lay the potential of European war. The configurations of Charles' holdings, moreover, made such war almost inevitable. For on every frontier of expansion France was opposed by the Hapsburg Empire—on the disputed border of Flanders, along the Rhine corridor, in the Pyrenees, and in Italy. It was inevitable that Francis would try to break through the Hapsburg "ring of steel" that threatened to crush him. The weakest point was Italy. Charles had inherited from his Spanish grandfather the Aragonese hold upon the Kingdom of Naples, but only disputed claims to lands in northern Italy. It was to forestall such claims that Francis seized Milan in 1515, taking up once more the traditional policy of France in Italy. Thus Charles found his conflict with Francis already begun when he mounted the throne of Spain.

The first of several wars between Charles V and Francis I actually broke out in 1521. Backed by an alliance with England and the papacy, Charles retook Milan in the spring of 1522. But the tenacious Francis held on elsewhere, and Charles was running out of money. The war dragged on with both parties maneuvering for allies and resources. Then, in the winter of 1524, the balance swung in favor of Francis. An imperial invasion of France failed ingloriously. Charles' allies were restive, especially the new Medici pope Clement VII who, while still formally in alliance with Charles, negotiated a secret treaty with Francis. In mid-winter Francis crossed the Alps once more to press his advantage. That advantage turned into ruin, for in the Battle of Pavia his army was destroyed and Francis himself was captured and taken prisoner to Madrid. After almost a year of confinement, genteel but nonetheless real, the captive French king was induced to sign the Treaty of Madrid, bringing a formal end to the war. The terms of the treaty were moderate considering the diplomatic advantage that Charles had. Francis abandoned his claims in Italy and his rights in the Low Countries and the Duchy of Burgundy.

Despite his most solemn pledges, Francis repudiated the Treaty of Madrid as exacted from him by force, and within three months had joined the pope and several other Italian powers in an alliance against Charles called the League of Cognac. Again Charles was seriously threatened, not only in his western lands but by the Turks on the eastern flank of the empire. In the summer of 1526 the Turks advanced far into Hungary to Mohacs, where they annihilated the forces of the Hungarian king, Louis II, who died in the battle. Ferdinand of Hapsburg, Charles' brother and his regent for Germany, took advantage of this disaster to claim the Hungarian crown. A native Hungarian party opposed the Hapsburg claim and the two parties engaged in a civil war for what remained of Hungary. The leader of the Hungarian nationalists even allied himself with the Turks on the very eve of a renewed Turkish advance. The Turkish wave rolled through Hungary scarcely meeting resistance, but was finally broken by the heroic defense of Vienna and, as the winter of 1529 approached, the Turks withdrew.

Meanwhile, Charles had moved to break the League of Cognac. He saw the scheming Clement VII as the evil genius of this alliance and, while he bitterly attacked the pope's lack of faith and general unfitness for spiritual office, he encouraged the Italian enemies of the papacy to attack Rome itself. As Clement took refuge in the papal fortress of the Castel Sant' Angelo and his city was overrun, another disaster for the papacy was in the making in northern Italy. The imperial forces there had been held in frustrating inaction while diplomatic negotiations were drawn out and, more to the point, they had not been paid; moreover, there seemed little likelihood that they would be. In this dangerous situation the renegade Duke of Bourbon, one of Charles' commanders, took the initiative, put himself at the head of the hungry and mutinous army, and marched on Rome. They reached Rome early in May 1527, and took the almost defenseless city by storm. Their commander was killed and his troops began the sack of Rome. Its first fury lasted eight days and its horrors are almost unparalleled: murder, robbery, and rape. Parts of the city caught fire. Churches were ravished and ransacked. Many of the Germans among the heterogeneous imperial forces were already Lutheran, and to the natural barbarism of the sixteenth-century mercenaries they added their violent anti-Catholic sentiments. The occupation of Rome lasted almost a year. In the wake of devastation came the plague. Rome was almost depopulated. The papal states had been carved up by both the friends and enemies of the papacy. Whether or not Charles V, the European champion of Catholicism, actually ordered the sack of Rome is purely academic. He allowed it and accepted the political and diplomatic advantage that it gave him. The demoralized pope sued for peace on the emperor's terms. Francis I of France stood in diplomatic isolation with the alternative either of accepting terms or of facing invasion. In the Peace of Cambrai (1529) Charles' terms again were not as harsh as they might have been. The papacy was restored and Francis was held substantially to the provisions of the earlier Treaty of Madrid.

The Peace of Cambrai held for seven years and, as we shall see, left Charles free to move more strongly against the Lutheran menace in Germany. But again, neither the pope nor Francis could afford to have Charles overshadow Europe. The religious problem had by this time become so complex and so serious that only a general council held any hope of dealing with it on a European scale. The pope, as always, was opposed to the whole conciliar principle, and once more he approached his old ally, Francis I. In 1533 another secret treaty was struck between them. By its terms Francis was to back Clement in his hostility to the proposed council, while the pope was to support the ambition of Francis to create a strong, French-dominated state in northern Italy.

The death of Clement VII in 1534 and of a restored Sforza duke of Milan in 1535 opened the Italian question once more. In the spring of 1536 Francis openly moved to establish himself in northern Italy; the third war with Charles began. The new pope, Paul III, was much less eager than his predecessor to maintain the active alliance with Francis. Henry VIII of England, while hostile enough to Charles, was far too involved in his domestic affairs to give any comfort to Francis. In this crisis "The Most Christian King" of France allied himself with the heretical Lutheran princes of Germany, and even with Suleiman and the Ottoman Turks. All the old issues of territory between Charles and Francis were raised once more, but neither monarch could really press the war to a con-

TITIAN. *Charles V. 16th century.*

EL GRECO. *Cardinal Don Fernando Nino de Guevara.* c. 1600.

Above: LUCAS VORSTERMAN. *Ignatius of Loyola*. 17th century.
Left: LUCAS CRANACH THE ELDER. *Portrait of Martin Luther*. 16th century.
Below: HENDRIK HONDIUS. *John Knox. 17th century*.

Above: FRANCOIS CLOUET.
Francis I. c. 1525 – 30.
Right: John Calvin.

clusive victory. Both were hard-pressed for funds and, with the urging of the pope, a truce was arranged at Nice in which both Charles and Francis accepted the *status quo* at the opening of the war. Francis even joined Charles and the pope in a league against his sometime allies, the Turks.

But once more the basic causes that had produced three wars between France and the Hapsburg Empire remained unresolved; and once more Francis dragged his nation into war, in 1542. This time, while Italy was inevitably involved, the decisive action concentrated on the northern and eastern frontiers of France, where Francis was seriously threatened. But Charles could not press for a victory because of the instability of the diplomatic situation in Italy and Germany. Thus he wearily concluded still another truce with Francis, the Peace of Crépy (1544) where the same empty promises were exchanged. This truce, followed by the death of Francis I three years later, gave Charles V a temporary advantage in his long struggle with France.

Charles seized this opportunity to move decisively against the Turks, both in eastern Europe and in the Mediterranean. He was also able to take a harder line toward the Lutheran princes in Germany who had for so long enjoyed the protection afforded by Charles' preoccupation with France. And finally, Charles was able to force the assembling of the general council that the papacy had so steadfastly blocked, the epochal Council of Trent (1545–63).

In France Francis I had been succeeded by his son, Henry II, who was as threatened by the Hapsburg power as his father had been; he adopted for himself the policy which, after nearly forty years, had become traditional. Henry allied himself with the leading Protestant princes, thus forcing Charles V to woo the very men he wished to crush and to conclude a religious peace with them. At the same time Henry was negotiating with the Turks, which resulted in a strengthened Turkish drive in Hungary and the Mediterranean. With the tacit support of the pope, a French army struck again at Italy; and with the active support of the German princes, another moved upon the eastern frontier in Luxemburg and Lorraine. Imperial defenses held, and imperial arms and diplomacy neutralized the French alliances.

As the war turned in his favor Charles V, weary of war and negotiation, worn out by illness, disappointment, and compromise, began to divest himself of his empire. In a series of abdications (1555 and 1556) he surrendered Spain, his holdings in Italy, and the Low Countries to his son, Philip; and the empire with the German and eastern lands of his house to his brother, Ferdinand, who had already spent many years as Charles' regent in Germany. These dispositions made, Charles sailed for Spain to end his days in the monastery of Yuste.

In the meantime the last French war was coming to a close. The French were seriously defeated on the Flemish frontier at St. Quentin and Gravelines, and peace negotiations were already beginning. The resulting Peace of Cateau-Cambrésis (1559) marks the end of an era: the borders of the Netherlands were substantially restored and Spanish supremacy in Italy was recognized. Thus, nearly half a century of war had gained France scarcely a foot of land and, more important, had done little or nothing to remove the Hapsburg threat that haunted the French monarchy. But the events surrounding the Peace of Cateau-Cambrésis marked a fundamental change in the alignment of European affairs. The division of the Hapsburg Empire set its several parts in various directions. Shortly after the peace settlement Henry II of France was killed in a jousting accident, and France was dropped into a long generation of domestic war. The religious and economic policies of Philip II of Spain increasingly alienated the Low Countries, and within ten years he was faced with a full-scale revolt there which eventually robbed him of the most economically valuable portion of his inheritance and involved him in the futile and expensive wars of the Reformation. Also, some five years before Cateau-Cambrésis Charles V had signed a peace with the Lutheran princes that recognized both their religion and their territorial sovereignty.

Luther, Lutheranism, and the Princes

For forty years the almost continuous wars with France had prevented Charles V from moving effectively against Lutheranism. By the end of his reign the boundaries of Lutheran Germany were well-established and Lutheranism had spread to Scandinavia and along the southern shores of the Baltic into Slavic Europe. During the same period the petty dynastic policies and narrow secularism of the papacy had prevented a militant revival of Catholicism and such spiritual-ecclesiastical reform as might alone have countered the spread of the reformed doctrines. The Catholic Counter Reformation, which came with the approach of mid-century came too late to win Germany back to the church. Finally, in the years since the condemnation of Luther at the Diet of Worms, Lutheranism had made an entente with the temporal powers of northern and central Germany, and the destinies of the new reformed religion were inseparably joined with the forces of German politics.

Even before the Diet of Worms a "Lutheran party" had already begun to form. From the beginning Luther was protected by the personal political prestige of Frederick the Wise. In the so-called Reformation Tracts of 1520—*An Address to the Christian Nobility of the German Nation, The Freedom of the Christian Man,* and *The Babylonian Captivity of the Church*—Luther had issued a kind of German national manifesto. His arguments appealed, at the same time, to the princes with their long fight for political independence; to the urban middle class with its monetary sensitivity; to the humanists with their reforming demands upon the church; and to the common people of Germany who were beginning to feel the stirrings of nationalism. By the time the long-awaited papal condemnation of Luther was published in Germany, Luther had been transformed into the national champion of Germany against the "foreign domination" of the papal hierarchy. The old ghosts, not only of German secular rebellion but of German episcopal independence, had been awakened once more. At the Diet of Worms Luther was virtually elevated to a national popular hero, and a significant minority of the princes and at least two of the electors stoutly defended him. His name was associated in the next year with a revolutionary uprising known as the Knights' War. Then came the Peasants' Revolt. The peasants assumed that Luther was their natural leader but, as we have seen, he repudiated them. His action in this was probably an immediate and emotional response to radicalism rather than a calculation of socio-political philosophy. Luther really had no such philosophy. Nonetheless, and for whatever personal reasons, Luther's religious revolution did not become a social revolution. The Lutheran party was dominated by the territorial princes and by the sober, conservative middle class of the cities; Lutheranism was becoming a state religion.

By 1526 the Lutheran party comprised the state of Saxony under John, the brother of Frederick the Wise; the nearby state of Hesse with its Landgrave Philip; the important state of Prussia, which had been held by the Teutonic Order until its grandmaster declared himself Lutheran and secularized the order, becoming its duke. Other ecclesiastical lords followed his example, and in many secular states church property was confiscated. A great many prosperous German cities, as well as several smaller states, had become Lutheran.. Their motives were as mixed as the threads of the Reformation, but their common religion and their common danger gave them a certain unity. After the condemnation of Luther and the Diet of 1521 the Lutheran states drew togther into a league and, by the time of the Diet of Speyer (1526), they were in a strong position. They were able to oppose the enforcement of the Edict of Worms and force Ferdinand, the emperor's brother, to accept the principle that each state should determine the religion it wished to follow. This uneasy truce continued, for the emperor was immediately plunged into his second French war.

By 1529, with Charles' victory over the French alliance, the Catholic imperial party in Germany was able to take a stronger position on the Lutheran question. As the Diet met once more in Speyer, the Catholic majority was able to demand the enforcement of the Edict of Worms, the abolition of Lutheran innovations, and the resignation of the privileges granted three years before. The Lutheran princes lodged a formal "protest" (the general term "Protestant" derives from this incident). The common danger from the Turks, however, turned the edge of religious hostility for the moment. In 1530 the whole complex religio-political problem was laid before the emperor himself at the full-dress meeting of the Diet in Augsburg. In the face of growing imperial strength, the Lutherans presented the famous Augsburg Confession. It was the work not of the truculent Luther but of his learned younger colleague, Philip Melanchthon, and was a distinctly conciliatory statement of Lutheran belief. It tried to minimize the essential differences in belief between the old church and the new. But even at its most conciliatory, Lutheranism was unacceptable to the ultra-Catholic party that religious antagonism had thrust into a dominant position. There was much theological haggling at Augsburg, but the ultimate decision of the Diet rejected Lutheranism entirely. The Lutheran princes were directed to recant under threat of arms.

They withdrew to form an open military alliance, the Schmalkalden League, which included nearly all the Lutheran states and cities of Germany. There was some desultory fighting between individual states, but Charles V had promised a general council to consider all the religious questions; and the Turks were threatening once more. A nervous truce held Germany together as Charles was involved once more with the Turks, the French, and the pope. It was only after the Peace of Crépy (1544), ending his fourth war with Francis I, that Charles was able to turn to Germany again, this time with the long-deferred, full-scale war against the Schmalkalden League. The league began to fall apart immediately: one of its important members defected to the emperor and others were more concerned about their own lands than the common defense. In the spring of 1547, at Mühlberg in Saxony, Charles defeated the Elector of Saxony; shortly the leading Lutheran princes were in his

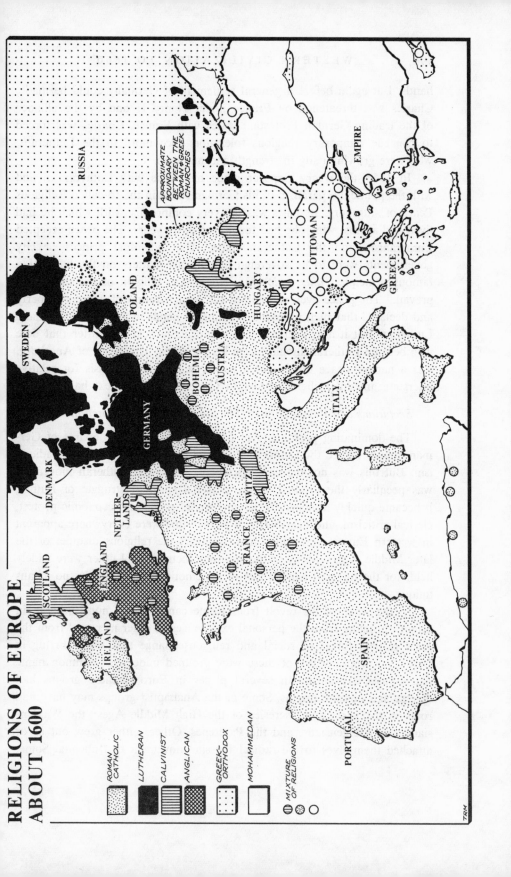

RELIGIONS OF EUROPE ABOUT 1600

RUSSIA

EMPIRE

OTTOMAN

GREECE

SWEDEN

DENMARK

POLAND

BOHEMIA

GERMANY

AUSTRIA

HUNGARY

NETHER-
LANDS

SWITZ.

FRANCE

ITALY

SCOTLAND

ENGLAND

IRELAND

SPAIN

PORTUGAL

APPROXIMATE
BOUNDARY
BETWEEN THE
ROMAN & GREEK
CHURCHES

ROMAN
CATHOLIC

LUTHERAN

CALVINIST

ANGLICAN

GREEK-
ORTHODOX

MOHAMMEDAN

MIXTURE
OF RELIGIONS

TRM

hands. But again before a general settlement of Germany could be made, Charles was threatened by France under Henry II and by the alliance of the leading German Protestant states with France. Charles was forced to concede temporary religious toleration once more to the Lutherans, who were growing daily in strength and numbers.

In 1555 the weary emperor made his peace with Lutheranism and with the political separatism of his German states in the so-called Religious Peace of Augsburg. Its basis was the very compromise with which he had lived and against which he had fought for thirty years. The peace accepted Lutheranism and the Lutheran states. The individual princes or city governments were to be sovereign in religious matters on the basis of a famous principle, *cuius regio eius religio,* "the religion of the ruler shall prevail." The peace even recognized the secularization of church property and declared that such property in Lutheran hands in 1552 should remain Lutheran. But it also declared that any ecclesiastical lord after that date who became Lutheran should resign his benefices. The Peace of Augsburg, was a narrow peace but it was a peace. It became the basis for relative interstate and interreligious order in Germany for the next half century.

Sectarians and Revolutionists: The Spread of the Reformation

The dominating personality of Martin Luther and the course of German politics turned the Lutheran Reformation away from its early radicalism. But this was not the case elsewhere. While the Lutheran movement was peculiarly the product of the personal spiritual struggle of Luther, it became quickly attached to the currents of social and economic protest, clerical criticism, and near-heretical pietism that were everywhere apparent in western Europe and which had produced the religious disquiet of the later Middle Ages. Many of the spiritual doctrines of Luther were widely held, for the tortured experiences of his emotional life were by no means unique.

In the wake of his revolt from Rome came others, non-Lutheran in origin, springing from the personal experiences of other men and from the great restless forces of social and religious change that were stirring in Luther's Europe. Many of these were grouped under the common name Anabaptists. Appearing in several places in Europe, these groups had diverse and obscure origins. Some of the Anabaptist groups may have had roots in the widespread heresies of the High Middle Ages: the Waldensians, the Albigensians, and the Paterenes. Others either grew out of or attached themselves to the radical Hussite movement of Bohemia. Some, in the Rhine cities and the cities of the Low Countries, were clearly associated with populist protest movements. Some were pacifist or quietist in temper; many were guided by the popular conception of Biblical and Apostolic poverty, which turned easily into material communism. Some believed in direct revelation and allowed themselves to be led by wild-eyed "prophets." Nearly all of them rejected the authority of the state, whether by implication or outright revolution. All of them shared the idea of adult baptism (*ana*-baptist, "re-baptized") as a symbol of Christian regeneration suspiciously like the Albigensian idea of purification.

Many of these Anabaptist ideas were woven through the history of Christianity: nearly all of them had been rejected at one time or another by both religious and secular authority. They had invariably been associated with peasant, proletarian, or popular unrest wherever they appeared. This continued to be the case in the sixteenth century. The radical protest of the German Peasants' Revolt was Anabaptist in temper and, as we have seen, conservative opinion, both Lutheran and Catholic, aligned against the peasants. In the Diet of Speyer, where the Lutheran princes protested the restriction of their freedom of worship, those same princes joined the Catholics in a harsh condemnation of the Anabaptists.

They were declared outlaws to be hunted down like animals; their sects were stamped out in Saxony, in Switzerland, in Bohemia, and in the Low Countries with torture, murder, and fire. But where one cult was destroyed another sprang up. An Anabaptist sect appeared in the Westphalian city of Münster, preaching the end of the world. It spread through the masses of the city, who rose in joyous revolution against the city government. In 1534 one of the leaders of the revolution declared himself king of this "Kingdom of Münster." In the following months the Münster Anabaptists practiced community of goods and polygamy and, in their frenzy, broke not only with conventional religious practice but rejected the canons of society. The city was laid under siege by its bishop with the cooperation even of Lutheran authorities; was finally taken after sixteen months of Anabaptist rule. The defenders were killed with every refinement of torture, but their ideas survived, for they had deep roots in European society.

Many of the small Reformation sects, such as the Mennonites, and such later submovements as the English Independents, Diggers, and Fifth Monarchy Men were essentially Anabaptist—and they rehearsed the history of Anabaptist persecution. In Bohemia, Switzerland, and the Low Countries, Anabaptist ideas persisted and joined with other local religio-social causes to prepare the way for the revolutions which were yet to come to these regions.

The Reformation in England

The English Reformation, like that of the continent, was part of the travail which created modern western civilization. Yet it is distinctly set apart from its continental counterpart because the initiative did not come from the protests of the masses or from the conscience of a clerical reformer, but from the crown.

The course of the English Reformation was inseparably connected with the fortunes of the Tudor dynasty. Its founder was the Henry Tudor who had defeated the Yorkist usurper Richard III at Bosworth and founded his new monarchy, like William the Conqueror, upon the right of conquest. Yet Henry Tudor—or Henry VII (*1485–1509*)—was not really made of such heroic stuff. He more nearly resembled his contemporary fellow monarchs Louis XI of France and Ferdinand of Aragon. Like them he preferred diplomacy to war and economic substance to princely show. Henry VII inherited a nest of troubles in his own realm and his chief concerns were domestic. His victory over Richard III marked the end of the long civil war between the rival houses of Lancaster and York, the Wars of the Roses. But it took more than half his reign before the claims of the war were finally settled. There were pretenders who could gain the support of France or Burgundy or Scotland; yet Henry was able to cope with both the pretenders and their foreign support. One of the pretenders was such a transparent fraud that when he was captured Henry did not even extend him the courtesy of execution. Instead, he was put to work amid the pots and pans of the royal kitchen.

Henry VII founded his dynasty upon solid popular support. The people were weary of senseless feudal conflict in which they had no stake. The articulate, influential, and growing English middle class in particular craved peace and stable government. Furthermore, the recent wars had removed many of the most troublesome feudatories who might have stood in the way of the new dynasty. Thus an England already beginning to be dominated by its middle-class economic interests found in Henry VII a king whose interests were also essentially middle class and economic.

Henry was a careful and tight-fisted monarch. He drastically overhauled the royal financial system and capitalized on public confidence by moving against the remnants of feudal privilege, turning them into crown revenues. In every possible way he encouraged the economic interests of English merchants, extending privileges to their companies, imposing favorable tariff laws, and supporting them against the competition of foreign commerce. Indeed, this economic concern was the principal basis of what foreign policy Henry VII had. He entered negotiation with Charles VIII of France on the eve of the French invasion of Italy with the purpose of allowing himself to be bought off by a handsome settlement. He arranged a marriage alliance between his son and the princess Catherine, one of the daughters of Ferdinand and Isabella of Spain, and thus increased the continental prestige of his new dynasty—and at little or no cost. In 1506 he arranged a commercial treaty with the Low Countries so advantageous to England that shortly the Flemish began to call it the *Intercursus Malus,* "Wicked Treaty." Henry's economies, his fostering of trade, and his sound money policies confirmed the support of the merchant class. They were, by and large, more interested in stable government than in parliamentary right—and so was Henry.

He called Parliament as seldom as possible and almost always with the assurance of commons' support, for he seldom asked for money and "lived of his own." Henry VII was able, at the same time, to be a popular monarch and to create the basis of English royal absolutism. He surrounded himself with counselors of humble birth who would be completely dependent upon the crown and thus faithful to it. As his agents in Parliament, as his judges and legal advisers, these men—often able and often unscrupulous—served the king's cause against the nobility. Like the great English medieval kings, Henry VII was a "Lion of Justice." He tightened the common law and the administration of justice at every level. He created the famous court of Star Chamber (later to become infamous under the Stuarts) as an administrative court operating outside the safeguards of the common law. There is no better evidence of the growing Tudor absolutism than this court; and there is no better evidence of Tudor popularity than its general acceptance by the people, who tended to look upon it as a "quick and easy way" with criminals, stiff-necked nobles, and corrupt officials.

At his death Henry VII left a peaceful, prosperous, and obedient realm —and a full treasury. He was succeeded by his son, Henry VIII (*1509–1547*). The new monarch was young, handsome, and accomplished. The rival dynastic claims that had clouded the early years of his father's reign had been dispelled, for Henry VIII was heir to the claims, through inheritance, of both Lancaster and York as well as to his father's accomplishments. Probably the most learned ruler of his time, Henry VIII was a good Latin scholar and could argue theology as glibly as a canon. He was the intimate of the leading English humanists and a friend and patron of Erasmus, and he shared with these a concern for the reform of religion and the church. Young Henry's broad learning and ready wit made a happy contrast with the sourness and narrow piety of his father. The contrast was equally marked in other areas.

The new king was as ambitious for glory as his father had been for solvency. And England, now solvent, was ready to welcome a show of royal magnificence and fustian. Where the father had pursued a cautious, calculating, and limited foreign policy, the son pursued a policy as bold as it was vague. He envied the glory of the great medieval kings, and since their glory had been won in war against France, Henry turned his own ambitions toward this traditional enemy. He played directly into the capable hands of Pope Julius II and Ferdinand of Aragon. He joined them against France in 1511 and 1512, reviving the English royal claim to the French throne. This splendid enterprise, viewed from either Rome or Madrid, was a minor, diversionary action in the game of Italian-Spanish politics, and Henry VIII was a useful pawn. It was a role Henry did not relish; he joined a counterleague in the following year and invaded northern France himself. Again he found he had been used, this time by the Emperor Maximilian as well as by Ferdinand. His victories in France were of no consequence and, in the meantime, northern England had been invaded by the Scots. They were beaten at Flodden Field, but Henry had been burned in his ambition for foreign glory.

At this point began the career of Thomas Wolsey (c. 1475–1530). This ambitious and unscrupulous cleric had made himself indispensable to Henry in the management of the last French war. And in the years following 1515 Wolsey became the king's right hand. More and more of the management, particularly of foreign affairs, became Wolsey's; and along with responsibility came honors and wealth until, at the apex of his career, he was archbishop and cardinal, and even aspired to the papacy. For nearly fifteen years Wolsey dictated the role of England in the complex diplomacy of the continent. Both Francis I and Charles V needed the support or at least the neutrality of England in their long and bitter conflict. Wolsey saw that, with comparatively little cost or involvement, England could hold the balance between the two great continental powers. But even this modest role was costly, and Parliament began to grumble at the expense. Henry resorted to arbitrary taxation and forced loans, and was faced with sullen resentment from his favored middle class and an open rebellion in part of the country.

As the Hapsburg-Valois wars on the continent swung into their second round, following the Treaty of Madrid (1526), Henry VIII became increasingly involved in the domestic problem that was to dominate the rest of his reign. He had been married for more than twenty-five years to Catherine of Aragon, widow of his older brother, and the Spanish princess who had been the prize of Henry VII's diplomacy. Of the several children Catherine had borne, only a daughter, Mary, had survived infancy. The years passed quickly and Catherine was approaching the time when she would bear no more children; Henry was almost forty; and there was no male heir. He was faced with a bitter prospect. There was no precedent for a reigning queen and, unless a prince were born shortly, there might be an infant succession. As Henry worried about this dynastic question, a demure young lady of the court, Anne Boleyn, caught his royal eye. Love and policy coincided and in 1527 Henry VIII began to negotiate for a divorce in order to marry Anne who would, he was confident, bring him the son he so desperately needed.

While the church had no doctrine of divorce as such, there was ample precedent for the dissolution of royal marriages by the pope for dynastic reasons. Normally Henry's request would have posed no problem. But in 1527, within a month after Henry had declared his desire for divorce, Rome was invaded by the army of Charles V. Pope Clement VII was a virtual prisoner of the man whose aunt Henry sought to reject! The emperor was further annoyed at what he chose to consider the perfidy of Henry VIII in the recent wars with France. The pope could not afford to flaunt the will of the nearby emperor for the sake of a distant king. The divorce was delayed. Henry turned to Cardinal Wolsey to manage this as he had managed the other business of the king. But Wolsey had no desire to offend the pope he hoped to succeed and was deeply involved in his own game of ecclesiastical politics.

Delays continued and Henry's short temper flared. Wolsey was suddenly dismissed as chancellor and disgraced. The direction of affairs in Italy made it obvious that no divorce would be granted. Henry began a concerted attack upon papal jurisdiction in England. In 1529 he summoned the Parliament that was to sit for seven years and be known as the Reformation Parliament. This body, at the king's request, enacted into law broad reforms of clerical abuses which were at the same time a trenchant attack upon papal revenues and privileges. It sanctioned the king's demand that the clergy recognize him as head of the English church. In 1532 Henry was able to get the appointment of a sympathetic cleric as Archbishop of Canterbury, Thomas Cranmer (1489–1556). In the following year Cranmer, now the leading ecclesiastic of an independent national church, declared Henry's previous marriage invalid; married Henry VIII and Anne Boleyn; and installed Anne as queen; thus preparing the way for "legitimate issue." But Anne betrayed her husband's hopes, for her "issue" was not a boy, but a girl, the future Queen Elizabeth.

In little more than two years Anne Boleyn was executed for her crimes —the chief of which had been her failure to supply Henry with his heir. Yet in pursuit of that heir he had already cracked open the door to the Reformation in England. It had been more than a decade since Luther had defied the pope and the emperor at Worms. Germany was divided and warring over the bitter religious issues. The Reformation had flamed up in a dozen places on the continent and the "new learning" of Lutheran doctrines had begun to penetrate England. The same broad anticlerical sentiment, the same popular criticism of church abuses, the same growing sentiment of nationalism to which Luther had appealed in Germany rose in England to approve the actions of Henry VIII. And Henry shrewdly directed popular approval through resort to Parliament. At every point he sought the sanction of Parliament and thus of the people. In 1534 Parliament passed the Act of Supremacy, making Henry the supreme head of the English church and the heir, in England, of the powers and privileges of the pope. In the same year it passed the Act of Succession, settling the crown upon the heirs of Anne and officially removing any doubt of legality in the divorce-marriage proceedings. Then came the Act of Treason to silence any opposition to the king's religious reforms. In 1536 and 1539, again with parliamentary sanction, Henry moved to dissolve the monasteries and distributed their lands and wealth, thus securing solid support for his revolution from those who now held former church property.

While Henry was willing to break with the church and confiscate its temporalities, he was not willing to break with Catholic doctrine; and this was probably the case with the majority of Englishmen. In an earlier day Henry had attacked Luther for his innovations and had gained from the pope the title "Defender of the Faith," which he continued to carry with no apparent sense of contradiction. In 1536 he summoned the clergy into convocation and called upon them to define orthodox doctrine. In

1539 he made the resulting Catholic doctrinal orthodoxy a matter of law. At his insistence Parliament passed the Statute of the Six Articles. This statute made it a serious, even a capital, offense to deny any of the articles.

The Henrican Reformation was the "Kynge's Busynes," the product of his ruthless will. To it he was willing to sacrifice his greatest lords, his most loyal servants, and his most humble subjects. Wolsey was ruined and died in disgrace in 1530; in 1535 Thomas More, the great English humanist and chancellor, was executed for his refusal to take the Oath of Supremacy; with him died John Fisher, the revered Bishop of Rochester; for the same offense a company of English Carthusians were executed. In 1540, Thomas Cromwell, one of Henry's must trusted henchmen, was executed under the Act of Treason, as much for his political failures as for his beliefs. Adamant Protestants as well as adamant Catholics died for their faith.

Yet, despite his indomitable will, Henry VIII was unable to stop the course of the Reformation when it had gone as far as he wished. Throughout the rest of his reign and despite his most severe measures, a distinctly Protestant sentiment continued to grow, especially among the significant middle class of the cities. There were doctrinal Protestants, even among Henry's highest church officials, and he was constrained to permit the translation of the Bible into English in 1536 as well as certain portions of the service. From whatever motives, this was a concession definitely Protestant in flavor. Yet the king managed to enforce his limited concept of Reformation until his death.

The domestic situation he had created was the preoccupation of his last years. He ruled in England with increasing despotism. Abroad he continued to shift his loyalties with the fortunes of the continental wars, his chief motivation being to prevent a Catholic imperial invasion of his realm. The vexing problem of the succession that had triggered the break with Rome continued. In 1536, after the execution of Anne Boleyn, Henry married Jane Seymour, who died little more than a year later with the birth of a son, the future Edward VI. Henry was married briefly to the German princess Anne of Cleves in 1540, as part of an abortive foreign alliance. Again in 1540, at the behest of his subjects, Henry married once more, this time Catherine Howard. Within two years the indiscretions of this lady brought her to the block. Catherine Parr, a shrewd and worldly widow, was the last of Henry's queens, and managed to outlive him.

Despite his arbitrary rule, his evil temper, and his selfishness, Henry

VIII never lost the affection of his people. He remained, though grossly fat, lame, and prematurely old, their "Bluff Prince Hal." To the end he maintained that same well-calculated alliance with Parliament that had assured the permanence of his Reformation. He fixed the order of succession and Parliament approved it. It is ironic that, in the end Henry VIII had to face both the painful alternatives—a minority succession and a female succession—that had estranged him from Catherine of Aragon twenty years before. Edward was a weak and sickly child; the other two surviving children were Mary and Elizabeth. Henry and his Parliament determined that Edward and his heirs should rule, and that, in the event of Edward's death without issue, the crown should pass to Mary, then to Elizabeth, and finally to the line of Henry's sister, Mary. Shortly before his death in 1547 Henry created, again with parliamentary sanction, a council of regency to rule for the young Prince Edward (*1547–1553*).

Despite the care with which Henry had chosen the regents for his son, the inevitable contest began immediately for the domination of the young king, the council, and the nation. For the first three years of Edward's reign the leading figure of the council was the king's uncle, the Earl of Hereford, who took the titles Duke of Somerset and Lord Protector.

Somerset's supremacy was a prize of doubtful worth. The treasury was nearly exhausted, and from the countryside came rumblings of rebellion. The encouragement that Henry VII and Henry VIII had given to commerce and industry had placed a premium on wool. As a result, capitalistic landlords turned increasingly to sheep raising to supply the demand for this staple commodity; and this led to the "enclosure" of land for sheep grazing. Thousands of peasants and small landowners were ruined by the growth of the enclosure movement. The labor problem was further aggravated by the breakdown of the guild system and the encroachment of "cottage" manufacture and piecework, again under the pressure of a growing capitalism, especially in the woolen industry. The thousands of workers who could not be immediately absorbed into this new system of production added their cries to the popular unrest. Another cause of hardship was the slow and steady growth of inflation. This was a tendency all over Europe as the precious metals Spain imported from the "New World" infiltrated the economy and depreciated the value of coins. In his last years Henry VIII had added to this trouble by systematic debasement of the English coinage. The weight of inflation bore hardest upon those whose wages were small and, of course, upon the many who could no longer command wages at all.

Hostilities with both France and Scotland still smoldered. In an ill-advised invasion of Scotland, Somerset drove the Scots directly into another alliance with France, sealed by the marriage of James V's daughter, Mary (Queen of Scots), to Francis, the heir to the French throne. Then shortly France declared war upon England.

Thus the regency, insecure at best, was faced with both foreign and domestic problems that might have taxed the most secure of monarchs. The council turned for support to the people, as represented in Parliament, with a bid for popular and financial support. The result was not the strengthening of the regency but the wholesale introduction of the Reformation into England. To the regency, as to Henry VII and Henry VIII, the most important class in the realm was the substantial, commercial middle class. This class had grown vastly in significance under Henry VIII and it was the class most competently and vocally represented in commons. It was the only faction of Parliament that had a clear, common interest as a group. The English merchants—as opposed to the provincial towns-men, the country gentry, or even the nobility—had close ties. Because they were concentrated in southeastern England, their continuous business relations gave them an opportunity to form a common body of opinion and prejudice. They were probably the most liberal and enlightened group in England—and, they were generally disposed toward Protestantism. Thus, the popular concessions of Somerset and the regency were concessions to this group.

There were, moreover, strong forces at work to give these concessions a specific Protestant, reforming shape. A strong "Lutheran" party had formed in England, despite the stringent repressive measures of Henry VIII. This group dominated the intellectual atmosphere of London and the nearby cities. It included distinguished foreign scholars and theologians as well as many learned Englishmen. And in the council of regency, Thomas Cranmer, the Archbishop of Canterbury, had long been the ardent spokesman of the reforming intellectuals. Throughout Henry VIII's later years Cranmer had been a pronounced "reformer"; with the old king removed, Cranmer became the chief architect of the English Reformation. In the first parliamentary session of 1547, the punitive statutes of Henry VIII, such as the Treason Act and the Six Articles, were removed. In the same year Parliament and the council decreed the abolition of images from the churches, ordered the use of English in the church service, and dissolved the chantries, the last substantial financial resource of the old church. At the same time marriage of the clergy was authorized. Within two years the first Book of Common Prayer was issued. This was largely the work of Cranmer and it was filled with the spirit of Protestantism. Because of its nature as a public document and the uniformity of its use, it became a powerful instrument of the Reformation.

In two years practically the whole program of Henrican Catholicism had been abolished and England had joined the Reformation. But in 1549 the regency faced a serious rebellion. In the backward country regions Catholicism was still strong. Even the reforms of Henry VIII had met resistance there, especially in the northern and western counties. Furthermore, these regions were hard-hit by the economic troubles of the time. Religious and economic discontent merged with a dozen other grievances to create a widespread popular uprising. It began in Devon and Cornwall, triggered by the appearance of the Prayer Book, but it was directed primarily against the enclosures. Peasants from the countryside and the wretched laborers of the western towns joined the movement as it rolled eastward, finding a leader in Robert Kett. The rebellion became serious enough to threaten London and the regency. But even more it threatened the vested interests of the powerful country gentry and the urban middle class. Somerset had some sympathy for the rebels and little force to put against them. He temporized; in so doing he lost the confidence of the class to whom he had made concessions in religion for his failure to protect their social and economic interests. The growing dissatisfaction of the council joined the general protest and Somerset was forced to step down.

His place was taken by the Earl of Warwick, his chief opponent in the council. Warwick, soon known as the Duke of Northumberland, was a conscienceless and self-seeking politician. He took a strong stand against the peasant rebels, which was enough to destroy their already weakened force. Once in power, Northumberland openly and flagrantly courted the propertied classes. He encouraged enclosures and made peasant protest tantamount to treason. He restored peace by virtual surrender to the Franco-Scottish alliance. He allowed the Reformation to move rapidly toward Protestant extremism. In 1552 a second Prayer Book was issued, more explicitly Protestant than the first. In the following year came the "Forty-two Articles," which spelled out the new reformed doctrines as law. Among the provisions of the articles were the denial of transubstantiation, a Lutheran-like concept of faith, and a rejection of the sacramental theory.

Behind the scenes the government was corrupt and arbitrary; state finances were in disorder. Furthermore, the young king was dying, and with him the means of Northumberland's supremacy. The scheming duke appealed to Edward's genuine religious sentiment to set aside the succession of his Catholic half-sister, Mary, as provided by Henry VIII's will. He further persuaded Edward to assign the crown to Lady Jane Grey, who was related to the Tudors through the line of Henry's sister, Mary. When the succession was assured Northumberland arranged a marriage between his own son and Lady Jane Grey. The plot was hatched.

Northumberland counted heavily upon the Protestant sympathies of the nation, but he seriously miscalculated the strength of the Tudor myth and the dead hand of Henry VIII. When, in the summer of 1553, young Edward died, Northumberland hastened to install Lady Jane Grey, but Princess Mary, daughter of Henry VIII and Catherine of Aragon, claimed the crown and called upon the nation to support her. Mary's Catholicism, while certainly unpopular, was outweighed by the legality of her claim and by the prospect of the civil war that surely loomed ahead. The people of England overwhelmingly endorsed Mary; she entered London in a moment of triumph she was never to forget. Northumberland was tumbled from his place shortly to be executed along with the unfortunate young girl who had been his pawn.

Mary Tudor was already a midddle-aged woman—plain, grim, and embittered. Through twenty years of uncertainty and danger she had clung obstinately to her Catholic faith until it was the cardinal fact of her character; it became the cardinal fact of her reign. The Catholic partisans who had been silenced, imprisoned, or exiled during the Protestant reign of Edward came out of hiding to surround the new queen. She demanded of her first Parliament in 1553 the complete restoration of Catholicism. Parliament consented to return to the doctrinal Catholicism of Henry VIII, but beyond this it would not go either to restore church property or accept the primacy of the pope.

Mary changed her tactics. With the Emperor Charles V, her cousin, she negotiated a marriage alliance between herself and his Spanish son, Philip. Even her Catholic counselors advised against the marriage on political grounds, and there were popular uprisings in protest against it. But Mary persisted; if she could not restore her nation's faith by domestic action, then she would restore it by foreign force. Backed by the threat of force, Mary bludgeoned Parliament into a reluctant restoration of papal headship. The religious pendulum was swinging back. In the face of increasing unpopularity, Mary forced the restoration of the laws against heresy. The persecutions began, slowly at first, then with mounting fury until nearly three hundred people had burned at the stake, including Archbishop Cranmer, and Mary had become "Bloody Mary." She had hoped to break the Protestant temper of her people, but once more the blood of the martyrs was the seed of the church. The whole nation was in turmoil. There were fresh outbreaks of rebellion at each new spate of executions.

Then, as if to compound the hatred of the people, Mary was persuaded by her Spanish husband to send an English force to assist him against France. Both the cost and the cause of this war were insufferable to England. The French retaliated against Mary's dispirited and ill-supported troops and took the port of Calais in 1558. The loss of this English doorway to the continent was a damning symbol of Mary's failure as a monarch. The glory of Edward III, the Black Prince, and Henry V had faded completely. To Mary's humiliation was added the realization that she and her nation had been used by Spain, and that her own exalted Catholic faith had made her a party to the venality of papal and Spanish politics. Before the end of 1558 Mary Tudor died, knowing that her Catholic restoration had finally failed. The nation turned once more to the will of Henry VIII and to his lone surviving heir, Elizabeth.

CALVINISM AND THE CATHOLIC REACTION

Lutheranism, the Anglican revolt, and even the various "splinter" movements of the continental Reformation were closely tied to ethnic, national, regional, or class interests. It was only with the rise of Calvinism that the Reformation gained an internationalism and universality to set against the ancient, ecumenical claims of traditional Catholicism.

Switzerland and the Background to Calvinism

In the middle years of the sixteenth century the reformer John Calvin (1509–1564) made the Swiss city of Geneva a "Protestant Rome," the center from which his doctrines would go out to sects and congregations all over western Europe. Yet, long before Calvin came to Geneva the

Reformation had reached Switzerland and the way had been prepared for him.

Before the turn of the sixteenth century the Swiss confederacy was in fact a free state within the loose association of the German Empire. The Swiss were proud of their independence and the freedom they enjoyed had attracted many humanists to Switzerland. The cities of Bern and Basel were flourishing centers of humanistic studies. The latter was the favorite residence of the great Erasmus and a center of the European book trade. As the Reformation became a violent, revolutionary movement, reformers of every stripe fled to Switzerland, bringing their doctrines with them. The ideas and protests that stirred the early sixteenth century crowded into Switzerland. And in Switzerland itself the social tensions produced by the antagonism of city aristocracies and commons, of town and country, of peasant and landlord, added to the ferment of the Reformation.

The work of Huldrich Zwingli (1484–1531) represented the first wave of the Swiss Reformation. Zwingli was a native Swiss, born in a mountain village in German-speaking eastern Switzerland. He began to study for the priesthood but, as happened to many another bright young man in the opening years of the sixteenth century, his studies took him outside the traditional scholastic channels into the "new learning" of Humanism, especially to the works of Erasmus. In 1506 Zwingli received his first pastorate in the village of Glarus, and for the next several years advanced steadily through one position after another until, in 1518, he was appointed to the important city church of Zürich. During this time Zwingli had come, like Luther, to insist that religion be based solidly upon Scripture. But his approach to Scripture was still that of the humanist scholar rather than the radical reformer—Erasmian rather than Lutheran. This changed in 1519, after Zwingli had narrowly escaped death from the plague. His intellectual doubts led him before long into initiating a full-fledged Reformation. Ironically, though he shared Luther's notions on faith and works, other of Zwingli's ideas set him at bitter variance with the Lutherans.

Zwingli went beyond Luther in rejecting the idea of the Mass and the Eucharistic interpretation of the Lord's Supper. He maintained that this was only a memorial to which neither mystery, power, nor magic were attached. Zwingli also went beyond Luther in developing the latter's implicit idea of predestination to the point where it, rather than faith, became his cardinal doctrine. Before long Zwingli's convictions led to positive acts of religious revolution. In 1522 he refused to honor the abstinence of Lent; in the same year he married. He attacked traditional religious rituals as non-Biblical and, with them the whole traditional structure of the church, including indulgences, pilgrimages, saints, relics; even taxes, fees, and temporalities.

These reforming ideas stemmed from many sources. Some were Lutheran, some Anabaptist, some humanistic, and some merely the expression of general protest. As Zwingli preached and his doctrine spread, it was bitterly debated. In many areas the rapidly forming Zwinglian movement was enthusiastically adopted. In others, particularly the conservative forest cantons, the people clung to the old faith. The peculiar federal structure of Switzerland forced the Reformation to break not along national or regional lines, as in England or Germany, but along local lines. Communities accepted or rejected the reformed religion on the basis of community decision after public debate and disputation. In this way, the nearly unique political freedom of Switzerland added to the Reformation the significant feature of community, and thus congregational, sovereignty. Zwingli's Reformation spread rapidly through Switzerland. Like-minded men joined him, in some cases contributing their ideas of reform to the existing Zwinglian doctrines.

These doctrines began to lap over into southern Germany, and Catholic Europe was faced with the dangerous prospect of a Protestant alliance. This was indeed the hope of Landgrave Philip of Hesse (1509–1567), who had become the chief political leader among the Lutheran princes. As the Peace of Cambrai (1529) threatened to release the emperor from his involvement with France, Philip of Hesse desperately tried to forge such a Protestant alliance. At his insistence Zwingli and Luther, each backed by a party of divines, met at Marburg in 1529. Zwingli was willing to cooperate on many points, as were several of the Lutheran leaders. But Luther himself was adamant in his refusal to accept Zwingli's interpretation of the Lord's Supper. The "Marburg Colloquies" were a failure; each party went its own way and the hope of multiparty Reformation in Germany was lost. The failure of the Lutheran-Zwinglian entente forced the Swiss Reformation to take another direction, to face the French west rather than the German east. Zwingli himself was killed in a battle between Zürich and the Catholic cantons at Kappel in 1531. But by this time reform agitation was rapidly gaining ground in several cities of French-speaking western Switzerland. The French refugee reformer, Guillaume Farel, had already begun the work to which Calvin would give final form.

The French Origins of Calvinism

The Swiss Reformation was powerfully influenced by a number of reforming tendencies that originated in France and, perhaps more significantly, by the fact that these tendencies were ultimately rejected in France and forced to seek another locus. On the eve of the sixteenth century most of the conditions for a religious Reformation were present in France, as in western Europe generally. The French clergy were as corrupt as the German; the abuses that scandalized Luther also scandalized Lefevre d'Étaples, Budé, and Briçonnet. There was widespread hostility to these abuses and to the temporal crassness of the church. The old heresies were still very much alive in France, and they were being fed by the general discontent caused by the rapid economic and social changes of the period. French humanists, as we have seen, were fully as critical of conventional religion and as much bent on reform as any group in northern Europe. But the political conditions that had allowed and even encouraged religious revolution elsewhere were very different in France. In the German domains of the Holy Roman Emperor, the fragmentary character of imperial government and the relative self-determination of local towns and regions had allowed the Hussites, the various Anabaptist groups, the Swiss, and the German reformers to develop. The Lutheran movement blended with the strong tradition of princely sovereignty in Germany. In England, while a powerful popular monarchy existed, political necessity made common cause with popular protest to create a nationalistic Reformation. In contrast to imperial Germany, France was the most strongly centralized nation in Europe. In contrast to England, the French crown had already won most of the national-ecclesiastical control for the sake of which Henry VIII was constrained to break with Rome. Since the Pragmatic Sanction of Bourges (1438) the French kings had held substantial control over the church in France. This control was further extended by the political maneuvering of Francis I and Leo X which resulted, in 1516, in the Concordat of Bologna. Thus, on the eve of the Reformation the higher clergy in France were almost all appointed by the crown, and papal jurisdiction in France was sharply limited. The French church was a national church within the community of international Catholicism.

In the early years of the sixteenth century several groups of enlightened clergy were working for the reform of the church, men who were the spiritual descendants of the great reforming conciliasts that France had produced in the fifteenth century. Most of them were humanists of Erasmus' stamp, and they enjoyed the support of the crown. Their guiding spirit was the reforming Christian humanist Lefevre d'Étaples (1455–1537). He and his followers advocated doctrines of faith and love remarkably similar to those of Luther. Lefevre translated the New Testament into French in 1523 and it was widely used. One of his pupils, Guillaume Briçonnet, became Bishop of Meaux and his bishopric became a haven for the Christian-humanist spirit. Specific reforms, which might well have brought a genuine Reformation to the French church, were begun. But the revolutionary teachings of Luther had already begun to filter across the frontiers from Germany and his books were widely read. Orthodox opinion, led by the conservative and influential University of Paris, condemned the Lutheran doctrines. The Parlement de Paris, the highest judicial authority in France, also condemned them, and the king followed. The church and the state closed ranks against opinions that threatened them both and the distinction between legitimate reform and heretical revolution was lost. The government began persecutions against several active Lutheran agitators and sympathizers. Under pressure and suspicion many reformers renounced their reforming principles and many fled the country. Some defied persecution and drifted across the line into heresy. There were inflammatory incidents: the desecration of a venerated statue of the Virgin in 1528; local uprisings in the name of religion by several worker groups, especially in the cloth towns along the Flemish border; and finally, in the fall of 1534, the posting of a number of blatantly Protestant placards all over Paris, one even attached to the door of the royal bedchamber. In the next few days unorthodox opinion of every degree was condemned. "Lutherans," whether simple, pious Waldensians, humanist reformers, or social revolutionaries, were hunted down, tortured, hanged, and burned. At the same time their "Most Christian" King was in active political alliance with the Lutheran princes of Germany, and even with Suleiman, the Turk.

A number of expatriate French humanists and reformers fled to French Switzerland. Chief among them was Guillaume Farel (1489–1565). He had been one of the pupils of Lefevre d'Étaples and one of the friends of Briçonnet at Meaux. But his radical opinions put him at odds with even this liberal group and he went to Basel in 1523. He preached and taught in several cities along the upper Rhine in southwestern Germany and Switzerland. His own views blended with the reforming movements already flourishing there. By 1531 he had broken completely with traditional Catholicism and attracted a considerable following. In the next several years Farel led the militant point of the Reformation into the strategic city of Geneva in western Switzerland. He managed to identify his cause with the sentiment of local political independence at a moment when the Catholic alliance of Charles V threatened that independence. There was a general uprising, not only in Geneva but in the surrounding districts, against Catholic authority and the property of the church. On May 21, 1536, the people of Geneva officially accepted the tenets of the Reformation in a public oath. Farel had led Geneva to this point. In mid-summer of the same year Jean Calvin arrived in the city.

Calvin (1509–1564) was born in Noyon, a small cathedral town in Picardy. His father was a notary of some learning and some means, connected with the financial operation of the cathedral. At fourteen, after basic studies in Noyon, Calvin was sent to the University of Paris, his way paid by a small benefice from the cathedral of Noyon. The University of Paris was still wracked with the strife between the "ancients" and the "moderns" that Erasmus had seen there twenty-five years earlier. Calvin was exposed both to "modern" Humanism and "ancient" Scholasticism. He preferred the former and was well on his way to becoming an accomplished humanist. Near the end of his university studies, probably at his father's insistence, Calvin entered the school of law at Orléans, where he ultimately took a degree. At the same time he continued his humanistic studies, learning Greek and having at least an exposure to Hebrew. About this time he published his first book, a commentary on the *De Clementia* of the Roman philosopher Seneca. It was a typically humanistic work, concerned with classical moral values and, by implication, considering Christianity as a moral-philosophic system. This writing might well have launched Calvin into the career of a professional humanist. Instead, it was both his first and his last work of this sort. For, shortly after its publication, Calvin passed through the experience of personal conversion which turned him toward the Reformation.

This was the most crucial change in Calvin's life, and the most obscure. We know nothing of its immediate cause, only that his conversion was sudden. Certainly religious change and church reform were the leading concerns of the day, and Calvin's training had led him to these concerns along the path followed by many northern humanists before him. We know that his circle of friends included a number of humanists with strong reforming views. But it is also possible that his break with the church was, if not caused, at least hastened by, a more personal experience. Shortly before his conversion his father had died under excommunication from the church, possibly for his religious views, probably for manipulation of church funds. In any case, Calvin joined the ranks of the reformers.

At this time he had already left Orléans and returned to Paris, where he became a member of the liberal reforming party of religious humanists condemned by the university and the Parlement. As the persecutions increased and Calvin's personal religious views became more sharply defined, he abandoned Paris and fled the disintegration of the Reformation in France. Early in 1535 he settled in Basel. It was in that city in the following months that Calvin completed the first edition of his *Institutes of the Christian Religion,* the work that was to be expanded and elaborated for the rest of his life and which was to become the most comprehensive system of Protestant theology. Just as this book was finished the aged Erasmus died in the same Swiss city—the old order giving way to the new.

When the *Institutes* was finished Calvin left Basel, traveled briefly in Italy, and once more in France. On his way to Strassburg he passed through Geneva and met Farel. That fiery and impetuous reformer convinced Calvin to stay with him and work for the reformed cause. In August of 1536 Calvin settled with Farel in Geneva. The two men moved too far and too fast in their reforming schemes. They issued so many ordinances against sin, misbehavior, blasphemy, and even harmless pleasures, that the city council, with the same public procedure that welcomed the Reformation to Geneva, banished its zealous prophets in 1538. For the next two years Calvin preached and taught in the reformed city of Strassburg and came to know the religious leaders there. He rapidly became an important figure among the reformers and a powerful public spokesman. Meanwhile, in Geneva the tumult of religious factions continued until, in 1541, the weary city officials asked Calvin to return. Geneva was finally ready to accept the governance of Calvin and of God.

Theocracy and Theology: Calvin in Geneva

The reforms of government and society that Calvin instituted in Geneva during the next twenty years established the classic patterns of the Protestant "City of God" and the "Protestant Ethic." Both were reflections of Calvin's systematic theology, which was worked out in intricate detail during the same span of years. Calvin's theology was eclectic, and little in his system was unique. Like most of the other

Protestant thinkers, Calvin depended upon the Bible as his ultimate authority, giving it a strict and literal interpretation. Like them, too, he rejected nearly every vestige of Catholic tradition—the cults of saints and relics, the sacramental system, purgatory, indulgences, and the whole concept of hierarchy from pope to parish priest. Calvin derived from Luther the concepts of justification by faith and the priesthood of believers. He followed Luther in his acceptance of Baptism and the Holy Supper as the only sacraments that had Scriptural basis. But, unlike Luther, he divested even these of their sacramental quality. They did not convey grace, nor of themselves could they remove sin; they were symbolic only. Calvin, in this regard and particularly in his rejection of transubstantiation, was deeply influenced by the teachings of Zwingli and the Strassburg reformers.

Like Luther, Calvin was overwhelmed by the power and majesty of God and by fear of Him. The sovereignty of God was the basis of the Calvinist system. God was the creator of the world and man, the ever-living, immaculate, unknowable ruler. He had created man in the perfection of his own image. But man, by the original sin of disobedience, had corrupted his sublime nature and passed on his resulting total depravity to all mankind. Man could offer his faith to God; he could take some comfort in Christ's promise of salvation. But his salvation lay ultimately not with himself but with God. Thus was derived the characteristic Calvinist doctrine of election. Since God was omniscient, eternal, and omnipotent, He must know every individual man's fate, whether to be damned or saved; and He must have known it from before the beginning of time, since both time and man are his creations. To know and to will are the same in the mind of God and so, by His will and knowledge, God has chosen among the multitude of men, some to be saved and some to be damned. Calvin's exalted notion of God forced upon him this iron logic of predestination—and he did not hesitate to accept it.

Fully as characteristic of Calvinism as the doctrine of predestination, was Calvin's concept of ethic. While man could not know the will of God and could not alter it by his behavior, Calvin nonetheless insisted upon the most strenuous morality on the part of the Christian. The elect were not merely "called to forgiveness"; they were "called unto holiness." And holiness was manifested in a grim, humorless, puritanical righteousness, a characteristic Calvinism carried with it wherever it went.

Calvin's conception of God and man was set within the framework of church and state. He shared with Wyclif, Hus, and Zwingli the notion that the "Holy Catholic Church" is the "whole number of the elect," the invisible company of the saved, the living, the dead, and the unborn. But, for practical purposes, since men cannot know which of their fellow men belong to this elect company, Calvin defined the church as an association composed of all "who by confession of faith, regularity of conduct, and participation in the sacraments, unite with us in acknowledging the same God and Christ." Calvin went to the Scriptures and to the primitive church for his model. Pastors and teachers of religion were to be elected by the whole community; yet, while thus elected, these spiritual leaders were still "called of God" to be the agents of His will for the community. Ecclesiastical sovereignty, however, remained with the whole community. Again, wherever Calvinism was carried it retained this strong sense of community or congregational exclusiveness and independence, of in-group charity and discipline. The state was closely related to the church in this community sense. Indeed, Calvin revived in other terms the medieval doctrine of the two swords, for he saw the state as the civil counterpart of the church. It was the duty of the state to cooperate with the church and to enforce its will. In this cooperation of church and state lay the basis of Calvin's theocracy, the rule of God over the Christian community.

By the time Calvin came to Geneva the basic framework of his theology was complete. He gradually came to overshadow Farel and, with his triumphant return from exile in 1541, Calvin was the unofficial master of the city of Geneva. He set about to make it a model of the Christian community, conceived in terms of his theological system. Within a month of his restoration in 1541, Calvin proposed a set of regulations that became the basis of the civil-ecclesiastical constitution of Calvinist Geneva. They were called the *Ecclesiastical Ordinances*. The ordinances established four councils for the government of church and state: the first comprised the ministers who were elected from the community, called the Venerable Company; the second group was the teachers of doctrine; the third was the consistory, a disciplinary body of far-reaching authority, consisting of twelve elders appointed by the city council; and finally, the council of deacons was established to assume the responsibility for public charity.

This interlocking order of the community was the extension both of Calvin's system and of his own personality. He exerted a powerful influence upon the councils that the ordinances established. The ordinances reflected in detail the sense of sin so marked in Calvin; he saw sin not only in the violation of moral law but in every pleasure or frivolity. The death penalty was decreed for heresy and adultery, and severe punishment was attached to blasphemy and idolatry (this latter included the traditional celebration of the Catholic Mass). There were regulations against dancing, card-playing, and theater. Grave suspicion was attached to any niceties of dress or grooming, extravagant hairdos or excessive jewelry. Officials were indefatigable in their pursuit of sin and sinners—their calling was from God himself and the moral health of their fellow men depended upon their vigilance. The result was a fearful tyranny over the individual that could always be sanctioned by the "word of God."

The force of Calvin's terrible will and the moral zeal of his officials clamped tight upon Geneva. Those who resisted were branded libertines; they were persecuted; some even executed; and a great many left the city. The others conformed; Calvin would tolerate no deviation. In 1543 a humanist-theologian was banned from the city for his views on Biblical poetry; another was banished for his criticism of the doctrine of predes-tination. A simple citizen who was suspected of agitation against the tyranny of the city's government was arrested, tortured, and finally exe-cuted. The most famous victim of Calvinist persecution was Michael Servetus, a Spanish theologian, humanist, and physician. Servetus held radical theological views—he rejected the trinity, predestination, and the eternal divinity of Christ. He wandered about the continent and was con-demned by Catholic officials. Finally, he dared to appear in Geneva and, at Calvin's insistence, he was arrested. After a lengthy trial Servetus was burned at the stake in 1533. The wheel of intolerance and brutality had come full circle from the burning of Catholic heretics to the burning of Protestant dissenters—all in the name of religion.

For more than twenty years Jean Calvin was the living spirit of his reforms in Geneva. Thin and slight, he favored the sober dress of the academic, which suited the manner of the censorius schoolmaster that clung about him. Calvin was reticent and reserved about his private life, and we have no such ingratiating portrait of Calvin the man as we have of Luther. Calvin was a commanding personality without being an at-tractive one. Despite his frail health he was a prodigious worker: he preached and taught and was almost continuously involved in the gov-ernment of his city. His writings, in addition to the massive *Institutes,* included sermons, tracts, commentaries, and a huge volume of letters to and from practically every significant figure in the Protestant world— in all, more than fifty heavy volumes.

From Calvin's Geneva a constant stream of zealous preachers and missionaries went out to preach the reformed doctrines. Throughout

Europe triumphant Calvinism seized upon local movements and protests and transformed them. The Huguenot movement in France, the Reformed Church of the Low Countries and Germany, the English Puritans, and the Scottish Presbyterians, as well as a dozen splinter sects in other places, were all varieties of Calvinism. Calvin himself actively supported these sects and, to a degree, they all bore his personal stamp. Many of their leaders—Scotland's John Knox, for example—came to Geneva and under the direct influence of Calvin. By the time of his death Calvin's Reformation was solidly established and militant Calvinism assumed the burden of hostility to the Catholic faith and the Catholic powers. With the second half of the sixteenth century, the wars of religion were resumed once more, not on a local, regional, or even an exclusively dynastic basis, but generally and across the whole continent of Europe.

The Counter Reformation

Protest against the church, its abuses, its secularism, even its doctrines, had finally come to violent revolution in the Protestant Reformation. This revolutionary, schismatic crisis shattered the unity of western Christianity and, in its militancy, seemed to threaten the very existence of the traditional pattern of Christianity. Yet, in the face of this crisis, as through the centuries of its prior history, Catholicism rallied. It struck back at the divisive force of the Reformation and began to attack those very abuses within its own ranks that gave to the Protestant reformers their most effective arguments. This far-reaching and significant Catholic revival is called the Counter Reformation. Yet this term, like many conventional labels, is not entirely descriptive. It implies that the Catholic revival which came in the second half of the sixteenth century was a response, a reciprocal reaction to the Protestant Reformation. While this was certainly the case in part, there were other, equally significant sources of vitality within Catholicism itself. Millions of people, whole regions and classes throughout Europe, remained loyal to the old church. Protestantism made little appeal generally to the conservative peasantry. While humanistic criticism, humanistic books, and humanistic education had been mighty contributing factors to the coming of the Reformation, the great majority of European intellectuals of the "new learning" remained Catholics. This was true also of most of the conventional universities and their faculties, involved as they were by tradition with the church and the scholastic system. Even the liberal, urban middle class, the strongest support of the Protestant movement, did not universally embrace the new doctrines, and many highly urbanized areas remained Catholic.

The sentiments for reform, moreover, which had been such a potent factor in the Reformation, continued to be expressed with new urgency within the church itself. Even at the height of the secularized Renaissance papacy there were highly placed churchmen working for reform. Many Catholic princes were concerned with restoring the vitality of the old faith. But the deep and desperate involvement of the papacy in the business of the world was the most serious impediment to general and systematic Catholic reform. For a moment, after the death of Leo X in 1521, there was hope of papal reformation. The conclave, under the pressure of Emperor Charles V, elected a pious and learned Dutch cleric as Adrian VI. Like so many of the northern reformers, Adrian was a product of the Brethren schools and the orthodox University of Louvain. He had never lost his fervent pietism through a long and distinguished ecclesiastical career. He had been tutor and counselor to Charles V and had gone with him to Spain, where he had ruled as Charles' regent during the uncertain early years of his Spanish reign. Adrian's pontificate, however, was too brief—less than two years—and the papacy too well established in the pattern of Alexander VI, Julius II, and Leo X to be easily changed.

At his death, in 1523, Adrian was succeeded by another Medici, Clement VII, and the papacy was dedicated once more to its familiar concerns. But time was running out and the temper of Catholic reform was strengthening. By the time of Clement's death, in 1534, his playing at politics and his concern with temporalities had cost Rome the terrible sack of 1527 and the loss of half of Europe to the Reformation. With the accession of Alexander Farnese as Paul III (*1534-1549*) the Renaissance papacy came to an end, and the church entered upon the age of the Counter Reformation. Adrian VI had been a foreigner from the barbarous north and his zeal for reform was greeted with hostility and contempt. But Paul III came from a background more familiar and congenial to his cardinals. A man of taste and learning, he was a product of the best of Renaissance thought and training. Moreover, he had already spent a lifetime at the papal court and was universally respected for his knowledge of the church. Dedicated to the new spirit of reform, he was a man who could translate that spirit into positive action. He appointed to the College of Cardinals the most distinguished and upright men in the church, chosen from all over Europe. He appointed a papal commission which, in 1537, produced a frank and comprehensive catalogue of church abuses, on the basis of which far-reaching reforms were immediately put into effect.

At the other end of the ecclesiastical scale the same sentiment for reform produced a rash of new religious orders—the Sommaschi, the Barnabites, the Ursulines, the Theatines, the Capuchins, the Oratorians, the Carmelites, and, the most significant of all, the Society of Jesus, or the Jesuit order. The Jesuit order was shaped by a single personality, Ignatius Loyola (1491–1556), one of the most important figures of the sixteenth century. Loyola was a Spaniard, born in the mountain kingdom of Navarre. His family was of the lower nobility and he was, as a young man, passionately dedicated to the military, knightly, crusading tradition of his class and his nation. Loyola took service in the army of Charles V and was wounded in the leg during the fighting along the northern frontier in the first French war. When he recovered from the shock of his wound, the leg had to be broken and reset, and the protruding bone sawed away. As he lay in delirium, so near death that last rites were given him, Loyola passed through a profound experience of conversion. He vowed to dedicate his life to God and as he recovered his health the resolve deepened. He subjected himself to the customary austerities and undertook the works of charity that usually follow such a conversion.

In 1523 Loyola visited the Holy Land. Returning to Spain he prepared himself for university studies and then entered the University of Alcala. From there he went on to Paris and the same College de Montaigu where both Erasmus and Calvin had been students before him. The same iron will that had carried him through the agonies of his sickness supported him in the almost equally agonizing labors of learning. He had been trained as a soldier, not a student; and he had to start his education as a middle-aged man. But he rose from the scholar's bench of the common school to become the archetype of the learned, razor-sharp Jesuit theologian. Even before his work at Paris was finished he had attracted a small company of men like himself and they pledged themselves and each other to poverty and chastity. They resolved to go to the Holy Land as missionaries but, when this could not be done because of the Turkish wars in the Mediterranean, Loyola went to Rome and placed himself and his companions at the service of Pope Paul III. This was one of the most fruitful meetings in the history of the church. The reforming pope judged the temper of Loyola and saw the potential of his growing band. In 1538 the Jesuit order was officially formed, with Loyola as its first general.

Despite his conversion, Loyola had never ceased to be a soldier, and the Society of Jesus was organized as an army of God. Loyola infused the order with his own chivalric, crusading spirit, imposing on it a formal structure which marks him as one of the great organizing geniuses of his age. The foundation of the order was the individual dedication and burning zeal of its members. Loyola wanted every Jesuit to know, as he had known, the intimate experience of personal conversion. To this end he wrote the *Spiritual Exercises,* one of the most remarkable pieces of mystic literature ever produced. It owed much to such popular devotional works as the *Imitation of Christ* of St. Thomas à Kempis and the writings of other mystics; it owed much also to the profound personal mysticism of Loyola. But it owed most of all to the purpose for which Loyola wrote it—to be a practical handbook of mystic conversion. Through its several parts the reader is led to know the horror of sin, the promise of Christ, and finally the reality of His Resurrection. Furthermore, as he comes to "know" these things in a conventional sense, he begins to know them in the mystic's sense of illumination until, at the last stage of the exercises, the reader achieves the vision of God. After this, he descends once more, like Plato's philosopher-guardian, into the market place of men. The study of this book and the application of its exercises became the basis of Jesuit training. From this beginning novices went on to further discipline and a truly formidable regimen of education. They took the customary vows, but in addition, a soldier's vow of absolute obedience to the pope. Upon the completion of training the individual Jesuit took his place in a vast and highly articulated order. Each house had its rector, each district its governor, and the whole order its general. Throughout its structure the organization was military and the discipline absolute.

Despite its rigors and its extremely high standards of admission, the Society of Jesus grew rapidly. No agency was more effective in promoting the Counter Reformation. The Jesuits founded schools and colleges which were for centuries among the most advanced and effective in the world. In other colleges and universities Jesuit scholars dominated higher studies in a dozen fields. Learned Jesuit preachers and confessors penetrated down to the individual parish congregations to introduce a new moral discipline and doctrinal purity. In the other direction, Jesuit confessors and spiritual advisers became the familiars of Catholic courts all over Europe, where they exerted a profound influence upon politico-religious policies. At every level of their activity Jesuits were the articulate champions of the new, invigorated, and reformed Catholicism. All along the Protestant frontiers the Jesuits vigorously led the Catholic forces to reconquests: they penetrated Switzerland, strengthened the ancient Rhine bishoprics which were badly shaken by the Reformation, consolidated the gains of the church in southern Germany and in the Austrian Hapsburg lands. They were instrumental in restoring Catholicism to Poland, where Lutheranism had begun to make gains. By the middle of the century the Jesuits had spread their influence literally all over the world. They took up the challenge of paganism as they did that of heresy. Jesuit missionaries followed the Spanish and Portuguese conquerors and traders into the Americas and Asia.

The idea of a reforming general council of the church had been an important political issue throughout the early sixteenth century. The French king, Louis XII, had used the threat of a council as a bludgeon against the papacy; Charles V did the same thing. There was much popular demand for a council. Many people, both Catholic and Protestant, felt that Christian unity still might be restored through a council that would include representatives of the reformed sects. But the whole question of the council became mired in the politics of the Hapsburg-Valois wars. Paul III, in 1545, finally summoned the long-awaited council at Trent, on the border between Germany, France, and Italy. By this time it had become clear that the Protestants would not accept a council on either political or doctrinal grounds. Francis I of France, also for political reasons, withheld his support; Charles V was more interested in the political implications of church reform than in reform itself; even the Catholic clergy were divided on the issues of the council, and there was much suspicion and hostility. Under such inauspicious circumstances the Council of Trent held its opening sessions. In 1547 the council was adjourned. Despite the continued irritation of politics and the constant threat that the council would split into hostile parties, it was called into session once more in 1551–52. The final sessions were delayed still another decade and the Council of Trent closed with the sessions of 1562–63.

During the nearly twenty years covered by the council the reforming work of Paul III had been continued by Julius III (*1550–1555*), Paul IV (*1555–1559*), and Pius IV (*1559–1565*). The traditional opposition of pope and council was destroyed by the reforming initiative of these popes, and the Council of Trent set the seal of the church upon the work of reform that was already transforming Catholicism. Thus, the decrees of the Council of Trent may be said to represent a summation of the Counter Reformation. Catholic orthodoxy, after a half century of alternate hostility and conciliation, rejected the reformed sects completely and repudiated their cardinal doctrines. The decrees of Trent reaffirmed traditional Catholicism on the traditional bases as the only form of Christianity. The church rested upon the authority of Scripture and upon the equally valid traditions of the church. There were decrees on the sacraments, transubstantiation, faith and works, clerical celibacy, and the hierarchy under papal headship. The work of the papal Inquisition, strengthened by Paul IV, was extended and confirmed at Trent. The council also authorized the publication of an *Index of Prohibited Books* as a measure against the spread of heresy. There was hardly a point of dispute which the Council of Trent did not handle, and its decrees tended to supplant previous statements on all these points.

SUGGESTIONS FOR FURTHER READING

≈⅀

General Works

*R. H. Bainton, *The Reformation of the Sixteenth Century* (Boston: Beacon Press, 1952).

H. J. Grimm, *The Reformation Era 1500–1650* (New York: Macmillan, 1954), an unusually comprehensive and systematic survey.

*E. H. Harbison, *The Age of Reformation* (Ithaca: Cornell University Press, 1955).

H. Holborn, *History of Modern Germany*, vol. I, *The Reformation* (New York: Knopf, 1959).

*G. L. Mosse, *The Reformation* (New York: Holt, 1952).

New Cambridge Modern History, Vol. II, *The Reformation*, ed. by G. R. Elton (Cambridge: Cambridge University Press, 1958), probably the best general work on the Reformation.

Preserved Smith, *The Age of the Reformation* (New York: Holt, 1920), still one of the best general works; balanced, sane, and wise.

Political and Social History

*S. T. Bindoff, *Tudor England* (Baltimore: Penguin, 1952), mature and lively narrative.

K. Brandi, *The Emperor Charles V* (London: Jonathan Cape, 1939), the best work on Charles.

P. Champion, *Louis XI,* tr. and adapt. by W. S. Whale (New York: Dodd, Mead, 1929), a standard biography.

H. W. Chapman, *The Last Tudor King* (New York: Macmillan, 1959).

G. R. Elton, *England Under The Tudors* (New York: Putnam, 1955).

————, *The Tudor Revolution in Government* (Cambridge: Cambridge University Press, 1953), one of the best revisionist works on the Tudors.

C. W. Ferguson, *Naked to Mine Enemies: The Life of Cardinal Wolsey* (Boston: Little, Brown, 1958).

F. Hackett, *Francis I* (Garden City, N. Y.: Doubleday, 1935), popularized biography.

D. B. Wyndham Lewis, *King Spider* (New York: Coward-McCann, 1929), a fine literary biography of Louis XI.

G. Mattingly, *Catherine of Aragon* (Boston: Little, Brown, 1941), vivid and highly readable.

R. B. Merriman, *The Rise of the Spanish Empire* (New York: Macmillan, 1918–34), Vols. II-IV, massive standard work.

T. M. Parker, *The English Reformation to 1558* (Oxford: Oxford University Press, 1950).

A. F. Pollard, *Henry VIII* (London: Longmans, 1951), on old, standard book.

*M. Powicke, *The Reformation in England* (Oxford: Oxford University Press, 1961).

*H. F. M. Prescott, *Mary Tudor* (New York: Macmillan, 1962).

C. Read, *The Tudors* (New York: Holt, 1936).

*R. H. Tawney, *Religion and the Rise of Capitalism* (Baltimore: Penguin, 1947), a popularization of the Weber thesis.

M. Weber, *The Protestant Ethic and the Spirit of Capitalism,* ed. by T. Parsons (New York: Scribner, 1930), a famous and much-disputed thesis.

Reformers and Counter Reformers

*R. H. Bainton, *Here I Stand: A Life of Martin Luther* (New York: Mentor, 1955), probably the best and most readable biography of Luther.

————, *Hunted Heretic: The Life and Death of Michel Servetus, 1511–1553* (Boston: Beacon Press, 1960).

*John Calvin, *On the Christian Faith: Selections from the Institutes, Commentaries, and Tracts,* ed. and intro. by J. T. McNeill (Indianapolis: Bobbs-Merrill, 1957), a particularly good collection.

————, *On God and Political Duty,* ed. and intro. by J. T. McNeill (Indianapolis: Bobbs-Merrill, 1950), selections.

————, *The Institutes of the Christian Religion,* ed. by J. Allen (Philadelphia: Westminster, n.d.), 2 vols., the official American edition of this basic work.

P. Dudon, *St. Ignatius Loyola* (Milwaukee: Bruce, 1949), an official and scholarly Jesuit biography.

O. Farner, *Zwingli the Reformer* (New York: Philosophical Library, 1952).

G. Harkness, *John Calvin, The Man and His Ethics* (New York: Holt, 1931).

H. Holborn, *Ulrich von Hutten and the German Reformation* (New Haven: Yale University Press, 1937).

P. Hughes, *Rome and the Counter-Reformation in England* (London: Burnes and Oates, 1942).

*F. E. Hutchinson, *Cranmer and the English Reformation* (New York: Collier, 1962).

S. M. Jackson, *Ulrich Zwingli: The Reformer of German Switzerland* (New York: Putnam, 1900).

P. Janelle, *The Catholic Reformation* (Milwaukee: Bruce, 1951).

Martin Luther, *Reformation Writings,* tr. and ed. by B. G. Woolfe (New York: Philosophical Library, 1953–56), 2 vols.

————, *Table Talk* . . . ed. and intro. by T. S. Kepler (New York: World, 1952), the collection of Luther's fascinating "kitchen" conversations.

J. Mackinnon, *Calvin and the Reformation* (London: Longmans, 1936).

J. T. McNeill, *The History and Character of Calvinism* (Oxford: Oxford University Press, 1954).

E. G. Schwiebert, *Luther and His Times,* (St. Louis: Concordia, 1952).

*Paperbound edition. In the case of reprint editions, publisher and date of publication given will be that of reprint rather than the original.

⚹ 14 ⚹

Dragon Seeds:
The Wars of the Reformation

DYNASTIC AMBITIONS and intrigues had long been the cause of bitter conflicts throughout Europe. By the middle of the sixteenth century the Reformation had added an equally potent cause, involving much of Germany and central Europe in religious wars. In the next century political and religious issues joined to produce a number of devastating conflicts, out of which the modern state system of Europe was forged.

REVOLT IN THE NETHERLANDS

Prelude and Provocation

With the abdication of Charles V in 1556 his son, Philip II (*1556–1598*), received not only Spain but the Netherlands (the Burgundian inheritance of the House of Hapsburg). The seventeen provinces that made up the Netherlands had been pulled together by the aggressive dukes of Burgundy and their Hapsburg heirs into a loose federation. For two centuries the provinces had been ruled by "outsiders," French or German lords, and their resources had been used to pursue alien aims. Among the provinces themselves there were conflicts of interest that served to keep them divided and suspicious of each other. Some were commercial and industrial states, like Flanders and Holland, dominated by their flourishing cities and fed by world trade; others were conservative and backward agricultural states, like Groningen and Friesland. Although the ruling dynasties had created a form of overall political organization, the individual provinces had managed to retain a large part of their autonomy, protected by a complex of provincial privileges. Even under Charles V the jealously independent provinces remained the most significant political units in the Netherlands.

Although the Netherlands were far from being a nation in any political sense, a growing sense of cultural and ethnic community was beginning to stir by the mid-sixteenth century, encouraged by two factors. First, there was general resentment—and at least one open rebellion— because for forty years the prosperous Netherlands had been taxed by their foreign rulers to finance the latter's own dynastic wars. Second, a long tradition of religious protest further alienated large portions of the Netherlands population from their rulers, who were fervent defenders of Catholic orthodoxy.

In the later Middle Ages the Netherlands had already spawned a number of protest movements. At one extreme the depressed workers of the cities had risen in spasmodic rebellions closely connected with social-revolutionary heresies. At the other extreme, throughout the same period the Netherlands had produced a number of influential religious mystic and pietistic Catholic reform movements—including Geert Groote's Brethren of the Common Life. By their implied criticism of the church, these reform movements had been almost as damaging to the prestige of the church as the openly heretical movements. Later the Netherlands had become the home of a learned Christian Humanism—of the tradition that nurtured Erasmus. It should be said, however, that the Netherlands also contained strongholds of scholastic orthodoxy—such as the University of Louvain. Moreover, a large element of the population remained staunchly attached to the orthodox church. Then came the influence of Luther.

The impact of Luther's Reformation on the Netherlands was strengthened by the fact that Luther was in bitter political conflict with Emperor Charles V, ruler of the Netherlands. As the Lutheran movement spread across the Rhine into the Netherlands, it found sympathetic ground. Orthodoxy, championed by Charles V, fought back with persecution, including a special Inquisition for the Low Countries, established by Charles in 1522. In spite of this—indeed, partially because of it—imported Lutheranism enjoyed considerable success, drawing on the deep springs of native dissent. In the heavily urban and industrial areas, Lutheranism

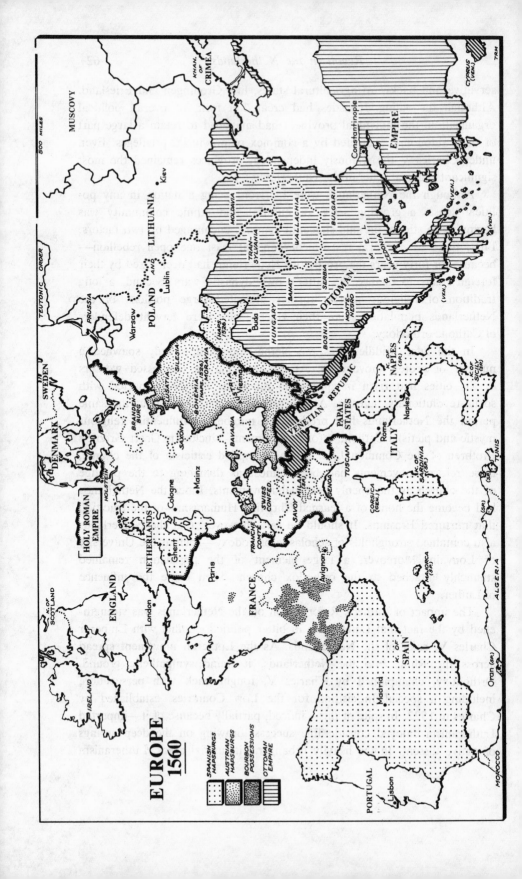

EUROPE
1560

SPANISH HAPSBURGS
AUSTRIAN HAPSBURGS
BOURBON POSSESSIONS
OTTOMAN EMPIRE

HOLY ROMAN EMPIRE

500 MILES

MUSCOVY

KHAN. OF
CRIMEA

Kiev

LITHUANIA

TEUTONIC ORDER

PRUSSIA

Warsaw

POLAND AND

Lublin

SWEDEN

DENMARK

HOLSTEIN

BRANDEN-
BURG

SAXONY

LUSATIA

SILESIA

BOHEMIA
(HAPS MORA)

MORAVIA

BAVARIA

(HAPS 1526)

Vienna

Buda

HUNGARY

MOLDAVIA

TRAN-
SYLVANIA

BANAT

WALLACHIA

SERBIA

BOSNIA

MONTE-
NEGRO

BULGARIA

MACEDONIA

RUMELIA

OTTOMAN

Constantinople

EMPIRE

ENGLAND

K. OF
SCOTLAND

IRELAND

London

NETHERLANDS

Ghent

Cologne

Mainz

SWISS
CONFED.

MILAN
(SP.)

SAVOY

GENOA

TUSCANY

VENETIAN REPUBLIC

(VEN.)

(VEN.)

(VEN.)

(VEN.)

CYPRUS
(VEN.)

PARIS

FRANCE

FRANCHE
COMTÉ

Avignon

CORSICA
(GEN.)

PAPAL
STATES

Rome

ITALY

Naples

K. OF
NAPLES
(SP.)

K. OF
SICILY
(SP.)

K. OF
SARDINIA
(SP.)

SARDINIA
(SP.)

MAJORCA
(SP.)

TUNIS

SPAIN

Madrid

PORTUGAL

Lisbon

MOROCCO

Oran (SP.)

ALGERIA

TRM

assumed the radical Anabaptist form, and although the socio-economic extremism of the Anabaptists was unacceptable to the majority of dissenters, Anabaptist ideas remained to nourish further heresies even after the sect itself had been broken. As state persecution increased, resistance stiffened. But until the 1550's dissent lacked organized form. Lutheranism had failed to gain either the broad social approval or the official political support that had made it so successful in Germany. The Anabaptists had alienated all but the most radical opinion, while the various sacramentarian, pietistic and vaguely "Protestant" groups were divided on a great range of issues.

Ultimately, organization and a common cause came not from Luther's Germany but from Calvin's Geneva. The missionaries from the "Protestant Rome" made their way down the Rhine into the Netherlands. From the beginning, Calvinism blended well with native reform ideas, while Calvinist theology helped the Dutch reformers crystallize their own ideas into a positive program. The Calvinist principle of congregational and community organization was highly congenial to the Netherlands' tradition of particularism, while the Calvinist sense of divine purpose provided a common bond for the several forms of Dutch protest. The logic and clarity of the intellectual structure of Calvinism appealed to the literate and responsible middle class as no other form of Protestantism had.

Through the long reign of Charles V the growing forces of popular revolt in the Netherlands were held in check. Charles needed the financial support of the provinces for his imperial wars and paid for it with political concessions. As a result, although popular resistance against Charles' state-supported religious policies mounted, it did not break out in open violence. Charles was a Fleming himself, born in Ghent, and the people of the Low Countries tended to regard him as one of their own and to forgive him much. Charles, for his part, also had a certain sentiment for his fellow countrymen. This rapport was becoming strained, however, toward the end of Charles' reign. It was destroyed altogether in the decade following his abdication.

The new king, Philip II, was a Spaniard in a sense that Charles, for all his Spanish sympathies, had never been. Philip had grown up in the fanatic orthodoxy of Counter Reformation Spain. He saw himself not only as a monarch, but as a divine monarch, the champion of religion, more Catholic than the pope. This exalted self-image produced the two leading motifs of Philip's policy—an insistence upon unquestioning political loyalty and rigid intolerance for every form of religious deviation.

Further, Philip was temperamentally incapable of the kind of compromise that his father had been forced to live with for forty years.

As soon as he was able to settle the issues that held over from the last French war, Philip left the Netherlands, never to return. But he had already established the policies that his agents were to carry out, to the eventual ruin of Spanish interests there. Philip's religious policies raised immediate protest, and the persecutions were increased. There were fears that local inquisitions would be replaced by the more severe Spanish Inquisition. The edicts of the Council of Trent were published and approved by the government. The regent council began to move toward the creation of a series of new bishoprics, which would make religious control more effective.

The people of the Netherlands were as fearful of the political as of the religious consequences of Philip's policies, since his methods of enforcing orthodoxy threatened their hard-won political rights and privileges. The powers of the regents tended to infringe those of the estates; the creation of the new bishoprics would do the same. Perhaps the most galling indignity of all was the quartering of a large body of Spanish troops in the Low Countries—a clear sign of Philip's seriousness of purpose.

Resistance and protest came from every level of society. The native nobility, who had been overwhelmingly loyal to Charles, were offended by their exclusion from the government. Several of those who retained official positions refused to enforce the edicts of persecution. Philip's alienation of the nobility formed them into a more cohesive force than they had ever been, and a more hostile one. In 1566 some four hundred nobles presented a petition of grievance to the council of regency. The petition was ignored but the temper of the council was clear enough. One of the courtiers contemptuously referred to the assembled nobles as "beggars." This term rapidly became the proud badge of an opposition party, shortly to become the party of rebellion. On the heels of this protest by the nobles came outbreaks of popular violence that spread from town to town throughout the country. These outbreaks were stridently anti-Catholic: mobs broke into churches, destroyed sacred relics and shrines, and broke statuary and windows.

The Spanish Initiative

In the face of such overt hostility Philip II dismissed the regent, his natural sister, Margaret of Parma, and appointed in her stead the Duke of Alva. Alva was a close adviser to the king, an important Spanish noble, and a general of formidable reputation. Furthermore, he was in complete sympathy with the religio-political policies of the crown. Alva came like a conqueror into a foreign country, at the head of ten thousand Spanish troops, with both orders and intentions to stamp out opposition of every sort. His rule was tantamount to martial law. He ignored and stifled the ancient privileges of the states; he created the Council of Troubles— called the Council of Blood by the people—as his chief instrument of repression. Under its processes hundreds of people were condemned to death and their property confiscated. He seized and publicly executed two of the leading spokesmen of the nobility, the counts of Egmont and Hoorn. Other nobles followed them to the scaffold and still others fled the country, leaving their estates to be confiscated. It is a comment upon the insensitiveness of Spanish rule that these men, who were as offended as Philip himself by the religious excesses of the people and who might easily have been won back to the support of the king, were brutally and needlessly put aside.

The Duke of Alva added to his religious and political repression a ruinous economic policy. Planning to make the people pay for their own persecution, he imposed a series of taxes—a ten per-cent sales tax, a five per-cent tax on the transfer of property, a one per-cent general property tax. These threatened to wipe out the margin of profit on which the industry and commerce of the Netherlands depended. Philip II was willing to sacrifice the prosperity of one of the most productive areas of Europe for the sake of political and religious conformity.

The imposition of these unrealistic taxes pushed protest across the line into open rebellion. Armed resistance seemed suicidal against Alva's forces, so the rebels turned to the sea. A conglomerate naval force was drawn together, made up of fishing boats, merchantmen, and pirate ships, and manned by fugitive Netherlanders both noble and common. Collectively they took the defiant name, "Sea Beggars." They harried Spanish shipping, raided coastal stations, and committed their share of atrocities. But they were the only effective force against Spanish arms in the Low Countries. In 1572 the Sea Beggars suddenly captured the coastal town of Brill. It was of no particular economic or strategic value but this "victory" had important morale value. It represented a counterblow to Spanish oppression and, at a crucial time, stiffened native resistance everywhere. Despite the network of forts that Alva had spread across the land and his threats of reprisal, city after city closed its gates to the Spanish forces; and the Sea Beggars continued to win victories.

As the unequal contest took this turn, the Netherlands found a leader in William of Nassau, Prince of Orange (1533–1584), called William the Silent. As a young man he had been one of the court favorites of the emperor Charles. He had been an important public official, *stathouder* (governor) of several provinces, and a responsible, moderate supporter of royal government. As oppression mounted he became increasingly hostile. He had fled the Council of Blood and lost his Dutch estates. But he had lands and friends outside the Netherlands. Early in the revolt he had raised an expeditionary force in Germany that was beaten by Alva and by its own inadequate resources. Nonetheless, William had become the focal point of Dutch resistance. Shortly after the capture of Brill, William of Orange returned to the Netherlands to become head of the provisional, revolutionary government.

The Duke of Alva had failed in every particular and, in 1573, he was replaced as Philip's regent by Luis de Requeséns, a noble Spaniard as well-intentioned as he was incompetent. His appointment did nothing to change the course of the war. The Spanish still held the country at large and the Beggars held the sea. While the Dutch could not meet the Spanish in battle they could defend their cities behind walls and dikes. Year after year the country districts were ravaged and reprisals taken against the helpless people; and the Spanish position in the Low Countries grew worse with every year. In 1576 the Spanish troops—ill-led, unpaid, and inured to brutality—mutinied. They stormed a number of peaceful towns and finally attacked the great commercial city of Antwerp. In the course of the "Spanish Fury" thousands of people were murdered. Houses, docks, warehouses, and factories were vandalized; the whole city was so ravaged that it never recovered its former prosperity. The sack of Antwerp galvanized the Dutch cause. All seventeen provinces, despite their wide differences and parochial hostilities, united under the Pacification of Ghent, signed November 8, 1576. They seized the powers of government; reversed the persecution edicts; and restored the confiscations of the past twenty years. The Dutch now had not only a common leader in a common cause, but the beginnings of a common government.

The Failure of Spain

To this crisis Philip II sent his illegitimate half-brother, Don Juan of Austria, probably the most renowned military hero of his generation. Four years before he had commanded the Spanish fleet at Lepanto and dealt the crucial blow to Moslem sea power. But his great personal prestige was not enough to cope with the Dutch crisis. He needed Philip's support and this did not come. Don Juan was forced to recognize the Pacification of Ghent and to dismiss the Spanish troops. He was trusted by neither Philip nor the Dutch. The revolt continued. It gained reluctant support from Elizabeth of England and the doubtful advantage of the intervention of the Duke of Anjou, brother to the French king, who hoped for some profit from his help.

In 1578, on the death of Don Juan, Philip appointed as his successor Alexander Farnese, Duke of Parma, and supported him heavily with arms. Parma was an able general and a skillful diplomat who began immediately to repair the Spanish position in the Netherlands. He was able to take advantage of the bitter religious differences that still weakened the common cause of the rebels. The ten southern provinces had remained predominantly Catholic and, with some justification, had come to fear the Protestant intolerance of their northern neighbors more than the politico-religious oppression of their Catholic king. The Duke of Parma induced them to abandon the Pacification of Ghent and form themselves into the Union of Arras (1579). Within a short time the signatory states accepted Philip's rule once more and were confirmed not only in their religion but their traditional political privileges. (These provinces went on to become the Belgium of modern history.) In the face of this disastrous defection and the increased military pressures of Parma, the seven remaining northern provinces formed the Union of Utrecht (1579). Its guiding force was William of Orange. For a time William accepted for the states of the union the nominal headship of the irresponsible Duke of Anjou, hoping thereby to gain active French support. But in 1581 the states declared their independence from Spain and made William of Orange their statholder with the right of succession in his family. Three years later William was assassinated. He had been the soul of Dutch resistance, and the leaderless young state faced the reinvigorated forces and diplomatic skill of the Duke of Parma.

Parma pushed his advantage to the utmost, shrewdly combining military strength and politic clemency. In the year following the death of William of Orange, Parma's forces besieged a whole string of strategic cities along the southern frontier of the new Dutch union—from Bruges and Ghent to Brussels, Mechlin, and Antwerp. The city governments, one after another, appealed desperately for help from the north, but there was little or no help to be had. Then, one after another, the cities fell, until, with the capitulation of Antwerp in the late summer of 1585, the duke was in a position to launch a direct, all-out attack upon the states of the Union of

Utrecht. Moreover, he had consolidated his previous gains. Parma, if not Philip II, had profited from the experience of Alva's terrorism and realized that it had failed as a policy. Therefore he held out to the beleaguered cities promises of restored local privileges, freedom from military occupation, and economic concessions—if they returned to Catholicism and obedience to their king. These were powerful arguments, especially since Catholic sentiment remained strong in most of these cities. Most of all, in city after city, Parma kept his pledges. The people south of the rivers had fought against political rather than religious tyranny, and as the political situation improved under the Duke of Parma, they fell away from the revolt.

The desperate northern provinces in the meantime had turned once more, as a last resort, to the policy that William of Orange had pursued, seeking the support of a foreign power. They appealed again to France, though with all the reluctance that came from centuries of French menace to the Netherlands. After a precious year of negotiations, while Parma's position steadily improved, the French king, Henry III, pressed by his own domestic troubles, refused aid to the Dutch. They turned then to England and the scheming, hard-bargaining Elizabeth. For her intervention and her consequent break with Spain she demanded the control of two access ports in Holland and a voice in the internal affairs of the Dutch. They were in no position to haggle. Elizabeth gave as little aid as possible and encumbered that with the leadership of her perennial favorite, the Earl of Leicester.

With no substantial foreign aid and with the steady advance of Parma the destruction of the revolutionary Dutch state seemed certain. But though her friends had almost ruined her, her archenemy saved her. In 1587–88 Philip II suddenly diverted his attack from the Netherlands to England and France. Philip had reached the end of a long and exasperating negotiation with England. He had failed both in his initial design to marry Elizabeth and in subsequent plots to have her assassinated. His chief pawn was removed when Mary Stuart, the captive Scots queen, was executed by Elizabeth in 1587. On Elizabeth's part, the open breach with Spain was marked by English intervention in the Low Countries. Philip ordered the preparation of his "Invincible Armada," which sailed in the early summer of 1588. Parma was ordered to divide his forces and prepare to have a large body of his troops picked up by the Armada for the expected invasion of England. The troops were ready, but the great Armada was destroyed by the English fleet, its remnants finished off by storms in the

North Sea. Another portion of Parma's troops, under his own command, was diverted to northern France, where complex and lengthy negotiations had finally broken down, involving Philip in a politically costly and unsuccessful intervention in France's religious wars.[1] This diversion of Spanish forces to France cost Philip the initiative that Parma had won for him in the Low Countries.

The Netherlands United

As Spanish pressure lessened, the revolutionary states of the Netherlands transformed themselves into the Dutch Republic under the leadership of the statesman Johan van Oldenbarneveldt (1547–1619), and of Maurice of Nassau (1567–1625), the son of William of Orange and one of the most notable generals of his age. Maurice trained an army that became as formidable on land as the Beggars of his father's generation had been at sea. Gradually he began to win back the borderlands to the south and east, which defined the new republic of the seven northern provinces. The patience and skill of Oldenbarneveldt meanwhile gave the republic its civil form.

The Dutch Republic bore a striking resemblance to the Swiss confederacy; its leading principle was that of "states' rights," the individual provinces retaining a major portion of their sovereignty, the central government governing as little as possible. This stemmed, both in fact and in theory, from the medieval, Burgundian tradition that had first formed the Netherlands: the particular, individual state privilege had been the most overriding issue for which the long war with Philip had been fought; and in victory the separate states maintained their old rights. In theory, the deposition of Philip II by the States-General in 1581 had caused the sovereignty to revert to the individual provinces that had come to form the new republic.

The apparent structural weakness of the Dutch Republic was offset by three factors: the dominant position of the province of Holland, the prestige of the House of Orange, and the wealth of the Netherlands.

Holland was the largest, the most populous, and the most prosperous of the states, and Oldenbarneveldt was the head of Holland's provincial government. In this capacity he represented Holland in the States-General. His grasp of policy and political leadership enabled him to advance the cause of his nation without disservice to his own province.

1. See pp. 640-41; 663-64.

Perhaps an even more important bridge between the individual provinces and the collective state was the House of Orange. William of Orange had been clearly the champion of a national principle; his son continued that championship. While the legal, constitutional authority of this family might be limited to the stathoudership of one or of several of the provinces, the successive members of the house tended to be sovereigns in fact if not in name. In the course of the seventeenth century the family of William the Silent became officially the royal family of the Dutch.

The sound economic base on which the Dutch Republic rested was a final factor in offsetting the constitutional weakness of the state. Since the days of the Sea Beggars the ships of the Netherlands had dominated the trade of the Atlantic coast, and in the early days of the war the Dutch rebels had defeated the Spanish navy. As the rebellion succeeded, this naval supremacy became the source of a substantial income for the fledgling republic. The enterprising Dutch merchants, even at the height of their war for survival with Spain, continued their profitable carrying trade with Spain. In 1586 edicts were issued against "trading with the enemy," but the trade continued, nonetheless. Much more important, the prolonged state of war with Spain made Spanish shipping fair game until the middle of the seventeenth century, and the Dutch were able to make serious inroads upon the overseas trade with the New World and the Orient, which before had been so nearly a Spanish-Portuguese monopoly. In 1602 this wholesale depredation was organized by the formation of the Dutch East India Company, one of the most successful merchant corporations of all time.

The war on land as well as at sea was turned eventually to the economic advantage of the Dutch. The most repeatedly devastated region of the Netherlands was the strip of territory south of the great rivers on the southern boundary of the republic; and this was precisely the region in which the wealth of the Netherlands had previously been concentrated. Such great centers as Antwerp and Bruges were conquered and reconquered, sacked, besieged, and blockaded until their prosperity was ruined. Furthermore, as these regions were reclaimed by Spain and by Catholicism they rapidly lost their Calvinist minority, with serious economic consequences. While the great majority of the people in the southern provinces were Catholic, a significant number of the urban middle class were Calvinist. When they migrated to the states and cities of the north they took with them their skills, their economic connections, and their capital. Thus, on the eve of the seventeenth century the Dutch Republic was ready for its golden age of wealth and culture.

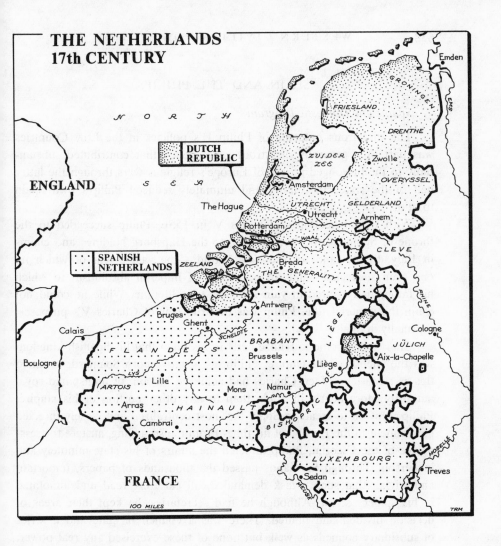

THE NETHERLANDS
17th CENTURY

DUTCH
REPUBLIC

SPANISH
NETHERLANDS

ENGLAND

FRANCE

100 MILES

NORTH SEA

Emden

GRONINGEN

FRIESLAND

DRENTHE

ZUIDER ZEE

Zwolle

OVERYSSEL

Amsterdam

The Hague

UTRECHT

GELDERLAND

Rotterdam

Utrecht

Arnhem

WAAL

CLEVE

ZEELAND

Breda

THE GENERALITY

RHINE

Antwerp

Bruges

Ghent

SCHELDTE

BRABANT

LIÈGE

Cologne

JÜLICH

Calais

FLANDERS

Brussels

Liège

Aix-la-Chapelle

Boulogne

LYS

Lille

ARTOIS

Mons

Namur

BISHOPRIC OF LIÈGE

Arras

HAINAULT

Cambrai

MOSELLE

LUXEMBOURG

Treves

Sedan

MEUSE

TRM

By 1590 Spain had tacitly recognized the loss of the Dutch provinces. The Duke of Parma was followed by a series of ineffectual dynasts neither able nor willing to carry on a losing war. Philip II's grand design for a Spanish-Catholic hegemony of Europe was falling apart even before his death in 1598. In 1609, after lengthy negotiation, peace was gained on the basis of the Twelve Years' Truce. This represented, for all practical purposes, the recognition of Dutch independence. The Dutch used the next forty years of peace to confirm their economic leadership of Europe. In 1648, at the general peace settlement of Westphalia following the Thirty Years' War, Spain, by that time reduced to a hopelessly second-rate power, finally granted formal independence to the Dutch.[2]

2. See p. 685.

SPAIN AND THE PHILIPS

Spain: The Domestic Program

The disastrous outcome of Philip II's policies in the Low Countries was part of a generally disastrous royal policy that contributed substantially to the prolonged misery of Europe's religious wars through the latter half of the sixteenth century and ultimately reduced Philip's own Spain to ruin.

With the abdication of Charles V in 1556, Philip succeeded to the throne of Spain, to the Netherlands, to the Hapsburg holdings and claims in Italy, to the lands of the New World[3]—the vast extent of which no one even suspected—and to the dream of imperial absolutism to which his father had aspired in vain for most of a lifetime. While he could not claim the imperial title, Philip was the true heir of Charles V's purposes, especially in Spain.

Charles had come to realize early in his reign that his Spanish kingdom was the anchor of his empire. Philip, as a native-born Spaniard, assumed this as a matter of fact. Charles had achieved his aim of undisputed royal authority more nearly in Spain than in any other portion of his empire. Philip went on to create in Spain the most centralized and closely directed government in the Europe of his time. From the sprawling, austere fortress-palace of the Escorial, Philip directed the affairs of his state minutely and in person. Through his hands passed the thousands of papers, important and trivial, that such a task demanded, all carefully read and annotated in his spidery script. Although he had secretaries, he kept their areas of decision divided and limited. There was a council of state and a series of subsidiary councils as well, but none of these exercised any real power. They were merely extensions of Philip's personal authority. He drew his officials from the lower nobility and carefully limited what powers were left to the great magnates.

The Spanish church was completely integrated with this system of government. This was a Spanish tradition reaching back into the long history of the Crusades, and more immediately to the policies of Ferdinand and Isabella and of Charles V. Philip II controlled every important ecclesiastical appointment in Spain; papal bulls were invalid in Spain without his approval, and he permitted no appeals to Rome from Spanish ecclesi-

3. See p. 724ff.

astical courts. At times he unceremoniously confiscated clerical wealth. And all this aroused scarcely a dissenting murmur from the papacy. The popes of the Counter Reformation were markedly different from their ambitious predecessors, and their own ambitions took a different form. On the one hand, they tended to consciously withdraw from active temporal and political concerns; on the other hand, they were so wholeheartedly concerned with reform and the church's battle against heresy that they tended to accept the championship of Philip II, in spite of the risk that his growing political influence represented.

On Philip's part, his control of the Spanish church derived from his notion of the sanctity of royal absolutism rather than from any opposition to the church itself. Indeed, he was a fanatic Catholic, spending long hours in prayer and agonizing penance. He unhesitatingly supported the doctrinal reforms of the Council of Trent and was personally concerned about further reform of the church in Spain. Nothing short of complete uniformity of belief and practice would satisfy him. It is for this reason that Philip encouraged the extension of the Spanish Inquisition.

This institution was modeled upon the Papal Inquisition of the High Middle Ages and dedicated, like its model, to the eradication of heresy. It had been created by Ferdinand and Isabella as an instrument for the conversion of the Spanish Moors and Jews and had been, from the beginning, as much a political as a religious agency. Under Philip it was more centralized, efficient, and powerful than ever before. Through the Inquisition Philip continued the assault upon the Jews and the Moriscos, which resulted finally in their being driven out of Spain entirely. But the Inquisition dealt not only with such overt forms of religious deviation as these. Every whisper of heresy reached it; and in the atmosphere of Counter Reformation Spain the definition of heresy was infinitely extended. Every intellectual was suspect. Every new idea had to be carefully tested, whether it pertained directly to spiritual matters or not. Nor were churchmen, even of the highest rank, exempt from inquisitorial questioning. Even Ignatius Loyola was called before it. The records of the Inquisition contain the name and trial record of virtually every literate and creative Spaniard of the period. The meager beginnings of Spanish Protestantism were crushed out along with every other deviation from Catholic purity. The goal of religious uniformity was reached—but at the cost of a closely circumscribed intellectual conformity that robbed Spain of some of her richest talent and set the tone of the Spanish "golden age."

It was the ambition of Philip II to extend throughout his dominions, throughout Europe, and even the world, the same royal absolutism and religious uniformity that he achieved so strikingly in Spain; and at any cost. The stubborn resistance of the Dutch was, as we have seen, a major blow to Philip's larger designs. Not only was it a shocking example of rebellion in his own inherited lands, but in many ways it was the key to the general failure of Philip's policies for the preservation of a Catholic Europe. For, by their revolt, Philip was not only denied the support of the strategic Low Countries, but was forced to commit troops and money to the war there instead of elsewhere.

Philip's French Policy

Philip's failure in the Netherlands was intimately connected with the failure of his French policy. The Treaty of Cateau-Cambrésis (1559), by which Philip concluded the last of his father's wars with France, seemed to presage a new era of good feeling. The wars of the Reformation in Germany and the Turkish menace on the eastern frontier of Europe had split the Hapsburg Empire and relieved the pressure that had caused half a century of French anxiety. Charles V had already formalized this split by the division of his lands. Thus, at long last, France drew close to Spain. Under the terms of the treaty the recently widowed Philip was married by proxy to the child princess Elizabeth of Valois, and Philip and Henry II agreed to adopt a joint policy of opposition to Protestantism and heresy in their lands. In the same year Henry II was killed in a jousting accident, leaving his foreign queen, Catherine de Médicis (1519–1589), to rule for his minor sons. This was the signal for the outbreak of bitter religious hostilities, which assumed first the proportions of a civil war, then of a war that threatened to involve most of Europe.

Philip II was constrained to support the French radical Catholic party headed by the powerful ducal family of Guise. The need for this support became more urgent as the Huguenot (Protestant) party gained the upper hand early in the war and an entente threatened between the French Huguenots and the Calvinist rebels of the Netherlands.[4] We have already seen how desperately William of Orange worked for such an arrangement. Furthermore, the active intervention of England was a distinct possibility and Philip, as the self-appointed leader of European Catholicism, saw a giant Protestant alliance beginning to form. This became more than a threat when the titular leader of the Huguenots, Henry of Navarre, was married to a sister of the French king, Charles IX, in August of 1572.

4. See p. 633.

At best this was a move of reconciliation; at worst it was the first step toward a Protestant succession in France. The marriage festivities signaled the famous St. Bartholomew's Day Massacre, in which some three thousand Protestants were slaughtered in Paris and thousands more throughout France. Most of the Huguenot leaders were killed. The pope and Philip II were overjoyed; but the Catholic rejoicing was premature, for the senseless brutality of St. Bartholomew's Day, committed in the name of fanaticism and narrow partisanship, transformed the war of religion into a full-scale civil war for the control of France.

Philip II watched the fluctuating progress of that war. In 1584 the long dreaded specter of a Protestant succession rose once more. The Valois line was running out and it became apparent that Henry of Navarre—now the avowedly Protestant leader of the Huguenots—would succeed to the throne. Philip II intervened on behalf of the Catholic League. We have already noted what a decisive effect this intervention had in weakening the Spanish position in the Low Countries. Moreover, the intervention of a foreign power in the affairs of France, added to the arrogance of the Catholic leaders and the war-weariness of the French people, turned the tide. After a nominal submission to Catholicism, Henry of Navarre was hailed as Henry IV. Philip II, as insensitive to the national temper of the French as he was to that of the Dutch, persisted in championing what was a lost cause in France, now clearly *his* cause rather than that of any French party. The French Catholic League collapsed and Philip had lost another round in his battle to maintain a Spanish-Hapsburg-Catholic hegemony of Europe.

The Failure against England

The same grand design that led Philip II to his loss of the Low Countries and his diplomatic and military failure in France also involved England. The thread of his English policy ran back to Mary, the Catholic daughter of Catherine of Aragon, whom Henry VIII had divorced with such momentous consequences. In the midst of his last war with France, in 1554, Charles V had arranged a marriage between his son Philip and Mary Tudor of England. Mary's eagerness to restore her religion in England made her the tool of Hapsburg power politics. But the reluctant and inglorious role that England played in the war against France made it clear that military alliance would not bring England into Charles' imperial net. Mary's barrenness killed the hope of a Hapsburg dynastic succession in England.

When Catholic Mary was succeeded by Protestant Elizabeth, the probability of another strongly Protestant power in northern Europe arose. This was as much the hope of the continental Protestants as it was the dread of Philip II. And Elizabeth played on both the hope and the dread. Her chief aim was to restore the order and prosperity of her nation and the religious issue was secondary. Thus, she gave secret aid to the continental Protestants, particularly the Dutch, but refused to support them openly and so break with Spain. At the same time she remained cordial to Philip and even encouraged a marriage proposal from him.

In many ways the key to Elizabeth's foreign relations was her cousin Mary Stuart, Queen of Scots. Mary was descended from the Scots marriage of Henry VIII's sister. But the diplomatic purpose behind that marriage had failed to materialize and, in the course of the sixteenth century, Scotland renewed more strongly than ever its medieval alliance with France. A result of that alliance was the marriage of the princess Mary with the son of Henry II of France who became Francis II. This connection with France was even more significant because, through her mother, Mary was closely connected with the Guise family in France. The imminent end of the Tudor dynasty with Elizabeth made Mary as important to England as she was to France, and as much so to Philip of Spain. While Mary was an ardent Catholic, the possibility of her uniting the claims of Scotland, England, and France in her person or heirs held a serious menace to Philip's political plans for, in such an event, he might face a rejuvenated and strengthened France in a renewal of the French-Hapsburg duel. Thus Philip's religious and political programs came into serious conflict—a situation of which Elizabeth was quick to take advantage. Francis II died in 1560 and Mary returned to Scotland. Six years later she was forced to flee Scotland, discredited by her personal behavior and pursued by the thunderings of John Knox. She came to England and the "protection" of her cousin Elizabeth.

At this point the diplomatic balance shifted in Philip's favor. There was no longer any danger that Mary would become the cornerstone of a political alliance among France, England, and Scotland directed against Hapsburg interests. But there was a chance that Mary might replace or succeed Elizabeth and restore Catholicism to England—a coup for Philip both on political and religious grounds. Thus Mary Stuart became the center of an intricate web of intrigue, every strand of which led back to Madrid. Time after time Elizabeth was endangered. Furthermore, in 1585 Philip openly allied himself with the Catholic-Guise party in France. Elizabeth could no longer equivocate; if Philip succeeded in paralyzing

France, the struggling Dutch Republic would be next, and then Elizabeth's own England. She intervened on the continent and then, in 1587, ordered the execution of Mary Stuart. Philip's alternatives had been systematically reduced until, if he wanted England, he would have to invade it. He prepared his vast Armada, one hundred thirty ships and twenty-four thousand men, to take the stubborn island. The preparations were slow, careful, and expensive, and harried by damaging English raids. Finally, in July of 1588 the Armada sailed, only to be destroyed in one of the great, dramatic reversals of European history. The time that Elizabeth's diplomacy had won had been well spent in bolstering England's strength. The defeat of the Armada marked the end of Spain as a major sea power. Although the Anglo-Spanish war continued until 1604, it was largely in the form of individual sea engagements—the famous English Sea Dogs preying on the almost defenseless Spanish shipping, and growing rich on the loot from the New World.

The Decline of Philip's Spain

Philip had set out to win the supremacy of Europe—and he had failed. In the revolt of the Dutch he lost one of the most prosperous parts of his inheritance; his attempt upon England had ended in disaster; his French policy had been completely repudiated and, under Henry IV, France was preparing to assume the place in Europe's affairs Philip had tried for in vain. His Catholic militancy had everywhere confirmed rather than reversed the advances of Protestantism. The extravagance of his ambitions had robbed him even of the victories he might have had.

By the middle of his reign the Counter Reformation papacy had come to dread the consequences of his policy and had pulled back its support. It was the same fear of secular domination that had, time and again in the reign of Charles V, placed the pope on the side of France. Philip had joined Venice and the papacy in the great crusading push against the Turks in the Mediterranean as Islam seemed once more on the march under Selim II (*1566–1574*). Philip's half-brother, Don Juan, in command of a fleet of more than two hundred ships, crushed almost the entire Turkish navy in the Battle of Lepanto (October 7, 1571). It was one of the great, decisive victories of modern war. But Philip's forces, money, and energy were too widely dispersed for him to take advantage of the victory. It is ironic that he should have failed in this, for the most deep-seated tradition of his nation was the tradition of the crusade. With one concerted blow Philip might have leveled the Ottoman Empire and destroyed the political center of Islam. But he could not strike the blow.

In 1578, with the death of King Sebastian of Portugal, Philip claimed that kingdom. But he was never really able to rule it and its cost was greater than its profit to Spain. By the middle of the next century it had shaken off the claims of Philip's heirs.

In the long run, Philip II's greatest mistake was probably his failure to develop a sound economic program to support his expensive political ambitions. He was unable to see that in his age, as never before, wars were won, allies gained, and policies implemented by money; and even more important, that sound money flowed from a sound domestic economy. Nor was he alone among his fellow monarchs in this. Europe as a whole was still a generation away from the general acceptance of the need for a national economic policy. But in other countries the growth and activity of private business and financial interests had been sufficient to lay the foundations of national prosperity. This was not the case in Spain, which had never been a rich country and which was still predominantly agricultural rather than commercial.

In the course of Philip's reign a series of crises undermined even the basic agricultural order. Sheep-raising and the consequent enclosure of land encroached on farming with the same unfortunate results that had been earlier evident in England. But Spain lacked the means that England had found to adjust to this change. As Spanish agriculture was pushed to the wall, grain production fell off to such an extent that grain became the most crucial item of Spanish import. In the early 1570's Dutch ships practically closed the north Atlantic coast to Spanish shipping. The bulk of Spain's imported grain came from the Baltic to the Low Countries and was shipped from there in Dutch vessels. Thus Spain was forced to depend upon the commerce of her enemy, forced to pay exorbitant prices, and to pay them in silver since she was the victim of an unfavorable balance of trade. In this way large amounts of silver from the New World passed unproductively through Spanish hands and into the European money market.

This ruinous tendency could not be reversed, for Spain had virtually no economic middle class to challenge foreign enterprise. Religious fanaticism systematically ruined the Moriscos and the Jews, who were economically the most productive minorities in Spain.. Heavy taxes, forced loans, royal oppression, and the deterioration of the Near Eastern trade just as systematically ruined the prosperity of Spain's Mediterranean cities that had begun to flourish in the High Middle Ages. Even the sheep-raising, which might have been the basis for national recovery, was largely concentrated in the hands of the economically sterile nobility.

From such a shaky foundation Philip II had launched his great political and religious crusade and, as that crusade failed year after year, its economic burden bore down upon Philip's own impoverished nation. Spain, Italy, and the Mediterranean could no longer carry even the part of that burden that they had under Charles V. The Netherlands, upon which Charles had always been able to depend, were in successful revolt from Philip; the German-Austrian lands, for what little support they might have given, were in other hands, involved in other troubles. Furthermore, Philip had inherited from Charles V a crushing imperial debt of seventy million ducats (some two billion dollars in current values). He ignored it and set out to complete his father's work with even more costly wars and policies.

The silver and gold from the New World, which had begun to flow into Spain in the middle years of Charles' reign, became a glittering flood under Philip. This created the impression of boundless wealth, in Europe as well as in Spain. In reality it was the final curse of Philip's economy. A large portion of it went to the Dutch in trade and to the Dutch, English, and French in piracy. Another large portion went to the great private banking houses that held the crown debts of Spain. But the interest on these debts increased at such an astronomic rate that Philip could never keep up with them. The remaining wealth of the New World, which Philip jealously restricted to Spain, flooded the Spanish economy to produce the chronic inflation that dealt a final blow to the development of a sound domestic economy. When Philip died in 1598 he left to his heirs not only the shambles of his foreign policy, but a hopelessly bankrupt nation.

Philip II was an able, dedicated, and honest king. But he was completely blind to the powerful forces at work in the new Europe of his time. Yet the failure of his policies, so obvious to us today, was singularly unapparent to his contemporaries, most of all to his royal successors in Spain. His very prestige commended Philip's program to his successors; and Philip III (*1598–1621*) and Philip IV (*1621–1665*) continued to expend Spain's dwindling energies upon the same policies that had cost Philip II so dearly.

They involved Spain in the Thirty Years' War largely because of Hapsburg family interests and religious concerns. As that war broadened into a general European war, Spain came into conflict with the rising

Above: PETER PAUL RUBENS. *The Triumphal Entry of Henry IV into Paris.* c. 1600.
Right: Queen Elizabeth I.

OPPOSITE
Above: Workshop of Leone Leoni. *Philip II of Spain.*
Below: Workshop of François Clouet. *Henry II, King of France.* 16th century.

power of France. On the old battlegrounds of northern Italy and the Spanish Netherlands, French and Spanish forces met once more. But this time it was no contest of equals. A greatly weakened Spain faced the France of Cardinal Richelieu, perhaps the greatest diplomatist produced by his nation, and the armies of France, as well-provisioned, trained, and led as any in Europe. In 1643 the fortress of Rocroi in the Spanish Netherlands was taken and the Spanish army that held it defeated in one of the most spectacular and decisive battles of the Thirty Years' War. With this French victory the last shred of Spanish military prestige disappeared. In an even more important sense Spain had already been by-passed by France and most of the rest of Europe. The religious and imperial motives that had prompted the policies of Charles V and Philip II had given way to the "modern" dynastic and political considerations which the Peace of Westphalia revealed. Spain was virtually isolated in the new Europe to which she really did not belong and in the face of a dangerous war with France. In 1658 a series of campaigns in the Spanish Netherlands by the great French general Turenne ended Spanish resistance. Peace negotiations began, which culminated in the Peace of the Pyrenees (1659).

THE ENGLAND OF ELIZABETH THE GREAT

The Elizabethan Domestic Settlement

We have already seen something of England's involvement in the tangled affairs of the continent in this period. Unlike Philip II of Spain, whose pursuit of his European policy overrode his domestic concerns, Elizabeth subordinated foreign affairs to the internal affairs of her state. This was as much a matter of necessity as of choice. In the five years of her predecessor's reign, England had been brought to the brink of ruin. Mary's participation in Philip II's war against France had been a costly failure, in material terms and in the loss of national prestige. The government was almost bankrupt, the tempo of the national economy much slowed. Most demoralizing of all was the profound religious strife that divided the nation.

For ten years England had been torn by religious discord, first under Protestant Edward, then under Catholic Mary; and each had demonstrated the divisive effect of religious extremism. The lesson was not lost upon the new queen, who had survived both previous reigns. Elizabeth was committed to being a Protestant; her very legitimacy and consequently her claim to the throne rested upon this. But while she was a Protestant by necessity, she was a politician by choice. She realized that the great majority of her people were neither fanatic Protestants nor fanatic Catholics, and that this majority desired religious peace and public confidence more than doctrinal purity of either stamp. Thus Elizabeth conceived her religious policies in essentially political and social rather than religious terms, and her so-called religious settlement was devised accordingly.

Her church was to be first of all a national church; to this end she adhered to the partnership her father had so solidly established with Parliament. In the first year of her reign, Parliament enacted the Act of Supremacy and the Act of Uniformity. The Act of Supremacy repealed the Catholic legislation of Mary, broke the tie with Rome once more, and named Elizabeth "the only supreme governor of this realm, as well in all spiritual or ecclesiastical things or causes, as temporal." The Act of Uniformity reversed the radical Protestantism of Edward's reign, authorized the second Book of Common Prayer—significantly revised in the direction of moderation—and established a religious norm for all services and beliefs. These acts were followed by the Thirty-Nine Articles, which defined the fundamental beliefs of the English church. They were a modification of Cranmer's earlier Forty-Two Articles and the modifications were designed to blur rather than emphasize the sharp and irritating distinctions between Catholic and Protestant. Elizabeth was in the process of creating a church that would not rest upon distinctions but upon unanimity, one which loyal Englishmen of varying shades of religious opinion might find acceptable. And the great majority of the English people followed her. Only the most extreme religious partisans were excluded from the Elizabethan church.

The general support of Elizabeth's religious settlement stemmed as much from national as from religious motives. The disasters of Mary's Catholic reign had made the average Englishman identify the interest of his nation with hostility to Spain and to Roman Catholicism; the shape of European affairs in the opening years of Elizabeth's reign gave him little reason to alter his judgment. Philip II of Spain was following closely the Hapsburg policies of his father, which meant an inherited enmity toward England. Philip's great crusade for a Spanish-Catholic domination of Europe had already begun.

Closer to home, Mary Stuart, the Scots queen, had been married to the young King Francis II of France, and this dynastic union freshened the long-standing alliance between France and Scotland, to England's peril. Mary Stuart was descended from the collateral Tudor line of Henry VIII's sister; she was a Catholic and, in the eyes of Catholic Europe she, rather than the Protestant and "illegitimate" Elizabeth, was the proper queen of England. Mary listed among her titles "Queen of England." Thus England and Elizabeth were directly involved in the Hapsburg-Valois rivalry which had kept Europe in turmoil for almost half a century. It became the policy of Elizabeth to play these dynastic powers against each other. The dangerous game began almost immediately.

Elizabeth's first opportunity came with the course taken by the Scottish Reformation. In Scotland, as in Germany, the Reformation took a strong, popular-nationalistic turn, which focused its hostility upon the French attachments of the Scottish crown. One of its most outspoken leaders for a generation had been John Knox, who had led revolts, endured prison, the slave-galleys of the French fleet, and finally exile—in Calvin's Geneva. There Knox found the embodiment of the reform toward which he had been moving; when he returned to Scotland in 1559 he came as the prophet of Scots Calvinism, which was to be known as the Presbyterian movement. Knox was a militant prophet and under his lash the Scots rebelled against the Catholic-French regents of their absent queen. Elizabeth of England supported this popular rebellion—though it offended her royalist sensibilities and might well drive Catholic France and Catholic Spain into alliance against her. But Elizabeth was willing to take the latter risk in the hope of destroying the Franco-Scottish alliance that threatened her more immediately. It was a chance well taken. In the next year (1560) Francis II died and Mary Stuart returned to her hostile and suspicious Scots. The Franco-Scottish alliance had collapsed and France was already deeply involved in the prolonged agony of the Wars of Religion. As the fortunes of France fell, the balance of continental power shifted to Spain, and Elizabeth turned to the menace from this quarter.

The Menace of Spain

As long as there had been a serious threat that Mary Stuart might become the means for an alliance of France with Scotland and England, Elizabeth had had little to fear from Philip II, for he was more clearly menaced by the political danger in such a union than by the Protestantism of Elizabeth's England. Indeed, he had proposed an entente with England in the form of a marriage alliance with Elizabeth; she tactfully demurred. But by 1568 the situation had changed radically. With the political danger of France mitigated, Philip could turn his full attention to his program for the Catholic reconquest of Europe. At this very time, and with genuine reluctance, Elizabeth was becoming the leading figure in European Protestant politics. She had given support to the Protestants in Scotland, in France, and to Philip's rebellious subjects in the Low Countries. In each case she had been compelled by political rather than religious motives; she was striking at the political capabilities of France and Spain. It was almost incidental that this was done through the support of dissenting Protestant groups. Still Elizabeth did not want open war with Spain, knowing that England was not prepared for the costs and risks of such a war. For this reason she shrank from accepting the aggressive leadership of European Protestantism that was urged on her by the French Huguenot leaders, by William of Orange, and by many of her own counselors. She much preferred the wiles of diplomacy. For thirty years she trimmed her policies to the changing pattern of events on the continent—the war of factions at the French court, the progress of the Dutch revolt, the shifting relations of the German states. Through this whole time her foreign policy was conspicuously inconsistent with everything but the welfare of England. But by 1585 the exigencies of continental politics forced Elizabeth to take direct action.

She openly intervened in the Dutch revolt, openly challenged Philip II of Spain, and at long last publicly identified herself with revolutionary Protestantism. In the meantime, the anti-Catholic and anti-Spanish sentiment of her nation had grown to fanatic proportions. The English people felt a close kinship with the Huguenots of France and the Dutch Calvinists. The valiancy of their struggle and the reports of Catholic atrocities sharpened English hatred of Spain and Spanish-flavored Catholicism.

This popular hatred and suspicion came to bear upon the figure of Mary Stuart, Elizabeth's guest-captive. Long before, in 1568, Mary had been forced to flee Scotland and seek Elizabeth's protection. While Mary no longer had any actual political power, she was still a potent threat to Elizabeth because of her Catholic claim to the English throne. While Elizabeth had pursued her complex "cold war" on the continent, Mary had become the center of a series of Catholic-Spanish plots in England, directed toward the assassination of Elizabeth and the succession of Mary with the support of a Spanish invasion. Each of these plots was unraveled and frustrated by the tireless vigilance of Sir Francis Walsingham, the queen's somber, dedicated, Protestant secretary.

In 1586 the most daring of these plots was revealed. It was clearly traced to Philip II and Mary Stuart was undeniably implicated in it. Elizabeth ordered her execution, which took place early in the following year.

The removal of Mary Stuart, plus Elizabeth's open hostility to Spain on the continent, brought Philip II into war with England. As long as England supported the Dutch rebels and the French Huguenots, Philip's entire European program was threatened. The hope of a Catholic succession in England had died with Mary Stuart. In the spring of 1588 the Armada sailed from Spain to its destruction in the Channel and the North Sea. The English defeat of the Armada was the vindication of Elizabeth's foreign policy. For thirty years she had forestalled a shooting war. She had kept her enemies divided, her friends alive, and frustrated myriad domestic plots. She had bought the precious time her people needed to prosper and recover.

In conjunction with her foreign policy, Elizabeth had encouraged the privateering enterprise of English seamen, largely at the expense of Spanish and Portuguese shipping. Indeed, the war with Philip had begun on the Spanish Main and along the coast of Africa long before the Armada sailed. Such men as Sir John Hawkins, Sir Martin Frobisher, and Sir Francis Drake, as early as the 1560's, had begun to run trade into the closed Spanish colonies of the New World and to make highly profitable raids on the Spanish treasure fleets. In 1577 a small fleet under Drake sailed along the coast of Central and South America, through the Straits of Magellan and up the western coast of the New World to California, plundering Spanish forts all along the way. As escape closed behind him Drake, with his customary daring, struck out across the Pacific and, after three years, returned to England from around the world, his lone remaining ship loaded with treasure and with the pride of his nation. Such exploits virtually founded the myth of English seamanship. At the same time they contributed mightily to the growing English prosperity. It was the confidence and experience of these Elizabethan "sea dogs" that gave England her victory over the Armada.

The Founding of English Prosperity

In the years following 1588 the general European conflict and the maritime war against Spain flowed together. Each year an English fleet put to sea to harass Spanish trade and bring home the profits of legal piracy. In 1591 Sir Richard Grenville, commanding the *Revenge*, held off the entire Spanish fleet in the Azores Islands. In 1596 Essex and Raleigh led a plundering expedition against the Spanish port of Cadiz, burning the city and destroying the fleet anchored there. These men and the trade they carried and preyed upon were the products of a new economic age. The wealth of western Europe, its stores of precious metals, its centers of trade and production, had begun to shift to the shores of the north Atlantic, away from the Mediterranean, which had been the center of European economic life since classical times. This shift had been taking place over several centuries until, by the seventeenth century, the English found themselves no longer located at the outer edge of the world but very near its center.

England's prosperity and the daring achievements of her mariners against a powerful enemy gave Englishmen a new sense of national destiny, fostered and supported by Elizabeth's policies. In addition to encouraging the privateering of her sea dogs, she developed a systematic maritime policy: she encouraged ship-building, sea-borne trade, and large-scale fishing. The privileges of the foreign merchants—so conspicuous in the economic life of England a half century before—were withdrawn to allow greater opportunities for English merchants. Elizabeth followed up the hesitant beginnings that her father and grandfather had made in exploration. It was in Elizabeth's reign that the foundations of the British Empire were laid. Largely at the insistence of her merchants, Elizabeth began to couple exploration with the granting of monopolies and the chartering of companies, principles already established in England's dealings in the continental wool trade. She encouraged the Moscovy Company, which had been founded shortly before the beginning of her reign, and the Eastland Company, founded somewhat later, both designed to compete with the Baltic trade of the weakened Hanseatic League. Other such companies were established to trade with the Near East and, in 1600, the British East India Company was founded, to become, like the Dutch East India Company, one of the most successful commercial enterprises in the world.

The burgeoning of English foreign commerce was only partly due to the general shift of center in the European economy. Equally significant was the expansion of England's domestic economy. By the time of the Armada this had reached new heights, with direct encouragement from the crown. Backed by public confidence and the unity born of the overwhelming threat from Spain, Elizabeth was able to carry through sweeping reforms in English economic life. She drastically overhauled the coinage system; she devised fairly successful methods for dealing with unemployment and pauperism; and she encouraged the development of domestic industry by granting monopolies. The execution of these reforms was aided by underlying economic trends both in England and on the continent. For example, the temporary hardships caused by the coinage reform were partially offset by an unprecedented influx into England of precious metals acquired by the capture of Spanish treasure ships and by trade. The evils of the enclosure movement—so severely felt during the three preceding reigns—began to be offset by the growth of English industry and the consequent absorption of the labor force displaced by enclosure. Moreover, the general rise in population and the growth of cities increased the demand for food, and this, in turn, encouraged the return of a considerable amount of acreage to crop production.

A direct boost to the development of English industry came from the effects of the religious wars on the old centers of economic activity in France and the Low Countries. On the urging of her counselors, Elizabeth invited thousands of skilled craftsmen, particularly in the cloth industry, who had been uprooted by these wars to immigrate to England, where they contributed substantially to the development of industry. Simultaneously, of course, England benefited from the crippling of trade and manufacture in the continental regions, such as Flanders, which had become battle grounds. Even the threat of being drawn into the continental wars herself proved a positive stimulus to England's economic growth, for it prompted a movement toward national self-sufficiency. Many new "defense industries" were thus established: the mining of coal and ore, factories for arms and naval stores, cannon foundries, and gunpowder mills. The men who founded these industries and invested in the growing maritime trade dealt the final blow to the restrictions imposed on economic development by the medieval guilds. Elizabethan England acquired the capitalistic structure of finance, business, industry, and commerce that had already ushered in the modern age on the continent.

In the closing decades of Elizabeth's long reign, England enjoyed a prosperity it had never known before. The merchants and gentry who had been the loyal supporters of the Tudor dynasty for a century were wealthy, comfortable, and confident. The blessings of material well-being had filtered down even to the lowest classes of the realm. Houses, furniture, clothing, and ornament of greater charm and convenience were to be seen everywhere. The queen and her thronging court were the mirror of ever more extravagant fashions. Englishmen of every degree felt a livened sense of national destiny and, furthermore, a destiny being fulfilled before their eyes. The queen was the living symbol of her nation—of its greatness, its prosperity, and its purpose. The dangers and uncertainties that clouded the early years of her reign had been dispelled. England's golden age was at hand—one of the most magnificent of European culture periods. Yet one major domestic issue, unresolved questions that held over from the religious settlement, continued to raise problems for Elizabeth.

The Breakdown of the Religious Settlement

The problem of the English Catholic minority, which held over from the reign of Mary and which had seemed so threatening in the early days of Elizabeth's reign, had been largely resolved. Many of the most intractable Catholics had chosen to leave for the continent, where they lived in exile communities and longed and plotted for the day when both they and their faith might be triumphantly returned home. Most of the English moderate Catholics remained in England and conformed, however reluctantly, to the religious law of the land. Their compromise was encouraged by their patriotism and by the comparative leniency with which Elizabeth's religious program was enforced.

Yet a small and bitter group of militant Catholics remained. They endured the spite and suspicion of their neighbors. They paid their recusant fines and taxes, harbored foreign priests, and risked their lives and fortunes to practice their religion. And many of them lent their support to the series of plots against the queen's life, plots to "raise the countryside" to support a Spanish invasion, and conspiracies with the Catholic Irish to open a "back door" to Spain. This clandestine political activity of the discredited Catholic party further embittered the English anti-Catholic, anti-Spanish temper, for Catholicism, foreign or domestic, was hopelessly identified with Spain, the great national enemy. Moreover, the door to religious compromise had been finally closed by the reformed papacy. In 1570 a bull of condemnation had been published declaring Elizabeth deposed and her subjects freed from obedience to her. Under such circumstances, the popular English reaction was to consider the old Catholic faith tantamount to treason. In 1571 Parliament declared it treasonable to hold that Elizabeth was not the rightful sovereign. The property of Catholics who had fled the country was confiscated. As the national temper grew and the Catholic-Spanish menace to England became more pressing, the laws against Catholics became more stringent. In spite of the best efforts of the Counter Reformation—perhaps because of them—England was and remained staunchly Protestant.

The extreme Protestants had disapproved of the moderation of Elizabeth's official religion as thoroughly as the extreme Catholics. But, again, all but the most intractable of them had accepted the queen's settlement and submerged their private views for the sake of the war effort and national unity. Yet, those private views remained and were reinforced. The Protestants who had fled the Catholic revival of Queen Mary (the so-called Marian exiles) had come in contact with the severe and vigorous forms of continental Calvinism. A great many of these exiles found a source of strength and purpose in the Calvinist doctrines, and with their return after Elizabeth's accession they introduced these new religious views into England. There was considerable popular support for them. Much in the religious background of the English Reformation was congenial to Calvinism, and it was continually reinforced by outside influences. There was almost no barrier to the passage of religious ideas from Scotland into England, and the Scottish Reformed Presbyterian movement evoked broad popular sympathy. English sentiment was also sympathetic to the reform movements of the continent. The steady stream of Dutch and Huguenot refugees added to the Calvinist flavor of English Protestantism. Furthermore, Calvinist ideas flowed freely into England with the propaganda and counter propaganda of war and diplomacy. Just as it was impossible to separate hostility to Spain from hostility to Catholicism, so it was difficult to separate the financial and military support given to the religious parties in France and the Low Countries from support of the ideas and beliefs for which they fought.

The effect of these various strong Protestant-Calvinist influences was to "unsettle" the Elizabethan settlement. From early in Elizabeth's reign there had been grumblings about such "Romish" vestiges as clerical vestments, symbolism, and ritual. There was opposition to the ideas of uniformity of service and episcopal control. There were bitter controversies over freedom of conscience, congregational sovereignty, the use of the Prayer Book, Bible reading, and a score of other particular issues. And against this sort of separatist tendency the state and the established church began to move with greater severity. This hostility tended to crystalize a number of groups, each with its own peculiar insistence, upon this or that practice at odds with official usage. Those who advocated congregational independence or "separation" from episcopal domination were called Separatists. They differed in little but name from another faction, the Presbyterians. A somewhat more radical group holding the same general principles was founded by Robert Browne—the Brownists. Their program opposed not only episcopal control of the church but tended to oppose the time-honored principle of the crown's control of religion. There were other factions and splinter-groups that held still more radical views on the sovereignty of conscience and proposed a great range of lunatic social and political schemes. Many of these groups were secret; most of them were small; and, while they tended to distrust each other and quibble over details of belief and practice, they began to be called the Puritans. For, in one way or another, they all wanted to "purify" the established church. They were all opposed in some degree to the hierarchical structure of the church and they were all more or less Calvinist in their theology and ethics. In this broad sense the Puritans were becoming an increasingly vocal minority in the last years of Elizabeth's reign.

The great majority of Englishmen regarded these Protestant extremists with distaste, suspicion, and some alarm, not so much for their religious views as for the political implications they obviously held—implications of rebellion, popular sovereignty, community of goods, and general social disorder. The separation of religion and politics was as impossible in the England of Elizabeth as in the Spain of Philip—indeed in Europe as a whole. Thus Parliament legislated against Puritan agitators as well as against Catholic "traitors." In 1593 the Conventicle Act was passed to restrain the meetings of extremist Puritan congregations, and this was followed by other harassing legislation. The acts were indifferently enforced. Puritan sentiment continued to grow and grumble against both state and church. It was largely the personal popularity of the old queen that forestalled serious domestic trouble during her last years.

Other issues inevitably attached themselves to the rapidly spreading religious unrest. For all her popularity, Elizabeth was dogmatic and arbitrary. In the halcyon decade of the 1590's, when the threat of Spain seemed removed forever, the harsh measures of economic and social control that had been in the national interest a generation before seemed despotic. There were troubles with Parliament, with the merchants and merchant companies. Indeed, the sentiments of political and social, as well as of religious discontent, tended to originate in the merchant class. This class was concentrated in the cities of the urbanized southeast of England, especially London. Their common business interests drew them together and their proximity made the flow of opinion easier. They were more clearly a "class" than any other in the realm. Moreover, under the Tudors, they had come to play an important role in the realm. They had every intention of continuing to do so. A strong wind of change had long since begun to blow when, at last, in the spring of 1603, the aged Elizabeth died quietly in her bed.

FRANCE AND THE WARS OF RELIGION

In many ways the key to international developments on the continent in the second half of the sixteenth century is to be found in the immobilization of French power as a result of that country's involvement in a prolonged and bitter domestic war of religion. Spain, England, and the Dutch Republic were thus freed to pursue their policies without fear of effective intervention by France.

The Religious Crisis

In the spring of 1559 the negotiations to end the last Hapsburg-Valois war had been concluded in the Peace of Cateau-Cambrésis.[5] The peace was woven of complex concessions by all the parties to the war. It was by no means a victory for France; but it represented at the same time an admission by Charles V that France had succeeded in preventing the consolidation of his encircling Hapsburg Empire. Henry II had brought his father's (Francis I) foreign policy to this qualified victory and once the treaty was signed this somber, orthodox king turned to what he considered his most serious domestic problem, the growing Protestant heresies. Since 1549 he had battled this menace with the weapons of royal absolutism: the courts, close control of the press, outlawry, and a special commission known as Le Chambre Ardente ("the burning court") for its ruthless procedures against religious dissenters. One of the consequences of the Peace of Cateau-Cambrésis was an understanding between Henry II and Philip II of Spain to make common cause against heresy in their respective lands. This new era of understanding was sealed in a royal marriage between the recently widowed Philip and one of the daughters of Henry II. It was in the celebrations attending the wedding that Henry was fatally injured in a jousting accident only a few weeks after the signing of the peace. He left his state, his policies, and the still unresolved issue of religion in the hands of his Italian wife, Catherine de Médicis, and a family of weakling children, the eldest of whom was scarcely more than a boy. Catherine, a foreigner, inexperienced in government, despised by many of the highest nobility, and distrusted by still more, was to be the focal point of France's chaotic fortunes for the next twenty years.

Even before the death of Henry II, the religious problem in France was

5. See p. 592.

rapidly turning into a political problem. Henry's predecessor, Francis I, as we have seen, was not unduly hostile to the early French reform movements. But as they inevitably came to advocate the destruction of the established church and the consequent overturn of order, Francis turned against this incipient Reformation. What cause had he to sanction a religious revolution? The crown virtually controlled the resources of the French church; it was a valuable and traditional source of order; and, perhaps most important of all, an attack on the church might well suggest an attack on the state. Francis' decision was certainly in keeping with the sentiments of most Frenchmen, but was based more on political than on religious considerations. This is confirmed by the repeated alliances of the "Most Christian" and Catholic king of France with the Lutheran princes of Germany and even, from time to time, with the Turks, in the course of his prolonged wars with Emperor Charles V.

In the crises of war, Francis could not afford to have the religious loyalties of his own nation divided. Furthermore, he needed the alliance of the papacy, though no more than the papacy needed him. United against their common Hapsburg enemy, Francis I and Pope Leo X arranged a pact, the Concordat of Bologna (1516); this was essentially a financial deal by which the papacy allowed Francis virtually unlimited control of the French church in return for military-political support against Charles V. The concordat paid some deference to religious issues, but it was mainly an economic and political instrument. Its effects were disastrous, for it insured that the already scandalous condition of the French church would be even more scandalous as its offices became the spoils of the state. All the traditional abuses of centuries, including simony, pluralism and absenteeism, were multiplied. Francis I had thus turned away from the Reformation and at the same time had cynically disregarded the insistent demand for church reform that was one of the most inflammatory, popular issues of his century.

Under these circumstances the infant Protestant movements in France grew to maturity. They were originally a varied group—from the pietism of the reformers of Meaux and the intellectualism of the French Erasmian humanists all the way to Anabaptist-like social-action groups. With the pressure of increased persecution, French Protestantism not only grew but became unified; and the unifying force was Calvinism, still predominantly French though exiled in Geneva, and still carrying enormous appeal for Frenchmen. French refugees fled to the Calvinist communities of Switzerland and Germany; from Geneva hundreds of capable, Calvinist-French missionaries poured back into France to assist the Protestant cause and organize the churches. By 1559 French Calvinism had grown virtually to be a state within a state following the politico-ecclesiastical policies of Calvin and responding to the pressures of persecution. In that very year, epochal in so many ways, the Calvinist party held its first national synod in Paris, secretly and under the very nose of the hostile government. This assembly adopted a rigorous confession of faith, drawn up by Calvin himself, and approved a "discipline" that amounted to a constitution for this underground religious community. The synod became the coordinating agency for a religious and ecclesiastical organization that had been growing for a decade into a flexible, tough, purposeful network of Calvinist congregations, representing perhaps as many as half a million people from nearly every level of society.

The movement drew its greatest support from the business and professional middle class—the merchants, artisans, lawyers, the university people, many of the lower clergy, and the literate who were so susceptible to the intellectual appeal of Calvinist propaganda. But it was also supported by a significant segment of the nobility, particularly in the south of France, where the movement was generally strongest and where the embers of the great medieval heresies had never been quite trampled out. As religious dissent gave way to religious war in the second half of the sixteenth century, the leadership of the Calvinist cause shifted to a handful of these noble and even princely houses. Their motives were no more completely religious than were those of the Protestant princes of Germany. Many were, of course, sincere and devout converts. Others saw an opportunity to join liberty of conscience with political independence. By 1559 the French Calvinists were already more than a religious group, if not yet a full-fledged political party, and they already bore the party name of Huguenots. In that year the death of Henry II and the succession of his immature son, Francis II, raised politico-religious factionalism to the level of national crisis.

The Wars of Religion

A coterie of the highest nobles of the realm stood next to the throne; and they were bitterly divided on the issue of religion. Antoine, king of the little Pyrenean principality of Navarre, and head of the House of Bourbon, was a Huguenot. So was his brother, the Prince de Condé. Antoine was weak and indecisive; but his family stood next in line for the throne should the line of Valois run out. Condé was reckless, hot-headed, and proud; a brilliant partisan, but neither a statesman nor a leader. Gaspard de Coligny was both; and a dedicated Huguenot as well. He was a distinguished soldier and admiral of France who had been elevated to prominence in the train of his uncle, Anne de Montmorency, the constable of the realm, head of the French military establishment, and devoted servant of the crown and of its faith. This was a family divided by the cause of religion.

FRANCE AND THE HAPSBURGS

FRANCE	HAPSBURGS
CHARLES VIII *(1483-1498)*	
LOUIS XII (Orleans) *(1498-1515)*	MAXIMILIAN I *(1493-1519)*
FRANCIS I (Angoulême) *(1515-1547)*	CHARLES V *(1519-1556)*
HENRY II *(1547-1559)*	AUSTRIAN BRANCH / SPANISH BRANCH
FRANCIS II *(1559-1560)*	FERDINAND I *(1556-1564)* / PHILIP II *(1556-1598)*
CHARLES IX *(1560-1574)*	MAXIMILIAN II *(1564-1576)* / PHILIP III *(1598-1621)*
HENRY III *(1574-1589)*	RUDOLF II *(1576-1602)* / PHILIP IV *(1621-1665)*
HENRY IV *(1589-1610)*	

Opposite the Huguenot lords stood the family of Guise, rich in lands, offices, and talent—and dedicated to Catholicism in both purse and conscience. The family had risen to a preeminent position in France through the favor of Francis I and Henry II. Duke Henry of Guise was a brilliant soldier, a hero of the Franco-Hapsburg wars, and the captor of Calais. His younger brother was the most powerful churchman in France, the Cardinal of Lorraine, and one of the most eloquent champions of Catholicism. Their holdings were immense in eastern France, and their connections tied them not only to the French royal family but to the throne of Scotland and to its queen, now Queen of France as well through the succession of her husband, Francis II.

These were the factions that crowded in upon the boy king, Francis, and the queen mother, Catherine de Médicis. In the face of seemingly insurmountable problems of state finance, social and religious discord, and myriad other complex problems Catherine, with her son in train, turned to the Guises, who were more than willing to accept the burdens of hard and unpopular decisions in return for almost unlimited influence over the crown. The opposition party, desperate in the face of this move, was led by Condé into a series of foolish conspiracies that might have thoroughly discredited their cause. Then, after less than two years of rule, the weak young king died.

His brother and successor, Charles IX, was not yet ten years old, and the complete creature of his possessive mother. His accession gave Catherine a splendid opportunity to play politics. She sincerely hoped that by dominating the king she could bridge the dangerous factionalism for which she was in part responsible. She tried to force some sort of religious compromise upon the parties, and succeeded only in alienating both Huguenot and Catholic extremists. Throughout the country both parties made menacing gestures of civil war. The fears of the Catholics drove them, in 1561, to form a Catholic League under the leadership of the Guise cardinal and the old and loyal Constable Montmorency. The league marked the emergence of a Catholic political party, dominated still by the family of Guise, but freed of the stigma of a court faction. In the militant and well-organized Huguenots and in the Catholic League France possessed the two parties of a potential civil war, and only a defenseless boy king between them. In this tense atmosphere any incident could set off open conflict.

In the spring of 1562 the Duke of Guise attacked a Huguenot meeting at the town of Vassy. Some two hundred people were killed or wounded by his guard. From this beginning, atrocities and rumors of atrocities multiplied. Then the forces that the Catholic League had gathered suddenly descended upon Paris and seized the person of the king and the queen mother. The league leaders could now claim that they fought for the protection of the king against the Huguenot rebels. The Guises, in the name of the king and with Catherine's reluctant cooperation, turned for help outside France to Philip II of Spain. As a countermove, the Huguenots turned to Elizabeth of England and their German fellow-Protestants. But neither party got much help from its allies, who were all seriously occupied with other affairs and all of whom, moreover, were much more concerned with the dismemberment of France to their respective advantages. Even without substantial help, the war continued to smolder, and incident followed inflammatory incident. Both Antoine of Navarre and the Duke of Guise were killed. The war became a series of sporadic "wars"—engagements, massacres, desecrations—punctuated from time to time by faithless truces. All the savagery of civil war was compounded with religious intolerance on both sides. By 1570 the country was exhausted, the state finances in incredible chaos, and all parties ready for peace. The Spanish alliance of the crown and the Catholic League were becoming more odious to every element in France. The Huguenots cried out in horror against the persecutions by Alva in the Low Countries. Even the more moderate Catholics saw that the success of Philip's Dutch policy would reestablish the Hapsburg menace to France. An increasing number of moderate Catholics were clamoring for peace and the restoration of order, regardless of the religious question. The Peace of St. Germain-en-Laye (1570) was signed.

Despite the impasse to which the war had come, the treaty was a clear advantage to the Huguenots. They were granted amnesty and the right to hold free religious services within certain restrictions; they were given a number of fortified cities; the status of a virtually independent state, which they had had for years in fact, was recognized by treaty. Much of the credit for the treaty must go to Gaspard de Coligny. In the course of the war he had emerged as the leader and the conscience of the Huguenot party, a figure comparable to William of Orange in the Low Countries. The arrogance and narrow partisanship of the Guise faction had discredited them, and Coligny had become the voice to which the king and Catherine de Médicis listened. He counseled not only the interests of his party, but the interests of his nation. The recognition of the Spanish menace was largely due to his promptings. The treaty of peace was to be sealed and the new directions of French foreign policy to be inaugurated by a series of marriage alliances. One was to be with Elizabeth of England, another with the Austrian Hapsburgs, and one even with Philip II of Spain, once more a marriageable widower. But the most important of these royal marriages was that between the Valois princess, Margaret, and the young Huguenot king, Henry of Navarre, the heir of the Bourbon line.

In the months between the signing of the treaty and the summer of 1572, the mercurial temper of the court changed once more. Henry, the new Duke of Guise, was bitterly resentful at the concessions the Huguenots had received, at his own loss of influence at court, and at the advancement of his personal enemy Coligny. Catherine de Médicis was also becoming disenchanted with the Huguenots and feared Coligny's influence over her son. For these and probably other reasons, Catherine turned to the Guises once more. The marriage of her daughter with Henry of Navarre took place in Paris, in August of 1572. In the midst of the celebrations a Guise assassin attacked Coligny but succeeded only in wounding him. The king was enraged at this assault upon his favorite. Catherine and the Guises saw themselves about to be exposed. In an audacious move the queen convinced her weak-willed son not only that Coligny was a danger to him, but that the whole Huguenot party was about to erupt in rebellion once more and that his own life was being threatened. The king then gave his assent to one of the most incredible plots of an incredible century.

Practically all the leaders of the Huguenot party were in Paris for the royal wedding, and Catherine and the Duke of Guise planned to murder them all! At the ringing of the church bells at dawn on August 24—St. Bartholomew's Day—all over the city bands of assassins fell on the unsuspecting Huguenots. The wounded Coligny was dragged from his bed and murdered by the Duke of Guise himself. The fanatically Catholic street mobs of Paris joined in the slaughter. In all, perhaps three thousand people were slain in this bloody frenzy. The plotters had hurriedly coordinated their plans with other cities, where similar slaughter took place and perhaps twenty thousand Huguenots throughout France were killed. The pope ordered special celebrations of joy in Rome and in Madrid Philip II laughed outright when the news was brought to him.

In domestic terms the unbelievable folly of this mass murder brought open war once more—but with a significant change. The Huguenots threw over even the pretense of loyalty to the crown and fought openly for freedom and the control of France. New leaders rose from the Huguenot masses and new strength from their deep moral outrage. The whole south of France became an armed state. The treachery of the queen and her Guise co-conspirators soured the temper of most moderates, who moved to support the Huguenots in the interests of the whole nation. In the midst of this turmoil Charles IX died, in 1574, to be succeeded by his younger brother, Henry, who had been installed as King of Poland and left that bankrupt throne only a jump ahead of a revolution to become Henry III of France.

The new king was no more competent than his brothers and lacked the resources with which to counter Huguenot strength. In 1575 his younger brother went over to the rebel party, to be followed early in the next year by Henry of Navarre who, since the massacre, had been kept close to the court and forced to accept Catholicism. He now openly declared himself a Calvinist once more and became the leader of the Huguenots. Henry of Navarre's escape coincided with the Peace of Beaulieu (1576), a virtual capitulation of the crown to the Huguenots. They were granted complete freedom of religion, save only in Paris and a handful of Catholic strongholds. This was the result of St. Bartholomew.

Once more, as before, the liberal terms of the peace alienated the extreme Catholic party. And again, under the lash of the Guises and with the Catholic spirit of the Counter Reformation running high, an almost spontaneous revival of the Catholic League took place throughout France. Henry III, like Francis II before him, was caught between two armed forces and constrained to choose between them, for the crown had no party of its own. He chose the Catholic League, in spite of its renewed domination by the Guises, because it claimed the support of most of the French people. Desultory war followed for almost a decade, with France divided and bankrupt, and government hobbled. In 1584 the Duke of Anjou, the king's brother and sole remaining son of Henry II, died. With him died the Valois line, for Henry III was childless. The Huguenot leader, Henry of Navarre, the Bourbon heir, was next in line of succession.

Confronted by this disaster, the Catholic League allied itself with Philip II of Spain, presenting the paradox of a national party allied with a foreign power against the interests of its own state. Philip was delighted; for once his religious and political causes coincided. He could neutralize an ancient enemy in France and advance the cause of orthodoxy—all at comparatively little cost. As the fortunes of the league rose, those of Henry of Guise rose too. He had the support of Philip of Spain and of the papacy. He was "King of Paris" and to all intents and purposes, King of France. Henry III, with no support left, called the Estates-General into session. While it met the king had both the Duke and his brother, the Cardinal of Guise, assassinated. As the St. Bartholomew's Day Massacre had unified the Huguenots against the crown, this act of desperate and criminal folly did much to unify the nation, Catholic and Protestant, against the crown. It produced a rash of political theories justifying rebellion against tyranny. Henry III turned to the only leader of authority and respect who remained, Henry of Navarre, and joined with him to march on Paris, held by the Catholic League. During the siege of the city, Henry III was assassinated by a Catholic zealot in the spring of 1589. His last act was to commend the succession of his Bourbon cousin. Catherine de Médicis had predeceased her last royal son by several months. Thus, through a maze of assassinations, massacres, and civil war (the "War of the Three Henrys") Henry of Navarre had become Henry IV (*1589–1610*) of France.

One serious problem remained, however. The people of France, with all their detestation of the Valois, were still overwhelmingly Catholic and could not accept their new king as long as he remained Huguenot. His religion still divided his country and perpetuated the wars. Henry fought as best he could against the Catholic League, treating it as the rebel force it was in fact. Meanwhile, the Protestant succession had brought a crisis in French foreign affairs. Philip II of Spain, already in alliance with the Catholic League, claimed the French throne by right of his marriage to Elizabeth of Valois and orthodoxy, and sent an army under Parma across the northern frontier to assert his claim. At this point, Henry IV announced his conversion to Catholicism, with the famous dictum, "Paris is worth a Mass." No matter how nominal or perfunctory his conversion, it was enough and the nation rose to support him. His conversion deprived the Catholic League of the reason for its existence. It was now merely a rebel faction in league with the national enemy, rather than defender of the faith of most Frenchmen. Similarly, Philip II lost his provocation for invading France and was revealed as a Hapsburg dynast rather than a Catholic crusader. In 1594 Henry IV was welcomed to Paris with hysterical enthusiasm and in the following year approved by the papacy.

Henry IV and the Restoration of France

In Henry IV the lots of war had shaken out the best man among the leaders of his generation. When he marched into Paris in 1594 Henry was just over forty years old, vigorous, seasoned, and dedicated to the reconstruction of his nation and its monarchy. Years of war had sharpened his natural intelligence into realistic shrewdness. He was a quick and sure judge of men and had a flair for dealing with people of every station. The task that faced France in the closing years of the sixteenth century had found its master in Henry IV.

A generation of war had left France prostrate. National finances, which had never recovered from the expensive wars of Francis I and Henry II, had been thrown into such confusion by the wars of religion that the government was literally bankrupt. The crown had for years been unable to pay its *rentes* against the national debt; there was scarcely a single government official whose salary was current; from the mid-1570's the state had progressively defaulted on its debts until private bankers refused to extend further credit, even at usurious interest. Furthermore, the economic resources on which the health of national finance depended were seriously depleted. The uncertainties of war and credit had practically destroyed commerce. Many cities in which economic production was concentrated had been occupied and sacked in the course of the wars until the French industrial plant was in shambles. The country districts had suffered from the devastation of armies and marauding bands of soldiers. Fields lay uncultivated; farm villages were deserted. France lived from day to day in the anticipation of famine. The paralysis of finance had, of course, completed the ruin of the central government. The ineptitude of three Valois kings had allowed the initiative in national affairs to pass, first to the factions of court and then to the parties of the civil war until the national unification that the great medieval kings had fostered was all but destroyed.

Such were the problems that faced the new king. The very completeness of the national ruin was a source of strength to him. For Frenchmen of all parties had come to realize that the very existence of France was at stake. And they conceded that a strong and capable monarchy was the only immediate solution. In part, this widespread conviction came from the confidence that Henry IV inspired. His heroic struggle against the leaguers and their Spanish allies had aroused a patriotic regard for the crown which men had not been able to indulge for nearly forty years. And Henry used his popularity to increase public confidence on every side: he surrounded himself with officials drawn from every level of society, but most conspicuously from the business and professional middle class. They were rich and poor, Protestant and Catholic; but they were all his men and he ruthlessly demanded their loyalty. The worthless and expensive court favorites were seen no more at court. Henry began the reconstruction of the system of government under department heads, who collectively composed a royal council. He subordinated every agency in the state to "the king in council." The Estates-General was not once summoned. The traditional advisory function of the high nobility was quietly bypassed. The Parlements were firmly directed to register the edicts of the crown and readily did so. Henry IV, by his will, his personal prestige, and popularity, was re-creating the machinery of royal absolutism that Richelieu and Louis XIV would use so impressively.

Much as the effectiveness of Henry IV depended upon the personal qualities of the king, it was almost equally dependent upon the economic policies of his greatest minister, Maximilien de Bethune, the Duke of Sully (1560–1641). Sully was a sour and righteous Huguenot. Despite his religious principles, he had amassed a great personal fortune during the years of war. Henry IV put Sully's financial abilities to his own use and that of the nation. He put into the hands of his minister a combination of powers that amounted to the economic management of the state. Sully's talent was neither brilliance nor originality; it was simple honesty and Puritanical thrift. His reforms were not directed at creating new devices of economy, but at making the old ones work.

With the backing of the king, Sully cut court expenses to the bone, mercilessly dispensing with the fantastic expenses of court favorites and hangers-on. He bought back the precious rights and immunities that three weak kings had frankly sold for momentary profit. The system of tax farming, by which a large portion of the state's taxes were collected by private individuals who had purchased the right, was too deeply entrenched for Sully to do away with. But he eliminated as many abuses as he could from the system and prosecuted the most notoriously corrupt of the tax farmers. He introduced bookkeeping and auditing reforms and stopped the petty theft and graft that incompetence encouraged. On the larger front Sully began the repair of roads and waterways and the construction of canals. Backed by the king's personal interest in the revival of agriculture and industry, Sully's reforms began to stir the French economy to life once more. Part of Sully's success may be attributed simply to the restoration of peace and public confidence in the crown.

In many ways Henry IV's most significant contribution to the stability of France was his religious policy. This was most dramatically revealed in his Edict of Nantes (1598). This document marked the end of the Wars of Religion in probably the most constructive religious settlement of the sixteenth century. Henry had been both a Huguenot leader and a Catholic leader but, like his great contemporary, Elizabeth I of England, he was more essentially a politician than a zealot for any religious cause. The Edict of Nantes was thus, first of all, a very realistic political document. It was a recognition of the fact that the Huguenots were, under Henry as they had been for a generation, a tightly organized, armed minority—a state within a state. The edict recognized the religious and legal basis of that state. Huguenots were granted freedom of conscience and private exercise of their religion as well as its public exercise everywhere but in Paris and its immediate vicinity. They were to enjoy all civil rights, including the right to hold the highest public offices. They were, furthermore, allowed to retain most of the armed towns that they held at the end of the last war. By these sweeping concessions Henry IV bound up the great wound that crippled his country and returned to its loyal service a significant minority of its most useful and industrious citizens.

As Henry slowly restored the unity and prosperity of France, he also had to deal with France's international involvements. In the same year as the Edict of Nantes, Henry finally brought to an end the war with Spain, which held over from Philip's interference in behalf of the Catholic League. By 1598 Spain was clearly in the role of an aggressor, fighting against the growing unity and strength of France. Everywhere on the continent Philip II's grandiose plans were toppling: the Dutch had defied him successfully; the English and the Dutch had practically captured control of the Atlantic coastal waters; and with the recovery of France that nation gradually regained its central position on the continent. In the course of the sixteenth century the roles of Spain and France had been reversed. The Bourbons, with Henry IV, succeeded to the enmities as well as to the throne of the Valois. But the dreaded Hapsburg enemy was no longer the specter it had been to Francis I in the opening years of the century. The grandson of Henry IV would finally set a member of his own house upon the throne of Spain. Europe was entering the age of French ascendancy.

As the power of Philip's Spain declined, Henry IV mobilized the new strength of France for an aggressive role in European affairs. In 1609 he was preparing to carry the initiative to the Hapsburgs on the German frontier. Then, in the spring of 1610, as his army stood ready to move, Henry IV was assassinated by an insane school teacher and Catholic fanatic. "[It] is one of the bitterest ironies of fate that the most tolerant and enlightened of seventeenth-century kings should have perished at the hands of a religious maniac."[6] France was to wait almost twenty years for the successor to Henry's policies in the person of Richelieu.

6. David Ogg, *Europe in the Seventeenth Century* (London: Black, 1948), p. 77.

SUGGESTIONS FOR FURTHER READING

≈⋉

H. M. Baird, *The History of the Rise of the Huguenots of France* (New York: Scribner, 1900), 2 vols., basic work.

———, *The Huguenots and Henri de Navarre* (New York: Scribner, 1886).

J. B. Black, *The Reign of Elizabeth* (Oxford: Clarendon Press, 1936), probably the best general account of the Elizabethan period.

P. J. Blok, *History of the People of the Netherlands,* Part III, *The War with Spain* (New York: Putnam, 1898–1912), best general work on the Low Countries.

B. Chudoba, *Spain and the Empire 1519–1643* (Chicago: University of Chicago Press, 1952), dealing with Philip's continental policies in light, particularly, of the Hapsburg family alliance.

G. R. Elton, *England under the Tudors* (London: Methuen, 1955).

S. L. England, *The Massacre of St. Bartholomew* (London: Long, 1938).

P. Geyl, *The Revolt of the Netherlands* (London: Williams and Norgate, 1932), brilliant analysis.

A. J. Grant, *The Huguenots* (London: Butterworth, 1934).

E. H. Harbison, *Rival Ambassadors at the Court of Queen Elizabeth* (Princeton: Princeton University Press, 1940), excellent for the complexities of Elizabethan foreign policy.

M. A. S. Hume, *Philip II of Spain* (London and New York: Macmillan, 1897), the best of the older biographies of Philip.

D. G. Loth, *Philip II of Spain* (New York: Brentano, 1932).

*G. Mattingly, *The Defeat of the Spanish Armada* (Boston: Houghton Mifflin, 1962).

R. B. Merriman, *The Rise of The Spanish Empire,* Vol. IV, *Philip the Prudent,* cited for Chap. 13.

*J. E. Neale, *The Age of Catherine de Medici* (New York: Barnes and Noble, 1958).

*———, *Queen Elizabeth* (Garden City, N. Y.: Anchor, 1957), the best short biography of Elizabeth.

W. F. Oakeshott, *Founded upon the Seas* (Cambridge: Cambridge University Press, 1942), the rise of English naval supremacy.

*F. C. Palm, *Calvinism and the Religious Wars* (New York: Holt, 1932).

A. F. Pollard, *The History of England, 1547–1603* (London: Longmans, 1934).

D. B. Quinn, *Raleigh and the British Empire* (London: English Universities Press, 1947).

Conyers Read, *Mr. Secretary Cecil and Queen Elizabeth* (London: Jonathan Cape, 1955).

———, *Mr. Secretary Walsingham and the Policy of Elizabeth* (Oxford: Clarendon Press, 1925), 2 vols., a fascinating "key" biography of this period.

R. Roeder, *Catherine de Medici and the Lost Revolution* (Garden City, N. Y.: Doubleday, 1939), detailed and absorbing study of this complex subject.

*A. L. Rowse, *The England of Elizabeth* (New York and London: Macmillan, 1950).

———, *The Expansion of Elizabethan England* (London: Macmillan, 1955).

H. D. Sedgwick, *Henry of Navarre* (Indianapolis: Bobbs-Merrill, 1930).

———, *The House of Guise* (Indianapolis: Bobbs-Merrill, 1938).

J. W. Thompson, *The Wars of Religion in France* (Chicago: University of Chicago Press, 1909).

R. Trevor-Davies, *The Golden Century of Spain, 1501–1621* (New York: Macmillan, 1937).

C. V. Wedgwood, *William the Silent* (New Haven: Yale University Press, 1944).

J. A. Williamson, *Sir John Hawkins, the Times and the Man* (Oxford: Clarendon Press, 1927).

O. Zoff, *The Huguenots* (New York: Fischer, 1942).

*Paperbound edition. In the case of reprint editions, publisher and date of publication given will be that of reprint rather than the original.

❧15❧

The Eve of Modern Europe

THE THIRTY YEARS' WAR

Prelude to War

Through the second half of the sixteenth century the German states—like France, England, and the Low Countries—had been torn by wars of religion. Then, in the opening years of the seventeenth century, they became enmeshed in the most sustained and devastating of all the religious conflicts—the Thirty Years' War.

Its causes reached back in a tangled skein to the tentative and unsatisfactory religious-political settlement that Charles V had concluded with the German princes in 1555. Charles' dealings with the Lutheran states had been closely bound up with the course of the Hapsburg-Valois wars, and even the limited victories he had been able to claim in Germany had been neutralized by French diplomacy. On the other hand Charles' unrelenting hostility to the Lutheran princes had helped to unify and spread the Lutheran movement. Thus, by 1555, the Emperor faced a coalition of almost solidly Protestant German states. Even his own family lands in central Europe had been penetrated by the reformed doctrines, and his foreign enemies were once more courting the Germans. At Augsburg in 1555, the Emperor's brother, Ferdinand, his regent for Germany, met with the princes for a settlement of the religious issues. It was a capitulation to reality. Princes and cities that were Lutheran were to receive legal recognition and freedom of worship. But the so-called Religious Peace of Augsburg left two important issues unresolved. The first was the status of Calvinism, which was gaining rapidly in Germany, but which neither the Catholic nor the Lutheran princes were willing to recognize under the peace. The second was the so-called "ecclesiastical reservation," a clause appended to the treaty documents which stated that any ecclesiastical lord who became Lutheran should forfeit his lands and titles. German Calvinism continued to grow and German princes, lay and clerical, continued to secularize church lands. But, even with its serious limitations, the Religious Peace of Augsburg became the basis of a restive peace in Germany for a generation.

The abdication of Charles V and the division of the empire tended to set the German Hapsburgs on a different course from that of their Spanish cousins. Ferdinand I (*1556–1564*) and his son Maximilian II (*1564–1576*) were far too concerned with the restoration of their own lands to be much involved in the great Counter Reformation religious and political crusade of Philip II. Necessity further dictated a somewhat more conciliatory attitude toward their Protestant subjects because of the continuing threat of Moslem penetration of eastern Europe. Moreover, the German Protestants were not just a religious minority. They were a strongly organized and legally recognized body, and the German Hapsburgs were compelled to deal with them. Finally, the imperial powers in themselves, without the support of Hapsburg strength outside of Germany, were sharply circumscribed by the imperial constitution and the long tradition of German state-ism. The religious settlement helped strengthen the claims to sovereign independence among the German princes, both Catholic and Protestant.

In the period of comparative peace that followed the religious settlement the Protestant states began to feud with each other over the extension of Lutheran doctrines. The second generation of Lutheran preachers and scholars were striving to devise a new Protestant orthodoxy, and in their factional fights became as intolerant of each other as of their common enemy. But as traditional Catholicism gained new vitality and direction under the spur of the Counter Reformation, the Protestant states tended to draw together once more. To this confused situation the growth of Calvinism in Germany added yet another complication.

Calvinism had begun to spread into Germany in the middle of the sixteenth century, and while it had not been recognized by the Augsburg settlement, by 1559 a number of important princes had become Calvinists. They clamored in vain for the same rights that their Lutheran fellow princes enjoyed; the entrenched Lutherans steadfastly refused to recognize them. Despite this hostility, Calvinism continued to grow, particularly in the states of western Germany, where the influence of the Swiss, the French, and the Dutch Calvinist movements was strongest. By the early seventeenth century a solid corridor of Calvinist German states extended from the Rhine Palatinate north through Anhalt, Nassau, Cleves, Jülich, Berg, Kassel, and finally in north-central Germany to the great electoral state of Brandenburg, whose elector, John Sigismund (1608–1669), declared himself a Calvinist upon his accession. The hostility of the Lutheran princes to Calvinism further split the effectiveness of the German Protestants, and even the advance of the Counter Reformation was not enough to unite Lutherans and Calvinists in defense of their common religious purposes. In the latter part of the sixteenth century Bavaria was reconquered for Catholicism and its dukes appointed themselves the German champions of the church. At the same time the Counter Reformation made gains in the Hapsburg-German states and Protestant privileges began gradually to be withdrawn. In this inflammatory situation a series of incidents, trivial in themselves, moved Germany toward open war.

In 1606 a religious riot broke out in the little city of Donauwörth near the Bavarian border. The Catholic Emperor Rudolf empowered the Catholic Duke Maximilian of Bavaria to intervene and, in order to protect the religious rights of an almost nonexistent Catholic minority, Maximilian promptly confiscated the city and declared it Catholic. The whole procedure was a clear violation of the terms of the Augsburg settlement.

By 1608 the religious issues had become so heated that the Imperial Diet of that year was completely disrupted. The Protestant delegates spearheaded by the Calvinist elector, the Count Palatine Frederick IV, withdrew from the Diet to form the Protestant Union. It comprised most of the Calvinist states and many Lutheran ones, with the important exception of Saxony and the powers that moved in the Saxon circle. The union was, nonetheless, a focus for German Protestantism and the nucleus of a Protestant war party in Germany. In turn, Maximilian of Bavaria, the acknowledged leader of the German Counter Reformation, promptly organized a Catholic League with himself at its head. The league seemed the more necessary in view of the signing of the Twelve Years' Truce (1509) between the Netherlands and Spain, which meant that the west German, predominantly Calvinistic members of the Protestant Union might well count upon strong support from the Dutch. Maximilian's Catholic League, widely supported by the embattled west German Catholic states and backed by the considerable financial and military resources of Bavaria, rapidly became the nucleus of a Catholic war party.

In the same year, 1609, these parties nearly came to war over another incident, the succession to a handful of small Rhine states—Jülich, Berg, Cleves, Mark, and Ravensburg. The several claimants to one or another of these states enlisted the aid of the two great military unions. They in turn sought alliances with the great powers of Europe. Spain, the Empire, France, England, and the Dutch Republic were all arming for war and there were even some clashes of troops. The assassination of Henry IV of France removed a key figure in the complex of alliances and the hostilities sputtered out. But for this the Thirty Years' War might have started in the Rhineland. As it was, however, the outbreak of the war was deferred until 1618 and the incident that triggered it was the disputed succession to Bohemia.

Bohemia had become a pawn in the ugly domestic strife among the various princes of the House of Hapsburg. The insane emperor, Rudolf II, in a desperate attempt to protect his authority from his ambitious brother, Matthias, had made such liberal concessions to the Bohemian Protestants as to give them religious self-determination. This was confirmed in the so-called Letter of Majesty of 1609. While Matthias did succeed his brother as emperor in 1612, the rising star of the German Hapsburgs was the young Ferdinand, Duke of Styria. He had grown up and been educated by the Jesuits in the part of the Hapsburg estates where the Counter Reformation had taken deepest root. He was shrewd, vigorous, and a fanatic Catholic. Ferdinand was the obvious family choice to succeed Matthias as emperor. With this intention Matthias began to concentrate the territorial possessions of their house in Ferdinand's hands.

In 1617 Matthias commended Ferdinand to the Bohemian estates. The Bohemian electors, in spite of the obvious danger to their religious freedom, accepted this dedicated Catholic as their king. Admittedly, Ferdinand pledged himself to uphold the Letter of Majesty guaranteeing religious freedom, but even the most naive might have anticipated his intentions. In the following year, again with the urging of Emperor Matthias, the Hungarian Diet proclaimed Ferdinand King of Hungary. The stage was now set for the imperial succession and, upon the death of Matthias in 1619 Ferdinand stood forth as a candidate. Again, despite the obvious danger to their religious position, the Protestant electors could not agree upon a common basis of opposition and, on August 28, 1619, they joined their Catholic colleagues in unanimously electing their most implacable enemy as Emperor Ferdinand II. Meanwhile, the Thirty Years' War had already broken out in Ferdinand's own Bohemia.

The Bohemian Insurrection and the Spread of the War to Germany (1618-1629)

Almost immediately after electing Ferdinand king in 1617, the leaders of the Bohemian estates had become alarmed at the consequences of this action. As Ferdinand set out to restore Catholicism, the estates, on the initiative of a radical Protestant nobleman, Count Heinrich von Thurn, protested the invasion of their liberties to Matthias, who was still emperor. Matthias refused to honor the protest and Ferdinand began to enforce Catholic reforms. Priests were sent out into every district of the state, among a predominantly Protestant population. Protestant lands were alienated by the crown to Catholic foundations. Protestant towns were compelled to concede rights to Catholics. Finally, in March 1618, Protestants were forbidden to hold meetings.

This edict inspired the leaders of the Protestant nobility to open revolt. With a band of armed retainers, accompanied by a street mob, and headed by Thurn, they marched on the palace at Prague. In the absence of Ferdinand, his regents had to face the rebels. Heated words led to blows and two of the most hated of the royal councilors, as well as a harmless secretary, were unceremoniously heaved out a window of the palace. They fell some fifty feet into the moat below and miraculously escaped with their lives.[1] This "Defenestration of Prague" was the first act of open violence in the war.

Thurn and his associates set up a revolutionary government, enacted a radical Protestant program, assembled an army, and marched on Vienna. This bold action galvanized anti-Catholic, anti-Hapsburg sentiment throughout Europe. Ferdinand, still archduke at this time, seemed seriously threatened by this chain reaction of uprisings against him. In fact, these were more noisy than effective. Ferdinand successfully defended Vienna, and was even able to make some headway against the confusion in Bohemia.

As the likelihood of Ferdinand's election to the imperial title increased, the revolutionary estates of Bohemia made plans to secure substantial aid. This came from two quarters: in Hungary, the Transylvanian prince,

1. The Catholic account of this remarkable incident held that the three men were saved by the intervention of the Virgin Mary and borne up on the wings of angels. The Protestant account held that they had fallen into a pile of soft and rotting manure.

Bethlen Gabor, suddenly rose in revolt against the Catholic Hapsburgs; in the Rhenish Palatinate, the young Calvinist elector Frederick V (1596–1632) appeared as another potential ally. The Bohemian revolutionary estates offered the crown of Bohemia to him, and after some deliberation Frederick accepted. This was a significant coup for the rebels, for not only was he the leader of the Protestant Union, but also the son-in-law of James I (who had succeeded to the English throne in 1603, following the death of Elizabeth) of England. The Bohemians counted heavily on the support that these associations implied, as did Frederick himself. But they were soon disappointed. James I had troubles enough of his own in England and no sympathy for rebellion against legitimacy, even Hapsburg legitimacy. And the Protestant Union was neither an aggressive nor an effective instrument. Moreover, Frederick V was a thoroughly uninspiring young man with not the slightest grasp of political realities. Thus he became the luckless victim of his friends' bad advice. The chief of these was Christian of Anhalt, a radical Calvinist noble and the leading firebrand of the Protestant Union.

Frederick's election to the Bohemian throne took place just two days before Ferdinand's election to the empire, and the new emperor lost no time in using his new position as a means of marshaling support for the recovery of his Bohemian lands. By the time the young Elector Frederick left Heidelberg for Prague, two months later, the Catholic and Protestant powers of Europe had lined up in support of one or the other of the rival claimants in Bohemia. But Ferdinand had the advantage of being able to draw on support that was close at hand: the Catholic League and Maximilian of Bavaria. This he had bought by a secret agreement, whereby Maximilian might assume Frederick's electoral dignity when the latter was defeated and deposed.

In the spring and summer of 1620 the Catholic League forces, under the experienced, harsh, and devout General Tilly, slowly marched toward Bohemia on Ferdinand's behalf. In November this army met the undisciplined Bohemian forces under Thurn and the Prince of Anhalt at the Battle of White Mountain, near Prague, the first major battle of the Thirty Years' War. The Catholic forces swept the field and Maximilian of Bavaria took Prague. Frederick V and his family had already slipped away to begin a life of begging and plotting that would continue for most of the rest of the war. At the time of Frederick's accession, the Jesuits had contemptuously labeled him a "Winter King" who would melt with the coming of the summer sun. They were not far wrong.

The imperial, Catholic League victory at White Mountain punctured the Bohemian rebellion, which soon collapsed. Bethlen Gabor had already been forced to capitulate in Hungary. The neutrality of Saxony had been bought by the promise that its ruler might occupy disputed territory on the Bohemian frontier. Now the grim work of retaliation began in Bohemia. Prague was turned over to the mercies of the army; the leaders of the revolt were hanged; there were wholesale confiscations of land and the Protestant nobility of Bohemia was rooted out completely. The whole country was placed under military occupation. Catholicism was reinstated under the direction of the Jesuits and the schools transferred to Jesuit control. All political as well as religious liberties were revoked and Protestants by the thousands were forced to leave Bohemia. The same sort of measures were enforced in the various subsidiary provinces of Bohemia and to a somewhat lesser degree in Hungary.

The Bohemian revolt was over. But now Ferdinand was confronted with the need to honor his secret agreement with Maximilian. Bohemia had been, in a sense, a local Hapsburg problem. The transfer of Frederick's electoral office to Maximilian was something else; it would involve all Germany and the constitution of the Empire, and it would certainly arouse the concern of the great powers of Europe. But if Ferdinand would gladly have reneged on the agreement, Maximilian, who had invested money and men in the recovery of Bohemia, was not about to allow the emperor to cancel his debt. Thus, before Frederick could return to Heidelberg or the diplomats work out a compromise, the emperor transferred the electoral title to Maximilian. Simultaneously the forces of the league invaded the Palatinate from one end while Spanish-Hapsburg forces from the Low Countries invaded it from the other. This turn of events forced the Protestant powers of Europe to move. At long last England's James I was prepared to support the cause of his distressed son-in-law; and a continental champion—but one of doubtful virtue—appeared in Christian IV of Denmark, who was more interested in extending his own authority into Germany than in defending either the lands of Frederick or the honor of Protestantism. Spain, in the meantime, with the end of the Twelve Years' Truce, was once more at war with the Dutch and cooperating with the Bavarian, imperial, and league forces to hold the Rhine corridor. The Bohemian revolt had set the match to a full-scale European war.

In the face of the competent and experienced Catholic armies of Spain and the league, the Protestant cause was in the care of Christian of Denmark on the one hand and a motley of mercenary commanders on the other. Despite the obvious military capability of the Catholic armies, Emperor Ferdinand was desperately struggling to free himself from dependence upon Maximilian of Bavaria. At this juncture in the war one of its most colorful and controversial figures appeared, Albrecht von Wallenstein (1583–1634). Wallenstein was a Czech nobleman who had foreseen the course of events in Bohemia and sided with the emperor. He had been rewarded with enormous holdings from confiscated Protestant lands and, by his own shrewdness and financial acumen, had created of them a personal state comprising one-fourth of Bohemia. In 1625 he offered Ferdinand a private army, financed and provisioned by himself. The emperor had no choice but to accept; and with his acceptance he loosed upon the empire the most rapacious and cold-blooded mercenary of modern warfare. The pitiful forces of the Protestants were caught between the league army and the Spanish on the Rhine and Wallenstein, marching from the east. What little help had come from the non-German powers quickly withered. Neither the English nor the Dutch gave substantial aid and in 1626 the Huguenot problem in France demanded the full attention of that government. In Germany, Wallenstein and Tilly routed the Protestant armies and punished those states and princes who had backed them.

By 1629 the fortunes of Ferdinand and the empire were at their peak. He had humiliated the Danish king and overawed practically all of northern Germany. Wallenstein, in the name of the emperor, held the German side of the Baltic with a force of nearly a hundred and forty thousand men. Ferdinand could dictate his terms within the empire as no emperor since Barbarossa. Once more the war might have ended, as in 1620. But with the intoxication of victory Ferdinand issued the Edict of Restitution as a precondition for peace. This document spelled out the doom of Protestantism throughout Germany. It called for the restoration of all lands taken by Protestant powers since 1552 and denied official recognition to Calvinism as a religion. The Peace of Lübeck, which came shortly after the edict was published, was guaranteed to be no more than a truce; for the position the emperor had taken on restitution made genuine peace impossible both in Germany and in Europe.

The Intervention of Sweden and the Broadening of the War

With the Edict of Restitution and the Peace of Lübeck the war in Germany had been going on for a decade, spreading like a brush fire from region to region. The Catholic and imperial forces had consistently held the military advantage. Complete victory had been denied them mainly because of diplomatic considerations and the chronic poverty of the emperor. With the rise of Wallenstein and the shift in European diplomacy in the 1620's, even these problems seemed about to be resolved. At this point, beleaguered German Protestantism gained its first great military champion in Gustavus Adolphus, King of Sweden (*1611–1632*).

Gustavus Adolphus had carefully watched the course of events in Germany. He had been tempted to intervene as early as 1625. But he had first to secure the position of Sweden in the north. Since the age of seventeen, when he had become king, Gustavus had assumed and now nearly completed the task of his royal house. The dynasty of Vasa, from the mid-sixteenth century, had struggled to make a place for Sweden in the Baltic, first against the German Hansa and then against the emerging power of Russia, and lately—since 1621—against Poland. Gustavus Adolphus had conducted the Polish war and brought it to a successful conclusion on the eve of his intervention in Germany. In the process he had forged his nation into a total machine for war. He had reorganized Sweden's finances and civil administration. He had reorganized and modernized the military system, introduced an efficient scheme of conscription, and introduced new weapons and tactics. He was himself a superb, confident, and seasoned commander. An admirer of the great Dutch soldier, Maurice of Nassau, he had hired Dutch professional soldiers to help train his men and advise him on technical matters.

Only when he was ready did Gustavus Adolphus launch his invasion of northern Germany, for he looked on this offensive as part of a greater design. A devout Lutheran, he saw it as his duty to rescue his fellow Lutherans in Germany from the destruction they seemed to face. At the same time, as King of Sweden and master of the Baltic, he saw the opportunity to pull together the battered and vacillating states of northern Germany into a great Protestant empire under his command and to crush the Catholic House of Hapsburg.

In the summer of 1630 Gustavus Adolphus landed on the Baltic shore of Germany. He had secured his Polish flank, as we have seen, and by a lightning thrust had forced a treaty from the still demoralized Christian IV of Denmark. But then, for almost a year, the Swedes were stalemated because the German princes they had come to save distrusted the motives and feared the energy and strength of Gustavus Adolphus. The Catholic imperial forces were also temporarily immobilized. The issues raised by the Edict of Restitution had upset the always precarious relations between Emperor Ferdinand and his general, Wallenstein. Wallenstein, supremely disinterested in the religious issues and harboring imperial ambitions of his own, had opposed the edict on the grounds that it was bad politics. The emperor, convinced of the rightness of his religious position and worried about Wallenstein's independence, had insisted upon the edict and had dismissed Wallenstein from his service. This action was favorably received by Maximilian and the Catholic League, who had long clamored for Wallenstein's dismissal. But it also meant that at the very time that Gustavus Adolphus landed in Germany the emperor lacked the resources with which to meet him, while the master of the greatest army in Europe watched from the sidelines of his Bohemian estates and waited for the emperor's inevitable call.

In the course of this temporary respite, the war spread by diplomacy. Cardinal Richelieu,[2] who had assumed control of French foreign policy, took up his nation's old fight against Hapsburg encirclement. He was most interested, of course, in the Spanish-Hapsburg menace on his own immediate frontiers in Italy and the Spanish Netherlands; but he saw in the Swedish invasion of Germany a chance to keep the emperor occupied and thus forestall the "family alliance" between the German and Spanish Hapsburgs that always remained a dangerous possibility. In January 1631 he struck a treaty with the Swedish king, granting him a handsome subsidy to keep his army in Germany. Thus did a "war of religion" make political bedfellows of a Lutheran king and a Catholic cardinal.

In the spring of the same year the war began to move again. The strategic city of Magdeburg declared for Gustavus Adolphus and closed its gates to the Catholic League army, which had cautiously moved north flanking the Swedes to the east. The city was besieged by the league army. Gustavus Adolphus, chaffing to relieve Magdeburg, found his way barred by the two Protestant electors of Saxony and Brandenburg, who stubbornly maintained their neutrality and refused to allow Gustavus Adolphus passage across their lands. Violation of their neutrality might incur the hostility of the other Protestant princes, a risk Gustavus could not afford to take. Finally Magdeburg fell and was mercilessly sacked by the army of the Catholic League. Overnight the horror of the sack became the rallying cry for German Protestantism, and at last pushed the German princes into joining the Swedes. The decision was helped along by the emperor's bungling of his relations with Saxony. From the beginning of the war the Saxon elector had tried to keep out of the conflict of parties and had

2. See pp. 686ff.

maintained a position based on the imperial constitution. Up to this point his neutrality had been as valuable to the emperor as his active support would have been. But faced by the drawing together of Protestant forces, the emperor now demanded religious capitulation from Lutheran Saxony and moved troops in to force his ultimatum. Saxon neutrality was thus rudely ended and the elector driven into the arms of the Swedes.

In September 1631 the Swedish army under Gustavus Adolphus met the league army under Tilly at Breitenfeld in Saxony. It was a great pitched battle and it was won decisively by the Swedish king. This victory made him the undeniable champion of the Protestant cause; the great crusade had finally begun. With his Saxon allies guarding his flank and line of march, Gustavus struck south across Germany, heading straight for Bavaria. He shrewdly saw that Maximilian of Bavaria was the real head of German Catholicism and the paymaster of its armies. If he could be brought to terms, the emperor would be helpless. As Gustavus Adolphus fought his way toward Bavaria his name became a legend. He was the "Golden King," the "Lion of the North," the "Messiah"! By the winter of 1632 the Swedish army was deep in Bavaria. Munich was menaced, the league army defeated, and Tilly its commander dead. The Saxons had taken Prague, occupied most of Bohemia, and Austria was threatened.

The emperor prayed and fasted, but there was only one thing for him to do—recall Wallenstein. Wallenstein's price was complete control of the military, the revocation of the Edict of Restitution, and a decisive voice in imperial affairs. It was a heavy price to pay, and the implications of Wallenstein's demands were ominous. But Ferdinand had no choice. The Saxon forces, weak at best, and impossibly strung out to the south from Saxony to Austria, were easily intimidated by Wallenstein. The remnants of the league army, fleeing north from their defeat at the hands of the Swedish king, joined Wallenstein, whose forces were growing daily. He recruited and trained a vast army as he moved slowly from Bohemia into Saxony. From distant Bavaria Gustavus Adolphus saw his line of supply and retreat menaced by Wallenstein. He had no choice but to turn back and seek battle, the sooner the better, for Wallenstein's army lacked the training and spirit of his own. In the fall of 1632 Gustavus began to withdraw from Bavaria toward his Baltic base, giving the impression that he intended to avoid a battle and seek a defensive position for the winter. So Wallenstein concluded, and began to disperse his men and horses to forage. Then suddenly, on November 16, 1632, Gustavus struck, at Lützen in Saxony. It was a hard and desperately fought battle. The Swedes ultimately won, but at a cost worse than defeat. Gustavus Adolphus was killed.

The emperor had paid almost as dearly as the Swedes, for once more he was the virtual captive of the enigmatic Wallenstein. With Gustavus Adolphus removed and the Protestant cause faltering, Wallenstein's position was stronger than ever, as was his lust for power. The Emperor feared —and with every good reason—that Wallenstein, virtual dictator of northern Germany, would conclude a separate peace with the great powers of Europe in exchange for some recognition of sovereignty. Wallenstein's ultimate plans remain a mystery; possibly they were never fully worked out. In any case, the emperor connived at his assassination and, in 1634, Wallenstein was struck down by a clique of his officers. Within two years the two greatest military figures of the Thirty Years' War had been removed. As a sort of epilogue to this middle passage of the war, six months after the death of Wallenstein, the reassembled imperial army defeated the Protestant forces in Nordlingen. The war was at a draw.

In 1635 the major German parties agreed to the Peace of Prague. Once more it was a peace of exhaustion and did little more than reassemble the religious and territorial map of Germany along reasonably realistic lines. But it was the most that Germany could expect.

In the past decade suffering, death, famine, and pestilence had spread in the wake of the war. Mammoth armies had confiscated the crops and burned the fields and villages of peasants. Their work had been completed by the jackal bands of mercenaries and bandits who roamed at will, plundering what was left to the peasants, murdering for a handful of pennies or food, and often for no good reason at all. Whole regions were laid waste and practically depopulated. In some districts the miserable peasants ground chaff to make bread; their women and children fingered through manure on the chance of turning up a kernel of grain. An English traveler reported finding villagers lying dead with grass in their mouths. Once great cities had been fought over, besieged, and looted by first one protector and then another. The aggressions of Maximilian of Bavaria had not been able to spare his own Bavaria; the constitutional neutrality of the Saxon elector had not saved Saxony. Bohemia had been ground into the earth. Germany was ready for peace, no matter how equivocal the terms. But it was no longer a German war. Sweden had invested her men, her faith, and the life of her king. France and Spain, on opposing sides, had invested money and diplomatic commitments. These international involvements all carried demands for compensation. Thus, as the war entered its last phase, it became the first great international political conflict of modern time.

The International War and the International Settlement

The dominant Protestant power in Protestant Germany was Sweden. But the Swedish position was impossible. The great Gustavus Adolphus had been succeeded by his young daughter, Christina. The reigns of government, however, were in the hands of his faithful and able minister, Axel Oxenstierna, who was almost fanatically dedicated to the policy and the memory of his king. Sweden was so heavily committed in Germany that Oxenstierna felt he could not simply withdraw while any hope of gain remained. Thus the Swedes doggedly held on to the strip of territory between the Baltic coast of Pomerania and the Rhine valley. The drainage of Swedish resources continued and the ravishing of Germany went on as before, while the initiative clearly passed in the last years of the war to France and Richelieu.

Since 1631 Richelieu had tried to make the war in Germany an instrument of his anti-Spanish, anti-Hapsburg policy. He had skillfully used the Swedish attack on the Rhine valley and Bavaria to occupy the long-disputed eastern provinces of France. By 1635 he was in alliance with Sweden and a handful of German Rhine states, with Savoy in northern Italy, and with the Dutch Republic. Each of these called for different commitments from France, and the French allies each hoped for some separate benefit. But they had all been manipulated by the great French diplomatist for the chief purpose of bringing pressure on his Spanish enemy. In 1635 France formally declared war on Spain. At this point the Thirty Years' War shifted decisively from religion to politics. Richelieu, a cardinal of the Catholic church, was in alliance with the Lutheran Swedes and the Calvinist Dutch. Both Catholic France and Catholic Spain regularly ignored the wishes of the pope, and even papal policy was more clearly motivated by politics than by religion. The great crusade of Gustavus Adolphus had degenerated into a scramble for territory to gain compensation for Sweden in alliance with France. The clear threat to Hapsburg dynastic interests everywhere had driven the two branches of that house together for the sake of political survival.

In the course of the next five years France, with Swedish help, confirmed her hold on the Rhine and continued to exert pressure on the Spanish Netherlands. Gradually France took not only the political but the military initiative from the former combatants. In 1643 the strategic

Above, left to right: Albrecht von Wallenstein. Oliver Cromwell. 16th century.

PHILIPPE DE CHAMPAIGNE. *Triple Portrait of Richelieu.*

Riciulina.   Metzetin

Above: JACQUES CALLOT.
Two Clowns, from the
series *Balli di Sfessania*.
1622.
Below: PAUL PONTIUS
*Gustavus Adolphus, King
of Sweden*. 17th century.

fortress of Rocroi on the frontier of the Spanish Netherlands became the scene of one of the most decisive and spectacular French victories under the brilliant French general, Condé. The myth of Spanish military supremacy finally died on that battlefield. Meanwhile, the Swedes kept up their pressure in Germany, gradually forcing the German states, Denmark, and Hungary either into alliance or advantageous neutrality. The Austrian Hapsburgs were almost completely isolated. The only one of the original Catholic powers in the Thirty Years' War that remained unbroken was Bavaria. In 1646 the Swedes and the French, under the French marshal Turenne and the Swedish general Wrangel, invaded Bavaria and brought Maximilian to terms. Once more he defected and again, in the spring of 1648, Bavaria was invaded and occupied. While Bavaria fell into the common ruin of Germany, the powers had already met to conclude the general European Peace of Westphalia, ending the Thirty Years' War.

When the final documents of the peace were signed in October 1648, negotiations had been going on for more than five years. In 1641 it had been agreed by France, Sweden, and the new Emperor Ferdinand III that two separate congresses should convene in the Westphalian cities of Münster and Osnabrück to consider the problem of ending the war. Their task was incredibly complex. The religious issues that had become obscured by war and politics once more asserted themselves. Most of the European powers were represented by sizable delegations, and there was endless quibbling over precedence and etiquette. Indeed, this was why the negotiations took place in two cities: the French and Hapsburg delegates met at Münster, the Swedish and imperial negotiators at Osnabrück. All documents had to be duplicated and communications established between the double diplomatic staffs at the two parleys. Old animosities were still raw and sentiments of national pride extremely sensitive. Time after time talks were held up, sometimes for months, while some key delegate nursed injured feelings or waited for instructions from home. Moreover, the fact that the war was still being fought inevitably influenced the deliberations, since the representatives of the combatant powers would be belligerent, submissive, or evasive with each new battle report. Domestic issues in Sweden, France, the Empire, and among the German states contributed their part to slowing or accelerating the progress of the conventions. In spite of these almost insuperable barriers, the terms of the peace were painfully hammered out by compromise, concession, and as a last resort, by common sense.

The territorial settlements of the Peace of Westphalia were so significant that the map of modern Europe may be said to have been drawn there. The emperor regained the traditionally Hapsburg Upper Austria to add to the southeastern and Balkan lands of his house. He retained the crown of Bohemia, which now became hereditary in his line. The Duke of Bavaria was permitted to retain the electorate that Ferdinand II had transferred to him early in the war, and the Upper Palatinate to which it pertained. But to compensate the family of the unfortunate Elector Frederick, a new electorate was created for his son and a portion of his family holdings restored. The other German imperial states were confirmed in their sovereignty. One of them, Brandenburg, was significantly enlarged, owing to the diplomatic finesse of Frederick William, "The Great Elector," (1620–1688) in his support of the French. He emerged from the peace with a large and wealthy state, centered upon the muddy, squalid, wood-built town of Berlin, his capital, and spread across northern Germany. It was the substance from which the kingdom of Brandenburg-Prussia would eventually be created.

As a result of these settlements, the medieval Holy Roman Empire disappeared as an effective force in European politics and was replaced by two hostile constellations of states, clustering around Hapsburg Austria in the south and the new Hohenzollern Brandenburg in the north. This division tended to be confirmed by the religious settlement; essentially the terms of the Religious Peace of Augsburg of 1555 were renewed and broadened. The problem of secularized church lands, which had not been adequately settled by that peace, was arbitrarily pegged to the year 1624. All lands either Catholic or Lutheran in that year were to remain so. There were the inevitable inequalities and cruelties of any arbitrary settlement, but this decision did generally reflect the actual territorial distribution of faiths. Furthermore, the emperor was not forced to grant religious toleration in his own lands. This tended to drive what Protestant population remained there to migrate and settle in the north. Calvinism was at long last officially recognized in the religious settlement. The Elector of Brandenburg, whose house had favored Calvinism from time to time, opened his lands to Calvinists as well as to displaced Lutherans. Thus, in a few years, the hostility of Brandenburg and Austria was crystalized along religious as well as political lines.

Sweden received western Pomerania and several other pieces of nothern Germany, sufficient to redeem a portion of Gustavus Adolphus' dream. His country remained mistress of the Baltic and a major force in north German politics. France, in fuller measure than Sweden, achieved the territorial goals that had kept her in the war. She gained practical control of the left bank of the Rhine, which French troops actually held at the end of the war. And, because of the dominant military position of France, the rest of the territorial settlements were pretty much to her liking—or there would have been no settlements. As a codicil to the peace, Switzerland's independence, a fact for centuries, was legally recognized. By a separate treaty, signed almost a year before the general peace was concluded, Spain recognized the Dutch Republic.

Perhaps the best indication of the new spirit of Westphalia is the fact that all the powers, both Catholic and Protestant, systematically ignored the claims, the advice, and the protests of the papacy. Pope Innocent X refused to sanction any part of the peace; but this did not affect the secular parties. The medieval papacy died along with the medieval empire as a determining factor in European politics.

The Peace of Westphalia was as significant for what it left undone as for what it did. The treaties were filled with the equivocations and reservations so dear to diplomacy; and they contained the germs of a dozen wars. Many questions were left unresolved. The creation of an expanded Brandenburg rudely introduced a new power factor into German politics. The attempts to "round out" the lands of this state and establish its borders were to lead to the wars of Frederick the Great. The position of Sweden in Germany and the Baltic prepared the way for the wars of Charles XII. The attempts to maintain or improve the position of France along her Rhine frontier were to lead, more or less directly, to all the wars of Louis XIV. Finally, two of the major combatants, France and Spain, were still at war and would be for another decade. The Peace of Westphalia was thus both an ending and a beginning.

THE ASCENDANCY OF FRANCE

While France had been deeply involved in the Thirty Years' War in Germany, that conflict was never more than secondary to the basic concern of French foreign policy—Spain and the Spanish-Hapsburg Empire. This concern predated the Thirty Years' War by a century, and persisted for more than a decade after its close. The Bourbon kings inherited the hostilities of their Valois cousins; France continued to be threatened in the seventeenth century by the danger of Hapsburg encirclement on every landward frontier. This Bourbon-Hapsburg enmity was the most important underlying factor in the complex of western European relations on the eve of modern history. Its eventual resolution in favor of France placed that nation at the head of European affairs and European civilization in the reign of Louis XIV. This achievement, however, was not the work of kings, but of two great French ministers of state, the cardinals Richelieu (1585–1642) and Mazarin (1602–1661).

The Rise of Richelieu

The assassination of Henry IV in 1610 destroyed his plan for an immediate intervention in European affairs. His ultimate intention was to set France in a strong position on the Rhine between Spanish Italy and the Spanish Netherlands. This plan seemed doomed by his death, for his successor was his ten-year-old son, Louis XIII. For the next fifteen years the young king was at the mercy of warring factions. Their strife not only ruled out the pursuit of Henry IV's foreign ambitions, but almost wiped out the domestic gains he had so painfully made for France.

The queen mother and regent, Marie de Médicis, became the focus for all the enemies of royal order. She allowed herself to be led and flattered by the Spanish ambassador, by a household of Italian fortune hunters, and by a clique of greedy and irresponsible French nobles. Spain profited by a double-marriage alliance of Louis XIII and his sister with the Spanish Hapsburgs. An Italian rake, Concini, gained a personal ascendancy over the queen. The nobles gained a chance once more to indulge their taste for power and wealth at the expense of the crown. There was no middle ground between monarchy and anarchy. The French historical experience had, as we have seen, created no institution such as the English parliament or even the German Diet, by which the affairs of state could be influenced by the will of any large segment of the people. An abortive meeting of the French Estates-General in 1614—the last before the French Revolution—made this abundantly clear. If there was to be government it must be the government of the king; and when the king was weak or immature, then royal government was in the hands of favorites.

In 1617 Concini's influence was undermined by that of a vacuous noble named Luynes, who gained the affection of the young king. Concini was assassinated and the queen mother exiled from court. She escaped and determined to risk civil war to regain control of her son. This was the crisis that brought Richelieu forward. The son of a minor noble house and the bishop of an obscure see that was hereditary in his family, he had risen in the service of the queen mother and had accompanied her into exile. Now, as civil war threatened, he represented her in negotiations with Luynes and brought about the reconciliation of the queen and her son. For this politic service he was rewarded with a cardinalate.

In 1624 he became a member of the Council of State. Before the year was out the king had named him first minister and the lifelong association of these two unlikely partners had begun: Richelieu, the commanding, sinister, almost disembodied intelligence; Louis, the bumbling, uncertain, loutish devotee of the hunt. The king had only enough grasp of affairs to know that Richelieu was indispensable to him; and this was sufficient for Richelieu. Thus began his life's work: to make the king supreme in France and France supreme in Europe. The obstacle to the latter was Spain; to the former, the French nobility.

In many ways the problem of domestic supremacy was the more pressing. The French nobility was the most idle, arrogant, and potentially dangerous in Europe. The memories of the civil and religious wars of the last century were still fresh, and the brief stability of Henry IV's reign had not been enough to break the back of aristocratic independence. This remained for Richelieu. Almost immediately the nobles began to conspire against him. In 1626 the king's younger brother, Gaston Duke of Orléans, lent himself to a plot to displace Richelieu. It was discovered and crushed. Then in 1630 the queen mother, who now found herself increasingly isolated from her son by Richelieu's influence, prevailed upon Louis to dismiss his minister. But a private conference with the king restored him to favor. The affair was closed with what Richelieu dryly called the "Day of Dupes." The queen mother fled to Brussels and the arms of the Spanish. Two years later the Duke of Montmorency, Marshal of France and one of the greatest of the French nobles, led a rebel force across the frontier from the Spanish Netherlands; he was defeated, captured, and executed. In 1641 another royal favorite, the Marquis of Cinq Mars, who had entered into negotiations with Spain, was discovered and executed.

These plots clearly revealed that the leading French nobles were willing to betray and perhaps destroy their nation for the sake of personal independence or even simply for influence at court. This worked in Richelieu's favor, for each conspiracy merely strengthened his position. Out of the folly of his enemies he fashioned the Bourbon absolutism. For weeding out the conspirators, he was able to strike not only at the court circle but at the great families who ruled as governors in the provinces. One by one they were cut down to be replaced by loyal crown servants drawn largely from the middle class, and called *intendants*. At the same time Richelieu was creating a powerful legal and administrative machinery— his own courts and councils—to facilitate his work of centralization. France was slowly being reduced to instrument in the hands of its cardinal-master.

Important as was Richelieu's consolidation and unification of France, his more important work was in the realm of foreign policy. He was, in a sense, making the king supreme in France *in order to make* France supreme in Europe. The death of Henry IV and the chaotic regency that followed had tended to obscure the Franco-Spanish enmity that had flared up in the last years of the religious wars. But, as Richelieu came to power, the Hapsburg fortunes were on the rise once more and the danger to France was increasing daily. With the early 1520's the war in Germany had moved from Bohemia to the Rhine valley, and the Spanish-Dutch conflict had opened again after the expiration of the Twelve Years' Truce. These two wars were closely related through the family alliance of the Austrian and Spanish Hapsburgs, and both had come to focus on the Rhine corridor.

The southern Netherlands were the base from which Spain operated against the Dutch. Dutch naval supremacy had endangered the Spanish supply line through the narrow seas and, as maritime England drew close to the Dutch Republic, Spain was compelled to depend almost entirely upon supply by land. This was possible only by way of the Rhine corridor that connected the Spanish Netherlands with Spanish Italy and the Mediterranean. Thus, Spanish diplomacy encouraged Emperor Ferdinand II in his condemnation of the Elector Palatine, and strove constantly to bring imperial force to bear upon the lower Rhine against the Dutch and the potential Dutch allies in northwestern Germany. Spanish troops and supplies were fed to the German war as well as to the Spanish Netherlands by the Rhine route. If the Hapsburgs continued to command this route their victory seemed certain; and with victory came the isolation and encirclement of France. Therefore, control of the Rhine became the chief aim of Richelieu's foreign policy. This Hapsburg lifeline ran through the Alps and into Germany by way of the narrow gut of the Valteline valley that lay between Switzerland, Venice, and Milan. Its arch-strategic value was appreciated by Spain, which tried to dominate it from Milan. But it was also appreciated by Richelieu and by Venice, which was endangered in Italy by every accretion of Spanish power. Thus France and Venice allied themselves in 1624, to "protect" Protestant

Swiss control of the valley. This represented Richelieu's opening move against the Hapsburgs. But, at this early point in his ministry, he was still not strong enough to enforce his foreign policy. He had not yet quelled the opposition of the French nobility and, at this crucial time (1626) he was faced with a Huguenot rebellion that forced him to deal with Spain and abandon his strong position in the Valteline.

The Huguenot problem was a serious distraction from Richelieu's chief concern, one that cut across both his foreign and his domestic policy. The death of Henry IV had been an obvious threat to the religious and political freedom of the Huguenots. They began to tighten their organization and prepare for hostilities. As in the days of the religious wars, the Huguenot party sought foreign alliances with England and even with Spain. For many Huguenot nobles, the danger to their party served only to mask personal ambition and greed. By 1626 the government found itself in the midst of a full-scale Huguenot rebellion. Its centers were the armed towns that the Huguenots had been granted, and none was more important than the port city of La Rochelle, through which foreign aid, especially from England, could be poured into the Protestant camp. Richelieu himself took charge of the siege of this city. For almost a year La Rochelle held out, but at last, closed in by land and the harbor blocked, it capitulated. Within a few months the other centers of resistance surrendered. Richelieu, who had conducted the war with cold savagery, addressed the problem of peace with equal coldness. He was not concerned with punishing, but with making use of the rebels. By the Pardon of Alais (1629) the Huguenots were allowed to retain their freedom of religion while they were forced to give up their status as an independent political party. They were no longer to hold fortified towns or have their party organization. By this statesmanlike solution Richelieu was able to disarm a dangerous internal power and, at the same time, command the loyalty of a significant and productive minority of the French people.

The Huguenot interlude, for all its happy solution, had cost Richelieu dearly in another quarter. He had been forced to relinquish the French position on the Valteline. Now he had to find another way to block the Rhine. At this moment the war in Germany was turning to his advantage. The rise of Wallenstein had served to free the emperor from his dependence upon Spain, and thus split the dangerous Hapsburg family alliance. Richelieu was already busily intriguing with any power or powers that might take the initiative against the enemies of France.

He negotiated with the Protestant Christian of Denmark in the north and the Catholic Maximilian of Bavaria in the south. Then, in 1630, Gustavus Adolphus intervened in the cause of German Protestantism and, in Paris, Richelieu exulted at finding a champion capable of destroying the Hapsburg menace for him. While Richelieu and the Swedish king neither trusted nor really understood each other, their mutual needs drove them together. Richelieu needed the military initiative Gustavus was willing to take; Gustavus needed French money in order to maintain his army in Germany. The Treaty of Bärwalde was signed between Richelieu's representatives and the Swedish king in 1631. By its terms Gustavus was to keep a substantial army in Germany in return for a French subsidy of four hundred thousand *thalers*. He was to attempt to restore the empire to its prewar internal boundaries. Richelieu was careful to stipulate that the Catholic religion would not be interfered with. He hoped that Maximilian of Bavaria and the other German Catholic princes could be brought over through their fear of the emperor's strengthened position and obvious imperialist intentions. Such an alliance, hand in hand with his Swedish treaty, would have isolated the emperor and made Richelieu master of Germany.

He was especially eager for this solution in Germany, for his hopes in northern Italy were on the upswing once more, and he might be able to catch both Spain and Austria in one complex diplomatic net. In 1627 the Duke of Mantua had died, leaving a disputed succession to this strategic little north Italian state. Two candidates appeared, one with French and the other with Spanish support. Richelieu intervened at the crucial moment when the Hapsburg emperor was being threatened by Gustavus Adolphus and secured the succession of his candidate. It was a daring stroke and a calculated risk, but it paid off; and in 1631, six months after his treaty with Gustavus, Richelieu signed another treaty whereby he gained possession of one of the key Mantuan fortresses.

While Richelieu could claim to be the master of the European chessboard, the very complexity of his game and the mobility of the pieces kept the situation always uncertain. His one great miscalculation was to underestimate Gustavus Adolphus. He understood his patriotism and territorial ambitions, but he was incapable of understanding the almost spiritual feeling that Gustavus had about the Protestant cause. The Swedish decision to attack Bavaria upset the French calculation completely, for Richelieu wanted to maintain his alliance with both powers.

Before he was compelled to make an unhappy choice between his allies, Richelieu's diplomacy was saved by the emperor's recall of Wallenstein, which forced Gustavus to quit Bavaria in order to face Wallenstein in Saxony. The death of Gustavus at Lützen (1532) removed the greatest figure of the Thirty Years' War—but it also removed a serious obstacle to Richelieu's program. As the affairs of Germany returned once more to stalemated equilibrium, Richelieu moved toward the objective that had always been concealed in his German diplomacy, French control of the Rhine. In the fall of 1633 he sent French troops into Lorraine. Then he allied himself with the Archbishop of Trier and forced now-embattled Sweden to surrender control of Alsace. He had effectively blocked the lifeline of Spain. In February 1635 he concluded a full-scale treaty with the Dutch Republic, and three months later formally declared war on Spain. The latent hostility of Bourbon and Hapsburg had finally come into the war, but only when Richelieu was prepared for it to.

Unfortunately for a continent tired of war, French arms were not equal to the support of French diplomacy. Spain was still a powerful state, even in decline, and her armies still among the most experienced and best disciplined in Europe. It was not until the spring of 1643 at Rocroi, on the borders of the Low Countries, that a French army decisively defeated a major Spanish force. This battle was in many ways the culmination of Richelieu's foreign policy and the definite mark of Spain's decline among the nations of western Europe. Richelieu was not permitted to enjoy his triumph. He had died five months before Rocroi, in December 1642.

Mazarin, the Regency, and Domestic Crisis

The impetus of French arms was sufficient to carry Richelieu's policy through to the Peace of Westphalia, and by 1648 the reins of French government were in the hands of Richelieu's successor, Cardinal Mazarin.

Louis XIII had followed his great minister to the grave within half a year. Once more France had a minor king in the five-year-old Louis XIV, and a foreign queen mother as regent, the Hapsburg Anne of Austria. In an attempt to forestall the trouble that a regency would almost surely bring, Louis XIII and Richelieu had appointed a council to advise the regent, which was representative of the royal house, the high nobility, and the officialdom of the government. The council was torn by strife from the beginning. Its two leading figures were the old intriguer, the king's uncle, the Duke of Orléans, and the Prince of Condé. The only thing on which they agreed was their hatred of Mazarin. Their suspicions of him were well-founded, for he and the queen mother had already begun the intimacy on which he was to build his power (there was even a persistent rumor that they were secretly married). Anne, with Mazarin behind the scenes, played upon the jealousies and ambitions of the councilors. She convinced Condé and Orléans that she was going to dismiss Mazarin and that she would allow them a major share in her regency—if they would petition the Parlement de Paris to dissolve the council and make her sole regent. They eagerly complied and immediately Anne made Mazarin first minister. It was another "Day of Dupes."

The man who thus replaced Richelieu as the power behind the French throne was an Italian ecclesiastic (Guilio Mazarini) who had risen in the papal diplomatic service. He had come to Paris as a minister of the pope in 1634 and caught the eye of Richelieu. Mazarin had represented Richelieu in the complicated and tedious negotiations over the Mantuan succession. His success won him a cardinalate. Since that time he had been the obvious heir to Richelieu's policies and, with the dismissal of the council, he took up Richelieu's position. It is another measure of Richelieu's greatness that he saw his successor in Mazarin, for the two men were temperamentally poles apart: Richelieu, cool, austere, remote; Mazarin, garrulous, devious, almost fawning in his manner, and endlessly deceitful. But, in his own way, Mazarin was as dedicated to the goals that Richelieu had set for France as Richelieu himself—and as successful in achieving them.

At the beginning of his ministry Mazarin faced, as had Richelieu, a rash of plots and intrigues to depose him, and he was equally successful in putting them down. But unfortunately, the petty personal grievances of a handful of high-born plotters stirred a deeper and more fundamental unrest. France was in a desperate financial condition. Richelieu's foreign wars and diplomatic subsidies had been expensive. Furthermore, he had failed consistently to give adequate attention to financial administration or to keep Sully's fiscal machinery in repair. He had raised taxes and sold monopolies and offices recklessly. Mazarin inherited this problem and, like Richelieu, he ignored it. More than this, he set out to enrich himself, his relatives, and his servants at the expense of the nation. It seems incredible that this man could have had such a great sense of responsibility in most areas of government and so little in this one. He and other highly placed officials manipulated the national credit structure for their personal gain and at the expense of the *rentes,* the government debt annuities.

Public confidence was shaken and public protest formed quickly in the vocal middle class, whose security was most obviously threatened. Only the successful progress of the foreign wars prevented an explosion.

In 1648, as the war was drawing to a close, the Parlement de Paris proposed extensive reforms in the financial administration of the country. The proposal was widely supported by the other organs of government. In the summer of 1648 the government was presented with a list of demands, largely for financial reform, but so sweeping as to remove the power of the purse from the hands of the monarchy. The regent and the cardinal yielded for the moment; then they struck back, arresting and imprisoning the leaders of the protest. This treachery touched off the explosion: Paris rose in the rebellion which is known as the *Fronde*. This term derived from the name given to street gangs who threw mud at passers-by; but like many derisive terms, it came to refer generally to protest against the abuses of government.

The first stage of this incipient rebellion has been misnamed the Fronde of the Parlements, or the Constitutional Fronde; actually it never deserved to be thus dignified. While some of its leaders may have had a genuine commitment to constitutionalism, most of them were not seriously concerned with principles of justice or liberty. The Fronde was, at its very best, an economic rebellion led by men who feared for their financial security. Further, the Parlement that took the lead was a narrow and restricted court of law, not a body either representative of the nation or capable of exerting national leadership. The Fronde was a parody of a revolution. But with Paris in arms and the disturbances likely to spread, it was nevertheless a serious danger to the government. The end of the Thirty Years' War enabled the government to direct the brilliant and popular General Condé to besiege Paris.

As the government's position became stronger, that of the besieged rebels weakened. The leadership of the Fronde was appropriated by the same group of nobles who had long opposed Mazarin. Whatever constitutional flavor the movement had ever possessed was quickly lost. The leaders of the Parlement treated for peace and the government was happy to make concessions. In the spring of 1649 the gates of Paris were opened for the reentry of the court. But the Fronde was not finished. The Parlement had lost its chance to make a revolution, but the nobility who had seized the movement were not so ready to relinquish an advantage. They decided that their best chance lay in wooing Condé, hero of the war and siege, by showing him that his alliance with the court was not in his best interest. Working on his ambition—inflated by his recent successes to the point where he saw no place for himself short of head of state—his conspiring relatives and fellow nobles succeeded in winning him over to their plans. But Mazarin, forewarned of the rebellion brewing in the court, struck suddenly and arrested Condé and the other rebellious princes.

This action triggered the second Fronde, or the Fronde of the Princes, which broke out in the spring of 1650. The temper of the rebel princes had spread to their fellow nobles in the provinces. The smoldering resentments that had been stifled since the days of Richelieu flared up once more, and the French nobility made its last significant bid for independence from the crown. Enough confusion of principle remained to attract a certain amount of popular support. Mazarin was sufficiently hated by nearly every class for the prince to use his eminence as a rallying point for a general rebellion. The court was in a hard position. Not only the rash Condé but the sober Turenne defected, and with them practically the whole army. In virtually every province great noble families seized control of affairs once more. The leading nobles were treating with Spain, willing as always to betray their country in return for personal preferment.

In this mounting crisis Mazarin retired from France and the princely party gained the day. The leaders, released from prison, called a convention at the Luxembourg Palace and proposed to place themselves at the head of the government. But once in a position of command, the inherent jealousies and conflicting interests of the *frondeurs* soon revealed them as a selfish faction inimical to the national interest. The middle class and the Parlement rallied to the court. By the end of 1651 Mazarin had returned and Turenne had deserted the rebel cause. In the following year the leading nobles, now in open alliance with Spain, and with Spanish armies once more invading France, saw their revolution collapse in the face of massive national opposition. On October 21, 1652, the queen and Louis XIV, now declared of age, entered Paris in triumph. Some of the rebel leaders fled; others were imprisoned; all were discredited. Where Richelieu and Mazarin had failed, the nobles had finally succeeded in destroying their own political effectiveness. Moreover, they had taught Louis XIV a a lesson he would never forget. When he solemnly reentered his capital in October 1652, he was dedicated forevermore to the principle of monarchical absolutism.

The Conclusion of the War with Spain

The breaking of the Fronde placed Mazarin in control of France once more. The concessions that the government had been forced to make were quickly revoked, and the provinces recalled to order. Secure again, Mazarin turned once more to the problem of Spain. The war between France and Spain had continued after the general settlement of Westphalia. But that settlement necessitated the realignment of French alliances and offered new alternatives to Mazarin. In a way the situation was greatly simplified. The German states were neutralized and the empire divided from Spain. To confirm the balance of power in Germany Mazarin allied himself with the Rhine states as a makeweight against the emperor. Sweden, France's old ally in Germany, still managed to keep a finger in German politics, but was more concerned with her Baltic affairs. The Dutch Republic was out of the war, and to replace this ally Mazarin managed in 1655 to bring England into line against Spain. Cromwell's government had revived the old national anti-Spanish sentiment; English commercial elements welcomed an alliance that would open French markets to them; and Mazarin pledged not to harbor the exiled Stuarts.

With Spain thus carefully boxed in, Mazarin proposed a marriage between young King Louis XIV and the Spanish heiress, Maria Theresa, eldest daughter of Philip IV. It was a brilliant stroke; it would not only ensure French supremacy over Spain, but supremacy over western Europe as the successor of Spain. The implications were not lost on the Spanish ambassadors, and Spain balked. But Mazarin had both time and strength. He tightened his hold along the Rhine and his ties with Cromwell's England. With the latter he launched a joint campaign against the Spanish Netherlands. As success followed military success, Spanish diplomatic resistance flagged. In the fall of 1658 Spain agreed to the marriage proposal, which was finally signed after endless haggling a year later as the Peace of the Pyrenees.

It was a settlement second only in significance to the Peace of Westphalia. It formally ended the war between France and Spain. France as the dominant party to the treaty was confirmed in most of her border conquests on the previous half-century. Maria Theresa renounced her claim to the Spanish succession and Spain agreed, in exchange for this renunciation, to pay an enormous dowry of half a million crowns. (The fact that this dowry was never paid became the basis for the French claims forty years later in the War of the Spanish Succession.) For the moment it was peace and victory, both military and diplomatic, for Mazarin's France. In the summer following the signing of the peace Louis XIV and Maria Theresa were married in one of the most splendid ceremonies of the century. Mazarin had completed the work of Henry IV and Richelieu. He died in the spring of 1661, and the personal reign of Louis XIV began.

STUART ENGLAND: REACTION, REVOLUTION, AND COMPROMISE

The Estrangement of King and Parliament

The death of Elizabeth marked the passing of an era. She was the last of the direct Tudor line and her successor had long been designated in the King of Scotland, James VI, of the House of Stuart, the descendant of the Scots marriage of Henry VIII's sister. James became James I of England (1603–1625). Any ruler who followed Elizabeth would have had a difficult task. After a reign of almost half a century she had become a living legend. Moreover, her prestige had masked rumblings of discontent in her later parliaments and with her death several long-suppressed issues came to the fore. James was not the man to deal with them effectively.

The new king had an initial disadvantage in being a Scot, for English hatred of their northern cousins had become almost a part of the national faith. Furthermore, James had neither an engaging manner nor prepossessing appearance. He was arbitrary, stubborn, and pedantic; he seemed to lack completely that gift for sensing the temper of the people which the greatest of the Tudors had so surely possessed. James I did not have the makings of a popular king. What is more, he had no desire to be one, for James brought with him to the English throne the doctrine of divine right, which was to serve his house so badly in the century to come. This doctrine had already taken shape on the continent largely because of the extension of religious dispute into war and politics. James had accepted it completely and had every intention of applying it in England, where he confidently expected to rule without restraint of any sort, accountable only to God.

Armed with this foreign doctrine—predictably unacceptable to many of his new subjects—James pitted himself against the two major issues that had come to the fore following Elizabeth's death. The first arose from the growing strength of those unwilling to accept the state religion. The second, soon to become intertwined with the first, stemmed from the growing demand of Parliament for a more significant role in royal government.

The Elizabethan religious settlement was, as we have seen, a broad doctrinal compromise inspired more by political than purely religious considerations. While it was acceptable to most Englishmen, it excluded, at one end of the scale, the most extreme Catholics and, at the other, the most extreme Protestants. Although these groups had suffered some disabilities, especially the Catholics, they had been tolerated in fact and continued to exist through Elizabeth's reign. The very dogmatism that had kept them outside the Elizabethan church nourished their conviction that they were right.

The English Catholics were still a significant minority in spite of popular hostility, which tended to identify them with Spain, plots, and treason. But the war with Spain was past and the Catholics looked to James to rescind the penal laws that made them second-class citizens. With his usual vacillation and poor sense of timing, James first made some concessions to the English Catholics and then withdrew them. Both moves he made from principle. He removed the "church-going fines" which they had been compelled to pay out of a genuine feeling for justice and humanitarianism. Then, when he saw how eagerly and in what number the Catholics availed themselves of their new liberty, he feared the consequences of his indulgence and reimposed the fines. In the fall of 1605, as the Parliament was about to open its session, a large cache of gunpowder was discovered in the basement of the building where the session would meet. Investigation revealed that this "Gunpowder Plot" was an elaborate and far-reaching Catholic conspiracy to seize the government. The reaction to its discovery was immediate and savage. The plot was crushed and all the popular fear and suspicion of Catholics came flooding back, along with a host of even more severe anti-Catholic laws. In spite of the fact that the plot was directed in part against the king, James was never able to shake a popular suspicion that he was pro-Catholic. Nor did he do much to counteract this false impression, though in fact he was as militantly opposed to Catholic doctrine as any Puritan divine.

Despite the furor over the "Gunpowder Plot," the English Catholics were not a serious threat at this time. On the other hand, the Protestant extremist groups—the Puritans—had been growing in number and significance and were rapidly becoming the most important socio-religious group in the realm. Puritanism was essentially Calvinistic. During the religious troubles of Edward and Mary in the last century, militant Calvinism had penetrated England from the continent and had been grafted to the vague populist Protestantism that had grown up after Henry VIII's break with Rome. From these beginnings English Puritanism had grown in many directions and manifested itself in a number of splinter sects, which tended to elevate one or another point of theology and wrangle with each other as bitterly as with "outsiders." But whatever particular beliefs the various Puritan sects held, they held them dogmatically and arbitrarily. All of them wanted to "purify" the church, but no two groups could be found to agree on what precisely was to be purified first among the lingering "Poperies" of the established worship. But beneath such diversities Puritanism had a common base on the bedrock of Calvinist morality. Whatever else the Puritan believed, he was convinced of the reality of sin. He saw its evidence everywhere and tried with all his might to combat it in himself and in his loose-living neighbors. This resulted in the harsh, humorless bigotry that was the most obvious identifying mark of the Puritans. They studiously avoided fashionableness in dress or grooming, affecting "sad-coloured and simply cut clothes" in homespun fabrics; they larded their speech with Biblical words and phrases; they saw the work of Satan in even the most innocent pastimes and pleasures. In all, they wore the sin of spiritual pride as the badge of their convictions.

Like the Catholics, the Puritans looked to the new king for aid and reform. Almost immediately upon his arrival in England James was presented with a lengthy petition drawn up by a great number of Puritan clergymen, calling for a number of reforms in the established church. Again, James was not hostile to the idea of church reform in itself. He called a conference to debate the various issues before him, the so-called Hampton Court Conference. In the course of the discussions one of the Puritan disputants made an inadvertent reference to "presbyters." This was an extremely touchy issue with James, who had suffered from the meddling of the Presbyterians in Scotland. He had no intention of allowing any vestige of Presbyterianism in England. In a rage he dismissed the whole conference and denied the petition.[2] From then on James was

2. Almost the only good thing that came out of the petition was James' authorization for a new translation of the Bible, which was finished in 1611, the famous King James Version.

convinced that all Puritans by their attack on the established church threatened his divine absolutism. For their part, the Puritans relinquished any hope of furthering their aims through the king. Thus began the process by which the Puritans would be converted from a religious to a revolutionary political party. In the first two years of his reign James had driven the Catholics to an abortive revolution and alienated the Puritans beyond all hope of reconciliation.

He had little better success with Parliament. By 1611 he had alienated his first Parliament almost as completely as he had the Puritans. Indeed, his mishandling of the religious issues carried over into his relations with Parliament to pile discord upon discord. Fundamentally, James had no understanding of the historic role of Parliament nor of the processes of English government. The whole idea of representative participation in government seemed an encroachment upon the Godly business of "kingscraft." In the first session of his first Parliament James clashed with the Commons on a range of issues that crystalized their basic antipathy. The Commons stated the case of Parliament in a document modestly titled, *The Apology of the House of Commons to the King.* It began with the dissimulating statement that their "Most Gracious Sovereign" had been "greatly wronged by misinformation," and went on to correct it:

> With all humble and due respect to your Majesty, . . . we must truly avouch, first, that our privileges and liberties are our right and due inheritance, no less than our very lands and goods. Secondly, that they cannot be withheld from us, denied, or impaired, but with apparent wrong to the whole state of the realm.[3]

The *Apology* then set forth a considerable list of further parliamentary rights, extended to include the "free choice" of members by "the shires, cities, and boroughs of England," that those elected "during the time of the parliament, as also of their access and recess, be free from restraint, arrest, and imprisonment," and "that in parliament they may speak freely their consciences without check or controlment."

The sessions of the next six years were as stormy as the first. In 1614 James called his second Parliament. He tried, without conspicuous success, to intimidate the voters and rig the election. He asked for revenues; the members asked for redress of grievances. James dissolved the Parliament, which had sat for exactly two months and had passed not a

3. E. P. Cheney, *Readings in English History* . . . ,new ed. (Boston: Ginn and Co., 1935), pp. 428-29.

single bill. It has been called the "Addled Parliament." Several of the most outspoken leaders of the house were arrested and imprisoned.

Yet James' absolutist victory was more apparent than real. He was happy enough to rule without Parliament, but he was neither happy nor able to rule without money, and this is precisely what he was forced to do. The fixed income of the crown had been diminished by the growing inflation of the sixteenth century. James, furthermore, had no head for finance and loved to keep a luxurious court with a retinue of expensive favorites as befit his station. It was his financial straits which had compelled him to call the Parliament of 1614. When he failed to gain his "supply" from the truculent house he resolved, supply or not, to rule without Parliament; and he did so, until 1621. During this time he tried every expedient to solve the monetary problems that were approaching crisis proportions. His demands and exactions served only to harden the hostility between the king and his people. The domestic impasse was finally broken by the crisis of foreign affairs.

In the early years of James' reign the continental powers were moving toward another round of wars. The crucial factor was once more the threat of Hapsburg domination. And once more the anti-Hapsburg, anti-Spanish sentiment of the English people was revived. The war issue in England came to focus upon the question of the Rhine Palatinate and the fate of its elector, Frederick V, in the opening phase of the Thirty Years' War.[4] Frederick was married to the daughter of James I, the popular and lovely Princess Elizabeth; Frederick was, furthermore, the nominal leader of German Protestantism; and finally, he seemed to be leading the fight against the Hapsburgs. On every score the English people were enthusiastic for his support. Here was an issue that could unite the nation and the king as nothing else could. But James, with his usual wrongheadedness, threw away his chance.

Since the beginning of his reign James had been favorably disposed to Spain. He saw no reason to continue hostilities and had favored a marriage alliance with this great continental power. While, in terms of cold diplomatic logic this was not a bad course, in terms of national temper and tradition it was an impossible one. Hostility to Spain was too deepseated in the English national experience. Furthermore, the continued state of hostility left English privateers and maritime companies free to prey on the almost defenseless Spanish shipping. James' stubborn courting

4. See p. 675.

of Spain added materially to his unpopularity. In addition he was thoroughly used and duped by Spanish diplomats. The Spanish talked peace and alliance, fed James' ego and pompous theories, and encouraged his estrangement from his people—while Spanish troops moved on to the Palatine frontier. Only when the Palatinate fell did James realize the consequences of his pro-Spanish policy, and prepared to go to war. It was a popular cause and the Parliament James summoned in 1621 was ready to bury all past grievances and support him.

Under the circumstances it took almost unbelievable ineptitude for the king to alienate his people. But this he did. He asked Parliament for a large money grant to conduct the war. The parliamentary leaders respectfully asked him how it was to be used. He refused to tell them. Certainly he was within the letter of his right as commander-in-chief, but it was hardly a politic action. The Parliament, however, was still willing to support him and granted a token subsidy as proof of good faith. Then in the months that followed the worst suspicions of the parliamentary leaders were confirmed. What money had been granted was put in the hands of irresponsible and arrogant court favorites whose misuse of royal monopolies was already a national disgrace. And James came once more under the malign influence of the Spanish ambassador. The king failed to see what was obvious to every other court in Europe: that the Hapsburgs, whether the Spanish or the Austrian branch, were a common menace, and that their policies and their wars were family undertakings. While still trying to raise forces for intervention in the Palatinate, James entered actively into a negotiation with Spain for a marriage alliance for his son Prince Charles. These confusions and contradictions in English foreign policy naturally delighted Spain and understandably frustrated Parliament. Parliament tried to force the issue by proceedings of impeachment against the most obnoxious of royal favorites and monopolists, by insisting on a war with Spain, and by advising the king to seek a Protestant bride for Prince Charles. This James regarded as an insufferable invasion of his royal prerogative. Once more he dissolved Parliament with feelings more bitter than ever on both sides.

At this juncture a bizarre incident took the initiative out of the king's hands. Prince Charles decided, on an impulse, to travel to Spain to press his royal suit and see his intended bride. Accompanied only by his close friend George Villiers, an emptyheaded court favorite who had been made Duke of Buckingham, the gallant prince made his way to Spain. The whole affair was like a grotesque romantic comedy. The Spanish court was caught by surprise and made hasty arrangements to entertain the royal guest. There were embarrassing incidents of all sorts. Charles wanted to see his bride but was put off with excuses and long-winded theological discussions. Then one night he leaped over her garden wall only to have her flee from him in horror. It became obvious even to Charles that there would be no Spanish marriage. He could not afford to renounce his state religion and this was pleaded as an indispensable condition of the marriage. Convinced that the Spanish had made fools of his father, himself, and his nation, Charles returned to England. James' foreign policy, such as it was, lay in ruins; and Charles was prepared to lead a war against Spain.

The prince found himself a popular hero with unlimited support. The Parliament of 1624 was a war parliament. Charles and Buckingham had virtually seized the management of the king's affairs. While the warlike bluster went on, a more appropriate marriage alliance was being sought with France, the great continental enemy of Spain. It was arranged for Charles to marry Princess Henrietta Maria, the sister of Louis XIII. But once more the religious issue was raised. In France Richelieu was not yet firmly in command of royal policy and could not risk the danger of such a marriage alliance without demanding protection for English Catholics. To the great majority of the Catholic French the memories of the religious wars were still too fresh. In England James, pressed by Charles and Buckingham, accepted the marriage on Richelieu's terms and appended to the understanding a secret agreement for Catholic toleration. This impossible treaty was almost the last act of "the wisest fool in Christendom." He died in 1625, before the marriage he had arranged could be celebrated later in the same year.

From Estrangement to Rebellion

Charles I (*1625–1649*) succeeded his father on a crest of popularity that James had never known. But Charles was attractive largely by contrast to James. None of the basic issues that had divided the king from the representatives of his people for more than twenty years had changed. Charles was as obstinate as his father precisely on the point of royal absolutism, and Parliament began to be disenchanted with its new sovereign before the first sessions of 1625 had ended.

By the time this session met, several points of irritation had already been established, the most important of them being the conduct of the war. The supply granted the previous year, little as it was, had been squandered. Now Charles wanted more money; Commons balked; they wanted a naval war to strike directly at Spain, not the expensive, unfamiliar, inglorious venture into the business of troops, supplies, mercenaries, and subsidies, which was the kind of war Charles wanted on the continent. Their dissatisfaction came to focus upon Buckingham. He had, after all, engineered the French marriage that was viewed suspiciously by the Commons. He had advocated the policy of intervention in collusion with Richelieu, and he was the chief spokesman for the king. As the criticism of Buckingham mounted, Charles intervened and dissolved the Parliament. But the probing and questioning had revealed two things: Buckingham was the real author of royal policy, and Charles was willing to throw away the confidence of Parliament and the hope of a successful war to preserve his favorite.

With neither parliamentary sanction nor money, Charles and Buckingham recklessly continued the course of their foreign policy. Buckingham, hoping to gain popular support, organized a naval expedition to strike at the Spanish port of Cadiz, as Raleigh had done in the previous century. This expedition was as badly managed and as disastrously unsuccessful as the continental intervention of 1624. And, to add to the confusion, England began to drift toward war with France, ironically enough due to Buckingham, who had originally engineered the Anglo-French alliance in his enthusiasm for war against Spain. Having first made concessions to Richelieu to secure the treaty, Buckingham then began to regret the bargain. When France refused to change the terms, his sensitive honor was affronted. Then the Huguenots rebelled against Richelieu and the cardinal added insult to injury by asking the English to honor the marriage agreement by supplying naval support to be used against the Huguenot city of La Rochelle. This brought the crisis of Anglo-French relations to a head.

At this point Charles' second Parliament met and began impeachment proceedings against Buckingham. Again Charles dissolved the Parliament and saved Buckingham. With his war still to fight and no parliamentary grant, Charles resorted to a forced loan, demanding of the parliamentary constituencies contributions equivalent to what Parliament *should* have granted him. He found solid resistance almost everywhere. By this time relations with France had deteriorated completely; Buckingham was now as ardent for war with France as he had been before for alliance. In response to the French demand for help against La Rochelle, Buckingham instead personally led a naval expedition to the relief of that beleaguered city. It was hoped that this blow for the Huguenots would recoup the reputation of the crown and the favorite. Instead it was another disastrous failure.

A generation earlier the touchy domestic constitutional and religious issues of James' reign had led into the tangle of foreign policy. Now the foreign policy of Charles and Buckingham led back into domestic strife. The Puritan element in Parliament, as in the country at large, had greatly increased. The Puritan leaders had never trusted James on religious questions—and trusted Charles even less. They deeply resented the French marriage alliance. They saw the continental military failures of Charles and Buckingham as desertion of their fellow Protestants. They interpreted the bungling of the Spanish war as some sort of toadying to Popery. They thoroughly disapproved the elegance and what they regarded as the immorality of the court circle. The consistent failure of the government to favor their religious cause in any way made them darkly suspicious of every policy, foreign or domestic, however innocent. They found a justification for their suspicions and hostilities in the so-called New School of theology, a counter-Puritan movement that had begun within the English church. In previous years the theology of the established church had absorbed considerable Calvinist elements. The New School reversed this trend by favoring more ritual in the service, and in general fostering a Henrican Anglo-Catholic, as opposed to a Calvinistic, point of view on most ecclesiastical and religious questions. This group had been growing in significance and had found considerable support from both James I and Charles. The Puritans saw the favors accorded the New School as nothing less than concessions to Catholicism, further evidence of the crown's Catholic sympathy. The Stuart religious policy had forged the Puritans into a party whose leaders were the most prominent spokesmen against the government. They had been joined by a great many others who were not necessarily Puritan in religion but who opposed the crown on constitutional questions. It was this broadened political and religious Puritanism which had come to dominate the Parliament in the reign of Charles.

Parliament's persistent denial of financial support forced the king and Buckingham to increasingly despotic measures to support their war effort, making the success of that effort even more unlikely. The forced loan was such a measure, and was regarded by its victims as "taxation without representation." Many who opposed it were imprisoned. But the forced loan failed and its failure left Charles without adequate funds to pay the soldiers who had been recruited for continental service. As an expedient, they were billeted on the civil population. The civilian protests that followed were peremptorily handled by military courts, which the government justified by the existence of a state of war. These bitter popular grievances came to a head in the Parliament of 1628, which followed hard upon the failure of Buckingham's expedition to La Rochelle.

Parliament immediately drew up the Petition of Right, one of the most important of English constitutional documents. It dealt not only with abuses but with the fundamental human rights that Parliament now knew to be threatened. The chief demands of the petition were: protection of the people from arbitrary taxation, from arbitrary imprisonment, from military billeting, and from the imposition of martial law. The petition, sweetened by the offer of a substantial money grant, was offered to the king. He could accept it or dissolve Parliament. He accepted it and it became part of the law of the land, amid wild demonstrations of popular approval. There were bonfires and street dances. Couriers took the news to every corner of the realm. But it was no real victory over the king, for he rejected the theory it represented. Because these concessions had been wrung from him, Charles did not feel bound to honor them—as was soon to become obvious.

While the government prepared to spend its new-found substance on another campaign against La Rochelle, an event occurred more damaging to Charles I than a dozen petitions of right. Buckingham was assassinated by a madman; Charles lost his closest friend, adviser, alter ego, and, in a curious way, his most important protector. By Buckingham's arrogant usurpation of the royal prerogative he had pushed the king into the background. Thus the angry force of popular opinion had been directed largely at him rather than the king. Even most of the leaders of Parliament were still loyal to Charles and felt him to be the victim of bad advice. But the removal of Buckingham left Charles virtually unprotected from his people's hostility. Within a year Charles dismissed Parliament once more (1629) and entered upon the eleven years of personal rule during which he would complete the alienation of his people and lay his country open to civil war.

Charles began his personal rule by having several of the most outspoken leaders of Parliament arrested for their opposition to him in the house—thus clearly violating the point of Parliamentary free speech that the Stuart absolutism had already made so sore an issue.

The decision to rule without Parliament, however, ended the folly of Charles' foreign policy, for he could no longer afford war. Indeed, the war debts and the cost of his court made it almost impossible for him to afford peace. Since Charles had no intention of calling Parliament he resorted to a long series of ingenious financial expedients to supply himself with money. He demanded, for example, the so-called forest fines. The king disputed the legality of ownership of lands that had once been royal forest. Some of the land so challenged had been in private hands for centuries, but in order to legalize the possession the owners were compelled to pay substantial fines. Charles skirted the monopolies law and granted new and lucrative monopolies whose recipients then victimized the public with their prices, often of basic commodities.[5] But the most famous of these royal exactions was ship money. This was based upon a medieval precedent by which coastal towns provided ships or their money equivalent for the defense of the realm in time of national peril. Charles used this precedent to impose a tax upon the coastal towns, then upon the inland towns. A man named John Hampton refused to pay on the grounds that this was an illegal tax imposed without Parliament's consent. He lost in the courts but the Hampton ship money case became another symbol of national opposition to the king.

Charles' highhanded way of raising money was only one of the causes of growing opposition to him. Even more offensive to the nation were his religious policies. We have already mentioned that he favored the New School, the "high church" group which came to be known as Anglican. The tenets of this group pleased his own sense of religious propriety and dignity. Moreover, its theology tended to support—at least by implication—the royal absolutism to which Charles was dedicated. Thus his support of the Anglicans was a way of striking at the political as well as religious principles of the Puritans. Finally, it is important to realize that Charles was a typical seventeenth-century prince committed to the notion of religious uniformity. Consequently, his favoring of the Anglicans represented more than a declaration of personal preference—it raised an issue of national significance.

In 1633 Charles elevated the leading spirit of the New School, Bishop William Laud, to the archbishopric of Canterbury. With the king's firm backing and the sanction of such courts as Star Chamber

---

5. One such was a monopoly on soap, which was granted to a group of Catholics prominent at court. It was called Popish Soap and the Puritans were convinced it would not only corrupt the body but the soul as well. See G. M. Trevelyan, *England under the Stuarts* (London: Methuen and Co. Ltd., 1949), p. 133.

and the Court of High Commission,[6] Laud began a program of uncompromising enforcement of religious uniformity. The Laudian reforms not only offended the most zealous Puritans, but that increasing number of Englishmen who were being driven to support the Puritans for various reasons. Laud took a position so extreme that it was acceptable only to the barest minority of the nation. The Puritans became convinced that he was deliberately paving the way for the restoration of Catholicism. While this was probably not Laud's intention, there was a germ of truth in the Puritan suspicion. The influence of the French-Catholic queen had been instrumental in reviving the fortunes of a Catholic court faction, which worshiped openly by the old forms. Charles personally had no great objection to the Catholic worship and this permissiveness flowed out from the court into the land.

It was Charles' attempt to impose the Laudian reform on Scotland that brought about the crises which led to his overthrow. English relations with Scotland had been in limbo since the first year of his father's reign. James I had tried to effect a formal union between the two countries whose king he was, but a suspicious Parliament rejected the act of union. Nonetheless, James loved the title King of Great Britain and, indeed, a union of sorts did exist. But the Scots clung stubbornly to their independent tradition, and particularly to their Presbyterian religion. When Charles ordered the imposition of Laud's church reforms in Scotland (1637), the Scots rose in armed rebellion against the Anglican Prayerbook and the episcopal system in what is known as the First Bishops' War. It was actually the first blood of the great civil war shortly to come. Without funds adequate for peace, Charles now faced a serious war. The only thing left was to call Parliament in the hope that the nation would rally to the war cause and forget the grievances that had piled up for a decade.

Charles had miscalculated again. The people as a whole felt more sympathy for the religious position of the Scots than for that of Charles and his archbishop. And, whatever they may have felt toward the Scots, their own grievances were uppermost in their minds. District after district elected the most outspoken critics of the government, the Puritans and parliamentarians who had suffered imprisonment and indignities at Charles' hands. Faced by such a hostile assembly, Charles had no re-

6. While such courts had been used by the Tudors, they had been used largely with public support. Now they were used against the public interest and will and their doubtful constitutional status was quickly called into question.

course but to dismiss the session after scarcely three weeks. Thus ended the Short Parliament and Charles still lacked the supply necessary to raise an adequate army.

A hastily assembled force, pressed into reluctant service, ill-armed, untrained, and unprovisioned, dissolved as the warlike Scots army moved across the northern frontier in the Second Bishops' War. England lay open to attack with an enemy already across the border and no means of defense. In the fall of 1640 Charles summoned the Parliament that was to sit, in one form or another for almost twenty years, to sanction the revolt of the English nation, the execution of a king, and finally the restoration of the Stuart monarchy. It was aptly called the Long Parliament.

This time there was no tug of war over supply and grievance. The king at last gave up the initiative and Parliament seized it. Almost its first act was to strike down by legal action the chief agents of the king. One of the most notorious of them, the brutal Lord Strafford, was condemned to execution. Archbishop Laud was impeached, imprisoned, and later executed. Then the Parliament rushed through a series of laws to preserve its position—a provision for regular sessions, with or without royal summons, the provision that Parliament could not be dissolved without its own approval, the abolition of the special royal courts that had served the Stuart tyranny so well. But on the question of religious reform the Parliament divided. There was general hostility to Laud's reform program but no general agreement on what should replace it. Here the religious Puritans and their political allies tended to split. A large moderate party was content with the basic English church and wished to go no farther in the "reformed" direction.

With division in Parliament growing more bitter, another military crisis arose: the Irish rebelled. If they were to be put down an army would have to be raised. But could it be entrusted to the king? Would this not restore by arms the very absolutism that Parliament was trying to destroy by legislation? The radical, largely Puritan party insisted that parliamentary control was essential. The moderates contended that this would simply replace a royal with a parliamentary tyranny and were driven back to support the king—many, it is true, only with the greatest reluctance. Parliament thus divided almost equally between Puritan-parliamentarians and Episcopal-royalists. The issue of the Irish revolt was forgotten for the moment, but it had served to catalyze the parties of the English Civil War.

The Civil War

In the early summer of 1642 the revolutionary party in Parliament presented the king with a bill of propositions tantamount to an ultimatum. They asked for parliamentary control of the military, parliamentary control of church reform, and virtual guardianship of the crown. If Charles planned to remain king he had no choice but to reject these proposals. This he did, and the breach between king and Parliament was complete. The king withdrew to Nottingham, followed by a substantial number of the Parliament. The remaining members formed a revolutionary government and began to raise arms.

Thus began the English Civil War. Though often called the Puritan Revolution, it was by no means simply a "war of religion." Like the Thirty Years' War on the continent, the English revolution was a war over political and constitutional as well as religious issues. For precisely this reason it cut across lines of class and region. The high nobility

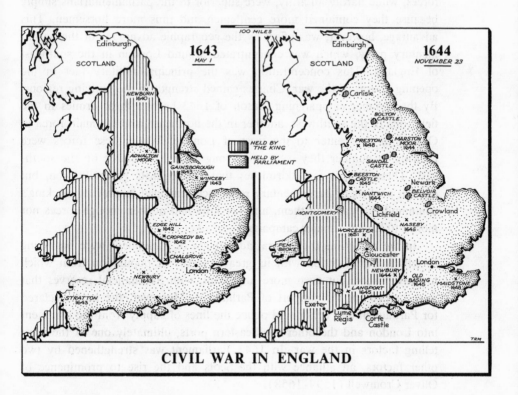

CIVIL WAR IN ENGLAND

generally fought for the king. The townsmen, who were heavily Puritan, generally fought for Parliament. The country gentry were deeply divided. Many fought for the king but many had been representatives of districts, some even of towns, and thus tended to go with Parliament. Men of every class divided on the religious issue. Some of the king's most out-spoken critics on constitutional grounds still supported him out of loyalty to the established church or fear of religious radicalism. There were great and wealthy noblemen who fought for Parliament, townsmen who fought for the king. None of the terms or party names that were hurled back and forth—Puritan, Cavalier, Episcopalian, or Independent—really defined either party.

Hostilities opened slowly, for both sides had to feel their way. England had no standing army to declare for one party or the other. The long financial duel between crown and Parliament had attenuated both the number and discipline of the reserve forces of militia, as the Scots crisis had clearly revealed. Thus both sides had to form armies. The royalist forces, while hardly an army, were superior to the parliamentarians simply because they contained more gentlemen and thus more horsemen. This advantage, however, was offset by the geographic advantage of the parlia-mentary party, which was concentrated around London in the southeast of England. This concentration was the principal military fact in the opening phases of the war. Charles gained strength in the outlying regions. By the summer campaigning season of 1643 he had three armies in the field; one in the southwest, another in the northeast, and his main force at Oxford in the center to the west of London. While these forces were growing in number they were not strong enough to march on the south-east. There were a few skirmishes that the royalists generally won, but enough pockets of parliamentary resistance remained to prevent the king's commanders bypassing them, and the king had neither enough forces nor money to launch a major campaign.

In the meantime the natural advantages of Parliament were beginning to tell. It held London with its great reserves of population from which to draw forces, but even more important, with its financial reserves that were tapped for the support of Parliament. Moreover, the navy declared for Parliament and thus could police the lines of supply from the continent into London and the other southeastern ports, ultimately one of the most telling factors in the war. In 1643 Parliament was strengthened by two other factors, an alliance with the Scots and the rise to prominence of Oliver Cromwell (1599–1658).

The pact with the Scots was called the Solemn League and Covenant. By its terms a religious understanding was reached with the Presbyterian Scots. They joined the parliamentarians in prosecuting the war and put their invaluable military forces into the cause of the rebellion. But of even greater importance to Parliament, 1643 and 1644 brought Cromwell into the forefront of the war. He was a Puritan squire from the eastern counties who had sat through the frustrating parliamentary sessions leading up to the war. He had fought in several of the early engagements and had trained the best regiment of cavalry in the parliamentary army, by infusing his men with an indomitable sense of religious purpose. They were psalm-singing crusaders, willing to submit to the iron discipline of command, willing to learn the hard lessons of tactics from a stern chief, because they believed in the righteousness of what they did. They were soon to be called the Ironsides and their pride of spirit gradually permeated a large portion of the Parliamentary forces. Cromwell himself became cavalry commander for the regional army of the Eastern Association. The proof of Cromwell and his soldiery first came at Marston Moor, the greatest pitched battle of the civil war, in which Cromwell slaughtered the best force Charles had. It was from that battle that he wrote, "God made them as stubble to our swords."

On the heels of military victory the parliamentary cause seemed about to be lost in council. The parliamentarians had begun to splinter on religious and political questions, and the haggling of the civilian leaders threatened to destroy the military. At this point Cromwell, capitalizing on his considerable prestige, persuaded Parliament to overhaul the command of the armies and to press the war to its conclusion. Largely on his recommendation the military forces were consolidated into one large, well-paid, and well-trained force—the New Model Army, of which Cromwell himself shortly became the moving spirit. In the summer of 1645 the New Model Army overwhelmed the chief remaining force of the king at Naseby. Within a few months the last scattered bands of royalists had been defeated and the last strongholds taken. Charles I, out of money and out of support, surrendered to the Scots.

With the restoration of peace it looked as if Charles, though defeated, might still profit from the division of his enemies. Again the religious issue was paramount. The parliamentary leaders had moved almost completely to the Presbyterian position and were advocating a Presbyterian state church. Those who wanted no such conformity, Presbyterian or otherwise, found their only remaining support in Cromwell and the army, which gradually became the champion of the "Independent" party. Thus the victors divided. Charles I, still king notwithstanding his defeat, could have seized the initiative from either party, for both the Parliament and the army proposed alliance with Charles and terms for his restoration. Had Charles been willing to lend the sanction of his royal legitimacy to either party he might have been restored. Instead he tried to play them off against each other. Failing in this, he allied himself with the Scots, promising a Presbyterian church in return for their support. In the eyes of the Puritans Charles was now not only false to religion, but the enemy of his country. The Scots were defeated in a brief second round of civil war and the completely discredited king was captured. The army now commanded the situation.

In the winter of 1648 the army overawed Parliament and excluded the pro-Presbyterian members. The remnant of the Parliament that remained was the "rubber stamp" of the army. This so-called Rump Parliament proposed the execution of the king. What was left of the House of Lords violently opposed it. The Commons rejected the authority of the Lords, abolished that body completely and, in the name of the people, ordered the execution of "that man of blood, Charles Stuart." On January 30, 1649, he was beheaded.

The Failure of the Commonwealth

By dying Charles I did more for the cause of monarchy in England than he had ever done in life. The profoundly shocking Act of Regicide symbolized for the vast majority of Englishmen the ruin of their revolution. In less than a decade it had passed from populist revolt to military oligarchy. When the Long Parliament had been summoned, its members carried with them the protest of a whole nation against the abuses of the Stuart tyranny. But on the issue of open revolution against the crown, two-thirds of the Lords and more than one-third of the Commons chose to support the king. Religious dissension had further reduced the size and the representation of Parliament. The exclusion of the Presbyterian members had produced the Rump, which represented the army and which was guilty of the execution of the king. Thus the government which was declared a Commonwealth in 1649 was a minority government; it had neither the political nor the religious support of the people. It owed its existence to the military, on which it would further depend for its survival. Moreover, it was immediately called on to face enemies both close at hand and abroad.

The Puritan victory in England triggered a wholesale revolt in Ireland. The Irish, already in rebellion at the opening of the civil war, had thrown their lot with Charles in exchange for his promise of Catholic toleration. This "betrayal" by the king had done great damage to the royalist cause in the course of the war, and had crystalized all the fanatic hatred of English Protestantism against the Irish. In 1649 the Irish declared the son of the dead king, King Charles II. Cromwell, at the head of an expeditionary force, invaded Ireland. Within little more than a year he had subdued virtually the whole island. Tens of thousands of Irish were excluded from amnesty, imprisoned, executed, or transported. Settlements were broken up to destroy their sense of community, and their people dispersed throughout the country. Estates were confiscated. The most savage religious regulations were strictly imposed.

While the Irish campaign was in full swing the former Scots allies of the English Puritans also seized the opportunity for revolt. The Scots had earlier been willing to deal with Charles I in exchange for his hollow promise to establish Presbyterianism in England. They made much the same bargain with his son. In 1650 and 1651 Cromwell once more defeated the Scots, who were then forced to treat. The Scots settlement, because it was not complicated by the Catholic problem, was much more generous and enlightened than that in Ireland.

The wars of the Commonwealth in Ireland and on the Scots frontier were largely wars of religion and politics, but it was principally pounds and shillings that led to the larger conflicts with the Dutch and with Spain. From the beginning of the troubles between James I and his parliaments the Puritan middle class had advocated an aggressive naval policy. During the civil war the navy had deserted the king for Parliament. The control of the seas around England and the free flow of trade had been one of the important strengths of the parliamentarians in the war. With its end the Puritan merchants continued to press for naval strength. This was necessary for several reasons. France had been brought to the verge of war by the success of the English revolution, and French markets were closed to English goods. This meant that England had to be prepared to defend her coasts; it meant also that the English had to gain economic compensation elsewhere—from the growing number of colonies.

These had been greatly expanded, especially in New England, by the steady Puritan migration in the years leading up to the civil war. The war, however, had carried over to the New World and the southern colonies such as Virginia and the colonies of the West Indies had remained royalist. These, unfortunately, were the only English colonies with a substantial export trade. Thus, the Puritan government found it imperative to bring them back into line. This was done by enforcing a virtual blockade on the colonies.

What would have been otherwise simply a colonial issue was complicated by the role of the Dutch in world trade. The Navigation Act of 1651 was superficially a restriction of English colonial trade to English vessels. But it was equally a blow at the Dutch carrying trade. By mid-century these two great Atlantic naval powers were already on the eve of conflict. On the sea the Dutch had seized the initiative from Spain and ruined the trade of the Spanish Netherlands. The lapse of a strong English naval policy under the first two Stuarts had left the Dutch without a rival at sea until the Puritan Commonwealth challenged them by passage of the first Navigation Act. For two years (1652–1654) the first of a series of Anglo-Dutch naval wars was waged. It seesawed back and forth, finally ending with a slight advantage to the English. But it was shortly to be opened once more, and to be carried on through much of the remainder of the century.

The colonial issue led not only to the Dutch war but to a war with Spain, which followed immediately. It was, in a way, a political smoke screen set up by Cromwell. He hoped that a war with Spain, the traditional enemy of England, would arouse popular enthusiasm for his increasingly unpopular, minority government. The attack was directed at the cluster of rich Spanish colonies in the West Indies and was, to a degree, successful. The naval operations were supplemented by a show of military force on the continent to back up Cromwell's diplomatic maneuvering, not so much against Spain as against the Dutch. Cardinal Mazarin in France needed help in forcing a peace with Spain. Pressure could be most readily exerted in the Spanish Netherlands: it was in this connection and in this region that the strange alliance was made between the French cardinal and the English Puritan. Both gained what they wanted: the cardinal kept the pressure on Spain, while Cromwell's forces seized the town of Dunkirk, which could be used as a threat against the Dutch. In all, the foreign policy of the Puritan government was as successful as it was vigorous. But it could not gain popular support for a government that most Englishmen regarded as naked military despotism.

The Commonwealth government had been imposed and was maintained by the army. Only the Rump Parliament survived as the last vestige of legitimacy. But, after the series of purges that it had suffered, this body was no longer even remotely representative of the nation's will. At the same time this remnant of Parliament was as unsatisfactory to the army as to the people at large, though for an entirely different reason. In the years of the war the army had gradually become the focal point for the most radical religious and political thought. Puritan in origin, these radical views represented the transfer of Puritan religious separatism to politics. And now the army demanded a new, popularly elected Parliament. Cromwell, however, knew that a Parliament thus elected would reject the Commonwealth, the army, and perhaps even the gains of the civil war. But pressure from the army forced him to dissolve the Rump Parliament in 1653 and to call a new one. Because he had to restrict its membership severely to protect the Commonwealth, it was no more representative and no more satisfactory to any party than the Rump had been. The only alternative left was a strong one-man rule—and the only man for the job was Cromwell. Thus the Commonwealth was succeeded by the Protectorate, with Cromwell as Protector. The English revolution had found its reluctant Napoleon.

The Protectorate was established under a written constitution, the Instrument of Government, which had been drawn up by the leaders of the army, the first such document in English history. In addition to the executive power of the Protector, it called for a representative Parliament. This body was elected and immediately opposed both the fact and the theory of the Protectorate. Despite the severe restrictions of suffrage and the rejection of a great many unfavorable members, even the Parliament expressed the well-nigh universal dissatisfaction of the people with the government. The only thing the government could do was dissolve Parliament. Thus ironically, Cromwell laid his own government open to precisely the charge that he and his supporters had levied against the government of Charles I—failure to respond to the will of the people.

The resistance of the Parliament was the resistance of the nation, and the Protectorate began to break down. Elected officials defied laws not sanctioned by Parliament. There were the old protests about taxation, about representation, and, of course, about religion. And Cromwell moved another step toward despotism. The country was divided into military districts, each under the command of a general and ruled by martial law. Twice more Cromwell tried to deal with parliaments and each time the protests were stronger and the parliaments were dissolved. By his death in 1658 it had become clear, even to the most fanatic champions of governmental reform, that England's experiment with military despotism had failed as utterly as the experiment with parliamentarian democracy.

Briefly Cromwell's son Richard was invested with his father's powers. But he lacked both his father's ability and will. Richard quickly abdicated in the face of a mounting sentiment for restoration of legitimate monarchy. With the removal of "Tumbledown Dick," a large group of civil leaders represented the desire for restoration. They gained the cooperation of one of the few remaining popular army commanders, General George Monk. With Monk's troops supporting each move, the Rump Parliament was recalled in 1660, forced to dissolve itself, and call a convention Parliament. Meanwhile Prince Charles, the son of the executed Charles I, had issued a declaration from his exile in Holland, expressing his willingness to accept his father's crown and to cooperate with Parliament.

On May 1, 1660, the convention accepted this declaration and proclaimed the Restoration in Charles II. On May 29 the new king stepped from his barge onto the London docks amid such a transport of rejoicing as England had not seen in a long and harrowing generation. The beginning of the new reign was officially back-dated to the death of Charles I. But this delicate fiction could not conceal the changes that divided the England of Charles I from that of Charles II. While the nation had rejected the corruption of democracy as decisively as it had rejected the excess of monarchy, it demanded the preservation of that handful of basic principles that had been the real issue of the civil war. The king was to be "king in parliament." This partnership, which had been a desperate revolutionary demand in 1640, became a part of the English constitution in 1660. In the same way were the principles of personal liberty of the citizen and freedom of conscience preserved. England had by no means established a completely constitutional government, but she had taken a long stride toward it.

Milton, Last Voice of the English Renaissance

While the "rule of saints" had proved unacceptable in almost every way to the majority of Englishmen, the Puritan experiments in religion and government had produced the last great spirit of the English Renaissance in John Milton (1608–1674). Milton was the son of a middle-class Puritan family. His father was a man of learned tastes, and from his earliest youth the young Milton was exposed to literature. He went to the famous St. Paul's School and on to Cambridge at seventeen. At this stage of his life his religion expressed itself in a rigid personal austerity that was coupled with an almost irreligious love of poetry. He was privileged to know the last generation of the great Elizabethans (they called themselves "the sons of Ben," after the poet and humanist Ben Jonson). John Milton was one of them in the spirit of his early writings, which reveal him as a lyric poet of great style and a humanist of astonishing learning. But he was a Puritan, and shared with his coreligionists the profound spiritual disquiet that tends to make the Puritan a revolutionary.

In 1638 Milton visited Italy, as young English humanists had been doing for two centuries. Word reached him there of the drift of English affairs toward war and he hastened home. For the next fifteen years Milton devoted himself almost exclusively to the cause of the Puritan revolution. In its service he estranged his wife and daughters, imperiled his personal security, and gave up his eyesight. He lamented no part of his sacrifice, not even his eyes. In a sonnet addressed to a friend he says:

> What supports me, dost thou ask?
> The conscience, friend, to have lost them overplied
> In liberty's defence, my noble task,
> Of which all Europe talks from side to side.

If not "all Europe" certainly all England talked of Milton, for he was the most successful and aggressive of the host of pamphleteers who sprang up in the course of the civil war. The work of Milton in this cause was particularly needed. The Puritans were not generally given to literature, except to long dreary sermons and sermonizing tracts. The Elizabethan literary spirit had lodged in the cavalier and episcopal cause. Thus, in the war of words and creeds the Puritans were hard pressed. But Milton was as brilliant as he was dutiful, and a whole library of treatises poured from his study, one after another—*Of Reformation, Or Prelatical Episcopacy, The Reason of Church Government, Aeropagitica* (a defense of the freedom of the press).

In the crisis following the execution of Charles I, Milton continued to support the radical Puritan cause. He was made Latin secretary to the new government and redoubled his already prodigious literary output. He wrote thousands of letters, some of them tracts in themselves. He answered the charges that were brought in increasing numbers against the state, and continued his polemical writings. It was in this time (1652) that he became finally blind. In the last years of the Protectorate, even when it was obvious that the revolution had been lost, Milton never wavered in its defense. Even after the Restoration was an accomplished fact he wrote some of his most substantial polemics, attempting to preserve the theory and the spirit of the cause whose practical fortunes were ruined. Much of this work was done in semiretirement, which his health forced upon him after 1655. At the time of the Restoration he was sought out by the new government, briefly imprisoned, and made to pay a stiff fine, but finally allowed to return to a secluded private life.

It was only in these years that Milton returned to poetry, to produce his greatest works, *Paradise Lost, Paradise Regained,* and *Samson Agonistes.* Even in these works the Puritan had not given place to the poet, but had simply changed his mode. *Paradise Lost* and *Paradise Regained* are Protestant epics. In the opening lines of *Paradise Lost* Milton states the purpose of his work in the traditional epic's prelude-prayer:

> And chiefly thou, O Spirit, that dost prefer
> Before all temples the upright heart and pure,
> Instruct me, for thou know'st . . .
>
> . . . what in me is dark,
> Illumine; what is low, raise and support;
> That to the height of this great argument
> I may assert eternal Providence,
> And justify the ways of God to men.

These great epics are taken from the traditional lore of the Old Testament that the Puritans loved so well, and subjected to the transforming influence of Milton's intellect and sense of poetic form. The story is simple, the war in heaven between God and Satan, the Fall of Satan, the Temptation and Fall of man, the promise and fulfilment of Redemption. But on this simple framework Milton erected his mighty and complex allegorical epics. In his own time they were little noticed. England had passed on to the gay trivialities of the Restoration and most Englishmen were happy to be rid of Puritan theology. But in the judgment of time Milton's poetry pleads the cause to which he devoted his life more eloquently than all his polemics. It is his poetry that raises Milton to a place second only to Shakespeare in English literature.

THE EXPANSION OF EUROPE

In the century and a half between the eve of the Reformation and the end of the religious wars the people of Europe had enough energy left over from killing each other in the names of their several religious faiths to spread their maturing civilization to the ends of the earth—to explore, exploit, plant colonies, and stamp the image of Europe upon other continents. The age of the Reformation and the dawn of modernity was also the great age of European expansion.

The Explorations

In the High Middle Ages Europe began to shake off the restrictions of localism and isolation that had been so characteristic of medieval life. With the revival of towns and trade, the great pulsations of exchange began to be felt once more. The Crusades and the European reconquest of the Mediterranean were crucial to this development, for the single most important key to the economy recovery of Europe was the control of the Mediterranean. In the later Middle Ages, as in ancient times, this great inland sea was the broad highway of international trade. And in this later time, as in antiquity, it was dominated by Italy.

The Italian merchant cities, as we have seen, profited most signally from the Crusades. They gained trading monopolies in the reconquered lands of the east at the expense of the Moslem powers and the Byzantine Empire. The force of the Crusades was added to their own increasing naval strength until such cities as Venice and Genoa were able, by the fourteenth century, to dominate Mediterranean commerce. This meant that their ships made contact on the coasts of Syria, at the mouth of the Nile, and in the Black Sea with the western end of the ancient caravan routes and Asiatic water-roads that had carried the goods of the east for centuries. This trade in spices, silk, perfumes, medicines, rare woods, and metals, which were produced in the Far East, western Europe was willing to pay premium prices for. It was a trade in luxuries, some of which were in such demand—spices and medicinal herbs, for example— as to be practically necessities. Pound for pound it was the most valuable trade in the world, and the wealth it brought to Italy provided in large part the material basis of the Italian Renaissance.

As long as the Mediterranean controlled the access to this eastern trade and as long as the Italian merchant cities controlled the Mediterranean the nations of the Atlantic seaboard were denied direct participation in it and were at the mercy of Italian prices. It was the attempt to circumvent this Italian monopoly that was the primary reason for the age of exploration. But, at the same time, a great many other factors contributed to it. The suicidal conflicts between the leading Italian states in the fourteenth and fifteenth centuries weakened them disastrously. The conquests and expansion of the Ottoman Turks began to encroach upon the Levantine trade of Italy, and the Mongol disturbance in Asia disrupted the caravan trade. At the same time the nation-states of western Europe were beginning to assume their modern forms. The economic middle class throughout Europe played an important role in this development. Merchants, industrialists, and entrepreneurs created a new foundation for the European economy, based upon domestic trade and manufacture of basic goods. A new complex of production and exchange was coming into existence in the body of continental Europe. But the lure of the east retained its magic, and the expanding economy of Europe created a surplus wealth, some portion of which could be invested in the adventure of exploration. Yet it was not one of the great states of western Europe that initiated the age of exploration, but the relatively minor state of Portugal.

Much, indeed most, of the credit for Portugal's remarkable achievements in exploration belongs to a younger son of the Portuguese royal house, Prince Henry the Navigator (1394–1460). In spite of this title, Prince Henry was not himself a navigator, but rather the enthusiastic patron and organizer of a generation of bold Portuguese exploits in seamanship. Portugal, at the opening of the fifteenth century, was simply another of the several Iberian kingdoms that had been formed in the course of the Christian reconquest. It had been only recently secured from absorption in the growing state of Castile by the military and political skill of King John I, Prince Henry's father. The struggle with Castile and continuing Spanish hostility tended to cut Portugal off from the trade of the Mediterranean. This and the native poverty of the country forced the Portuguese to turn to the sea, which was their western frontier. Prince Henry took the initiative in this move. In 1415 he encouraged his father to attack and seize Ceuta, a strategic point on the Atlantic coast of North Africa. With this as a forward base and with Henry's constant support, a number of Portuguese expeditions followed each other down the coast of Africa, each time pushing farther south. This work was furthered not only by necessity and princely patronage, but by a remarkable misconception of the world's geography and an equally remarkable series of improvements in marine technology.

In the time of Prince Henry, world geography was still visualized in Ptolemaic terms, and the ancient estimates of global distance were much shorter than was the actual case. This tended to make the early explorers more confident. Their confidence inspired their seamanship and their seamanship tended to inspire technical improvements. In the course of the fifteenth century the *carrack,* or full-rigged ship, replaced the oar and sail galley for open-water transit. Greater number and variety of sails made them more maneuverable, and new principles of construction made them more comfortable, spacious, and seaworthy. There were rapid improvements in cartography that were brought about by greater knowledge of the shape of the continents, the development of modern mathematics, and the insistent demands of exploration. There were parallel improvements in navigational instruments, amounting to a technological revolution. All these not only made possible the discoveries of the Portuguese but the discovery (or rediscovery) of the Americas and the circumnavigation of the world half a century after the death of Prince Henry.

The Portuguese kept before them the hope that Africa was really a gigantic peninsula which they could ultimately sail around. If this were true, then the riches of the east could be reached directly from western Europe by sea. There were a number of other motives—the possibility of attacking the Turks from the rear, the zeal to convert heathen peoples to Christianity, the legends of gold and treasure more fabulous even than those of the eastern trade, and simply the fascination of the unknown. But the overriding motive was the water route to the Indian Ocean and direct access to the Oriental trade. In 1488 Bartholomeu Diaz discovered the tip of South Africa, and in 1497 and 1498 Vasco da Gama rounded the Cape and reached the western coast of India. Da Gama was followed by others who began to piece together a Portuguese commercial empire in India and the Far East. Expeditions under Alfonso de Albuquerque founded a string of fortified points from the East Indies to the Persian Gulf. By the second decade of the sixteenth century the Portuguese had taken the lead in the spice trade and the repercussions were felt throughout Europe. It was this competition from the Portuguese halfway around the world that dealt the death blow to Italian commerce—not the fall of Constantinople to the Turks in 1453, as was long held to be the case.

The opening of the Portuguese water route to the east ended once and for all what might be called the "era of the inland sea" in world commerce. In Europe the shift of trade and finance to the Atlantic coast was completed, but not to the entire advantage of the Portuguese. Despite the enormous profits of the spice trade, the route around Africa was long and hard. Furthermore, Portugal did not have the financial machinery or business class to exploit her trade. Financial control began to slip into the hands of the Dutch and Flemish merchant companies and bankers, and the Portuguese spice trade swelled the profits that were making the

Captain John Smith and His Map of New England, from Smith's *Description of New England*. 1616.

Low Countries the economic hub of Europe. In the meantime, Spain had followed the lead of Portuguese exploration and was rapidly overtaking her in the opening years of the sixteenth century.

The story of Spanish exploration begins with the impetus of Portugal and with the voyages of the most famous of all explorers, Christopher Columbus, or more properly, Cristoforo Colombo (1446–1506). A native of Genoa, he had virtually grown up in the sea trade and as a young man was already a skillful and well-qualified sea captain. The exploits of the Portuguese explorers and the geographic speculation that their voyages aroused, fired his imagination. Perhaps as early as 1474 Columbus had already formulated the idea of reaching the east by sailing westward. It was, if a daring plan, not an unreasonable one. Contrary to some of the "Columbus mythology," knowledgeable people no longer believed that the earth was flat and had not done so for centuries. There was even some speculation about a "New World." A great many people, both practical sailors and book-learned scholars, believed that Japan and the Spice Islands lay only a few thousand miles beyond the Azores (actually, their estimate was about half the distance to the New World).

For nearly twenty years Columbus laid his plans before one prospective patron after another. Several Italian states, including his own Genoa, turned him down. The King of Portugal refused because his own men were already exploring the African route. Finally Columbus appealed to the monarchs of Spain. That country had been only recently united after centuries of struggle, and Ferdinand and Isabella were more than eager to make a place for their new nation in the European community. Moreover, the accomplishments of neighboring Portugal tempted them to similar efforts. If Columbus' assumption should prove correct, then Spain would have found another route to the riches of the east, perhaps a quicker and more profitable one than the Portuguese. The Spanish monarchs agreed to support Columbus and on August 3, 1492, the famous expedition of the *Niña,* the *Pinta,* and the *Santa Maria* sailed from the port of Huelva. After touching the Canary Islands, the fleet sailed on westward in September.

In less than six weeks Columbus made land in the Bahamas of the West Indies. He claimed the land in the name of his patrons and gratefully called it after the Holy Saviour, San Salvador. He thought that he had reached the fringe islands of the East Indies, which is why he called the native inhabitants Indians. He headed three more expeditions in 1493, 1498, and 1502, which claimed more islands and the coast of South

America. Columbus, for all his achievement, never realized that he had discovered a new world. With each expedition he confidently expected to come upon the great cities of the east that he thought must lie just beyond the next island or over the coastal range. Two years after his last voyage Columbus died, missing even the honor of having his discoveries named after him. The New World he had not recognized was named rather after an Italian cartographer, Amerigo Vespucci, who was among the first to publicize the thesis that it was indeed a New World and who himself sailed with several subsequent expeditions.

As Spanish exploration began to have results, the two great "colonial" powers of Spain and Portugal agreed to divide the non-European world between them to assure each a sphere of influence where their explorers had staked their claims. In 1493 Pope Alexander VI, as arbitrator, set a line of demarcation down the mid-Atlantic to divide the claims of Portugal to the east of the line from those of Spain to the west. This arrangement was modified the next year by a treaty that moved the line some distance farther west. This was later to give the Portuguese a legal basis on which to claim Brazil and the Spanish the Philippine Islands on the other side of the globe.

The discoveries of Columbus contributed to the fever for further discovery. In 1500 Pedro Álvares Cabral led a Portuguese expedition that touched the coast of Brazil to establish Portugal's claim there. Another Portuguese expedition pushed through the East Indies and out on the Asiatic edge of the Pacific while Balboa laid claim to its American shores, having crossed the Isthmus of Panama in 1513. Fernando Magellan in 1519, still seeking the western route to the Indies, sailed around the tip of South America and across the Pacific. While most of his expedition was lost and he himself killed by natives of the Pacific islands, one ship completed the journey via the Portuguese route around Africa and returned to Europe. After three years of incredible adventure this little vessel completed its voyage around the world.

The success of Spain and Portugal prompted England and France to attempt similar ventures. As early as 1480 English merchant companies began to send expeditions, but these failed to discover western land. Then, in 1497, again under the sponsorship of private companies, Giovanni Caboto (1450–1498), an Italian captain who had settled in the port of Bristol, led the first successful English expedition. He (John Cabot) discovered and claimed for England the northern coast of North America. In the following year he led another expedition as far south as Chesapeake Bay. His sons and others followed up these voyages. In the next generation another Italian seaman, the unsavory adventurer and pirate Giovanni da Verranzo, sailed for France into the New World and staked a French claim to portions of the North American coast. Between 1534 and 1541 the Frenchman Jacques Cartier penetrated the St. Lawrence and established a settlement which he called King's Mountain, Montreal. But neither the French nor the English explorations yielded many immediate results. Like the Spanish, they were seeking an alternative route to the Far East; but all attempts to find a northwest passage came to nothing. Moreover, the wild and inhospitable shores to which both French and English explorers came seemed to offer no hope of profit. The French made a few tentative settlements in what was to be Canada, but they were unsuccessful and the disheartened colonists returned home. The English made no attempt to settle in their new world for almost a century. As France and England became deeply involved in their own domestic troubles in the course of the sixteenth century, the beginnings of exploration and colonization were almost forgotten; Spain and Portugal were left to exploit the more salubrious parts both of the old and the new worlds that their explorations had opened.

The First Age of Colonization

By the early sixteenth century both Spain and Portugal were already passing beyond the stage of exploration into settlement and exploitation. From the beginning, the Portuguese had found it necessary to establish colonies as they went—coastal stations along the African coast and "factories" or fortified depots in India and the Indies. In west Africa they had pushed inland from a fortified base to take the gold from the hinterland of the "Gold Coast." In Guinea, the Congo, and Angola they established bases for the slave trade, for which they gained papal authorization. On the subtropical islands of the Atlantic and in the New World empire of Brazil they founded plantation colonies worked by the African slaves delivered there by their ships. By the middle of the sixteenth century the plantations of Brazil were exporting marketable quantities of tobacco and a large portion of the world's sugar.

During the same period Spain outstripped the Portuguese to become, by the end of the century, the greatest colonial power in the world. Early returns from Spanish exploration in the New World had been most unpromising. There was no easy route to the eastern trade. The natives were low-level savages. Spanish parties scoured thousands of miles of coastline

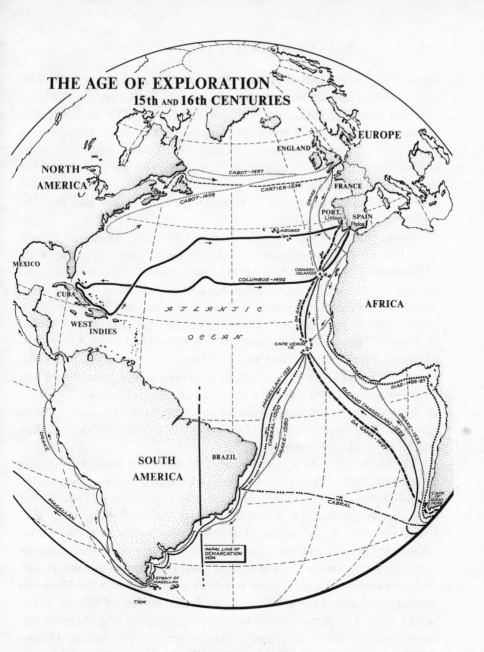

THE AGE OF EXPLORATION
15th AND 16th CENTURIES

EUROPE

NORTH
AMERICA

ENGLAND

CABOT-1497

CABOT-1498

CARTIER-1534

FRANCE

PORT.
Lisbon

SPAIN
Palos

AZORES

MEXICO

CUBA

WEST
INDIES

COLUMBUS-1492

CANARY
ISLANDS

AFRICA

A T L A N T I C

O C E A N

CAPE VERDE
IS.

DA GAMA

DIAZ-1486-87

MAGELLAN-1521

CABRAL-1500

DRAKE-1580

ELCANO (MAGELLAN)-1522

DA GAMA-1497

DRAKE-1522

DRAKE

SOUTH
AMERICA

BRAZIL

CABRAL

CAPE
OF
GOOD
HOPE

MAGELLAN

PAPAL LINE OF
DEMARCATION
1494

STRAIT OF
MAGELLAN

TRM

and found nothing but jungle and more savages on the mainland of their
New World.

Then Hernando Cortez (1485–1547), a soldier who had gained experience in the conquest of the islands and the mainland coast, led a small
expedition inland from the site of Vera Cruz to discover the fabulous
Aztec Empire of central Mexico and the material riches for which the

Spanish had so far looked in vain. The Aztecs had created a high order of civilization and undreamed-of wealth. It was the latter, the stocks of gold and silver, not the culture, that attracted Cortez. With incredible daring and confidence he set about the conquest of the Aztecs. He had some three hundred men and sixteen cavalry. But the fear and superstition of the Aztecs and the discontent of their subject people played into the conqueror's hands. After some preliminary skirmishing and tentative negotiation Cortez, reinforced by another expedition from Cuba, took the Aztec capital in 1521.

Farther to the south another military adventurer, Francisco Pizarro (c. 1470–1541), was gathering an expedition to probe into the body of South America, from which he had heard rumors of another high and wealthy civilization. In 1531, at the head of a small band, Pizarro penetrated to the capital of the Incas in Peru. It was an even more cultivated, more highly organized, and richer civilization than the Aztec. Within three years Pizarro had conquered Peru as Cortez had Mexico.

These two conquests laid the foundations for the Spanish colonial empire of the New World. There were, of course, further explorations and more *conquistadores* of the stamp of Cortez and Pizarro to carry the claims of Spain to the tip of South America and far into the interior of North America. They were all after gold and silver. The fantastic riches of Peru and Mexico had fired their zeal.

The same riches, to a large extent, determined the pattern of Spanish colonialism. Unlike Portuguese colonialism in Asia, which was commercial, Spanish colonialism in South America was exploitative. Thousands of Spaniards sought the New World in search of gold and silver, which they found not only in the stores of treasure they looted from the native empires of Mexico and Peru, but in the mines that were the source of that treasure. In Peru especially, mines were discovered by the middle of the century that supplied silver in greater abundance than the European economy had ever known before. Spanish exploitation of mineral riches spread to the exploitation of the native peoples and the land. Many things contributed to the almost feudal pattern of Spanish colonialism. Despite their numbers, the Spanish in the New World were a distinct minority and, moreover, a minority who looked upon themselves as military conquerors and thus superior to the natives. Production and shipping of the precious metals was most profitably carried on under monopoly grants. In addition, huge grants of land were made to individuals and companies and were held almost as principalities. As the Spaniards in the New

World turned to agriculture, they concentrated on the most profitable export crops such as sugar, tobacco, or indigo, which could best be grown on plantations worked either by African slaves or enslaved native peoples. This socio-economic system was the more easily managed because it was essentially the same as that before the Spaniards came; both the Inca and Aztec empires had exploited subject peoples in the creation of their magnificent civilizations. Thus the Spaniards, in conquering Mexico and Peru, became their successors and for most of the New World peoples Spanish rule merely represented a change of masters.

The system of colonial government was much the same as the socio-economic system and closely related to it. The authority of the crown in Spain, the most complete in Europe, was extended into the New World. The king's authority stemmed down through two viceroyalties, New Spain comprising Mexico, the Central American and island holdings; and Peru, comprising most of the continental South American lands. There were further subdivisions down to the local *alcaldes* (mayors) of village settlements and garrison commanders. The clearing house for all the affairs of the New World was the Council of the Indies, which stood in the same relationship to the crown as the several other councils of state that were the administrative and advisory bodies subordinate to the Spanish king. Like the other councils, the Council of the Indies was closely directed by the king and narrowly circumscribed in its authority. Most of the difficulties of the colonies, the abuses of power, the brutal exploitation of native peoples, the maddening slowness of every governmental process, must be attributed to the cumbersome machinery of the Spanish state, which forced every decision, virtually every scrap of official paper, through the hands of the king.

Just as the state and the church were nearly synonymous in Spain, so they were united in the New World. Christian missionaries had earlier followed the Portuguese into Asia but, excepting such spectacular individuals as St. Francis Xavier, the church had succeeded only indifferently in converting the swarming millions of Asiatics. Both Portugal and Spain were much more successful in spreading their faith in the New World. From the time of the first western discoveries the papacy had sanctioned the conquests and settlements in America. The new spirit of the Counter Reformation that was stirring in Catholic Europe was carried to the New World. The great missionary orders such as the Franciscans and Jesuits sent their brethren out side by side with the conquerors. Indeed, what ameliorating humanity is to be found in the story of the *conquistadores* must be attributed to the influence of these missionaries. Frequently they blazed the trails of further conquest as their zeal to convert the Indians led them, often alone and unprotected by anything except their faith, into the most remote regions of America. As the government of the New World took shape the church was brought under it in the form of a state-church. Latin America was to be Catholic America as well.

Colonialism and the Mercantile System

The behavior of the colonial powers in the New World reflected both the absolutist political theories that prevailed in monarchical Europe and, the economic twin of absolutism, the mercantile theory. Mercantilism had developed gradually as the kings of the emerging European national monarchies gathered into their hands the many threads of national sovereignty—including control of national economic policies. We have noted earlier the close association of the kings and the towns in the High Middle Ages. As the kings slowly won their dominant position in early modern times, they appropriated the economic philosophy of the medieval towns and applied it to their national states.

The essence of this philosophy—whether for town or state—was protection and regimentation. In the state it brought about the notion of complete governmental regulation of the national economy. One of the aims of this regulation was the achievement of national self-sufficiency. Each state aspired to be completely in control of its own interests in every sphere. Inevitably, this policy led to a chronic state of hostility, either hot or cold, among nations. Each nation saw its own prosperity in exclusive terms and, furthermore, each nation viewed its own prosperity as having to be gained at the expense of other nations. Thus, in large terms, mercantilism was "war by other means"—economic means.

The mercantilist end of national self-sufficiency was to be achieved by a number of policies that formed the framework of the system: government protection for native industry and commerce, a favorable balance of external trade, and the stockpiling of precious metals. While virtually all European nations subscribed to these general economic principles, Spain especially extended them to her colonial empire in Latin America to become the most "perfectly" mercantile power in Europe in the sixteenth century.

Spanish economic and political policies toward the American colonies can be properly understood only in mercantilist terms. Spain regarded the colonies as an outlet for Spanish goods and thus practically forbade any other power to trade with them. But the backward state of Spanish industry made it impossible for her to provide the necessities that were demanded by the colonies, and wholesale smuggling resulted despite the most dreadful penalties and reams of laws and regulations against it. At the same time Spain forbade the export of any colonial goods directly to other powers. But this prohibition was also regularly violated. Spain was especially concerned with monopolizing the gold and silver of the New World and took elaborate precautions to protect her treasure fleets. Nonetheless, millions of dollars worth of bullion was taken every year by daring pirates —French, Dutch, and English. Thus all Spanish attempts to structure and control the bursting new economy of the Americas failed. As Spain was the most nearly perfect mercantile power in the sixteenth century, by the seventeenth she was the comparably perfect illustration of the failure of mercantilism as a system. The riches of the New World became for Spain literally an embarrassment of riches.

The North Atlantic Powers

By the seventeenth century Spain had been challenged as a colonial power by the Atlantic seaboard nations to the north, especially the Dutch Republic, England, and, to a lesser degree, France. These powers came fully into the business of overseas colonies by way of their European wars.

We have already seen that Dutch naval power was the decisive factor in the success of the revolt against Spain.[7] In the early seventeenth century the Dutch were able to carry the war from the waters of the European coastline to the Spanish colonies and treasure fleets of the New World and into the heart of the Spanish-Portuguese trade empire of the east. Daring and well-armed Dutch fleets struck at the spice trade in the last decade of the sixteenth century. In 1602 Dutch merchants formed a chartered company, the Dutch East India Company, to consolidate their economic efforts in the Indies. It rapidly became the greatest corporation of the century. The Dutch were able to strike with ever greater success and profit against the moribund trade empire of Portugal. With sturdier ships, heavier guns, and powerful financial backing, Dutch fleets swept the eastern seas of naval opposition. By mid-century they had gained control of the trade and many of the factories of the East Indies, from which they were not dislodged until the present century.

The Dutch attempted a similar exploitation of North America. But

7. See p. 631.

here the European wars of the Dutch against the English in the mid-seventeenth century worked to the advantage of the English. After a scant half century in the New World, following the exploration of Henry Hudson (1609), the English won the Dutch colonies as part of the loot of war and New Amsterdam became New York.

The British had long since begun their own settlement of the New World. The tremendous expansion of England under Elizabeth included not only the privateering of the sea dogs but the planting of permanent colonies, which continued to flourish in the opening years of the seventeenth century. Under crown grants the Virginia colony was established in 1607, to be followed by other establishments in the islands of the West Indies and along the eastern shore of what would be the United States. The most important of these for the future of English colonialism in the New World were the New England colonies. Their rapid growth was tied once more to the unsettled politics and wars of Europe. New England was virtually populated by Puritan refugees in the years preceding the English civil war, and they stamped their faith indelibly upon their newly adopted land.

In the meantime, English merchants had followed the Dutch into the preserves of Spain and Portugal in the East. In 1600 the British East India Company was formed and by mid-century had staked out economic claims on the Indian mainland to match those of the Dutch in the Spice Islands. All through the century the Anglo-Dutch hostilities were fought out with local savagery in the east as in the home waters.

The French followed the Dutch and the English into piracy, imperialism, and finally colonial settlement in the New World. But France came late. The wars of religion, the heavy French involvement in continental politics, and the emphasis upon national centralization and monarchial absolutism worked against French colonialism. The Anglo-French contest for North America is part of a later story. In the mid-seventeenth century the New World, like the Old, stood on the verge of the modern era.

SUGGESTIONS FOR FURTHER READING

General Works

*G. N. Clark, *Early Modern Europe, from about 1450 to about 1720* (Oxford: Oxford University Press, 1960).

————, *The Seventeenth Century* (Oxford, Clarendon Press, 1929), organized topically with interesting chapters on such things as philosophy, commerce, armies, navies, law, finance.

C. J. Friedrich, *The Age of the Baroque 1610–1660* (New York: Harper, 1952), probably the best cultural history of the period.

New Cambridge Modern History, some material in Vol. II, but the volumes that pertain most to this period are still in preparation.

*D. Ogg, *Europe in the Seventeenth Century* (New York: Collier, 1962), straightforward, largely political history of the continent.

*B. Willey, *The Seventeenth Century Background* (Garden City, N. Y.: Anchor, n.d.), largely philosophy and intellectual history.

Political History

A. Bailly, *The Cardinal Dictator: A Portrait of Richelieu* (London: Jonathan Cape, 1936).

G. Davies, *The Early Stuarts* (Oxford: Oxford University Press, 1937).

C. Firth, *Oliver Cromwell and the Rule of the Puritans in England* (New York: Oxford University Press, 1953), the best study of Cromwell.

J. H. Hexter, *The Reign of King Pym* (Cambridge: Harvard University Press, 1941).

M. Roberts, *Gustavus Adolphus* (New York: Longmans, 1953), 2 vols.

G. M. Trevelyan, *England under the Stuarts* (New York: Putnam, 1949), probably the best one-volume work on the subject; stylistically somewhat "old fashioned."

H. R. Trevor-Roper, *Archbishop Laud* (London: Macmillan, 1940).

F. Watson, *Wallenstein, Soldier under Saturn* (London: Chatto and Windus, 1938).

C. V. Wedgwood, *The King's Peace, 1637–1641* (London: Macmillan, 1955), the first volume of a large-scale, comprehensive reevaluation of the English civil war.

————, *The King's War* (London: Macmillan, 1958), the second volume of the study on the civil war.

————, *Oliver Cromwell* (London: Duckworth, 1939).

*————, *Richelieu and the French Monarchy* (New York: Collier, 1962), one of the best short works on the period.

*————, *The Thirty Years War* (Garden City, N. Y.: Anchor, 1961), the best general account of the subject.

The Exploration

W. C. Abbot, *The Expansion of Europe* (New York: Holt, 1918), 2 vols.

*J. B. Brebner, *Explorers of North America* (London: Black, 1933).

C. H. Haring, *The Spanish Empire in America* (Oxford: Oxford University Press, 1947).

F. A. Kirkpatrick, *Spanish Conquistadores* (London: Black, 1934).

*J. A. Mason, *Ancient Civilization of Peru* (Baltimore: Penguin, 1957).

S. E. Morison, *Admiral of the Ocean Sea* (Boston: Little, Brown, 1942), the best work on Columbus.

*————, *Christopher Columbus, Mariner* (New York: Mentor, 1956), a recast of much of the material of the earlier work.

W. Notestein, *The English People on the Eve of Colonization* (New York: Harper, 1954), a fine social history of the immediate background of the American colonies.

*C. E. Nowell, *The Great Discoveries and the First Colonial Empires* (Ithaca: Cornell University Press, 1954).

*L. B. Packard, *The Commercial Revolution* (New York: Holt, 1927).

C. M. Parr, *So Noble a Captain* (New York: Crowell, 1953), Magellan and his time.

J. H. Parry, *Europe and a Wider World 1415–1715* (London: Longmans, 1949).

W. H. Prescott, *History of the Conquest of Mexico* (New York: Dutton, n.d.) 2 vols., classic work.

*————, *History of the Conquest of Peru*, ed. and abr. by V. W. Von Hagen (New York: Mentor, 1961).

E. Sanceau, *Henry the Navigator* (London: Hutchinson, 1945).

H. See, *Modern Capitalism, Its Origin and Evolution* (London: Douglas, 1928).

G. C. Valliant, *The Aztecs of Mexico* (Garden City, N. Y.: Doubleday, 1941), probably the best work of its scope on the subject.

*W. Von Hagen, *Realm of the Incas* (New York: Mentor, n.d.).

*Paperbound edition. In the case of reprint editions, publisher and date of publication given will be that of reprint rather than the original.

Epilogue

In looking back over the long span of time covered by this book, one is struck by the persistence of certain relationships among men and between men and their environment: the struggle for power, the struggle for possessions, the effort to control and harness nature, the attempt to understand and control the supernatural, and, forming a constant theme, war in the name of various causes.

The struggle to achieve and maintain power—control over other human beings—appears with the earliest subspecies of civilization and, in one form or another, has continued ever since—whether manifested in the "divine" power of the Egyptian Pharaoh, the constitutional power of the Roman consul, the usurped power of the feudal baron, or the representative power of the seventeenth-century English parliamentarian. For power may be wielded by individuals, legitimate monarchs, usurpers, constitutional magistrates, or by cliques and classes. It may be clothed in institutional forms as varied as the Mesopotamian and Egyptian divine monarchies, the medieval papacy, or the Florentine Renaissance patriciate. The struggle to achieve and maintain power may be barely perceptible, as in the stable political setting of ancient Egypt; at other times it may become the dominant theme of a period, as in the chaotic final century of the Roman Republic. It may, and usually does, have economic overtones.

The struggle to possess goods—the economic conflict—also appears with the earliest civilizations which, by their very nature, seem founded on economic inequality. But almost from the very beginning the economic conflict is more complex than the desire of the "have-nots" to *share* in in the wealth of the "haves." For if the manifestoes of reformers call for a happy state in which all shall have enough and none shall want, historical facts suggest that much more frequently what the "have-nots" want is not equality but supremacy, the very supremacy that the proprietary group is determined to keep. This pattern is so general that something of value may be found out about every society above the level of savagery from an examination of the nature of its economic conflict—of the forces contending to control its material life and the methods and means employed to do so.

Almost as persistent as the effort to achieve power over other men has been the effort to control nature. This too is a matter of power, but power in the technological sense of energy. The extent to which it can harness the driving forces of nature determines a great deal about the form and nature of any civilization. Perhaps nothing so much distinguishes the modern world from past civilizations as the revolution in the utilization of physical energy during the past century—steam power, electricity, atomic and cosmic energy. The mechanical contrivances remain much the same, and even Archimedes, for instance, would not be completely baffled by the modern machine. It is the extension of man's control into the realm of energy that is the innovation. This development is part of the history of technology that began when our first dim-witted, slack-jawed ancestor closed his fingers around a stone or tree limb and lifted it to strike a blow. By this much he extended the reach and leverage of his arm and the efficiency of his hand. From that time to this men have continued their struggle to reach farther and better and more quickly, to get more of the work of the world done with greater dispatch.

At the other end of the scale from the material and the natural lies the supernatural. Here too we have evidence that man tried from the earliest times to understand and control the many forces that he could not explain in natural terms. The attempt has gone on and been entered upon by theologians, philosophers, and scientists as well as ordinary people. In many cases we have discovered not more about supernature, but that what we once attributed to it can in the light of increased knowledge be rather attributed to nature. But while the frontier of the supernatural has been constantly pushed back, the last mysteries remain. Perhaps they always will. Can we know the nature of God more clearly than Moses or Socrates?

Can we explain the existence of evil and sin in the world more cogently than Augustine or Calvin?

As men have contended with the forces of nature and supernature, so they have for a variety of causes contended with each other. An inordinate amount of men's energy has been devoted to the systematic killing of each other. Indeed, the few generations in man's history that have been free of war stand out as remarkable for that reason alone. It is more common to see the resources of talent and wealth marshaled behind "war effort," to see technology suborned to its service, intellectual abilities harnessed to its strategy and justification, and to see the power of the supernatural evoked in its cause. Perhaps the very constancy and intensity of man's dedication to war has at last in our own time brought the possibility of a world without war. It is certain that technology has now brought us to the point where we actually can destroy every living thing on our planet, and perhaps the planet itself. It remains to be seen whether men will heed the warning that their own destructive inventiveness forces upon them. If they do not there will be no more need of history and no more history—the "argument without an end" will have ended.

This brings us to the qualification that must be kept in mind when we consider the so-called "constant themes" in history. For while the discourse of history is made up of such words as "war," "state," "king," and "people," we must remind ourselves that these words have somewhat different significance within different historical periods. There is obviously a great difference in the nature and consequences of the Peloponnesian War and World War II. There are equally important differences in the significance of other terms. The failure to recognize these distinctions can lead to a very false reading of the past. Think for a moment of the term, "the people." In the centuries since the French and American revolutions this term has come to be associated with such notions as popular rights, mass voting, widespread literacy, and a popular press. But this complex meaning would have been inconceivable to a feudal baron, to Sargon of Akkad, or even to such champions of "popular" rights as Pericles or the Gracchi.

How often have we heard the ancient Athenian democracy praised and compared to our own as if the two were as similar as father and son. Yet how untrue this is. The Athenian concept of democracy carried in its very definition that very undemocratic notion of privilege and, indeed, in the great age of Athenian democracy the possession of a democratic constitution was often regarded as the badge of tyranny. The ancient political philosophers tended to regard democracy with suspicion, as a form of government that lacked the necessary ingredient of responsibility. Similarly, the student of history will recognize the vast differences that separate the Ancient Near East state of the Bronze Age and Calvin's Geneva, though both may be described as "theocracies"; the differences that separate the Egyptian Pharaoh from Louis XIV, though both ruled by "divine right."

But whether we talk of patterns and themes in history or of its vast individuality and the uniqueness of historical events, we must remember that history is made by men, and that its ultimate wonder stems from the virtually endless variety of human thought and action. We are part of that variety, and when we study history we hold up a mirror to ourselves.

Index

Index

737

SOURCES OF ILLUSTRATIONS

PLATE 1. Above: British Information Service; below: French Government Tourist Office.

PLATE 2. Above: British Information Service; below: Courtesy of the American Museum of Natural History.

PLATE 3. Above: Courtesy of the Oriental Institute, University of Chicago; below: The Metropolitan Museum of Art, Rogers Fund, 1943.

PLATE 4. Above: The Metropolitan Museum of Art, Dodge Fund, 1931; below: The Louvre.

PLATE 5. Above: The Metropolitan Museum of Art, Dodge Fund, 1911; below: The Louvre.

PLATE 6. Above: Arab Information Center; right: The Louvre.

PLATE 7. Royal Consulate General of Greece. Press and Information Service.

PLATE 8. Above: British Information Service.

PLATE 9. Italian Cultural Institute.

PLATE 10. Left: Assessorato Turismo—Spettacolo; below: The Metropolitan Museum of Art, Rogers Fund, 1906.

PLATE 11. Above: Delphi Museum.

PLATE 13. Above: Capitoline Museum; below: The Granger Collection.

PLATE 15. Left, top: The Metropolitan Museum of Art, Rogers Fund, 1912; left, center: Conservatori; left, below: Capitoline Museum.

PLATE 17. Italian State Tourist Office.

PLATE 19. Above: Art Reference Bureau; below: The Metropolitan Museum of Art, Bequest of Mary Clark Thompson, 1926.

PLATE 20. Above: Art Reference Bureau; below: The Metropolitan Museum of Art, Gift of Henry G. Marquand, 1897.

PLATE 22. Above: The Metropolitan Museum of Art, Fletcher Fund, 1925.

PLATE 23. Above: The Louvre; below: French Cultural Service.

PLATE 24. Bildarchive Foto Marburg/Art Reference Bureau.

PLATE 25. British Information Service.

PLATE 27. Above: Musée de Bayeux; below: Italian Information Center.

PLATE 28. Italian Information Center.

PLATE 29. Caisse Nationale des Monuments Historiques.

PLATE 30. Above: The Granger Collection; below: Caisse Nationale des Monuments Historiques.

PLATE 31. Italian Cultural Institute.

PLATE 32. Caisse Nationale des Monuments Historiques.

PLATE 33. Caisse Nationale des Monuments Historiques.